DEVELOPMENT POLICY AS PUBLIC

To Roland and Julia

Development Policy as Public Finance

CLIVE BELL

OXFORD
UNIVERSITY PRESS

OXFORD
UNIVERSITY PRESS

Great Clarendon Street, Oxford OX2 6DP

Oxford University Press is a department of the University of Oxford.
It furthers the University's objective of excellence in research, scholarship,
and education by publishing worldwide in

Oxford New York

Auckland Bangkok Buenos Aires Cape Town Chennai
Dar es Salaam Delhi Hong Kong Istanbul Karachi Kolkata
Kuala Lumpur Madrid Melbourne Mexico City Mumbai Nairobi
São Paulo Shanghai Taipei Tokyo Toronto

Oxford is a registered trade mark of Oxford University Press
in the UK and in certain other countries

Published in the United States
by Oxford University Press Inc., New York

British Library Cataloguing in Publication Data

Data available

Library of Congress Cataloging in Publication Data

Bell, Clive, 1943–
Public finance and development policy / by Clive Bell.
p. cm.
1. Economic development–Finance. 2. Economic policy. 3. Finance, Public.
I. Title.
HD75 .B455   2003   338.9–dc21   2002192561

ISBN 0-19-877366-8 (hbk.)
ISBN 0-19-877367-6 (pbk.)

1 3 5 7 9 10 8 6 4 2

Typeset by Newgen Imaging Systems (P) Ltd., Chennai, India
Printed in Great Britain
on acid-free paper by
Biddles Ltd., Guildford & King's Lynn

Preface

This book has its remote origins in a course of lectures on project appraisal for M.A. students that I first held at Vanderbilt some fifteen years ago. A little earlier, I had begun to teach public economics at both the undergraduate and graduate levels, partly in response to gentle but firm nudging from departmental chairmen, but also because of a growing conviction that development economics needs to draw more heavily and systematically on the advances in knowledge made in public economics, particularly where the formulation and analysis of development policy is concerned. For if governments do have a developmental role to play—other than simply holding the ring for the private sector to go about its business in an orderly way—then development economists should take the economics of government seriously in its own right. In the ensuing years, my lectures on development and public economics became increasingly intertwined, as I struggled to realize this synthesis and to exploit the resulting economies of scope in teaching. The topics bearing on development policy, though scattered about over several courses, now ranged far beyond project appraisal, and the students who served as guinea pigs were mostly second-year Ph.D. candidates, so that the treatment of the material also became more formal. There matters lay, without any further plans, until the summer of 1991, when Pranab Bardhan invited me to contribute the volume on development policy in this series.

Shortly thereafter, I had my first taste of what turned out to be a long stint of teaching in the *Hauptstudium* of the German system, first at Regensburg University, and later at Heidelberg. Comparisons of the Anglo-Saxon and German systems are not easy to make, and can be invidious; but it is generally fair to say that the level of the *Hauptstudium* is broadly comparable to a good Anglo-Saxon M.A. In my experience, the better German students compare favourably with their Anglo-Saxon counterparts, and I have pitched the level of the courses accordingly. The lectures themselves slowly evolved into a three-semester cycle (four hours per semester) in Development Economics, the second and third parts of which deal with policy as public finance, broadly interpreted. The writing of the first full draft finally caught up with the lectures in the winter of 2001.

One inevitably accumulates many debts over such a long drawn-out process. In the early stages, I gained much from extensive discussions with

Edward Buffie, whose work on trade and liberalization has been influential in the drafting of the chapters on those topics. Through discourses that go back well over two decades, Shantayanan Devarajan, T. N. Srinivasan, and Nicholas Stern have also exerted a strong influence on my way of thinking about the problems of development policy. Students at Johns Hopkins, Vanderbilt, Regensburg, and Heidelberg kept me on my toes all the while, especially in forcing me to explain things clearly and to justify treating them in a particular way. To the extent that the text is clearly and persuasively written, it is to them that readers should direct their thanks. I wish to mention in particular certain of my assistants and doctoral candidates at Heidelberg: Carsten Fink, Stefan Klonner, Ramona Schrepler, Dagmar Völker, and Ansgar Wohlschlegel. Two anonymous referees made a number of valuable suggestions, which resulted in important improvements, not only in the details of certain arguments, but also in the structure of the whole text. To all of the above I am deeply grateful, while clearing them of all responsibility for any surviving errors of opinion or analysis.

Permission to use the following published material has been kindly granted by the copyright holders.

Cambridge University Press: Tables from E. Ahmad and N. H. Stern (1991), *The Theory and Practice of Tax Reform in Developing Countries*, Cambridge: Cambridge University Press.

Elsevier Science: A table from Ahmad & Stern (1984), 'The Theory of Tax Reform and Indian Indirect Taxes,' *Journal of Public Economics*, 25: 259–298.

The World Bank: Two tables from C. Bell, P. Hazell and R. Slade (1982), *Project Evaluation in Regional Perspective*, Baltimore, MD: The Johns Hopkins University Press 1982; one table from R. Dornbusch and A. Reynoso (1993), 'Financial Factors in Economic Development', in R. Dornbusch (ed.), *Policymaking in the Open Economy*, New York: Oxford University Press; extensive parts of C. Bell (1990), 'Reforming Property Rights in Land and Tenancy,' *World Bank Research Observer*, 1990; data from the World Bank's Development Indicators (1998) have been used to construct various figures.

I owe a quite different, and altogether larger debt to my children, to whom this book is lovingly dedicated.

Clive Bell
August 2002

Contents

Introduction

Development policy is such a broad subject that radical exclusions must be made if a coherent body of material is to be both carefully treated and crammed within a single pair of covers. The corset is provided by two central questions in public economics, namely, how to raise and spend revenues well, in the specific sense of promoting development. Under any reasonable definition of development, these questions are certainly norm-ative. Yet, whether something has been done 'well' in this context must also be judged in relation to what is actually feasible. Given the inability—or unwillingness—of governments to make lump-sum transfers, the design of policy in practice is inherently concerned with considerations of the second-best. This awkward fact besets the analysis of interventions in all areas of policy, be it international trade or small-scale finance, and it runs through the entire book.

No text on this subject would be complete without a serious attempt to deal with the role of international trade, and this is precisely the point of departure. As just argued, however, much more is involved than a discus-sion of the importance of trade as a possible engine of development. For taxes on international trade are a leading source of government revenue in many poor countries, so that trade and taxation are closely intertwined. Chapter 1 gives an account of theory that reflects this interplay, paying close attention to the claim that free trade is best and the possible sources of market failure that threaten to undermine it. There is a marked emphasis on the gains from trade that arise from the opportunity to obtain produ-cer goods—above all, investment goods—from abroad on better terms than through domestic production. This places the discussion where it properly belongs, namely, in the realm of economic growth, where it is joined by the so-called 'infant industry' argument. How best to promote domestic industries, when there is a case for doing so, is analysed in the light of the actual instruments at the government's disposal and whatever distortions may have entrenched themselves in the economy. Viewed in this way, the protective effects of tariffs can be seen as an unavoidable side-effect of the need to raise revenue when other instruments are lacking.

Chapter 2 deals, in a nutshell, with the practice and effects of protection-ism in less developed countries in the second half of the twentieth century. It begins by sketching the trade policies governments have actually pursued in that period. One pattern that occurs quite frequently is a so-called escalated structure of protection, in which consumer goods are subject to stiff tariffs or tight quotas, but producer goods are let off rather lightly. The next step is to assess how damaging such policies have been, where the yardstick is provided not only by the ideal of first-best, but also by practicable alternatives. A widely used method is to build a computable general equilibrium model of the economy, calibrate it, and run the required comparative statics experiments. For expositional purposes, the essentials are captured by a simple 2×2 model of a small, open economy. This yields results which suggest that the damage done, expressed as a proportion of GDP at world prices, is very modest, a finding wholly in keeping with those produced by its full-scale brethren. An alternative line of approach is to investigate the relationship between 'openness' and economic growth econometrically, using both time-series and cross-section data. This has yielded rather mixed findings.

Dismantling protection—more formally, the liberalization of trade—is the topic of Chapter 3. Whether such moves yield gains or losses in welfare turns out to hinge not only on whether GDP at world prices rises or falls as a result, but also on whether the deviations of relative domestic prices from their world price counterparts are reduced in a particular way. As in any second-best setting, distortions in other markets, especially that for labour, play an important role in determining the outcome. When they are so firmly rooted in the political–economic structure that a direct attack upon them is not to be contemplated, a devaluation may be necessary as an indirect freeing stroke.

This discussion of trade sets the stage for a systematic treatment of taxation and its reform, in Chapters 4 and 5, respectively. With an eye on actual practice, both historical and contemporary, the emphasis is on indirect taxes and how difficulties of administration influence the choice among various tax instruments. The question of how to incorporate considerations of distributive justice is now addressed directly within the admittedly orthodox framework of the Bergson–Samuelsonian social welfare function, which serves not only as a necessary element of the theory of optimal commodity taxation, but also as the basis for the evaluation of reforms of policy throughout the remainder of the book. The said theory and the principal results are set out in some detail, thereby providing both a benchmark against which to measure the performance of actual tax systems and a vital piece of apparatus for cost–benefit analysis. This excursion into theory is complemented by a simple method of calculating the effective tax rates on goods that arise from the tangled mixtures of tariffs, excises, surcharges, and sales taxes that are commonly employed in practice, the results of which usually yield ample ammunition for proponents of reform.

What, then, are the essential elements of such a programme? Two principles are advocated as desirable guidelines, rather than hard and fast rules: the first is that taxes should be broadly based, so as to keep individual rates low (but by no means necessarily uniform); the second is that intermediate goods should not be taxed. As a very first step, therefore, all quotas on imports should be replaced by tariffs. Then, once the administrative capacity is established, taxes on international trade should be abolished in favour of taxes on domestic use, regardless of a good's origins. Matters now become less straightforward. For, in view of the virtual impossibility of imposing compliance on the legions of small-scale producers in the unregulated sectors of the economy, in which consumption out of home production can be important, a value-added tax (VAT) with extensive coverage will remain a distant prospect. This motivates the application of the theory of piecemeal tax reforms to find (possibly 'local') changes in existing rates that will improve welfare without causing a loss to the Treasury.

Seigniorage and public debt are generally thought of as macroeconomic topics, but no account of public finances would be complete without them, and they are taken up in Chapter 6. Both involve dynamic considerations, seigniorage through the impulse it gives to inflation, and debt through its shifting of tax liabilities into the future. Both have their place in the government's array of instruments, but both involve temptations that carry substantial risks. Issuing additional currency typically requires only an acquiescent central bank. A prudent resort to the printing press when real incomes are growing will normally yield a modest inflation tax (on real balances) at strikingly low administrative costs and for a small deadweight loss. Lack of restraint, however, will soon put the economy on the path to high inflation, with the possibility of a hyperinflation—and all its woeful legacies—as the end result. The situation with debt is similar. Putting off tax payments until tomorrow makes eminently good sense when exercised in moderation and real incomes are growing. To overdo it is to invite a slide into fiscal instability, as tax revenues are devoured by the need to service the debt. Governments that fail to get their fiscal affairs in order through an adept mixture of taxation and budgetary stringency are forced to steer a course between this particular pair of Scylla and Charybdis. A few have even managed to taste the experience of both.

A dynamic setting can harbour other dangers that threaten the success of attempts at economic reform, two prime examples of which are addressed in Chapter 7. The first is the familiar problem of 'time incon-sistency', whereby certain incentives that are at work at the outset cease to matter later on, and so make it rational for the government to go back on an original declaration of policy. The second is that there may be a self-fulfilling expectations equilibrium in which the government does not willingly reverse a reform introduced earlier, but rather is forced to do so because the public is persuaded at the outset that the reform is not sus-tainable and acts accordingly, thereby bringing about the very conditions under which a reversal is unavoidable. It is on the second possibility that the chapter concentrates, in variations that span a reduction of tariffs, the introduction of a limited value-added tax to replace taxes on trade, and capital flight. Devising measures to rule out such equilibria—or at least to make the chances of a reversal seem slim—is evidently important, but perhaps the best one is not to launch reforms under the duress of a crisis.

Most of the second half of the book is concerned with the evaluation of 'projects', be they particular programmes of public expenditure, construed in the widest sense, or private undertakings. There are two reasons for devoting so much space to a topic that seems to have passed out of aca-demic fashion—unsurprisingly, it never found favour among actual policy makers. First, social cost–benefit analysis can and should be employed to impose a relentless discipline on decisions concerning how public funds are spent, both directly in the form of projects and indirectly through the approval of private ones, in a wide range of circumstances. For this pur-pose, the central concept of a shadow price must be exactly defined and the complete set of such prices must be estimated for practical use. Second, it turns out that shadow prices are also indispensable to the evaluation of any economic reform when producer prices deviate from shadow prices. It will be clear from the foregoing paragraphs that this latter state of affairs is the norm rather than the exception.

Chapter 8 provides a general introduction to this topic, the approach being kept strictly intuitive. The starting point is to lay out how a rational businessman, as a private agent, should evaluate the profitability of a pro-ject, as set out in any textbook. This general procedure is largely applicable to the social evaluation of projects, but with one vital difference: doing the calculations at market prices may yield the 'wrong' decision, in the sense of reducing rather than increasing welfare relative to choosing the relevant alternative. For, in practice, there are a variety of reasons why market prices almost invariably fail to measure social scarcities. To be sure of arriving at the right decision, therefore, one must use the 'right' prices, namely, shadow prices. One way of estimating them is to use partial

equilibrium analysis; but on closer examination this proves to be unsatisfactory. Hence, one turns perforce to procedures in which the shadow
prices of all goods and factors are mutually and simultaneously determined. The one adopted here closely follows that advocated by Little and
Mirrlees (1974), in which the world prices of traded goods play a central
role. It is presented at this point in a somewhat 'cookbook' fashion, with
a sketch of how it can be extended to evaluate the social profitability of
private projects.

The stage is thus set for a rigorous treatment of the subject in Chapter 9.
The groundwork involves defining what is meant by a small project, which
then yields, as a set of special cases, the shadow prices of all goods such
that each correctly measures the social scarcity of the good in question,
drawing on the discussion of Bergson–Samuelsonian welfare functions in
Chapter 4. Defined in this way, shadow prices permit the decentralization
of public decisions about projects, just as market prices yield an allocation
of resources through decentralized private decisions. The second step is to
set out a formal method for estimating the complete set of shadow prices,
choosing a framework that lends itself to (comparatively) simple exposition, without being unduly restrictive. All this is done and discussed in
considerable detail, in the course of which it becomes clear that shadow
prices need not be independent of the policies being pursued. The possibility that there is an intimate link between projects and policies introduces
an additional complication: a policy reform that is worthwhile on its
own merits—assessed at shadow prices, of course—should be undertaken
without regard to any project whose fate depends on the reform in question,
whereas any project must stand or fall by its social profitability under the
policy reform.

For all the generality of the approach laid out in Chapter 9, its application in practice requires a number of extensions of the basic framework.
As in standard textbooks on microeconomic theory, these have to do
with the date, the place, and the state of nature in which a commodity is available. These are the topics of Chapters 10–12, in that order. To
introduce time is to introduce discounting and hence that crucial variable,
the social discount rate. Its estimation involves answering the question:
where are the funds for projects coming from? The alternatives range
from reductions in private consumption or investment, the shelving of
other public sector projects, and additional taxation, to borrowing, especially from abroad. The process of estimation itself can run the gamut
from back-of-the-envelope calculations to the construction of fully blown,
many-period, general equilibrium models.

Space matters because the pattern of trade among locations depends on the pattern of transportation costs. Indeed, the 'natural' protection afforded by transportation costs can easily exceed that arising from tariffs and regulations, and may be so large as to rule out trade altogether, whether foreign or domestic. The presence of significant internal transportation costs means that what are normally thought of as (pure) exportable and importable goods must, in fact, be treated as mixtures of internationally traded goods and the non-tradable services of the transportation sector, a fact that must be correctly taken into account when estimating all shadow prices. Big transportation projects alter both patterns of trade and relative prices, market and shadow alike. High transportation costs also induce large swings in the domestic prices of tradables in response to internal shocks, such as droughts, pests, and floods.

The vagaries of nature, the unknown future course of world prices, and human fallibility in designing, constructing, and running plants and equipment all ensure that the stream of payoffs to a project is a stream of random variables. That is to say, both the technical performance of a project and the environment in which its returns are realized are subject to uncertainty, which holds also for the vector of shadow prices. Three important questions arise. First, how does the uncertainty surrounding these variables translate into uncertainty about a project's social profitability? Second, how are shadow prices to be estimated when the economy is beset by uncertainty? Third, in the event that the social profitability of a project is uncertain, is the use of a decision criterion based on expected values justifiable? These questions are addressed in detail in Chapter 12, where the institutional arrangements for spreading and sharing risks turn out to have a decisive influence on the answers to the second and third questions.

The discussion of big transportation projects in Chapter 11 also raises a general question: what happens if a project is 'large' in the sense of having a measurable impact on market prices and household incomes? This question is an especially awkward one, for it casts doubt on the validity of using shadow prices derived from an analysis of the effects of small changes, and hence also on the decentralization of decision making that they permit. Chapter 13 attempts to provide a defensible and practicable solution to this apparent conundrum. The basic idea is to combine two frameworks. For those goods or factors whose market prices would change appreciably, there is an appeal to the standard apparatus for analysing equilibrium in individual markets, in which consumers' and producers' surpluses naturally appear. For all the rest, there are just the shadow prices, estimated in the usual way. Making these frameworks compatible bedfellows is not an entirely straightforward business, and the details of the splicing are set out at length. Such an approach is evidently defensible only when at most two or three market prices would be substantially affected by a project; for the burden of the implicit assumptions of *ceteris paribus* rises rapidly with the number of such cases. Otherwise, there is nothing for it but to undertake a full-scale general equilibrium analysis.

At first sight, the last two chapters—on the land question and small-scale credit—fit less obviously into this scheme of things. Yet, both are examples of economic reforms in the broad sense of the term, and so fall under the rubric of evaluation advocated above. In defence of these particular choices to illustrate what is involved, suffice it to say that, first, both topics are evidently important, dealing as they do with rural inequality as well as with allocative efficiency, and second, I am familiar with them.

Land reform, the registration of plots, and the regulation of tenancy all involve property rights. The motives for changing the form of such rights and the distribution of claims to them are usually twofold: first, to improve welfare through redistribution alone, and second, to improve incentives and the efficiency with which resources are allocated. It should now be clear that it is invalid to evaluate such proposals at market prices. Indeed, to the extent that cropping patterns, techniques of cultivation, and aggregate income would change substantially—as the advocates of reform are keen to claim—the reforms in question should be treated as 'large' projects in the sense of Chapter 13. How to do this is set out at some length in Chapter 14. At the same time, one must not lose sight of the fact that land reform is a politically highly charged subject. The political economy of such reforms is discussed in some detail, both in historical perspective and with the aim of assessing the chances of success in the present.

Small-scale credit has become *à la mode* in policy-making circles, perhaps in part because making subsidized loans to the poor poses a far less obvious threat to the existing social order than does reforming property rights in land. In fact, attempts to drive the traditional moneylender out of business, or at least to curtail the scope of his operations, are of long standing. One widespread measure was to compete with him directly by pushing organized banking into rural areas. The evidence suggests that he has accommodated quite well to this challenge, the banks rarely being up to the job of providing credit at low effective costs, and that credit designated for the needy has often gone to the well-to-do. Newer initiatives, such as the *Grameen Bank*, have sought to overcome both of these drawbacks. Whether they have actually done so, or promise to do so, at a tolerable cost to the Exchequer is strongly debatable. In any event, none of these programmes may be exempted from an evaluation at shadow prices.

This overall schema will not please everyone. Nothing is said about population, health, nutrition, and education, and while distributional considerations are certainly not forgotten, they serve here largely as hand-maidens in the task of evaluating economic reforms. Technology and industrial policy get equally short shrift, as do private foreign investment and privatization. The framework of Chapters 8–13 can be jigged so as to address some of the questions that arise, but it seems fair to say that, so used, it will often operate rather like a procrustean bed. The reader will search in vain for a discussion of the environment and that nebulous concept, sustainability. Even within the realm of public economics itself, there is nothing to be found in this text on social security, insurance, and disaster relief. In omitting these topics, I deny not their importance, but rather my ability to handle them satisfactorily.

To close, a brief word on how this text can be used. There is probably too much material even for a two-semester sequence. One broadly based course would comprise Chapters 1–13. If time is especially short, one could focus directly on public economics, namely, Chapters 4–13, with Chapter 1 providing the essential underpinnings where trade is concerned. Another variant would be to pare down the detailed treatment of cost–benefit ana-lysis by dropping Chapters 10–12 in order to accommodate the applications to land reform and small-scale finance. There are exercises to all chapters, many of which are fairly demanding and quite time-consuming. It is essen-tial that students tackle them on their own and then discuss their solutions in class. At this point, it is also usual to say that the text will be suitable for able undergraduates in their final year, presumably in the hope of increas-ing sales. I will go no further than this: such students should profit from a careful reading of the less technical parts of most chapters, but rather few will have the time and experience to make a serious attempt at mastering the tougher sections, let alone the exercises.

1. International Trade: Theory

In *Capital and Growth*, Hicks (1965) writes, 'Underdevelopment economics is a [...] practical subject which must expect to call upon any branch of theory [...] which has any relevance to it. If there is any branch of theory which is especially relevant to it, it is the Theory of International Trade' (pp. 3–4)—authority indeed to begin with a chapter on trade in a book dealing with development policy.[1] We begin, therefore, with a very brief account of received theory, paying close attention to the claim that free trade is best. Since the theoretical basis for this claim can be regarded as involving an appeal to the first fundamental theorem of welfare economics, any attempt to refute its validity as a prescription for policy must concentrate on the possible sources of market failure. Those of particular interest in the context of development policy include non-convexities in production, which often spell trouble for the assumption of perfect competition. Especially important are externalities in production, which undermine the theorem even under competitive behaviour. These, and their remedies, are taken up in Section 1.2, with special reference to the so-called 'infant industry' argument.

The development of many industries, infant or otherwise, also faces hurdles erected by the government itself, in the form of interventions that are not aimed at the relief of market failure, but rather have some other motivation, such as raising revenue or favouring a particular interest group. The distortions caused by interventions of this kind are said to be *policy-imposed* (Bhagwati, 1971), in contrast to those arising from market failure. One important example in practice is provided by the government's influence on wage setting in certain sectors of the economy, a topic which is addressed in Section 1.3.

In general, the right countervailing measures to deal with market failure or potentially damaging interventions that are fixed features of the policy-making landscape will depend on what fiscal instruments are actually at the government's disposal. The discussion of remedies will introduce the *principle of targeting*, according to which a distortion should be attacked as closely as possible to its source and financed by non-distortionary means, in order to avoid causing distortionary losses elsewhere. Lump-sum transfers are the essential auxiliary means here, and without them, the principle

---

[1] In an aside, he directs the interested reader to Hicks (1959, 1964).

is no longer secure. A great deal therefore depends on whether the government can actually employ lump-sum taxes; for if it is unable to do so, departures from free trade may form part of the (second-best) package of measures. It is an awkward fact of life that governments are very reluctant to impose lump-sum taxes, preferring instead to resort to distortionary means to raise revenues and distribute subsidies.[2] The public finance aspects of trade policy are briefly taken up in Section 1.4, in the form of the question of whether a sound case can be made for the taxation of international trade.

1.1. Received Theory

If a country faces parametrically given world prices $p^* = (p_1^*, \ldots, p_m^*)$ for all tradable goods, international trade offers it the opportunity of exchanging one such good for any other at the fixed ratio defined by their world prices. In effect, trade is a technology whereby one such good can be produced from any other under constant returns to scale (CRS). In examining the effects of introducing such a technology on output and welfare, it is important to distinguish between those of a once-and-for-all nature and those involving a permanent change in the economy's rate of growth, these being labelled henceforth as 'level' and 'growth' effects, respectively.

1.1.1. The Static Gains From Trade

Beginning with the domestic economy, suppose that: (i) the country's markets are complete and all agents act on the assumption that none has any measurable influence over prices; (ii) the technologies for the domestic production of all goods are convex; and (iii) consumers' preferences are continuous, locally non-satiated, and convex. Under autarky, therefore, not only will a competitive equilibrium exist, but it will also be Pareto-efficient. The introduction of free trade can be viewed as involving nothing more than an addition to the set of available technologies, and hence an enlargement of the production possibility set. Since its introduction preserves the convexity of both, any resulting competitive equilibrium that arises under the above conditions will also be Pareto-efficient.

---

[2] The international trade fraternity sometimes shies away from the public finance aspects of the questions at hand. As an introduction to their treatment of distortions and policy instruments, Bhagwati *et al.* (1998), for example, write, 'Nor will we consider questions of second-best analysis which arise from not being able to utilize lump-sum transfer...' (p. 286). For a fine survey of the literature on precisely this problem, see Dixit (1985).

It remains to be shown that free trade is superior to autarky. As a preliminary, we invoke the vital assumption that the government can make unrestricted lump-sum transfers, so that all the conditions required for the validity of the second fundamental welfare theorem are satisfied. We sketch the argument heuristically in two steps. Starting from the competitive allocation under autarky, let each individual's chosen consumption bundle become his endowment in an exchange economy, but now with the additional opportunity to trade at world prices. As each and every individual can still obtain the bundle he chose under autarky by simply consuming it, none will be worse-off; and if any international trade actually takes place, at least one individual must be strictly better-off, as a simple matter of revealed preference. At the second step, we must relax the assumption that domestic production remains unchanged in the face of these new opportunities. If international trade actually occurs in equilibrium in the fictive exchange economy just described, the vector p^* will not be the same as the corresponding price vector ruling under autarky, so that some marginal rates of transformation (MRT) under autarky will no longer be equal to consumers' marginal rates of indifferent substitution, and the equilibrium of the fictive exchange economy will not be Pareto-efficient, there being further potential gains from reallocating resources in domestic production. Given the availability of unrestricted lump-sum transfers, these gains can be realized in a competitive allocation without anyone being worse-off than he was in the fictive exchange equilibrium, from which it follows that the said competitive allocation under free trade is strictly Pareto-superior to any competitive allocation under autarky, and hence to any allocation under autarky.[3]

In view of the fact that lump-sum transfers may be impracticable, it is important to ask whether this result will continue to hold in their absence. Suppose, therefore, that the government's choice of instruments is confined to taxes and subsidies on goods and factors, albeit without any restrictions on the individual rates. If, under free trade, there exists a set of taxes and subsidies such that each and every consumer attains the same level of utility he enjoys under autarky, while the government's net revenue remains non-negative, then the desired result indeed holds. One policy that comes immediately to mind in this connection is to leave consumers facing autarky prices under free trade, but to confront producers with

---

[3] If preferences or the production possibility frontier are not smooth everywhere, the MRS and the MRT will not be defined at the corresponding 'kinks', and the claim must be weakened to: 'free trade is not Pareto-inferior to autarky', in order to allow for the possibility that the allocation sticks fast at a kink.

world prices p^* for goods. Dixit and Norman (1980: 79–80) prove that the government's net revenue is indeed non-negative in this case. As they remark, however, there is an important caveat: If there are fixed factors specific to industries, and if there are CRS in production only when these factors are included in the lists of inputs employed by the firms in question, then pure profits, if any, will accrue to such factors. The absence of any restrictions on tax rates is therefore equivalent to the ability to tax the profits of different industries at unrestrictedly different rates, which casts the assumption in a somewhat different light. In any event, the taxation of pure profits will arise again in Section 1.4 and again in Chapter 4.

So much for the ranking of free trade and autarky. There is, however, a still stronger claim that can be proved under the above assumptions, namely, that free trade is superior to any other alternative. For present purposes, it is unnecessary to formulate the argument in its full generality, the underlying logic being most easily grasped in the special case where there are just two produced goods, both of which are fully tradable, and a single representative consumer. We assume that both the technology and preferences are nicely smooth, with all factors being necessary in production and all goods likewise in consumption. Given the assumption that the technologies for producing the goods domestically are convex, the production possibility frontier (PPF) will be concave, and it is drawn as strictly so in Fig. 1.1.[4] Consider any feasible vector of outputs $y = (y_1, y_2)$. This can be transformed into any consumption bundle $x = (x_1, x_2)$ satisfying

$$p^*x \leq p^*y \tag{1.1}$$

through the CRS 'technology' offered by international trade at the parametric prices p^*, the weak inequality allowing for free disposal. The case where Eqn (1.1) holds as an equality defines the so-called availability line at domestic output y and world prices p^*. It is clear that given any y, there will be gains from international trade, except in the unlikely case where the marginal rate of indifferent substitution (MRS) at the output bundle in question just happens to be the same as the exchange ratio (p_1^*/p_2^*). As drawn, Fig. 1.1 depicts the usual case, in which there are such gains, with the arbitrary choice of y falling on the PPF in order to make the point that efficiency in production does not suffice to ensure a full optimum.

---

[4] If the technologies exhibit CRS and are identical up to a scalar multiple, the PPF will be linear, a claim that the reader should prove.

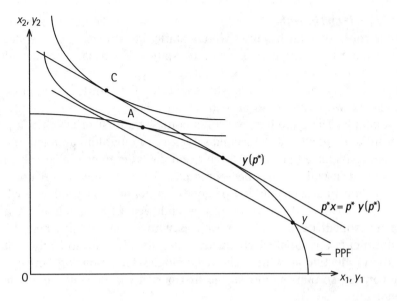

Figure 1.1. The superiority of free trade: the standard case

Among all feasible vectors y, we must now establish which is optimal, given that trade at prices p^* is an option. In the absence of satiation in consumption, the global optimum is attained on that availability line which is farthest from the origin, that is, on that line corresponding to the output vector for which the value of output at world prices, p^*y, is maximal, say $y(p^*)$. The latter is attained if and only if the $|\text{MRT}|$ in domestic production at $y(p^*)$ is equal to the exchange ratio (p_1^*/p_2^*), as depicted in Fig. 1.1. Given the availability line through $y(p^*)$, the representative consumer's welfare is maximized when he obtains the bundle denoted by point C. Turning to decentralized allocations, since consumers and producers face the price vector p^* under free trade, it follows that in any resulting competitive equilibrium,

$$|\text{MRS}| = |\text{MRT}| = p_1^*/p_2^*, \tag{1.2}$$

which is precisely the necessary and sufficient condition for a social optimum under the assumptions listed above. For reference, the competitive equilibrium under autarky is also depicted, namely as point A, where $y^A = x^A$ and

$$|\text{MRS}^A| = |\text{MRT}^A| \neq p_1^*/p_2^*,$$

with the consumption bundle C being strictly preferred to A.

1.1.2. Trade and Growth

The account thus far has been wholly static; but it is readily extended to cover more than one period. Since our purpose here is to set out ideas and principles, two periods will suffice to begin with: the first may be thought of as the present and the second as the future, at the close of which the world comes to an end. In all other respects, too, things are kept simple. There are but two commodities, the first of which is a pure consumption good and the second serves as an input into production. The former is assumed to be non-storable and the latter to be usable only after the period in which it has been produced. Let $y_i(t)$ and $x_i(t)$ denote the output and final consumption of good i in period t, respectively, where $x_2(1) = x_2(2) = 0$. The economy is endowed with an initial stock of the investment good, $z_2(1)$, as well as with labour in each period. All endowments are supplied completely inelastically, but are fully mobile across productive activities. The technologies for producing both goods are convex, so that the PPF in the first period will be concave. Let it be denoted by

$$\psi[y_1(1), y_2(1); z_2(1), L(1)] = 0, \tag{1.3}$$

where $L(1)$ is the economy's endowment of labour in period 1. Since, under autarky, $x_1(1) = y_1(1)$, the locus $\psi(\cdot) = 0$ represents all efficient pairs of consumption and investment (which equals savings) in that period.

For simplicity, let inputs of the investment good be wholly used up in current production, that is, let capital take the circulating form. Then $y_2(1)$ is the stock thereof available to firms for use in period 2. Since the world comes to an end thereafter, only good 1 will be produced in the second period, and then in the amount

$$y_1(2) = f_1[z_2(2), L(2)], \tag{1.4}$$

where the production function $f_1(\cdot)$ is assumed to have all the relevant well-behaved properties, namely, that it is strictly increasing, smooth, and concave, with both inputs being necessary in production. Since $L(2)$ is exogenously given, $f_1(\cdot)$ will be strictly concave in $z_2(2)$ [$= y_2(1)$] alone. Under autarky, the set of all feasible inter-temporal consumption vectors is therefore given by

$$S^A = \{(x_1(1), x_1(2)): \psi[y_1(1), y_2(1); z_2(1), L(1)] \leq 0,$$
$$x_1(1) = y_1(1), x_1(2) = y_1(2) = f_1[y_2(1), L(2)]\}, \tag{1.5}$$

which is clearly convex under the above assumptions. The upper boundary of S^A is none other than the consumption possibility frontier (CPF^A) under autarky in this two-period setting. Given a representative consumer whose preferences can be represented by the utility function $u[(x_1(1), x_1(2)]$, the associated competitive equilibrium can be obtained by solving the following problem:

Let a benevolent dictator choose $(x_1(1), x_1(2), y_1(1), y_1(2), y_2(1))$ so as to

maximize $u[(x_1(1), x_1(2)]$

subject to $((x_1(1), x_1(2)) \in S^A, (x_1(1), x_1(2)) \geq 0.$ (1.6)

All of the above elements are laid out in Fig. 1.2. The PPF in period 1 is drawn in the NE quadrant. Any point thereon is an efficient pair of feasible choices in consumption and investment in period 1. With investment, $y_2(1) = z_2(2)$, so chosen, the output of the consumption good in period 2 is determined by the production function represented by the curve $f_1[z_2(2), L(2)]$, as depicted in the NW quadrant. Using the 45° line through the origin in the SW quadrant, this value of $y_1(2)$ is projected onto the SE quadrant, where, together with the associated level of consumption in period 1, it forms a point on the CPF^A. The optimum is depicted as point A, where an indifference curve is tangent to the CPF^A. The corresponding point on the PPF in period 1 is denoted as point B. This allocation will arise as a competitive equilibrium, in which the |MRS| at A is equal to one plus the rate of interest and the absolute value of the slope of the PPF at B will be the price of the consumption good in terms of the investment good in period 1, a claim that the reader should check.

Now let the economy face trading opportunities in goods in period 1 at the relative world price (p_1^*/p_2^*). Without loss of generality, and also plausibly for less developed countries (LDCs), in which the producer-good sectors typically have relatively high costs, let (p_1^*/p_2^*) be larger than the relative domestic price that would rule under autarky, that is to say, the country has a comparative advantage in producing the consumer good in period 1. Since the world comes to an end at the close of period 2, no country will produce the investment good, and hence there will be no international trade, in that period. Following the same steps in the heuristic argument with which we began this section, let production in the first period remain at B, and draw the availability line with slope (p_1^*/p_2^*) through B, which is denoted as BB'. By projecting any point lying on BB', first, onto the NW quadrant to yield $y_1(2)$, and thence onto the SE quadrant, it is immediately clear that, for any given level of availability of

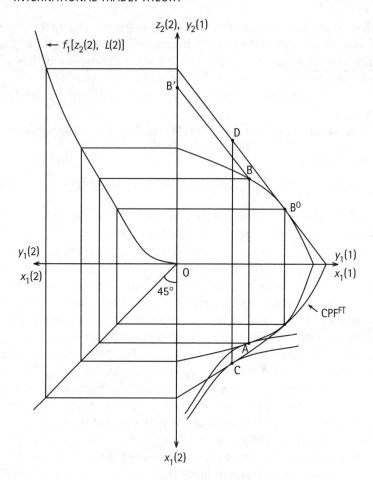

Figure 1.2. Allocations under autarky and free trade in a two-period setting

good 2 for use in period 2, and hence for any given level of consumption in period 2, consumption in period 1 will be higher by trading the consumption good for the investment good in period 1 than by utilizing the domestic transformation possibilities exhibited by the PPF to the NW of B.

Proceeding to the second step, in which production is free to vary, what, then, is the global optimum? Observe that in the presence of trading opportunities at parametric prices, decisions concerning current production and savings become separable; for by maximizing the value of output at world prices in period 1, the highest availability line in that period is attained, from which an appropriate bundle of the consumption good in period 1 and the input of the producer good in period 2, $z_2(2)$, can then be chosen, where $z_2(2)$ is now the algebraic sum of the domestic output and imports of good 2 in period 1. Stated precisely, the optimization process involves, first, choosing the output vector $(y_1^0(1), y_2^0(1))$, which is depicted as point B^0 in Fig. 1.2, where an availability line with slope (p_1^*/p_2^*) is tangent to the domestic PPF under autarky,[5] and then solving the following problem:

Choose $x_1(1), x_2(2), y_1(2)$, and $z_2(2)$ so as to

$$\text{maximize } u[(x_1(1), x_1(2)] \tag{1.7}$$

subject to: the availability line through B^0 in period 1,

$$p_1^* x_1(1) + p_2^* z_2(2) = p_1^* y_1^0(1) + p_2^* y_2^0(1), \quad (x_1(1), z_2(2)) \geq 0, \tag{1.8}$$

and the ensuing availability of consumption in period 2,

$$x_1(2) = y_1(2) = f_1[z_2(2), L(2)]. \tag{1.9}$$

The constraints (1.8) and (1.9) generate the CPF in the presence of trading opportunities at world prices, which is drawn as CPF^T in Fig. 1.2. It has just one point in common with CPF^A, namely, that corresponding to B^0 itself, and it dominates CPF^A everywhere else. Since A lies inside CPF^T in the presence of trading opportunities at p^*, it follows that A is not optimal under free trade, there being feasible consumption pairs that are strictly preferred to it. The optimal consumption vector is depicted in Fig. 1.2 as C, which results from the choice of the bundle D on the availability line through B^0. As depicted, investment is higher, and consumption lower, in period 1 under free trade than under autarky; but the normality of consumption in both periods implies that consumption could be higher in both.

While intuitively illuminating where the relationship between the set of inter-temporal consumption possibilities and trade is concerned, the two-period model has the drawback that it does not permit one to distinguish between transitory and permanent effects on the growth rate of the economy. Nor does such a distinction become possible by stretching out the number of periods when the horizon remains finite; for there can be no steady-state growth path so long as the horizon is finite. In order to deal with this question, we must therefore turn to an infinite-horizon setting.[6] What follows draws heavily on Srinivasan (2000).

[5] Complete specialization is also a possibility, of course, but for the purposes of exposition, nothing essential hinges on assuming an interior solution.

[6] If the horizon is long enough, the Turnpike theorem tells us that the growth path will remain in the neighbourhood of the von Neumann ray most of the time, so that comparisons of the rates of growth associated with the said rays under autarky and free trade, respectively, would be sensible.

Consider the Cass (1965)–Koopmans (1965) model, in which a single intermediate good is produced under CRS by means of capital and labour, output per worker, y, being a neoclassically well-behaved function of capital per worker, $f(k)$. Each unit of this intermediate good can be transformed into either one unit of current consumption or one unit of investment, in both cases at no cost, so that under autarky the |MRT| between the consumption and investment good is unity. The population is growing at the steady rate n and capital is subject to radioactive decay at the rate δ. A benevolent dictator is assumed to choose a consumption path $x(t)$ so as to maximize the welfare functional

$$W = \int_0^\infty e^{-\rho t} u(x(t)) \, dt, \tag{1.10}$$

where ρ is the pure rate of time preference and the felicity function $u(x)$ is assumed to be strictly concave. Under autarky, the sum of $x(t)$ and gross investment per worker, $z(t)$, will be equal to the current output of the intermediate good, so that the scarcity constraint on the dictator's problem is

$$x(t) + z(t) = f(k(t)), \tag{1.11}$$

where gross investment may be used to augment the capital stock per worker, as well as to equip new entrants into the workforce and make good the depreciation on the existing capital stock:

$$z(t) = \dot{k}(t) + (n + \delta)k(t), \tag{1.12}$$

and the value of $k(0)$ is given. It can be shown that the solution to this problem converges asymptotically to a steady-state path along which the economy grows at the rate n, with capital and consumption per worker taking the (constant) values satisfying

$$f'(k^{*A}) = (n + \delta + \rho) \tag{1.13}$$

and

$$x^{*A} = f(k^{*A}) - (n + \delta)k^{*A}.\text{[7]} \tag{1.14}$$

---

[7] Observe that k^{*A} will be smaller that the so-called 'golden-age' value, which corresponds to the case where the level of consumption per head in the steady state is maximized, if and only if $\rho > 0$.

Equation (1.13) states that the marginal product of capital in the steady state covers not only the depreciation of that stock and the requirement that each of the additional workers also be equipped with k^{*A}, but also the opportunity cost of investment that arises from the pure impatience to consume. The intuition for this result is as follows. The level of gross investment per head in any steady state is $(n + \delta)k$. Since $f(k)$ is strictly concave and satisfies the Inada conditions, it will intersect the line $(n+\delta)k$ at just one positive level of k, say k_1, as depicted in Fig. 1.3. Hence, consumption per head cannot grow without bound; and in a steady state, it will be positive if and only if $k < k_1$. Consider, therefore, a small unit increase in the steady-state value of k, which is realized by a once-and-for-all reduction in x of one unit. This investment will yield a permanent change in the level of consumption per head in the amount $[f'(k)-(n+\delta)]$. Given that such small changes have no effect on the marginal utility of consumption, the present value of this stream when discounted at the rate ρ is proportional to $[f'(k) - (n + \delta)]/\rho$. Hence, the said investment just breaks even if and only if $[f'(k) - (n + \delta)]/\rho = 1$, a simple rearrangement of which yields Eqn (1.13). Equation (1.14) then follows at once from Eqn (1.11), x^{*A} being depicted in Fig. 1.3 as the vertical line segment AC.

Now suppose that the consumer and investment goods can be traded at parametric world prices, with each unit of the former costing p^* units of the latter, where $p^* > 1$ in keeping with the case depicted in Fig. 1.2. In the face of these trading opportunities, the economy will therefore have a comparative advantage in the consumption good: the whole of the current output of the intermediate good will be transformed into the latter and an appropriate amount will be exported in exchange for the investment good. For any given level of k, the availability lines for consumption and gross investment corresponding to autarky and free trade, respectively, will be as depicted in Fig. 1.4, and Eqn (1.11) will be replaced by

$$x(t) + (1/p^*) \cdot z(t) = f(k(t)). \qquad (1.15)$$

Starting from any value of $k(0)$, the optimal path will once more converge to a steady-state in which the economy grows at the rate n, now with values of capital and consumption per worker satisfying

$$f'(k^{*T}) = (n + \delta + \rho)/p^* \qquad (1.16)$$

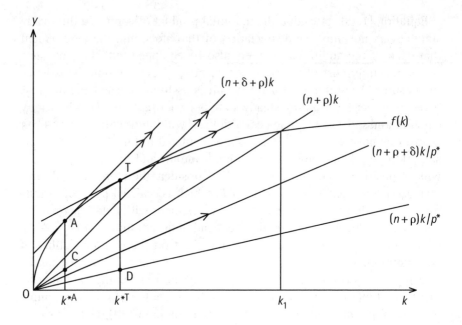

Figure 1.3. Steady states under autarky and free trade

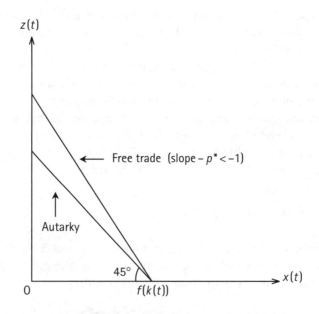

Figure 1.4. Feasible pairs of consumption and gross investment under autarky and free trade

and

$$x^{*T} = f(k^{*T}) - \left[(n + \delta)k^{*T}\right]/p^*. \tag{1.17}$$

The intuition underlying Eqn (1.16) is exactly analogous to that underlying Eqn (1.13), the only change being that with the economy possessing a comparative advantage in the consumption good, a permanent increase in k of one unit now requires a once-and-for-all reduction in consumption per head of only $1/p^*$ (<1) units, while yielding a permanent increase in consumption per head in the amount of $[f'(k) - (n + \delta)/p^*]$. Comparing Eqns (1.13) and (1.16), it is seen that the common factor $1/p^*$ arising from this advantageous opportunity induces a higher steady-state value of k than under autarky.[8] It is also clear from Eqn (1.16) that k^{*T} is increasing in p^* in the regime where $p^* \geq 1$. Differentiating Eqn (1.17) w.r.t. p^* and using Eqn (1.16), we obtain

$$\frac{dx^{*T}}{dp^*} = \frac{\rho}{\rho^*}\frac{dk^{*T}}{dp^*} + \frac{(n + \delta)k^{*T}}{p^{*2}} > 0,$$

so that the level of consumption per head in the steady state is higher under free trade than under autarky, where x^{*T} is depicted in Fig. 1.3 as the line segment TD. Under the above assumptions, therefore, the introduction of free trade produces a level effect, but not a permanent growth effect.

As noted above, the assumption that is responsible for the absence of a growth effect is that any neoclassically well-behaved technology $f(k)$ satisfies the (upper) Inada condition $\lim_{k\to\infty} f'(k) = 0$. As k rises indefinitely, the gross social pay-off to further increases therein must eventually fall below the critical level $(n+\delta+\rho)$ under autarky, a result that access to free trade does not overturn in a qualitative way, although the critical level falls to $(n+\delta+\rho)/p^*$. One way of freeing the economy from a stationary, long-run condition in per capita terms is to impose a positive lower bound on the marginal product of capital, a simple formulation of which is

$$f(k) = g(k) + \beta k, \tag{1.18}$$

where $g(k)$ is well behaved and β is a positive constant. Beginning with autarky, if $(n+\delta+\rho) > \beta$, then Eqns (1.13) and (1.14) will continue to hold; but if $(n + \delta + \rho) < \beta$, then the optimum path will involve unbounded

---

[8] Srinivasan (2000) analyses the case where $p^* < 1$, so that the country specializes in the investment good. In this case, free trade will have no effect on the steady-state value of k, the term $1/p^*$ no longer appearing on the RHS of Eqn (1.16).

growth in k and x. Suppose, for example, that $u(x)$ takes the isoelastic form $x^{\eta+1}/\eta + 1$, where $\eta \leq 0$. It can then be shown that k and x will eventually grow at the steady rate $[\beta - (n+\delta+\rho)]/|\eta| > 0$. Access to trade modifies the above condition for unbounded growth in k and x to occur; for, with the relevant $|MRT|$ between consumption goods and investment goods being p^* rather than unity, the opportunity cost of an additional unit of current consumption in terms of investment at any level of k is now p^*, and the critical condition becomes $p^*\beta = n+\delta+\rho$. If, as assumed here, the economy has a comparative advantage in the consumption good ($p^* > 1$), and if the condition $p^*\beta > n + \delta + \rho > \beta$ holds, then the 'technology' offered by trade raises the net pay-off to saving sufficiently strongly that, whereas k and x would converge to stationary values under autarky, they will grow without limit under free trade. In the case where $u(x)$ is isoelastic, k and x will grow at the rate $[p^*\beta - (n+\delta+\rho)]/|\eta|$ in the steady state. With the positive floor β under the marginal product of capital, the introduction of free trade can therefore have quite radical growth effects on the optimal growth path, and the theme 'Trade and Growth' is no misnomer.

The importance for long-run growth of being able to obtain investment goods on advantageous terms through trade also emerges in a quite different setting examined by Srinivasan (2000). This is the Fel'dman (1928)–Mahalanobis (1955) planning model, in which each good is produced under CRS by means of capital alone.[9] It therefore possesses a feature common to models in which growth does not peter out, namely, that the returns to at least one reproducible input do not go to zero as its use becomes indefinitely large, Eqn (1.18) being one such simple representation. In Srinivasan's variation of the Fel'dman–Mahalanobis model, the consumption and investment goods sectors each produce two 'intermediate' goods of each type, and aggregate consumption and investment, respectively, are both Cobb–Douglas indices whose elements are the corresponding pair of intermediates. Capital, once installed, can be shifted, but only within each of the two sectors. Under autarky, all four goods will be produced domestically; for both types of each good are necessary to produce the corresponding aggregate. With a fixed proportional allocation of the stream of aggregate investment between the domestic consumption and investment good sectors, the introduction of free trade in consumption goods alone produces only level effects in the long run, with the economy specializing in the production of one of them and trading some of it for

---

[9] One may think of the capital–labour ratio being fixed in each line of production, with an indefinitely large reserve army of labour to draw upon in the background.

the other. Free trade in investment goods, however, induces an increase in the economy's long-run rate of growth, the underlying reason being analogous to the condition $p^* > 1$ analysed above. For by specializing in the right investment good and trading appropriately for the other, it is always possible to increase the index of aggregate investment for any given level of the capital stock in the investment goods sector, relative to autarky. With a fixed proportional allocation of the stream of gross investment between the two sectors, the assumption that the marginal product of capital is constant in all lines of production then yields a permanently higher rate of growth of the investment goods sector, and hence of the economy as a whole.

Pulling all these results together, one is led to the conclusion that, since the logic underpinning them is unassailable, any departure from free trade must be justified with reference to plausible departures from the assumptions on which the results rest. Even then, it should be emphasized that some departures might not, by themselves, suffice to overturn the desirability of free trade when the government has the right instruments at its disposal. The basis for this assertion will become clearer in the sections that follow.

1.2. Market Failure

As noted in the introduction, the claim that free trade is best can be thought of as involving an appeal to the first fundamental theorem of welfare economics. Any attempt to refute it will therefore involve market failure in one form or another. We confine ourselves to the possible sources of market failure that seem most pertinent to development policy.

1.2.1. Non-convexities in Production
One consequence of non-convexities is that a competitive equilibrium may not exist, with some agents able to act in the knowledge that they possess some, perhaps considerable, influence over prices. This can come about, for example, if there are increasing returns to scale in particular lines of production and transport costs are so high as to provide domestic firms with a comfortable measure of 'natural' protection from foreign competition. Certain branches of transportation, power, and communications come to mind at once in this connection, and we shall take up this important case in some detail in Chapters 11 and 13. There are also circumstances in which it is plausible to assume that competitive behaviour will prevail, but the

non-convexity has its source in the absence of certain markets: external effects without clear property rights constitute an important example. That being so, a competitive equilibrium—should one exist—will not, in general, be Pareto-efficient. In keeping with the theme of this chapter, the emphasis in what follows will be on goods that are, in principle at least, readily tradable. The particular case where there are economies of scale external to the firm itself, and firms are numerous, will be discussed in some detail.

One aspect of technology which naturally comes to the fore in discussions of development policy, especially in relation to industry, is learning-by-doing: today's infant is supposed to be given a helping hand, so that it can reach vigorous maturity. There are basically two ways in which such learning can come about. Drawing upon studies of the airframe industry in the Second World War, Arrow (1962) proposed that the marginal cost of production depends on the total number of units ever produced. Kaldor (1962), noting the intellectual challenge involved in reading just one of Arrow's papers, formulated an alternative, in which marginal cost depends on the length of time elapsed since the very inception of production. Each surely captures an important element of the truth. At the beginning of a production run of a new item, managers and workers will have the blueprints to guide them and the machinery for the assembly line, as well as a stock of past experience of a general kind; but the exact details of how best to lay out, schedule, and execute the work at hand must be learned by actually doing it. If practice indeed makes perfect, successive units will be produced faster and with less waste. All this involves time, of course, but the key point is that the tasks are repeated over and over again. Over the longer run, however, new products must be introduced and old ones modified, perhaps with accompanying changes in the production process. The success with which this can be done surely depends heavily on the stock of past experience embodied in the managers, engineers, and workers. More importantly still, from the development perspective, is the fact that success breeds success through the accumulation of experience. Ordering and assimilating the knowledge so gained takes time rather than the mere repetition of a set task.

Now consider the case of an entrepreneur who wants to start up a line of business in which neither she nor anyone else in the economy has any direct experience. Despite this drawback, such a project might be not only technically feasible, but also actually profitable, even at world prices—provided there is a pool of engineers and skilled workers to draw upon, and all parties exert themselves sufficiently strongly to slide well down the learning curve. That being so, then in a world of complete markets, and with all relevant information being symmetrically held, what this entrepreneur needs is the services not of a lobbyist to obtain a protective tariff, but rather of a bank to finance both the physical investment in plant and equipment, and the investment in learning needed to achieve profitability over the long run. This rather pat conclusion invites the rejoinder that no economy on earth enjoys a complete set of markets, and that LDCs are especially far removed from this ideal, a fact that has much to do with the costs of acquiring information and enforcing contracts. Indeed, both adverse selection and moral hazard arise quite naturally in the example discussed here. A bank would have to worry about attracting the 'right' sort of entrepreneurs in the first place and then giving them adequate incentives to perform well in establishing and running the business. Such problems plague even economies with well-developed financial systems, as the Savings and Loan debacle in the United States in the 1980s vividly demonstrates.

To compound matters, the above account of learning-by-doing points to another kind potential market failure. To the extent that the process of learning generates knowledge and skills that are not specific to the firm in question, an externality will arise. For through the very act of producing, the firm enlarges the pool of qualified engineers, managers, and workers available to other firms, both existing and potential, yet without being able to appropriate the associated rents thereto. Stated in this way, the problem has a classical ring to it, with a classical remedy, to be discussed in Section 1.2.2.

Learning-by-doing is not the only source of positive externalities in production. It is often asserted that firms in related branches of industry frequently exhibit a strong tendency towards spatial agglomeration, which leads to economies through the attraction of common suppliers and a pool of skilled workers. When a firm joins the agglomeration or expands its existing production therein, it deepens the common pooling, and hence reduces the other firms' costs. This possibility, which was first analysed by Marshall (1920), involves an externality to the individual firm which is specific to the industry. Since individual firms are unable to capture the external benefits arising from their activities, each is likely to produce too little from the social point of view.

In one formulation, the strength of the external effects of agglomeration depends on the aggregate inputs of capital, K, and labour, L, employed in the industry in question, and manifests itself as an efficiency factor ϕ in the production function at the level of the individual firm. The output of the ith firm is, therefore,

$$y_i = \phi(K, L) \cdot f(k_i, l_i), \quad \forall i, \tag{1.19}$$

where k_i and l_i are its choice of inputs of capital and labour, respectively, and $f(\cdot)$ is assumed to exhibit the usual well-behaved properties, including CRS. Let the firm face parametric prices (p, r, w) for output and inputs, and let it take the input decisions of other firms as given. If the firm also takes prices as parametrically given, the first-order conditions for its profits to be a maximum are

$$p \cdot [(\partial \phi / \partial K) f(\cdot) + \phi(\cdot) \partial f / \partial k_i] - r = 0 \tag{1.20}$$

and

$$p \cdot [(\partial \phi / \partial L) f(\cdot) + \phi(\cdot) \partial f / \partial l_i] - w = 0, \tag{1.21}$$

where the terms involving the derivatives of $\phi(\cdot)$, which are positive, reflect that part of the effect of firm i's activities on collective efficiency which i itself internalizes. What this calculus ignores, of course, is the effects of changes in ϕ on the output, and hence on the profits, of all other firms. Given that firm i is small, the change in the industry's aggregate profits induced by a marginal (unit) increase in k_i at i's (private) optimum is, using the envelope theorem, $\left[p \cdot (\partial \phi / \partial K) \sum_{j \neq i} f(k_j, i_j)\right]$. Assuming that there are no other departures from the conditions needed to ensure a first-best allocation, the first-order conditions for a social optimum are, therefore,

$$p \cdot \left\{ (\partial \phi / \partial K) \left[\sum_{j \neq i} f(k_j, l_j) + f(k_j, l_j) \right] + \phi \cdot (\partial f / \partial k_i) \right\} - r = 0, \quad \forall i \tag{1.22}$$

and

$$p \cdot \left\{ (\partial \phi / \partial L) \left[\sum_{j \neq i} f(k_j, l_j) + f(k_j, l_j) \right] + \phi \cdot (\partial f / \partial l_i) \right\} - w = 0, \quad \forall i. \tag{1.23}$$

A comparison of Eqns (1.22) and (1.23) with their counterparts (1.20) and (1.21) reveals at once that the individual firm employs too little capital and labour, relative to the social optimum.

In the present setting, we can go a step further; for in the absence of appropriate intervention, the competitive equilibrium will induce an allocation that does not even lie on the PPF. In order to see this, observe that under the above assumptions, the economy will be productively efficient if and only if the marginal rate of technical substitution (MRTS) is the same everywhere. Suppose, therefore, that whereas industry 1 is not subject to such externalities, so that ϕ_1 is a constant, industry 2 is characterized by them. By virtue of the assumption that all firms in each industry have access to the same CRS technology, the necessary and sufficient condition for productive efficiency is

$$\frac{\partial f_1/\partial L_1}{\partial f_1/\partial K_1} = \frac{(\partial \phi_2^0/\partial L_2) \cdot f_2(K_2, L_2) + \phi_2^0(\partial f_2(K_2, L_2)/\partial L_2)}{(\partial \phi_2^0/\partial K_2) \cdot f_2(K_2, L_2) + \phi_2^0(\partial f_2(K_2, L_2)/\partial K_2)}, \qquad (1.24)$$

where the RHS is the expression obtained by dividing Eqn (1.23) by Eqn (1.22) and the superscript 0 denotes that ϕ_2 is evaluated when the employment of capital and labour in the industry take their socially optimal levels. Under perfect competition, however, the |MRTS| in industry 2 is equal to the wage–rental ratio as given by Eqns (1.20) and (1.21), so that

$$\frac{\partial f_1/\partial L_1}{\partial f_1/\partial K_1} = \frac{(\partial \phi_2/\partial L_2) \cdot f_2(k_i, l_i) + \phi_2(\partial f_2(k_i, l_i)/\partial l_i)}{(\partial \phi_2/\partial K_2) \cdot f_2(k_i, l_i) + \phi_2(\partial f_2(k_i, l_i)/\partial k_i)} = \frac{w}{r} \quad \forall i,$$

$$(1.25)$$

from which it is clear that condition (1.24) will not, in general, be satisfied, even in the case of a symmetric competitive equilibrium.

We are therefore left with an awkward question: in the face of failures in other markets, does free trade remain best? The question is awkward because we have entered the terrain of the second best, where the only general result is that partial movements towards fulfilling the conditions needed to support a first-best allocation may bring about Pareto-inferior allocations. The question will be taken up in the following sections. For the present, we note that whilst the rejoinder to the effect that markets are not complete is telling, it is not decisive.

1.2.2. Remedies

We begin by taking up the above examples of market failure. In earlier times, it was often argued that if private sources were unable or unwilling to finance new industrial undertakings, then the government should step in. The main instruments at its disposal for this purpose include issuing directives concerning the allocation of credit by existing banks, their nationalization, and the establishment of state-owned industrial banks. The argument for such interventions, if they are to be successful, must rest on the premise that the government and its agencies are better able to solve the informational problems that defeated private lenders, a premise whose general validity seems doubtful to the point of beggaring belief. In this case, to rush in where banks feared to tread is to run a strong risk of substituting government failure for market failure. The question of whether free trade is still best, conditional on the nature of the financial markets, remains open however.

The remedy for the unsatisfactory outcome in the case where individual firms generate externalities and behave as price-takers is well known, but also highly demanding of information. Let the vectors k^0 and l^0 satisfy Eqns (1.22) and (1.23). Then the government should grant firm i a specific (Pigouvian) subsidy in the amount $\left[p(\partial \phi^0/\partial K)\sum_{j\neq i}f(k_j^0, l_j^0)\right]$ on each unit of capital it employs and a like subsidy in the amount $\left[p(\partial \phi^0/\partial L)\sum_{j\neq i}f(k_j^0, l_j^0)\right]$ on each unit of labour, both financed, of course, by lump sum taxation. When the option of free trade is available, it should be fully embraced, with consumers and firms in industries not subject to such externalities facing (undistorted) producer prices, a subset of which is the vector of world prices p^*. This result is illustrated in Fig. 1.5

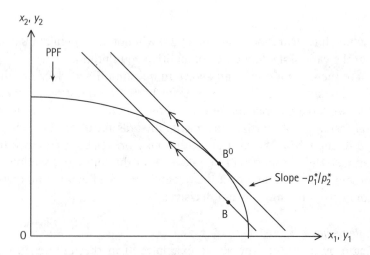

Figure 1.5. The inferiority of free trade in the absence of intervention when there are Marshallian externalities in industry

for the case of two tradables, where good 2 is subject to such external-ities and all firms therein are identical, so that the production subsidy is the same for all. In the absence of intervention, a competitive allocation arises at point B, which lies in the interior of the production possibility set and to the SE of the optimum B^0, where the slope of the PPF is (p_1^*/p_2^*), as required for the attainment of a full optimum. The optimal corrective subsidy induces an expansion of industry 2 at the expense of industry 1 to yield the domestic output vector denoted by point B^0.

Finally, it is important to note that free trade may itself offer a partial remedy for certain failures of competition that arise under autarky. For the opportunity to buy and sell a product at its world price, when open to all, places a precise limit on what firms can charge for it. Thus, were market power to be a problem under autarky, this fact would actually enhance the importance of free trade as a policy option.

1.2.3. Monopoly Power in International Trade

If an economy has some measurable influence over the world price of a good that it exports or imports, and if, as is perhaps natural, the government cares only for the welfare of its own citizens, then it should exploit the economy's market power by imposing a suitably chosen (optimal) export tax or tariff, respectively. That is to say, it should deliberately engineer a departure from the conditions needed to sustain allocative efficiency from a global point of view. This point was estab-lished over a century ago by Bickerdike, and there is no need to labour it here.

1.3. Policy-imposed Distortions

Departures from condition (1.2) arise not only because markets fail, but also because governments intervene in the economy in ways that are not motivated by the desire to correct some existing distortion. The two leading examples are interventions in factor markets, especially that for labour, and the use of distortionary taxes in order to raise revenue. Following Bhagwati (1971), the ensuing distortions will be called *policy-imposed*, as distinct from the *market-determined* distortions discussed in Section 1.2. We concentrate here on the labour market, the use of distortionary taxes being taken up in its own right in Section 1.4.

A salient feature of labour markets in developing countries is that the wage rate for unskilled workers who hold jobs in the urban, formal sector is usually at least twice what their unskilled counterparts earn working in agriculture. Various reasons have been advanced to explain this wage gap, but there is fairly general agreement that the government plays a central role in its determination, both directly as the leading employer in the formal sector and indirectly as a mediator between private employers and the trades union. That some governments are dependent on the unions for political support, and that most governments think twice before doing anything that might well bring the unions' members onto the streets, suggest that the said gap is the outcome of a complex of political and institutional factors rather than an exogenous act of regulation. For the purposes at hand, however, it will be simplest to treat it as the latter; for an endogenous gap in wages adds a difficult twist to the analysis that would take us rather far afield.

To illustrate what is involved, suppose that there are just two goods, both of which are tradable at parametric prices, and that, initially, the only distortion in the economy is an unalterable regulation of the labour market that brings about a fixed, proportional gap between the wage rate ruling in the two sectors: $w_2 = \lambda w_1$, where the factor of proportionality $\lambda > 1$. Given this intervention, any competitive allocation will be productively inefficient, regardless of whether others factors are mobile. For, assuming incomplete specialization, the value of the marginal product of labour at world prices will not be the same in the two sectors, so that the value of national income measured at world prices can be increased by shifting labour from the unregulated to the regulated sector.

How should this be accomplished in a decentralized fashion, and is a full optimum attainable? If lump-sum taxes are available, the answers to these questions are contained in Fig. 1.1. The full optimum is reached when firms, in aggregate, choose the production vector $y(p^*)$. Let the value of the MPL at world prices at $y(p^*)$ be m^*. In order to induce this vector of outputs, the government must arrange things such that firms in both industries face a net marginal cost of labour in the amount m^*. Since the gross marginal cost of labour to firms in industry 2 at the output level $y_2(p^*)$ is λm^*, the net marginal cost will be m^* if those firms receive an *ad valorem* wage subsidy in the amount $(\lambda - 1)/\lambda$. This result illustrates the principle of targeting once more: given that an unavoidable intervention in the labour market raises the real cost of labour to firms in industry 2, the right solution is to tackle the problem at source by means of an offsetting distortion, in the form of a subsidy which suitably reduces the said cost, and which is financed by a lump-sum tax in order to avoid any further distortionary effects.

1.4. Public Finance

We now turn to the awkward fact that, for various reasons, governments cannot, or will not, resort to lump-sum taxes under virtually any circumstances. That being so, it appears dangerous to appeal to the principle of targeting. For if distortionary taxes must be employed to finance an attack on an existing distortion, a balance must be struck between the relief of the latter and the possible damage wrought by the former. We have now entered the realm of optimal tax theory, wherein the principles are clear, but the ensuing results do not always yield precise and general prescriptions as to which instruments should be used to attain the (constrained) optimum.

We begin by asking whether there is any reason a priori why international trade should not be taxed, given that raising revenue in some distortionary fashion or other is unavoidable. Observe that the question is being posed completely independently of whether there is any merit in the arguments for the state to further so-called 'infant industries', as discussed in Section 1.2. (It is in the latter context that the tariffs on imports and levies on exports come in for so much trenchant criticism in the literature on trade and development.) The central result here is due to Diamond and Mirrlees (1971), which may be summarized as follows: in order to rule out lump-sum taxes, suppose that taxes can be levied only on households' net trades with the rest of the economy. If there are CRS and perfect competition everywhere, then in the absence of any limits on tax and subsidy rates,[10] production efficiency in the aggregate is optimal. This implies that all firms should trade at producer prices, that is, at world prices for tradables; so that indeed trade should not be taxed. Revenue should be raised instead by taxing domestic consumption. If there are limits on rates, productive efficiency will not be desirable in general, but it remains the case that trade taxes will not form part of the (constrained) optimal package (Dixit, 1985: 338).

The basic intuition here is that a tariff on the import of a good effectively confers a subsidy on each unit of it that is produced domestically and imposes a tax in the same amount on each unit consumed domestically. For, by definition, the level of imports is equal to the difference between domestic consumption and production, so that imposing a tariff t on each unit imported is equivalent to levying a tax of t on each unit

---

[10] If there are decreasing returns in the private sector, so that pure profits will arise, then it is also required that all such profits can be taxed away (Stiglitz and Dasgupta, 1971).

consumed and paying a subsidy of t on each unit produced at home. This inherent linking of the two rates is in itself undesirable, but it is not the tariff's only drawback. The tax base is the level of imports, which is usually far narrower than that offered by consumers' aggregate net trades in the commodity in question. Financing the same level of the subsidy on production by taxing aggregate net consumption can therefore be achieved through lower rates, and hence, in many circumstances, with a smaller attendant deadweight loss. A further consideration is that the main burden of a tariff is likely to fall upon the consumers of the good in question, be they firms or households. If the principal argument for a production subsidy is to correct for the sort of externalities that were the focus of Section 1.2, which ramify extensively throughout the economy, then it is hard to defend this particular and highly selective way of financing it (Ahmad and Stern, 1991).

The thrust of the argument thus far is that tariffs fully deserve their poor reputation; so that, in attempting to justify their widespread use, one seems to be driven back to a line of defence in third-best territory, namely, that collecting taxes on international trade makes far less demanding claims on administrative capacity than does the collection of taxes on domestic transactions. Cursory reflection on the state of public administration in many developing countries in relation to the task of dealing with legions of small-scale producers who keep few, if any, records suggests that this defence is to be taken seriously. This conclusion is reinforced by the history of taxation in what are now developed countries, from which a similar picture emerges. The caveat is that taxes tend to be like habits: once acquired, they are difficult to change. Hence, one would not want to undermine the long-run development of the whole tax system by basing it on the tax authorities' currently feeble capacities. On the contrary, strengthening such capacities is an important step in furthering tax reform, a point to which we shall return in Chapter 5.

For the present, however, the appeal to administrative factors carries considerable practical weight. It seems useful, therefore, examine the extreme case where the only taxes available are those on international trade. This problem can be solved using the formal apparatus of optimal tax theory in the usual way (see, e.g. Dixit, 1985: 339-40). It should be noted that there is no reason whatever why the optimal tariffs that so emerge will be uniform, a fact which should serve as an antidote to some of the stronger claims in favour of uniformity that have appeared in the applied literature on trade and development.

1.5. Summary

The claim that free trade is best can be viewed in two ways. The first is as essentially a corollary of the two fundamental theorems of welfare economics. For the moment, let the assumptions that underpin their validity be granted. Then, starting from autarky, adding the opportunity to trade in two or more goods at parametrically given world prices is equivalent to introducing additional CRS technologies for producing them. When properly and fully exploited, this opportunity will, in general, yield a Pareto-improvement over autarky or, indeed, any other departure from free trade. In contrast to the standard textbook exposition of this result, which involves two or more tradable consumption goods, the emphasis here has been placed on the case where the home country specializes in producing consumption goods and exports them in exchange for investment goods; for this is surely the relevant case for the overwhelming majority of LDCs. The introduction of free trade in the textbook case yields only 'level' effects on welfare. Access to investment goods on better, parametric terms through international trade, however, can lead to a permanently higher rate of growth of the economy. The impact of free trade may even be strikingly qualitative: an economy facing the ultimate fate of a stationary level of consumption per head under autarky can be released onto a path along which consumption per head grows indefinitely at a steady rate.

The second way of viewing free trade is as a possible element of an optimal package of policies when one or more of the assumptions necessary for the validity of the two said welfare theorems is violated. In keeping with our central theme, we began with externalities in the form of learning-by-doing and (positive) economies of agglomeration, both of which bear on the so-called 'infant industry' argument. The first-best policy involves Pigouvian subsidies to correct the externalities, lump-sum taxes to finance them, and a rigorous adherence to free trade. This package reflects the principle of targeting, in that the distortion ensuing from the externalities is attacked at source with an optimal counter-distortion. The same principle applies if the source of the trouble is the very decision-making process that generates policies, to the extent that the resulting choices are simply distortionary. One important example is the set of interventions whose aim is to regulate the wage rate in the organized sectors of the economy above the level that would otherwise rule.

The principal example, however, is the wholesale resort to distortionary taxation, whose practical importance can hardly be overemphasized.

A salient feature of the first-best package described above is that such taxation makes an appearance in an essential, if administratively very demanding, form. Suppose, more plausibly therefore, that lump-sum taxes are not available to finance the corrective subsidy. Is there then a case for protective tariffs to channel subsidies to deserving infant industries in particular, or for taxes on international trade to raise revenues in general? The answer to these questions remains a decisive 'no'—provided it is possible to choose domestic consumption as the tax base, even when there are restrictions on the tax or subsidy rates that can be imposed on individual commodities. This fundamental result in (second-best) optimal tax theory leaves advocates of taxes on international trade in the seemingly rather awkward position of having to defend them on the grounds that they are comparatively easy to collect. Both the history of taxation in now developed countries and the quality of public administration in today's LDCs tell us, nevertheless, that this argument is not to be lightly dismissed, and we shall take it up again in Chapters 4 and 5.

Recommended Reading

Readers who need to brush up on trade theory have the choice between the more classical approach of Bhagwati *et al.* (1998), and the largely unswerving use of duality theory in Dixit and Norman (1980). The relationship between trade and growth is extensively treated in Grossman and Helpman (1991). Its classical origins are insightfully revealed and analysed by Maneschi (1998).

Exercises

1. Consider the two-period model in Section 1. The technology for producing good i domestically in period t can be represented by the form

$$y_i(t) = \frac{A_i z_{2i}(t) L_i(t)}{z_{2i}(t) + L_i(t)}, \quad i, t = 1, 2,$$

where $z_{2i}(t)$ is the amount of the investment good employed in industry i in period t. Recalling the notation in the text, let the economy's endowments be $z_2(1) = L(1) = L(2) = 1$. If $A_1 = 8$ and $A_2 = 4$, show that the domestic PPF in period 1 will be

$$y_1(1) + 2y_2(1) = 4,$$

and then derive the CPF under autarky. If the representative consumer's preferences over consumption in the two periods take the form

$$u = \log_e x_1(1) + (1/2) \cdot \log_e x_1(2),$$

derive the competitive allocation under autarky, taking care to find all prices.

Now suppose that both goods are tradable at the parametric relative price $(p_1^*/p_2^*) = 3/2$ in period 1, and that the whole world comes to an end at the close of period 2. Find the competitive allocation under free trade, and compute the gains from trade in this setting in the form of the equivalent variation (EV) using consumption in period 1 as the numeraire. The allocations under autarky and free trade should be depicted graphically.

[It is possible, though somewhat tedious, to obtain the allocations in algebraic form, which can then be solved using a hand calculator. This the reader is strongly urged to do; but if his patience fails, he should find the solutions numerically using a package such as Maple.]

2. Consider a three-sector variant of the Fel'dman–Mahalanobis model in which each good is produced by means of capital alone under CRS. The output of the consumption good 1 at time t is

$$y_1(t) = ak_1(t),$$

where k_1 is the installed capital stock in that sector and a is the (constant) output–capital ratio. This good never enters international trade. Goods 2 and 3 are intermediate goods, whose domestic technologies are identical:

$$y_i(t) = k_i(t), \quad i = 2, 3.$$

When combined in a symmetric Cobb–Douglas aggregate, they yield new capital (investment) in the amount

$$I(t) = [x_2(t)x_3(t)]^{1/2},$$

where $x_i(t)$ is the amount of good i (=2, 3) used to produce investment. Newly produced capital can be freely allocated among the three sectors. Once installed, capital in sector 1 becomes fixed, but existing capital in sectors 2 and 3 can be shifted without cost between them. The allocation of capital within the two producer goods sectors is always chosen so as to maximize the level of current aggregate investment, but the allocation of the latter between the consumption goods and the producer goods sectors is fixed, the proportion $0 < \mu < 1$ going to sectors 2 and 3 combined.

(a) If the combined capital stock in sectors 2 and 3 at time t is $K(t)$, find the level of $I(t)$. Hence, or otherwise, show that in the absence of depreciation, the whole economy will eventually grow at the steady rate $\mu/2$ under autarky.

(b) The capital goods sectors are now opened up to free trade at world prices $p_2^* = 1$ and $p_3^* > 1$. Show that the steady-state growth rate is $(\mu/2)\sqrt{p_3^*}$ in this case.

(c) Comment on these results in the light of the debate over the role of trade in development.

3. An industry produces a fully traded good and is comprised of n identical firms, each of which perceives its cost function to have the form

$$c(y_i) = y_i + y_i^2/2, \tag{3.1}$$

where y_i is the output produced by the firm in question. Show that the industry's supply schedule is

$$Y(p) = \begin{cases} n(p - 1) & \text{if } p > 1, \\ 0 & \text{otherwise,} \end{cases}$$

where p is the producer price.

Now suppose that, in fact, there are Marshallian externalities at work, whose effects are such that the individual cost functions take the form

$$c(y_i, Y) = y_i + \left(\frac{n}{2\sqrt{n^2 + Y}} \right) y_i^2, \tag{3.2}$$

but the firms still conjecture that (3.1) rules. Comment briefly on (3.2) and derive the social marginal cost of production for the industry as a whole.

The domestic demand schedule for the industry is

$$X(q) = 20 - q,$$

where q denotes the consumer price. Let $n = 10$, which we assume to be large enough for firms to behave as if they had no influence on prices.

(a) Find the competitive equilibrium of the industry in the case where the economy is free of any policy-imposed distortions and the world price of the good is 2.

(b) If lump-sum taxation is possible, find the optimal production subsidy.

(c) As a final variant, suppose instead that the government were to impose a specific protective tariff in the same amount as the optimal production subsidy in part (b), with lump-sum transfers being employed to bring about a balanced budget.

Compare all three allocations, ranking them from the welfare perspective and depicting them in the familiar price–quantity space.

4. A competitive industry exhibits the *private* cost function

$$c(Y) = Y + Y^2/2,$$

where Y is the industry's total output. Such production by individual firms generates an externality that is internal to the industry in question, with the result that the social marginal cost of production is given by

$$\gamma(Y) = 1 + Y/2.$$

The economy is otherwise undistorted. The domestic demand for this good is given by

$$X(q) = 6 - q,$$

where q denotes the consumer price. The world price of the good is 2.

(a) Find the first-best taxes and the resulting improvement in social welfare over the competitive outcome in the absence of intervention.

(b) The second-best alternative involves a corrective subsidy that is financed exclusively by a sales tax on the good in question. Find the optimal levels thereof and the resulting improvement in welfare in this case.

(c) Consider a third-best optimum, in which production subsidies are not possible, but a protective tariff and lump-sum rebates of revenues are. Repeat part (b).

Illustrate your solutions graphically in each case.

2. International Trade: Practice

Just as there is a body of received theory, so there is also a received account of the trade policies pursued by almost all developing countries after the Second World War, or liberation from colonialism, whichever came later. According to this account, the collapse of commodity prices, the stagnation of international trade, and the rise of protectionism during the Great Depression had cast a pall over the prospects of exporting in the post-war period. This 'lesson' of interwar history was reinforced by the timely appearance of the Prebisch–Singer hypothesis, which holds that poor countries, as exporters of primary products and importers of manufactures, are subject to secular forces that progressively worsen their commodity terms of trade (Singer, 1950; Prebisch, 1951). A closely related consideration was the association between industrialization and levels of living. Viewed from the capitals of the 'South', surrounded as they were by agrarian backwardness, the source of the 'North's' wealth was seen to be its industrial base, now fully recovered from idleness in the Great Depression and the devastation of war, and growing rapidly. Taken together, these diverse elements seemed to constitute a compelling case in favour of promoting not only industry in general, but also the production of import substitutes in particular. Thus persuaded, governments of various stripes set about implementing a strategy of import substitution (IS) with a will.

As a rule, the easier stages of this process, which involve the production of the simpler sorts of consumer goods such as textiles, were undertaken first. The harder task of mastering the production of more complex industrial producer goods was usually, and sensibly, deferred. Only in the larger countries, where the pool of locally available skills and the domestic market for such outputs promised to be large enough, was there a serious early attempt to lay the foundations of a complete industrial structure.[1] Even in the latter cases, of course, large-scale imports of industrial producer goods continued to be necessary.

The packages of policies employed to implement IS-strategies in various countries were usually variations on a common design, whose elements are described in Section 2.1. The variations can be characterized in terms of the 'structure of protection' they yield, whereby some activities are favoured at

[1] The classic example is India's Second Five-Year Plan (1956–61), whose formal underpinnings are laid out in Mahalanobis (1955).

the expense of others. A commonly used measure of the protection enjoyed by an activity, namely, the effective rate of protection, is defined and critically discussed in Section 2.2. What ultimately matters, of course, is the damage done by pursuing such policies, an assessment of which is tackled in two quite different ways. Section 2.3 deals with model building on the theoretical basis offered by Section 1.1, with free trade as the benchmark. The alternative approach is to examine the empirical relationship between measures of openness and economic performance, particularly that between exports and growth. This is taken up in Section 2.4.

2.1. Protectionist Policies

How were IS-strategies actually put into effect? To make domestic production at the easy stages profitable, stiff tariff barriers were erected against imports of the goods in question, whereas the imports of intermediate inputs and machinery needed to produce them were subject to more modest duties, if any. So arose a so-called escalated structure of protection. When tariffs alone did not suffice to dull the edge of foreign competition, there was a resort to quotas, whose levels were often progressively reduced in concert with the expansion of domestic capacity, sometimes to the point of an outright ban on imports. Quotas were rarely auctioned, however, and the resulting competition for the rents associated with import licences attracted resources away from other uses. Indeed, the time and effort devoted to filing applications and lobbying, as well as the payment of bribes, all privately rational though they may be, fall into the category of what are called directly unproductive profit-seeking activities (DUPAs). Nor was this the end of the story; for measures aimed at making the domestic production of certain goods more privately profitable normally have the effect of attracting foreign investment into the sectors concerned. Such tariff-jumping was not always desired, however, the rents generated by protection being often viewed as the rightful preserve of national business interests and the trades union. Thus, regulations to hinder such investment were often imposed, sometimes in the form of limiting foreign shareholders to a minority stake in enterprises in particular branches of the economy.

To compound matters, the promotion of IS-activities in the above fashion necessarily involves putting export activities at a disadvantage, to the extent that the cost of producing exportables is driven up by higher prices of imports and their domestic substitutes. Direct subsidies, including access to credit at favourable rates, to IS-activities are also not unknown, and when granted, they must be financed. In many poorer less developed countries (LDCs), agriculture constitutes an important part of the tax base as well as being the economy's leading source of export earnings, so that the need for revenues to subsidize IS adds to the burden of disincentives weighing on exporters.

It is sometimes asserted that there is also a macroeconomic aspect to policies of this kind, inasmuch as such regimes are often associated with overvalued exchange rates. Here, one must guard against making the stronger assertion that protectionism causes such overvaluation. It is true that, *ceteris paribus*, an overvalued rate keeps down the cost, in domestic currency, of imported inputs, which is clearly advantageous to all users of those inputs. By the same token, it also puts downward pressure on the domestic currency prices of the outputs produced by protected sectors when protection is confined to an exogenous tariff. That this latter effect is absent in the face of a binding quota is surely one factor underlying the use of quotas in IS-regimes. The sectors producing exportables are, of course, effectively taxed, to the extent that they too face prices in domestic currency that are correspondingly lower. In this situation, an economy can be said to experience a shortage of foreign exchange in the sense that there is excess demand for foreign currency at the prevailing nominal rate, as tends to happen when there is a reliance on exchange rate pegs and the monetary authorities pursue sufficiently expansionary policies. It should be quite clear from the national accounts identities, however, that such a shortage must be laid at the door of inadequate domestic savings. Here, the real source of the problem is lax fiscal policy, which is bound up, in turn, with a resort to seigniorage (see Chapter 6). For a plethora of interventions aimed at raising profits in selected sectors is perfectly compatible with zero excess demand for foreign currency when the government balances its books through taxation alone, as is assumed in the (standard) exposition of the real models in Chapter 1. What can be said is that if macroeconomic policy is such as to bring about an overvalued exchange rate, and if the government shies away from grasping the mettle of a nominal devaluation, then the pressures to restrict imports by further tightening quotas may be well nigh irresistible. Bowing to the inevitable will intensify the protectionist regime, but there should be no confusion about the direction of causation.

To sum up the received account, while the first step down the protectionist path may have been the comparatively innocuous introduction of selected tariffs, the next step involved the much more damaging imposition of quotas, attended by their rents and incentives to behave in rent-seeking ways. At length, the economy is hobbled by a tangle of taxes and regulations, which errors in macroeconomic policy cause to bind all the more tightly. This is essentially the story which unfolds in one variation or another in the classic and influential country studies of protection-ism that were published in the 1970s (Little et al., 1970; Balassa, 1971; Bhagwati, 1978).

2.2. A Measure of Protection

While the outline is clear, the reader might be ill satisfied with a general description of protectionist policy, preferring instead to have quantitative measures of the degree of protection. This is where most practitioners will reach into their tool bag and pull out that trusty measuring rod, the effective rate of protection (ERP).

We begin with a case that excludes certain complications. Let all goods be fully tradable. Some may be subject to taxes on trade, but none to quantitative restrictions, so that the domestic price of good i is

$$p_i = (1 + t_i)p_i^*,$$

where t_i denotes the tariff rate if good i is imported, and the subsidy rate if it is exported. The nominal rate of protection (NPR) of good i is simply t_i. The technology available to domestic firms in all branches is assumed to be of the Leontief type and to exhibit constant returns to scale (CRS). Let the amount of the ith good (kth factor) needed to produce one unit of good j be denoted by a_{ij} (l_{kj}), and the unit activity vector in industry j by $(a_j; l_j) = (a_{1j}, \ldots, a_{mj}; l_{1j}, \ldots, l_{fj})$. The value added generated by this unit activity at domestic prices is $(p_j - \boldsymbol{p}\boldsymbol{a}_j)$; at world prices, it is $(p_j^* - \boldsymbol{p}^*\boldsymbol{a}_j)$. The associated ERP is defined to be the ratio of the former to the latter minus one:

$$\text{ERP}_j \equiv \left[(p_j - \boldsymbol{p}\boldsymbol{a}_j)/(p_j^* - \boldsymbol{p}^*\boldsymbol{a}_j) \right] - 1 = \frac{p_j - \sum_{i=1}^{n} p_i a_{ij}}{p_j^* - \sum_{i=1}^{n} p_i^* a_{ij}} - 1. \quad (2.1)$$

If the ERP is positive, then the factors employed in producing the good in question will enjoy greater nominal remuneration than they would under free trade, and conversely if the ERP is negative. Observe that if a good is produced by means of primary factors alone, the EPR is equal to the nominal *ad valorem* tariff on the good in question.

We now ask what pattern this index is likely to exhibit under a system of escalated protection, since this supposedly characterizes the tariff structure adopted by most LDCs. To this end, it is useful to rewrite Eqn (2.1) as

$$\text{ERP}_j = \frac{t_j p_j^* - \sum_{i=1}^n t_i p_i^* a_{ij}}{p_j^* - \sum_{i=1}^n p_i^* a_{ij}}. \tag{2.2}$$

As a benchmark, consider the case where there is a uniform tariff, or a uniform export subsidy at the same rate, as the case may be.[2] It is clear from Eqn (2.2) that the ERP in all sectors is equal to the uniform nominal rate. If, however, the nominal rate varies across goods, then it is clear that the sectors that are subject to the highest rate enjoy an ERP which exceeds their nominal rate, whereas the converse must hold for those subject to the lowest rate. No claims can be made for intermediate cases without further assumptions about the vectors p^*, t, and $(a_1, \ldots, a_n)$.

A numerical example will be helpful to illustrate the process of escalation. Suppose the unit activity vector in the textile industry requires one unit of cotton, 0.1 units of imported spare parts to keep the machinery running, and one unit each of the services of machinery and labour. Let the world prices of textiles, cotton, and spares be 100, 30, and 300, respectively. At these prices, the value added yielded by the unit activity would be 40 (= 100 − 30 − 0.1 × 300). The government now imposes tariffs on textiles and spares at the rates of 50 and 20 per cent, respectively. The unit value added at the resulting domestic prices is 84 (= 150 − 30 − 0.1 × 360), so that Eqn (2.1) yields the finding that the textile industry enjoys an ERP of 110 per cent, or over twice the nominal rate.

The special case just dealt with lends itself to clear exposition, but it is sorely in need of extension if the method is to be promoted for practical use. Three thorny questions arise at once. First, how is one to treat non-tradables? Second, what happens if substitution in production is possible? Third, how are inputs of factors to be valued in the presence of distortions, including those in factor markets? Taking up these questions in turn, one possibility is to combine non-tradables with domestic factors, thereby leaving Eqn (2.1) formally unaltered, but at the cost of destroying the interpretation of effective protection in terms of the rewards to the factors employed in the activity in question. Indeed, the very meaning of the index is far from clear in this case. An alternative is to break down non-tradable inputs into their tradable and factor components, so that the terms entering Eqn (2.1) now represent the direct and indirect tradable

---

[2] Some goods, after all, must be exported in order to pay for imports.

content of the unit activity in question. The omission of the factor content of the non-tradable inputs from the numerator and denominator alike is consistent, but also rules out any interpretation of the ERP index as a measure of the implicit subsidy granted to the factors directly employed in the said activity. This decomposition is, moreover, both straightforward and theoretically unproblematic only if the technology is Leontief, as assumed above.

This leads us to the second question. If substitution in production is possible, then the unit activity vectors will depend on prices, and hence on the vector of tariffs, which raises the question of whether the vector $(a_j; l_j)$ appearing in Eqn (2.1) should be that which would be chosen at world prices, or that which is chosen, and actually observed, in the protected regime. Unfortunately, the former is theoretically correct if the aim is to use the ERP as an index of how badly resources are misallocated. Thus, the practitioner is badly torn between simplicity and rigour. If conscience demands rigour, then there is nothing for it but to undertake a full-scale general equilibrium analysis, in which case the ERP index will have become the fifth wheel of the coach.

The question of how inputs of factors should be valued in the presence not only of distortions in the domain of international trade, but also of those encountered in factor markets and those arising from taxation in general, introduces a raft of additional considerations. Dealing with them requires a unified treatment, which is taken up at length in Chapters 8–11.

Such theoretical complications aside, the list of problems encountered in applying even the simple method in practice is by no means exhausted; for quotas and overvalued exchange rates have yet to be brought into the reckoning. Quotas can be dealt with by an appeal to the concept of the equivalent tariff, which is just the difference between the domestic and world prices of any good subject to a quota, and hence will be positive whenever a quota binds. This simple arithmetic has obvious attractions, which make it the dominant approach in practice; but the underlying reasoning is not watertight. For if a quota binds, the good in question is effectively a non-tradable at the margin for all increases in net domestic demand. Thus, whilst the equivalent tariff suffices to describe the configuration of market equilibrium in the presence of a quota, it can do little to aid in the task of analysing the system's comparative statics.

The conclusion is, therefore, a bleak one: when calculated in the simple way that commends it to practitioners, the ERP index is, in general, so flawed that no use should be made of it; and when it is correctly calculated, it is simply superfluous.[3] In the later chapters on shadow prices, we shall develop a method that is (largely) proof against these criticisms, albeit much more demanding of intellectual effort, time, and data. It remains the case, however, that there is a vast body of empirical studies of effective protection, about whose findings something should be said.

In a well-known work on trade and employment, Kreuger (1983) makes extensive use of ERP indices in developing her case that export-promotion (EP) strategies are superior to those based on IS. In doing so, she draws on studies of twelve countries at various points in time between 1958 and 1973,[4] each case (country-period) being classified as an example of an EP, IS, or moderate (M)IS trade strategy. The average ERP for manufacturing ranges from −1 per cent in South Korea (one of the two EP cases), to 19, 27, and 33 per cent in Colombia, Thailand, and Indonesia (three of the four MIS cases), respectively, all the way up to 356 per cent in Pakistan (1963 and 1964) and 384 per cent in Uruguay. The range within each case is also large, spanning the extremes of −15 to 82 per cent in Korea and −19 to a giddy 5400 percent in Indonesia (ibid.: Table 3.1, 34).

It is interesting to note that where tariff-escalation is concerned, the picture that emerges from Table 3.3 (ibid.: 37), in which ERP values are reported by end-use, is hardly a ringing confirmation of the 'standard' account. Brazil clearly conformed to it in 1958, with rates on consumer, intermediate, and capital goods of 242, 65, and 53 per cent, respectively, and arguably still in 1967, with 66, 39, and 52 per cent. In the cases of Thailand (1973) and Argentina (1969), however, the pattern is exactly the reverse, the rates being 19, 25, and 77 per cent and 96, 127, and 162 per cent, respectively. Of the remaining cases, Pakistan (1970 and 1971) is closer to Brazil's pattern, Colombia and South Korea to the reverse, and Tunisia lies somewhere in between.

Some selected estimates for the late 1970s appear in World Bank (1987: 89). By 1978, South Korea had installed a strongly protectionist regime in favour of rice farmers, with an ERP index for the primary sector of 77 per cent, whereas that for manufacturing remained low, at 5 per cent. Brazil's primary sector (excluding mining), in contrast, was more heavily burdened than in the mid 1960s, with an ERP of −24 per cent, but manufacturing also made do with the much more modest rate of 23 per cent. The Philippines had moved some way towards neutrality; but Colombia had slipped further

---

[3] For a thorough and critical treatment of effective protection, see Bliss (1987).

[4] Brazil (1958, 1963, 1967), Chile (1967), Colombia (1969), Indonesia (1971), Ivory Coast (1973), Pakistan (1963 and 1964, 1970 and 1971), South Korea (1968), Thailand (1973), Tunisia (1972), and Uruguay (1965). For the original sources, see Kreuger (1983: Table 3.1, p. 34).

into a protectionist stance, with rates of 39 and 55 per cent for the primary and manufacturing sectors, respectively. In Nigeria, where oil had come to dominate the primary sector, the pattern was reminiscent of Latin America in the 1960s.

2.3. The Costs of Departures from First-best

How damaging have such policies been? In order to answer this question, we now appeal to standard static theory, with free trade as a benchmark. As it stands, the account in Section 1.1.1 does not go far quite enough. For although the ranking of policies is clear, it is not obvious whether their performance, as measured by an index of social welfare, is strikingly different. Obtaining estimates of the gaps that separate them requires that the model be applied and empirically calibrated to the actual situation of interest. Well-established practice involves choosing sufficiently flexible forms to represent the technologies and preferences, and then proceeding to do some sensitivity analysis on the values of the parameters in order to allow for the fact that arriving at satisfactory econometric estimates thereof is often difficult. Highly simplified though it is for expository purposes, the structure set out below yields results that are arguably of the right order of magnitude.

Consider a small, open, 2×2 economy in a static setting with a single representative consumer. In the light of Sections 2.1 and 2.2, sectors 1 and 2 should be thought of as agriculture and industry, respectively, where the model will be so calibrated that good 1 will be exported in equilibrium. The economy's factor endowments, of capital ($\bar{K}$) and labour ($\bar{L}$), are given and supplied completely inelastically; they are also completely mobile across sectors. The technologies for producing goods domestically exhibit CRS and all the other 'well-behaved' properties needed for simple exposition:

$$y_i = f_i(K_i, L_i), \quad i = 1, 2, \tag{2.3}$$

where (K_i, L_i) is the bundle of inputs employed in sector i. If factor prices are sufficiently flexible, then both factors will be fully employed in equilibrium:

$$K_1 + K_2 = \bar{K} \tag{2.4}$$

and

$$L_1 + L_2 = \bar{L}. \tag{2.5}$$

Since both factors are supplied completely inelastically, a uniform tax on both factors or on total consumption will effectively serve as a lump-sum tax (see Section 4.3), so that some restrictions on what taxes are at the government's disposal are needed if we are to proceed further. In view of the fact that a substantial share of agricultural output will be consumed by farmers themselves, it will be assumed that the production and consumption of good 1 is taxable only indirectly through an *ad valorem* tax, t_1, on exports. Hence,

$$p_1 = q_1 = p_1^*/(1 + t_1), \tag{2.6}$$

where p_1 and q_1 denote, respectively, the producer and consumer price of good 1. The use of capital and labour in sector 2 can be taxed (or subsidized) at the *ad valorem* rates t_r and t_w, respectively, so that the government can impose differences in the marginal cost of employing factors across sectors. Taxes (or subsidies) on the production of good 2 are also assumed to be possible. If taxes on international trade in good 2 are ruled out, it follows that

$$q_2 = p_2^*; \tag{2.7}$$

but p_2, in contrast, is effectively a policy variable, being determined by a suitable choice of a tax or subsidy on the production of good 2.

The wage rate in sector 1 is assumed to be perfectly flexible; but that in sector 2 is subject to regulation in such a way as to bring about a constant proportional wage gap, with $w_2 = \lambda w_1$, as in Section 1.3. How is this wage gap to be reconciled with the assumption of full employment? For if workers are fully mobile across sectors, all will seek the better-paying jobs in sector 2. The answer is that firms choose how many jobs to offer at the going prices, and those workers who suffer the disappointment of being turned away at the factory gate are assumed here to take up employment at once in sector 1.[5] The real possibility that some of them may decide to stay unemployed instead, in the hope of improving their chances in the next round of job offers, is addressed at length in Chapter 9, albeit within a rather different structure. In any event, full employment of both factors is ensured in the present setting if at least one of the production functions satisfies the lower Inada condition with respect to each of the factors, though neither production function need do so with respect to both.

Firms maximize profits, taking all prices as parametrically given. Since all have access to the same CRS technologies, the first-order conditions in

---

[5] If lump-sum taxes are available, then, as already noted in Section 1.3, the first-best allocation can be attained by means of a suitably chosen wage subsidy.

each sector are

$$p_1 \partial f_1 / \partial K_1 = r, \tag{2.8}$$

$$p_1 \partial f_1 / \partial L_1 = w, \tag{2.9}$$

$$p_2 \partial f_2 / \partial K_2 = (1 + t_r)r, \tag{2.10}$$

and

$$p_2 \partial f_2 / \partial L_2 = (1 + t_w)\lambda w, \tag{2.11}$$

where a unit of capital yields the (net) rental r to its owner wherever it be employed, and the wage rate received by a worker in sector 1 is denoted by w. Households derive their incomes solely from the earnings of their factor endowments. In aggregate, therefore,

$$M = r\bar{K} + w(L_1 + \lambda L_2), \tag{2.12}$$

all of which is spent on the two goods in question. Given the preferences of the representative household, its income M and the consumer prices q, the ordinary (Marshallian) demand functions

$$x_i = x_i(q, M), \quad i = 1, 2, \tag{2.13}$$

are derived in the usual way.

In order to complete the model, we lay out the government's accounts. In the absence of foreign borrowing or grants, the fact that all private income is spent implies that the government must balance its books currently. The simplest and most insightful way of writing this condition follows from the observation that Walras' law then requires that the value of exports at world prices be equal to the value of imports at world prices. Since both goods are tradable, we have

$$p^*(y - x) = 0, \tag{2.14}$$

that is to say, the value of output at world prices equals the value of consumption at world prices.

Given world prices p^*, the factor endowments $\bar{K}$ and $\bar{L}$, and taking the labour market 'regulation' described by λ as an unalterable feature of the policy landscape, the system (2.3)–(2.14) can be solved for the policy described by the vector (p_2, t_r, t_w, t_1), not all elements of which are necessarily independent of one another. Some cases of particular interest are as follows:

(a) Free trade, no distortions: $\lambda = 1, p_2 = p_2^*, t_r = t_w = t_1 = 0$. Under the above assumptions, this case yields a first-best allocation, and so provides the benchmark against which to judge the performance of several alternatives in the presence of the (fixed) distortion in the labour market. In view of the convenient normalization of both world prices to unity, a natural way of expressing the equivalent variation (EV) is as a percentage of the value of GDP at world prices in case (a).

(b) A proportional wage-gap: $\lambda > 1$, $p_2 = p_2^*$, $t_r = t_w = t_1 = 0$. In general, the economy will not be productively efficient; for the regulation in question causes the wage–rental ratio, and hence the marginal rate of technical substitution (MRTS), to differ across the two industries.

(c) A proportional wage-gap, with one or more countervailing distortions. The variants include a subsidy on wages or production in order to offset the high unit cost of labour to firms in sector 2, financed by a combination of a tax on the use of capital in that sector and an export tax on good 1.

(d) A proportional wage-gap, with a protective tariff on good 2: $\lambda > 1$, $t_2 > 0$. In this case, Eqn (2.7) is replaced by

$$p_2 = q_2 = (1 + t_2)p_2^*. \tag{2.7'}$$

Such systems do not possess closed-form solutions, except in very special—and empirically rather uninteresting—cases, so we must resort to numerical methods. For this purpose, specific functional forms for the technologies and preferences are needed. We adhere to standard practice by choosing CES-forms for both:

$$y_i = A_i \left[\alpha_i K_i^{-\rho_i} + (1 - \alpha_i)L_i^{-\rho_i} \right]^{-1/\rho_i}, \quad i = 1, 2$$

and

$$u = \left[\beta x_1^{-\rho_c} + (1 - \beta)x_2^{-\rho_c} \right]^{-1/\rho_c},$$

whereby the homothetic character of the latter carries the rather unrealistic assumption that all income elasticities of demand are unity.

The parameter values constituting the 'base case' are as follows. Round figures for the factor endowments and world prices may be chosen for convenience, since the efficiency factors A_i may be selected independently to yield an allocation that respects the broad shape of things. Here, they are chosen in the light of the factor endowments and world prices such that good 1 will be exported under conditions of free trade, a configuration for which some tinkering with all the values thereof may be needed. Let

Table 2.1. Output, consumption, prices, and welfare in selected variants

	(a) Free trade, no distortion	(b) Wage distortion	(c) Countervailing distortion $t_w = -0.4$, $t_r = 0.2, p_2 = p_2^*$	(d) Protective tariff $t_w =$ $t_r = 0, p_2 =$ $q_2 = 5p_2^*/4$
Output (y)	(1.326, 0.412)	(1.706, 0)	(1.510, 0.220)	(1.199, 0.524)
Consumption (x)	(1.044, 0.696)	(1.024, 0.682)	(1.079, 0.651)	(1.199, 0.524)
Prices ($p = q$)	(1, 1)	(1, 1)	(0.906, 1)	(0.820, 1.25)
Factor prices (r, w)	(0.487, 0.626)	(0.357, 0.675)	(0.373, 0.590)	(0.520, 0.490)
Labour (L_1, L_2)	(1.739, 0.261)	(2, 0)	(1.869, 0.131)	(1.703, 0.297)
Capital (K_1, K_2)	(0.488, 0.512)	(1, 0)	(0.715, 0.285)	(0.296, 0.704)
EV*	0	1.84	0.53	2.88

*The EV is expressed as a percentage of the value of GDP at world prices in the first-best allocation.

$(\bar{K}, \bar{L}) = (1, 2), p^* = (1, 1)$, and $A_1 = A_2 = 1$. The empirical evidence points to a value of the elasticity of substitution in manufacturing that is somewhat below unity, but one in agriculture that is much higher, with unity as a lower bound; correspondingly, let $\rho_1 = -1/3$ and $\rho_2 = 1$.[6] The former sector is more capital-intensive in poor countries, so we choose a value of α_1 that is significantly smaller than α_2, say $\alpha_1 = 0.25$ and $\alpha_2 = 0.75$. Food and manufactures are also unlikely to be particularly good substitutes in consumption, but for convenience, the choice of utility function falls on Cobb–Douglas ($\rho_c = 0$). The lion's share of total expenditures goes on food, and the value of β is selected accordingly, at 0.6.

The associated values of all relevant variables in equilibrium for the benchmark of first-best and the various alternatives corresponding to the above restrictions on taxes are set out in Table 2.1. In keeping with one stylized fact, the proportional wage gap, λ, is set at 2 in cases (b)–(d). In case (c), the values of the tax rates levied on the use of factors in sector 2 have been chosen so that firms in both sectors face the wage–rental ratio w/r, as can be checked by substitution into Eqns (2.10) and (2.11). The reason for this choice is to induce efficiency in production, so that the resulting allocation will lie on the production possibility frontier (PPF). Since such choices are not, in general, self-financing, the value of the export tax on good 1, and hence the domestic price of good 1, is determined endogenously. It should be remarked that three decimal places have been chosen in order to make the sizes of certain differences clear, the need for which is itself a conclusion of sorts.

[6] Recall that the elasticity of substitution is $-1/(1 + \rho)$.

Beginning with cases (a) and (b), whereas the loss in welfare due to the regulation of the wage rate in sector 2 turns out to be very modest, the EV being just under 2 percent of GDP valued at world prices, the regulation's effect on the allocation of resources between the two sectors is dramatic, leading to complete specialization of production in good 1.[7] In case (c), the countervailing distortion in the form of the subsidy on wages in sector 2, when combined with the fairly stiff tax on the use of capital in that sector needed to bring about the same net wage–rental ratio in both sectors,[8] does something to offset the competitive disadvantage imposed by the regulation. Even with the additional help of the (endogenous) export tax on good 1 at the rate of almost 10 per cent, however, the output of good 2 is just over half of its level under free trade in the absence of the distortion in the labour market. Relative to case (b), the EV is reduced by almost three-quarters—an interesting and useful demonstration of how more distortions can be better than fewer.

Case (d) has the singular feature that there is no trade at all. This is no accident, but rather an instance of a result that holds whenever there are just two goods, even in the presence of differences in factor prices of the kind treated here. In order to prove this rather odd-looking result, observe that if the only taxes in the system fall on trade, then $p = q$. CRS and perfect competition in both sectors together imply that $py = M$, where $M = qx$ by virtue of all income being spent at prices q. Since Eqn (2.14) must also hold in equilibrium, it follows that if there are just two goods, then $x = y$. In the particular example chosen here, the (exogenous) choice of a protective tariff of 25 per cent on good 2 must be combined with an export tax on good 1 at the rate of 22 per cent, in order to induce $x = y$ at the price vector $p = q = (0.82, 1.25)$. The government raises no revenue if $x = y$, of course; but both elements of the tax vector must still be appropriately chosen. Case (d) demonstrates once more the key role played by lump-sum transfers in the 'standard' account: tariff revenues are wholly rebated to households in the form of lump-sum subsidies, so that the government raises no net revenue. Given the restriction that net revenue be zero, however, the imposition of a tax on any transaction must be offset by subsidies to others. In the two-good system considered here, which wholly conforms to the textbook case, imposing a tariff while

---

[7] In this particular example, therefore, the allocation of resources in production happens to be efficient, all factors being employed in sector 1 in the face of the regulatory intervention in the labour market.

[8] The net wage–rental ratio in sector 2 is $(1 + t_w)\lambda/(1 + t_r)$. Hence, $t_w = -0.4$ and $\lambda = 2$ imply that $t_r = 0.2$.

denying the government the use of lump-sum transfers is possible only if there are no transactions to tax.[9] It is also noteworthy that the costs of imposing autarky are very modest, the EV being just under 3 per cent of the value of GDP under free trade.

An understandable reaction to such simple, small-scale models is that they have their pedagogic value and yield useful qualitative insights, but their quantitative results are not to be taken very seriously. We turn, therefore, to the findings from their large-scale cousins. Clarete and Whalley (1987), for example, estimate that the elimination of all tariffs, quotas, and export taxes in the Philippines in 1978 would have increased GNP by 5.2 per cent—all well and good, but hardly overwhelming. For Cameroon, Devarajan and Rodrik (1991) arrive at estimates of the costs of protection in 1980 that are more in line with the illustrative results obtained above, namely, about 1 per cent of GDP if perfect competition rules everywhere, and rising to double that amount in the case of monopolistic competition in certain sectors, albeit with the whole structure set up so that all of the distortions pull in the same direction. Much recent work along these lines has been concerned with the gains from trade generated by the Uruguay Round. That the estimates thereof for LDCs, as reported in Martin and Winters (1996), are still smaller confirms the general thrust of earlier findings. When such accomplished practitioners of the art of CGE model building have laboured so hard, and yet produced estimates of this order, there are grounds for asking what all the fuss is about.

2.4. Openness and Growth

The inescapable conclusion to be drawn from Section 2.3 is that, viewed purely statically within the standard framework, the costs of protectionist policies have been small—for most countries, at most two or three years of economic growth.[10] It would be wrong on this basis alone, however, to dismiss the criticisms of protectionism as much ado about nothing; for it is possible that other mechanisms are at work that hinder growth in a protectionist regime over the longer run. One such mechanism was discussed at some length in Chapter 1, namely, the transformation of consumption into investment goods through international trade rather than through domestic

---

[9] For an extensive treatment of this matter, see Gersbach and Haller (2001). Note that the result does not extend to the case of three or more goods, where additional degrees of freedom arise, but it remains the case that not all taxes on trade can be chosen independently of one another.

[10] It should be conceded that the capitalized value thereof amounts to a significant sum.

production. A failure to exploit this advantageous opportunity will almost certainly have adverse transitional effects and could result in a permanently lower rate of growth, with extremely adverse effects on welfare over the long run. In this case, it is really imports of producer goods that drive the process, with exports playing an enabling role (Rodrik, 1999). When this mechanism is at work, the case for promoting exports therefore rests on the argument that exports are a necessary element in a process for converting domestic savings into investment in an efficient way. By the same token, promoting IS in the producer-good sectors is strongly counterproductive. In any event, a more rapid growth of exports may lead to a more rapid growth of GDP if the rate of investment (measured in efficiency units) also rises thereby.

A second mechanism emphasizes the potential spillovers that arise from many exporting activities. The need to compete in world markets, it is argued, imposes unrelenting pressure on all the firms involved to improve the quality of their products and the efficiency of the processes used to produce them. In order to compete, these firms and their workers must learn, and to the extent that the firms cannot fully appropriate the know-how so gained, an externality arises. It follows that exports of such goods should be promoted, where it is clear that the argument applies much more plausibly to industry than to agriculture. In contrast to the first mechanism, exports not only play the leading role, but are also desirable in themselves, in the sense that, all else being equal, their social value exceeds their private value. What the two mechanisms have in common is the claim that promoting exports can, under the right circumstances, result in faster growth.

A related and, in some ways, even stronger claim is that the more 'open' the economy—in respect of trade, investment, and ideas—the faster is its rate of growth. A particular form of this claim is that a policy regime free of bias against exports, often called an 'open' development strategy, promotes more rapid growth than an 'inward' (IS) strategy, a claim presumably predicated on the existence of a link between the degree of openness so defined and the growth of exports. This claim found especially strong expression in the *World Development Report* in 1987, which is written as if the issue were settled as a matter of empirical fact. Testing such claims empirically is beset by various problems, however, not the least of which is the fact that the theoretical advances in this field are quite recent.[11] In keeping with the importance of these claims, a great deal of effort has

---

[11] Perhaps the seminal work concerning the theoretical relationship between trade and growth is Grossman and Helpman (1991).

gone into the empirical side of the enterprise over the past thirty years or so, with an increasingly heavy use of econometric techniques. What follows is necessarily a rather selective account, from which most of the finer econometric points have been omitted.

2.4.1. The Extent of Openness

We begin with simple description. The account in Section 2.1 certainly leaves the impression that LDCs have pursued policies which have reduced their foreign trade, at least relative to a continuation of the *status quo ante* ruling in the early 1950s. We shall not attempt to deal with this counter-factual. Nor shall we try to construct measures of the 'openness' of an economy's policy regime.[12] We content ourselves instead by describing the extent to which LDCs have become more or less open with respect to foreign trade over the past forty years, as measured by the ratios of exports and imports to GDP. For country i at time τ, these ratios are denoted by $e_{i\tau}$ and $m_{i\tau}$, respectively. It should be noted that $e_{i\tau}$ is almost invariably less than $m_{i\tau}$, by virtue of the net inflows of official and private capital into LDCs that mark the post-war period. Although there is data going back to 1950 for some countries, the group is rather small and dominated by developed countries, and its comparability leaves much to be desired. By 1960, the group had become much larger, with LDCs much more heavily represented, and the influence of the UN's standard system of accounts had started to take hold in most offices of statistics. Reconstruction following the Second World War in Europe was also largely complete, trading patterns had settled down, and the process of liberation from colonial rule was well underway. For these reasons, 1960 has much to commend it as the base year for a comparison with the state of affairs in 1995.

The values of e_i and the so-called trade ratio $(e_i + m_i)$ for the subset of eighty-two countries for which data is available, sixty of which were classified as LDCs in 1960,[13] are presented in the form of histograms in Figs 2.1a–d. The levels of the two indices in 1960 are displayed in Figs 2.1a and c, and the pairwise differences between their respective values in 1960

---

[12] Constructing measures of openness where policies are concerned involves inherent difficulties. Tariff rates are at least measurable, but the inevitable use of averages, even for groups of products, is problematic. Quotas and regulations are still less tractable, though indices of their incidence are constructed by some agencies (see Rodrik, 1999: Table 1.2, for a comparative picture of the situation in the early 1980s and 1990s). Employing such measures as regressors in econometric analysis is certainly not for the squeamish.

[13] South Korea and Saudi Arabia fell into this group in 1960, but had been elevated to the status of 'developed' by 1995.

and 1995 in Figs 2.1b and d. The purpose of taking the pairwise differences is, of course, to describe the changes over time more precisely by
ridding them of (country) fixed effects. In 1960, the average values of
e and $(e + m)$ were about 24 and 50 per cent, respectively. There was

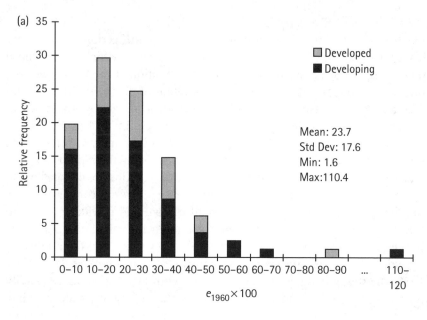

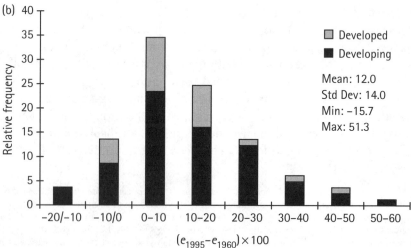

Figure 2.1. Continued

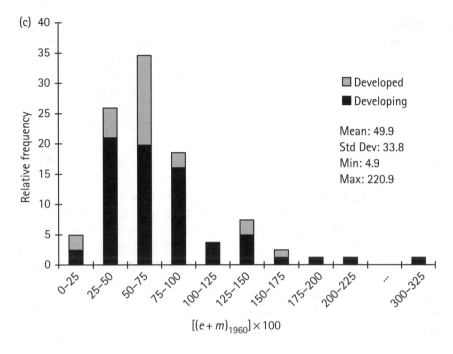

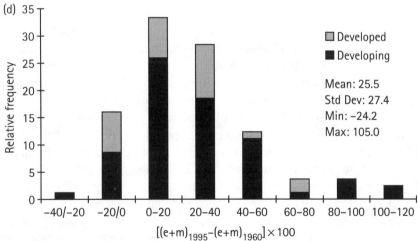

Figure 2.1. (a) Exports as percentage of GDP, 1960. (b) Changes in the ratio of exports to GDP, 1960–95. (c) Trade ratios, 1960. (d) Changes in trade ratios, 1960–95

Source: World Bank (WDI, 1998). The sample comprises fifty-nine observations for developing, and twenty-three observations for developed countries, as defined in World Bank (WDI, 1998).

considerable dispersion in both indices, as one would expect in such a heterogeneous group, though the difference between developed and less developed countries as subgroups was not especially large. It is clear from Figs 2.1b and d that, by these measures, both groups of countries became much more open over the period in question: at about 12 and 26 per cent points, respectively, the mean values of the differences in the two indices are almost exactly half the values of their mean absolute levels in 1960. That the great majority of countries were moving in the same direction can be seen from an alternative depiction of these indices. In Figs 2.2a and b are plotted, respectively, the values of e_i in 1960 against those in 1995 and the corresponding values of the trade ratio $(e_i + m_i)$. Not only is the correlation strong in each case, but most points also lie above the 45° line through the origin. For all the battery of protectionist measures which governments deployed in this period, the outcome in the majority of countries was fuller integration into the system of international trade.

2.4.2. Exports and Growth

It is well established that periods of rapid growth in the world economy were also periods in which international trade expanded at an even faster clip, whereas slow growth was accompanied by a sluggish expansion of trade (Lewis, 1980). It seems that virtually all countries were carried along, to some extent at least, on the same current, though the part played by their individual trade policies is not revealed thereby. We now take up the question of whether there is an empirical relationship between exports and economic growth, and if so, whether there is a clear direction of causation. A substantial literature[14] addresses these questions, but has yet to yield a definite answer where the matter of causality is concerned.

We begin, as before, with simple description. Figure 2.3 is the scatter-plot of the rate of growth of GDP against the rate of growth of exports for a group of forty-six countries over the period from 1960 to 1995. It is clear that the rates are correlated; indeed, as exports typically comprise about one-third of GDP, it would be surprising if they were not, a point made by Michaely (1977) in connection with yet earlier studies by Emery (1967), Maizels (1968), and Kravis (1970). Michaely proposed to deal with this difficulty by employing the growth rate of the ratio e instead of the growth rate of exports. As Heller and Porter (1978) pointed out, however, this solution is impaled on the same identity, namely,

$$Y \equiv (C + I + G - M) + E \equiv Z + E, \tag{2.15}$$

[14] The references that follow in the text may be consulted for further contributions.

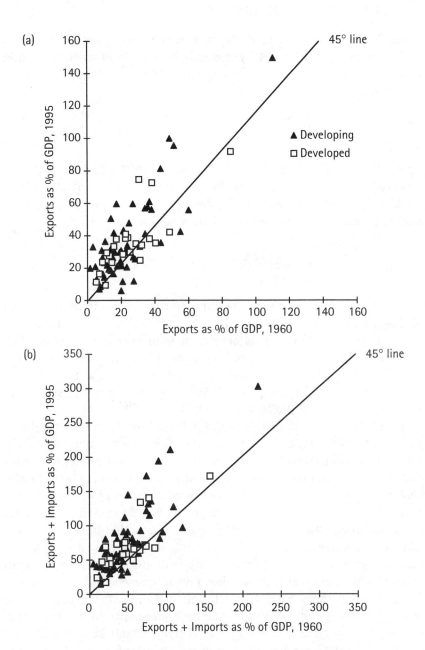

Figure 2.2.

Source: World Bank (WDI, 1998). The sample comprises fifty-nine observations for developing, and twenty-three observations for developed countries, as defined in World Bank (WDI, 1998).

where Y denotes GDP and Z the sum of the components of that part of final demand that is met by domestic output. In order to show this, we differentiate (2.15) w.r.t. time and obtain the following expression in growth rates:

$$\frac{\dot{Y}}{Y} \equiv (1-e) \cdot \frac{\dot{Z}}{Z} + e \cdot \frac{\dot{E}}{E}, \qquad (2.16)$$

from which it is clear that one is almost certain to find a correlation between the growth rates of output and exports when e is about one-third, which is the average for the sample reported in Fig. 2.1. A simple rearrangement of (2.16) also yields, however,

$$\frac{\dot{Y}}{Y} \equiv \frac{\dot{Z}}{Z} + \frac{e}{1-e} \cdot \left(\frac{\dot{E}}{E} - \frac{\dot{Y}}{Y} \right), \qquad (2.17)$$

and since $(\dot{E}/E - \dot{Y}/Y)$ is the growth rate of e, it is plain that Michaely's proposal is still beset by the same problem—indeed more so, for $e/(1-e) > e$. One way of skirting it is to examine the correlation between the growth rate of exports and that of Z, the residual component of GDP. The associated Spearman rank correlation for Michaely's sample of forty-one LDCs over the period 1950–73 is 0.452, which is significant at the 1 per cent level (Heller and Porter, 1978: 192).

What is one to make of this finding? Heller and Porter are careful to point out that arriving at the 'correct' correlation does not imply that one is about to employ a correct test of the presence of a causal relationship. This word of caution went unheeded in some quarters. Balassa (1978) and Feder (1983), for example, were mainly concerned to control for cross-country differences in the growth rates of factor inputs. To establish whether a particular interpretation of a correlation between the growth of output and exports would survive such a control, they proceeded to extend a standard growth accounting framework by introducing the growth rate of exports as an additional regressor. Employing somewhat different reduced forms,[15] both authors found the coefficient on the growth rate of exports to be positive and highly significant, and both succumbed to the temptation to draw the conclusion that they had thereby established a causal link running from the growth of exports to the growth of output. In focusing on the strong possibility that important variables might be omitted, they

---

[15] Whereas Balassa (1978) simply adduced a reduced form, Feder derived his from a two-sector framework, in which exports yield an external effect on production in the rest of the economy.

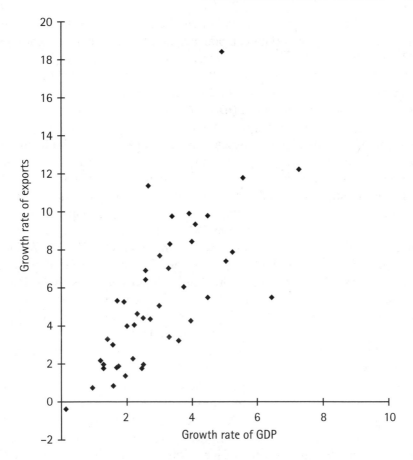

Figure 2.3. Growth rates of GDP and Exports, 1960–95

Source: International Statistical Yearbook, 1998 (nominal data), International Financial Statistics Yearbook, 1984 and 1998 (deflators for 1960).

had overlooked the more fundamental points raised by Michaely and Heller and Porter.

Just how dangerous it can be to draw conclusions based on correlations or the introduction of 'plausible' regressors into the growth accounting framework is nicely demonstrated by Sheehey (1990). Why, it might be asked, should we stop at exports when there are other components of GDP that plausibly generate positive externalities or spill-overs? Indeed, to be on the safe side, one should also test whether 'implausible' components, such as private consumption, conform to prior expectations. Sheehey first calculates Spearman rank correlation coefficients between the growth of aggregate output and various components thereof, both on the expenditure side and by sector of origin. Exports come out well, but private consumption and manufacturing do even better. An unpromising start, but matters get worse. The next step, in view of (2.15) and (2.16), is to subtract the contribution of each component to GDP in order to yield a variable analogous to Z, and then to compute growth rates once more. The corresponding Spearman rank correlation coefficient is now statistically insignificant in the case of exports, a finding that contradicts Heller and Porter's (1978). Only in the case of three sectors of origin, namely, manufacturing, utilities, and services, is the said coefficient significant at conventional levels. As a final step, Sheehey runs growth-accounting regressions using both Balassa's and Feder's specifications, with the growth rate of each component of GDP taken in turn as the additional regressor. The coefficients thereon turn out to be highly significant in all cases. These findings add up to a devastating attack on much of the literature dealing with this issue. As Sheehey writes in conclusion, '... it should be stressed that these results in no way overturn the case for an export promotion strategy. They merely indicate that a large body of evidence that is supposed to demonstrate the superiority of this strategy has no bearing on this controversy' (p. 115).

Some other approach is needed, therefore, if the aim is to establish whether there exists a causal relationship between the growth of exports and that of output. One such alternative appeals to the concept of 'causality' in econometrics. In essence, the idea is to establish whether the preceding movements in one variable influence the current movement of another. If this is indeed the case, it is said that the former series (Granger-)causes the latter, where the converse may also hold simultaneously. In the present context, one begins by estimating an equation for the rate of growth of output at time τ using some set of past values thereof as regressors:

$$\hat{y}_\tau = a + \sum_{i=1}^{M} \alpha_i \hat{y}_{\tau-i} + u_\tau, \tag{2.18}$$

where u_τ is an i.i.d. disturbance term and $\hat{y}_\tau \equiv (Y_{\tau+1} - Y_\tau)/Y_\tau$. The number of lags, M, is chosen so as to minimize a particular criterion function. The next step is to discover whether the fit yielded by Eqn (2.18) can be improved by introducing lagged values of the rate of growth of exports as additional regressors; so one then estimates

$$\hat{y}_\tau = a + \sum_{i=1}^{M} \alpha_i \hat{y}_{\tau-i} + \sum_{i=1}^{N} \beta_i \hat{e}_{\tau-i} + u_\tau, \tag{2.19}$$

where $\hat{e}_\tau \equiv (E_{\tau+1} - E_\tau)/E_\tau$ and N is determined similarly to M, given M from the first stage. If the introduction of these additional terms improves the fit, then 'causality' from the growth of exports to that of output has been duly established. It is then interesting to examine the sign of the sum of the estimated coefficients, $\sum_{i=1}^{N} \beta_i$, in the expectation that it will be positive. To complete the story, one then reverses the roles of output and exports, and thereby tests whether changes in output 'cause' changes in exports.

This is the approach adopted by Bahmani-Oskooee et al. (1991), who thereby refine an earlier contribution of Jung and Marshall (1986). The latter analyse a group of thirty-seven countries; but only in four do they find evidence of a link running from exports to output. Bahmani-Oskooee et al. take a group of twenty LDCs, in which the series range from 24 to 37 years. In ten cases, there is no evidence whatever of causality from the growth of exports to that of output. In the remaining ten, the F-statistic is significant at the 5 per cent level in only three cases: the Dominican Republic, Paraguay, and Peru, with the sum $\sum_{i=1}^{N} \beta_i$ being negative for the latter pair. The darling cases, Taiwan and South Korea, pass muster only at the 10 per cent level, as do Indonesia and Thailand. Turning to the converse direction, the split is thirteen to seven against causation from output to exports. In the latter seven, only in the case of Indonesia, Nigeria, and Thailand is the F-statistic significant at the 5 per cent level, with the sum of the estimated coefficients being positive for the latter pair. In the case of Korea, the sum is positive too, but only at the 10 per cent level. Bahmani-Oskooee et al. attempt to construe their findings as providing 'some support for the export-led growth hypothesis...' (p. 414); but the interpretation that output leads exports seems equally admissible. Most readers will probably settle for the Scottish verdict of not proven.

To close this section, it should be remarked that how best to interpret the correlation between the rates of growth of output and exports is closely bound up with the acrimonious controversy about the right trade strategy that has run through the literature on this topic. In contrast to the 1987 *World Development Report*'s bold assertion of the superiority of an 'open' strategy, the above reading of the evidence adduced in its favour suggests that the case is far from compelling, even if one ignores the work based on the time series approach. The fact that the main reservations were already well-known, and that the awkward findings in Jung and Marshall (1986) were available to the *Report*'s authors at the time of writing, leaves the impression that, on this particular score, scholarly prudence had fallen victim to the demands of an institutional agenda. In this connection, it is noteworthy that in a recent essay, Srinivasan (2000), a tireless campaigner for open development strategies in the broad sense, is deeply reluctant to place much weight on the results of such regressions, on the grounds that there are such serious problems with the quality of the data, and so much latitude in the choice of sample, time period, and specification, that any 'finding' can be overturned. Instead, he prefers to rest the empirical case for an open strategy on the classic variety of cross-country studies referred to above, with their detailed analyses of individual cases. Given the strong element of judgement, however tempered and careful, that enters into such studies, it seems fair to conclude that important aspects of the nature of the relationship between trade and growth are still issues on which reasonable people can differ.

2.5. Summary

From the middle of the twentieth century onwards, most LDCs began to pursue a strategy of import substitution in which domestic industry was promoted at the expense of the primary sector, especially agriculture. The main reasons for doing so ranged from a deep 'export pessimism' born of the inter-war experience to a conviction that rapid industrialization is the key to a high standard of living, with an occasional hint that an industrial sector might be a merit want. The battery of measures employed for this purpose included not only protective tariffs and quotas, which were tightened as needed to maintain domestic profitability, but also restrictions on foreign investment, which were designed to keep the ensuing rents at home. As time passed, the whole system of taxes, subsidies, and regulations often took on an impenetrable and partly contradictory character, and it was only towards the end of that century that widespread and serious efforts were made to dismantle at least part of the structure that had been progressively erected in earlier decades. Yet despite all this, most economies became more open, as measured by their trade-to-GDP ratios, between 1960 and 1995.

When confronted with such a set of thoroughgoing interventions, economists are wont to try to quantify them in the form of an index. The

commonly used measure in this case is the so-called effective rate of protection, which is obtained by taking the difference between an activity's
value added at domestic and world prices, respectively, and then normaliz-
ing it by the latter. For all its prominence, especially in practical work, the
ERP suffers from a number of grave defects. In order to accommodate non-
tradables and substitution in production, a full-scale general equilibrium
analysis is needed. This, once accomplished, renders the ERP superfluous.
There is, moreover, no place in this index for the effects of distortions
arising outside the sphere of international trade, such as those connected with taxes on consumption or imperfections in factor markets. These
theoretical drawbacks aside, the calculation of the index is considerably
complicated in practice by the presence of quotas, other regulations, and
an overvalued exchange rate. For none of these problems is there a fully
satisfactory solution outside a full-scale general equilibrium analysis.

To measure the 'extent' of protection is one thing; but what ultimately
counts is the damage wrought by protectionist policy, and here the EPR is
of no use. A natural way of evaluating an economic policy is to measure
the resulting gain or loss in welfare relative to a well-defined alternative.
The 'standard' account in Section 1.1 suggests that the right reference case
is free trade, and that the right way to address the question is to use general equilibrium analysis. This is indeed the approach adopted by many.
In order to show how it is implemented, it suffices to set out a static 2×2
model of the textbook sort. The next steps are to list the particular policy
instruments at the government's disposal, to select values for the endowments and parameters associated with the choice of functional forms, and
then to solve the system for the particular policy variant of interest. What
are arguably 'plausible' values yield estimates of the costs of protection
that are strikingly small—of the order of 1 or 2 per cent of GDP at world
prices. Perhaps just as striking is the fact that these estimates are very
close to those yielded by carefully estimated, large-scale models featuring
numerous goods, an array of factors, and diverse households.

An alternative line of approach is to discard static theory and, prompted
by the dynamic factors considered in Chapter 1, to examine instead
whether there is an empirical relationship between the growth of exports
and that of GDP. Testing for such a relationship runs up against at least
two difficulties. First, exports usually comprise a substantial proportion
of GDP, so that their growth rates are virtually bound to be positively
correlated. Secondly, there is the need to establish the causal direction
in any such statistical relationship. It seems fair to say that the correlation is well established, though it does not always survive after suitable

adjustments have been made to deal with the first difficulty. More troubling still is that various other components of GDP perform even better as regressors in growth-accounting frameworks. Attempts to draw inferences about the causal direction have centred, quite naturally, on the use of certain techniques in time-series econometrics. These, too, have yielded a rather meagre harvest for protagonists of open trade regimes. In the great majority of cases, the growth of exports fails to 'lead' that of GDP at conventional levels of significance, and 'reverse causation', from GDP to exports, also crops up.

Recommended Reading

The path-breaking studies of protectionism in the post-war era are Little *et al.* (1970) and Balassa (1971). A pioneering study of the relationship between the trade regime and employment is Kreuger (1983). For a somewhat more sceptical view of 'open' trade regimes, see Rodrik (1999).

Exercises

1. Consider a small, open economy in which perfect competition rules everywhere, except in the labour market. An exportable (good 1) is produced by means of unassisted labour alone, the labour–output coefficient being constant at unity. The world price of good 1 is unity and exports are subject to an *ad valorem* tax of 25 per cent. Two goods are imported ($i = 2, 3$); neither is produced domestically. Good 2 is wholly consumed; good 3 is used solely as an input into the production of good 4. The world prices of goods 2 and 3 are unity and two, respectively. Good 2 is subject to a tariff of 100 per cent, good 3 to none. Good 4 is a non-tradable. The technology is Leontief, the (unit) input vector being

$$a_4 = (0.1, 0, 0.3, 0; l_4 = 0.5).$$

There is full employment, but the wage rate in sector 4 is regulated to a level that is twice that ruling in sector 1, in which the wage is determined under perfect competition. Find all domestic prices, including wage rates.

Consider the following proposal to produce good 2 on a small scale at home, namely, with the unit activity vector

$$a_2 = (0, 0.2, 0.3, 0.1; l_2 = 0.4).$$

If the wage payable is the regulated wage, is the project profitable at market prices? What ERP would the project enjoy, if undertaken? Repeat the analysis for the case where the unit input vector for sector 4 is

$$a_4 = (0.1, 0, 0.3, 0.1; l_4 = 0.5).$$

Comment on your choice of how to treat and value non-tradables and the factors needed to produce them. Repeat your analysis for the case where the said project could be replicated on a large scale.

2. Derive the allocations in cases (a) and (b) of Table 2.1 analytically. Using Maple or a similar package, confirm the allocations in cases (c) and (d). Failing such programming skills, use a hand calculator to verify that all details of the latter allocations are indeed correct, up to rounding errors. [Hint: In cases (a) and (b), first principles can be used to simplify the problem. If these are not apparent, it will suffice to write out a system of six equations, which are formulated so as to respect the full-employment conditions for labour and capital. These can then be further reduced and solved. The demand side of the story can be derived independently. In cases (c) and (d), however, there is an endogenous tax on good 1, so that eight equations now need to be solved simultaneously, and a numerical procedure is needed.]

3. Repeat the analysis of the computable 2×2 model in Section 2.3 when the value of ρ in sector 2 is 0.25 instead of unity. Comment on the differences between both sets of results, and compare them in turn with those obtained for the two-period model in Exercise 1.1.

3. International Trade: Liberalization

The path away from protectionism toward an open trading regime has turned out to be a rocky one, and those travelling it have experienced many a setback along the way. Just how tortuous is revealed by Little *et al.*'s (1993) wide-ranging study of eighteen LDCs over the period between 1965 and 1990.[1] They identify no fewer than twenty-six episodes of tightening and thirty-three of liberalization for the group in question (ibid.: Table 9.1, pp. 266–7), an assessment based on the changing course of quotas, tariffs, and the taxation of exports in each. This was, of course, a rather turbulent period in the world economy. The Bretton Woods system of fixed exchange rates broke down, triggered by the floating of the dollar in 1971. The first of the two oil shocks and a general boom in commodity prices followed in 1973–74, the second oil shock in 1979–80, oil prices collapsed in 1986, and there were sundry sharp movements in the prices of other primary commodities. The first oil shock also ushered in half a decade of plentiful foreign credit at low real rates of interest, as the commercial banks recycled the surpluses racked up by OPEC's members. Buffeted by adverse terms-of-trade shocks, most LDCs seized eagerly on this opportunity to borrow, perhaps in the hope that the shocks would be temporary, but more likely as a way of postponing the painful adjustments required if they turned out to be permanent. These countries were therefore in a vulnerable position when the second oil shock was compounded by the pursuit of rigorously restrictive monetary policies in the United States and other OECD countries, which caused real interest rates to rise to historically very high levels and precipitated the debt crisis. Rates began to fall only in 1984, declining from their peak of 6–7 per cent to about 4 per cent by 1987 (ibid.: 103).

In such an environment, any attempt to isolate the effects of liberalizing measures on output, employment, and welfare must be counted as a hazardous undertaking. Many of these effects make themselves felt only over the medium to long run; but as noted above, governments changed course so frequently in response to other exigencies that there are ample confounding factors to bury the evidence. Indeed, the life expectancy of an attempted liberalization appeared to be bound up with the course of external events and whether sound policies had been pursued in other

---

[1] Argentina, Brazil, Cameroon, Chile, Colombia, Costa Rica, Côte d' Ivoire, India, Indonesia, Kenya, South Korea, Mexico, Morocco, Nigeria, Pakistan, Sri Lanka, Thailand, and Turkey.

areas. Central aspects of trade policy were subordinated, in large part, to the demands of macroeconomic management. In episodes of tightening, which were usually responses to balance-of-payments difficulties, the choice of instrument commonly fell on quotas, whereby goods were moved from a 'free' to a 'restricted' list. Under liberalization, goods were shunted in the reverse direction (ibid.: 264), occasionally with the palliative of higher tariffs. Liberalization was often preceded, or accompanied, by a devaluation.

It is not our purpose here to go into the particular empirical details of this period of economic history, but rather to employ the tools of comparative statics the better to understand its various elements, albeit presented in a highly simplified form. This is an essential step, both to make sense of the historical record and to guide future attempts at reform. We begin, in Section 3.1, by laying out a model of a small, open economy, which serves as the basis for the entire chapter. It also yields a proposition that states sufficient conditions for a change in any policy to improve welfare: first, that it yield an increase in the value of GDP at world prices, and second that it compress consumer prices in a particular way. In order to apply the model to the issues at hand, Section 3.2 introduces the important, and realistic, assumption that wage rates are imperfectly flexible, which both complicates and enriches the analysis of changes in trade policy. Reductions in tariffs are dealt with in Section 3.2, and a relaxation of quotas in Section 3.3. The results thereof are then put to work in analysing situations wherein an improvement in the trade balance is required, possibly with the economy labouring under 'import starvation'. This is the topic of Section 3.4. Given the importance of the product-wage in determining employment and output, one is drawn to examining the effects of reducing distortions in the labour market. This is taken up in Section 3.5, which serves as a preliminary to the vital topic of devaluation in Section 3.6. The latter requires an important extension of the basic model to include money.

3.1. Ranking Policies

By and large, the questions that concern us in this chapter can be addressed satisfactorily without bringing non-tradable goods into the picture. Their exclusion yields a valuable and welcome simplification. For if all goods are traded and the economy is small, it turns out that the effects of changes in policy on economic welfare hinge crucially not only on whether distortions are reduced in a suitable way, but also on whether output valued at world prices increases or decreases.

Recalling the notation of earlier chapters, let p_i, q_i, x_i, and y_i denote the domestic producer price, consumer price, consumption, and (net) output of good i, respectively. A formal statement of the assumptions to be employed is:

Assumption 1. All goods are tradable on world markets at the parametric prices p^*.

Assumption 2. There is a single representative household, whose preferences are locally non-satiated, strictly quasi-concave, and smooth, with representation $u = u(x)$. All goods are both normal and necessary in consumption.

Assumption 3. The household treats consumer prices as parametrically given.

Assumption 4. The economy possesses an endowment of F units of foreign exchange.

Assumption 5. The government returns all net revenues to the household.

Some brief comments are in order. First, the analysis is confined to a single period, so that A5 can be taken to imply that all income is consumed. This restriction can be relaxed by the usual device of dating all variables and writing down the budget constraints in a suitable way. For present purposes, however, there is little to be gained from such a generalization, dynamic considerations being postponed to Chapter 7. Second, the endowment of foreign exchange may be interpreted as a (fixed) amount of foreign aid or borrowing ($F > 0$), or of foreign lending ($F < 0$), in any period. Equivalently, it is the deficit on the trade account. Third, the government's net revenues include the surpluses or losses of state-owned enterprises. Observe that thus far, no appeal has been made to the possibility of using lump-sum taxes to effect transfers between the private and public sectors.

The following two conditions must be satisfied in any equilibrium. First, given any vector of consumer prices, q, and disposable income, Y^d, the household is at its optimum. Since preferences are smooth and all goods are consumed in strictly positive amounts, the first-order conditions yield the familiar condition that the |MRS| between any pair of goods be equal to the ratio of their prices:

$$u_i/u_j = q_i/q_j \quad \forall i,j \ (i \neq j), \tag{3.1}$$

where u_i denotes the derivative of $u(x)$ w.r.t. x_i. Second, however taxes be levied and the resulting revenues rebated to the private sector, Walras' law implies that

$$p^*x = p^*y + F, \tag{3.2}$$

that is to say, the value of consumption at world prices is equal to aggregate value added at world prices plus the endowment of foreign exchange.
For any given q, the set of consumption vectors satisfying Eqn (3.1) is the
corresponding income-expansion path in the space of x, where it should be
recalled that only relative prices matter. If all goods are normal, the projec-
tion of this path onto the plane defined by (Ox_i, Ox_j) will be upward-sloping
for all pairs $(i, j; i \neq j)$. Similarly, for any given vector $(p^*, p^*y + F)$, condition (3.2) defines the upper boundary of the set of all feasible consumption
vectors, which is the plane with normal p^* that passes through the point
$(y_1 + F/p_1^*, y_2, \ldots, y_n)$. It follows at once that the intersection of the said
sets is a unique, positive consumption vector, x^0 say.

The case of two goods is depicted in Fig. 3.1, where, for convenience,
it has been assumed that $F = 0$. The income-expansion path is the locus
$OE(q)$; the upper boundary of the feasible set is the straight line with slope
$-(p_1^*/p_2^*)$ that passes through the point A, which denotes the pair (y_1, y_2).
They intersect at the point C, which denotes the bundle (x_1^0, x_2^0), where
the indifference curve through C has slope $-(q_1/q_2)$. Given the bundle of

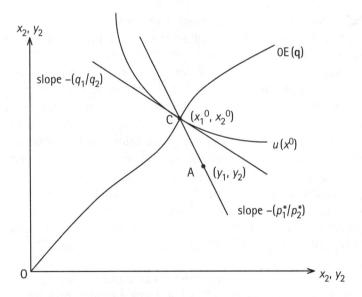

Figure 3.1. Production and consumption when all goods are traded

outputs y and the opportunity to trade at prices p^*, the line passing through AC is the availability line for the economy.

The first result is immediate. An increase in (p^*y+F) with q unchanged will yield a strictly preferred allocation, since by virtue of A2, both elements of x^0 increase as one moves outwards along a given expansion path. The second result follows from the fact that since the normal to the indifference curve at x^0, namely $\nabla u(x^0)$, is proportional to q, an improvement in welfare is possible, in principle, whenever $q \neq p^*$ and there is some substitutability in consumption. An improvement is realized if the divergence between q and p^* is reduced in a suitable way, provided whatever measures bring about a desirable change in q do not also reduce (p^*y+F). In the case of two goods, any divergence between p^* and q may be reduced as follows. Suppose, without loss of generality, that $q_2/q_1 > p_2^*/p_1^*$, as depicted in Fig. 3.1. It is clear that any measures that reduce q_1/q_2 while preserving $q_2/q_1 \geq p_2^*/p_1^*$, and that do not diminish $(p^*y + F)$, will improve welfare. For the expansion path that corresponds to the new q will intersect the line though AC at a point to the NE of C such that the point in question is preferred to C.

The first result generalizes at once to the case of more than two goods. The second, unfortunately, does not. That is to say, it does not follow that by taking any pair of goods whose relative consumer price diverges from the corresponding relative world price and then reducing the gap between them, one will bring about a preferred allocation. The reason is that changes in the relative consumer price of any pair of goods will, in general, affect the consumption of other goods, a complication that cannot arise when there are only two goods. Observe, however, that the above argument in the case of just two goods involves preserving the initial rank ordering of their domestic and foreign relative prices. Armed with this insight, let all goods be ranked according to the ratio of their consumer to their respective world prices, and consider a reform whereby the consumer price of the good whose said ratio is greatest is reduced until its ratio equals that of the second-ranked good. Symmetrically, one can also start at the other end with the good whose ratio is lowest, and raise it until the second lowest ratio is reached. The process is then continued in the same way, from the 'outside in', as it were. Such a combined reform of consumer prices will be called a 'concertina' reform.

The question to be answered is this: for any given vector $(p^*, p^*y + F)$, will such a reform improve welfare? A sufficient condition to answer it in the affirmative involves augmenting A1–A5 by a further restriction on preferences:

Assumption 6. All goods are Hicksian substitutes: $\partial x_i^h / \partial q_j > 0 \, \forall i, j \, (i \neq j)$, where x_i^h is the compensated demand for good i.[2]

Lemma. *If A1–A6 hold and the vector $(p^*, p^*y + F)$ is fixed, then any 'concertina' reform will improve welfare.*

Proof. The proof that follows deals with the case of three goods, which has the advantage that geometry can be used to convey the basic intuition. It will become clear that the generalization to more than three goods is straightforward. We proceed in steps.

Step 1. The availability set in the space of x is now the plane defined by $p^*x = p^*y + F$, the relevant subset of which is a triangle whose vertices lie on the coordinate axes, as depicted by FGH in Fig. 3.2. Without loss of generality, let $q_3/p_3^* > q_2/p_2^* > q_1/p_1^*$. Let the initial equilibrium be at point C, which lies on the ovoid-shaped intersection of the associated indifference surface with FGH. This ovoid-shaped curve, $\psi(x) = 0$, all points within whose boundary are strictly preferred to C, can be represented in differential form as follows. On any indifference surface, we have, by definition,

$$\mathrm{d}u = \nabla u(x) \cdot \mathrm{d}x = 0.$$

At the same time, changes in x must leave it on the upper boundary of the availability set, which may be written in differential form as

$$p^* \cdot \mathrm{d}x = 0.$$

At point C, moreover, the gradient vector $\nabla u(x)$ is proportional to q, the factor of proportionality being the Lagrange multiplier associated with the consumer's budget constraint. It follows that both $q \cdot \mathrm{d}x = 0$ and $p^* \cdot \mathrm{d}x = 0$ are satisfied at C. Eliminating $\mathrm{d}x_1$, we obtain the slope of the ovoid-shaped line at C when projected onto the plane (Ox_2, Ox_3):

$$\left. \frac{\mathrm{d}x_3}{\mathrm{d}x_2} \right|_{\psi=0, \mathrm{C}} = -\frac{(q_2/p_2^*) - (q_1/p_1^*)}{(q_3/p_3^*) - (q_1/p_1^*)} \cdot \frac{p_2^*}{p_3^*} < 0 \tag{3.3a}$$

---

[2] Given the output vector y, A6 implies that the excess demand for the good with the highest ratio of the domestic to the world price is a net substitute for all other goods, which is a requirement for the validity of an analogous, well-known proposition in the theory of tariff reform. For an exposition and references, see Bhagwati *et al.* (1998: chapter 35).

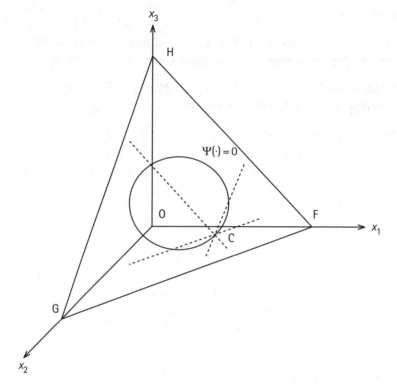

Figure 3.2. The availability set and a 'concertina' reform under Assumption 6

by virtue of the assumption that $q_3/p_3^* > q_2/p_2^* > q_1/p_1^*$ is satisfied. Analogous expressions hold for the pair of goods 1 and 2, as well as for the pair 1 and 3, where

$$\left.\frac{\partial x_3}{\partial x_1}\right|_{\psi=0,C} > 0, \tag{3.3b}$$

$$\left.\frac{\partial x_2}{\partial x_1}\right|_{\psi=0,C} < 0. \tag{3.3c}$$

Hence, C must lie in the segment of $\psi(\cdot) = 0$ as depicted in Fig. 3.2.

Step 2. The dashed lines through C on the plane FGH are parallel to the respective sides of the triangle. That parallel to GH, for example, may be expressed in differential form as

$$\left.\frac{dx_3}{dx_2}\right|_{dx_1=0} = -\frac{p_2^*}{p_3^*}, \tag{3.4}$$

and analogously for the other pairs. A comparison of Eqns (3.3a)–(3.3c) with Eqn (3.4) in the light of the condition $q_3/p_3^* > q_2/p_2^* > q_1/p_1^*$ yields

$$\left|\frac{\mathrm{d}x_2}{\mathrm{d}x_1}\right|_{\psi=0,C} > \left|\frac{\mathrm{d}x_2}{\mathrm{d}x_1}\right|_{\mathrm{d}x_3=0}, \quad \left.\frac{\mathrm{d}x_3}{\mathrm{d}x_1}\right|_{\psi=0,C} > 0 > \left.\frac{\mathrm{d}x_3}{\mathrm{d}x_1}\right|_{\mathrm{d}x_2=0},$$

$$\left|\frac{\mathrm{d}x_3}{\mathrm{d}x_2}\right|_{\psi=0,C} < \left|\frac{\mathrm{d}x_3}{\mathrm{d}x_2}\right|_{\mathrm{d}x_1=0},$$

so that the dashed lines parallel to FG, FH, and GH intersect $\psi(\cdot) = 0$ at C as drawn.

Step 3. Consider now a piecemeal reform under which the domestic price of good 3 alone is reduced by an amount that preserves $q_3/p_3^* \geq q_2/p_2^*$. Such a reform will increase the compensated demand for good 3 and, by A6, reduce the compensated demands for goods 1 and 2, the utility level in question being that attained at C. Since the reform also preserves the weak inequality in both Eqns (3.3a) and (3.3c), the resulting compensated demand vector, when viewed from a direction normal to the plane FGH, will lie within the arc formed by the dashed lines through C parallel to GH and FH. It follows that the expansion path associated with the post-reform consumer price vector will intersect the plane FGH within the said arc.

Step 4. By examining the arc with apex C formed by the dashed lines parallel to FH and FG, an exactly analogous argument establishes that welfare will also be improved by an *increase* in q_1 alone that preserves $q_2/p_2^* \geq q_1/p_1^*$.

Step 5. In order to complete the proof, we need to examine the case where $q_3/p_3^* = q_2/p_2^*$. A comparison of Eqns (3.3a) and (3.4) reveals that the dashed line through C parallel to GH is then tangential to $\psi(\cdot) = 0$ at C. From Step 4, it is clear that welfare can be improved by increasing q_1 while preserving $q_3/p_3^* = q_2/p_2^* \geq q_1/p_1^*$. When there are more than three goods, however, it will be necessary to reduce (or increase) the consumer prices of two or more goods in concert as the whole price vector is progressively compressed in 'concertina' fashion, so we consider the effects of reducing q_3 and q_2 in such a way as to preserve $q_3/p_3^* = q_2/p_2^* \geq q_1/p_1^*$. This will clearly have the effect of reducing the compensated demand for good 1, as desired. In order to prove that welfare will improve as a result, it suffices to show that the compensated demands for goods 2 and 3 will both increase, which is proved as follows.

Since $q_3/p_3^* = q_2/p_2^*$, we have

$$dx_2^h = \left(\frac{\partial x_2^h}{\partial q_2} + \frac{p_3^*}{p_2^*}\frac{\partial x_2^h}{\partial q_3}\right) dq_2.$$

Recalling that the compensated demand function for the ith good is the corresponding derivative of the expenditure function and that said demand function is homogeneous of degree zero in q, we have $q \cdot (\partial x_i^h/\partial q) = 0$ for all i. For good 2, therefore,

$$\frac{q_1}{q_2}\frac{\partial x_2^h}{\partial q_1} + \left(\frac{\partial x_2^h}{\partial q_2} + \frac{p_3^*}{p_2^*}\frac{\partial x_2^h}{\partial q_3}\right) = 0,$$

where the fact that the reform preserves $q_3/p_3^* = q_2/p_2^*$ has been used once more. Since $\partial x_2^h/\partial q_1 > 0$, , it follows at once that the reform in question will indeed increase the compensated demand for good 2. By symmetry, the same holds for good 3. □

Remark 1. If there are four goods, for example, the first stage of a full concertina reform will yield $q_4/p_4^* = q_3/p_3^* \geq q_2/p_2^* = q_1/p_1^*$ and, by virtue of the lemma, an improvement in welfare. Successive concertina reforms will do likewise. In the case of a full concertina reform, domestic prices will be a scalar multiple of world prices, $q = ep^*$. Since only relative prices matter in this setting, the resulting allocation will be efficient given $(p^*, p^*y + F)$.

We turn finally to the effects of changes in policy. Let s denote the vector of policy parameters. In general, all endogenous variables will depend on s, although some may be independent of one or more elements thereof. The foregoing results may be summarized as follows:

Proposition 3.1. *Let the goods be numbered in ascending order according to their ratios $q_i(s')/p_i^*$ under policy s'. Given assumptions A1–A6, s will be a superior policy vector to s', in the sense that $u[x(s)] > u[x(s')]$, if all of the following conditions hold and at least one of the first three does so as a strict inequality:*

(i) $p^*y(s) \geq p^*y(s')$;

(ii) *there is some positive integer h such that*

$$q_{n-h+1}(s')/p_{n-h+1}^* \geq q_n(s)/p_n^* = \cdots = q_{n-h+1}(s)/p_{n-h+1}^* \geq q_{n-h}(s')/p_{n-h}^*;$$

(iii) there is some positive integer l such that

$$q_l(s')/p_l^* \leq q_1(s)/p_1^* = \cdots = q_l(s)/p_l^* \leq q_{l+1}(s')/p_{l+1}^*;$$

(iv) and that there are no changes in the consumer prices of all other goods.

Condition (i) states that the value of GDP at world prices be no lower under policy s than under s'; and the remainder state that s have the effect of compressing consumer prices, 'concertina' fashion, at the two extremes, so allowing for the possibility that the ratios of domestic to world prices may be unified at the top and bottom of the scales under s. Inspection of Fig. 3.1 suggests that these conditions may be loosely interpreted as involving an income and substitution effect, respectively, of a switch from one policy to the other, the substitution effect being induced by a reduction in one or more of the distortions among consumer prices. If any of these conditions is violated, then further analysis is needed to rank s and s'. It should be emphasized that nothing has been said about whether there is efficiency in production or about the forms of taxation or regulation that the government chooses to employ. In this respect, Proposition 1 is fairly general, though condition (iv) is evidently restrictive.

We now proceed to employ this proposition in settings where protection is accompanied by distortions in the labour market. The snag here is that although a piecemeal reform that satisfies the conditions of Proposition 1 will bring about an improvement in welfare if it does not result in a reduction in GDP at world prices, such a reduction cannot be ruled out in the face of a labour market that is regulated or insufficiently flexible. It should be emphasized that the same holds in the case where protection is completely dismantled.

3.2. Reductions in Tariffs When Wages are Rigid

We begin with the case where liberalization takes the form of a cut in tariffs. As noted in the introduction, this usually occurs at the last stages of the 'loosening' process of an attempted reform; but it turns out to be somewhat easier to analyse than the relaxation or outright abolition of quotas, which usually constitute the early stage. For present purposes, a two-good model has much to commend it. In addition to simplicity, it permits a straightforward application of Proposition 1; for a reduction in the difference between the domestic and world prices of either good will lead to an improvement in welfare if GDP valued at world prices does not fall. Rather more structure is needed, of course, to which end assumptions A1–A6 are supplemented by:

Assumption 7. Each good is produced under CRS by means of labour and a sector-specific form of capital K_i ($i = 1, 2$). Both production functions are smooth and satisfy the Inada conditions.

Assumption 8. The markets for goods are perfectly competitive.

Assumption 9. All three factors are supplied completely inelastically. Labour is perfectly mobile across sectors.

Assumption 10. The only form of distortionary taxation is an *ad valorem* tariff, t_2, on imports of good 2. Under the prevailing cost and demand conditions, good 2 is indeed imported, and the resulting revenues are rebated to households in the form of lump-sum transfers.[3]

Assumption 11. The wage rate ruling in the protected sector, w_2, is fixed exogenously at such a level that the labour market clears only when the wage rate in sector 1, w_1, is lower than w_2. In the short run, moreover, w_1 is also rigid downwards.

It follows from A7 and A9 that both goods will be produced domestically. In view of A10, goods 1 and 2 will also be referred to as the export and import good, respectively. A10 also implies that consumer prices will be equal to domestic producer prices. Observe that, although sector 2 enjoys a protective tariff, it is also burdened with a wage rate that exceeds the level that would rule in the absence of distortions in the labour market. Without further assumptions, therefore, it cannot be asserted that the output of good 2 will be greater under a protective tariff than under free trade. We shall return to this point shortly. Finally, the assumption that w_1 is rigid downwards in the short run implies that open unemployment can emerge during periods of adjustment to changes in policy.[4]

3.2.1. Equilibrium

Given that there is a tariff on good 2, it is natural to select good 1 as numeraire, with the normalization $p_1 = q_1 = p_1^* = 1$. The domestic price

---

[3] Recall from section 2.3 that with just two tradable goods and with all taxes to be rebated, there will be no trade at all if lump sum transfers cannot be used. Given the focus of this chapter, the availability of such transfers is, therefore, a welcome simplification. Matters become much more awkward in the absence of such transfers, and are postponed until the chapters on taxation.

[4] Support for this assumption is found in Little *et al.* (1993): 'In no country are prices and wages completely flexible downward…, less [so] in more urbanized or industrialized countries' (p. 101).

of good 2 is

$$p_2 = q_2 = (1 + t_2)p_2^*. \tag{3.5}$$

To complete the price vector, we note that under conditions of full employment, w_1 must be such that the derived demand for labour in sector 1 is equal to the residual supply thereof after firms in sector 2 have chosen their offers of employment at the regulated wage rate w_2. Let

$$L_2^0(w_2, p_2, K_2) \equiv \arg\max_{L_2}[p_2 f_2(L_2; K_2) - w_2 L_2].$$

In order to clear the labour market, therefore, w_1 must satisfy

$$w_1 = p_1 \partial f_1(\bar{L} - L_2^0; K_1)/\partial L_1, \tag{3.6}$$

where $\bar{L}$ is the economy's total endowment of labour. The above assumptions on the technology ensure that Eqn (3.6) has a unique, positive solution:

$$w_1 = w_1(p, w_2; K, \bar{L}). \tag{3.7}$$

In the absence of any distortions in the labour market, A7 yields a production possibility frontier (PPF) with the usual 'well-behaved' properties. Even in the presence of a wage gap ($w_2 > w_1$), however, the output vector will lie on the PPF whenever there is full employment. The output vector that rules in the case where $w_2 = w_1$ will be such that the absolute value of the slope of the PPF there (namely, the $|MRT_{12}|$) is equal to the domestic price ratio p_1/p_2. The said vector is denoted as point B in Fig. 3.3, where B lies on the expansion path OE(q) by virtue of $p = q$.

In the face of a wage gap, however, domestic production will lie at some point to the SE of B, at point A, say. In order to establish this claim, observe that profit maximization at prices (p, w) implies that

$$p_i \partial f_i/\partial L_i = w_i, \quad i = 1, 2. \tag{3.8}$$

Since capital is immobile and $L_1 + L_2 = \bar{L}$ holds everywhere along the PPF, we have

$$|MRT_{12}| = \left(\frac{\partial f_2/\partial L_2}{\partial f_1/\partial L_1}\right)_{L_1+L_2=\bar{L}}. \tag{3.9}$$

Using Eqns (3.5) and (3.8) in Eqn (3.9), we obtain, in equilibrium,

$$|MRT_{12}| = \frac{p_1^*}{p_2^*(1 + t_2)} \cdot \frac{w_2}{w_1}, \tag{3.10}$$

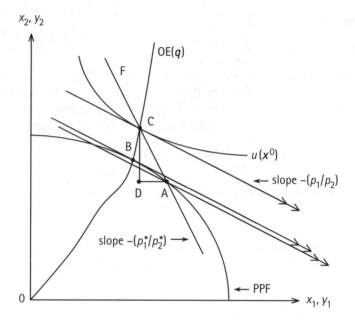

Figure 3.3. Equilibrium when there is a tariff and a wage gap

which exceeds p_1/p_2 if, and only if, $w_2 > w_1$. As drawn, the |MRT| at point A is less than the world-price ratio (p_1^*/p_2^*), which corresponds to the case where $(w_2/w_1) < (1+t_2)$: here, the tariff outweighs the proportional wage gap $(w_2/w_1)-1$ in determining how the allocation of labour is pulled away from that which would rule under free trade, the production point under the latter lying to the SE of A.

The value of gross domestic product at domestic prices is denoted by

$$y(\boldsymbol{p}, w_2; \boldsymbol{K}, \bar{L}) \equiv p_1 y_1(p_1, w_1(\cdot); K_1) + p_2 y_2(p_2, w_2; K_2), \qquad (3.11)$$

where $y_i(p_i, w_i; K_i)$ is the aggregate supply function of firms in sector i and w_1 is given by Eqn (3.7). This value added is distributed to households in the form of wages and the (quasi-)rents accruing to the fixed factors.

In order to complete the picture, we turn to the private sector's consumption decisions. The representative household's total income is the sum of gross domestic product and the rebate of tariff revenues, where the latter are denoted by

$$T \equiv (p_2^* - p_2)(y_2 - x_2). \qquad (3.12)$$

The household chooses a consumption vector x so as to

maximize $u(x)$

subject to the budget constraint

$$qx \leq Y(p, w_2; K, \bar{L}) + T \equiv Y^d, \tag{3.13}$$

where the household takes q, w_2 and Y^d as parametrically given. (Recall that $p = q$ under the above assumptions.) By A2, this problem has a unique, positive solution, which is denoted by $x^0(q, Y^d)$. We are not quite home, however, because T depends upon x_2. Although, in this particular model, production is independent of domestic demand, income and domestic demand are mutually and simultaneously determined. In order to find x^0 and Y^d, observe that Eqns (3.5), (3.11), and (3.12), and $p_1 = q_1 = p_1^*$ yield

$$Y^d = p^*(y - x) + qx,$$

so that Eqn (3.13), which will hold as a strict equality at the optimum, may be written as condition (3.2), with $F = 0$. That is to say, the trade account is balanced at world prices, which is simply a restatement of Walras' law, the household possessing neither foreign assets nor access to foreign borrowing opportunities. Condition (3.2) is depicted in Fig. 3.3 by the availability line AF, whose absolute slope, p_1^*/p_2^*, exceeds that of the household's budget line, p_1/p_2, by virtue of the tariff $(t_2 > 0)$. All consumption bundles lying on AF are available to the economy through international trade.

The condition needed to determine where on AF the equilibrium is located is that the household choose $x = x^0(q, Y^d)$. This choice lies on the income-expansion path associated with prices $q (=p)$, namely, OE(q). The intersection of OE(q) with AF, namely, point C, is the consumption bundle x^0. The segment AC is the associated trade vector, AD units of good 1 being exported in exchange for CD units of good 2.

In order to check this result for consistency, observe that the household's perceived budget line in the absence of the transfer T is the line with slope $-(p_1/p_2)$ that passes through the production point A. With the trade vector AC, the transfer amounts to $(p_2^* - p_2)(y_2 - x_2)$, where the tax wedge $(p_2^* - p_2)$ is represented by the difference between the slopes of the two lines that pass through A, and the amount imported, $-(y_2 - x_2)$, is CD. Hence, the household's budget line is the line through C with slope $-(p_1/p_2)$. Faced with the corresponding disposable income, Y^d, and prices q, however, the household will indeed choose C; for, by definition, the first-order conditions are satisfied everywhere on the expansion path OE(q).

3.2.2. A Reform

This is the state of affairs when the government, perhaps prodded by the World Bank and the IMF, decides to embark on a process of liberalization. In this simple model, liberalization takes the form of a cut in the tariff on good 2. As we will now demonstrate, this move may actually reduce welfare, even when the labour market has had time to adjust in full and the offending tariff has been abolished altogether. The reason for this dismaying possibility is that the economy is initially beset not by one, but by two distortions. The reduction, or outright removal, of the trade distortion will leave the distortion in the labour market wholly free to do its work in undermining efficiency, as measured by the value of GDP at world prices.

We analyse this reform employing a technique that will also prove to be useful in the following sections. Recalling Section 3.1, the market equilibrium may be represented as the solution to the (artificial) planner's problem

$$\underset{x|p}{\text{maximize }} u(x) \quad \text{subject to: Eqns (3.1) and (3.2),} \tag{3.14}$$

the purpose of whose introduction here is to bring the envelope theorem into play. The associated Lagrangian is

$$\Phi = u(x) + \mu(q_1 u_2 - q_2 u_1) + v[p^*(y - x) + F]. \tag{3.15}$$

Using the envelope theorem and recalling Eqn (3.5), we obtain the effect of a reduction in the consumer price of good 2 on economic welfare:

$$-\partial \Phi^0/\partial q_2 \equiv -\partial u^0/\partial q_2 = \mu u_1 - v p^*(\partial y/\partial p_2). \tag{3.16}$$

It is clear from Proposition 1 that both the dual variables μ and v are positive. For an increase in F with no change in domestic consumer prices will induce an outward movement along an unchanged income-expansion path, so that v is positive. Likewise, in the absence of a change in $(p^*y + F)$, a decrease in q_2 $(=p_2)$ that preserves $q_2 \geq p_2^*$ will improve welfare.

It should be emphasized that apart from the condition $p = q$, Eqn (3.16) has been derived without any reference to the forms of distortions, if any, that afflict the economy in question. In the present case, a cut in the tariff on good 2 will reduce p_2 and q_2 in the same proportion, so that welfare will improve if the value of GDP at world prices does not fall. If its value should fall, then problem (3.14) must be solved to obtain μ and v, whereupon Eqn (3.16) is used to evaluate $\partial u^0/\partial p_2$.

3.2.3. The Short Run

The cut in the tariff reduces p_2, to p_2' say, and hence causes output and employment in sector 2 to contract. Since w_1 is assumed to be inflexible downwards in the short run, output and employment in sector 1 are not immediately affected by the reform, so that open unemployment emerges. (Those who do keep their jobs enjoy the windfall of an increase in the real purchasing power of their wages; but distributional considerations have been suppressed by the assumption of a representative household.) The contraction in production is depicted in Fig. 3.4 as the vertical downward movement of the production point from A to A', through which passes the availability line in the presence of the lower tariff, which is denoted by A'F'. Taken by itself, this effect of the reform brings about a fall in welfare in the short run.

What pulls in the other direction is the reduction in the consumer price of good 2. That this may not be enough to offset the reform's adverse effect on GDP valued at world prices is seen at once by considering the case where the goods are strict complements in consumption, so that the position of the income-expansion path is independent of domestic prices. The reform then results in the consumption vector represented by the

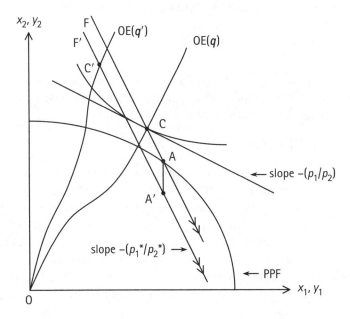

Figure 3.4. A cut in the tariff: the short-run effects

intersection of OE(q) with the availability line A'F', which lies below AF. By continuity, it follows that the reform will reduce welfare in the short run for all sufficiently small values of the elasticity of substitution in consumption. If, however, the said elasticity is large, then the reduction in q_2 will induce a substantial anticlockwise rotation of the expansion path, to OE(q') say, which may be so large as to bring about an equilibrium that lies to the NW of point C. The case depicted in Fig. 3.4 is such that the net effect of the reform is indeed an improvement in welfare, C' being preferred to C.[5] In general, however, the effect of the reduction in the tariff on welfare is ambiguous in the short run.

3.2.4. The Longer Run

After sufficient time has elapsed, and the reform has taken on at least the appearance of permanence, it is plausible that the labour market will clear through a reduction in the wage rate in the unprotected sector. The output vector will lie on the PPF once more, but now to the SE of A, since output in the protected sector will remain at the level established in the short run. Thus, the equilibrium output vector will be the intersection of the PPF with the horizontal through A', as depicted in Fig. 3.5. The question to be settled is whether this recovery leaves output valued at world prices at a higher level than that ruling before the reform. For any y, we have

$$\frac{\partial (p^* y)}{\partial p_2} = p_1^* \frac{\partial f_1}{\partial L_1} \cdot \frac{\partial L_1}{\partial p_2} + p_2^* \frac{\partial f_2}{\partial L_2} \cdot \frac{\partial L_2}{\partial p_2}.$$

Recalling Eqn (3.9), and that $\partial L_1 / \partial p_2 + \partial L_2 / \partial p_2 = 0$ at full employment, it follows that the value of GDP at world prices will increase as a result of a (small) cut in the tariff on good 2 if and only if

$$p_1^* / p_2^* > |\mathrm{MRT}_{12}(y)|. \tag{3.17}$$

If Eqn (3.17) also holds after any reform, however large, then that reform will result in an increase in GDP at world prices. Such case is depicted in Fig. 3.5, where the combined effect of the changes in producer prices and wages is to shift production to the point A'' and consumption to C''.

If there were no distortions in the labour market, condition (3.17) would always hold when $t_2 > 0$, so that any movement towards free trade in this two-good setting would then always improve welfare. In the face of a sectoral wage gap, however, this claim cannot be made, for the usual

---

[5] In order to avoid unnecessary clutter, the line through C' with slope $-p_1/p_2'$ has not been drawn.

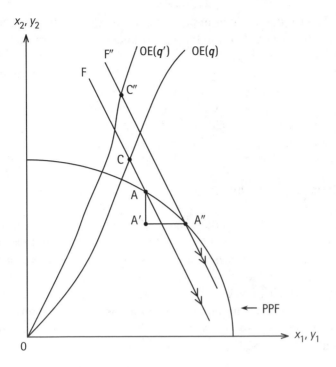

Figure 3.5. A cut in the tariff: the long-run effects

second-best reasons. Using the first-order conditions (3.8) to substitute for the values of the marginal products, a simple rearrangement yields the following expression for the change in GDP at world prices

$$\frac{\partial(p^*y)}{\partial p_2} = \left[-\frac{p_1^*}{p_1}w_1 + \frac{p_2^*}{p_2}w_2\right]\frac{\partial L_2}{\partial p_2}. \tag{3.18}$$

Recalling that $p_1^* = p_1$, we have the following result:

$$-\partial(p^* \cdot y)/\partial p_2 \gtrless 0 \quad \text{according as } w_2/w_1 \lessgtr (1 + t_2). \tag{3.19}$$

That is to say, a cut in the tariff will lead to an improvement in welfare if the tariff rate exceeds the proportional wage gap. If the converse holds, Eqn (3.16) will yield an ambiguous result where the effect of the reform on welfare is concerned. We have already seen that the elasticity of substitution in consumption plays a crucial role here. In particular, if the goods are poor substitutes and the level of protection is modest, a cut in the tariff is likely to reduce welfare. In practice, (w_2/w_1) is commonly in the region of two, if not higher, which implies that protective tariffs must be of the order of 100 per cent if the reform is to generate an increase in GDP at world prices, and so ensure that an improvement in welfare results when tariffs are cut. One should, of course, be wary of jumping to conclusions; for non-tradables have been omitted from the analysis. It is clear, however, that proponents of such liberalizing measures should also exercise due caution when making claims about the improvements those measures will bring about.

3.3. A Relaxation of Quotas

Quantitative restrictions on the imports of consumer goods are not usually relaxed in practice until the later stages of the liberalization process, and when they are loosened, offsetting tariffs are often introduced in order to dull the edge of foreign competition. Here, we confine the analysis to an economy in which there are initially quotas on imports of all consumer goods, but no tariffs. The public finance aspects of the reform are kept out of the picture by an appeal to lump-sum transfers when needed. The model laid out in Eqns (3.5)–(3.13) is easily adapted for this purpose. A10 is modified to read:

Assumption 12. Imports of good 2 are subject to a binding quota Q_2, and the domestic price is such as to clear the market.

Hence, Eqn (3.5) is replaced by the requirement that $p_2(= q_2)$ satisfy

$$y_2(p_2, w_2; K_2) + Q_2 = x_2^0(q, Y^d), \tag{3.5'}$$

where

$$Y^d = Y(p, w_2; K) + (p_2 - p_2^*)Q_2. \tag{3.13'}$$

The quota-rents in the amount $(p_2 - p_2^*)Q_2$ accrue either to the government through an auction, with the proceeds then rebated in the form of a lump-sum transfer to the private sector, or by importers who enjoy the receipt of licenses to import up to the amount Q_2 at the world price and then the right to sell off the said amount in the open market at the price p_2. In the case of a single, representative consumer, it does not matter which mechanism is in force. The difference between the domestic and world price implies an equivalent tariff rate of $(p_2/p_2^*) - 1$.

There are two ways of relaxing this quota. The first involves a preliminary step, in which the quota is replaced by its equivalent tariff. Under the above assumptions, this will leave the allocation of resources unchanged, except that all quota rents will now accrue to the government, if they did not do so before. This step is followed by a cut in the tariff, which brings us back to Section 3.2. The level of imports of good 2 in the resulting equilibrium can be dubbed the new quota without altering anything of substance. As will be argued in Section 5.1, this reform has much to commend it when there is a premium on government income. It is not, however, the course that governments always choose to take.

Consider, therefore, the second case, where the quota is simply increased. If it is lifted altogether, or is so substantially relaxed that it ceases to bind, producers and consumers alike will face the world price vector p^*. The results of this reform are exactly those derived in Section 3.2 for the case where the initial tariff is wholly abolished. If, however, the quota is relaxed somewhat, but continues to bind, then the new equilibrium must be found. Applying the envelope theorem to Eqn (3.15) once more, we have

$$\partial \Phi^0 / \partial Q_2 \equiv \partial u^0 / \partial Q_2 = [-\mu u_1 + v p^* \cdot (\partial y / \partial p_2)] \cdot (\partial p_2 / \partial Q_2), \quad (3.20)$$

a comparison of which with Eqn (3.16) reveals that the effect of a change in a binding quota is identical (up to a scalar multiple) to that of the negative of the change in its equivalent tariff. The only question to be settled, therefore, is whether an increase in a quota always results in a reduction in the equivalent tariff.

The answer is contained, implicitly, in Eqn (3.5′), total differentiation of which yields

$$\frac{\partial y_2}{\partial p_2} \cdot dp_2 + dQ_2 = \frac{\partial x_2^0}{\partial q_2} \cdot dq_2 + \frac{\partial x_2^0}{\partial Y^d} \cdot dY^d,$$

where dY^d is obtained by total differentiation of Eqn (3.13′). The partial equilibrium part of the story is clear: the supply of good 2 is increasing in its own price ($\partial y_2 / \partial p_2 > 0$) and the demand for it is decreasing in the same ($\partial x_2^0 / \partial q_2 < 0$), implying that p_2 falls as Q_2 rises. The spoiling factor is the income effect, $\partial x_2^0 / \partial Y^d$, which is positive and weighted by the change in aggregate income at domestic prices. To show that it does not outweigh the other, partial equilibrium effects, we proceed as follows. Dividing through by $dp_2 (= dq_2)$ and using the Slutsky equation, we obtain

$$\frac{dQ_2}{dp_2} = -\left(\frac{\partial y_2}{\partial p_2} - \frac{\partial x_2^h}{\partial q_2}\right) - \left(x_2^0 - \frac{dY^d}{dp_2}\right)\frac{\partial x_2^0}{\partial Y^d}, \quad (3.21)$$

where x_2^h is the Hicksian (compensated) demand for good 2, and

$$\frac{dY^d}{dp_2} = \frac{\partial Y^d}{\partial p_2} + \frac{\partial Y^d}{\partial Q_2} \cdot \frac{dQ_2}{dp_2}.$$

Recalling Eqns (3.11) and (3.13′), we obtain

$$\frac{\partial Y^d}{\partial p_2} = p_1 \frac{\partial Y_1}{\partial w_1} \cdot \frac{\partial w_1}{\partial p_2} + p_2 \frac{\partial y_2}{\partial p_2} + y_2 + Q_2$$

and

$$\frac{\partial Y^d}{\partial Q_2} = p_2 - p_2^*.$$

Substituting into Eqn (3.21), noting that $x_2^0 = y_2 + Q_2$, and rearranging, we obtain

$$\left(1 - (p_2 - p_2^*)\frac{\partial x_2^0}{\partial Y^d}\right) \frac{dQ_2}{dp_2}$$

$$= -\left(\frac{\partial y_2}{\partial p_2} - \frac{\partial x_2^h}{\partial q_2}\right) + \left(p_1\frac{\partial y_1}{\partial w_1} \cdot \frac{\partial w_1}{\partial p_2} + p_2\frac{\partial y_2}{\partial p_2}\right)\frac{\partial x_2^0}{\partial Y^d}$$

$$= -\left(1 - p_2\frac{\partial x_2^0}{\partial Y^d}\right)\frac{\partial y_2}{\partial p_2} + \frac{\partial x_2^h}{\partial q_2} + \left(p_1\frac{\partial y_1}{\partial w_1} \cdot \frac{\partial w_1}{\partial p_2}\right)\frac{\partial x_2^0}{\partial Y^d}.$$

Since both goods are normal, $\partial x_2^0/\partial Y^d > 0$ and $p_2 \cdot \partial x_2^0/\partial Y^d < 1$, so that the expression in brackets on the RHS is positive. Recalling that w_1 is non-decreasing in p_2 (by virtue of labour being drawn out of sector 1 in response to an increase in p_2 over the longer run), we have the desired result that the price of good 2 is decreasing in the import quota thereon.

3.4. Adjustment and Import Starvation

As noted in the introduction to this chapter, the fate of attempts to liberalize trade is often bound up with macroeconomic events, chiefly balance-of-payments difficulties, whatever be their origin. Confronted with the need to reduce the deficit on the current account, governments tended, at least until a decade or so ago, to react to such difficulties by imposing tighter quotas on imports (Little et al., 1993: 264). Tackling the outgoings in this way, however, usually has an impact on the incomings side of the account;

for tighter quotas induce changes in relative prices and hence, in general, changes in output. This possibility is especially acute in a case of some practical importance, namely, where production requires inputs of imported intermediate goods for which there are no close domestic substitutes. A cut in the supply of such imports will normally reduce output, an effect which is called 'import starvation'. This can take on grave proportions. For if the net output of tradables valued at world prices falls and the level of domestic consumption thereof, similarly valued, fails to do so at least *pari passu*, then the value of net exports at world prices will also fall, and the initial trouble will deepen.

The situation at the outset, then, is one in which $p^*x > p^*y$, the difference ($F > 0$) being financed either by drawing down reserves of foreign exchange, or by borrowing abroad. The essentials are captured in Fig. 3.6: at the prices p and q, respectively, firms choose the net output vector denoted by point A, the representative household selects the consumption bundle C, and the resulting trade vector is AC. We now suppose that this state of affairs cannot continue indefinitely. At some point, foreign exchange reserves will have been exhausted and foreign credit will be

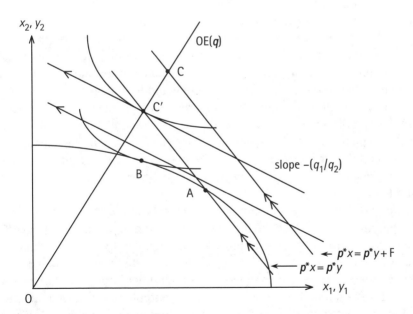

Figure 3.6. Adjustment at constant domestic prices and a complete ban on imports compared

withdrawn. Even with a moratorium on repayments of debt, the condition $p^*x = p^*y$ (equivalently, $F = 0$) must hold in any equilibrium that is ultimately established.

One possibility is for the government to choose a set of policies such that p and q remain unchanged, which, under many circumstances, will be accomplished by leaving things alone. In this case, there will be no changes in output, but consumption will beat a retreat along $OE(q)$ until the bundle C' is reached: imports are smaller and exports are larger. This policy is contractionary neither in the short, nor in the long run; nor is there any import starvation, only the scarcity implied by the constraint (3.2), with $F = 0$. It is painful only to the extent of the income effect caused by the withdrawal of F, and that pain will be mitigated by an accompanying liberalization that fulfils the conditions of Proposition 1. It is important to note that this claim holds even in the presence of non-competitive imports of intermediate goods; for if net output does not change, consumption valued at world prices will fall by the amount F.

In the above story, the private sector learns to live within its means when confronted with the loss of F without any attendant changes in the economic environment (by A5, the government is always virtuous, in this respect at least). In keeping with what commonly happens, let us now suppose instead that the government obscures matters by imposing binding quotas. This cannot stave off the need to save F, relative to the *status quo ante*. What it certainly can do, however, is to intensify the misery of that adjustment; for we are now in Section 3.3 once more, but on a reverse course. To make the point plain, let there be no half measures: all imports are banned, with non-competitive imports being assumed away. The result will be autarky ($x = y$), so that $p^*x = p^*y$ is now satisfied, an allocation that is depicted in Fig. 3.6 by point B. Foreign exchange in the net amount F has certainly been saved, but at the cost of the gains from trade that are realized under the alternative denoted by the production–consumption pair (A, C').

We now reintroduce non-competitive imports of intermediate goods into the picture, which are denoted by good n. Let the input thereof needed to produce one unit of output in industry j be denoted by $a_{nj}(j \neq n)$ and let $a_n = (a_{n1}, a_{n2}, \dots, a_{n,n-1})$. In order to illustrate what is involved, consider the case where there is a complete ban on all other imports, but good n is free of any quotas. Let the vector of *gross* outputs in all other industries bar n be denoted by $z(n)$, so that the net output (equals imports) of good n is $-a_n \cdot z(n)$ and other goods in the value of $p_n^*(a_n \cdot z(n))$ must be exported to finance it. In this case, there is no import starvation. Now suppose that, in a veritable fit of regulatory zeal, the government goes a step further and imposes a binding quota on imports of good n. Then the industries that use them intensively will tend to contract relative to $z(n)$, as the domestic price rises to reflect the quota rent. If the value of GDP at world prices falls as a result, then the situation will deteriorate further. This is a true case of import starvation, and a self-inflicted one at that. As a policy, it may be likened to the allied bombing campaigns aimed at 'strategic' industries in the Third Reich during the Second World War, with the notable difference that the said quota is likely to be altogether more destructive of industry, while wreaking its effects almost exclusively on home territory.[6]

To sum up, it is readily conceded that policies aimed at cutting private consumption are politically difficult, and that, for most of the population in poor countries, such cuts are especially painful. The fact remains, however, that the loss of the resources represented by F makes an adjustment of some kind unavoidable. Some ways are less damaging than others, would governments but choose them.

3.5. A Reduction in the Regulated Wage

The important, and potentially spoiling, role of the distortion in the labour market prompts the question of whether a countervailing devaluation should accompany the cut in tariffs or the loosening of quotas, the idea being to reduce the product-wage in the protected sectors, along with the level of protection. One cannot, strictly speaking, address this question in the model as it stands; for it lacks money. What can be done, however, is to consider the effect of a reduction in w_2 as an intermediate step towards the extension that follows in Section 3.6, in which agents do hold a financial asset.

Applying the envelope theorem to Eqn (3.15), we obtain

$$\partial \Phi^0 / \partial w_2 \equiv \partial u^0 / \partial w_2 = v p^* \cdot (\partial y / \partial w_2), \tag{3.22}$$

so that the question boils down, once more, to whether the reform, in the shape of a cut in the product-wage in the protected sector, induces an increase in GDP valued at world prices. If the economy is already at full employment, the resulting expansion of output in the protected sector will

[6] For a fine treatment of one of the most important of such raids, see Middlebrook (1985), who approaches his subject by drawing heavily on the personal accounts of those who survived, aircrew and civilians alike.

be accompanied by a fall in output in the other sector. By an argument analogous to that yielding condition (3.19), we obtain

$$\partial u^0/\partial w_2 \gtreqless 0 \quad \text{according as } (w_2/w_1) \lesseqgtr (1+t_2).\tag{3.23}$$

That is to say, a cut in the regulated wage will lead to an improvement in welfare if the labour market distortion, as measured by the proportional wage gap $(w_2 - w_1)/w_1$, is greater than the trade distortion, as measured by the *ad valorem* tariff t_2; in the converse case, welfare will fall. Since only the product-wage (w_2/p_2) matters to firms, the effects of changes in p_2 and w_2 on output are opposite in sign; and in the absence of changes in consumer prices, the analysis is complete.

3.6. Devaluation

Money is introduced into the story in a very simple way. The capital account is closed and high-powered money is the only financial asset private agents are permitted to hold. Thus, exporters must sell their earnings of foreign currency to the central bank at the going exchange rate, and importers can settle their bills only by buying foreign currency from that source. The central bank is assumed to pursue an accommodating policy, in that it offers to swap domestic for foreign currency at a fixed exchange rate, to the extent that its reserves permit. The bank has an initial reserve of F dollars, the public initially holds $\bar{M}$ units of domestic currency, and the exchange rate is e units of domestic currency per dollar.

In order to avoid the unnecessary analytical complications attending quotas, we return to the setting of Section 3.2. With domestic currency as the natural choice of numeraire, the domestic prices of the goods are given by

$$p_i = q_i = (1+t_i)ep_i^*, \quad i = 1, 2,\tag{3.24}$$

where we retain the assumption that $t_1 = 0$. The wage rates are now nominal, whereby the assumption that w_2 is exogenously fixed is now more obviously at variance with the extensive indexation of wages in the regulated sector in many countries at various times, a fact that we gloss over.[7]

---

[7] Not too much should be made of this simplification. In most of the Latin American countries studied by Little *et al.* (1993), for example, real wages declined substantially in the 1980s. 'This does not mean that nominal wages were instantaneously flexible downward. [...] Inflation in a depressed real economy led to a fall in real wages' (p. 101).

In the foregoing sections, where the wage is fixed in terms of good 1, a cut in t_2 will lead to a contraction of output and employment in sector 2 in the short run. Here, in contrast, such a cut in the protective tariff can be offset by a devaluation, that is, by an increase in e. Consider, in particular, the case where the devaluation is fully offsetting, in the sense that the product $(1 + t_2)e$ is held constant. Such a devaluation will leave the product-wage in sector 2 unchanged, so that firms therein will not alter their production plans. Given that w_2 is so indexed, therefore, the accompanying devaluation will accomplish what wage commissions are apparently unable to do. Any devaluation will, however, increase the domestic price of good 1. Hence, if w_1 is sticky in the short run and if the currency is devalued under conditions of full employment, the initial result of a fully offsetting devaluation will be excess demand for labour in the economy as a whole. Firms in sector 1 will bid up the nominal wage w_1, but if the latter lies below w_2 at the point where the labour market clears once more, then the package will have the virtue of leaving the allocation of resources in production undisturbed, even in the short run. A more modest devaluation will fail to take all of the sting out of a cut in the protective tariff, in which case the package will produce results qualitatively like those already derived in Section 3.2.

In order to complete the production side of the picture, we examine the effect of a devaluation alone on the value of GDP at world prices. If the economy is at full employment and there is a wage gap, then sector 2 will expand at sector 1's expense, even without an adjustment in w_1. Noting that at full employment, $dL_1 + dL_2 = 0$, we have

$$p^* \cdot (\partial y / \partial e) = \left(p_1^* \frac{\partial y_1}{\partial L_1} - p_2^* \frac{\partial y_2}{\partial L_2} \right) \frac{\partial L_1}{\partial e},$$

where $\partial L_1 / \partial e < 0$ by virtue of $\partial L_2 / \partial e > 0$. Recalling Eqns (3.8) and (3.24), a simple rearrangement yields

$$p^* \cdot (\partial y / \partial e) = \left(w_1 - \frac{w_2}{(1 + t_2)e} \right) \frac{\partial L_1}{\partial e}. \tag{3.25}$$

In effect, we have arrived at condition (3.19) once more:

$$\partial (p^* \cdot y) / \partial e \gtrless 0 \quad \text{according as } (w_2 / w_1) \lessgtr (1 + t_2)e, \tag{3.26}$$

where the initial value of e may be normalized to unity. This result is as expected, since a fall in the product-wage in sector 2 is engineered here by a devaluation.

We now turn to consumption. In the one-period setting to which this chapter is confined, preferences are assumed to take the additively separable form[8]

$$U(\mathbf{x}, M) = u(\mathbf{x}) + \phi(M/P),\tag{3.27}$$

where P is the price index that corresponds to the subutility function $u(\mathbf{x})$,[9] M/P is the public's stock of real money balances, and $\phi(\cdot)$ is an increasing, strictly concave, and twice-differentiable function that also satisfies the lower Inada condition. In such a formulation, the assumption that preferences are so separable is rather strong, but defensible. The property that the MRS between goods is independent of real money balances will be especially advantageous in the two-period setting analysed in Chapter 7.

The household's problem is to choose $\mathbf{x}$ and M so as to

$$\text{maximize } U(\mathbf{x}, M) \quad \text{subject to: } \mathbf{q}\mathbf{x} + M \leq Y^{\mathrm{d}} + \bar{M},\tag{3.28}$$

an interior solution to which is ensured by the foregoing assumptions. The associated first-order conditions are

$$u_i - \lambda q_i = 0, \quad i = 1, 2,\tag{3.29}$$

$$\phi' - \lambda P = 0.\tag{3.30}$$

As starting point, we require an equilibrium in which the household desires to hold cash balances in exactly the amount of its initial endowment $\bar{M}$ thereof. Given $\mathbf{p}^*, t, e$, and Y^{d}, this amount is obtained as follows. Analogously to Section 3.2, one solves $u_1/u_2 = q_1/q_2$ and $\mathbf{q}\mathbf{x} = Y^{\mathrm{d}}$ to obtain the optimal bundle $\mathbf{x}^0$ under the condition that initial money balances are exactly maintained ($M = \bar{M}$), whereupon λ follows from Eqn (3.29). Substituting this value of λ into Eqn (3.30) yields an M^0 such that exactly Y^{d} is indeed spent on the consumption of goods. By setting $\bar{M} = M^0(\mathbf{q}, Y^{\mathrm{d}})$, we obtain the desired equilibrium. Observe that in any such equilibrium, the trade account will be in balance, that is, $\mathbf{p}^*\mathbf{y} = \mathbf{p}^*\mathbf{x}$; for if the private sector has no net transactions with the central bank, it must be spending exactly the amount of its foreign currency earnings from exports on imports.

---

[8] For a vigorous defence of putting the stock of money into the utility function, see Feenstra (1992).

[9] Given some reference level of utility u, and two price vectors $\mathbf{q}^1$ and $\mathbf{q}^2$, let $C(\mathbf{q}^1, u)$ and $C(\mathbf{q}^2, u)$, respectively, denote the minimum cost of attaining u at the said prices. Then the Könus price index is defined to be $P \equiv C(\mathbf{q}^2, u)/C(\mathbf{q}^1, u)$, where $\mathbf{q}^1$ is the reference price vector (see Diewert, 1988).

The next step is to examine the effects of a devaluation and a cut in the protective tariff, respectively, on the demand for money, changes in which play the decisive role in determining whether the policy described above is sustainable. Note that

$$q = e(p_1^*, (1 + t_2)p_2^*)$$

and

$$Y^d = e\left[(p_1^* y_1 + (1 + t_2)p_2^* y_2) + t_2 p_2^*(x_2 - y_2)\right].$$

A pure devaluation will scale up the domestic prices of goods. In doing so, it will also scale up the price index P, and hence reduce the household's endowment of real balances, $\bar{M}/P$, in the same proportion. With nominal wages behaving as assumed above, such a devaluation will also bring about changes in output. It will not, therefore, be neutral, in the sense of simply scaling up both q and $(Y^d + \bar{M})$. The same evidently holds for a cut in t_2 that is accompanied by a fully offsetting devaluation, as defined above. In both cases, there will be a change in the household's demand for cash balances.

Suppose, first of all, that the demand for cash is higher in the new equilibrium. Given the central bank's accommodating stance, the additional demand will be met by the issue of additional currency, which the private sector must purchase out of its foreign exchange earnings from exports in the process whereby the new equilibrium is established. Since the trade account is balanced $(p^*y = p^*x)$ in both equilibria, both the stock of high powered money and the central bank's reserves of dollars will be higher in the equilibrium that rules after the devaluation. If, however, the demand for cash falls, then the central bank will have to draw down its initial reserves, the level of which may not be able to sustain the policy of offering unrestricted swaps of foreign for domestic currency at a fixed exchange rate.

We now consider this latter, awkward possibility in greater detail. Substituting for λ from Eqn (3.30) into Eqn (3.29), we obtain

$$u_i - (q_i/P) \cdot \phi'(M/P) = 0, \quad i = 1, 2. \tag{3.31}$$

It is clear that a devaluation will leave the ratio (q_i/P) unchanged, both rising in the same proportion. The following assumption will yield a welcome simplification where changes in the overall scale of consumption is concerned.

Assumption 13. The subutility function $u(x)$ is quasi-homothetic.

We begin with the case where $u(x)$ is homogeneous of degree one with respect to the displaced origin that defines the 'subsistence' bundle in the space of x. Given A13, the derivatives $u_i (i = 1, 2)$ will then depend only on the ratio of the excess of x_1 over the 'subsistence' level for good 1 to the excess of x_2 over its corresponding level. Since a devaluation will leave relative (goods) prices unchanged, A13 also implies that the u_i will also be unaffected thereby. It then follows from Eqn (3.31) that M/P will be invariant to a devaluation. That P is proportional to e yields the result that M will increase in response to a devaluation, both in the immediate aftermath, when $\bar{M}$ reflects the conditions of the previously ruling equilibrium, and over the longer run, when all variables will have adjusted to the new level of the exchange rate. In the case where $u(\cdot)$ is strictly concave, there are two possibilities. If the scale of consumption falls following the devaluation, then the u_i will rise, and hence M/P will fall. Since P is proportional to e, however, the demand for cash (M) will still rise if neither $u(\cdot)$ nor $\phi(\cdot)$ is too strongly concave. If the scale of consumption should rise, however, then M/P, and hence M, will increase. To sum up, in the static framework employed here, a devaluation will normally lead to an improvement in the central bank's reserves. As we shall see in Chapter 7, however, this reassuring finding does not necessarily carry over to a many-period setting.

It remains to examine the effects of a devaluation on welfare—assuming that the initial foreign exchange reserves suffice to finance the transition. Recall that the equilibrium of the economy must lie on the expansion path corresponding to (q, P) in the space of (x, M), a condition which is implicitly defined by rewriting the first-order conditions as Eqn (3.31). Appealing once more to the (artificial) planner's problem (3.14), the associated Lagrangian may be written as

$$\Phi = U(x, M) + \sum_{i=1}^{2} \mu_i [u_i - (q_i/P)\phi'] + v[p^*(y - x)]. \tag{3.32}$$

The envelope theorem yields, after a little manipulation,

$$\partial U^0/\partial e = -\sum_{i=1}^{2} \mu_i \left[\phi' - \left(\frac{e}{P} \cdot \frac{\partial P}{\partial e} \right) \cdot \left(\phi' + \phi'' \cdot \frac{M}{P} \right) \right]$$

$$\times \frac{(1 + t_i) p_i^*}{P} + v p^* \cdot (\partial y/\partial e), \tag{3.33a}$$

where use has been made of Eqn (3.24). In addition to the familiar effects of a devaluation on the value of GDP at world prices, we have terms that arise from the fact that a devaluation increases P. It has been established in Section 3.2 that v is positive. That μ_1 and μ_2 are positive follows from an examination of the household's budget constraint $qx + M \leq Y^d + \bar{M}$. In the absence of a compensating change in Y^d, it is seen that a scaling up of q will cause the feasible set in the space of (x, M) to contract everywhere but the extreme point $(0, 0, Y^d + \bar{M})$, which is never an optimum under any plausible assumptions about preferences.

Equation (3.33a) is rather unwieldy, so to simplify matters, we appeal to A13 once more. This implies that $(e/P) \cdot (\partial P/\partial e) = 1$; so that Eqn (3.33a) then specializes to

$$\partial U^0/\partial e = \sum_{i=1}^{2} \mu_i[\phi'' \cdot (M/P)](1+t_i)(p_i^*/P)| + vp^* \cdot (\partial y/\partial e). \quad (3.33b)$$

Since ϕ is strictly concave, it follows that even if a devaluation does bring about an increase in the value of GDP at world prices, this outcome will not suffice to ensure that welfare will improve. The intuition here is that a devaluation reduces the initial value of real money balances, and hence the size of the household's opportunity set, at a stroke.

Given that a devaluation and a cut in the protective tariff pull in opposite directions, it is interesting to return to the reform considered in Section 3.2, that is, a reduction in t_2 without a compensating devaluation, but now with the twist that money has made an appearance. By the envelope theorem, we have

$$\frac{\partial U^0}{\partial t_2} = \sum_{i=1}^{2} \mu_i[\phi' + \phi'' \cdot (M/P)]\left[(1+t_i)\frac{ep_i^*}{P^2} \cdot \frac{\partial P}{\partial t_2}\right]$$
$$- \mu_2(ep_2^*/P) \cdot \phi' + vp^* \cdot (\partial y/\partial t_2). \quad (3.34)$$

The third term on the right-hand side (RHS), namely, the effect on GDP at world prices, is familiar from Section 3.2. The first and second terms represent the effects of an increase in t_2, and hence in q_2 and P, on the household's welfare through its holding of money balances. If $\phi(\cdot)$ is isoelastic, the term $[\phi' + \phi'' \cdot (M/P)]$ will be positive, in which case the algebraic sum of the first and second terms may take either sign. Observe, however, that $\partial P/\partial t_2 = (\partial P/\partial q_2) \cdot (ep_2^*)$ and the fact that $(q_2/P) \cdot (\partial P/\partial q_2) < 1$, together with Eqn (3.24), imply that the algebraic sum of the terms involving μ_2 is negative, whereas the substitution effect, which involves the terms associated with μ_1, pulls in the other direction. On balance, since P must fall if one price falls and no other rises, it seems likely that a cut in the protective tariff will increase welfare if it also induces an increase in GDP at world prices.

We close with a remark about the central bank's foreign currency reserves. As noted above, if the public reduces its holdings of money following a devaluation or a liberalization of tariffs, then under the assumption that the central bank pursues an accommodating policy at a fixed exchange rate, the reserves will be drawn down. If the flight out of money is strong enough, it may precipitate a foreign exchange crisis, in the sense that the initial reserves are insufficient to sustain the exogenously determined change in the exchange rate or, in the case of changes in tariffs alone, to defend the existing rate. Should this occur, the government would be forced to change course, perhaps to the extent of doing a full U-turn. In a world in which the private sector has full information, however, the very possibility of such a change in course in response to a crisis may be self-fulfilling, even when the initial level of reserves, viewed statically, is adequate; for the private sector's behaviour in the expectation of a subsequent reversal of course may induce the very crisis that makes the reversal inevitable. To address this problem properly, we need at least two periods, with the possibility that absorption can be switched between periods. If the public is persuaded that reforms in the present will be reversed under pressure in the future, then there may indeed be a surge in consumption in the present, financed by the drawing down of real balances on such a scale as to precipitate a crisis that does force a reversal of policy. We have now entered the realm of dynamic analysis, a theme which is taken up in Chapter 7.

3.7. Summary

A reading of the post-war experience leaves the strong impression that whereas LDCs found no difficulty in erecting an extensive system of barriers to international trade, the task of dismantling it in a progressive way was often beyond them. One reason for this was surely that numerous attempts to liberalize the trade regime were made during two decades, namely 1970–90, in which the world economy went through a series of upheavals whose effects on poor countries were mostly adverse. In such circumstances, the fate of trade reforms was often determined by the need to deal with macroeconomic shocks. Yet serious failures in macroeconomic policy, including the failure to provide in advance for adversity, surely played an important role in this history.

There is, however, another, quite simple reason why an apparently sensible reform in one sphere of the economy is later reversed, namely, that it turns out to be damaging. This can certainly happen if the reform in question is undertaken when intractable distortions are at work in other spheres, as is often the case in practice. Given such second-best considerations, what guidance does theory offer as to when a partial reform will indeed improve welfare? In the case of a small open economy in which all goods are tradable, it suffices that a reform satisfy two conditions. The first is that the value of GDP at world prices not fall. The second is that the reform induce changes in the ratios of domestic to world prices of goods that conform to the so-called 'concertina' pattern, whereby the top ratio is squeezed to the second, then both to the third, and so forth, leaving all other ratios unchanged. Symmetrically, those at the bottom, if they change at all, must be compressed upwards in an analogous way.

The measures undertaken to liberalize trade in practice often broadly conform to the required pattern, with the top tariff rates being cut, and quotas being relaxed and replaced by moderate tariffs. The snag is that there are good grounds for supposing that introducing such measures may reduce GDP at world prices, especially in the short run. For if the protected sectors face a rigid product-wage, they will contract, and those thrown out of work may not find employment elsewhere if that segment of the labour market also functions inflexibly. An important complicating factor here is the fact that one of the main alternative employment opportunities is often in the (unprotected) agricultural sector, an option which is of limited worth unless workers are geographically mobile. Given the costs of moving, the newly unemployed may well stay put in the towns, especially if they are persuaded that the reform will soon be reversed and that being on hand will then improve their chances of getting back their old jobs. Even over the longer run, however, it is not a foregone conclusion that seeing the trade reform through will induce an increase in GDP at world prices. For although wages, employment, and output in the unprotected sectors may adjust, the erstwhile heavily protected sectors now have a smaller compensating advantage to offset the burden of the high regulated wage. Once the point is reached where the effects of the two distortions on output in the latter sectors are exactly offsetting, then further cuts in tariffs will cause GDP at world prices to fall.

This rather sobering result illustrates the dangers of piecemeal reform. The obvious corollary—that the labour market, in particular, should be reformed at the same time—is, however, in the nature of a long-term political project, so that some immediate, indirect means are needed. The natural choice here is a nominal devaluation of the currency—provided the regulated wage is not fully indexed. Yet that is not the end of the matter: introducing money also brings new considerations into the reckoning. First, it must be established whether the central bank possesses enough foreign reserves at the outset to defend the announced exchange rate; for the private sector's initial holdings of cash are available to supplement the purchasing power of current income. In the static setting of this chapter, it has been shown that this requirement is very likely to be met. Second, by increasing the price level, a devaluation reduces the value of real balances at a stroke, so it may reduce welfare even if it yields an increase in GDP at world prices. In the latter case, the longer the time horizon, the more tolerable this once-and-for-all cost will be.

Recommended Reading

An insightful account of the comparative experience of liberalization may be found in Little *et al.* (1993). A valuable formal treatment is provided by Buffie (2001).

Exercises

1. Consider the model in Section 1. Let there be two goods, whose world prices are both unity. Good 2 is initially subject to a protective tariff, t_2, at the rate of 150 per cent, with all revenues being rebated to households in the form of a lump-sum transfer. The domestic output vector is $y = (2, 1)$ and $F = 0$. Let the household's preferences take the form

$$u(x) = x_1 x_2 / (x_1 + x_2).$$

Find the domestic consumption vector, the size of the rebate, and total income.

  If t_2 were reduced to 50 per cent and y remained unchanged, determine the values of all endogenous variables in the resulting equilibrium and compute the associated equivalent variation. Repeat your calculations for the case where the said tariff is abolished completely. Depict all three allocations in the space of goods.

2. We turn to Section 3.2, making a small change in the household's preferences in exercise 1:

$$u(x) = x_1 x_2 / (3x_1 + x_2).$$

The technologies in the two sectors can be represented by

$$y_1 = 2L_1^{1/2} \quad \text{and} \quad y_2 = 3L_2^{1/3},$$

respectively. Let the economy be endowed with 5 units of labour, and let the world prices of both goods be unity, with sector 2 enjoying a protective tariff of 150 per cent, the proceeds of which are rebated to households in lump-sum form. If the wage rate in sector 2 is regulated at the value two, find the wage rate in sector 1 and the values of all other endogenous variables.

Now suppose that t_2 is reduced to 50 per cent. Assess the effects of this reform both in the short and in the longer run. Repeat your analysis for the case where the reduction in the tariff is accompanied by a cut in the regulated wage to 1.5.

What would happen in the absence of the small change in $u(x)$? Interpret the tariff on good 2 in this case.

3. Consider the following variation. The marginal product of labour in sector 1 is constant and takes the value unity. The technology in sector 2 takes the form

$$y_2 = AL_2 / (1 + L_2).$$

If the wage rate in sector 2 is regulated so that its level is twice that ruling in sector 1, find an expression for the level of employment in sector 2 as a function of the domestic producer price p_2.

(a) Let the initial protective tariff on good 2 be 200 per cent, the proceeds of which are rebated to households in lump-sum form. In the case where $A = 5$ and the economy is endowed with 10 units of labour, find the levels of employment and output in both sectors. Repeat your analysis for the case in which the tariff is wholly abolished.

(b) If the representative household's utility function is

$$u(x) = 10 \ln x_1 + 4x_2,$$

does this radical reform improve welfare? Explain your conclusion.

4. We extend exercise 2 to Section 3.6. Instead of reductions in t_2, let there be a devaluation of 20 per cent. Find the resulting values of all variables

pertaining to production when the labour market has adjusted in full, and comment on your results in relation to condition Eqn (3.26).

5.   (a) Let the subutility function $u(x)$ in Eqn (3.27) take the form given in exercise 3.1. Derive the corresponding price index.

(b) Good 2 is initially subject to a protective tariff at the rate of 100 per cent, with all revenues being rebated to households in the form of a lump-sum transfer. The domestic output vector is $y = (2, 1)$, and $F = 0$, as in exercise 3.1. The latter are assumed to be fixed. The initial exchange rate is parity. This is the point of departure, where the price index P is defined to be unity.

Let the function $\phi(M/P)$ be isoelastic, with parameter one-half:

$$\phi = a(M/P)^{1/2}, \quad a > 0.$$

What value should the household's initial endowment of cash take such that this is indeed the value of cash balances the household would choose in the setting so described? (To be specific, choose a such that the velocity of circulation is 5.) What would happen if the currency were devalued by 20 per cent? If the value of output at world prices were to rise, how might things turn out?

4. Taxation

Even the so-called 'minimalist' state, whose only function is to defend the realm against foreign foes and maintain internal order and property rights, needs revenue, though in relatively modest measure. The 'developmental' state, in contrast, has requirements for funds of wholly different order. For in addition to ensuring law and order, it is supposed to provide the people with education, health, and at least some form of collective insurance against natural disasters. It is also charged with the task of furthering economic activity directly, by creating physical infrastructure, by subsidizing particular industries, and by writing and enforcing suitable regulations. Construed in the widest sense, the developmental state is also concerned with the distribution of well being among the population. So described, it appears that whereas the minimalist state need look no farther than a poll tax to finance its undertakings, the developmental state requires a more extensive range of instruments to achieve its ends.

In fact, the state has three ways of obtaining current revenue. First, it can enact, and attempt to enforce, laws to raise taxes. Second, it can exercise its right of seigniorage by issuing currency, thereby avoiding the need to write new tax statutes or to revise existing ones. Third, it can issue debt, provided there are foreign or domestic agents willing to accept its paper. In practice, governments resort to all three; but as the second and third are closely related and involve certain dynamic considerations, they are best treated on their own, a task taken up in Chapter 6.

The object of the present chapter, therefore, is to examine the tax instruments in some detail (Sections 4.1 and 4.3), to describe their relative importance as sources of revenue (Section 4.2), and to provide a brief account of the theory of taxation with an eye on the question of how these instruments ought to be used. The treatment of the latter is tailored to the demands of this volume and does not pretend in any way to be exhaustive, the emphasis being firmly on the taxation of commodities.[1] As there are several excellent texts on public economics, an extensive account of theory would, in any event, be superfluous. Section 4.3 deals with the preliminaries, starting with some key concepts and the equivalence of certain taxes, and complemented by a discussion of heterogeneity among individuals

[1] Fine surveys of taxation in the context of developing countries are provided by Ahmad and Stern (1989) and Burgess and Stern (1992).

and how to treat inequality among households for the purposes of social evaluation. Optimal commodity taxation itself is taken up in Section 4.4, followed by an exposition of the Diamond–Mirrlees model in Section 4.5. How far practice can depart from these well-established principles when taxes are imposed on intermediate goods is illustrated in Section 4.6 by an analysis of the taxes, nominal and effective, on commodities in Pakistan in the mid-1970s.

4.1. Tax Instruments

We begin by noting the obvious. First, an instrument cannot be used unless the authorities are in a position either to observe the relevant transaction or to place a reasonable presumptive estimate on its value, based on other observable information. Second, the ability to observe something in principle is, of course, not enough; there must also be the capacity to determine liability and then to collect the taxes due. Third, using whatever administrative capacity currently exists is costly, if only in the sense of there being an opportunity cost whenever a particular taxable transaction is pursued rather than another; and building up the capacity to expand collections involves direct costs. Such administrative capacity is seriously wanting in less developed countries (LDCs), and the fact that many enterprises keep no records of any worth to the tax collector exacerbates matters. Bearing these points in mind, we maintain the conventional distinction between (direct) taxes on factors and (indirect) taxes on commodities, examples of both having already made appearances in Chapters 1–3.

Where direct taxes are concerned, the easy pickings are to be found in the formal, regulated sectors of the economy. Large firms, domestic and foreign alike, can be subjected to corporation taxes, their distributions of dividends to withholding taxes, and their payments of wages and salaries to social security taxes and withholdings of income taxes. Since the formal sector of the economy is usually quite small, we appear to have a plausible and persuasive explanation of the fact that direct taxes commonly account for a small proportion of total revenues (see Fig. 4.3).

That first impressions can be deceiving, however, is nicely illustrated by the following historical examples. Taxes on real wealth were important sources of revenue in parts of medieval Europe: there was the 'hearth tax' in France and the *Vermögenssteuer* (a tax on real (property) wealth) in Germany, the latter surviving until 1997. The eighteenth century witnessed the introduction of the 'window tax' in Britain as a presumptive tax on wealth, one predictable effect of which is still visible in the form of bricked-up windows in country houses of the period. Perhaps the most striking case of all is the taxation of land in India, both under the Moghuls and their British colonial successors. The revenue unit was the village, from which an intermediary collected a particular, fixed amount—up to one-half of the normal level of gross output—in return for the right to use a tract of land tax-free (Habib, 1982: 240).[2] The British took over this system, modifying it in various ways as they progressively obtained control over various regions of the Indian subcontinent. As late as the turn of the nineteenth century, it yielded over one-half of all revenues, but by the eve of Independence in 1947, its share had sunk to just 7 per cent (Kumar, 1982: 929). In all these cases, the authorities had the wherewithal to observe, assess, and tax an important form of wealth. The successor states of the subcontinent are no worse placed in this regard; for the land records are maintained and the peasants, ever jealous of their landholdings, have every interest in seeing to it that the records are brought up to date when they acquire additional plots. Thus, some explanation other than a limited ability to observe what is going on and a limited capacity to administer matters must be sought for the fact that the land revenue now makes a negligible contribution to the Treasury, a matter to which we shall return.

These examples and arguments notwithstanding, indirect taxes contribute the lion's share of total taxes in LDCs. Collecting taxes on goods is comparatively easy when there are natural 'choke points', such as ports and factory gates, in the chain of transportation from producers to users. Goods that enter international trade or those produced by large firms are, therefore, natural targets. To give historical examples, customs duties were a very important source of revenue in Britain in the eighteenth century and in the United States in the nineteenth. Today, their contributions to the respective countries' Treasuries are negligible. In contrast, taxes on international trade continue to play a very important role in public finance in LDCs (see Fig. 4.3), whereby it should be emphasized that it is not uncommon for exports of primary commodities to be subject to duties or the pricing practices of state marketing monopolies. Similar considerations apply to the taxation of domestic production and consumption. Fully developed economies, with their systems of extensive record-keeping and capable bureaucracies, can enjoy the advantages of broadly based commodity taxes in the form of either a value-added tax (VAT) right down to

---

[2] Cited in Ahmad and Stern (1991: 15), which should be consulted for further discussion of land taxes in the subcontinent.

the retail stage, or comprehensive sales taxes. The governments of LDCs, administratively constrained as they are, must generally make do with excises on goods produced by large firms, perhaps supplemented by a VAT of limited coverage. The consequences of this restriction will be followed up later. For the present, we turn to a simple description of current practice.

4.2. The Level and Sources of Revenue

We begin with the level of central government revenue expressed as a proportion of GDP, which is a useful summary statistic of the state's claims on resources, even though it reflects both administrative capacity and the effort devoted to raising revenue. In the present context, some further insights may be yielded by examining how this, and related statistics, have changed over the course of time. In making such comparisons, it is desirable to rid the data of (country) fixed effects, so that one is driven to choose countries for which data is available for the same period, and here much is dictated by the sources that are ready to hand. Inevitably, the choice falls on the World Bank's *Development Indicators* (World Bank, 1997), which reports the position for the years 1980 and 1995. The sample that results from this principle of selection comprises thirty-nine countries classified by the World Bank as 'low-' and 'lower middle-income', and another twenty-three classified as 'high income', in the year 1995. Abusing terminology somewhat, these groups will be called LDCs and DCs, respectively.

The two distributions of the ratio of central government revenue to GDP for 1995 are depicted in Fig. 4.1.[3] It is clear that although there is a substantial overlap, governments in LDCs claim, on average, a much smaller proportion of their economies' GDP than do their counterparts in DCs, the simple averages being 19.8 and 31.9 per cent, respectively. Both averages were slightly higher than in 1980, by 0.8 and 2.7 per cent, respectively; but the overall changes are most clearly seen from the distributions of the countrywise differences, which are depicted in Fig. 4.2. These suggest a somewhat more mixed experience among LDCs than among DCs, though this could be merely sampling fluctuation.

Turning to the sources of central government revenue, the position for 1995 is depicted in Figs 4.3 and 4.4 in the form of pie charts, from which the heavy reliance of governments in LDCs on indirect taxes in general, and

---

[3] The distributions were smoothed as follows.

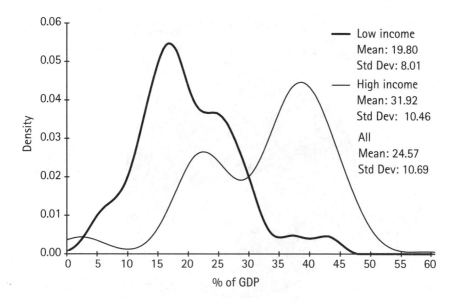

Figure 4.1. Central government revenue as percentage of GDP, 1995

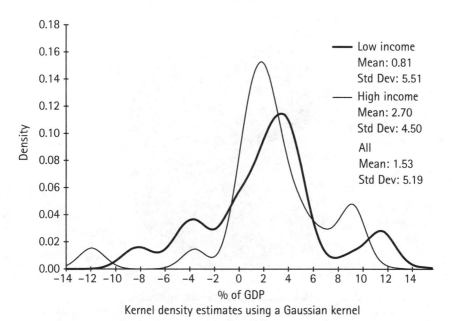

Kernel density estimates using a Gaussian kernel

Figure 4.2. Changes in central government revenue, 1980–95

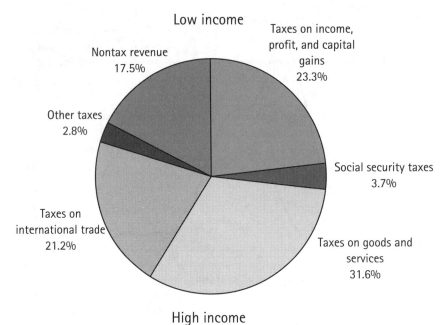

Low income

- Taxes on income, profit, and capital gains 23.3%
- Social security taxes 3.7%
- Taxes on goods and services 31.6%
- Taxes on international trade 21.2%
- Other taxes 2.8%
- Nontax revenue 17.5%

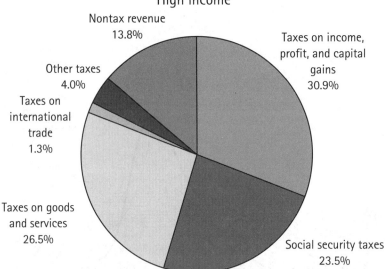

High income

- Nontax revenue 13.8%
- Other taxes 4.0%
- Taxes on international trade 1.3%
- Taxes on goods and services 26.5%
- Taxes on income, profit, and capital gains 30.9%
- Social security taxes 23.5%

Figure 4.3. Central government revenue

Source: World Bank's Development Indicators, 1995, Tables 4.12 and 4.14. What are labelled low-income countries in Figs 4.1–4.3 fall under the World Bank's definition of low- and low-middle-income countries.

on those on international trade in particular, is clear. What is interesting in this connection is that while the overall reliance on indirect taxes changed very little between 1980 and 1995, the importance of taxes on international trade therein declined substantially, by some six percentage points. In the light of the discussion in Section 1.4 and what will follow below, this shift might be construed as a small step in the right direction—though the usual reservations on second-best grounds continue to apply.

4.3. Optimal Taxation: Preliminaries

Before tackling optimal taxation, we must deal with some preliminary matters. The first is the equivalence between certain tax structures and the conditions under which they will hold. Second, there is heterogeneity among households in its various forms and its relation to inequality. Third, there is the problem of how to formulate social welfare for the purposes of evaluating policy when inequality matters.

4.3.1. Tax Equivalence

We begin with the case where households are endowed only with labour, which they allocate between employment at the wage rate w and time spent in leisure, the latter being denoted by l. Their earnings are wholly spent on

---

Only those countries for which complete data is available make up the sample. Thus the sample for the central government finance statistics consists of thirty-seven observations for low-income countries: Botswana, Burundi, Cameroon, Colombia, Congo (Dem. Rep.), Costa Rica, Dominican Republic, Ecuador, Egypt, El Salvador, Ethiopia, Gambia, Ghana, Guatemala, India, Indonesia, Iran, Jordan, Kenya, Myanmar, Nepal, Nicaragua, Pakistan, Panama, Papua New Guinea, Paraguay, Peru, Philippines, Romania, Sri Lanka, Syrian Arab Republic, Thailand, Tunisia, Turkey, Venezuela, Zambia, and Zimbabwe.

It consists of twenty-three high income countries: Australia, Austria, Belgium, Canada, Denmark, Finland, France, Ireland, Israel, Italy, Japan, Korea (Rep.), Netherlands, New Zealand, Norway, Portugal, Singapore, Spain, Sweden, Switzerland, United Arab Emirates, United Kingdom, and United States.

The sample for the central government revenue statistics consists of thirty-nine observations for low-income countries: Burundi, Cameroon, Colombia, Congo (Dem. Rep.), Costa Rica, Dominican Republic, Ecuador, Egypt, El Salvador, Ethiopia, Gambia, Ghana, Guatemala, India, Indonesia, Iran, Jordan, Kenya, Lesotho, Madagascar, Myanmar, Nepal, Nicaragua, Pakistan, Panama, Papua New Guinea, Paraguay, Peru, Philippines, Romania, Sierra Leone, Sri Lanka, Syrian Arab Republic, Thailand, Tunisia, Turkey, Venezuela, Zambia, and Zimbabwe.

The sample for the central government revenue statistics consists of twenty-four observations for high-income countries: Australia, Austria, Belgium, Canada, Denmark, Finland, France, Germany, Ireland, Israel, Italy, Japan, Korea (Rep.), Netherlands, New Zealand, Norway, Portugal, Singapore, Spain, Sweden, Switzerland, United Arab Emirates, United Kingdom, and United States.

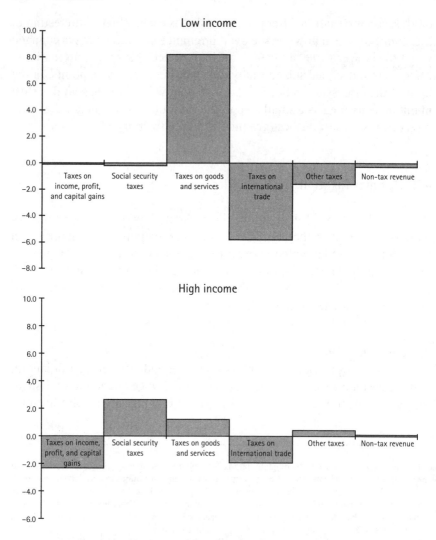

Figure 4.4. Changes in the composition of central government revenue, 1980–95 (in per cent)

a bundle of goods. In the absence of taxation, therefore, the expenditure–income identity of a household endowed with $\bar{L}$ units of labour is

$$px + wl \equiv w\bar{L}, \tag{4.1}$$

where x is the bundle consumed, p ($= q$) is the vector of producer (consumer) prices, and the opportunity cost of leisure is the wage rate. The market value of the endowment at the going wage, $w\bar{L}$, is usually referred to as the household's *full income*.

The first equivalence arises in the case where leisure is taxable. Suppose an *ad valorem* tax is imposed on the consumption of all goods and leisure at the uniform rate t. Then Eqn (4.1) becomes

$$(1+t)(px + wl) \equiv w\bar{L}, \tag{4.2a}$$

where it should be noted that the prices (p, w) that rule in the presence of the tax will differ, in general, from those that would do so in its absence. Rearranging Eqn (4.2a) as

$$px + wl \equiv w\bar{L} - [t/(1+t)]w\bar{L} \tag{4.2b}$$

reveals that, at any prices (p, w), the said flat tax leaves the household with the same budget set as would a lump-sum tax in the amount $[t/(1+t)]w\bar{L}$, so that the two taxes are equivalent.

The notion that leisure is directly taxable is best regarded as a useful thought-experiment. For on purely practical grounds, the authorities are restricted to taxing net transactions, and even that is possible only when the transactions are formally recorded as bookkeeping entries on which the authorities can lay their hands. The prime example is the payment of wages to workers in regulated employment, in which case, the taxation of labour supply, $\bar{L} - l$, is administratively feasible. With the tax base limited to net transactions, Eqn (4.2a) must be rewritten as

$$(1+t)[px + w(l - \bar{L})] \equiv 0, \tag{4.3}$$

a comparison of which with Eqn (4.1) reveals that a flat tax on all net purchases will leave the budget set unchanged and hence will yield no revenue.[4] More generally, let commodities and labour supply be taxed at different rates. Since the consumer price of good i is $q_i = (1 + t_i)p_i$, where t_i is the *ad valorem* tax thereon, Eqn (4.3) generalizes to

$$qx + (1 - t_w)w(l - \bar{L}) \equiv 0, \tag{4.4a}$$

----

[4] Since the household supplies labour, a tax on its net purchases thereof is equivalent to a wage subsidy at the same rate.

which states that the value of the household's net purchases at the prices $[q, (1 - t_w)w]$ is always zero. In other words, the value of the household's wage earnings after taxes is equal to its expenditures on all other goods. The assumption that only net transactions are taxable implies that the household's lump-sum income (but not its full income) is also zero, a point we shall take up below. By rewriting Eqn (4.4a) as

$$[q/(1 - t_w)]x + w(l - \bar{L}) \equiv 0, \tag{4.4b}$$

we obtain a second equivalence, namely, that when the tax base takes the form of all net transactions, the tax vector (t, t_w) is equivalent to the tax vector $[(t + t_w u)/(1 - t_w), 0]$, where u is a vector of ones of appropriate dimension. This is illustrated geometrically in Fig. 4.5 for the case where there is an aggregate commodity, $\bar{L}$ is normalized to unity, and the household takes all prices as parametrically given. Together with Eqn (4.3), a case where no revenue is raised, this second equivalence motivates the idea that the setting may be viewed as one in which a single commodity is not taxable. In the present case, the natural choice falls on labour.

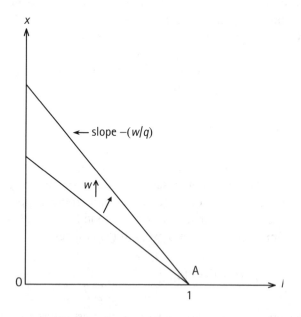

Figure 4.5. Budget sets when labour is the only endowment

Such a restriction accords nicely with the fact that the great majority of workers in LDCs are employed either within the family enterprise itself or by small firms under the terms of informal contracts, which the authorities lack the means to monitor and regulate. The equivalence yielded by Eqn (4.4b) tells us that the tax inspector's limited reach into this domain does not matter, so long as the consumer prices of all goods can be varied by taxes and subsidies. Yet the list of transactions that are, in effect, non-taxable does not end with labour supply. In the agricultural sector, a large share of output does not find its way into the market, being directly consumed instead by farmers and their families without the threat that the tax collector will place himself between the barn and the kitchen. The same holds for goods produced by family enterprises in other sectors of the economy, though the extent of self-consumption is usually much more limited in these cases. The upshot is that governments must resort to other, in some ways less satisfactory, instruments to raise revenue or to alter households' opportunity sets.

A third equivalence of considerable practical importance should be added, this time in connection with international trade. Suppose the economy is sufficiently small that the world price of a certain good can be taken as given. In the absence of a tariff, the domestic price to producers and consumers alike will be p^*, and in the presence of an *ad valorem* tariff at the rate t, it will be $(1 + t)p^*$. The tariff is therefore equivalent to an *ad valorem* tax on domestic consumption of the good at the rate t, coupled with an *ad valorem* subsidy on domestic production at the same rate (recall Section 1.4), a restriction whose drawbacks are partly offset by the administrative advantage that collection and disbursement occur automatically and simultaneously at the customs house. It should be observed that this third equivalence does not depend on any of the special assumptions made above: it is almost a matter of definition.

4.3.2. Inequality

We now turn to the issue of heterogeneity among individuals, with particular reference to inequality. As formulated above, the differences in endowments yield no differences in lump-sum income, which is always zero when only net transactions are taxable. The fact that there are only twenty-four hours in a day for rich and poor alike, and that the time spent in leisure pursuits is so bounded, suggest that while this form of heterogeneity has some expositional advantages, it is not especially satisfactory when it comes to representing the sources of inequality. It is more appealing to give all individuals the same endowment (of time), but to allow the wage rate to vary in order to reflect differences in productivity, whether innate or acquired. With identical lump-sum incomes of zero, individuals would then face different (relative) prices–and hence possess different budget sets. While all have the option of devoting themselves exclusively to leisure, high-wage individuals otherwise enjoy strictly superior opportunities in consumption. This formulation is depicted in Fig. 4.5, where $\bar{L}$ is normalized to unity for all individuals and the more productive individual's budget line is the steeper of the two drawn through the endowment point (1, 0), which is denoted by point A.

The next step is to extend the list of endowments. For present purposes, it will suffice to add just one, with the particular characteristic that it is supplied completely inelastically. If it commands a positive price in equilibrium, then any household that possesses this second endowment will have a positive lump-sum income. To be specific, this endowment may be thought of as land whose quality cannot be improved by any action of its owner. Let the income derived from this source be denoted by $\bar{M}$, so that Eqn (4.1) becomes

$$px + wl \equiv w\bar{L} + \bar{M}, \tag{4.5}$$

from which it is clear that the first equivalence established in Section 4.3.1 continues to hold. In the absence of all taxation, the associated budget set in the space of (l, x) is depicted in Fig. 4.6 for the case where there is an aggregate good, the extreme point A being the leisured existence described by the consumption bundle $(1, \bar{M}/p)$. The point B depicts the other extreme of unrelenting work $(0, (w + \bar{M})/p)$. Turning to the case where only net transactions are taxable, Eqn (4.3) becomes

$$(1 + t)[px + w(l - \bar{L})] \equiv \bar{M}, \tag{4.6}$$

so that a uniform tax on such transactions is now equivalent to a lump-sum tax in the amount $[t/(1 + t)]\bar{M}$. The resulting upper boundary of the budget set is obtained by a downward, parallel shift of the line AB in that amount. If, however, supplies of labour cannot be taxed, then a uniform tax at the rate t on all other consumption is equivalent to a flat tax on wage earnings at the rate $t/(1 + t)$ combined with a tax on lump-sum income in the amount $[t/(1 + t)]\bar{M}$. The upper boundary of the corresponding budget set is depicted in Fig. 4.6 as the line segment CD. Note that the

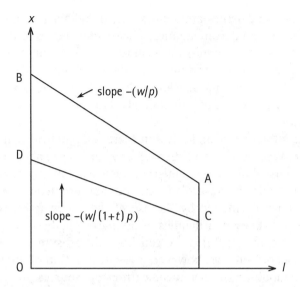

Figure 4.6. A second, inelastically supplied endowment, with a uniform tax on the bundle x

generalization of Eqn (4.4) is simply

$$qx + (1 - t_w)w(l - \bar{L}) \equiv \bar{M}. \qquad (4.7)$$

4.3.3. Social Welfare

In order to complete this account, we set out one way of evaluating economic policy in the presence of inequality, an approach that will provide the framework for most of this volume. Suppose individual h is endowed with one unit of labour and $\bar{M}^h$ units of lump-sum income, and that she faces parametric prices (q, w^h) for goods and labour, respectively. Let her indirect utility function be denoted by $v^h(q, w^h, \bar{M}^h)$. In order to evaluate the effects of taxation on welfare in a society of heterogeneous individuals, we appeal to the construct of a Bergson–Samuelsonian social welfare function, whose arguments are the individuals' (indirect) utilities:

$$V(q, w, \bar{M}) = W[v^1(q, w^1, \bar{M}^1), \ldots, v^h(q, w^h, \bar{M}^h), \ldots, v^H(q, w^H \bar{M}^H)].$$
$$(4.8a)$$

Even when labour supplies are not taxable, individuals' levels of welfare can be altered by taxing commodities, at least when net transactions occur. It is even possible that lump-sum incomes can be changed, not only by means of a poll tax or a tax on land (should either of those measures be politically possible), but also through grants, in the form of food or other rations, which could be conditioned on the household's demographic characteristics.

This looks all very nice and tidy, but there is a practical snag that must be addressed. We know rather little with any confidence about labour supplies, in the sense that the econometric evidence pertaining to households' choices over goods and leisure appears thin and problematic when asked to bear the burden entailed by the use of the above framework. There are also the well-known difficulties of taxing on the basis of wage rates, as opposed to earnings. What we can hope to measure reasonably well through household surveys, however, is the distribution of total expenditures on commodities, or net income from all sources. In the present framework, this is just the distribution of

$$qx = (1 - t_w)w(\bar{L} - l) + \bar{M} \equiv m,$$

where lump-sum income is measured net of any taxes on the endowment itself and includes the value of grants, if any. The amount in question is, sadly, neither fish nor fowl, being neither full income nor lump-sum income; but almost invariably, this is the measure that the data will force us to use. In that case, given that all households face the same prices of goods, Eqn (4.8a) takes the special form

$$V = W[v^1(m^1), \ldots, v^h(m^h), \ldots, v^H(m^H)]. \tag{4.8b}$$

4.4. Optimal Commodity Taxation

The fact that governments of LDCs rely heavily on indirect taxes as a source of revenue—and that they will continue to do so for a long time to come—makes it especially important that the structure of indirect taxes be well designed. In the brief treatment of optimal commodity taxation that follows, the emphasis is on principles rather than on precise numerical calculations.

In order to introduce the general approach, we begin with the simplest possible case: a partial equilibrium setting, in which a good is produced by a perfectly competitive industry under conditions of constant unit costs. The essentials are captured in the familiar price–quantity diagram, as

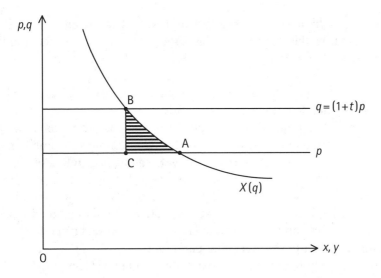

Figure 4.7. The deadweight loss of a tax when producer prices are fixed

depicted in Fig. 4.7. In the absence of taxation, the consumer and producer prices are identical, at the average (equals marginal) cost of production p. Assuming that the industry does not use its own output as an input (or, should it do so, that the ensuing tax is rebated), then the imposition of an *ad valorem* tax t thereon will result in the consumer price rising to $q = (1 + t)p$, so yielding revenue in the amount $R = (tp) \cdot X(q)$, where $X(q)$ is the ordinary demand function. The associated deadweight loss, as measured by net consumers' surplus, is the area of the shaded curvilinear triangle ABC, which, for sufficiently small t, is approximately equal to $(|X'(p)|/2) \cdot (tp)^2$. That is to say, ignoring all cross-effects, the deadweight loss arising from the taxation of a single good is increasing and quadratic in the tax rate. The expression $(|X'(p)|/2) \cdot (tp)^2$ can be rewritten as

$$\Lambda \equiv |\varepsilon| \cdot (pX) \cdot (t^2/2),$$

where ε is the own-price elasticity of demand in the untaxed equilibrium. Differentiating with respect to t, we obtain the marginal deadweight loss arising from an increase in t designed to raise one (small) additional unit of revenue:

$$\frac{\partial \Lambda / \partial t}{\partial R / \partial t} = |\varepsilon| \cdot t.$$

It follows that if the only thing that matters is efficiency, in the sense of minimizing the total deadweight loss of raising a fixed amount of revenue, then, *ceteris paribus*, goods should be taxed at rates that are inversely proportional to their own-price elasticities of demand. Considerations of equity aside, the assumption that all else is equal is not to be taken lightly, however; for the neglect of cross-effects is potentially very serious, and upon rectification, it turns out that the pursuit of efficiency alone will, in general, require departures from this 'rule'.

In this connection, it is sometimes claimed that uniformity of rates is best. False though it is in general, this claim is nevertheless (loosely) tethered to an approach that embodies a sound principle. As we shall see shortly, there exist certain circumstances, albeit restricted ones, under which the claim can be given a rigorous basis. It should also be said that the more widely accepted idea that tax systems should be broadly based, so that tax rates can be kept relatively low, surely owes something to the reasoning set out in the preceding paragraph.

The next step, therefore, is to examine the general case, in which both considerations of equity and cross-effects are accorded their proper place. The model chosen for this purpose is unswervingly simple. Suppose that transactions among producers are not taxed and that producer prices are fixed;[5] that neither labour supply nor lump-sum income is taxable; that all households face the same consumer prices; and that indirect tax rates can be varied without limit. Then the government can bring about any q by choosing a vector of taxes t such that

$$q = p + t. \tag{4.9}$$

If individuals can purchase as much as they please at the prices q, the (indirect) utility of individual h at her optimum will depend only on her lump-sum income and q, and the same will hold for her net demand for commodities, x^h. Hence, if the government has a social welfare function of the Bergson–Samuelsonian type, this function will take the form in Eqn (4.8a). The vector of individuals' aggregate demands for commodities is denoted by

$$X(q; w, \bar{M}) = \sum_{h-1}^{H} x^h(q; w^h, \bar{M}^h). \tag{4.10}$$

---

[5] A sufficient set of conditions for this to hold is as follows: (i) labour is homogeneous and the sole primary factor, (ii) the technology exhibits CRS in labour and all produced goods, and (iii) there is perfect competition. By the non-substitution theorem, therefore, the producer price of a good will be proportional to its unit direct and indirect labour content, which will be constant even in the face of substitution possibilities.

It is assumed that the government needs to raise a certain amount of revenue, R_0 say, the only source of which is indirect taxes. The government's problem, therefore, is to choose a vector of taxes t so as to

$$\text{maximize } V(q; w, \bar{M}) \quad \text{subject to } R(q) = tX(q) \geq R_0, \qquad (4.11)$$

where q and t are related by Eqn (4.9), producer prices being fixed by assumption. We write the associated Lagrangian as

$$\Phi = V(q; w, \bar{M}) + \lambda[tX(q) - R_0]. \qquad (4.12)$$

Note that under the above assumptions, choosing t is equivalent to choosing q. Assuming an interior solution, the first-order conditions are

$$\frac{\partial V}{\partial q_i} + \lambda \left[X_i + \sum_{j=1}^{n} t_j \frac{\partial X_j}{\partial q_i} \right] = 0 \quad \forall i, \qquad (4.13)$$

where the expression in brackets is the change in public revenue induced by a (small) unit increase in the tax on good i. At the optimum, λ measures the improvement in social welfare, as formulated in Eqn (4.8a), that would result if the government were to receive a grant in the amount of one unit of income from a source outside the economy.

We now examine the elements of Eqn (4.13) in more detail. Recalling Eqn (4.8a), we have

$$\frac{\partial V}{\partial q_i} = \sum_{h=1}^{H} \frac{\partial W}{\partial v^h} \cdot \frac{\partial v^h}{\partial q_i} = -\sum_{h=1}^{H} \left(\frac{\partial W}{\partial v^h} \cdot \alpha^h \right) x_i^h \quad \forall i, \qquad (4.14)$$

where the expression on the far right follows from Roy's identity, with $\alpha^h \equiv \partial v^h / \partial \bar{M}^h$ denoting individual h's marginal utility of income. In view of Eqn (4.14), it will be useful to define the quantity

$$\beta^h \equiv \frac{\partial W}{\partial v^h} \cdot \alpha^h, \qquad (4.15)$$

which is the social value placed on a (small) unit increase in income accruing to individual h. The vector $\beta = (\beta^1, \ldots, \beta^H)$ is therefore the appropriate set of weights for valuing small changes in individuals' incomes.

We turn next to the derivatives of the aggregate Marshallian demand functions. Using Slutsky's equation and summing over individuals, we have

$$\frac{\partial X_j}{\partial q_i} = \sum_{h=1}^{H} \left(s_{ij}^h - x_i^h \frac{\partial x_j^h}{\partial \bar{M}^h} \right), \qquad (4.16)$$

where s_{ij}^h is the derivative of individual h's compensated demand for good i with respect to the price of good j, and use has been made of the fact that the Slutsky matrix is symmetric: $s_{ij}^h = s_{ji}^h \, \forall i, j$. Substituting Eqns (4.14)–(4.16) into Eqn (4.13) yields

$$
-\sum_{h=1}^{H} \beta^h x_i^h + \lambda \left[X_i + \sum_{j=1}^{n} t_j \sum_{h=1}^{H} \left(s_{ij}^h - x_i^h \frac{\partial x_j^h}{\partial \bar{M}^h} \right) \right] = 0 \quad \forall i,
$$

which, noting that $X_i = \sum_{h=1}^{H} x_i^h$, may be rearranged as

$$
\sum_{j=1}^{n} t_j \sum_{h=1}^{H} s_{ij}^h = \sum_{h=1}^{H} \left(\frac{\beta^h}{\lambda} - 1 + \sum_{j=1}^{n} t_j \frac{\partial x_j^h}{\partial \bar{M}^h} \right) x_i^h \quad \forall i. \tag{4.17a}
$$

This is the so-called many-person Ramsey rule. In the special case where all individuals are identical, Eqn (4.17a) specializes to

$$
\sum_{j=1}^{n} t_j s_{ij} = \left[\left(\frac{1}{\lambda} - 1 \right) + \sum_{j=1}^{n} t_j \frac{\partial x_j}{\partial \bar{M}} \right] x_i \quad \forall i, \tag{4.17b}
$$

where the superscript h has become superfluous and β^h has been normalized to unity. Observe that dividing through by λ is equivalent to choosing government income as numeraire.

An interpretation of the various terms appearing in Eqns (4.17a) and (4.17b) will be helpful. Consider the thought-experiment in which the government transfers a unit of income to individual h as a lump-sum grant. If all individuals are identical, the social value of such a transfer will be unity and the associated direct cost, in terms of V, will be λ. With public income as numeraire, the net direct benefit yielded by this transfer will be $(1/\lambda) - 1$. On receiving the grant, however, the individual will spend it on the bundle $\partial x/\partial \bar{M}$, so that the government will claw back some of the transfer through the system of taxes (or incur additional expenditures should the individual decide to purchase goods that are subsidized) in the amount $t \cdot (\partial x/\partial \bar{M})$. Thus, the terms in brackets on the right-hand side (RHS) of Eqn (4.17b) can be thought of as the net social benefit yielded by the government making a unit, lump-sum transfer to any single individual drawn at random from a homogeneous group. If individuals are heterogeneous, so that Eqn (4.17a) is the relevant form, then the same interpretation applies to such a transfer to individual h, with the term $(\beta^h/\lambda) - 1$ replacing the uniform term $(1/\lambda) - 1$.

Turning to the left-hand side (LHS) of Eqns (4.17a) and (4.17b), suppose taxes are sufficiently small at the optimum, so that the derivatives s_{ij}^h may be taken as constants in any neighbourhood that just includes both p and $(p + t^0)$, where t^0 is the optimal tax vector.[6] Since, starting from $q = p$, the change in q is just t^0, it is then seen that the LHS of Eqns (4.17a) and (4.17b) is the reduction in the compensated demand for good i which is induced by the tax vector t^0. In the case where all individuals are identical, it is seen by dividing both sides of Eqn (4.17b) by x_i that the RHS becomes independent of i, leaving us with the special result that the optimum is attained by reducing all compensated demands in the same proportion. Thus, goods whose compensated demand schedules are inelastic should be relatively heavily taxed.

If individuals differ, however, this result must be modified; for there is the compelling fact that it is the poorer members of society whose consumption tends to be intensive in those goods, such as food, that are most inelastic in demand. This central point is reflected in Eqn (4.17a) as follows. We see from the RHS thereof that each and every individual's demand for any good is weighted by her particular net social 'benefit-factor', as expressed by the algebraic sum of the terms in brackets. These factors vary across individuals by virtue of differences both in the social weights, β, and in individuals' tastes, as manifested in differences in their marginal propensities to spend on goods. A relatively poor individual will (or at least should) be assigned a relatively high value of β, and hence, *ceteris paribus*, will have a relatively high weight. Dividing both sides of Eqn (4.17a) by the aggregate demand for good i, X_i, we have the result that, at the optimum, the proportional reduction in the compensated demand for any good, relative to the untaxed allocation, equals the sum of the thus weighted individual shares in the aggregate consumption of that good. Goods consumed intensively by the poor will, therefore, be more lightly taxed than in the case where considerations of equity play no role at all, that is, where $\beta^h = 1$ for all h. The optimum tax vector corresponding to the latter case fulfils the prescription for 'efficient' taxation only in this special sense.

The idea underlying the Ramsey rule is clear and appealing; but the reader can be forgiven for wondering whether the rule lends itself to practical implementation. The first difficulty is normative: the very use of a social welfare function, as formulated in Eqn (4.8), is not uncontroversial.[7]

---

[6] Recalling the example with which we began this section, the said reduction corresponds to AC in Fig. 4.7.

[7] For a wide-ranging assault on 'Paretian' welfare economics, see Rowley and Peacock (1975).

Yet suppose, whatever be one's misgivings, that such an approach is adopted. There is the immediate question of what form the function should take. Even to pose the question in this way may smack overly of technocratic manipulation, in which case one is confronted with the problem of how to engage decision makers in a discussion that would yield such a function implicitly? The second difficulty is a positive one, which cropped up in Section 4.3 in connection with labour supply: is there sufficient information to estimate the demand systems that are needed to implement Eqn (4.17a) without severe a priori restrictions on their forms? Deaton (1987), in particular, has voiced considerable scepticism that such estimation is possible. This leads, in turn, to the question of what the structure of commodity taxes would look like if commonly employed restrictions were indeed imposed.

A fairly general answer to the latter question is provided by Deaton and Stern (1986). Let households' preferences be separable in factor supplies and goods, so that changes in the former leave marginal rates of substitution among the latter unchanged, and let the subutility function for goods be quasi-homothetic, so that households' Engel curves for each good are parallel, though the intercepts may differ and thereby impart some heterogeneity into the system, in particular through variations in households' demographic composition. Now suppose further that the government is able to make optimal, lump-sum grants conditioned only on a household's demographic characteristics, and that it does so, financing them out of the proceeds of taxes on consumer goods. That being so, it can be proved that all goods should be taxed at a flat rate. In this case, there is a division of labour among the instruments: the grants tackle the task of redistribution and the commodity taxes raise the required revenue.

Given the underlying assumptions, this striking result provides an underpinning for the commonly encountered proposal that commodity taxes (including tariffs) should be uniform, apart from a suitable supplement of special excises on goods whose use clearly causes externalities, such as alcohol, tobacco, motor fuels, and the like. The snag is, of course, that administering grants based on demographic characteristics is not a trivial matter unless the economic system as a whole is well ordered and developed in the bookkeeping sense. To argue for uniform taxes on the grounds of administrative simplicity, therefore, is to wield a double-edged sword; for if administrative capacity is wanting, it is wholly unrealistic to expect that the grants will be optimally distributed. Even if this difficulty were set aside, there is no denying that the result rests on strong assumptions about preferences. For these reasons, the door remains open to variations in rates, though the practical difficulties of trying to administer a finely tuned system based on Eqn (4.17a), and the uncertainty that inevitably surrounds the econometric estimates of the demand parameters, suggest that a wise choice would be to settle for just two, or at most three, broad rates, zero being an obvious candidate for some goods. This matter will be pursued further in Chapter 5.

To complete this section, we must say something about the optimal taxation of commodities in relation to international trade. We saw in Chapter 1 that, administrative considerations apart, foreign trade should be taxed only to exploit the economy's monopoly power, if any, in world markets. Now that tax instruments and some aspects of tax theory have been discussed at some length, it may be helpful to provide a somewhat fuller account of the intuition for a result that was earlier more or less simply asserted. Consider, therefore, Fig. 4.8, which is a variant of Fig. 4.7 in which the domestic industry produces under increasing, as opposed to constant, marginal costs. In the absence of taxation, the amount $y(p^*)$ will be produced domestically and the excess domestic demand at that price, namely $X(p^*) - y(p^*)$, will be imported, as depicted by the segment AB. Suppose now that a certain amount of revenue is to be raised. If the tax base is domestic consumption and the amount to be raised is not too large, the

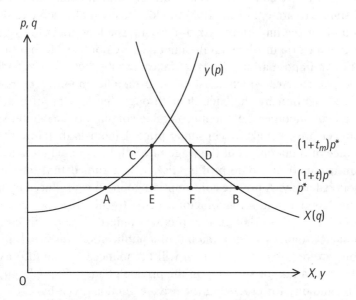

Figure 4.8. A tax on consumption and an import tariff that yield identical revenue

imposition of a suitable *ad valorem* tax thereon, at the rate t say, will raise the consumer price to $(1 + t)p^*$, while leaving the producer price at p^*, and hence domestic production unchanged at $y(p^*)$. Imports will fall *pari passu* with domestic consumption, and the associated deadweight loss is the small triangle whose height is tp^* and whose right-hand apex is B. If, however, the choice falls on the tariff, so that the tax base is imports, then the tariff rate must exceed t–indeed, it may not even be possible to raise the required amount of revenue if the initial level of imports is sufficiently small. Let such a tariff exist, and denote its value by t_m, as drawn in Fig. 4.8. At the common price $(1 + t_m)p^*$, domestic production is greater, and domestic consumption is smaller, than in the case where domestic consumption is the tax base. That the tax base in equilibrium, CD, shrinks on both counts causes the associated deadweight loss to be far larger, the respective contributions being the triangles ACE and BDF. As noted in connection with Fig. 4.7, all cross-effects have been neglected; but Fig. 4.8 reveals an essential element in the argument against tariffs.

4.5. The Diamond–Mirrlees Model

Given the frequent appeal in Chapter 1 to the results in Diamond and Mirrlees (1971), we complete this account of optimal commodity taxation with a simple treatment of the D–M model. This will also serve to prepare the ground for the important task of deriving shadow prices in Chapter 9.

Consider a world in which lump-sum taxes are not feasible, but the government can impose arbitrarily large taxes or subsidies on commodities–bar one, of course, which must be non-taxable in order to rule out lump-sum taxation by the back door through the levying of a uniform tax on all commodities. Let the non-taxable commodity be labour, so that its producer price equals its consumer price. Labour is therefore the natural choice of numeraire, but the wage rate will be denoted by w to avoid any confusion. If any pure profits arise, it is assumed that they can be wholly taxed away. A private consumption good (2) is produced by means of labour (good 1) and a fixed factor specific to each firm, which may be thought of as land, so that pure profits will indeed arise in this case. The government produces a fixed amount of a public good, for which L_0 units of labour are required. Its provision will be financed by the full taxation of profits and a tax (or subsidy) on the private good.

The technology for producing the private good is given by

$$y_2 = f(L_2), \tag{4.18}$$

where the production function $f(\cdot)$ is assumed to be strictly concave in labour inputs L_2 alone, to exhibit CRS in labour and the fixed factor, and to satisfy the lower Inada condition. Given perfect competition and CRS, the industry may be treated as a single firm that takes prices as parametrically given. Since firms trade at producer prices, their aggregate profits from producing good 2 are

$$\Pi_2 = p_2 y_2 - wL_2. \tag{4.19}$$

Under perfect competition, their choice of L_2 satisfies the first-order condition

$$p_2 f' = w, \tag{4.20}$$

so that the demand for labour depends only on the product-wage at producer prices:

$$L_2^0(p_2, w) = f'^{-1}(w/p_2). \tag{4.21}$$

Hence, the supply of good 2 at prices (p_2, w) is

$$y_2^0(p_2, w) = f[f'^{-1}(w/p_2)]. \tag{4.22}$$

Let there be a representative individual, whose continuous, locally non-satiated preferences over supplying labour (y_1) and consuming good 2 are assumed to be represented by the utility function

$$u = u(y_1, x_2). \tag{4.23}$$

He takes the prices w and q_2 as parametrically given. Since all pure profits are taxed away, the individual's problem is to choose y_1 and x_2 so as to

$$\text{maximize } u \quad \text{subject to } wy_1 - q_2 x_2 = 0. \tag{4.24}$$

Let $y_1^0(w/q_2)$ and $x_2^0(w/q_2)$ solve problem (4.24). The corresponding indirect utility function depends, therefore, only on the relative price (w/q_2), lump-sum income being zero in the face of a 100 per cent tax on profits:

$$v = v(w/q_2), \tag{4.25}$$

where $v(\cdot)$ is increasing in w/q_2.

The government's revenue from taxing consumption of the private good is $(q_2 - p_2)x_2^0$. Summing the two revenues together, namely, Π_2^0 and

$(q_2 - p_2)x_2^0$, and recalling Eqn (4.19), we can write the government's revenue constraint in the following form:

$$p_2 y_2^0 + (q_2 - p_2)x_2^0 = w(L_0 + L_2^0). \tag{4.26}$$

Since $y_2^0 = x_2^0$ in equilibrium, Eqn (4.26) reduces to the representative individual's budget identity:

$$q_2 x_2^0 = w(L_0 + L_2^0),$$

which is, in effect, a statement of Walras' law; for the government's books are also exactly in balance.

We can now state the government's problem as follows:

$$\underset{(p_2,q_2)}{\text{maximize }} v(q_2/w), \tag{4.27}$$

subject to the revenue constraint Eqn (4.26) and to the market-clearing conditions for the two private goods, namely, labour and good 2, respectively:

$$y_1^0(w/q_2) = [L_0 + f'^{-1}(w/p_2)] \tag{4.28}$$

and, from Eqn (4.22),

$$f[f'^{-1}(w/p_2)] = x_2^0(q_2/w). \tag{4.29}$$

The solution of problem (4.27) in the space of private goods is depicted graphically in Fig. 4.9. The (second-best) optimum must lie on the offer curve $[y_1^0(w/q_2), x_2^0(q_2/w)]$ corresponding to problem (4.24), which is drawn as OO'; and it must also lie in the feasible set for the economy as a whole. Given that L_0 units of labour will be employed in the production of the public good, the boundary of the feasible set of private goods is $G(y_1, y_2) = 0$, whose increasing, concave section to the left of the point $(L_0, 0)$ is $f(L_2) = f(y_1 - L_0)$. Since the individual becomes better off as he moves away from the origin along OO', the (constrained) optimum is point B, where OO' cuts the upper boundary of the feasible set for the last time. Hence, there is productive efficiency in the private sector, a feature of the allocation that is ensured by the government's ability to tax away all pure profits. The indifference curve passing through B is denoted by $v(q^*)$, the slope of which at B is w/q_2^*.

This allocation is reached as follows. The slope of $G(\cdot)$ at B is the ratio of the wage rate to the producer price of good 2, (w/p_2^*). For at these prices,

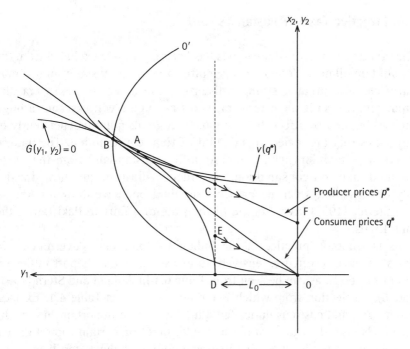

Figure 4.9. The optimum in D–M economy

firms will choose to produce at B, and as a result they will earn pretax profits (measured in units of good 2) in the amount of the vertical segment CD. The product-wage rate at consumer prices, (w/q_2^*), is the slope of the line OB, which, extended beyond B, is the consumer's budget line. At these prices, he does indeed choose B, and so the markets clear. As drawn, the good is subsidized ($p_2 > q_2$), the revenue from the tax on profits, CD, being more than enough to finance the production of the public good, the cost of which in units of good 2 is the segment DE, where OE has slope (w/p_2^*). The residual CE is exactly the amount needed to finance the subsidy $(p_2 - q_2)x_2^0$, given that households supply labour in the amount $y_1^0(w/q_2)$.

By way of comparison, the first-best optimum is also shown. This is point A, where an indifference curve is tangent to $G(\cdot)$, the boundary of the feasible set. As drawn, it involves more leisure and less consumption of good 2 than at the second-best optimum, which reflects the excess of profits over the costs of producing the public good. If profits alone were not sufficient to finance the latter, then good 2 would have to be taxed, and A would lie instead to the north-west of B.

4.6. Effective Taxes: Pakistan 1975/6

The taxation of intermediate goods has been rigorously excluded from the account up till now. Yet not only is it often an important source of revenue, but it can also produce strongly distorting effects. For to the extent that producers can shift them forward, taxes on inputs will cascade through the system, and so affect the prices of final goods quite independently of any taxes that are levied at the point of final consumption. The pattern of effective taxation may, therefore, differ substantially from the set of nominal taxes on consumption.[8] In order to illustrate just how drastically effective taxes can depart from nominal ones, we draw on Ahmad and Stern's (1991) investigation of the state of affairs in Pakistan in the mid-1970s.

As is common practice in the Indian subcontinent, governments in Pakistan have resorted extensively to excise taxes and import duties on producer goods, as can be seen from Table 6.1 in Ahmad and Stern (1991: 156-8), a selection from which is reproduced here as Table 4.1. Excises, surcharges, and customs duties fell quite heavily on important intermediate goods, as did customs duties and sales taxes on certain capital goods. There were also subsidies on three commodities (wheat, fertilizers, and agricultural machinery), all of which are reported in Table 4.1. Among non-tradables, only banking and insurance, gas, and other services (all reported here) were subject to nominal taxes.

So much for description. The first analytical task is to derive the set of effective tax rates that correspond to the nominal structure. For this purpose, we need a general equilibrium model in which the determination of prices will have a central place, yet which is simple enough to encourage its use in practice. Consider, therefore, a closed economy in which each and every good is produced under CRS by means of a Leontief technology, so that there is no substitution within a given line of production. Firms sell at producer prices p and buy at consumer prices q. Households, as producers of labour, sell their labour to firms at the after-tax wage rate, whereas firms buy at the before-tax wage rate of w (inclusive of employment taxes, if any). Let v_j be the value added in industry j when it produces one unit

---

[8] Such taxation may, moreover, have the effect of distorting resource allocation in production so heavily as to destroy any real hope that shadow prices will be even approximately proportional to producer prices. It turns out that this introduces additional complications into the elementary analysis of tax reforms presented in Chapter 5. These issues will be taken up in the chapters dealing with social cost–benefit analysis, once the foundations for such a treatment have been laid.

Table 4.1. Revenue collections on selected commodities, Pakistan, 1975/6 (millions of rupees)

Commodity	Excise	Surcharge	Sales (D)	Subsidies	Imports	Sales (M)
Wheat	0	0	0	−1209.3	0	0
Rice	0	0	0	0	0	0
Tobacco growing	88.8	0	0	0	5.9	0
Grain milling	0	0	0	0	0	0
Edible oils	588.6	0	0	0	11.5	0
Beverages	40.4	0	6.4	0	9.4	0
Cigarettes	1189.9	0	0	0	0	0
Cotton textiles (LS)	0	0	0	0	0.7	0
Cotton textiles (SS)	0	0	0	0	0	0
Fertilizer	0	321.5	0	−606.5	0	0
Petroleum	1073.7	163.2	0	0	320.0	0
Agricultural machinery	0	0	0	−24.4	0	0
Other non-elctr. machinery	0	0	0	0	431.1	95.4
Electrical mach.	0	0	0	0	303.9	72.5
Transport (LS)	0	0	4.0	0	513.3	166.2
Low-cost residential buildings	0	0	0	0	0	0
Luxurious residential buildings	0	0	0	0	0	0
Infrastructure	0	0	0	0	0	0
Electricity	0	0	0	0	0	0
Gas	0	321.0	3.2	0	0	0
Road transport	0	0	0	0	0	0
Rail transport	0	0	0	0	0	0
Phone, telegraph, and post	0	0	0	0	0	0
Banking and Insurance	10.7	0	0	0	0	0
Other services	32.0	0	0	0	0	0

Source: Ahmad and Stern (1991: 156-8).

of gross output. In the special case where labour is the only factor of production, for example, we have $v_j = w_j l_j$, where w_j is the wage rate in sector j and l_j is the input–output coefficient for labour. If product markets are competitive, producer prices will be equal to unit costs. For good j, therefore,

$$p_j = \sum_{i=1}^{n} q_i a_{ij} + v_j \quad \forall j,$$

where a_{ij} is the amount of the ith good needed to produce one unit of good j. This is compactly written as

$$p = qA + v, \tag{4.30}$$

where A denotes the technology matrix (a_{ij}). Since $q = p + t$, where t is the vector of taxes, we have

$$q = (v + t)(I - A)^{-1}. \tag{4.31}$$

In the absence of any taxes, producer prices would be equal to consumer prices. Denoting the price vector in this special case by p^0, we have

$$p^0 = q^0 = v(I - A)^{-1}, \tag{4.32}$$

so that a natural definition of the vector of effective taxes is

$$t^e \equiv q - p^0 = t(I - A)^{-1}. \tag{4.33}$$

That is, the effective tax on good i, t_i^e, is the difference between its consumer price in the presence of the tax vector t and its unit cost of production in the absence thereof. Observe that the vector v has been taken as fixed in the above derivations, which is equivalent to assuming that all taxes on goods are completely shifted forward. Ahmad and Stern comment briefly on the plausibility of this implicit assumption.

Imports are incorporated into the analysis by treating them as complementary to domestic factors: in the absence of any substitutability, they are non-competitive with domestically produced goods. Denoting the matrix of such import coefficients by A^m, Eqn (4.30) becomes

$$p = qA + v + (p^* + t^m)A^m,$$

or

$$q = (v + t + (p^* + t^m)A^m)(I - A)^{-1}, \tag{4.34}$$

where t^m denotes the vector of tariffs. Hence, the vector of effective taxes, relative to the case where $t = t^m = 0$, is

$$t^e \equiv (t + t^m A^m)(I - A)^{-1}. \tag{4.35}$$

The difference between t^e as defined in Eqn (4.35) and (t, t^m) measures the extent to which the taxation of inputs causes the levels of consumer prices to deviate from those that would rule in the case where the set of taxes (t, t^m) were levied only at the point of final consumption, as would happen under a value added or final sales tax.

In order to estimate t^e, Ahmad and Stern split the computation into three steps. The first involves solely the taxation of domestic production through excises, surcharges, and sales taxes, the associated vector of (nominal) taxes being denoted by t^d. In the present case, the ith element of the vector t^d is the algebraic sum of the corresponding entries in row i of Table 4.1, normalized by an appropriate index of the use of good i so as to yield t_i^d as a rate. In the second stage, imported inputs are included in v, and with them any import duties. Equation (4.35) then yields the vector of effective taxes t^e: as can be seen from Table 4.1, this differs markedly from t^d, most effective rates being 5–10 per cent higher than the nominal ones. In the third stage, the taxation of capital assets is brought into the reckoning in the same way, using an expression analogous to Eqn (4.34). The vector of effective taxes that arises at the third stage is denoted by the vector t^k. The resulting estimates of the vectors t^d, t^e, t^k, and the differences $(t^k - t^d)$ and $(t^k - t^e)$, all expressed as rates, are set out in Table 6.4 in Ahmad and Stern, the selection from which corresponding to Table 4.1 is set out here in Table 4.2.

It is noteworthy that the taxation of capital intensifies the degree of effective taxation, all elements of $(t^k - t^e)$ being positive and those for gas and electricity being strikingly large. It is also instructive to examine the three cases for which there are nominal subsidies on domestic production: 2.0 per cent on wheat, 26.7 per cent on fertilizer, and 7.9 per cent on agricultural machinery. In all three cases, the taxation of inputs (including capital) used in domestic production reduces the nominal subsidy by pulling strongly in the other direction—so much so, that in the case of agricultural machinery, there is a net effective tax of 2.9 per cent, and in the case of fertilizers, the effective subsidy, at 15.2 per cent, is sharply lower than the nominal rate. The only other good to enjoy a net effective subsidy is grain milling, to the tune of 4.8 per cent, which is a result of the subsidy on its main input, wheat. There are numerous cases in which the effective tax rate is much higher than the nominal one, including confectionery and bakery, beverages, textiles, clothing and footwear, paper and printing, a wide range of chemical products, cement, glass, metals and machinery, buildings, infrastructure, utilities, and transportation.

Table 4.2. Total effective taxes on selected commodities, Pakistan, 1975/6

Commodity	t^d	t^e	t^k	$t^k - t^d$	$t^k - t^e$
Wheat	−0.0200	−0.0179	−0.0136	0.0065	0.0043
Rice	0	0.0168	0.0233	0.0233	0.0065
Tobacco growing	0.1882	0.1953	0.1984	0.0103	0.0031
Grain milling	0	−0.0609	−0.0480	−0.0480	0.0129
Edible oils	0.0923	0.1228	0.1388	0.0465	0.0160
Beverages	0.0759	0.1519	0.1665	0.0906	0.0146
Cigarettes and tobacco prod. (LS)	0.7204	0.7669	0.7773	0.0569	0.0104
Cotton textiles (LS)	0.0222	0.0714	0.0949	0.0727	0.0235
Cotton textiles (SS)	0	0.0427	0.0596	0.0596	0.0169
Fertilizer	−0.2670	−0.1846	−0.1519	0.1151	0.0327
Petroleum products	0.3115	0.3407	0.3505	0.0390	0.0098
Agricultural machinery	−0.0785	0.0166	0.0289	0.1074	0.0123
Other non-electrical machinery	0	0.0641	0.0824	0.0824	0.0183
Electrical machinery	0	0.0821	0.0961	0.0961	0.0139
Transport (LS)	0.0032	0.0979	0.1125	0.1093	0.0146
Low-cost residential buildings	0	0.0664	0.0808	0.0808	0.0144
Luxurious residential buildings	0	0.0808	0.0954	0.0954	0.0146
Infrastructure	0	0.0762	0.1262	0.1262	0.0499
Electricity	0	0.0815	0.2160	0.2160	0.1344
Gas	0.4023	0.4158	0.5437	0.1414	0.1279
Road transport	0	0.0768	0.0836	0.0836	0.0068
Rail transport	0	0.0748	0.1108	0.1108	0.0360
Phone, telegraph, and post	0	0.0105	0.0345	0.0345	0.0240
Banking and insurance	0.0025	0.0335	0.0438	0.0413	0.0103
Other services	0.0030	0.0058	0.0157	0.0127	0.0100

Source: Ahmad and Stern (1991: 167–9).

A cursory glance at the higgledy–piggledy structure of these effective tax rates and their tenuous connection with the structure of nominal rates suggests two questions. First, was it really the government's intention to impose this particular pattern of effective tax burdens? Second, do there exist tax reforms that would improve welfare? One can, perhaps, hope to answer the second question. In the face of what appear to be strong forces making for distortions in production, it turns out that providing such an answer must be preceded by the estimation of a complete set of shadow prices. A rigorous examination of this question is therefore deferred until the groundwork has been laid in Chapter 9, but the presumption that a substantial improvement is possible must be strong. This example of a highly differentiated tax structure, whether it reflects some carefully laid-down plan or otherwise, also motivates a discussion of the merits of introducing a VAT, a possible reform that is taken up in Chapters 5 and 7.

4.7. Summary

What sort of tax structure should be used to finance development? In addressing this question, one is struck by the difference between what theory tells us is desirable and what governments usually choose to do. Lump-sum transfers provide a valuable benchmark, but are ruled out on practical grounds, thereby placing the discussion firmly in second-best territory. Whilst results of great generality are inevitably rather elusive, the essential features of a good tax structure are fairly clear. First, taxes on commodities should be broadly based in the interest of promoting efficiency. Second, to the extent that combined considerations of equity and efficiency argue for differentiation in rates, just two or three well-chosen values (of which one might be zero) will not do much worse than many. Third, exceptions should be made to deal with externalities, in the form of special excises on such goods as alcohol, tobacco, and fuels. Fourth, the fact that taxes on factors whose supply is very inelastic—land is the prime example—result in small deadweight losses is a compelling argument for imposing them, with the choice of rate(s) guided by the second point above.

In practice, these principles are widely honoured in the breach. Beginning with commodities, taxes are extensively levied on international trade instead of exclusively on domestic consumption. In both cases, there is often a plethora of nominal rates, whose structure reflects not studied calculations using the many-person Ramsey rule, but rather the haphazard accumulation of piecemeal decisions, in which lobbying doubtless played a part. Taxes on intermediate goods, which are usually undesirable on efficiency grounds, are both commonplace and rarely fully rebated. As their effects ramify through the stages of production, they induce a pattern of effective taxation that may depart radically from the nominal structure, and so serve to distort and obscure the position further. Turning to direct taxes, their overall contribution to the Exchequer is relatively modest, the statutory payers being enterprises and their employees in the regulated sector of the economy. Taxes on land are conspicuous largely by their (virtual) absence.

This state of affairs cries out for explanation. An immediate reaction is that it is the product of simple incompetence and a Byzantine political economy. Yet two crucial factors have been left out of the above account, namely, weak administrative capacity and the absence of bookkeeping practices in most of the informal sector of the economy, the former being a leading cause of the latter. When such capacity is especially scarce, the authorities will surely concentrate their attention on natural 'choke' points, such as ports, border crossings, and the gates of large factories, for the goal of broadly based taxation of final consumption is out of reach. (One might add that a resort to the printing press—an alternative we take up in Chapter 6—is also low on administrative costs.)

The history of taxation of now developed countries lends additional force to this explanation of the structure of indirect taxes in LDCs. The failure to tax land, however, has other roots, at least in South Asia; for both the Moghuls and, except towards the end of the colonial period, their British successors relied very heavily on the land tax. Yet what had been administratively routine from the sixteenth century to the early part of the twentieth was no longer politically feasible by Independence. It will not do, therefore, to seek refuge in the argument that the defects of today's tax structures can be laid wholly at the door of weak administrative capacity.

Two general conclusions suggest themselves. First, the development of a capable and honest system of tax administration is an essential complement to the formulation of sound development policy, and as such, is to be vigorously promoted. Second, even with the system as it is, there appear to be many promising opportunities to reform the structure of current taxes for the better. These will be explored in some detail in the chapter that follows.

Recommended Reading

The essential reference work on public economics is Atkinson and Stiglitz (1980). Where taxation in developing countries is concerned, a useful collection of theoretical contributions is to be found in Newbery and Stern (1987). A concise account with at least one eye on practice is Burgess and Stern (1992).

Exercises

1. We are interested in calculating the set of social weights (β^h) in a manner which reflects common practice when time and resources are particularly

scarce. Suppose all households have the same, homothetic preferences, that they spend all their income, and that all face the same consumer prices.

(a) Show that

$$x^h(q) = \left(\frac{M^h}{M^1}\right) x^1(q) \quad \forall h,$$

where M^h is the income of household h.

(b) If the utility function $u(x)$ is homogeneous of degree one in x, show that a suitable re-scaling of $u(\cdot)$ yields $\alpha^h = 1 \; \forall h$.

(c) Suppose the social welfare function takes the additively separable form

$$W = \left[\sum_{h=1}^{H} (M^h)^{1-\varepsilon} \Big/ (1 - \varepsilon)\right] \phi(q),$$

where ε is often termed the inequality-aversion parameter. If $M^1 = 1$ and β^1 is normalized to unity, find the value of β^h corresponding to $M^h = 5$ for each of the integer values $\varepsilon = 0, 1, 2, 3, 5$ and depict the functions $(M^h)^{1-\varepsilon}/(1-\varepsilon)$ graphically.

[N.B. $\lim_{\varepsilon \to 1} (M^h)^{1-\varepsilon}/(1 - \varepsilon) = \ln M^h$].

(d) Comment critically on the assumptions underpinning (b) and (c) in the light of standard (ordinal) consumer theory.

2. The aggregate demand function for an importable good is

$$X(q) = 12 - q,$$

where $X(q)$ denotes the amount demanded at the consumer price q. The domestic industry is perfectly competitive, the industry cost function taking the form

$$c(Y) = Y^3/12,$$

where Y denotes the level of domestic production.

(a) If the world price of the good is parametrically given at the value 3 and the government imposes an *ad valorem* tariff at the rate of 33 per cent, how much revenue will it raise and how large will be the attendant deadweight loss?

(b) Suppose, instead, that the same amount of revenue were to be raised through a sales tax. Find both the rate that must be imposed and the resulting deadweight loss. Depict all variables for parts (a) and (b) in a price–quantity diagram.

(c) Discuss, first, the likely robustness of your findings to the introduction of general equilibrium effects, and second, the political economy of the choice between the two taxes.

3. Consider the following Diamond–Mirrlees problem. There are n identical individuals, each of whom is endowed with one unit of time. There are two private goods, namely, leisure and corn, an individual's preferences over which take the form

$$u(x_1, x_2) = x_1^\alpha x_2^{1-\alpha}.$$

Corn is produced in the private sector by means of labour and a fixed factor, K, under conditions of CRS and perfect competition. The output of corn is

$$Y_2 = F(L_2; K),$$

where L_2 is the total amount of time supplied by individuals to the production of corn.

The government decides to produce Z_0 ($<n$) units of a public good, an activity that requires Z_0 units of labour (time). Leisure is not taxable, but a commodity tax can be imposed on the consumption of corn and profits can be taxed up to the rate of 100 per cent. Lump-sum taxes are not available. Subject to the requirement that it be able to finance the production of the public good, the government chooses taxes so as to maximize the welfare of a typical individual.

(a) Prove that the consumer price of corn at the second-best optimum is

$$q_2 = (1 - \alpha)/f(1 - \alpha - z_0; K/n),$$

where $z_0 = Z_0/n$ and $f(l_2) = F(L_2/n; K/n)$ and labour is the numeraire good. Hence, or otherwise, find expressions for the values of all variables in equilibrium.

(b) Depict your solution in the space of leisure and corn for the cases $f(l_2) = l_2^{1/2}$ and $f(l_2) = l_2^{2/3}$, when $\alpha = 0.5$, $Z_0 = 0.1n$.

(c) Find the first-best solution in each case when lump sum taxes are available and compare it with its counterpart in (b). [To make matters exact, calculate the equivalent variation in each case.]

4. Consider the following variant of exercise 4.2. The representative consumer's preferences now take the form

$$u(x_0, x_1, x_2) = v(x_0) + x_1 + \beta \ln x_2,$$

where x_0 is her consumption of the public good. The technology for producing the private good is given by

$$Y_2 = \sqrt{L_2}.$$

Find the optimum taxes for any given level of x_0 and illustrate the solution in the space of (x_1, x_2). Compare this second-best solution with the first-best in the case where $x_0 = n/4$ and $\beta = 1/2$.

5. Tax Reform

An important implicit assumption in much of the literature on optimum taxation is that the government can proceed to design tax structures without paying heed to those already in existence. It is rarely the case, however, that governments enjoy the advantage of starting anew with a clean slate. For the system of taxation reflects a society's political, social, and administrative history, as well as the constellation of influences and interests that vie with one another in the present. Some would argue, therefore, that the value of the results in that literature may lie more in their influence on how we think about the issues of taxation rather than in their provision of an apparatus to calculate optima. As Hahn (1973) puts it, 'Welfare economics is the grammar of arguments about policy, not the policy'. Yet a problem of pressing practical importance remains. For while such calculations themselves may be 'of dubious meaning' (ibid.: 106), it is still legitimate—indeed, it is essential—to determine whether improvements to existing tax structures can be found and implemented.

This task involves two questions. First, are the particular taxes currently in use the right ones for the job? Second, given the tax system as it stands, are there feasible improvements in welfare to be had by changing the structure of tax rates? These are broad questions indeed, and what follows is necessarily a selective account. In keeping with the importance of reforming trade policy and its connections with broadening the tax base, we begin with a discussion of proposals to replace quotas with tariffs (Section 5.1), the next stage being the abolition of tariffs in favour of a value-added tax (VAT) (Section 5.2). Answering the second question requires the use of the apparatus of optimum tax theory, not to compute the optimum, but rather—and more modestly—to establish which taxes should be raised and which lowered, the changes being perhaps of a strictly local nature. We shall examine how this can be done in Section 5.3, drawing upon an application of the theory to the reform of India's and Pakistan's systems of indirect taxes (Ahmad and Stern, 1984, 1991; Ahmad et al., 1984). In Section 5.4, we turn the question around by asking what values the marginal social weights for households with differing levels of total expenditure must take for the observed tax structure to be socially optimal. This so-called 'inverse optimum' problem can put the political economy that yielded the structure in question in a revealing—even unflattering—light. Section 5.5 deals with a reform of tariffs on importable intermediate inputs that are used to produce final goods whose domestic production is subject to stiff competition from smuggled items, with an application to Pakistan.

With an extensive treatment of social cost–benefit analysis to follow in later chapters, a general remark on the evaluation of economic reforms is called for at the outset, namely, that a tax reform has certain formal similarities to a public project. In both cases, the problem is to find directions of change that will improve social welfare. The ostensible difference is that whereas a tax reform is an intervention that affects prices directly, a public project is an intervention in the space of quantities, being a perturbation to the public sector's production plan. As we shall see, the shadow prices used to evaluate the social profitability of projects also play a key role in the evaluation of tax reforms when there are distortions in production.

5.1. Quotas into Tariffs

We saw in Chapters 2 and 3 that import quotas have been heavily used in the pursuit of import-substitution development strategies in the post-war period. This fact notwithstanding, they have little, if anything, to commend them. First, a binding quota on an importable renders the good non-tradable at the margin, so that the only connection between its domestic price and that ruling on world markets is that former exceeds the latter. Second, unlike a tariff, a quota generates no public revenues—unless it be auctioned, which rarely happens in practice. Given the pressing need for additional public income to finance development expenditures, this is a severe drawback. Indeed, the damage does not stop there. The very fact that the Treasury fails to appropriate the difference between amount that the quota fetches at the ruling domestic price and the cost of importing it generates a rent, for which private agents will compete and in which corrupt public servants and elected officials will seek to share. On these grounds, there is much to be said for abolishing all quotas in favour of tariffs, if only as a first step towards restructuring the tax system as a whole.

The weakest reform of this type is simply to transfer the existing quota rents to the government. This is accomplished by choosing a vector of equivalent tariffs, thereby leaving domestic prices unchanged.[1] That is to say, if the domestic price of good i is p_i in the presence of the quota, then

---

[1] This will hold only at the first round; for it is most improbable that private agents and the government will spend the quota rents in the same way.

the equivalent *ad valorem* tariff is defined to be

$$t_i^e = (p_i/p_i^*) - 1,$$ (5.1)

and the associated quota rent is

$$R_i^e = t_i^e p_i^* Q_i,$$ (5.2)

where Q_i is the (binding) import quota. The essentials are captured in the usual price–quantity diagram, as depicted in Fig. 5.1. The aggregate supply schedule, $Y_i(p_i)$, is identical to the domestic industry's supply schedule, $y_i(p_i)$, save that a horizontal segment of length Q_i is inserted into the latter at $p_i = p_i^*$, so that $Y_i(p_i)$ is simply a parallel displacement of $y_i(p_i)$ in the amount Q_i for all $p_i > p_i^*$. Formally,

$$Y_i(p_i) \begin{cases} = y_i(p_i) & \text{if } p_i < p_i^*, \\ \in [y_i(p_i), y_i(p_i) + Q_i] & \text{if } p_i = p_i^*, \\ = y_i(p_i) + Q_i & \text{if } p_i > p_i^*. \end{cases}$$ (5.3)

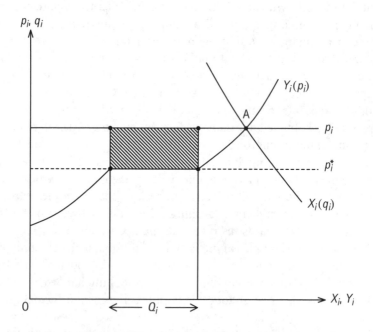

Figure 5.1. Output, demand, and price under a binding quota

The domestic demand schedule, $X_i(q_i)$, intersects $Y_i(p_i)$ at point A, where $p_i = q_i$ in the absence of any indirect taxes on good i. The absolute level of the tariff is $(p_i - p_i^*)$ and the quota rent is the shaded area.

Following the reform, Q_i is unlimited, but importers must pay the government $t_i^e p_i^*$ on each unit brought in. At the price $p_i = (1+t_i^e)p_i^*$, therefore, the aggregate supply schedule is now a horizontal line, and Eqn (5.3) becomes

$$Y_i(p_i) \begin{cases} = y_i(p_i) & \text{if } p_i < (1+t_i^e)p_i^*, \\ \in [y_i((1+t_i^e)p_i^*, \infty) & \text{if } p_i = (1+t_i^e)p_i^*. \end{cases} \tag{5.4}$$

The allocation is set out in Fig. 5.2, in which the associated tariff revenue is depicted by the shaded rectangle, whose area, by construction, is the same as the quota rent in Fig. 5.1.

Comparing the two configurations, it is seen that for any given vector of world prices and tariffs, domestic production becomes independent of domestic demand upon the abolition of quotas in favour of tariffs— provided there are no barriers to exports. Changes in world prices, at given tariffs, will affect both domestic production and consumption, whereas under a system of quotas, such changes affect only the size of the quota rents, so long as the quotas remain binding. To the extent that the domestic

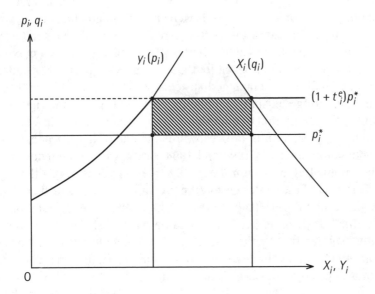

Figure 5.2. Output, demand, and tariff revenue

allocation of resources should respond to changes in relative scarcities in world markets, this also speaks for tariffs.

Zero-quotas are far from rare; in some protectionist regimes, indeed, they became almost the rule once domestic capacity had been built up to a level deemed to be adequate to meet domestic consumption at some notion of a 'reasonable' price. In such cases, the quota rent is also zero, and the equivalent tariff calculated in accordance with Eqn (5.1) is prohibitive.[2] If there is a premium on public income, the right course of action is to choose a tariff sufficiently modest that the good will be imported. The losers will be the owners of the fixed factors employed in the industries in question (who may be politically well organized), whereas consumers as well as the Treasury will gain. Such a shift in emphasis would also introduce the issue of wider cuts in tariff rates to include the equivalent rates on goods for which quotas were strictly positive before the reform.

An attempt at reform in this direction was made in India following the crisis that occurred in 1990 and 1991. Up to that time, India had arguably operated the most extensive system of regulation and licensing of foreign trade anywhere outside of the erstwhile socialist bloc. By the mid-1990s, the universal requirement of a licence to import had been replaced by a specific, albeit long list, which included not only items such as cereals, oil, and fertilizers, which are 'canalized' by state monopsonies, but also most consumer goods, on which total bans were maintained (Joshi and Little, 1996: 66). Quotas on all other goods were abolished, and tariff rates, which had been steeply raised in the 1980s, were also reduced. The simple average nominal rate stood at 125 per cent in 1990 and 1991, with a maximum of almost three times that level. In 1995, the maximum rate had fallen to 50 per cent, with the average perhaps close to 40 per cent (ibid.: 70).

In neighbouring Pakistan, a similar process had begun somewhat earlier, starting with a relaxation of quantitative restrictions in the mid-1980s and followed by a reduction in tariffs towards the end of that decade. Under a new policy announced in 1993 and 1994, tariffs were to be reduced from the then prevailing maximum rate of 92 to 35 per cent over a three-year period. The maximum rate fell to 70 per cent in 1994–5 and then further to 45 per cent in 1997 (Lahiri et al., 2000: 395). The expectation that the original target of 35 per cent would be reached shortly thereafter has actually been realized by the time of writing. It should be noted, however, that differences in tariff rates, even on the same good, have remained, with certain groups enjoying special rates (ibid.: 414).

---

[2] This is an egregious case of being on the wrong side of the so-called Laffer curve.

We close this section with a brief remark on another consequence of high tariffs and tight quotas, namely, the incentive to smuggle. Smuggling is a potentially important response to the existence of quota rents, whether they accrue to licence-holders or the government as customs revenue, and dealing with it is a burden on the government's administrative capacities. That lowering rates and simplifying the rules can both increase revenues and release officials from the task of chasing smugglers is beautifully illustrated by Jarvis's (1987) entertaining social history of smuggling in East Anglia in the eighteenth and first half of the nineteenth centuries. By 1760, the British government had established a list of some 800 dutiable luxury items, and added another 1300 over the next 50 years. Duties were very high, with matching criminal penalties for smugglers, including the noose. Yet smuggling was big business, depriving the Exchequer of 15–20 per cent of the statutory customs revenues according to some estimates. The Younger Pitt launched his reforms in 1784, under which duties were drastically reduced—that on tea, for example, from 127 to 12.5 per cent—without the Exchequer suffering any loss of revenue thereby. One is driven to the thought that policy makers might be more receptive to such reforms after reading a vivid account of social history than yet another memorandum from the World Bank, let alone a volume such as this.

5.2. Tariffs and Excises into a VAT

The next step along the path of reform is to broaden the tax base, from trade to domestic income or consumption, and to bring some order to the rather chaotic pattern of effective taxes that arises when producer goods are subject to excise taxes, as illustrated by the case of Pakistan in Section 4.6. The right instrument for this purpose, according to many scholars and the World Bank, is the VAT. A uniform tax on all output, with full credit for tax payments on non-factor inputs, is a flat tax on aggregate value added. If outlays on investment goods are also fully deductible, as is the case in the European Union, then the VAT is a flat tax on aggregate final consumption (excluding the value of leisure, of course). These tax-equivalences, with their 'neutral' overtones, are fundamental properties of the VAT, and its advocates make considerable play of them.

Implementing full coverage in practice is another matter, even in Europe. Reflecting on the practical experience with the VAT, Harberger (1993), a notable protagonist of the virtues of uniformity in all matters of taxation and protection, makes it clear that there are grave difficulties confronting any attempt to draw certain sectors into the system, particularly financial and certain other services such as health and owner-occupied housing; so that it is rare that more than half of GDP is actually covered (ibid.: 152). Sectors 'outside' the system pay no tax on what they produce, but usually cannot claim credits for the taxes on the inputs that they buy from sectors 'inside' the system. One of Harberger's main concerns appears to be the effects of incomplete coverage on total revenue. Here, it suffices to say that since the value of a firm's output almost invariably exceeds the value of its non-factor inputs, incomplete coverage will imply that, *ceteris paribus*, in order to raise a certain amount of revenue, the required tax rate must be that much higher than in the case of full coverage, with a heavier dead-weight loss as a very probable attendant effect. In what follows, however, we shall focus on the extent to which incomplete coverage endangers neutrality.

To this end, we return to the model used to compute effective taxes in Section 4.6. Consider, to start with, a comprehensive VAT, in which the outputs of all sectors are taxed at the uniform rate t and firms may subtract the taxes paid on the inputs they use when calculating their net liabilities at the output stage. Recalling the assumptions that there are constant returns to scale (CRS) and perfect competition everywhere, the price of good j is given by,

$$p_j = (1+t) \sum_{i=1}^{n}(p_i a_{ij} + v_j) - t \sum_{i=1}^{n} p_i a_{ij} \quad \forall j, \tag{5.5}$$

a rearrangement of which yields the vector of producer prices:

$$p = (1+t)v(I-A)^{-1}. \tag{5.6}$$

Thus, the price of each and every good is simply t per cent higher than the total (direct and indirect) value of its factor content. It is exactly this 'neutral' character of a VAT that so strongly commends it to many scholars.

So much for the VAT in principle. As noted above, the system's coverage is never fully comprehensive in practice, and in less developed countries (LDCs) very large parts of the economy will lie outside the tax net. In order to accommodate this fact, we partition the set of all sectors into those that are within and those that are outside the statutory tax net, which are denoted by S_1 and S_2, respectively. Equation (5.5) is replaced by

$$p_j = (1+t) \sum_{i=1}^{n}(p_i a_{ij} + v_j) - t \sum_{i \in S_1} p_i a_{ij}, \quad j \in S_1, \tag{5.7}$$

and

$$p_j = \sum_{i=1}^{n}(p_i a_{ij} + v_j) + t \sum_{i \in S_1} p_i a_{ij}, \quad j \in S_2. \tag{5.8}$$

Without loss of generality, we may renumber the sectors so that those within the tax system are numbered 1 to k, and those outside it from $k+1$ to n. Observe that the matrix A may then be partitioned into the form

$$A = \begin{bmatrix} A_{11} & A_{12} \\ A_{21} & A_{22} \end{bmatrix}$$

corresponding to S_1 and S_2, and the vectors p and v likewise. Equations (5.7) and (5.8) can therefore be compactly written as

$$(p_1, p_2) \begin{bmatrix} I - A_{11} & -(I + \hat{t})A_{12} \\ -(I + \hat{t})A_{21} & I - A_{22} \end{bmatrix} = ((1 + t)v_1, v_2), \tag{5.9}$$

where $(I + \hat{t})$ is a diagonal matrix of appropriate dimension, each of whose diagonal elements is $(1 + t)$. Solving for p, we have

$$(p_1, p_2) = ((1 + t)v_1, v_2)(I - A(t))^{-1}, \tag{5.10}$$

where

$$A(t) \equiv \begin{bmatrix} A_{11} & (I + \hat{t})A_{12} \\ (I + \hat{t})A_{21} & A_{22} \end{bmatrix}. \tag{5.11}$$

In order to compare the price vectors under comprehensive and incomplete coverage, we begin with the simplest possible example, namely, just two sectors. Let the tax be fully shifted forwards. Then Eqns (5.7) and (5.8) specialize to

$$p_1 = a_{11}p_1 + (1 + t)a_{21}p_2 + (1 + t)v_1$$

and

$$p_2 = (1 + t)a_{12}p_1 + a_{22}p_2 + v_2,$$

respectively. Solving for p, we have

$$p_1 = (1 + t)[(1 - a_{22})v_1 + a_{21}v_2]/|A(t)|$$

and

$$p_2 = [(1+t)^2 a_{12} v_1 + (1 - a_{11}) v_2] / |A(t)|,$$

where the determinant of the system is

$$|A(t)| = [(1 - a_{11})(1 - a_{22}) - (1+t)^2 a_{12} a_{21}].$$

The distortionary effects of changes in t are most easily seen by examining the relative price:

$$p_1/p_2 = (1+t)[(1 - a_{22}) v_1 + a_{21} v_2] / [(1+t)^2 a_{12} v_1 + (1 - a_{11}) v_2],$$

which is decidedly non-linear in t. In the absence of the tax, there is 'neutrality' by definition. It is readily seen that imposing a small tax rate does not necessarily increase the relative price of good 1, and that if t is sufficiently large and $a_{12} > 0$, a rise in t will always result in good 1 becoming relatively cheaper. It is left to the reader to explore this matter more fully (see exercise 5.2).

Having established the underlying intuition, we derive an expression for the vector (p_1, p_2) in the general case, where we make use of the fact that

$$(I - A)^{-1}$$

$$= \begin{bmatrix} D^{-1} & D^{-1} A_{12} (I - A_{22})^{-1} \\ (I - A_{22})^{-1} A_{21} D^{-1} & (I - A_{22})^{-1} (I + A_{21} D^{-1} A_{12} (I - A_{22})^{-1}) \end{bmatrix},$$

$$(5.12)$$

where $D = (I - A_{11}) - A_{12} (I - A_{22})^{-1} A_{21}$ (see, e.g. Intriligator, 1971: 488). Analogously, we also have

$$(I - A(t))^{-1}$$

$$= \begin{bmatrix} D(t)^{-1} & D(t)^{-1} (I + \hat{t}) A_{12} (I - A_{22})^{-1} \\ (I - A_{22})^{-1} (I + \hat{t}) A_{21} D(t)^{-1} & (I - A_{22})^{-1} (I + (I + \hat{t}) A_{21} D(t)^{-1} (I + \hat{t}) A_{12} (I - A_{22})^{-1}) \end{bmatrix},$$

$$(5.13)$$

where $D(t) = (I - A_{11}) - (I + \hat{t}) A_{12} (I - A_{22})^{-1} (I + \hat{t}) A_{21}$. Observe that the matrix $(I + \hat{t})$ scales up each and every element of any other matrix with which it is multiplied by the amount $(1 + t)$, so that the submatrices in question are strongly non-linear in t. Maintaining the assumption that all taxes are fully shifted forwards, which implies that v is independent of the tax structure and rates, a cursory comparison of Eqns (5.6) and (5.10) in the light of Eqns (5.12) and (5.13) reveals that even if the departures from comprehensive coverage are quite small, there are no a priori grounds for supposing that the associated departures from neutrality, as defined by

Eqn (5.6), are also small. Much depends on the density of inter-industry transactions across the statutory tax boundary defined by the partition of the production sectors into the subsets S_1 and S_2. Consider, for example, the extreme case in which there are no such transactions, that is, $A_{12} = 0$ and $A_{21} = 0$. The economy then happens to be productively decomposable with respect to the division of its sectors for statutory tax purposes, and it is immediately seen that

$$(I - A)^{-1} = (I - A(t))^{-1} = \begin{bmatrix} (I - A_{11})^{-1} & 0 \\ 0 & (I - A_{22})^{-1} \end{bmatrix}.$$

In this case, therefore, the price vector under incomplete coverage is

$$(p_1, p_2) = ((1 + t)v_1(I - A_{11})^{-1}, v_2(I - A_{22})^{-1}),$$

as elementary reasoning demands. If the elements of A_{12} and A_{22} are sufficiently large, however, then it is clear that the uniform statutory rate on sectors within the system will cascade throughout the system as a whole in a manner whose effects will be both non-uniform and non-negligible.

The activities lying outside the tax net in LDCs will include not only non-plantation agriculture, financial services, retail services, and professional services, but also small-scale enterprises in the rest of the secondary and tertiary sectors of the economy. Agriculture supplies the main raw materials for the food processing and textile industries, and the fact that the small-scale sector is outside the net also contributes to the density of transactions in A_{12} and A_{21}. It seems probable, therefore, that the departures from neutrality under a VAT, as it can actually be implemented in LDCs, will be substantial. Indeed, the vector of effective tax rates may exhibit a pattern not so very unlike the higgledy–piggledy structure in Pakistan that was discussed in Section 4.6. That being so, not too much should be expected of a VAT as a tax reform in the early phases. Rather, one should think of its introduction as an initial investment, whose pay-off will be realized as the system's coverage is progressively increased with the accumulation of experience and the growth of administrative capacity.

5.3. Reforming Commodity Taxes

We now take up the question of how existing tax rates should be changed, with special reference to commodity taxes. Our point of departure is a brief restatement of the model of optimum commodity taxation set out in

Section 4.4. We assume that producer prices, p, are fixed, that all individuals face the same parametric consumer prices, q, and that indirect tax rates can be varied without limit. Hence, given that transactions among producers go untaxed, the government can bring about any q by choosing a vector of taxes t such that

$$q = p + t. \tag{5.14}$$

The government is assumed to have formulated a social welfare function of the Bergson–Samuelsonian type, which may be written as follows:

$$V(q; \bar{M}) = W[v^1(q, w^1, \bar{M}^1), \ldots, v^H(q, w^H, \bar{M}^H)]. \tag{5.15}$$

The vector of individuals' aggregate commodity demands is denoted by

$$X(q; w, \bar{M}) = \sum_h x^h(q; w^h, \bar{M}^h). \tag{5.16}$$

It is further assumed that the government needs to raise a certain amount of revenue, R_0 say, and that indirect taxes are the only means of doing so. Hence, the government's problem is to choose a vector of taxes t so as to

$$\text{maximize } V(q; w, \bar{M}) \quad \text{subject to } R(q) = tX(q) \geq R_0, \tag{5.17}$$

where q and t are related by Eqn (5.14). The associated Lagrangian is written as

$$\Phi = V(q; \cdot) + \lambda[tX(q) - R_0], \tag{5.18}$$

whose first-order conditions are

$$\frac{\partial V}{\partial q_i} + \lambda \left[X_i + \sum_j t_j \frac{\partial X_j}{\partial q_i} \right] = 0 \quad \forall i. \tag{5.19}$$

Observe that Eqn (5.19) holds as an equality for all goods by virtue of the assumption that t is unrestricted.

Although this statement of the problem is a useful benchmark, it is not directly relevant for present purposes. Rather, we start from existing taxes and ask whether social welfare could be improved by changing them, while still satisfying the requirement that the revenue raised be at least R_0. In what follows, the analysis is restricted to 'marginal' reforms, the argument being based on derivatives, and hence on an implicit linearization of the system about an existing equilibrium.

Since producer prices are assumed to be fixed, differentiating w.r.t. t is equivalent to differentiating w.r.t. q. Suppose, therefore, that the tax on the ith good is increased slightly, so that there is a perturbation $(0, \ldots, dt_i, \ldots, 0)$ to the tax vector t. Recalling Roy's identity, this induces a change in $V(q)$ of

$$dV = -\sum_h \frac{\partial V}{\partial v^h} \alpha^h x_i^h \cdot dt_i = -\sum_h \beta^h x_i^h \, dt_i, \qquad (5.20)$$

where $\alpha^h \equiv \partial v^h / \partial \bar{M}^h$ and $\beta^h \equiv \alpha^h (\partial V / \partial v^h)$, the latter being the social value of an additional unit of (lump-sum) income accruing to individual h. The accompanying change in $R(q)$ is

$$dR = \left[X_i(q) + \sum_j t_j \partial X_j(q) / \partial q_i \right] dt_i. \qquad (5.21)$$

Suppose now that the government decides to raise one unit of revenue by raising the tax on the ith good. Setting $dR = 1$ in Eqn (5.21), the required increase in t_i is

$$dt_i = \frac{1}{(\partial R / \partial t_i)} = 1 \left/ \left[X_i(q) + \sum_j t_j \frac{\partial X_j(q)}{\partial q_i} \right] \right. . \qquad (5.22)$$

From Eqns (5.20) and (5.22), the marginal 'damage' inflicted on the private sector by raising an additional unit of public funds in this particular way is, therefore,

$$\lambda_i \equiv -\frac{\partial V / \partial t_i}{\partial R / \partial t_i} = \frac{\sum_h \beta^h x_i^h}{\left[X_i(q) + \sum_j t_j \partial X_j(q) / \partial q_i \right]}. \qquad (5.23)$$

More precisely, λ_i is the reduction in social welfare that would result from raising an additional unit of revenue by taxing commodity i more heavily.

At the full optimum, of course, all the λ_i must be equal. For suppose, on the contrary, that $\lambda_i > \lambda_k$ for some i and k ($i \neq k$). Then social welfare can be increased by reducing the tax rate on good i and increasing that on good k by a pair of (small) amounts that keep total revenue constant, in accordance with Eqn (5.22).

Although a comparison of the λ_i corresponding to any particular situation immediately tells us whether a feasible and desirable reform exists, the condition $\lambda_i \neq \lambda_k$ also implies the existence of a continuum of such reforms. For in the space of taxes, there will be a cone with its apex at the existing tax vector, within a small neighbourhood of which welfare is (locally) greater and the revenue constraint continues to be satisfied. In order to prove this claim, observe that the set of such tax reforms is defined by the conditions

$$dV = \nabla V \cdot \mathbf{dt} \geq 0 \tag{5.24}$$

and

$$dR = \nabla R \cdot \mathbf{dt} \geq 0, \tag{5.25}$$

respectively, where ∇V and ∇R are the respective gradient vectors[3] of $V(\cdot)$ and $R(\cdot)$ with respect to t, and $\mathbf{dt}$ is the vector of changes in taxes. In the case of marginal reforms, the vectors ∇V and ∇R may be treated as constants. The intersection of the two half-spaces thus defined itself defines a cone of directions of reform which are both feasible and desirable. Only if $\nabla V = \xi \cdot \nabla R$, where ξ is some constant, will no such direction exist; for such an equality implies, in turn, that the said cone will have collapsed into a single line: all the λ_i will then be the same, and the existing allocation will be an extremum.

The hyperplanes $\nabla V \cdot \mathbf{dt} = 0$ and $\nabla R \cdot \mathbf{dt} = 0$ define the set of all marginal reforms yielding constant welfare and constant revenue, respectively. In the case of just two taxable goods, each of these sets is a straight line, the intersection of which is the point depicting the initial tax vector, t_0. In Fig. 5.3, the lines are drawn as AA' and BB', respectively, and t_0 is denoted by the point 0', which is the origin of (dt_1, dt_2)-space. The shaded area AO'B contains the set of all feasible and desirable directions of reform, starting from 0'.

Full calculations have been carried out for India by Ahmad and Stern (1984) and for Pakistan by Ahmad et al. (1984). Households' demands for commodities were taken from household expenditure data and the existing taxes were estimated in the course of a detailed study of the tax system. In order to obtain the aggregate demand derivatives, $\partial X_j(q)/\partial q_i$, the authors drew upon econometric estimates of extended linear expenditure systems. The remaining elements of Eqn (5.23) are the weights β, which were derived from an additively separable, isoelastic form of $V(\cdot)$, with the normalization that β^1, the weight of the poorest class of household, be equal to

---

[3] $\nabla f(x) = (\partial f/\partial x_1, \ldots, \partial f/\partial x_n).$

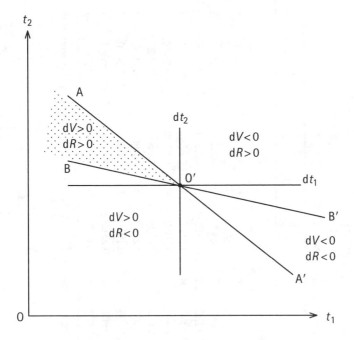

Figure 5.3. AO′B is the region of feasible and desirable reforms

unity. Hence, recalling the assumption that all households face the same consumer price vector q, we obtain

$$\beta^h = (m^1/m^h)^\varepsilon, \tag{5.26}$$

where the income m^h is defined in Section 4.3.2 and ε is a parameter whose value represents the social aversion to inequality.[4]

The results are set out in Tables 5.1 and 5.2, for India and Pakistan, respectively. Certain similarities are discernible. If neither government cared about inequality ($\varepsilon = 0$), or if both were of the view that the existing distribution of income is optimal, then both should impose heavier taxes on cereals, milk, meat, and eggs, while lightening the burden on clothing and other non-food items. With moderate aversion to inequality ($\varepsilon = 1$), the picture changes somewhat. The government of India should shift taxes from food (except milk) to non-food items (except fuel and light). The exceptions to such a shift are, in any event, almost unavoidable administratively, since it is very difficult to tax the home consumption of milk and

---

[4] See exercise 4.1.

Table 5.1. The marginal welfare losses of indirect taxes: India

Commodities	Effective taxes t^0	ε									
		0		0.1		1		2		5	
		λ	r	λ	r	λ	r	λ	r	λ	r
1. Cereals	−0.052	1.0340	8	0.8845	7	0.2377	2	0.0665	2	0.0047	2
2. Milk and milk products	0.009	1.0037	9	0.8320	9	0.1703	9	0.0353	9	0.0008	9
3. Edible oils	0.083	1.0672	6	0.9002	6	0.2163	4	0.0542	4	0.0027	5
4. Meat, fish, eggs	0.014	1.0532	7	0.8844	8	0.2058	6	0.0508	5	0.0028	4
5. Sugar and gur	0.069	1.0892	5	0.9156	5	0.2124	5	0.0508	5	0.0021	6
6. Other foods	0.114	1.1352	4	0.9561	3	0.2293	3	0.0588	3	0.0037	3
7. Clothing	0.242	1.2450	1	1.0204	1	0.1920	7	0.0378	7	0.0010	8
8. Fuel and light	0.247	1.1632	2	0.9887	2	0.2562	1	0.0708	1	0.0054	1
9. Other non-food	0.133	1.1450	3	0.9328	4	0.1729	8	0.0356	8	0.0014	7

Notes: ε is the inequality-aversion parameter, λ_i is the welfare loss generated by an increase in the tax on the ith good sufficient to raise one rupee in government revenue, r is the ranking of the λ_i for given ε. Twenty-eight household groups.

Source: Ahmad et al. (1984).

Table 5.2. The marginal welfare losses of indirect taxes: Pakistan

Commodities	ε									
	0		0.5		1.0		2.0		5.0	
	λ	r	λ	r	λ	r	λ	r	λ	r
1. Wheat	1.0423	14	0.7260	7	0.5235	2	0.2988	1	0.0964	1
2. Rice	1.0543	10	0.6975	12	0.4783	8	0.2484	8	0.0647	8
3. Other Cereals	1.0538	12	0.7219	9	0.5120	5	0.2848	3	0.0922	2
4. Pulses	1.0500	13	0.7221	8	0.5150	4	0.2889	2	0.0906	3
5. Meat and eggs	1.0092	17	0.6190	17	0.3964	16	0.1837	15	0.0392	14
6. Milk	1.0358	15	0.6742	14	0.4539	13	0.2263	10	0.0520	12
7. Veg., fruit, and spices	1.0196	16	0.6524	15	0.4360	14	0.2195	13	0.0568	10
8. Edible Oils	1.1089	5	0.7302	5	0.5000	7	0.2608	7	0.0704	7
9. Sugar	1.1859	4	0.7861	1	0.5402	1	0.2815	5	0.0735	6
10. Gur	1.0542	11	0.7270	6	0.5158	3	0.2825	4	0.0815	4
11. Confectionery	1.2035	2	0.7320	3	0.4622	11	0.2052	14	0.0370	15
12. Tea	1.0895	7	0.7306	4	0.5102	6	0.2768	6	0.0810	5
13. Other beverages	1.2875	1	0.7106	10	0.4086	15	0.1535	17	0.0211	17
14. Household items/fuel	1.0775	9	0.6853	13	0.4544	12	0.2240	12	0.0533	11
15. Clothing	1.0876	8	0.6990	11	0.4667	10	0.2320	9	0.0578	9
16. Rec. and Transportation	1.1004	6	0.6450	16	0.3958	17	0.1704	16	0.0324	16
17. Other non-food	1.1965	3	0.7407	2	0.4782	9	0.2245	11	0.0495	13

Notes: ε is the inequality-aversion parameter, λ_i is the welfare loss generated by an increase in the tax on the ith good sufficient to raise one rupee in government revenue, r is the ranking of the λ_i for given ε. Thirty-four household groups.

Source: Ahmad et al. (1984).

firewood when these are produced and consumed in rural areas. (Ahmad and Stern comment on this weakness in their scheme of aggregation.) The government of Pakistan, however, should still tax milk, meat, eggs, vegetables, and fruits more heavily than at present, while levying lower taxes on cereals, tea, and sugar. Other beverages, clothing, and non-food items should also be subject to heavier taxes. It is noteworthy that the general rankings in the case where the aversion to inequality is very high ($\varepsilon = 5$), which approximates the Rawlsian prescription of the maxi–min criterion for social welfare, differ little from those in the case where $\varepsilon = 1$. The ratios of the highest to the lowest groups of λ's are, however, much larger, indicating much larger social payoffs to (marginal) reforms when ε is large.

5.4. The Inverse Optimum Problem

Ahmad and Stern (1984) also address an important issue by posing the question in reverse: given the existing set of taxes, what must be the set of welfare weights β for those taxes to realize a social optimum? This question could be interpreted as follows: if the government is 'rational' and fully informed, so that the observed tax vector is 'optimal', what must be the vector of social welfare weights?

The first step is to rewrite the first-order conditions associated with problem (5.17) as

$$\sum_{h=1}^{H} \beta^h x_i^h = \lambda r_i \quad \forall i, \tag{5.27}$$

where $r_i \equiv \partial R / \partial t_i$. By a suitable rescaling of $V(\cdot)$, we may also normalize λ to unity, so that Eqn (5.27) may be written in matrix form as

$$\beta C = r, \tag{5.28}$$

where $C = (x_i^h)$ is the consumption matrix, the ith column of which is x_i. If there are exactly as many goods as groups of households, a condition that can always be brought about by appropriate aggregation, then the vector β may be 'recovered' from the data C and r by matrix inversion:

$$\beta = r C^{-1}. \tag{5.29}$$

The resulting vector of social weights for Indian households grouped by total per capita household expenditure is laid out in Table 5.3. It is hard

Table 5.3. Implicit weights by expenditure class: India

Per capita expenditure (Rs. per month)	0–25	25–32	32–40	40–45	45–55	55–70	70–90	90–150	150+
β		−126.4	171.4	53.9	−438.4	241.0	35.5	−80.7	18.9	−4.3

Source: Ahmad and Stern (1984).

to construe these estimates as reflecting anything but a perverse political economy, or at best a grave incompetence in formulating economic policy.

The vector $\boldsymbol{\beta}$ laid out in Table 5.3 is surely no mere artefact of the aggregation needed to 'recover' it. If there is no resort to aggregation, however, in which case the number of goods will almost certainly differ from the number of households, one can still ask whether Eqn (5.28) possesses non-negative solutions in $\boldsymbol{\beta}$, which seems a modest requirement to impose on the problem. The answer to this question turns out to be intimately linked to the existence of a Pareto-improving tax reform. The condition that household h be no worse off in the face of the reform $\boldsymbol{dt}$ is, using Roy's identity,

$$\sum_{i=1}^{n} \frac{\partial v^h}{\partial q_i} \cdot dq_i = -\alpha^h(\boldsymbol{x}^h \cdot \boldsymbol{dt}) \geq 0.$$

By virtue of Eqn (5.14) and the fact that $\alpha^h > 0$, this condition simply states that the cost of the bundle chosen before the reform, $\boldsymbol{x}^h$, be no higher at the post-reform prices $\boldsymbol{q} + \boldsymbol{dt}$, so that at least one price must be strictly lower. Since this condition must hold for all households, it may be compactly written as $\boldsymbol{Cdt} \leq 0$. The snag here is that reducing any consumer price will usually lead to lower net revenues, and a reform is deemed to be feasible only if net revenues do not fall. Hence, there exists a Pareto-improving reform that at the very least preserves current revenue if and only if the system of linear inequalities

$$\boldsymbol{C} \cdot \boldsymbol{dt} \leq 0 \quad \text{and} \quad \boldsymbol{r} \cdot \boldsymbol{dt} \geq 0 \tag{5.30}$$

possesses a solution.

The Minkowski–Farkas lemma yields an answer to both questions. It tells us that there are two mutually exclusive possibilities: either Eqn (5.28) possesses a non-negative solution in the welfare weights $\boldsymbol{\beta}$; or Eqn (5.30) holds, that is, there exists a Pareto-improving reform that does not involve a reduction in government revenue. Whenever the latter holds, as in Table 5.3, there is a chance of overcoming the real political difficulties of 'selling' a reform without mortgaging the future.

5.5. Intermediate Inputs

Taxes on intermediate goods, whether in the form of excises on domestic production or tariffs on imports, are an important source of both revenue and distortions, so they are natural targets for reformers. As already noted in Section 5.2, many have set their sights on the long-term goal of replacing both excises and tariffs with a 'comprehensive' VAT, and advocate introducing one of limited coverage as a stepping stone. Even the latter will involve a major administrative challenge, however, so it is also natural to ask what can be undertaken quickly through a piecemeal reform of the existing system. To see what is involved, we draw once more on an example from Pakistan (Lahiri *et al.*, 2000), with the additional twist that there is extensive smuggling of certain final goods.

Consider a small open economy that produces five tradables and a single public good. Goods 1–3 enter into final consumption only. Good 1 is not taxable and is the sole export. Hence,

$$p_1 = q_1 = p_1^*. \tag{5.31}$$

Good 2 is legally importable, but the tariff is so high and the borders are so porous that the smuggled item is cheaper and legal imports are zero. What can be thought of as the 'landed price' of the smuggled item is p_2^*. All items of good 2 are, in principle, subject to a general sales tax at the rate t, but smuggled items are assumed to escape the tax net entirely, so that

$$q_2 = p_2^*. \tag{5.32}$$

For domestic producers, however, there is no such escape, and since consumers can buy at the price p_2^*, the producer price is

$$p_2 = p_2^*/(1 + t). \tag{5.33}$$

Good 3, in contrast, is assumed to be proof against smuggling, so that

$$p_3 = (1 + t_3)p_3^*, \tag{5.34}$$

where t_3 is the *ad valorem* tariff rate, and the consumer price is

$$q_3 = (1 + t)(1 + t_3)p_3^*. \tag{5.35}$$

The list is completed by two intermediate goods, 4 and 5, both of which are subject to tariffs, but not to smuggling:

$$p_i = (1 + t_i)p_i^*, \quad i = 4, 5. \tag{5.36}$$

To place all this in its context, the main roles are played by good 2, which should be thought of as bicycles, and by good 4, which is the sheet steel for making them, among other things.

We now turn to public finance. The public good is produced in the public sector under CRS by means of good 1 alone, whereby one unit of the latter is needed to produce one unit of output. Hence, the cost of producing G units is simply $p_1^* G$. Since neither lump-sum transfers nor taxes on factors are available, such expenditures must be wholly financed by means of the sales tax and tariffs. Recalling that the derivative of the GNP function, $\Omega(p)$, w.r.t. the producer price of good i is the domestic supply of good i net of intermediate uses of that good, and that the derivative of the expenditure function, $e(q)$, w.r.t. the corresponding consumer price is the consumption thereof (see Sections A.5 and A.7), the requirement that the budget be balanced may be written as

$$p_1^* G = \frac{tp_2^*}{1+t} \cdot \frac{\partial \Omega}{\partial p_2} + t(1 + t_3)p_3^* \frac{\partial e}{\partial q_3} + t_3 p_3^* \left(\frac{\partial e}{\partial q_3} - \frac{\partial \Omega}{\partial p_3} \right)$$
$$- t_4 p_4^* \frac{\partial \Omega}{\partial p_4} - t_5 p_5^* \frac{\partial \Omega}{\partial p_5}. \tag{5.37}$$

The representative household has preferences over goods 1–3 and the public good. For any given level of provision G of the latter, let the household choose the consumption bundle $x^0(q, M, G)$ when faced with consumer prices q and endowed with income M. In the absence of lump-sum transfers and taxes on factors, aggregate private income will be equal to the value of GNP at producer prices. In the absence of local satiation, all income will be spent, so that at the household's optimum, we have

$$qx^0(q, M, G) \equiv e(q, G, u^0) = \Omega(p), \tag{5.38}$$

where u^0 denotes the value of the utility index at the optimum in question. The negative of the derivative of $e(\cdot)$ w.r.t. G is the marginal willingness to pay for the public good; for an increase in G permits a reduction in the expenditures on private goods needed to reach a given level of utility.

Given the household's preferences, the GNP function, and the restrictions on taxes set out above, the optimum second-best problem involves choosing a tax vector (t, t) and the provision G so as to maximize the indirect utility function $v(q, G, \Omega(p))$, subject to a balanced budget, Eqn (5.37), and the household's budget constraint in the form of Eqn (5.38). The piecemeal reform considered here, however, involves changes only in the tariff on good 4, all other taxes being viewed as fixed. That being so, we seek the effects of a change in t_4 on u^0, subject to Eqns (5.37) and (5.38). Observe that such a reform will have no effects on consumer prices, though it will affect Ω and the level of G. To simplify matters, Lahiri *et al.* (2000) assume that goods 2 and 3 and the public good are independent in consumption, or equivalently, that the marginal willingness to pay for the public good is independent of the prices of goods 2 and 3:

$$\frac{\partial^2 e}{\partial q_2 \partial G} = \frac{\partial^2 e}{\partial q_3 \partial G} = 0.$$

Differentiating Eqns (5.37) and (5.38) totally and rearranging, we then obtain, at length,

$$\left[\frac{\partial e}{\partial u^0} - \frac{1}{\theta}(t_3 + t(1 + t_3))p_3^* \frac{\partial^2 e}{\partial u^0 \partial q_3} \right] \frac{du^0}{dt_4}$$

$$= \frac{p_4^*}{\theta} \left(\frac{tp_2^*}{1+t} \frac{\partial^2 \Omega}{\partial p_4 \partial p_2} - \sum_{i=3}^{5} t_i p_i^* \frac{\partial^2 \Omega}{\partial p_4 \partial p_i} - (1 - \theta) \frac{\partial \Omega}{\partial p_4} \right), \qquad (5.39)$$

where the pure number

$$\frac{1}{\theta} - 1 \equiv - \left(\frac{1}{p_1^*} \frac{\partial e}{\partial G} + 1 \right) \qquad (5.40)$$

is to be interpreted as the proportional premium on public relative to private income, a quantity that will appear ubiquitously from Chapter 8 onwards. The intuition here runs as follows. Since the marginal cost of production of the public good is p_1^*, this must be the marginal willingness to pay for the same at the first-best optimum, in which lump-sum taxes are available. In this case, therefore, θ is equal to unity and the premium on public income is zero. In the absence of lump-sum taxes, however, the deadweight losses that arise from the use of distortionary taxes will yield a positive premium on public income. Citing a variety of sources, Lahiri *et al.*

(2000: 400) argue that a 25 per cent premium is to be regarded as 'normal' and values over 50 per cent as 'uncommonly high'. For Pakistan itself, Ahmad and Stern's (1991) estimates range from 15 to 101 per cent.

With this preliminary settled, we examine the various terms in Eqn (5.39). Beginning with those in brackets on the left-hand side (LHS), the derivative $\partial e/\partial u^0$ is the expenditure at prices q required to raise utility by an additional unit. Recalling that $\partial e/\partial q_3$ is the aggregate consumption of good 3, it is seen that $p_3^*(\partial^2 e/\partial u^0 \partial q_3)$ is the marginal expenditure on good 3, valued at the world price thereof, needed to raise utility by one more unit. The resulting increase in revenue from sales and tariffs on each unit thereof is $[t_3 + t(1 + t_3)]p_3^*$, which must be appropriately weighted in terms of private income, namely, by $1/\theta$. The terms in question have a negative sign by virtue of the fact that the revenue so raised will be used to increase the provision of the public good, and hence also the level of utility. In order to establish whether the entire expression in brackets is positive, observe from Eqn (5.35) that $q_3 = p_3^* + [t_3 + t(1 + t_3)]p_3^*$. Hence, if goods 1 and 2 are both normal and the premium on public income is sufficiently small, the said expression will indeed be positive.

We turn to the terms on the right-hand side (RHS) of Eqn (5.39). Recalling that $\partial \Omega/\partial p_i$ is the net domestic supply of good i, the corresponding second derivatives of Ω w.r.t. p_4 all have to do with the effects of an increase in p_4 (effected through an increase in t_4) on the revenues arising from the taxation of domestic production. The first term in brackets is negative; for an increase in the cost of sheet steel will reduce the domestic output of bicycles, and hence the receipts of sales taxes thereon. Where the production of goods 3 and 5 is concerned, such an increase in cost will also reduce production, so that imports will rise, and with them, tariff revenues: the terms are positive. As for sheet metal itself, an increase in its own price will lead to an increase in the level of its net domestic supply, with a corresponding fall in tariff receipts. The last term stems from the fact that since the increase in p_4 arises through an increase in the tariff rate t_4, it will also transfer income from the private to the public sector, the good being a net import. The transfer is desirable if, as is normally the case, $\theta < 1$. To sum up thus far, starting from some arbitrary policy (t, t), utility may be rising or falling in the tariff on good 4.

The final step, therefore, is to obtain empirical estimates of all of the derivatives on the RHS of Eqn (5.39). For this purpose, Lahiri et al. (2000) work with an isoelastic form of the demand for imports of good 4, choosing various specifications to deal with the possibility of unit roots and endogeneity. In doing so, they obtain the required cross-effects from the fact that $\partial \Omega^2/\partial p_i p_j = \partial^2 \Omega/\partial p_j p_i$ when the GNP function is twice-differentiable. The own price elasticity of demand for sheet steel turns out to pretty robust, at about -1.8, which implies that a reduction in the tariff rate from its 1997 of level of 45 per cent would yield an increase in revenue from this source. None of the cross-price elasticities is significant at conventional levels. Given the other prevailing tax rates, $t_3 = 0.3$, $t_5 = 0.4$, and $t = 0.25$, and the 'normal' value of $\theta = 0.8$, the optimal tariff turns out to be a subsidy of about 12 per cent. The intuition here is that by displacing domestic production, the smuggling of bicycles reduces the government's receipts from sales taxes. Since a cut in the cost of sheet steel will make domestically produced bicycles more competitive, it will therefore increase tax revenues through this back channel, and this effect turns out to be so strong that it is worth forgoing tariffs on the intermediate good altogether.

5.6. Summary

Tax reforms can be either sweeping affairs, in which the very basis of taxation is altered, or modest acts of fine-tuning a few rates. Even when the former are politically or administratively impossible, there is almost always plenty of scope for the latter sort of tinkering. In both cases, however, the aim is find directions of change that will yield an improvement in welfare without causing a reduction in revenues, or vice versa.

By their very nature, sweeping reforms are prone to have large-scale general equilibrium repercussions, and must be analysed accordingly. A compact account of the standard approach has already been given in Section 2.3, in which the connection between protection and taxation is very much at centre stage. The emphasis here is rather on what can be said without resort to such an apparatus. It is forcefully argued that quantitative barriers to international trade should be speedily dismantled and replaced with modest tariffs, thus generating public revenue while affording domestic industry a measure of interim protection. In doing so, the choice of rates should conform to the principles set out in Chapters 3 and 4. The next step is to broaden the tax base and bring some degree of uniformity to the pattern of effective taxes by switching the basis of taxation from international trade and the production of certain goods to domestic final use or consumption, thereby doing away with non-regulatory protection. In practice, this reform can be accomplished only over the long haul, so that a mixture of the two systems will have to be employed during the transition. In this connection, a VAT is bound to have rather limited coverage at first, as large areas of economic activity will remain beyond the tax collector's reach. On the basis of the model in Section 4.6, it is shown that the associated departures from tax 'neutrality' can be large, even when the effects of remaining tariffs and excises are left out.

There remains a wealth of opportunities to tackle 'marginal' reforms, in the sense of making small changes to the existing structure of rates. Beginning with the taxation of commodities entering final consumption, the apparatus is provided by the model of Section 4.4. Given the forms of the welfare function and households' preferences, the model can be set up to yield an estimate of the loss in private welfare caused by the increase in the tax on each good needed to raise one additional unit of revenue, starting from the status quo. Let the goods be ranked in ascending order according to this index of 'marginal damage'. Then by increasing the rates at the bottom of the list somewhat, while similarly reducing those at the top, one brings about an improvement in welfare without any loss in revenue. Since the analysis is 'local', in the sense of being locally linear, further steps must be accompanied by a recalculation of the index.

An interesting variation is to turn the question around: if the government is a 'rational' maximizer and the observed tax rates achieve its optimum, what is the marginal weight it must place on the total expenditure of each household type? The answer in the Indian case two decades ago is distinctly unflattering, the implicit weights of the lowest and fourth of nine expenditure classes being strongly negative, and that of the fifth being by far the largest.

Piecemeal reforms involving the taxation of intermediate inputs are, in general, inherently more complicated to analyse, for in the absence of rebating such taxes tend to work their way through the chain of production in a very uneven way. The presence of smuggling, especially of final goods, imparts an additional twist to matters; for if smuggled items escape taxation, taxing the inputs needed to produce them domestically robs the Exchequer of revenue at the consumption stage. In the case of Pakistan, for example, it has been estimated that given the drastic reduction in the smuggling of bicycles that would result, replacing the tariff on sheet steel with a modest subsidy would be optimal under the restriction that public goods be financed at the margin by tariffs and sales taxes alone.

Recommended Reading

For reflections on the experience of tax reform in developing countries, see Harberger (1993). Ahmad and Stern (1991) combine theory with an exhaustive application to Pakistan.

Exercises

1. A competitive industry produces an import-substitute under the protection of a fixed quota. The industry's cost function is

$$c(Y) = Y + Y^2/4.$$

The domestic demand function for the good in question is

$$X(q) = 10 - q.$$

(a) If the world price of the good is two, and the quota is also set at two, what is the quota-rent?

(b) Find the commodity tax on the good that would yield the same amount of revenue and compare the values of all variables in equilibrium in both cases, depicting your results graphically.

2. Consider the model of Section 5.2.

(a) Investigate fully the effects of changes in the tax rate on the structure of relative prices when there are two goods.

(b) In a four-good economy, sectors 1 and 2 may be thought of as agriculture and the 'informal', small-scale activities producing manufactures and services, respectively; and sectors 3 and 4 denote organized industry and tertiary activities, respectively. In the event that a VAT were actually introduced, the former pair would lie 'outside' the system, and the latter 'inside' it. The matrix A is

$$\begin{bmatrix} 0.10 & 0.15 & 0.10 & 0.01 \\ 0.05 & 0.05 & 0.01 & 0.01 \\ 0.15 & 0.05 & 0.20 & 0.10 \\ 0.03 & 0.02 & 0.15 & 0.10 \end{bmatrix},$$

and the vector of factor-input coefficients is

$$v = (1, 1.25, 0.5, 0.7).$$

Find the producer price vector that would rule in the hypothetical case of a uniform and universal VAT at the rate of t per cent.

(c) Repeat part (b) under the assumption that sectors 1 and 2 would lie 'outside' the system, choosing suitable values of t beginning at $t = 0.1$. Comment on your findings.

3. Consider a small, open, three-good economy in which perfect competition rules everywhere. Goods 1 and 2 are tradable, their world prices being

unity. Good 1 is produced domestically under CRS by means of labour alone, 1.25 units of which are needed for each unit of output. Good 2 is not produced domestically. Good 3 is non-tradable and is produced under CRS by means of a Leontief technology whose unit activity vector is

$$a_3 = (0.2, 0.2, 0.1; l_3 = 0.625).$$

Find the wage rate and all other prices in the following cases:

(a) No taxation.

(b) Exports of good 1 are subject to an *ad valorem* tax of 10 per cent, good 2 to a tariff of 50 per cent, and good 3 to an excise tax at the rate of 20 per cent.

(c) A universal VAT at the rate of 20 per cent.

(d) A VAT at the rate of 20 per cent, but with sector 1 lying 'outside' the system. Comment briefly on your results.

4. A small, open economy produces a single tradable, all of which is exported in exchange for two importables (goods 1 and 2), which are wholly consumed. The government raises revenue by means of tariffs on the latter. The private sector's preferences over goods 1 and 2 take the Cobb–Douglas form, with taste parameter α:

$$u(x_1, x_2) = x_1^{\alpha} x_2^{1-\alpha}.$$

(a) Prove that the corresponding indirect utility function is

$$v(q_1, q_2, M) = (\alpha/q_1)^{\alpha} [(1 - \alpha)/q_2]^{1-\alpha} M,$$

where q is the vector of consumer prices and M denotes the private sector's income

(b) Treating M as constant, prove that the reduction in welfare that would result if an additional unit of revenue were raised by increasing the tariff on good i is

$$v(q_1, q_2, M) \cdot (q_i/p_i^*) \cdot (1/M),$$

where p_i^* is the world price of good i. If the tariff *rates* are initially non-uniform, what should be done?

(c) Does this result provide any underpinning for recent proposals that developing countries should replace tariffs and excise taxes with a VAT?

(d) Assess briefly the practical value of the recent literature on the reform of indirect taxation in developing countries.

5. Consider the case of Stone–Geary preferences when there are two goods:

$$u(x) = (x_1 - \gamma_1)^{\alpha_1} (x_2 - \gamma_2)^{\alpha_2}, \quad \alpha_1 + \alpha_2 = 1,$$

where good 1 is a necessity ($\gamma_1 > 0$).

(a) Assuming an interior solution, derive the Marshallian demand for each good as a function of prices q and income M.

(b) A society is made up of two homogeneous groups ($h = 1, 2$) of equal size. The values of their preference parameters and income are:

$$\alpha_1 = \alpha_2 = 1/2 \quad \text{for both groups,}$$

$$\gamma_1^1 = 1, \quad \gamma_2^1 = 0, \quad \gamma_1^2 = 3/2, \quad \gamma_2^2 = 0, \quad M^1 = 2, \quad M^2 = 6.$$

Both goods are produced under perfect competition at constant unit costs. Good 1, being a necessity, is initially untaxed; good 2, however, is subject to an excise tax at the rate of 100 per cent. This yields the government exactly the revenue it needs. If the government has no aversion to inequality, show that it should reduce the excise on good 2 and introduce an excise on good 1. Is this particular direction of a reform also desirable when there is 'moderate' aversion to inequality? What is to be recommended in the Rawlsian case?

6. Seigniorage and Debt

A theme that recurs throughout this volume is the central role played by fiscal policy, not only as the handmaiden of development policy, but also as a source of problems. Following the treatment of taxation in Chapters 4 and 5, the purpose of this chapter is to complete the account of how governments finance their activities, a task that requires us to take up two further fiscal topics in their own right, namely, seigniorage and debt. Both open the door to profligacy, and each has a distinct dynamic flavour of its own.

When the government obtains revenue by the act of issuing additional currency, it is said to extract seigniorage. Like other means of raising revenue, seigniorage has its limits, of course, and the inflation that attends it may become politically unacceptable long before revenue from this source is maximized. This leaves the issue of public debt as the remaining way of covering any gap between public expenditures and receipts. As can be seen from Fig. 6.1, governments of all stripes in all continents have resorted to debt finance on a grand scale over the past two decades or more, with the consequence that, in many cases, simply servicing existing debt has become a heavy first charge on current revenues. The resort to debt therefore brings with it a new danger, namely, that fiscal instability will eventually ensue should the debt become sufficiently large. In a number of countries, this threat to fiscal stability has become very real.

The chapter begins with a treatment of seigniorage. This is followed, in Section 6.2, by an analysis of the financing of deficits, in which seigniorage and debt are drawn together through simple accounting. In Section 6.3, we deal with the dynamics of debt, using developments in India to illustrate how the principles involved can be applied in practice. The question of whether a continuation of past behaviour threatens to yield instability in the future is addressed econometrically in Section 6.4 using two quite different cases. The trajectory of India's debt since 1952 is investigated with the aim of establishing whether it portends trouble in the future should the government fail to mend its ways. In Brazil, in contrast, there was a heavy resort to seigniorage, with resulting high inflation, until the mid-1990s.

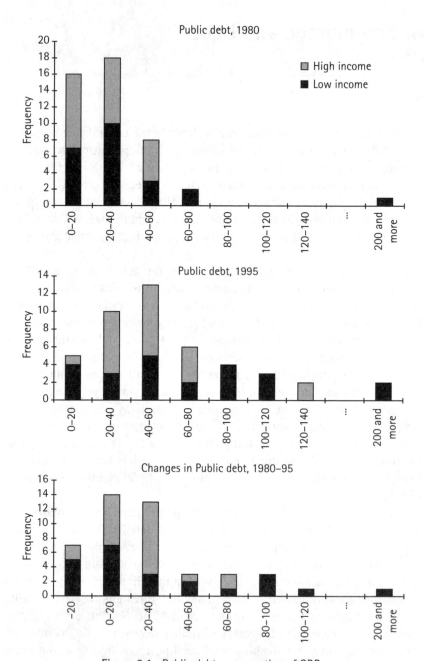

Figure 6.1. Public debt as proportion of GDP

Notes: Database: twenty-two high and higher middle income, twenty-three low and lower middle income countries, as defined by the World Bank (WDI, 1995).
Source: The International Financial Statistics Yearbook, 1998.

6.1. Seigniorage[1]

In earlier times, when the coinage was of precious metals, rulers (*seigneurs*) charged a fee (seigniorage) for minting it in response to private demand. If, as was almost invariably the case, the fee exceeded the cost of mintage, they turned a profit. Some, like Henry VIII of England, were so hungry for revenue that they resorted to debasing the currency, which was discovered, of course, with inflation as the inevitable consequence. With the advent of fiat money, not only were societies spared the costs of mining and smelting precious ores for this purpose, as well as those of the transportation and storage of specie, but governments' profit margins on issuing currency were raised, at a stroke, to almost the face value of the issue itself, the cost of operating the printing presses being negligible in comparison. With such attractions, seigniorage became a potentially important source of revenue indeed, and governments have continued to guard their monopoly rights to issue currency with understandable jealousy.

How large a source of revenue is set out for selected countries in Table 6.1, in which the columns labelled seigniorage are derived as follows. If the nominal stock of base money rises from M_{t-1} at the end of period $t-1$ to M_t at the end of period t, then, ignoring the cost of printing the banknotes, the government will have extracted seigniorage in the amount

$$S_t \equiv \Delta M_t \equiv M_t - M_{t-1}$$

in period t. Dividing through by the nominal value of GDP, $P_t Y_t$, where P_t is the price level in period t, we obtain the ratio

$$\sigma_t \equiv \Delta M_t / P_t Y_t, \tag{6.1a}$$

the values of which are reported in Table 6.1. For the 'Southern Cone' countries of Latin America–Argentina, Chile and, Uruguay–the average value of σ in the period from 1960 to circa 1978 was about 5–6 per cent of GDP. The relative importance of seigniorage as a source of revenue, as expressed by the ratio $S_t/(S_t+T_t)$, where T_t denotes the level of (fiscal) tax revenues in period t, varied considerably, however. It was a comparatively modest 18.3 per cent in the case of Chile, markedly larger, at 28.4 per cent, in Uruguay, and at no less than 45.9 per cent it was running neck and neck with tax revenues in Argentina. The attendant rate of inflation in all three countries would be intolerable, not only in contemporary industrialized

---

[1] This section draws extensively on Black (1992) and Kimbrough (1992).

Table 6.1. Seigniorage, growth, and inflation in selected countries in Asia and Latin America, 1960–86

Country	1960–78			1979–86		
	Growth	Inflation	Seigniorage*	Growth	Inflation	Seigniorage*
India	3.8	6.8	1.0	4.1	9.1	1.9
Korea, Rep. of	9.3	13.8	2.2	6.8	10.8	0.5
Malaysia	7.8	3.2	1.2	5.5	4.3	1.2
Pakistan	3.7	7.6	1.4	6.7	7.5	2.0
Philippines	5.7	8.4	0.8	1.2	17.9	1.1
Singapore	9.2	3.8	2.5	6.5	3.4	1.7
Argentina	3.3	57.2	6.2	−0.5	282.3	11.1
Brazil	8.3	36.5	3.2	4.2	131.3	2.4
Chile		88.9	5.5			
Colombia		15.0	1.8			
Mexico	6.6	8.0	1.6	2.7	55.3	5.4
Peru	4.6	15.2	2.6	0.8	91.0	8.4
Uruguay	1.9	51.7	4.8	0.5	54.4	4.8
Venezuela	5.6	3.3	1.1	−0.2	12.6	1.2

*As a percentage of GDP (see Eqn (6.2) in the text).

Source: Fischer (1982), updated by Dornbusch and Reynoso (1993).

societies, but also in the South Asian subcontinent. Elsewhere in Latin America, the levels of both inflation and seigniorage were more modest in the two decades leading up to the second oil shock, though they still lay, on average, somewhat above the respective norms for the Asian group. The years following saw the onset of rapid, if not hyper-, inflation in all the Latin American countries reported in Table 6.1, with the exception of Venezuela. There were striking increases in seigniorage in Peru, Mexico, and especially so in view of its starting level, Argentina. In Asia, the changes were modest and mixed in direction. Not that Indian governments by any means eschewed seigniorage as a source of revenue: over the period 1979–86, σ_t averaged just under 2 per cent, or about one-seventh of the central government's current tax revenues.

The variations in Table 6.1 raise three related questions: what is the upper limit on σ, what is the optimal value thereof, and how are these values related to inflation? As is the case for the taxation of any commodity, the answer depends heavily on the shape of the demand function—in this case, for money. In this connection, Eqn (6.1a) may be rewritten as

$$\sigma_t \equiv \mu_t \cdot \frac{M_{t-1}}{P_t Y_t} \equiv \mu_t \cdot \left(\frac{M_{t-1}}{M_t} \cdot \frac{M_t}{P_t} \cdot \frac{1}{Y_t} \right), \tag{6.1b}$$

where $\mu_t \equiv \Delta M_t/M_{t-1}$ is the growth rate of the nominal stock of base money, which can be thought of as the tax rate on the opening stock M_{t-1}. We see from the first part of the identity that σ_t is simply the product of the said growth rate and the ratio of the stock to nominal GDP in period t. The second identity contains the term M_t/P_t, which is the level of real balances at the close of period t. Now, the demand for real balances is normally assumed to be increasing in real wealth and decreasing in the nominal rate of interest, which is the rate wealth can earn when held in the form of interest-bearing paper as opposed to money. If money is neutral (or nearly so), then Y_t and the real rate of interest will be unaffected by changes in seigniorage (ΔM_t); but the ensuing changes in the inflation rate will affect the nominal rate of interest, and hence the demand for real balances. In particular, the increase in the inflation rate induced by an increase in seigniorage will induce households and firms to switch out of money into other, interest-bearing placements or, if interest rates are controlled, even into goods. That is to say, the tax base will shrink as μ_t rises. Since the demand for real balances is surely positive when seigniorage is zero, it follows from Eqn (6.1b) that σ_t is increasing in μ_t when μ_t is sufficiently close to zero. At higher values of μ_t, however, the tax base may shrink so fast in response to increases in μ_t that so-called 'Laffer' effects cannot be ruled out a priori. In this connection, it is interesting to note from Table 6.1 that after the second oil shock, σ_t was lower in Brazil than before, despite being accompanied by a near quadrupling of the inflation rate.

As for the numerical magnitudes of the maximum seigniorage that can be extracted, history provides some laboratory experiments in the form of the European hyper-inflations in the 1920s, in which governments were able to acquire 10 per cent or more of GDP by these means—and to wreak untold future damage thereby. In more recent times, this performance has been matched by Argentina (see Table 6.1). When, as they should be, such experiments are avoided, we are left to make inferences from econometric estimates of money demand functions. In the case of India, for example, Buiter and Patel (1992: 222) obtain an estimated upper bound on σ of just 6.6 per cent of GDP, on the assumption that the economy grows at the real rate of 4 per cent a year. This upper bound would, moreover, be approached only asymptotically as the inflation rate goes to infinity, there being no Laffer effects according to their estimates of the demand function for money. At the value of σ ruling in 1986 and 1987, namely 2.7 per cent of GDP, the same real growth rate implies a steady-state inflation rate of 21.2 per cent a year, a level reached just once and briefly since independence, and that experience was politically quite unacceptable. In contrast, the modest seigniorage of 1 per cent of GDP–the actual level ruling between 1960 and 1978–would be accompanied by a steady-state inflation rate of a mere 2.6 per cent a year. According to these estimates, therefore, the trade-off between inflation and seigniorage for India becomes painful even at low rates of seigniorage, so that not too much can be expected from this particular instrument in solving that country's deepening fiscal and indebtedness problems, a topic that is taken up in detail in Sections 6.3 and 6.4.

In order to pursue the relation between seigniorage and the rate of inflation more deeply, it is helpful to rewrite Eqn (6.1a) in the form

$$\sigma_t \equiv \frac{M_t/P_t}{Y_t} \left(\frac{\Delta(M_t/P_t)}{M_t/P_t} + \pi_{t-1} \right), \tag{6.2}$$

where $\pi_{t-1} \equiv (P_t - P_{t-1})/P_{t-1}$ denotes the rate of inflation. The first term in brackets is the rate of growth of real balances. All else being equal, this will be positive when aggregate real income is increasing, and the public's willingness to hold additional real balances with rising prosperity allows the government to extract seigniorage without necessarily inducing inflation. The second term is the rate of inflation, which, when multiplied by the tax base, namely, the current level of real balances, yields the inflation tax.

That these two components of seigniorage can pull in opposite directions to produce a disappointingly low net yield is nicely illustrated by Adam *et al.* (1996), whose analysis of Kenya, Ghana, and Tanzania covers the period 1971–93, the second decade of which saw programmes of financial liberalization in all three countries. The average values of σ were 0.2, 0, and 0.3 per cent, respectively, the pairs of components being (−0.07, 0.09), (−2.5, 2.5), and (−2.1, 2.4), with substantial fluctuations in all across subperiods (ibid.: Table 1, 536). With their populations growing at about 3 per cent annually, the average growth rates of aggregate real income, at 1.40, −0.12, and 2.83 per cent, respectively, were low; and all experienced substantial inflation, the average annual rates being 11.7, 43.9, and 21.4 per cent, respectively (ibid.: Table 3, 545).

Viewed against these averages, the above pairs suggest that if the aim was to maximize seigniorage, then all three governments pursued monetary policies that were too loose. In order to test this hypothesis, Adam *et al.*

estimate the demand for real balances as a function of Y, π, i, and the rate of return on foreign assets, and then use the resulting elasticities to calculate the (steady-state) rate of inflation which would yield maximal real seigniorage[2] at the rates of change of the remaining arguments of the demand function over the period in question. The resulting estimates are 15.4, 26.2, and 14.1 per cent, respectively, a comparison of which with the actual rates suggests that whereas Kenya could have extracted a little more seigniorage, both Ghana and Tanzania had overshot the mark, with Ghana landing up egregiously wide on the wrong side of the Laffer curve. As for the effects of financial liberalization, Adam *et al.* (1996: 549) go on to conclude that these can make revenue-raising from seigniorage more difficult in two ways. First, if they improve agents' abilities to substitute out of money, they will reduce the sustainable inflation rate at which seigniorage is maximized. Second, if they enable agents to reduce their money balances quickly, they will also limit the effectiveness of 'surprise' jumps in base money in the short-run. These points are well taken; but one should not overlook the fact that such liberalization may also lead to faster growth, and so increase the scope for raising σ via the demand for real balances at an unchanged rate of inflation.

So much for the maximization of seigniorage. To close this section, we sketch an account of the socially optimal level of seigniorage, as set out in Kimbrough (1992). Let i_t denote the nominal rate of interest in period t. Then, by writing out the government's budget constraint in present-value form, it can be shown that the (inflation) tax rate is $i_t/(1 + i_t)$ and that the associated tax base, denominated in goods and services, is the level of real balances, M_t/P_t. The reasoning behind this claim is as follows: if the government issues one more unit of currency in period t and uses it to reduce the stock of debt by one unit, then the cost of servicing the debt one period later will be smaller in the amount i_t, the present value of which is $i_t/(1 + i_t)$. Given that those who hold money also have the option of purchasing (one-period) bonds yielding i_t, but choose to hold M_t units of money in period t instead, a private individual's opportunity cost of holding a unit of currency at time t is also $i_t/(1 + i_t)$, so that the pair $[(M_t/P_t), i_t/(1 + i_t)]$ is a point on the aggregate demand function for real balances. Hence, the present value of the reduction in debt-service payments yielded by the stock M_t, when measured in goods and services,

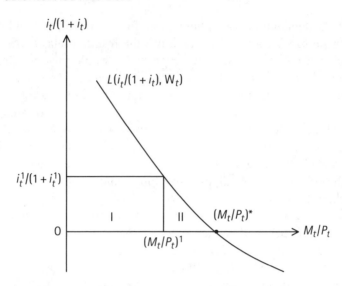

Figure 6.2. The inflation tax and the optimum quantity of money

is the product $[i_t/(1 + i_t)] \cdot (M_t/P_t)$. Equivalently, this is the yield of the inflation tax.

Consider, therefore, Fig. 6.2, which depicts the demand for real balances as a function, L, of $i_t/(1 + i_t)$ and the level of real wealth, W_t, which for the present is taken as given. Suppose the growth rate of the stock of base money is such that the nominal interest rate is i_t^1, so that agents choose to hold real balances in the amount $(M_t/P_t)^1$. The revenue so raised is depicted by the rectangle denoted by I and the associated deadweight loss by the adjoining curvilinear triangle II. When the nominal rate of interest is zero, real balances will take the value denoted as $(M_t/P_t)^*$, which is sometimes referred to as the 'optimum quantity of money'. At first glance, this seems to be a misnomer. For given that the alternative is to raise revenue through the use of distortionary fiscal instruments, to restrict seigniorage to the level yielded by setting the growth of the money supply such that the nominal rate of interest is zero implies choosing higher tax rates in the fiscal system than would otherwise be the case. Since the deadweight loss of seigniorage at very small nominal rates of interest is likely to be small, it appears that failing to employ this instrument somewhat more vigorously cannot be optimal (Phelps, 1973). More recently, this position has come under attack on the grounds that money is an intermediate good, and should not therefore be taxed in order to raise revenue (Kimbrough, 1986). Yet this latter prescription can itself be challenged on the grounds that such optimal second-best taxation is not possible, for the reasons discussed at length in Chapters 4 and 5. It also takes no account of the costs of collection, one of the attractions of seigniorage surely being the ease with which it can be administered. In any event, the chances that governments will heed this particular piece of advice seem to be decidedly slim.

6.2. Financing Deficits: Accounting

A government runs a so-called *primary* (non-interest) deficit when its outlays on consumption and investment exceed the algebraic sum of (fiscal) tax revenues, foreign grants and the receipts from the stock of public capital, including the net surpluses of public sector enterprises. As a rule, this is not the only item to be financed, for there is also the servicing of the current debt, of which there is usually a good deal. The principles of accounting being what they are, the sum of the primary deficit and current debt servicing obligations must be covered by some combination of printing money, taking on new debt, repudiating existing debt, and selling off public sector assets. Formal repudiation is, by its nature, a once-and-for-all event, and privatization usually proceeds in discrete steps. As such, neither fits readily into the framework used below, so a discussion of them is postponed until after the formal analysis is complete. What follows is based on Buiter and Patel (1992), albeit in a somewhat simplified form.

With financing of the current deficit thus restricted to printing money and taking on new debt, and assuming, for simplicity, that all debt has a maturity of one period, the budget identity of the consolidated public sector in period t is

$$A_t + (1 + i_{t-1})D_{t-1} + (1 + i^*_{t-1})(e_t D^*_{t-1}) \equiv (M_t - M_{t-1}) + D_t + e_t D^*_t,$$

(6.3)

where: A_t is the primary deficit; D_t and D^*_t are the levels of domestic and foreign debt, which are denominated in domestic and foreign currency, respectively; i_t and i^*_t are the corresponding rates of interest thereon; and e_t is the nominal exchange rate. It is assumed that D^*_t is measured net of foreign reserves, and that the latter also earn i^*_t. Dividing Eqn (6.3) by nominal GDP and rearranging terms, we obtain the normalized form thereof:

$$a_t \equiv \sigma_t + [d_t - (1 + i_{t-1})(P_{t-1}Y_{t-1}/P_tY_t)d_{t-1}]$$
$$+ [d^*_t - (e_t/e_{t-1})(1 + i^*_{t-1})(P_{t-1}Y_{t-1}/P_tY_t)d^*_{t-1}],$$

(6.4)

where

$$d_t \equiv D_t/P_t Y_t \tag{6.5a}$$

and

$$d_t^* \equiv e_t D_t^*/P_t Y_t \tag{6.5b}$$

denote the ratios of the values of domestic and foreign debt to nominal GDP, respectively, the latter being denominated in domestic currency. Let $\varepsilon_{t-1} \equiv (e_t - e_{t-1})/e_{t-1}$ and $\eta_{t-1} \equiv (Y_t - Y_{t-1})/Y_{t-1}$ denote, respectively, the rate at which the nominal exchange rate depreciates and the rate of growth of real GDP. Then Eqn (6.4) may be rewritten as

$$b_t \equiv \left[d_t - \left(\frac{1 + i_{t-1}}{(1 + \pi_{t-1})(1 + \eta_{t-1})} \right) d_{t-1} \right]$$
$$+ \left[d_t^* - \left(\frac{(1 + i_{t-1}^*)(1 + \varepsilon_{t-1})}{(1 + \pi_{t-1})(1 + \eta_{t-1})} \right) d_{t-1}^* \right], \tag{6.6}$$

where

$$b_t \equiv a_t - \sigma_t \tag{6.7}$$

is the proportion of nominal GDP that must be borrowed in period t to make good whatever part of the primary deficit is not covered by current seigniorage.

We now proceed in steps to express Eqn (6.6) in a more manageable form. If the rates of interest, inflation, and real growth in period $t - 1$ are sufficiently small, we may rewrite Eqn (6.6) as:

$$b_t \equiv [d_t - (1 + r_{t-1} - \eta_{t-1})d_{t-1}] + [d_t^* - (1 + r_{t-1} - \eta_{t-1})d_{t-1}^*]$$
$$- [(i_{t-1}^* + \varepsilon_{t-1} - i_{t-1})(1 + r_{t-1} - \eta_{t-1})]d_{t-1}^*,$$

where $r_{t-1} \equiv i_{t-1} - \pi_{t-1}$ is the real rate of interest on domestic debt in period $t - 1$ at the realized inflation rate π_{t-1}. Let

$$\delta_t \equiv d_t + d_t^* \tag{6.8}$$

denote the ratio of total (consolidated) debt to GDP in period t. Its behaviour is described by the first-order difference equation

$$\delta_t - (1 + r_{t-1} - \eta_{t-1})\delta_{t-1} - b_t$$
$$- [(i_{t-1}^* + \varepsilon_{t-1} - i_{t-1})(1 + r_{t-1} - \eta_{t-1})]d_{t-1}^* = 0. \tag{6.9a}$$

It would be evidently convenient if the terms involving d^*_{t-1} were to vanish, a necessary and sufficient condition for which is $[(i^*_{t-1} + \varepsilon_{t-1} - i_{t-1})(1 + r_{t-1} - \eta_{t-1})] = 0$. In practice, the expression $(1 + r_{t-1} - \eta_{t-1})$ will not stray far from unity. Hence, the said condition will be satisfied if, and only if, the nominal rate of interest on domestic debt is equal to that on foreign debt after adjusting for changes in the nominal exchange rate, as would certainly hold, for example, if the capital account were open and there were perfect foresight. In any event, should the terms involving d^*_{t-1} vanish, we would obtain the following, important special case of Eqn (6.9a):

$$\delta_t - (1 + r_{t-1} - \eta_{t-1})\delta_{t-1} - b_t = 0. \tag{6.9b}$$

If the said terms do not vanish, then the behaviour of the ratio of total debt to GDP will be influenced by terms that reflect the fact that the government enjoys some limited opportunities to arbitrage between foreign and domestic debt. In what follows, we shall assume them away; but the results derived below carry over readily enough by replacing b_t by the 'augmented' borrowing requirement

$$\tilde{b}_t \equiv b_t + [(i^*_{t-1} + \varepsilon_{t-1} - i_{t-1})(1 + r_{t-1} - \eta_{t-1})]d^*_{t-1}.$$

6.3. The Dynamics of Debt

A fundamental question that arises in connection with Eqn (6.9b) is whether, starting from a particular δ_0, a particular trajectory of borrowings $\{b_t\}_{t=0}^{t=\infty}$ yields a path of δ_t that has a finite upper bound, a special case of which arises when the system tends to a steady state. The answer to this question turns out to depend crucially on whether the real rate of growth of GDP exceeds the real rate of interest. If it does not, a solvency condition for the public sector must be introduced to deal with the consequences of an unlimited growth of δ_t as the horizon stretches out indefinitely. These cases are taken are taken up in turn.

6.3.1. Approaching a Steady State?
The state of affairs at time t depends on the initial value δ_0, a boundary condition to which the system is anchored, and the trajectories of a, r, η, and σ over the interval from zero to t. Accordingly, we solve Eqn (6.9b) backwards from time t to obtain an expression for the resulting value of δ_t.

Define $\rho_t \equiv 1 + r_t - \eta_t$. Then

$$\begin{aligned} \delta_t &= \rho_{t-1}[\rho_{t-2}\delta_{t-2} + b_{t-1}] + b_t \\ &= \rho_{t-1}[\rho_{t-2}[\ldots[\rho_0\delta_0 + b_1] + b_2]\ldots + b_{t-1}] + b_t \\ &= \left(\prod_{j=1}^{t}\rho_{t-j}\right)\delta_0 + \sum_{k=0}^{t}\left[\prod_{j=1}^{k}\rho_{t-j}\right]b_{t-j}. \end{aligned} \tag{6.10}$$

The first term on the right-hand side (RHS) of Eqn (6.10) is the accumulated value at time t of the original ratio of debt to GDP; the second is the accumulated value of further borrowings (each normalized by the current value of GDP) in the interval up to period t.

Inspection of Eqn (6.10) reveals that the behaviour of δ_t depends critically on the relationship between the real rate of interest and the rate of growth of GDP over the whole interval. If the latter exceeds the former in all periods, so that $\rho_t < 1 \; \forall t$, then the initial ratio of the debt to GDP will be progressively reduced from its starting level over the course of time, thereby permitting the government to resort to new borrowing without necessarily causing δ to grow, or, if the volume of borrowing is such that δ does grow, then without causing it to do so without bound. In the converse case ($r_t > \eta_t \; \forall t$), however, δ_t will indeed grow without bound— unless seigniorage exceeds the primary deficit by a sufficient margin over a long enough run of years, so making it possible to pay off enough of the original debt. It should be remarked that if $r_t < \eta_t$ over the long haul, then the economy will be dynamically inefficient, an issue that will be taken up in Section 6.3.2.

It is now natural to ask whether a continuation of current policies at time t will yield a steady state, in the sense that δ_t will approach an upper bound, perhaps asymptotically. To answer this question, we return to Eqns (6.9a) and (6.9b). As all variables take constant values in such a steady state, these equations yield, respectively, the following upper bounds:

$$\bar{\delta} \equiv [b + (\varepsilon + i^* - i)\bar{d}^*]/(\eta - r) \tag{6.11a}$$

and

$$\bar{\delta} \equiv b/(\eta - r), \tag{6.11b}$$

where the time subscripts on b, r, ε, and η may now be dropped without introducing any ambiguity. If borrowing is to continue indefinitely, that is to say, if the expressions $[b + (\varepsilon + i^* - i)\bar{d}^*]$ and b, respectively, exceed zero, then η must exceed r if δ is to approach a finite ceiling.

In order to illustrate how Eqn (6.11a) can be applied to establish whether an economy's public finances are threatened with long-term instability, we consider the case of India, which has been examined at some length by Joshi and Little (1994, 1996), taking the early 1990s as their point of departure. The first step in assessing the sustainability of current policies is to establish whether η will exceed r. Weighing the economy's record in the decade up to the early 1990s and other factors, Joshi and Little make what they call the 'prudent' forecast that GDP will grow in real terms at an annual rate of 6 per cent. Forecasting the real rate of interest involves the additional difficulty that the significant 'financial repression'[3] practised in earlier decades, which kept the real rate of interest on government debt low, was being dismantled as the result of certain reforms undertaken in the early 1990s, thereby raising r. Joshi and Little begin by putting its future value at 5 per cent p.a.–lower than, but somewhat alarmingly close to, η–thereby ensuring the relevance of Eqn (6.11a).

We now turn to the numerator, beginning with b. At 0.053, the value of a in 1990 and 1991 was substantial, raising the question of whether such a level of the primary deficit is indefinitely sustainable. How much of this gap can be covered by seigniorage? Here, Joshi and Little skirt the task of estimating the demand for real balances econometrically by employing Eqn (6.1b) in the following way. They note that the ratio of the money stock to nominal GDP has stayed roughly constant at 0.12 over a decade or more, and assume that it will continue to do so. With η forecast to be 0.06, a forecast of the future rate of inflation is now needed to produce a forecast of the rate of growth of nominal GDP. Given the widespread conviction in India that more rapid inflation entails rising inequality, the desired rate thereof is low. As a practical matter, however, the past record warns against allowing the wish to be father to the thought, so Joshi and Little settle for a forecast of 5 per cent p.a., thereby yielding the forecast that nominal GDP will grow at 11 per cent a year. If $M_t/P_t Y_t$ indeed stays steady at 0.12 in this configuration, then the stock of base money must also grow at 11 per cent a year, and the associated seigniorage rate is obtained from Eqn (6.1b):

$$\sigma = 0.11 \times 0.12 = 0.0132,$$

---

[3] The memorable phrase 'financial repression' was coined by McKinnon (1973) to describe how governments in most LDCs have, in his view, abused the financial system in order to generate resources for state activities in particular, and to influence resource allocation in general.

which is rather modest by the standards of the past couple of decades and so hints that the levels of the primary deficits run in the 1980s and early 1990s were unsustainable.

The final step is to deal with foreign borrowing. In order to arrive at an estimate of the relevant terms, Joshi and Little argue that the upper limit on foreign indebtedness for a large country like India is determined by the ratio of its exports to GDP. They follow this up by imposing an additional, independently determined upper limit of two on the ratio of foreign debt to exports. Coupled with the ratio of exports to GDP during the 1980s, namely about 0.1, this latter limit of two yields an implicit upper limit on the ratio of foreign debt to GDP of 0.2. Accepting this approach for the moment, any divergence between the future growth rates of GDP and exports will now come into play. On the same basis used to forecast η, they assume that exports will grow in real terms at 10 per cent annually. According to this export forecast, therefore, the ratio of exports to GDP will grow continuously at 4 per cent p.a., and hence also the upper limit on the ratio of foreign debt to GDP. Neither of these can hold in the long run, however. If, for example, the ratio of exports to GDP were to rise from 0.1 to 0.2, which—were it at all possible for India—would take a little less than 18 years at 4 per cent p.a., and if the factor two were used once more, then the corresponding upper limit on the ratio of foreign debt to GDP would double from its implicit level in the early 1990s to the value 0.4. Yet Joshi and Little themselves describe the (implicit) level of 0.5 in 1990/91 as 'absurdly high' (1996: 27). Their approach to establishing an upper limit on foreign debt is not, therefore, wholly consistent with their assumptions about the underlying growth rates of output and exports.

In any event, they call the value of the expression $e_t[(D_t^* - D_{t-1}^*) - i_t^* D_t^*]$ at the upper limit of foreign indebtedness 'the prudent level of foreign borrowing' (1996: 24, fn. 12). It is simply the excess of additional borrowing over interest payments at the limit in question. When normalized by GDP, let it be denoted by f, the value of which they reckon to be at most 1 per cent, of which only one half would be available to the public sector to finance its outgoings.

In order to carry through their analysis, Joshi and Little (1996: 28) use the equation

$$d_t - d_{t-1} = [a_t - \sigma_t - (f/2)] - (\eta - r)d_t, \tag{6.12}$$

which is Eqn (6.4) with the terms involving d_t^* and d_{t-1}^* replaced by f. To summarize: as initial values, in 1990–1 we have $a = 0.053$ and $d = 0.54$.

Joshi and Little's estimates of $f, \sigma, \eta,$ and r are 0.01, 0.0132, 0.06, and 0.05. In the steady state corresponding to these values, Eqn (6.12) yields

$$\bar{d} = [a - \sigma - (f/2)]/(\eta - r) = (0.053 - 0.013 - 0.005)/(0.06 - 0.05)$$
$$= 3.5,$$

which is completely absurd. On this basis, therefore, one can confidently assert that primary deficits on the scale of those in the 1980s and early 1990s are unsustainable.

An alternative approach is to take the 'current' value of d (0.54 in 1990–1) as the upper limit, and then to calculate the corresponding value of the primary deficit that would yield it. Setting the RHS of Eqn (6.12) to zero, this yields

$$a = 0.01 \times (0.54) + 0.013 + 0.005 = 0.0234.$$

As Joshi and Little doubt that the difference $(\eta - r) = 0.01$ is, in fact, sustainable, they assess the prudent level of the primary deficit to be at most 1 per cent of GDP, instead of the 2.3 per cent so obtained from Eqn (6.12).

A further alternative is to impose an upper limit not on the ratio of foreign debt to GDP, but rather on the ratio of all consolidated public debt to GDP, namely, on δ. The above values and Eqn (6.11b) imply that

$$\bar{\delta} = (0.053 - 0.013)/(0.06 - 0.05) = 4.0,$$

which is also absurd, so we calculate once more a prudent level of the primary deficit. When one examines the values of the ratio of debt to GDP in other countries, one can argue that the upper limit for $\bar{\delta}$ is perhaps one. In this case, Eqn (6.11b) yields

$$a = 0.01 + 0.013 = 0.023,$$

which is about the same as that derived in the previous paragraph.

In fact, the government of India has been able to keep the primary deficit within hailing distance of these levels only very intermittently over the past three decades. A mere glance at Fig. 6.3, which depicts the trajectories of two series of the ratio of India's total public debt to GDP, reveals that such a fiscal performance, if it lies at all within the government's grasp, cannot be expected any time soon.

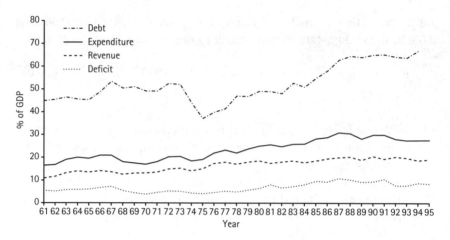

Figure 6.3. Debt and public finance in India, 1961–95

Source: Data for 1961–89 (Debt 1961–87) is taken from Burgess and Stern (EF No. 4, No. 45); for 1990–95 (Debt 1988–95) from the World Bank's Country Economic Memorandum.

6.3.2. Solving Forwards and Solvency

As indicated above, other issues arise when the real rate of interest exceeds the real rate of growth ($\rho > 1$). To see what is involved, we solve the system forwards recursively, starting in period t:

$$\delta_t = [\delta_{t+1} - b_{t+1}]/\rho_t$$

$$= [[\delta_{t+2} - b_{t+2}]/\rho_{t+1} - b_{t+1}]/\rho_t$$

$$= \lim_{k \to \infty} \prod_{j=0}^{k}(1/\rho_{t+j}) \cdot \delta_{t+k+1} - \sum_{k=0}^{\infty}\prod_{j=0}^{k}(1/\rho_{t+j}) \cdot b_{t+k+1}. \qquad (6.13)$$

The expression $\prod_{j=0}^{k}(1/\rho_{t+j}) \cdot \delta_{t+k+1}$ is the present value of the debt–GDP ratio $k+1$ periods on from t, discounted back to period t. We now impose the (transversality) condition

$$\lim_{k \to \infty} \prod_{j=0}^{k}(1/\rho_{t+j}) \cdot \delta_{t+k+1} \leq 0, \qquad (6.14)$$

which is the analogue of the requirement that public debt, expressed as a proportion of GDP, be non-positive at the close of a finite programme ($\delta_T \leq 0$). When Eqn (6.14) holds as an equality, Eqn (6.13) becomes the public sector's inter-temporal budget constraint, which is also the government's solvency constraint:

$$\delta_t + \sum_{k=0}^{\infty} \prod_{j=0}^{k} (1/\rho_{t+j}) b_{t+k+1} = 0. \tag{6.15}$$

The interpretation here is that, in the presence of the solvency constraint, any feasible borrowing programme starting at time t (the 'present'), $\{b_{t+k}\}_{k=0}^{k=\infty}$, must satisfy Eqn (6.15).

The reason for imposing Eqn (6.14) is the assumption that the economy is dynamically efficient, in contrast to the case where the rate of growth exceeds the real rate of interest forever. For if indeed $\eta_{t+j} > r_{t+j}$ for all j, as assumed in the discussion of the Indian case in Section 6.3.1, then Ponzi games would be possible: in principle, the government would have no difficulty in servicing existing debt out of growing output. By ruling out this possibility, we are assuming that starting from some t', there must be sequences $\{\eta_{t'+j}\}_{j=0}^{j=\infty}$ and $\{r_{t'+j}\}_{j=0}^{j=\infty}$ such that $\eta_{t'+j} < r_{t'+j}$: equivalently, that $\rho_t > 1$ for all $t > t'$. From Eqn (6.14), this implies that δ may grow without bound, a point to which we shall return shortly.

Returning to Eqn (6.15), this states that the debt at time t is exactly equal to the discounted stream of primary surpluses and seigniorage that accrue from t onwards. Given that there is some debt at time t, it follows that the algebraic sum of the primary surplus and seigniorage must be strictly positive in some future periods if Eqn (6.15) is to be satisfied. That is to say, imposing Eqn (6.14) is equivalent to imposing a measure of fiscal discipline at some stage in the proceedings. It is not, however, a particularly stringent requirement; for as we have just seen, solvency, as expressed by Eqn (6.15), is perfectly consistent with unbounded growth in the ratio of debt to GDP, as long as the latter grows at a rate smaller than $(r_{t+j} - \eta_{t+j})$ most of the time.

That such a concept of solvency should be such a weak requirement to impose on fiscal policy is, perhaps, all the more disquieting in the light of Section 6.3.1, where the condition $\eta > r$ emerged as essential to the existence of a steady state in which δ approaches a ceiling in the face of primary fiscal deficits that are not fully covered by seigniorage. The two conditions can be formally reconciled by noting that the price of fiscal stability in those economies whose governments are unable to run net surpluses (inclusive of seigniorage) is dynamic inefficiency. Yet such a reconciliation misses a telling point against the solvency condition when $\eta < r$, namely, that we have implicitly assumed that the government can, if needed, get its hands on the whole of GDP in order to service existing debt, and without reducing GDP in the smallest measure while so doing. This beggars belief. Buiter and Patel (1992: 186) put the point nicely:

> The reason why this remarkable fiscal high wire act [of sustaining an ever rising δ] may be possible is that our approach to solvency thus far has ignored the growing excess burden associated with ever-rising distortionary taxes and the rising real cost of extracting an ever-rising tax burden from the private sector. [...] If dead-weight losses ... or collection costs are an increasing and strictly convex function of the real tax rate or of the tax-GDP ratio, then only finite debt-GDP ratios are feasible.

The conclusion to be drawn from all this is that practitioners should anchor their calculations to sensible estimates of the upper bound of the debt–GDP ratio rather than to solvency conditions, even if dynamic inefficiency is an unavoidable implication.

6.4. Explosive Trends in Debt?

A closely related conclusion is that if a particular economy continues to behave as it has done in the past, then the series $\{\delta_t\}$ must contain neither a deterministic nor a stochastic trend if one is to rule out the possibility of fiscal instability in the future. Any hope of answering this empirical question rests heavily on the span of the available data series. We can continue with examination of the Indian case, for an unbroken series of her public domestic debt has been recently pieced together for virtually the entire post-Independence period by Rajaraman and Mukhopadhyay (1999). An interesting variation of the tax–seigniorage–debt nexus is provided by Brazil, as analysed by Issler and Lima (2000).

6.4.1. India

Rajaraman and Mukhopadyay's series for $\{d_t\}$ is depicted in Fig. 6.4, inspection of which suggests a somewhat unsteady track, with a tendency to increase, and perhaps with a hint of a structural break in the 1970s. The path's unsteady, meandering quality suggests that we should test for the presence of a unit root, together with a drift term to cover the possibility that the series has an upward trend. Consider, therefore, the autoregressive equation

$$\delta_t = \alpha + \beta\delta_{t-1} + \varepsilon_t,$$

which can be trivially rewritten as

$$\Delta\delta_t \equiv \delta_t - \delta_{t-1} = \alpha + (\beta - 1) \cdot \delta_{t-1} + \varepsilon_t, \qquad (6.16)$$

where α and β are constants to be estimated and ε_t is an i.i.d. disturbance term. If the 'drift' term α is positive, the system is said to possess a stochastic (upward) trend. In the special case where this year's value is equal to last year's plus ε_t, that is, where $\alpha = 0$ and $\beta = 1$, we have a random walk without trend. As can be seen from the estimates reported at the foot of Fig. 6.4, this hypothesis cannot be rejected. Yet inspection of δ_t's path suggests that the failure of the 'drift' term to be significant may be traceable to the possibility of a structural break in the middle of the 1970s, with α being zero up to the break and positive thereafter. This hypothesis can be tested using a method proposed by Perron (1989), in which the date of the break is varied exogenously. It, too, is rejected.

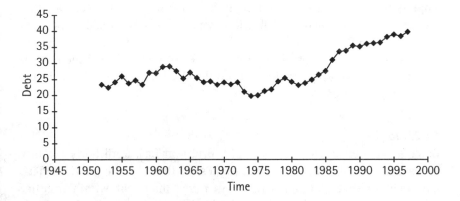

Figure 6.4. India's public domestic debt as a proportion of GDP: 1952–97
Source: Rajaraman and Mukhopadhyay (1999).
Two possible models (standard errors and *t*-values in parentheses):

1. *Model*: $\Delta\delta_t = \alpha + (\beta - 1) \cdot \delta_{t-1} + \varepsilon_t,$
   $\Delta\delta_t = 0.129883 + 0.009682 \cdot \delta_{t-1} + \varepsilon_t.$
   (1.201)   (0.043)
   (0.108)   (0.225)

2. *Model*: $\Delta\delta_t = \alpha + (\beta - 1) \cdot \delta_{t-1} + \gamma \cdot t + \varepsilon_t,$
   $\Delta\delta_t = 0.76001 - 0.042465 \cdot \delta_{t-1} + 0.033842 \cdot t + \varepsilon_t.$
   (1.267)   (0.056)   (0.024)
   (0.6)   (−0.756)   (0.1621)

A further possibility that the series also possesses a deterministic trend, so that time itself appears as a regressor:

$$\delta_t = \alpha + \beta\delta_{t-1} + \gamma t + \varepsilon_t, \tag{6.17}$$

which can be rewritten as

$$\Delta\delta_t = \alpha + (\beta - 1)\delta_{t-1} + \gamma t + \varepsilon_t, \tag{6.18}$$

where a structural break can be introduced in the same way. This possibility, too, is rejected. We are therefore left with the conclusion that the series lies on the very border of exhibiting explosive behaviour, with a unbounded variance in the limit as the sequence goes to infinity. This means that trying to muddle through, with halting, temporary attempts to restore fiscal discipline only under the pressure of acute events, is simply not an option if India is to avoid falling into an internal debt trap.

Rajaraman and Mukhopadhyay (1999) arrive at essentially the same qualitative conclusion using a structural time series model. The variant that performed best exhibits a trend whose level is stochastic, but whose slope is fixed, with a structural break in 1974. It yields the forecast that the ratio of internal debt to GDP will increase secularly from 41.8 per cent in 1998 to 56.5 per cent in 2014. As the authors note, the latter is not necessarily 'intolerably high, [but given the fixed slope] the time path of debt will not naturally stabilize at any level without a correction in the underlying fiscal parameters'.

6.4.2. Brazil

Brazil's experience since the Second World War has, until fairly recently at least, been quite different from India's, in that chronic public deficits have been financed through seigniorage rather than debt, with high inflation as the accompanying price to be paid. In their examination of this nexus over the period 1947–92, Issler and Lima (2000) go beyond the simple question of whether the debt is sustainable, and investigate both the role of seigniorage in securing fiscal equilibrium and the possibility that government expenditure is exogenous.

In essence, they use Eqn (6.9a), which may be rewritten to yield the change in d_t as that part of the deficit not covered by seigniorage:

$$\Delta d_t \equiv d_t - d_{t-1} \equiv (a_t - \sigma_t) + \hat{r}d_{t-1}, \tag{6.19}$$

where they make no distinction between internal and external debt, and $\hat{r} \equiv r_{t-1} - \eta_{t-1}$ is assumed to be constant. Whether the debt is sustainable, therefore, boils down to whether the series $\{\Delta d_t\}$ is stationary. Various unit-root tests reveal that, in contrast to India's, it is indeed so. This result implies that public expenditures (including debt service) are closely tethered to tax revenues (including seigniorage), with the two roughly in balance. Tests on these two series duly yield one unit root in each case, so that the next step is to test whether the series are cointegrated, with cointegrating vector $(1, -1)$ to reflect the fact that one balances the other. This null hypothesis cannot be rejected. In order to establish what role seigniorage played in bringing about this fiscal equilibrium, Issler and Lima remove seigniorage from the revenue series and then rerun the procedure. They find no cointegration in this case, which they interpret as evidence that seigniorage played a key role in maintaining fiscal equilibrium without a resort to additional debt.

Turning to 'causation', tests reveal that whereas expenditures are weakly exogenous for the cointegrating vector, revenues are not. At the same time, however, not only do expenditures Granger-cause tax revenues, but the converse also holds; so that expenditures are not strongly exogenous. Summing up, the authors characterize the policy regime between 1947 and 1992 as one of spend-and-tax, with seigniorage playing a central role in balancing the budget.

In a rather poignant postscript, Issler and Lima (2000: 146) draw attention to the fact that the so-called 'Real Plan' ushered in a new regime in 1994. Seigniorage receipts dropped sharply, expenditures continued to grow unabated, and apparently little was done to raise additional taxes, for the deficit reached 7 per cent of GDP in just 4 years. The bookkeeping 'slack' was taken up by public debt, whose level almost tripled in the same period. In a short space of time, Brazil had taken a giant stride towards joining India in the woes of Section 6.4.1.

6.5. Summary

When the excess of the government's current receipts from taxes and other sources over its outlays on consumption and investment do not suffice to service its current debt, it has just two options if it is to avoid a default on its outstanding debt: first, to print money, and second, to issue new debt. Both have their attractions—and drawbacks.

Extracting seigniorage involves virtually no direct costs at all in an age of *fiat* money, it can be varied without the need to rewrite existing law, and if prudently used, it can often yield substantial revenue without causing strong inflation. In those countries where the market for government debt is poorly developed, seigniorage is the only option. It can be overdone, however; for as higher inflation strengthens the flight out of domestic money into goods and other assets, the tax base in the form of real balances shrinks, and the resulting yield can fall. Contemporary history provides examples not only of a heavy resort to seigniorage, especially in Latin America, but also of 'overshooting', sometimes to the point where the yield is virtually zero. What, then, is the optimal rate of seigniorage? The theory of optimal, second-best taxation tells us that intermediate goods should not be taxed. This result has been seized on to argue that money should be issued only to satisfy the rising demand for real balances with economic growth. Yet the result's validity depends on the availability of other taxes, and in their absence the inflation tax comes back into the reckoning.

When the market for public debt is fairly well developed, the government has the option of issuing new debt in order to pay off the old, thereby shifting the burden of the taxes needed to finance it into the future. If both the economy and taxable capacity are growing, this alternative demands serious consideration. One approach to assessing the limits to debt policy is to establish whether the trajectory of borrowing implied by future fiscal policy and prudent seigniorage will result in a ratio of debt to GDP that approaches a tolerable upper bound. A necessary and sufficient condition for any finite upper bound to exist when borrowing is always positive is that the economy's real rate of growth over the long run exceed the real rate of interest on government debt. Even when this condition does hold, the associated ceiling may be absurdly high—some calculations for India in the early 1990s, for example, put it at three to four—which implies that a tighter fiscal policy is unavoidable. In the converse case, where the economy's real rate of growth over the long run is lower than the real rate of interest on government debt, a solvency condition for the public sector is required, under which the present value of the sum of the initial debt and the stream of future borrowings must be zero, so that fiscal surpluses must be run some of the time. That this condition does not necessarily rule out an unbounded growth in the ratio of debt to GDP ratio reveals it to be a weak reed on which to rest debt policy. The fact that steps to liberalize the financial system are likely to raise the real rate of interest by more than the real rate of growth simply reinforces the homespun conclusion that it is dangerous to possess the luxury of debt-finance without the accompanying virtue of fiscal discipline.

Recommended Reading

Accessible treatments of seigniorage are Black (1992) and Kimbrough (1992). Buiter and Patel's (1992) analysis of deficit finance is rewarding, but rather hard going.

Exercises

1. Show that Eqn (6.1b) may be written in the form

$$\sigma_t \equiv \Delta m_t + [(1 + \pi_{t-1})(1 + \eta_{t-1}) - 1]/[(1 + \pi_{t-1})(1 + \eta_{t-1})V_{t-1}],$$

where V_t is the so-called 'income velocity' of base money in period t, $m_t \equiv M_t/P_t Y_t \equiv 1/V_t$ is its inverse, and $\pi_{t-1} \equiv (P_t - P_{t-1})/P_t$ is the rate of inflation. Buiter and Patel's (1992) econometric estimation of the demand function for money yields the (approximate) steady-state form

$$V = 6.463 + 15.782\pi.$$

On this basis, compute the steady-state seigniorage that would result from the other assumptions employed by Joshi and Little, as set out in Section 6.3.1, and comment on the difference between this estimate and that obtained by the latter. Suppose, instead, that inflation were to set in at the higher rate of 8 per cent annually, which is somewhat closer to that realized over the period 1970–90. Repeat all calculations and comment on your results.

2. Consider the case where the real rate of interest exceeds the real rate of growth, so that the so-called solvency condition Eqn (6.15) comes into play. The point of departure is the beginning of period $t + 1$, the consolidated debt inherited from the past being δ_t. Suppose the economy will henceforth experience steady-state growth into the indefinite future, provided the right fiscal policy is pursued. Find an expression for b, as the 'right' steady-state fiscal policy.

Now consider the Indian case once more, as discussed in Section 6.3.1, but with $r = 0.06$ and $\eta = 0.05$. Taking the value of δ_t in the mid-1990s to be 0.7, find the associated steady-state value of the primary fiscal deficit and comment critically thereon in the light of the discussion in that section.

3. Show that if the real rate of interest takes the value of 5 per cent in the steady state, whatever be the rate of inflation, then the steady-state

demand for real balances in exercise 1 is

$$M/P = Y/(5.674 + 15.782i),$$

where i denotes the nominal rate of interest. Find the deadweight loss of seigniorage as a proportion of the revenue so raised at the inflation rates of 5 and 8 per cent, respectively.

4. Imagine that you are the country economist for Sri Lanka (or some other country of your choice) at some international organization. You are suddenly charged with the writing of a memorandum on the government's long-term finances, with special reference to fiscal stability. A friendly colleague reminds you that the IMF's *International Financial Statistics* contains numerous series, some of which are surely relevant. Your Division Chief, who has not forgotten her economics, expects to have a readable and well-structured draft on her desk the following morning.

7. Other Dynamic Pitfalls

The possibility that a lax debt policy will lead to a headlong march, or a series of stumbles, into fiscal instability was treated at length in Chapter 6. This is far from the only hazard that can await an economy in a many-period setting. Whilst there is no space here to deal with all the issues that arise, two others merit particular attention.

The first is 'dynamic' or 'time-inconsistency' (Kydland and Prescott, 1977), whereby at some point in time, it is no longer optimal to hold fast to a policy that was put into effect or announced in some earlier period, not because something unexpected occurred in the meantime, but rather because certain incentives, which were relevant for decisions in earlier periods, cease to have any effect in the present. Suppose, for example, that the government enacts a statute that abolishes the taxation of capital, with the expressed intention of raising saving and investment. If private agents are sufficiently persuaded of the permanence of this policy, they indeed might invest more than they would otherwise have done. Once the gestation period is over and the investment has taken a fixed form, however, a capital levy becomes a lump-sum tax and hence the best way to raise revenue. The government now faces the temptation, therefore, to renege on its earlier commitment not to tax capital, and if it were known that the world would come to an end at the close of the present period, it should indeed renege.

In fact, the world goes on, so that if the government were to succumb to this temptation, it would do considerable, perhaps even lasting, damage to its reputation. It is possible, though in view of the apparently high discount rates of those in office, doubtful, that the prospect of such damage will induce the government to keep its word. The alternative to this self-enforcing mechanism is for the government to enter into some form of binding commitment not to undo in the future what it has just written into the statute book. Again, this is much more easily stated as a desirable principle than credibly formulated in practical detail to persuade a sceptical public. Should the government actually renege, the task of rebuilding its reputation is likely to be long, drawn out, and very costly.

188 OTHER DYNAMIC PITFALLS

The main focus of this chapter, however, is on the possible existence of two or more self-fulfilling expectations equilibria, the inferior ones of which involve the subsequent reversal of a policy whose earlier introduction, viewed in a purely static way, made eminently good sense. An important case made a brief appearance at the close of Section 3.6, in which the central bank has a limited stock of foreign reserves. It is intuitively clear from the account sketched there that there are close formal similarities with the above example of dynamic inconsistency, inasmuch as the government would go back on an earlier undertaking should it rescind the reform in the future. The difference lies in the fact that in a setting where the reserves may run out, the government does not undo the reform because that has become the best choice among several alternatives from that point onwards, but rather because it is forced to do so as a result of the actions of a sceptical public, which render the original reform unsustainable when the public expects that the initial reserves will indeed run out.

The consequences of the very possibility of a reversal in policy will now be pursued in some detail in four variations. In Section 7.1, the economy has a fixed level of GNP at world prices and access to borrowing and lending opportunities at a parametric rate of interest in world capital markets. Thus, there is the scarcity implied by the economy's inter-temporal wealth constraint, but the economy cannot run out of foreign exchange in the sense just described above. In the second variant, we introduce precisely that latter possibility by ruling out foreign borrowing, while also allowing reforms to affect the level of output at world prices. For this purpose, we extend the model of Section 3.6 to two periods. In the third variant, the emphasis is on a reform aimed at raising revenues more efficiently rather than on dismantling protection as such. The example chosen for this purpose in Section 7.3 is the introduction of a value added tax (VAT) where, in contrast to Sections 7.1 and 7.2, lump-sum transfers are not available and a given level of public expenditures must be financed. Section 7.4 deals with various counter-measures that can be undertaken when a reform in some sphere of policy would, by itself, cause output at world prices to contract in the short run. The fourth variation (Section 7.5) returns to a setting in which capital is internationally mobile and private agents have the choice between a foreign placement and domestic investment, albeit with switching costs. Beliefs about the likelihood that a policy will be reversed influence this choice, and if those beliefs depend, in turn, on how much capital will be repatriated, then multiple equilibria are possible.

7.1. Costly Reversals of Policy

When the quantitative restrictions on imports of consumer goods are finally eased and any tariffs thereon reduced, a strong surge in purchases almost invariably follows. That such imports should rise is hardly surprising; for their relative prices have fallen and their quality is usually superior to the domestic products with which they directly compete. Yet the magnitude of the surge is often so large as to awaken the suspicion that other factors are at work. One possibility is that households are firmly persuaded that this 'last' stage of liberalization heralds an era of prosperity under an open trading regime. If, in the light of this rosy expectation, foreign credit is elastically available against future GDP (valued at world prices, of course), then part of the surge will reflect an individually rational, and socially desirable, smoothing of consumption. An altogether darker alternative is that households are not at all persuaded that the policy will last—understandably so, if they have lived through the episodes of loosening and tightening sketched in Chapter 3—and resolve to make hay while the sun shines.

What has exercised some economists whose work is primarily motivated by Latin America's problems is the question of whether an episode of liberalization is damaging precisely because it is temporary, quite aside from the static considerations treated in Chapter 3. A notable contribution in this vein is Calvo (1987), in which the representative household is assumed to be immortal, apparently to ease the task of analysing the effects of variations in the length of an episode. For present purposes, however, the question of whether temporary policies are costly can be addressed perfectly satisfactorily when the household's lifespan is just two periods, representing the present and future, respectively. We now extend the basic model of Chapter 3 accordingly, while specializing it in certain ways so that it largely conforms to Calvo's formulation. The references to assumptions are those set out in Chapter 3.

In a many-period setting, A1 is simply augmented to cover intertemporal trades in world capital markets:

Assumption 1′. The household has unlimited access to borrowing and lending opportunities abroad at the parametric rate of interest r^*. Obligations are always met.

The initial endowment F may now be thought of as a holding of foreign bonds, part or all of which can be sold to increase consumption in the present, or which can be supplemented by current savings and then used to increase consumption in the future.

The production side of the economy is drastically simplified to keep the spotlight focussed on the consumer's behaviour: A7, A9, and A11 are replaced by:

Assumption 7'. The value of GDP at world prices is constant, at Y^*.

The framework of assumptions is completed by specifying the household's preferences. In order to make the analysis comparatively tractable, we rule out substitution between goods within a period. This simplification is defensible inasmuch as such substitution plays a minor role in the present context, and its introduction would make for an increase in complexity out of all proportion to the additional insight it would afford.[1] Let $x(\tau) \equiv [x_1(\tau), x_2(\tau)]$ denote the household's consumption bundle in period $\tau(= 1, 2)$. The felicity function $u[x(\tau)]$ is therefore specialized to the form

$$u[x(\tau)] = u[\min(x_1(\tau), x_2(\tau)/b)]. \tag{7.1}$$

Rational consumers will choose bundles such that $x_2(\tau) = bx_1(\tau)$, so that we may speak of a composite consumption good, X units of which comprise the bundle (X, bX). Since such bundles are always feasible under the above assumptions, we may rewrite Eqn (7.1) as

$$u[x(\tau)] = U[X(\tau)], \tag{7.2}$$

where $U(\cdot)$ is assumed to satisfy the lower Inada condition. The cost of a unit of X is, by definition, the price index $P(\tau)$ associated with Eqn (7.1) (see Section 3.6, footnote 9). In the presence of the tariff t_2, we have

$$P = q_1 + bq_2 = p_1 + bp_2 = p_1^* + b(1 + t_2)p_2^*, \tag{7.3}$$

and in its absence, following complete liberalization,

$$P^* = p_1^* + bp_2^*, \tag{7.4}$$

where the assumption that the world price vector p^* is constant implies that the index τ may be omitted without ambiguity in defining these values.

---

[1] Calvo assumes that good 1 is not consumed, and good 2 not produced, domestically. As he notes in footnote 1 (ibid.; 247), the '[r]esults are essentially the same if exportables and importables are perfect complements'. The latter case better suits our purposes later in this chapter, and so is adopted.

The household's preferences over bundles $[X(1), X(2)]$ are represented by the additively separable form

$$W = U[X(1)] + \beta U[X(2)], \tag{7.5}$$

where β is the household's subjective discount factor.

It follows from Eqn (7.4) that output in each period yields a command over (Y^*/P^*) units of the composite good. In the space of $X(1)$ and $X(2)$, therefore, the economy's availability line is given by

$$P^*[X(1) + X(2)/(1 + r^*)] = [(2 + r^*)/(1 + r^*)]Y^* + F, \tag{7.6}$$

where the right-hand side (RHS) is the present value of lifetime wealth at world prices.

The benchmark is the benevolent dictator's problem

$$\text{maximize } W \quad \text{subject to Eqn (7.6).} \atop X \tag{7.7}$$

Under the above assumptions, problem (7.7) has a unique, interior solution X^0, which satisfies the familiar marginal condition

$$U'[X(1)]/U'[X(2)] = \beta(1 + r^*), \tag{7.8}$$

and is depicted as point C^0 in Fig. 7.1. As drawn, consumption exceeds output in period 1, the difference $[P^*X^0(1) - Y^*]$ being the value of the trade deficit at world prices. The output vector $(Y^*/P^*, Y^*/P^*)$ is depicted as point A, and the availability line VV includes the endowment F.

With the first-best allocation fully characterized, we turn to decentralized equilibria. The government draws up a policy programme at the beginning of period 1. We assume that half measures are ruled out, so that this involves choosing, for each and every period, between a tariff at the rate t_2 (>0) and none at all. In a two-period setting, there are thus four possible programmes, which are conveniently described by their associated vectors of price indices for the composite good. The set of policy programmes is then described by the Cartesian product

$$S = \{P, P^*\} \times \{P, P^*\}. \tag{7.9}$$

Let $P \equiv [P(1), P(2)] \in S$. We assume that the representative household has perfect foresight, that is, whatever be the government's announcements about what it intends to do, the household knows what the government

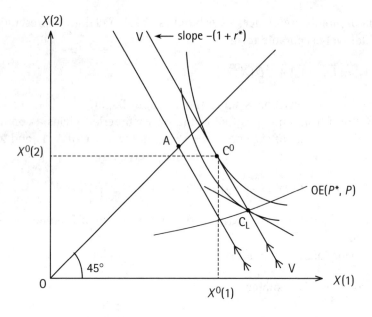

Figure 7.1. The costs of temporary policy (after Calvo)

will actually do. Given this knowledge, the household's lifetime budget constraint takes the form

$$P(1)X(1) + P(2)X(2)/(1 + r^*) \leq Y^d(1) + F + Y^d(2)/(1 + r^*), \quad (7.10)$$

where $Y^d(\tau)$ denotes the value of GDP at domestic prices plus the lump-sum rebate of tariff revenues, if any, in period τ. The household's decision problem is to

$$\underset{X|P \in S}{\text{maximize } W} \quad \text{subject to (7.10)}. \qquad (7.11)$$

The first-order necessary conditions, which are also sufficient under the assumptions employed here, are

$$U'(1) - \lambda P(1) = 0 \qquad (7.12)$$

and

$$\beta U'(2) - \lambda P(2)/(1 + r^*) = 0, \qquad (7.13)$$

where λ is the Lagrange multiplier associated with the constraint (7.10). It follows at once from Eqns (7.8), (7.12), and (7.13) that if the policy programme involves a constant tariff across periods, so that $P(1) = P(2)$, then a first-best allocation will result. That $[P^*, P^*]$ must yield this outcome is clear. That any pair $[P, P]$ does likewise is due to the fact that a tariff has no distortionary effects within a period when goods are perfect complements; and if it does not vary across periods, then the spot price of the bundle will not do so either, thereby leaving the inter-temporal price ratio undisturbed at its undistorted value $1/(1 + r^*)$.

We are left with the policy programmes of a 'temporary' character, in the sense that $P(1) \neq P(2)$. Here, condition (7.8) does not hold, so that the decentralized equilibria will be inefficient. The case that concerns Calvo (1987) is $[P^*, P]$, which may be called an episode of (temporary) liberalization. Substituting for P in Eqns (7.12) and (7.13), we obtain

$$U'[X(1)]/U'[X(2)] = \beta(1 + r^*)P^*/P < \beta(1 + r^*). \qquad (7.14)$$

The absence of the tariff in period 1 makes consumption in the present more attractive, all else being equal. With an unchanged availability line, consumption, and hence also the trade deficit, in period 1 is indeed larger than its first-best counterpart; savings are smaller in the same amount. This outcome is depicted as point C_L in Fig. 7.1. Larger though the trade deficit is, in no way does it signify the emergence of a crisis of any kind; for the equilibrium respects the inter-temporal opportunities described by the availability line. In this story, unlike the real world, loans are never in default or 'rescheduled', nor does the economy ever experience a shortage of foreign exchange independently of the scarcity expressed by Eqn (7.6).

Summed up in this way, there is surely something missing in Calvo's (1987) account of 'the costs of temporary policy', to use his apt title. It is empty of any interesting dynamics, and for each policy programme, there is but a single equilibrium. The costs that arise from the introduction of an unnecessary distortion, real though they are, properly belong in Chapter 3's catalogue of static cases. The root of the problem lies in $A1'$; for in a full-blown crisis, the opportunity to borrow at *any* rate no longer exists. What is needed, therefore, is a reformulation of the model such that a crisis, and hence a forced reversal of a declared policy, is possible, thereby also opening the door to imperfect credibility.

Before taking up this task, however, we complete the taxonomic treatment of Eqn (7.9) by examining the case $[P, P^*]$, whereby liberalization is postponed to period 2. Instead of Eqn (7.14), we have

$$U'[X(1)]/U'[X(2)] = \beta(1 + r^*)P/P^* > \beta(1 + r^*). \qquad (7.15)$$

The allocation is still inefficient; but relative to the first-best, consumption and the trade deficit are now lower and savings higher.

To close this section, a brief remark on credibility is called for. Given the assumption that households know exactly what the government will actually do in the future, it is superfluous for the government to make any announcements about its future intentions. There is no room, then, for credibility, or the lack thereof, to play a role in the proceedings. One can still ask, however, whether any of the above policy programmes could be plagued by time-inconsistency if lump-sum transfers were not available. A government in need of revenue in the future would eye bond holdings at the beginning of period 2 as a target; for a tax thereon would be lump-sum in nature at that point. Under the alternative $[P, P^*]$, savings would be higher than any other in the event that households were indeed certain that the government would not renege, in effect, by slapping a tax on wealth. For this reason, an announcement of $[P, P^*]$ would be greeted with some scepticism.

7.2. Self-fulfilling Expectations and Crises

In the light of the results just derived above, we now deny the economy the opportunity to borrow in world capital markets. Instead, an initial stock of foreign exchange offers the only means of consuming more than what is produced in any period. While withdrawing the opportunities set out in A1′, we loosen the straightjacket imposed by A7′; for it turns out the effects of a reform on the level of output play a key role in determining whether multiple equilibria can arise in the framework used below, namely, the model in Section 3.6 suitably extended to two periods. Some remarks on this extension are in order. It is assumed that currencies are storable, but goods are not. Currencies do not, however, bear any interest. The foreign reserves are in the possession of the central bank; but although the public is not permitted to hold foreign currency, it may exchange domestic for foreign currency in order to finance current imports. A crisis arises if the reserves are drawn down to such a level that current transactions with the rest of the world are seriously hampered, and so force a change in policy. The crucial question is whether, given a particular level of reserves, a crisis will indeed occur if that is what the public expects, whereas no crisis will arise if the public expects the announced policy to be maintained.

Suppose, therefore, that the economy is initially in a stationary equilibrium of the sort described in Section 3.6. The government then announces a cut in t_2, leaving the exchange rate unchanged. We seek to establish the possible existence of two perfect-foresight equilibria. In the first, the public is persuaded that the cut will be sustained in the second period, with the result that the cumulative demands on the central bank's reserves are tolerable. In the second equilibrium, the public expects the cut to be fully reversed in the second period, with a resulting run on reserves in the first period that brings them down to crisis level, and so induces the reversal.

To put matters precisely, we desire to establish whether both of the price vectors

$$p_R \equiv [p_1(0), p_2(0) - \delta_2; p_1(0), p_2(0)]$$

and

$$p_S \equiv [p_1(0), p_2(0) - \delta_2; p_1(0), p_2(0) - \delta_2]$$

can sustain a perfect foresight equilibrium, where δ_2 is the reduction in the price of good 2 that is induced by the cut in t_2, and the subscripts R and S denote that the policy is subsequently reversed and sustained, respectively. Under the assumptions of Section 3.2, the decline in output in the first period will be identical in both cases. In the second period, however, the outcomes will differ. A reversal will restore the *status quo ante*, namely, $y[p(0)]$, where $p(0)$ denotes the price vector that rules in the initial, stationary equilibrium, whereas a sustained reform will bring about $y[p_1(0), p_2(0) - \delta_2]$, as depicted by point A″ in Fig. 3.5. If, as one would hope, a sustained reform yields an increase in GDP at world prices in the second period, relative to the *status quo ante*, then such a success will be accompanied by a positive income effect on consumption in the first period, and so intensify the drawing down of foreign reserves. Weighing on the other side of the scales is the fact that, under a reversal of policy, consumption in the first period is relatively cheap; so that there is a substitution effect at work that is absent when the reform is sustained. These two effects tug in opposite directions, and their net outcome plays a key role in determining whether both p_R and p_S can support a perfect-foresight equilibrium.[2]

Recalling the form of the household's preferences in Section 3.6, namely, Eqn (3.25), the felicity function in Eqn (7.2) in Section 7.1 may be extended to

$$V[X(\tau), M(\tau)] = U[X(\tau)] + \phi[M(\tau)/P(\tau)], \quad \tau = 1, 2 \tag{7.16}$$

---

[2] We have already ruled out a third effect, namely, substitution between goods within a period, through the specialization of preferences in the form of Eqn (7.1).

and hence Eqn (7.5) becomes

$$W = V[X(1), M(1)] + \beta V[X(2), M(2)]. \tag{7.5'}$$

The household's budget constraints are

$$P(\tau) \cdot X(\tau) + M(\tau) = Y^d(\tau) + M(\tau - 1), \quad \tau = 1, 2, \tag{7.17}$$

where $[p(\tau), Y^d(\tau), M(0)]$ are parametrically given and known to all and sundry. We impose the condition $M(2) = M(0)$ to bring about stationarity. If the policy is fully reversed in the second period, imposing this condition will be quite valid; for we have ruled out the possibility of further adjustments in the stock of real balances in subsequent periods. If the cut is sustained, however, this restriction will not, in general, be correct. For, taken by itself, the fall in P will increase the value of real balances, and the changes in real income and consumption induced by a successful reform will presumably increase the demand for real balances. Since $\phi(\cdot)$ is strictly concave, these two effects will pull in opposite directions, with an unclear net outcome. We cut this Gordian knot by assuming that they are exactly offsetting.

The household's problem is to choose X and $M(1)$ so as to

$$\text{maximize } W \quad \text{subject to (7.17).} \tag{7.18}$$

The associated Lagrangian is

$$\Psi = W + \sum_{\tau=1}^{2} \lambda(\tau)[Y^d(\tau) + M(\tau - 1) - P(\tau)X(\tau) - M(\tau)]. \tag{7.19}$$

The first-order conditions with respect to the household's choice variables are[3]

$$\partial \Psi / \partial X(1) = U'(1) - \lambda(1)P(1) = 0, \tag{7.20}$$

$$\partial \Psi / \partial X(2) = \beta U'(2) - \lambda(2)P(2) = 0, \tag{7.21}$$

$$\partial \Psi / \partial M(1) = \phi'(1)/P(1) - \lambda(1) + \lambda(2) = 0. \tag{7.22}$$

Substituting for $\lambda(\tau)$, we obtain

$$\phi'(1) - U'(1) + \beta U'(2) \cdot [P(1)/P(2)] = 0. \tag{7.23}$$

---

[3] Henceforth, abusing notation somewhat, the arguments of functions are suppressed, leaving only the time index, τ, whenever no ambiguity would arise.

This implicitly describes the income-expansion surface corresponding to P in the space of $X(1), X(2)$, and $M(1)$, and may be written as

$$\psi[X, M(1); P] = 0, \tag{7.24}$$

a condition that must be satisfied in any equilibrium. Inspection of Eqn (7.23) reveals that: (i) for any given $M(1)$, the bundles $X(1)$ and $X(2)$ move in the same direction; (ii) for any given $X(2), X(1)$ and $M(1)$ move in the same direction; and (iii) for any given $X(1), X(2)$ and $M(1)$ move in opposite directions.

The next step is to derive the comparative static results for the vectors p_R and p_S, a task which will be accomplished using the (artificial) planner's problem:

$$\underset{X, M(1)}{\text{maximize } W} \tag{7.25}$$

subject to Eqn (7.24) and the conditions governing the availability and uses of foreign exchange in the economy as a whole:

$$P^* X(1) + M(1) = Y^*(1) + M(0) \tag{7.26}$$

and

$$P^* X(2) - M(1) = Y^*(2) + M(0), \tag{7.27}$$

where the exchange rate has been normalized to unity and $M(0) = M(2)$. The set of $[X, M(1)]$ satisfying Eqns (7.26) and (7.27) is a line in the space of $X(1), X(2)$ and $M(1)$, whose directional vector is such that: (i) for any given $M(1), X(1)$ and $X(2)$ move in opposite directions; (ii) for any given $X(2), X(1)$ and $M(1)$ move in opposite directions; and (iii) for any given $X(1), X(2)$ and $M(1)$ move in the same direction. It follows that the said line intersects the surface $\psi(\cdot; P) = 0$ just once, that is, the feasible set in problem (7.25) is a singleton. Hence, we need to consider only the constraints (7.24), (7.26), and (7.27) when analysing the effects of perturbations to the price vector $[p(0); p(0)]$.

We begin with the case of a reform whose failure is confidently anticipated, that is, households expect p_R, so that $P(2) = P(0)$. Differentiating Eqns (7.23), (7.26), and (7.27) totally and rearranging, we obtain

$$\begin{bmatrix} P^* & 0 & 1 \\ 0 & P^* & -1 \\ -U''(1) & \beta U''(2) P(1)/P(2) & \phi''(1)/P(1) \end{bmatrix} \begin{bmatrix} dX(1) \\ dX(2) \\ dM(1) \end{bmatrix} = \begin{bmatrix} [dY^*(1)]_R \\ [dY^*(2)]_R \\ \xi_R dP(1) \end{bmatrix},$$
$$\tag{7.28}$$

where

$$\xi_R \equiv \left[\frac{\phi''(1)}{P(1)} \cdot \frac{M(1)}{P(1)} - \beta \frac{U'(2)}{P(2)} \right] < 0, \tag{7.29}$$

and $[dY^*(\tau)]_R$ is the change in GDP at world prices in period τ induced by a decrease in the price of the composite good in period 1 that is then reversed in period 2. It is reasonable to interpret period 1 as what was called the short run in Chapter 3, in which case $[dY^*(1)]_R < 0$, where $Y^*(1) = Y^*(0)$ in the absence of any reform in period 1. Since the reversal of policy in period 2 restores the *status quo ante*, we have $Y^*(2) = Y^*(0)$, so that $[dY^*(2)]_R = 0$. Using Cramer's rule, the response of consumption in period 1 to such a cut in $P(1)$ is

$$-\left. \frac{dX(1)}{dP(1)} \right|_R = \frac{-1}{|A_R|} \left[\left(\phi''(1) \frac{P^*}{P(1)} + \beta U''(2) \frac{P(1)}{P(2)} \right) \left(\frac{dY^*(1)}{dP(1)} \right)_R - P^* \xi_R \right],$$

$$\tag{7.30}$$

where $|A_R|(<0)$ is the determinant of the matrix on the left-hand side (LHS) of Eqn (7.28). Whether consumption in period 1 rises or falls thus depends on whether the substitution effect represented by $P^* \xi_R$ outweighs the (adverse) income effect associated with $[dY^*(1)]_R < 0$,[4] relative to a continuation of the stationary equilibrium.

Given the assumption that the central bank is willing to exchange foreign for domestic currency as long as reserves last, it follows that the latter will fall in period 1 if the public's demand for money weakens. To be exact, Cramer's rule yields

$$-\left. \frac{dM(1)}{dP(1)} \right|_R = \frac{-P^*}{|A_R|} [U''(1) \cdot [dY^*(1)/dP(1)]_R + P^* \xi_R] < 0; \tag{7.31}$$

so that reserves always fall, despite the ambiguity surrounding the behaviour of consumption in period 1. The intuition here is that households will attempt to smooth consumption in the face of the temporary adverse shock to income, which they accomplish by drawing down their money balances. This effect is reinforced by the temporary cheapening of consumption in period 1, as represented by the term $P^* \xi_R$. The more ambitious the reform, as measured by the size of the cut in the tariff, the larger will be the reduction in $M(1)$, and hence the greater the strain on the central bank's foreign

---

[4] Since the reform involves a fall in $Y^*(1)$ that is induced by a fall in $P(1)$, $[dY^*(1)/dP(1)]_R$ is to be interpreted as a left-hand derivative, whose value is positive in this case. The sign of the right-hand derivative is unclear.

reserves. If the latter are insufficient to meet demand, the reform must be reversed.[5]

Given that such a 'bad' equilibrium exists, a second, 'good' equilibrium, in which the reform is maintained into the second period, can exist only if it entails a smaller demand for foreign currency in the first period than does the 'bad' one: equivalently, it must entail a smaller reduction in money balances. We begin by noting that when the price vector $\boldsymbol{p}_S$ rules, $P(1) = P(2)$, so that, from Eqn (7.23),

$$\xi_S \equiv \frac{\phi''(1)}{P(1)} \cdot \frac{M(1)}{P(1)}. \tag{7.32}$$

Although $[dY^*(1)]_R = [dY^*(1)]_S$, a permanent reform may induce a rise or a fall in the value of GDP at world prices relative to its initial level $Y^*(0)$, that is, $[dY^*(2)]_S$ may take either sign. Proceeding as before, we have

$$-\frac{dX(1)}{dP(1)}\bigg|_S = \frac{-1}{|A_S|} \left[\left(\phi''(1)\frac{P^*}{P(1)} + \beta U''(2) \right) \left(\frac{dY^*(1)}{dP(1)} \right)_S \right.$$
$$\left. + \beta U''(2) \left(\frac{dY^*(2)}{dP(1)} \right)_S - P^*\xi_S \right]. \tag{7.33}$$

Comparing the terms in braces on the RHS of Eqns (7.30) and (7.33), we see that the latter include a weaker substitution effect when the reform lasts, ξ_S replacing ξ_R, and the income effect associated with any difference between the value of GDP at world prices at the outset and in the second period. If the reform is indeed successful in raising GDP so measured, then this latter effect will pull in the direction of increasing consumption in period 1, and with it the public's demand for foreign exchange. At this stage, therefore, the existence of a second, 'good' equilibrium is still unsettled. Using Cramer's rule once more, we obtain

$$-\frac{dM(1)}{dP(1)}\bigg|_S = \frac{-P^*}{|A_S|}[U''(1)[dY^*(1)/dP(1)]_S$$
$$+ P^*\xi_S - \beta U''(2)[dY^*(2)/dP(1)]_S], \tag{7.34}$$

from which it is seen that all of the terms in brackets on the RHS will be negative, and hence that reserves will fall, if the reform brings about a long-term increase in GDP at world prices.

---

[5] The alternatives are to devalue the currency or impose exchange controls, neither of which will be considered here.

Since the demand for money falls in period 1 for all values of $P(1)$ in the interval $[P^*, P(0)]$ under the expectation that the reform will be reversed, a necessary condition for a 'good' equilibrium to exist for all reforms such that $P(1) \geq P'(\geq P^*)$ is

$$\frac{dM(1)}{dP(1)}\bigg|_R > \frac{dM(1)}{dP(1)}\bigg|_S \quad \forall P(1) \in [P', P(0)]. \tag{7.35}$$

Reaching a firm conclusion about whether condition (7.35) is fulfilled is complicated by the fact that, in general, the arguments of all the functions that are littered about in Eqns (7.31) and (7.34) take different values, even when the expressions are the same. The exception arises when one considers reforms sufficiently small as to render such differences negligible, with $P(1) \cong P(2) \cong P(0)$ in particular. In that case, some manipulation reveals that (7.35) holds if and only if

$$\frac{P^*}{P(2)} \cdot \frac{U'(1)}{U'(2)} \cdot X(2) - \eta(2) \cdot \frac{dY^*(2)}{dP(1)}\bigg|_S > 0, \tag{7.36}$$

where $\eta(2) \equiv X(2) \cdot U''(2)/U'(2)$ is the elasticity of the marginal utility of consumption of the composite good in period 2. By the strict concavity of $U(\cdot)$, $\eta(2) < 0$, so that (7.36) will always hold if the value of GDP at world prices in period 2 is no larger than its value when the reform is launched. If, on the other hand, $Y^*(2) > Y^*(0)$, then (7.36) may not hold.

This is a double-edged result for reformers. For under any reasonable definition, a successful reform of this sort should result in a long-term increase in GDP at world prices, which makes the existence of a second, 'good' self-fulfilling expectations equilibrium less likely, given the same initial level of reserves. The fate of a successful reform in this sense must therefore be taken up in more detail. From Eqn (7.3), we have $dP(1) = b dp_2$. Multiplying through by $bp_2/Y^*(2)$, condition (7.36) may be written as

$$\left(\frac{bp_2}{p_1 + bp_2}\right) \cdot \left(\frac{P^* X(2)}{Y^*(2)}\right) \cdot \frac{U'(1)_R}{U'(2)_S} - \eta(2)\varepsilon(2) > 0, \tag{7.37}$$

where $\varepsilon(2)$ is the long-run elasticity of GDP valued at world prices with respect to p_2. Observe also that $U'(1)_R$ refers to period 1 in the case where the reform is temporary, and $U'(2)_S$ to period 2 in that where it is sustained. Given the temporary surge in consumption in the former, it is plausible that the two derivatives do not differ markedly, even if the reform results in an increase in GDP at world prices. If, as is also plausible, the changes in the stock of high powered money are small relative to GDP, then $P^*X(2)$ will be approximately equal to $Y^*(2)$. Condition (7.37) then simplifies to

$$[bp_2/(p_1 + bp_2)] - \eta(2)\varepsilon(2) > 0.$$

Since $[bp_2/(p_1 + bp_2)]$ is the share of expenditures on good 2 in total expenditure, we have arrived at an interpretable, necessary condition for the existence of a second, 'good' equilibrium in the case where the reform is sufficiently small. What is clear is that, in combination, the desire for a smooth path of consumption, as measured by $|\eta(2)|$, and the long-run responsiveness of GDP at world prices to cuts in the protective tariff, namely, $|\varepsilon(2)|$, must not be too large if (7.35) is to hold. The intuition here is that the latter represents the effects of the reform on income in the future, and the former the extent to which households wish to enjoy such gains in the present.

We complete the argument as follows. For each and every reform in the interval $[P', P(0)]$, Eqn (7.31) implies that there is a corresponding initial level of reserves of foreign exchange, F say, such that for all smaller initial levels thereof, the expectation that the government will be forced to reverse course in period 2 because of a shortage of reserves at the outset will bring about just such a crisis: in short, a case of self-fulfilling expectations. Now consider the interesting case, in which the reform promises to be a success, in that it will eventually bring about an increase in the value of GDP at world prices, and suppose that it is not too radical, so that condition (7.37) may be employed. If preferences and the production structure are such that (7.37) is satisfied, then for all initial reserves smaller than, but sufficiently close to, F there also exists a second equilibrium, in which the reserves will suffice to maintain the reform into the future. Thus, we have established conditions under which a (small) liberalizing reform of protective tariffs in period 1 may be sustainable if that is what the public expects, but not so if it is persuaded that the government will reverse course under the pressure of a foreign exchange crisis.

7.3. The Introduction of a VAT

A number of countries have introduced a VAT in one form or another during the past two decades, and its adoption is under active consideration elsewhere. A central argument in its favour is that whenever efficiency is the main consideration in raising revenues, broadly based taxation is generally desirable, the basic intuition being that in the absence of any other distortions, the deadweight loss associated with a tax on a single commodity is increasing and approximately quadratic in the tax rate (Section 4.4). What concerns us here, however, is the possibility that the introduction or extension of a VAT may bring about both a shift in relative prices and an unintended, if temporary, reduction in output. If these are indeed among the consequences, then the sort of inferior, self-fulfilling expectations equilibria just discussed at length in Section 7.2 can also arise in connection with such a tax reform.

Consider, therefore, the common situation in which taxes on foreign trade are an important source of revenue and there is an escalated structure of protection. Since a tariff is both a tax on consumers and a subsidy to domestic producers, the rate needed to raise a given amount of revenue is higher than in the case where the tax base is the total consumption of the said items. The introduction of a VAT with a single rate chosen to yield an unchanged level of net revenue would, therefore, have the effect of making highly protected items relatively cheaper. If the labour market exhibits the distortions described in earlier chapters and employed in Section 7.2, then a temporary loss of output is also on the cards, so that the two stories begin to look quite similar. The final twist lies in the fact that agriculture's contribution to the Treasury, if any, usually takes the form of the taxation of exports. It is often proposed that the latter taxes be abolished, and since it is quite impossible to levy a VAT on legions of peasant producers, the only offset would be the replacement of subsidies on agricultural inputs by the VAT thereon, peasants being 'outside' the system. The rate required to produce the same revenue as before the reform would, therefore, be correspondingly higher.

The entire package would involve the abolition of taxes on trade in favour of a VAT to be levied on enterprises above a certain size and on importers of both competing goods and those goods that are not domestically produced at all. The net effect would be to reduce the relative prices of producer goods presently subject to protective tariffs, and to increase the relative consumer prices of most goods that would not be subject to VAT, the notable exceptions being agro-chemicals and fuel and power.[6]

In order to establish whether two perfect-foresight equilibria exist, we proceed using the framework of Section 7.2. In keeping with the present emphasis on the fiscal aspects of the problem, we do away with the convenient assumption that the government rebates any net revenues to households in the form of lump-sum transfers and introduce public

---

[6] As such, the package looks like some proposals that have been made for India.

expenditures on goods and services. Anticipating the notation of later chapters, these expenditures arise from the plan to purchase the bundle $-z$.

Before the reform is undertaken, the economy is assumed to be in the full employment equilibrium where producers and consumers face the same price vector

$$p(0) = q(0) = [(1 - t_1)p_1^*, (1 + t_2)p_2^*], \tag{7.38}$$

and the government raises revenue in the amount

$$R(0) = (t_1 p_1^*, -t_2 p_2^*)(y(0) - x(0)), \tag{7.39}$$

where there are *ad valorem* taxes on the export and import goods of t_1 and t_2, respectively. This revenue just suffices to finance the public consumption vector $-z(0)$:

$$R(0) = -p^* z(0), \tag{7.40}$$

where it should be noted that, once its internal transactions are netted out, the public sector effectively trades at world prices, and that the representative household's disposable income is equal to the value of its total consumption, namely, $q(0)x(0)$.

Under a VAT of the sort described above, producers would face world prices for outputs, whereas consumers would pay, in effect, an *ad valorem* consumption tax on the importable at the rate t_v:

$$p = p^* \tag{7.41}$$

and

$$q = [p_1^*, (1 + t_v)p_2^*]. \tag{7.42}$$

The reform is said to be revenue-neutral if t_v satisfies

$$t_v p_2^* x_2(q) = -p^* z(0) = R, \tag{7.43}$$

where $x_2(q)$ is the demand for good 2 at full employment when the producer price vector is p^*, that is, over the longer run and when all adjustments are complete. As argued above, since the tax base is likely to be broader under the (selective) VAT, it is plausible to assume that the imported good becomes (relatively) cheaper, that is,

$$1 + t_v < (1 + t_2)/(1 - t_1). \tag{7.44}$$

The next step is to consider the following pairs of two-period price vectors:

$$p_R \equiv [p^*; p(0)], \qquad q_R \equiv [q; q(0)]$$

and

$$p_S \equiv [p^*; p^*], \qquad q_S \equiv [q; q],$$

where the subscripts R and S denote that the reform is reversed and sustained, respectively. If condition (7.44) holds, it is clear that we have the same structure as in Section 7.2. If both pairs of price vectors can sustain an equilibrium, the output vector in the period immediately following the reform (period 1) will be identical in both cases. Under the assumptions of Section 7.2, the output of the importable will contract, while that of the exportable will be unaffected, so that the value of GDP valued at world prices will also fall.

If the government holds fast to its expenditure plan through thick and thin, despite the fact that actual revenue in period 1 is likely to fall short of $R(0)$ in both equilibria, then the qualitative analysis of Section 7.2 goes through unaltered. In summary, if the reform promises considerable gains in efficiency at full employment, in the sense that GDP at world prices rises substantially over the longer run, and if the public's preference for a smooth path of consumption is sufficiently strong, then consumption in period 1 under the price vector $[p_S, q_S]$ will be larger than that under the price vector $[p_R, q_R]$, despite the fact that consumption in period 1 is relatively cheaper under the latter. Under these conditions, therefore, the only equilibrium will the one in which there is a reversal of policy if the initial level of reserves is sufficiently small. Only if the said income effect and the desire for smooth consumption combined are sufficiently modest will there be two self-fulfilling equilibria.

The alternative is for the government to reduce its (implicit) claims on foreign reserves in period 1 by cutting current expenditures by at least the shortfall in current revenues relative to $R(0)$. Such a move clearly improves the chances that $[p_S, q_S]$ can support an equilibrium, and it may extinguish all chances that the economy will suffer a failed reform as a result of pessimistic self-fulfilling expectations. Whether sufficiently rapid and substantial changes in public expenditures are administratively and, even more to the point, politically possible is another question altogether.

7.4. Countermeasures

The temporary contraction of output in both of the preceding stories evidently makes the reform painful. It arises because of the assumption that wages are rigid downwards in the short run, an assumption that seems justifiable in the light of the evidence presented in Chapter 3. It is not an uncontroversial claim, however: dyed-in-the-wool 'new classical' scholars, in particular, would surely look it askance, and others might draw attention to the flexibility of labour markets in peasant agriculture, if that is the export sector. The first step, therefore, is to establish whether this assumption is necessary for the existence of two self-fulfilling expectations equilibria. Suppose, instead, that GDP at world prices were wholly insensitive to such reforms, even in the short run. Recalling Eqns (7.31) and (7.34), we see that the substitution effect, as represented by the terms $P^*\xi_R$ and $P^*\xi_S$, would remain, and since the former is absolutely larger than the latter, the argument would go through as before, with condition (7.36) holding always under this revised assumption.

Having secured our flanks against this particular criticism, we continue with the point that, for any given initial level of reserves, a contraction of output in the short run reduces the chances that a reform can be sustained over the longer haul. If the rigidity of nominal wages is the source of the problem, then a preceding or accompanying devaluation is perhaps the only means whereby the product-wage in the protected sector can be cut, as discussed in Section 3.6. In the present setting, a devaluation has the additional effect of reducing the public's real balances at a stroke,[7] and hence also the wherewithal to engage in the consumption-smoothing that contributes to the run on foreign reserves in the short run. For these reasons, a sufficiently large and well-timed devaluation almost surely belongs in any package of measures to liberalize trade.

The other essential element, obviously enough, is that reserves be sufficiently large at the outset. To launch a reform under the pressure of events, when reserves may already have fallen to low levels, is to invite failure. For this very reason, governments often seek balance-of-payments support from the IMF in conjunction with reforms of economic policy. Indeed, when private credit in world capital markets is no longer available, they

---

[7] When the pound was devalued in November 1967—an important event in the days of fixed exchange rates—the then Prime Minister, Harold Wilson, concluded his televised address to the British people with the memorable phrase, 'The pound in your pocket has not been devalued'. The public knew better.

have no choice in the matter, the price of getting the IMF's money being a ladle-full of its medicine.

We close with a remark on expectations and rigidity in the labour market. That workers in the protected sectors of the economy usually earn wages that carry a regulated premium is widely accepted as fact. If hiring practices therein are such that those fired in bad times are first in the queue to receive an offer of a job when things improve, or if physical presence plays an important role in determining who receives an offer (see Section 9.5.2), then those who are laid off following a reform will take good care to remain on hand if there are very good chances that the reform will not endure for long, and hence that their old jobs will soon reappear. Past failures will strengthen such expectations, and hence workers' reluctance to seek out jobs in the unprotected sectors of the economy, particularly if this means moving back to the home village, for example. In these circumstances, the reforms considered here will exert little or no downward pressure on the wage rate in the latter sectors in the short run, so that the assumption that wages are everywhere rigid downwards in the short run, while involving a certain abuse of language, has firmer logical foundations.

7.5. Investment

Over the longer run, the response of private investment to economic reforms surely has much to do with their ultimate success—provided, of course, that any new investments so induced are socially profitable. This consideration appears only very indirectly in Sections 7.2–7.4, in the form of changes in the value of GDP at world prices. An important reason for addressing investment in its own right is that the main result in the above setting depends on the assumptions that the only foreign asset always remains in the hands of the central bank and that the initial reserves cannot be augmented by inflows from abroad. The fact that the authorities in many countries have great difficulty preventing capital flight leads one to ask whether multiple self-fulfilling equilibria can arise when capital is mobile.

In order to answer this question, we give a brief account of Rodrik (1991). A risk-neutral individual possesses one unit of capital, which he can invest in foreign assets yielding a return of r^* or in domestic activities yielding r_i, where $i = 0$ and $i = 1$ denote, respectively, the situation before the reform is undertaken and afterwards. At the outset, he is invested only in the foreign asset. Placing savings initially and changing the form of investment subsequently both involve costs. In equilibrium, $r_0 \leq r^*$, where the (weak) inequality stems from the existence of hysteresis arising from these switching costs. It is assumed that a sensible reform will lead to an improvement in profitability: $r_1 > r_0$. Let all individuals share the same subjective probability π that a reform, once introduced, will be reversed in any period and, for simplicity, let a reversal be permanent.

The present value of his wealth when held indefinitely in the foreign asset is

$$V_0 = r^*/\rho, \tag{7.45}$$

where ρ is his subjective discount rate. If the reform leaves him unmoved, its reversal will not change his mind either. In order to obtain the corresponding (expected) present value of the alternative placement at home when made immediately after the reform, denote its value, when maximized, by V_1. Should the reform be reversed, the change in r, from r_1 back to r_0, and the presence of switching costs will reduce the expected present value of the domestic placement from that point onwards, to V_{1R}, say. Hence,

$$V_1 = [r_1 - \pi(V_1 - V_{1R})]/\rho,$$

or

$$V_1 = (r_1 + \pi V_{1R})/(\rho + \pi). \tag{7.46}$$

Let the once-and-for-all costs of switching back to the foreign placement be c_0, so that such a switch will occur if and only if $r_0 < r^* - \rho c_0$. It follows that

$$V_{1R} = \begin{cases} r_0/\rho & \text{if } r_0 \geq r^* - \rho c_0, \\ (r^*/\rho) - c_0 & \text{otherwise.} \end{cases} \tag{7.47}$$

The next step is to establish necessary and sufficient conditions for the individual to bring his capital back home. This is simply

$$V_1 \geq V_0 + c_1, \tag{7.48}$$

where c_1 denotes the associated switching costs. Substituting from Eqns (7.45)–(7.47), (7.48) may be rewritten as

$$r_1 \geq \begin{cases} r^* + (r^* - r_0)(\pi/\rho) + (\pi + \rho)c_1 & \text{if } r_0 \geq r^* - \rho c_0, \\ r^* + \pi c_0 + (\pi + \rho)c_1 & \text{otherwise.} \end{cases} \tag{7.49}$$

Since $r_0 \leq r^*$, it is clear that a necessary condition for (7.49) to hold is that the rate of return on the domestic investment in the presence of the reform exceed r^*. The upper branch corresponds to the case where the flow-equivalent of the costs of 'flight' exceeds the difference between the rates of return on foreign and domestic investments before the reform, so that repatriated capital stays put in the event of a reversal. In this case, repatriation will occur if and only if the weighted average of r_0 and r_1, where the respective weights are ρ and π, exceeds r^* by the flow-equivalent of the costs of repatriation. In the converse case, a reversal will induce 'flight', so that repatriation will occur following the reform if and only if r_1 exceeds r^* by the sum of the expected costs of the combined switch and the flow-equivalent of the costs of repatriation, as specified in the lower branch. In both cases, it is clear that for (7.49) to hold, the improvement in profitability promised by a reform must increase with the probability of a reversal.

If all individuals were identical, then for any given vector of rates of return, switching costs, the discount factor, and the probability of reversal, the corresponding reform would either leave all capital where it is abroad, or induce its wholesale return. Suppose, therefore, that individuals vary in some way, with respect to c_1 say, with a continuous distribution function F on the support $[0, \bar{c}_1]$. Define

$$\hat{c}_1 \equiv [r_1 - r^* - \pi c_0]/(\pi + \rho) \qquad (7.50)$$

and suppose that $c_0 < (r^* - r_0)/\rho$, so that the lower branch is relevant. Observe from the upper branch that $c_0 < (r^* - r_0)/\rho$ implies that no individual whose c_0 is at least as large as $(r^* - r_0)/\rho$ will repatriate his capital. Hence, if there are N individuals, the total amount repatriated will be

$$K = N \int_0^{\hat{c}_1} dF. \qquad (7.51)$$

We turn to the relationship between K and π which is implicitly defined by Eqn (7.51). Now,

$$\partial K/\partial \pi = Nf(\hat{c}_1) \cdot (\partial \hat{c}_1/\partial \pi), \qquad (7.52)$$

where $f(c_1)$ is the density function corresponding to F. In general, one would expect r_1 to be decreasing in K, so that substituting

$$\frac{\partial \hat{c}_1}{\partial \pi} = (\pi + \rho)^{-1} \left[\left(\frac{\partial r_1}{\partial K} \cdot \frac{\partial K}{\partial \pi} - c_0 \right) - \hat{c}_1 \right]$$

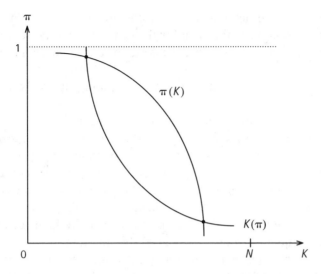

Figure 7.2. Multiple equilibria when capital is mobile

into Eqn (7.52) yields

$$\frac{\partial K}{\partial \pi} = -\frac{N[(c_0 + \hat{c}_1) \cdot f(\hat{c}_1)]}{[(\pi + \rho) - Nf(\hat{c}_1)(\partial r_1/\partial K)]} < 0, \tag{7.53}$$

as expected. Equation (7.53) implicitly defines the function $K = K(\pi)$.

The final step is to allow for the possibility that the magnitude of K also affects beliefs about the likelihood of a reversal of policy. Rodrik (1991) adduces various arguments that π is decreasing in K. If the equations $K = K(\pi)$ and $\pi = \pi(K)$ have more than one solution satisfying $K \in [0, N]$ and $\pi \in [0, 1]$, then the system will possess multiple equilibria. A case in which there is one 'good' and one 'bad' equilibrium is depicted in Fig. 7.2.

7.6. Summary

That a reversal of policy can be damaging when there is perfect foresight is clear enough from Section 7.1. In the absence of substitution among goods within a period, an early reform whose subsequent reversal causes the structure of inter-temporal prices at home to deviate from that ruling abroad for some, but not all, periods will result in losses when no other distortions are present. A delayed reform, on the other hand, can run into problems of 'time-inconsistency'. For if, in anticipation, agents were to save more in a form that could be subjected to a capital levy later on, the government would view this additional wealth as a natural source of revenue at the time in question. In the absence of a credible commitment not to impose such a tax, however, the promised reform would have limited, if any, effects on behaviour in the period leading up to the date of its announced implementation.

Beliefs about the future, then, influence actions in the present, and in so doing can be self-fulfilling. This is almost a truism, and yet it can undermine attempts to sustain reforms that, viewed statically, are moves in the right direction. The root of the problem is the possible existence of two, self-fulfilling expectations equilibria. In one, the public is quite convinced that the reform will be sustained and behaves accordingly, thereby ensuring that the conditions needed to sustain it actually hold. In the other, the public is equally strongly convinced that the reform will be reversed, makes its plans accordingly, and thereby precipitates the very conditions that make a reversal unavoidable. This possibility has been explored in three variants.

In the first, things have reached a pass where further foreign borrowing is out of the question and the only source of foreign currency other than export earnings is the initial reserves in the hands of the central bank. Private agents hold initial balances of domestic currency, which they can exchange for dollars in order to purchase imports. The reform involves a cut in a protective tariff, which, if later reversed, will make imports, and hence consumption, cheaper in the present relative to the future. This substitution effect will be reinforced by a desire to smooth consumption over time should real incomes rise while the reform is in force. If the movement out of domestic money is large enough in relation to the initial level of the central bank's reserves, the policy will become unsustainable, thereby validating the expectation that the tariff will be reimposed. The alternative is that the government is expected to stay the course, in which case, the substitution effect will not be at work and the reserves might suffice to bear out the expectation. The second variant is similar, the reform being the replacement of taxes on international trade by a VAT of incomplete coverage that is designed to raise the same amount of revenue. The results obtained lead to the conclusion that reforms should not be attempted as a last resort, when foreign exchange reserves and borrowing opportunities have been nigh on exhausted, but rather when such financing is ample. An accompanying devaluation, temporarily painful though it might be, will reinforce the position by reducing the value of real balances at a stroke.

The final variant deals with the effects of uncertainty about whether policy will be permanent on private investment when agents can invest either at home or abroad, albeit with switching costs in both directions. When the capital is already abroad, one goal of a package of reforms is to encourage its repatriation by raising the net returns to domestic investment. Under certain conditions, however, a reversal of policy will induce capital flight anew, should repatriation have occurred in response to the original reforms. In all this, private investors' beliefs about the probability of a reversal will weigh heavily on their choice of placement. If, at the same time, these beliefs also depend on the volume of capital that is repatriated, then multiple equilibria are possible.

Recommended Reading

Stern (1994) provides a useful survey of a wide range of dynamic issues in the theory of taxation. An extensive analysis of self-fulfilling crises in the context of trade liberalization is to be found in Buffie (2001). For a discussion of the influence of uncertainty about future policy on the behaviour of private investment, see Rodrik (1991).

Exercises

1. Consider the following special case of the model of section 7.5. Let c_1 be uniformly distributed on the interval $[0, \bar{c}_1]$, and let $r_1 = (2 - K/N)r^*$. Derive the function $K(\pi)$ and analyze its properties. Let beliefs about the likelihood of a reversal of policy take the simple form $\pi = 1 - aK/N, a \geq 1$. Establish necessary and sufficient conditions for there to exist exactly one or two self-fulfilling expectations equilibria, or none at all. Are all three possibilities plausible ones, and which strikes you as the most plausible, and why?

Repeat the analysis when c_0, not c_1, is the source of heterogeneity, whereby you may assume that $\rho \bar{c}_0 < r^* - r_0$. Compare the two cases critically.

8. An Introduction to Social Cost–Benefit Analysis

Planning of the all-encompassing sort that found expression in the formulation—albeit to a far lesser extent in the execution—of five-year plans has fallen into disfavour. It remains the case, however, that governments continue to spend a very substantial fraction of GNP, and it can hardly be otherwise in the future if they are to discharge their functions. Nor is it any less vital than before that public funds be well spent, in the sense of advancing economic and social well-being efficiently. As Little and Mirrlees (1974: 3) put it succinctly in planning's heyday, 'Projects are the building blocks [...]. The plan cannot be good if its constituent parts are faulty'. That applies with undiminished force to any analysis of public expenditure, regardless of whether there is a 'Plan'. What is usually called project appraisal or, more broadly, social cost–benefit analysis ought, therefore, to play a central role in the formulation of economic policy.

The questions that arise are practical and immediate. Should money be spent on extending the road or rail network, or on improvements to, and the maintenance of, what already exists? Is it better to build a multipurpose dam or a thermal power plant, where the latter might be accompanied by a programme of subsidized credit in order to encourage farmers to invest in tube wells? Or should more be spent instead on primary schools and health clinics? Such questions provide bones of sharp contention in the political arena; but it is essential that economists be able to provide good and persuasive answers to them. This holds, moreover, even if all the talk of allowing private firms to finance, build, and operate projects in sectors that have been almost exclusively reserved for the public sector, such as infrastructure and utilities, actually comes to something. For whether to let a private firm undertake a particular project is itself a question of the first importance, the answer to which will depend, in part, on the terms of the contract under which the project will be operated. Alternative contractual arrangements between the government and the firm are also available, and there is no reason to suppose a priori that there is nothing to choose between them where the general good is concerned.

The basic principle is readily stated, but a tall order to implement in practice: a project should be undertaken if, and only if, doing so will result in an improvement in social welfare, relative to the next best use of the same resources. In this chapter, we proceed intuitively and heuristically, with the aim of giving the reader a grasp of what is involved, while deferring a more rigorous and formal treatment to the chapters that follow.

8.1. The Private Project

It turns out to be enlightening to begin by asking how a (rational) businessman should set about evaluating a project. First, he needs a design, or 'blueprint', for the factory, process, or method. If properly specified, this will involve a minutely detailed description of what is to be done, and how and when it is to be done.[1] Uncertainty, in the form of possible deviations from the 'blueprint', now intrudes. What are the chances that the plant will work as designed? What other outcomes are possible, and what are their chances of occurrence?

Second, he must assess the markets for his outputs and inputs. What can be charged for the product? What will be the cost of labour and raw materials? What taxes or subsidies are payable, and are there regulations that will affect the costs of operation? Since the plant or equipment will normally have a physical lifetime exceeding a year, these questions concern not only current prices, but also those ruling in the future. The future being what it is, prices are not known with certainty; rather, like the chances that the plant will function in a particular way, they are conjectures in the businessman's mind, though they may be based, in part, on past experience and market forecasts.

Third, the businessman needs a decision rule, which will separate desirable from undesirable projects. The elementary textbooks tell us that the firm will (or should) maximize profits. Quite so, but long-lived projects present us with a difficulty: heavy costs are typically incurred early on, when the project is under construction, and net returns appear later, when the plant is complete and workers and management have learned how to make it work fairly well. To put it more formally, outwardly identical inputs and outputs appearing at different dates are really different goods, so that some way must be found to render them commensurate.

It is now widely accepted that, ignoring risk, the right way to render alternative streams of revenues and outlays comparable is to calculate their respective net present values (NPV). This involves valuing future outcomes

---

[1] There may, of course, be a variety of designs. If they are readily at hand, each must be evaluated. If not, the businessman must decide what resources should be devoted to discovering them, which is itself a project.

at their equivalents in the present. What exactly does this mean? Suppose, for example, the firm can borrow or lend as much as it pleases at 10 per cent annually. Then, for example, the sum of $110 when received or paid next year has exactly the same value to the firm as $100 received or paid today. If the firm obtains a dollar of revenue or incurs a dollar in expenses one year hence, the present value thereof is, therefore, (1/1.1) dollars, in the sense that the firm is prepared to pay at most (1/1.1) dollars today in order to obtain one dollar (with certainty) a year hence. In other words, the firm discounts future payoffs at the annual rate of 10 per cent. More generally, if the firm's discount rate is constant at r, the present value of a dollar received n years hence is $1/(1 + r)^n$ dollars. The rate r may, of course, vary over time. The discount rate will not, moreover, be the rate at which the firm can borrow if it is at all rationed in capital markets, or faces a rising cost of funds for other reasons. In principle, nothing is altered by these considerations where the use of discounting is concerned, although the practical difficulties of estimating r in these circumstances can be quite considerable.

The correct decision rule is now clear: accept all (compatible) projects that show a positive NPV at the appropriate discount rate, and reject those that do not. For by adopting this rule, the firm ensures that each and every activity makes a positive contribution to (discounted) profits, given the relevant alternative use of resources defined by the discount rate. The qualifier 'compatible' is introduced because undertaking one project may rule out others. If a tract of land is strip-mined for copper ore, for example, it cannot simultaneously be used for the grazing of sheep. Although both projects may be separately profitable, they clearly cannot be undertaken together. Similar considerations arise if there are limited technical and managerial skills so specific to the firm that acceptable substitutes cannot be obtained through the market.

We can now give a formal definition of the NPV of a project. Let $\Delta z(\tau)$ and $p(\tau)$ denote the vectors of *net* outputs[2] and their corresponding prices, respectively, of a project in year τ. We follow the convention that outputs are positive and inputs are negative, so that $\Delta z_i(\tau) < 0$ implies that the project uses more of good i in period τ than it produces. If the discount rate is constant, the NPV is defined to be

$$\text{NPV} \equiv \sum_{\tau}[p(\tau) \cdot \Delta z(\tau)/(1 + r)^{\tau}] \equiv \sum_{\tau}[B(\tau) - C(\tau)]/(1 + r)^{\tau}, \quad (8.1)$$

[2] For reasons that will become clear in the course of this chapter, we define a project as a change in an existing vector of net outputs. Hence the notation Δz.

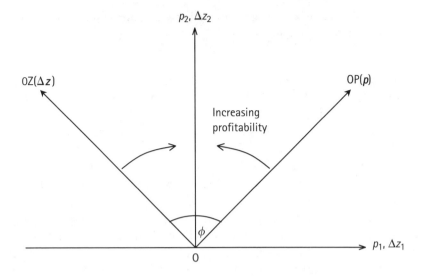

Figure 8.1. Profitability depends only on the relative directions of the net output and price vectors

where $p \cdot \Delta z \equiv \sum_i p_i z_i$, and $B(\tau)$ and $C(\tau)$ denote gross benefits and costs in year τ, respectively.

The formula can be illustrated graphically in the case of two commodities, where commodity one is an input and commodity two is an output. In Fig. 8.1, the 'blueprint' is represented by the vector $OZ(\Delta z)$ and the set of prices by the vector $OP(p)$. Note that the only thing that matters in determining whether the project is profitable is the direction of p relative to Δz, as measured by the angle ϕ: pure changes in scale have no effect on the sign of the NPV. A project becomes more profitable as ϕ falls, whether by Δz rotating clockwise, or p counterclockwise, or both. The former corresponds to the case in which the productivity of inputs rises, the latter to a favourable movement of output prices relative to input prices.

8.2. The Public Project and Social Profitability

In order to assess the social profitability of a project in the public sector, or of one undertaken by the private sector, we need to go through the same steps:

1. Draw up a 'blueprint' of the project, as expressed by the vector $[\Delta z(1), \ldots, \Delta z(T)]$, where the project will extend over T periods, including scrapping and the storage of any waste.

2. Ascertain or, where necessary, estimate the appropriate prices at which to value inputs and outputs.

3. Select a decision rule.

The first of these seems to be no different from its counterpart in a private calculation. We note, however, that one or more components of Δz may be the outcome of private decisions made in response to a public sector project; for example, peasant farmers will respond in a particular way to the provision of irrigation from public canals. In that case, Δz is not simply an engineering 'blueprint', and the relevant responses of private agents must be established through careful investigation. We shall deal with this matter in later chapters.

The second and third steps are interrelated. In the former, we must consider whether the market prices which are used in private calculations are appropriate when assessing the project's *social* profitability. In the latter, the decision rule reflects the objective of the entire exercise, so we are led to ask: is the notion of 'profit' appropriate in social evaluations? It will now be argued that it is, provided the calculation is made at the 'right' prices. Suppose the government has a collection of objectives and that it has preferences over these objectives which can be represented by a social welfare function (see Section 4.3.3). Suppose further that the *shadow price* of a commodity, π_i, is *defined* to be the resulting change in social welfare when the net supply of that commodity by the public sector increases by one unit.[3] If shadow prices so defined are used to value inputs and outputs, thereby yielding social profits or present value, then a project that makes a profit at those prices will necessarily increase social welfare, which is surely what the government wishes to accomplish; whereas one that makes a loss will necessarily reduce social welfare, a piece of information which is at least as valuable when it comes to making decisions.

There remains the task of estimating all shadow prices. Life would be straightforward indeed if shadow prices were equal to market prices. For the private businessman's calculus would always yield choices of projects that resulted in improvements in social welfare, and the technical analysts in the various ministries should also do their calculations at market prices, secure in the knowledge that the same decision rule would yield socially profitable choices among public projects. It is essential, therefore, to be clear about the conditions that must be satisfied if market prices are to

---

[3] It is sometimes computationally convenient to employ the concept of the *accounting ratio* of a good or factor, which is defined to be the ratio of its shadow to its market price, where the latter is the consumer or producer price, as appropriate.

measure social scarcities. Among the most important are the following:

1. *Full employment.* An involuntarily idle worker who obtains a job enjoys a net benefit over the combined loss of his leisure and unemployment income that results from his taking up employment. The profit-maximizing firm, however, looks only at the marginal cost of labour (including payroll taxes and any costs of retrenchment) when deciding how much labour to hire.

2. *Perfect competition.* That is, no agent has a measurable influence over prices, and there is profit maximization or utility maximization as appropriate.

3. The course of action under consideration must be 'small', in the sense that undertaking it will not lead to significant changes in market prices.

4. *Absence of external effects.* This rules out, for example, pollution and any gains from learning-by-doing that cannot be appropriated by the agent bearing the costs thereof.

5. *Absence of distortionary taxation.* If there are such taxes, a producer who sells a product for one dollar will not receive one dollar for it; for there will be a 'wedge' between the buyer's and seller's prices, respectively. In particular, if earnings from labour are taxed, there will be a wedge between the employer's marginal cost of hiring a unit of labour and the worker's marginal revenue from supplying it.

6. The distribution of income must be optimal, in the sense that the social value of an extra unit of income must be the same for all individuals. The use of private profits as a measure of social net benefit rests on the assumption that it is.

A brief reflection on these requirements in the light of the state of affairs in most countries suggests that the divergence between private and social costs (scarcities) may be considerable. If market prices do not reflect social scarcities, however, then a project which is privately profitable may not be socially profitable, and conversely (see Fig. 8.1 for such an illustration). The estimation of social scarcities, or shadow prices as defined above, is therefore a central task in social cost–benefit analysis. As we shall see, it is also a task that often involves considerable difficulties.

8.3. Estimating Shadow Prices: A Partial Equilibrium Approach

This approach is unswervingly in the Chicago tradition, its architect being Harberger (1972). We shall, of course, go well beyond Harberger's method in this and subsequent chapters; but it does have the considerable virtues of simplicity and pedagogic clarity. It also yields simple formulae for shadow prices, which are valid under certain restricted but important circumstances.

In the following example, there is a single departure from the necessary conditions listed above in Section 8.2. Consider a competitive market for a single commodity, on which a specific tax t is levied. By definition, the consumer price, q, is equal to the (net-of-tax) producer price, p, plus t. In the absence of government demand for the commodity, the market is in equilibrium when private demand, $D(q)$, is equal to supply, $S(p)$, with $q = p + t$. The essentials are depicted in Fig. 8.2, in which both the demand and supply schedules are linear, though that assumption is readily relaxed without altering the main result provided the changes in all variables are small. The equilibrium can be found as follows. Consider the supply schedule labelled $S'(q)$, which is a vertical translation of $S(p)$ in the amount t to reflect the fact that in the presence of the tax, the industry's supply at the producer price p is the same as at the consumer price $q = p + t$; for when firms sell to consumers at the price q, they actually receive the net price p, the difference going to the Treasury. Let the demand schedule intersect $S'(q)$ at the point A. Here, demand at the

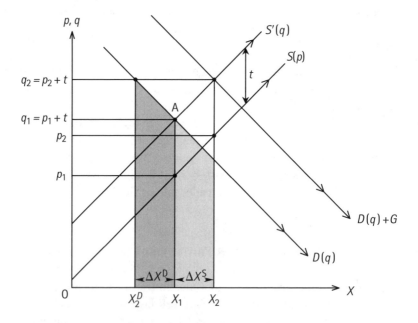

Figure 8.2. The effects of government purchases in a single market

consumer price q_1, namely, X_1, is equal to supply at the producer price p_1, so that the configuration (p_1, q_1, X_1) is the market equilibrium.

Now suppose the government enters the market and purchases an amount G at the ruling price, which it will use in some project. In order to accommodate G, the private sector adjusts as follows:

Private supply increases by

$$\Delta X^S = X_2 - X_1,$$

which is induced by an increase of $\Delta p = p_2 - p_1$ in the producer price.

Private demand decreases by

$$|\Delta X^D| = -X_2^D + X_1,$$

which is induced by an increase of $\Delta q = (p_2 + t) - (p_1 + t) = \Delta p$ in the consumer price, where $X_2^D = D(q_2)$. Note that the equality of Δp and Δq is a simple consequence of our assumption that the tax in question is a specific tax. These adjustments in the producer and consumer price yield $\Delta X^S + |\Delta X^D| = G$, where the components ΔX^S and $|\Delta X^D|$ are obtained from Δp $(= \Delta q)$ and the slopes of the supply and demand schedules, respectively.

There are three groups of agents to be considered: the government, producers, and consumers. In the Chicago tradition, the change in welfare is defined as the algebraic sum of the changes in government revenue, (net) consumers' surplus, and producers' surplus. In order to make the partial equilibrium computation that follows valid, a crucial assumption is now needed, namely, that except in the market under consideration, there are no other distortions (including those arising from taxation) anywhere else in the economy. In particular, any changes in net government revenue arising from the purchase of G units of the good in question are assumed to be financed by lump-sum transfers. That being so, the relevant changes are:

$$\Delta \text{ government revenue} = [t \cdot (X_2 - G) - p_2 G] - tX_1,$$
$$\Delta \text{ consumers' surplus} = -\Delta q \cdot (X_1 - |\Delta X^D|/2), \text{ and}$$
$$\Delta \text{ producers' surplus} = \Delta p \cdot (X_1 + \Delta X^S/2).$$

Observe that in calculating the net change in government revenue, no taxes accrue to the Treasury in connection with outlays by the spending ministries, which effectively trade at producer prices. Adding up and recalling that $\Delta p = \Delta q = p_2 - p_1$, we obtain the change in social welfare:

$$\Delta W = -q_2 G + t \cdot (X_2 - X_1) + \Delta p \cdot (|\Delta X^D| + \Delta X^S)/2. \qquad (8.2)$$

Noting that $\Delta X^S = X_2 - X_1$ and $G = \Delta X^S + |\Delta X^D|$, we may rewrite Eqn (8.2) as

$$\Delta W = -[(p_2 + p_1)\Delta X^S + (q_1 + q_2)|\Delta X^D|]/2. \tag{8.3}$$

The two terms on the right-hand side (RHS) of Eqn (8.3) correspond to the shaded trapezoidal areas in Fig. 8.2. The first is the increase in producers' total costs induced by the expansion of output from X_1 to X_2. The second is the absolute value of the change in consumers' surplus induced by the reduction in private consumption from X_1 to X_1^D. By definition, the shadow price of the good in question is the increase in welfare that results when the government supplies one unit thereof. (Equivalently, it is the reduction in welfare that results when the government uses one unit thereof.) Dividing Eqn (8.3) by G and letting G go to zero in the limit, so that p_2 goes to p_1, we obtain the shadow price of the commodity:

$$\pi \equiv - \lim_{G \to 0} (\Delta W/G) = p_1 \cdot (\Delta X^S/G) + q_1 \cdot (|\Delta X^D|/G). \tag{8.4}$$

Since $G = \Delta X^S + |\Delta X^D|$, π is a correspondingly weighted average of the supply and demand prices of the good. This is Harberger's well-known rule.

As empirical work on markets usually involves the estimation of supply and demand elasticities, it will be useful to express Eqn (8.4) in elasticity form, so that direct use can be made of such estimates. For sufficiently small G, we have

$$\eta^S = \frac{\Delta X^S}{X_1} \frac{p_1}{\Delta p} \quad \text{and} \quad |\eta^D| = \frac{|\Delta X^D|}{X_1} \frac{q_1}{\Delta q},$$

where η^S and $|\eta^D|$ are the absolute values of the elasticities of supply and demand, respectively. Hence, if t is sufficiently small, so that $p_1 \cong q_1$, a little manipulation yields the shadow price as the correspondingly weighted average of the producer and consumer prices

$$\pi = p_1 \cdot \frac{\eta^S}{\eta^S + |\eta^D|} + q_1 \cdot \frac{|\eta^D|}{\eta^S + |\eta^D|}. \tag{8.5}$$

Note that whereas Eqns (8.4) and (8.5) are valid only for small changes in G, Eqn (8.3) is valid for large changes when both schedules are linear, and it is readily modified to the case in which both are non-linear. Large changes will be tackled in detail in Chapter 13.

The derivation of the foregoing results is simple, given the definition of the shadow price. To some readers, however, the latter may seem rather puzzling in the light of how it has been derived; for nothing explicit has been said about what the government does with the G units once it has purchased them. The answer is that it 'disposes' of them, and at no cost; for otherwise, there would be further ramifications to be considered. In the converse case, where the government supplies a unit of a good, the corresponding thought experiment is that it produces the good at no cost out of thin air. Actual projects involve a stream of inputs (costless disposals) and, one hopes, at least one positive output (costless arrivals), and so are simple mixtures of a whole set of such thought experiments, one for each good as input or output. Provided the basic rule of accounting is applied consistently, with outputs having a positive sign, all will be well.

The above model is evidently very special, which invites the question: how robust are the results it yields to changes in the underlying assumptions? In one special, but empirically very important case, the answer turns out to be: quite robust indeed. The first step, however, is to derive a fundamental result using the partial equilibrium model.

8.4. The Shadow Prices of Tradables

Suppose that the country is a small player in international markets and the good in question can be traded at parametric world prices, there being no quantitative restrictions. Trade may, however, be taxed. The claim to be established is that the shadow price of a tradable is its free-on-board (f.o.b.) world price if the good is exported, and its cost-insurance-and-freight (c.i.f.) world price if imported.

Figure 8.3 depicts the case where the good is imported before the government makes its purchase of G units. The parametric world price is p^* and there is a tariff t, so that the domestic price of the good is $(p^* + t)$, the corresponding horizontal line representing a perfectly elastic supply of imports at the cum-tariff price $(p^* + t)$. Enjoying the fruits of protection, domestic firms produce the amount $X^S = S^d(p^* + t)$. In the absence of government purchases, equilibrium is established at point A, with $D(p^* + t) = X_1$ and imports of $X_1 - X^S$.

With a parametric world price and a fixed tariff, the domestic price will not be affected by the government's purchase of G units of the good. Under the usual assumption that the market in question is a small part of the economy, and that the project outlay on G is sufficiently small, the lump-sum tax needed to finance it will result in strictly second-order effects on the domestic supply and demand schedules. Domestic supply

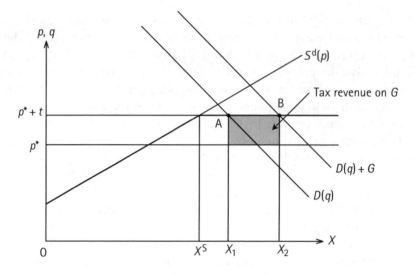

Figure 8.3. The case of an importable, with a parametric world price and a tariff

therefore remains unchanged at X^S, and private demand at X_1. Hence, the sole effect of the government's purchase in the amount $G(= X_2 - X_1)$ is to increase net imports of the commodity in question by that amount. The spending ministry lays out pG at domestic prices on this purchase, but the department of customs and excise collects tariff revenues in the amount of tG. As the domestic price is $p = p^* + t$, the government's net outlay is p^*G. By definition, therefore, the shadow price of the good is

$$\pi = -\Delta W/G = p^*. \tag{8.6}$$

We have therefore established that the shadow price of the commodity is its world (c.i.f.) price. An exactly analogous argument establishes that the shadow price of an exported good is its world f.o.b. price, a case that is depicted in Fig. 8.4. Taken together, these results constitute the so-called '*border price rule*'.

The case in which the government's demand is large enough to shift the good from being exported to a non-traded or imported status is depicted in Fig. 8.5. The shaded areas B and D sum up to the value (at world prices) of the net imports induced by G. The shaded areas A and C are, respectively, consumers' willingness to pay in order to avoid the reduction in the private consumption of the good and the value of additional resources drawn into domestic production. From the figure, it appears that the shadow price will

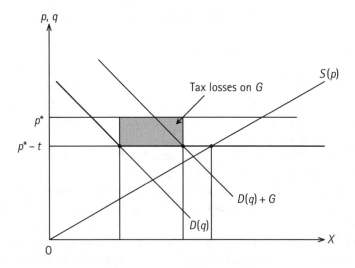

Figure 8.4. The case of an exportable, with a parametric world price and an export tax

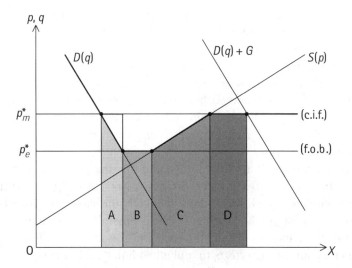

Figure 8.5. A government purchase large enough to induce a switch in the direction of trade, with p^*(c.i.f.) $>$ p^*(f.o.b.)

lie between the f.o.b. and c.i.f. prices. There is an important caveat where areas A and C are concerned, however, as will be seen in the following section. A full and rigorous treatment of this case will be taken up in Chapter 11, which deals with spatial considerations.

8.5. The Limitations of a Partial Equilibrium Approach

The nature of the assumptions that underlie the results derived in Sections 8.3 and 8.4 may not be fully apparent at first glance. It turns out that they are rather strong. As we shall soon see, relaxing them in the direction of realism will not only greatly complicate the analysis; with the very important exception of those for tradable goods, it will also overturn the results themselves.

We begin with Harberger's 'rule' and its graphical representation in Fig. 8.2. When the government purchases G units of the good in question, consumers' expenditure on other goods will change in response to the increase in its price. If other goods are taxed or subsidised, then there will be further changes in government income, which do not appear in the accounting leading up to Eqn (8.3). Similarly, if there is a response in the domestic supply of the good in question, resources will be drawn into, or out of, that industry, and if taxes on the use of factors vary across industries, there will be further effects on the government's net revenues. Again, these do not enter into Eqn (8.3). Thus, the existence of distortionary taxes elsewhere in the economy will, in general, invalidate Eqn (8.3), and hence the partial equilibrium formula (8.4). This argument applies a fortiori if lump-sum taxes are not available. For only by an extraordinary stroke of chance would the net change in public revenues ensuing from all general equilibrium effects be zero. Other departures elsewhere in the economy from the necessary conditions set out in Section 8.2 would also undermine the validity of a partial equilibrium approach—with one exception, to which we now turn.

Suppose some goods are fully traded and that the direction of trade does not alter in response to a project. Suppose also that the government finances its purchases of all such goods in exactly the same way, for example, by resorting to foreign borrowing, if that is possible, or by changing some set of tariffs or excises. Then, for each unit outlay of foreign currency, the general equilibrium effects that plagued Eqn (8.3) in the case discussed above will be identical, regardless of the tradable on which the currency is spent. Hence, the central conclusion of Section 8.4, namely, that the shadow price of a such tradable is its world price (c.i.f. or f.o.b. as appropriate), must be modified to read: the said shadow price is *proportional* to the world price, where the factor of proportionality depends on how the government chooses to finance additional expenditures, what other distortions are at work, and the whole gamut of tastes and technologies for producing goods. So reinterpreted, the so-called 'border price' rule is strikingly robust, which is one of its great attractions. The catch is that the factor of proportionality must be estimated, a task which is far from straightforward and which will occupy us at some length in later chapters.

In the case of non-tradables and primary factors, no such comparatively simple escape is possible. The same holds for those tradables subject to binding quotas, an all-too-common case in practice, and for those subject to idiosyncratic financing measures. The former are effectively non-tradable at the margin; the latter violate the uniformity of general equilibrium effects required to generate the modified border price rule stated above. Even if there were no other departures from the conditions needed to ensure that market prices measure social scarcities correctly, we would still be confronted with the need to derive rules for shadow prices in all these cases. The fact that other departures are common in practice is, of course, a complication with which we must deal.

The other feature of Harberger's formulation which is surely open to question (for some, it is simply objectionable) is the form of the social welfare function. By specifying this function as the algebraic sum of government revenue, consumers' surplus, and producers' surplus, Harberger is implicitly asserting that the existing distribution of income is optimal (or irrelevant). For many developing countries, in which the government's capacity to effect redistribution through the tax system is much more heavily constrained than in industrialized ones, such a specialization seems especially unattractive. In particular, the savings rate may well be suboptimal, and this may imply, in turn, that there should be a premium on government income relative to private income. Any scheme for estimating shadow prices should, therefore, admit considerations of equity in principle, even if the practical implementation thereof is controversial.

As a final comment before we embark on the task of deriving shadow prices that fully reflect these considerations, it should be said in Harberger's defence that he has always argued for the merits of simplicity in decision-making procedures and rules. The point is well taken, but it raises the question of whether any particular simplification will lead to errors that are so serious as to make it worthwhile to incur the cost of applying a more complex procedure. There is no set answer to that question: each case must be judged on its merits in the light of what rigour demands.

8.6. 'Cookbook' Rules

In order to complete this chapter, we need to lay out a set of rules that is fairly complete and in a form that lends itself to practical implementation, leaving rigorous derivations to later chapters. The basic formulae for shadow prices are presented here in an heuristic way, the idea being to acquaint the reader with the elementary intuition underlying the procedures for calculating shadow prices, as well as the formulae themselves, which are perfectly straightforward.

Consider a world in which there are many goods but only one non-produced factor, namely, labour. The goods are classified into those that will be fully traded under foreseeable policies and those that will not. Without loss of generality, let the goods be numbered such that the first m are tradables and the remaining n are non-tradables. In Sections 8.4 and 8.5, we have sketched a plausible argument that the shadow prices of the former are proportional to their respective world prices. For simplicity, we assume here that the factor of proportionality can be normalized to unity, the justification for which is left to Chapter 9. That being so, we have

$$\pi_i = p_i^*, \quad i \in T, \tag{8.6}$$

where T denotes the set of tradables.

We now turn to the shadow prices of non-tradables. In a competitive market economy, the producer price of a good is equal to its marginal (private) cost of production. In the light of Section 8.2, this suggests the following conjecture: the shadow price of a non-tradable good is equal to its marginal social cost of production. With this conjecture, we have

$$\pi_i = \sum_j \pi_j a_{ji} + w^* l_i, \quad i \in N, \ j \in N \cup T, \tag{8.7}$$

where N is the set of non-tradables, a_{ji} is the input of good j needed to produce an additional unit of good i, l_i is the complementary input of labour, and w^* denotes the shadow wage rate. If the technology vectors (a_i, l_i) are known, then, in view of Eqn (8.6), it is clear that Eqn (8.7) defines a system of n linear equations in $(n + 1)$ unknowns, the odd one over being the shadow wage rate. The final step, therefore, is to derive the latter, ideally in linear form, a step that involves a careful analysis of the labour market.

Consider what happens when the government hires a worker, who may receive a wage rate that exceeds what he was earning in his alternative employment, if any. Since he can no longer produce whatever he was producing before, the economy will, in the first instance, lose his output in that employment, and so incur an opportunity cost (valued at shadow prices, of course). That is not, however, quite the end of the story. For some other worker may take over his old job, and so on, until we finally arrive at the ultimate source of labour to the rest of the economy. This source may take the form of a pool of unemployed or underemployed workers, or a group of peasant farmers and tenants. The marginal product of labour (MPL) in this activity, valued at shadow prices, defines the real opportunity cost of labour to the economy. It should be noted in passing that the creation of one more job in the public sector may induce more than one worker in the 'source' sector to migrate elsewhere in search of other employment. Again, that is a complication we shall defer until Chapter 9.

In addition to the social opportunity cost of labour, there is also the possibility that hiring one more worker will commit the economy to greater private consumption, as would happen if the wage in public sector employment exceeds average earnings in the 'source' activity. This involves a cost, since the additional absorption of goods in consumption precludes them from being used in other activities. It also involves a benefit, however, since increases in private consumption (for the representative individual, at least) are surely socially valuable. Thus, if employing the said worker in the public sector increases private consumption, the net social cost thereof must be added to the social opportunity cost of labour in order to arrive at the shadow wage rate.

With this heuristic account as a basis, we have

$$w^* = m_0 \pi_0 + \left[\sum_{i \in \mathrm{N} \cup \mathrm{T}} (\pi_i / q_i) b_i - \theta \right] \cdot \Delta M, \tag{8.8}$$

where m_0 is the MPL in the 'source' sector, q_i is the consumer price of good i, b_i is the marginal propensity to spend on good i out of additional private income, where it is assumed for simplicity that all wages are spent ($\sum_i b_i = 1$), θ is the marginal social value of private consumption (with government income as the numéraire), and ΔM is the increase in private consumption arising from the creation of an additional job in the public sector.

The first term on the RHS of Eqn (8.8) is the social opportunity cost of labour. The second is the *net* social cost of any increase in private consumption that ensues from the creation of an extra job in the public sector. It comprises two parts. The expression $\sum_i (\pi_i / q_i) b_i$ is the cost, at shadow prices, of the bundle of goods purchased when total expenditure rises by one rupee, and is usually called the *consumption conversion factor* (or CCF). That the additional rupee of income is socially valuable is reflected in the presence of the term θ, with a negative sign to reflect the fact that it is beneficial to the recipient.

Given the necessary information, therefore, the system of $(m + n + 1)$ linear equations defined by Eqns (8.6)–(8.8) can be solved to yield the complete vector of shadow prices (π, w^*). The necessary information is: the vector of world prices, p^*; the technologies for producing non-tradables (a_j, l_j); the MPL in the 'source' sector, m_0; the marginal propensities to consume and consumer prices, (b, q); the increase in private consumption, ΔM; and the social valuation of an additional rupee of private consumption, θ. It should be emphasized that the solution of such a system necessarily involves, and takes account of, an extensive set of general equilibrium effects, though admittedly with strong underlying assumptions. Observe that in practical applications, it is sometimes easier to work with the so-called *accounting ratio* of a good or factor, which is the ratio of its shadow to its market price.

What, then, are the possible sources of the information so needed? Since we are dealing with small projects, viewed as perturbations to an existing equilibrium, it is the values of parameters at the margin that are relevant. If there are constant returns to scale, tax rates are constant, and wage rates do not vary, then the technical coefficients (a_j, l_j) will be constant for all j. Under these assumptions, the a_j can be computed from the relevant submatrix of any sufficiently detailed social accounting matrix (SAM). Estimates of the l_j will also require employment data by sector, the sources for which might also yield the required estimates of sectoral wage rates.

It is clear from Eqns (8.6)–(8.8), however, that much more is needed. The marginal propensities to consume out of income b and consumer prices q play an important role when shadow and market prices diverge significantly. At a pinch, b could be computed from a SAM if q were available; but this would involve the untenable assumption that all income elasticities of demand are unity. Access to the data from consumer budget surveys, which normally contain information on q, is really essential for this purpose, with econometric analysis to follow. Similarly, estimates of the world prices of tradables can be recovered from a SAM if taxes on trade are set out in sufficient detail. Yet an independent study of the taxation of foreign trade, coupled with references to the estimates published regularly by certain international organizations, would be preferable. Finally, the welfare parameter θ will not appear in any SAM and must be estimated by other methods. This will be one of our concerns in Chapters 9, 10, and 13.

8.7. Evaluating Private Projects

In order to complete this introduction, something must be said about the treatment of private projects. The following thought experiment provides a hint of how to proceed. A private firm applies for permission to undertake a project, the complete technical and financial details of which are contained in the documents accompanying the application. The Central Office of Project Evaluation (COPE), which is responsible for vetting public projects, then evaluates the proposal as if the project were to be undertaken in exactly the same way by the public sector (this is, after all, a thought experiment). The crucial point that remains to be dealt with is the fact that the after-tax profits the firm will make by trading at market prices will accrue, not to the Treasury, but to the firm's shareholders. Let the amount in question be Π. Then the private project may be construed as a 'pure' public project combined with a transfer of Π from the Treasury to the firm's shareholders.

We begin by recalling that the term $[\sum_i(\pi_i/q_i)b_i - \theta]$ in Eqn (8.8) measures the net social cost of an additional rupee of consumption by workers that arises from their receipt of a transfer of one rupee from the Treasury. Let the corresponding term for shareholders be denoted by ξ_K, where it should be noted that shareholders' spending habits are normally quite different from workers' and that there are grounds for arguing that an additional rupee of consumption enjoyed by the former is socially less valuable than if it were enjoyed instead by the latter. Analogously, let the social value of an additional rupee of savings by shareholders be θ_K, and let the fraction s_K of the 'transfer' be saved. Then the social 'profit' generated by a private project yielding the net output vector Δz, employing L workers, and yielding an after-tax profit of Π to the firm's shareholders is

$$\Delta W = \pi \cdot \Delta z - w^* L - [(1 - s_K)\xi_K + s_K(1 - \theta_K)]\Pi. \tag{8.9a}$$

In the special case where the shareholders are classically thrifty ($s_K = 1$), and public and private savings are judged to be equally valuable, Eqn (8.9a) specializes to

$$\Delta W = \pi \cdot \Delta z - w^* L, \tag{8.9b}$$

which is exactly the social profit generated by an identical public project without the 'transfer' to the shareholders.

It should be emphasized that whether the public sector is capable of executing the project so specified in practice is completely irrelevant to its social evaluation as a private project, unless a competing, incompatible public project is also under consideration.

8.8. Summary

The purpose of appraising projects is to sort out the good from the bad. For the private sector, the test is profitability at market prices. For the public sector, the criterion is whether social welfare, suitably defined, will improve or worsen. In a first-best setting, market prices measure social scarcities, in the sense that privately profitable projects will improve welfare, so that the so-called 'market test' will suffice. The world as we know it, however, is far removed from this ideal. Governments have no option but to resort to distortionary taxation; taxes and regulations are often tangled, with little prospect of sensible reform in the near future; some markets are imperfect or fail altogether for one reason or other; and inequality, in various forms, is indefensibly great. If the ultimate aim is to improve welfare under these conditions, the use of market prices, when they exist, to weed out bad projects is not only invalid but also foolhardy.

The task at hand, therefore, is to estimate the true social scarcities, or shadow prices, of resources under the conditions that actually prevail—or those that are expected to do so after all efforts at reform have been made. One approach is to derive the shadow prices of commodities through a partial equilibrium analysis of each market in turn, commodity by commodity. Upon close examination, the assumptions needed to make the analysis watertight prove to be so restrictive that the method must be judged unsatisfactory—with one notable and practically very important exception, namely, in the case where the good in question is tradable in world markets at a parametrically given price. The shadow price of such a good is its world price, f.o.b. or c.i.f. as appropriate, a robust result known as the 'border price' rule. The intuition here is that international trade at parametric prices offers the domestic economy in general, and the public sector in particular, a CRS technology for transforming one tradable into another, a point already emphasized in a related connection in Chapters 1 and 2.

By analogy, we arrive at the conjecture that the corresponding rule for non-tradable goods is that their shadow prices be equal to their respective marginal social costs of production, that is, marginal costs evaluated at shadow prices. This yields almost as many conditions (equations) as there are non-tradable goods, where the simultaneity of the conditions reveals the general equilibrium character of the approach.

In order to complete the system, it remains only to find the shadow prices of non-produced goods, or factors of production, above all that of labour. The shadow wage rate reflects two considerations. First, the employment of a worker on a project will normally reduce output elsewhere in the economy; when valued at shadow prices, this reduction is called the social opportunity cost of labour. Second, the worker in question (or rather his family or related group) may well earn more, in aggregate, as a result of gaining such employment, in which case, additional resources will be drawn into private consumption. This entails both a social cost, in that these resources are no longer available for other uses, and a social benefit, in that the family in question is better off. The said cost is the value, at shadow prices, of the additional basket of goods the worker's family consumes. The associated benefit is the social value of the extra income when viewed against the alternative of the Treasury holding on to the sum in question. The shadow wage rate is the sum of the social opportunity cost of labour and the net social cost of the additional consumption the worker's family enjoys as a result of his taking up the job on the project.

Thus completed, the system is then solved to yield the complete vector of shadow prices, whose mutual and simultaneous determination reflects the relevant general equilibrium effects in the setting under consideration. In this 'cookbook' form, the method is easy to implement both in principle and in practice—provided the necessary patience and care in obtaining and using the data are at hand.

Recommended Reading

The classic references are Dasgupta *et al.* (1972) and Little and Mirrlees (1974), where the latter is a greatly extended and revised version of OECD (1968). Although both were intended as 'manuals' in the broad sense of the term, neither reads much like the equivalent of a do-it-yourself handbook, and the associated debate in the *Oxford Bulletin of Economics and Statistics* (1972) is strictly for those who have a good grasp of the subject. A better starting point is the 'Introduction' in Layard and Glaister (1994), which is a useful collection of readings. Those who want a nuts-and-bolts account for practitioners should then read Squire and van der Tak (1975). This was intended as a manual for use in the World Bank; but the very approach was, and remains, quite alien to that institution's operational demands and internal incentives, and it never really took root (Little and Mirrlees, 1991).

Exercises

1. A perfectly competitive industry has the cost function

$$c(Y) = Y + Y^2/4,$$

where Y denotes the amount produced. It faces the market demand function

$$D(q) = 10 - q,$$

where q is the consumer price. Initially, there are no taxes on the good in question.

> (a) How much will be produced in equilibrium and at what price?
> (b) The government now imposes an excise tax of one rupee on each unit of output. Find all relevant variables in the resulting equilibrium, and the shadow price of the good in question in the presence of this tax.
> (c) The Ministry of Works now considers a project that would require two units of this good. What is the shadow cost of this expenditure, and why is it incorrect to use the shadow price derived in part (b)? State all necessary assumptions clearly and depict your analysis graphically.

2. As a variation on exercise 1, suppose, instead, that the good cannot be produced domestically. It can, however, be imported at the parametric world price of 3, subject to a 33 per cent tariff and a quota of 5 units altogether. The quota is distributed among importers administratively. Repeat parts (b) and (c) of exercise 1.

3. The entire demand for fertilizers in Ruritania is met by imports, which are subject to a tariff of 25 per cent. The market is competitive, and current domestic demand is 100 units at the going domestic price of 2 per unit.

The government now receives a proposal from a foreign firm to build a plant that will satisfy current local demand exactly. Apart from the plant itself, the process involves two inputs, namely, naptha, which can be imported free of tariff at a price of unity, and domestic labour, whose going wage rate is also unity. Each unit of fertilizer requires one unit of naptha and 0.1 units of labour. The plant would be constructed entirely of imported inputs, at a total cost of 500, again free of tariff, and would last for 20 years. The firm would finance the whole capital outlay.

Current tax law in Ruritania provides for straightline depreciation of capital goods over their normal lifetimes. Profits after depreciation are

taxed at a flat rate of 50 per cent, and all after-tax profits may be repatriated. The proposal is contingent on the continuation of the relevant
provisions of the present tax code, and it is assumed that the government
is able to give credible assurances that, should the proposal be accepted,
such would be the case.

The foreign corporation argues in its proposal that such a plant will save
the economy valuable foreign exchange.

    (a) Is this claim correct?

    (b) Whether the claim is correct or not, should the government accept the
proposal?

[The Central Office of Project Evaluation (COPE) has estimated the shadow
price of labour to be 0.75. If you need any further assumptions, state them
clearly and briefly discuss their plausibility.]

4. A private firm in a small open economy goes bankrupt and is taken
over by the state with the aim of saving the employees' jobs. Under state
management, it produces an annual output of 1000 units of a tradable good
(1) by means of an importable (2), a non-tradable (3), and labour, where the
input cost shares are given by (0.3, 0.3, 0.4), respectively. Good 1 is also
imported subject to a tariff of 25 per cent. All domestic prices are unity. The
current management is unable to do better than cover the variable costs of
production. Hence, the state remains saddled with the firm's outstanding
liabilities with the banks, which are also state owned.

    (a) If the 'accounting ratios' for the inputs are (0.9, 0.85, 0.75) and the
firm continues in business indefinitely, determine whether the takeover is
defensible.

    (b) A foreign firm now enters with an offer to invest the sum of 5000 to
renovate and restructure the plant, which would have a life of 20 years. The
investment would take the form of machinery imported free of tariff. The firm
would not assume the original bad debt, and it would be free to fire existing
employees without compensation in the course of rationalizing the firm's
operations. In response to a demand from the Ministry of Industry, it sets out
a detailed production plan, under which output would increase to 2000 units
annually, with the unit input vector

$$a_2 = (0, 0.3, 0.25; 0.15).$$

Profits net of depreciation are taxed at the rate of 40 per cent. Tax law
provides for straight-line depreciation over the life of the asset in question.
Should the government accept this offer?

    (c) Suppose that any workers made redundant would never find another
job, and that the law requires that, by way of compensation, such workers

must be paid an annual sum of one-half of their lost earnings over the life of the restructured plant. If the firm does not withdraw its offer under this condition, should the government change its decision? (The premium on public funds is 33 per cent and the consumption conversion factor is 0.85.)

5. A small island economy produces an exportable (good 1) and a non-tradable (good 3), both by means of CRS, Leontief technologies whose unit activity vectors are, respectively,

$$a_1 = (0,0,0;1) \quad \text{and} \quad a_3 = (0,0.4,0;1),$$

where good 2 is a non-competitive import and the last element in each vector is the labour-input coefficient. Both industries are competitive, but the wage rate payable in sector 3 is regulated, at twice the level ruling in sector 1. There is full employment of labour. The only barriers to trade are taxes on imports and exports, which are also the government's only source of tax revenue. The rates, which are levied on the invoice value in dollars, are 20 and 25 per cent, respectively; the world prices of goods 1 and 2 are both unity.

Households spend their incomes in the proportions $b = (0.4, 0.2, 0.4)$. The premium on public income is one-third.

(a) Determine all market and shadow prices, justifying all steps.

At the urging of the World Bank, the government now considers tourism as a means of improving the islanders' incomes. The following set of projects is put forward: the government would invest in the necessary public infra-structure (the airport, roads, sanitation, and the like), and foreign investors would finance and run the hotels. All these facilities would be built in one year and have an indefinitely long life. The corresponding investment vectors are, respectively,

$$K_d = (0, 100, 10; 15) \quad \text{and} \quad F_f = (0, 50, 5; 10).$$

The services provided by the hotels are produced by a process whose unit activity vector is

$$a_4 = (0.1, 0.2, 0.1; 0.4).$$

They will be priced on a cost-plus basis, with a mark-up of 25 per cent and workers receiving the regulated wage rate. Under a special provision of the law, all profits would be tax-free and freely remitted back to the foreign investors' home tax jurisdictions.

On the basis of experience with similar projects undertaken elsewhere, tourists are expected to allocate 40 per cent of their total expenditure to good 3 and the rest to hotel services.

(b) If the social discount rate is 10 per cent per annum, how much must tourists spend annually for the project to be socially profitable?

6. Rice in Ruritania is produced by small farmers during the monsoon season. Domestic production is insufficient to meet domestic demand, so rice is imported, subject to a protective tariff of 25 per cent. The country is small in relation to the world market for rice.

The government now decides that a move towards self-sufficiency is desirable. The Ministry of Agriculture draws up two mutually exclusive proposals for the exploitation of water resources so that a second crop of rice can be produced in the dry season. The first takes the form of a dam, the second involves a network of pumps. Both projects would take one year to build and would have the same economic life. Neither would so increase production as to displace imports entirely. The consulting engineers and farm management experts draw up the following estimates of costs and returns at market prices. In both cases, the government would bear all investment costs and the farmers all variable costs.

	Dam	Pumps
Investment costs		
Construction	1000	100
Machinery	100	600
Annual costs and returns		
Fertilizers	20	20
Diesel fuel	–	20
Output of rice	120	120

From studies of the households' budgets, it is reckoned that one half of additional farm income will be spent on rice, and the remainder on textiles. The COPE supplies the following information on shadow prices and other important parameters:

Accounting ratio for construction	0.7
Tariff on machinery	None
Tariff on diesel fuel	100%
Import subsidy on fertilizers	20%
Tariff on textiles	11%
The present value of an additional unit of public income received every year over the project's life	15.0
Premium on public income	33%

By taking public income as the numeraire and computing the social value of the vector of the changes in annual incomes (private and public) that would result from each of these projects, or otherwise, decide which, if indeed either, of them should be accepted. [Hint: set all domestic prices to unity, so that you can calculate the net change in government revenue associated with each proposal.]

Suppose floods occur on average every ten years, and that when they do so, crops worth 40 at market prices are destroyed. (The occurrence of flooding is an event that is i.i.d.) If the dam would eliminate this hazard, but the pumps would not, would your decision change?

9. Shadow Prices

Having prepared the ground with an intuitive account in Chapter 8, we now embark on the task of deriving shadow prices in a rigorous way. The main emphasis here is on capturing the general equilibrium effects that ensue from changes in public production and consumption, and on the relationship between shadow prices and economic policy, though some aspects of income distribution will also be treated as an integral part of the analysis.

The chapter opens with a formal statement of the problem, in the course of which the concepts of a 'small' project and the shadow price of a commodity are defined precisely. The case where the social welfare function takes a Bergson–Samuelsonian form is then pursued in some detail (Section 9.2). The derivation of the shadow prices themselves is accomplished using an extension of Bell and Devarajan (1983), underpinned by the general approach laid out in Drèze and Stern (1987). The basic model in Sections 9.3 and 9.4 is undeniably special in form, but lends itself readily to generalization, as we shall see both in Section 9.5 and in the chapters that follow. The particular topic taken up in Section 9.5 is the influence of a regulated wage in one or more sectors of the economy on the entire vector of shadow prices, whereby a crucial role is played by migrants' behaviour in the face of the opportunities that such a wage creates. It is shown that in this setting shadow prices are not, in general, proportional to producer prices, which illustrates the contention that shadow prices are not, in general, independent of the government's choice of policies. In Section 9.6, we examine how to evaluate economic reforms when shadow prices depart from producer prices, with an application to the reform of commodity taxes. To close the chapter, we show that if proposals to undertake certain projects are coupled to a reform of policy, then the projects must be evaluated separately from the reform itself, and at the shadow prices that would rule in the event that the reform were implemented.

9.1. The Principles of Shadow Prices

Evaluating a project essentially involves two steps. The first is to formulate a basis for ranking different states of the economy; for the ultimate question to be answered is whether undertaking the project in question is 'better' in some well-defined sense than the next best alternative. The approach chosen here is not especially restrictive, but it is also not wholly uncontroversial. We suppose that the social ordering of states of the economy can be represented by the continuously differentiable social welfare function

$$W = W(S_1, \ldots, S_m), \tag{9.1}$$

whose arguments may include the consumption and savings of various socioeconomic groups, as well as government income, perhaps with a distinction between what is committed for particular purposes and what is not, all at various points in time.

The second step is to estimate the project's effects on $S = (S_1, \ldots, S_m)$, and hence on $W(\cdot)$. In order to accomplish this, we begin by defining a project. Let the public sector's net supply of commodities be denoted by the vector $z = (z_1, \ldots, z_n)$, this being a summary statement of the public sector's transactions, including the production activities of state-owned enterprises. Physically identical commodities are distinguished, where appropriate, by the dates of their availability, so that n is defined accordingly.

Definition 1. A small project is a set of small changes in the components of z, namely,

$$dz \equiv (dz_1, \ldots, dz_n). \tag{9.2}$$

This definition treats a project as a disturbance to an economy in the form of a small change in the public sector's production plan. In general, the vector S will depend on all elements of z, although $\partial S_k/\partial z_j = 0$ may hold in particular cases.[1] The change in social welfare generated by the project dz is

$$dW(S) = \sum_{k=1}^{m} \frac{\partial W}{\partial S_k} \sum_{j=1}^{n} \frac{\partial S_k}{\partial z_j} \cdot dz_j. \tag{9.3}$$

A natural definition of the shadow price of commodity j (be it good or factor) is the change in social welfare that would result if the public sector's net supply thereof were to increase by one unit, with z otherwise

---

[1] Note that we have slipped in the assumption that S is differentiable in z.

unchanged. That is, the project $(0, \ldots, 0, dz_j, 0, \ldots, 0)$ yields the shadow price of commodity j as

$$\pi_j \equiv \frac{dW(S)}{dz_j} = \sum_{k=1}^{m} \frac{\partial W}{\partial S_k} \frac{\partial S_k}{\partial z_j}. \tag{9.4}$$

Under this definition, the change in social welfare induced by the project $\mathbf{dz} = (dz_1, \ldots, dz_n)$ is

$$dW(S) = \boldsymbol{\pi} \cdot \mathbf{dz}. \tag{9.5}$$

Hence, by using the (shadow) price vector $\boldsymbol{\pi}$ to value inputs and outputs, the government can rest assured that it is measuring the change in social welfare that would result from undertaking the project $\mathbf{dz}$.

Two things should be noted about this procedure. First, $\boldsymbol{\pi}$ is defined on the assumption that all other forms of intervention are optimally chosen within the limits imposed by the government's opportunity set both before and after the project is undertaken. As we shall see in this chapter, any failure to exploit opportunities to improve policy in other spheres will lead to a fundamental difficulty when using shadow prices to evaluate projects. Second, the shadow prices defined above decentralize public sector decision making: once the Central Office of Project Evaluation (COPE) has finished its business, individual ministries and enterprises in the public sector can get on with theirs without any further need of economic coordination in choosing among projects or production activities.

To sum up thus far, if we can obtain the derivatives $(\partial S_k / \partial z_j)$ using a suitably formulated model of the economy, and if defensible assumptions can be made about the form of $W(\cdot)$, then we are home. The principles themselves seem straightforward enough; but as we shall now see, implementing them in practice can involve some formidable difficulties.

9.2. The Social Welfare Function

Suppose aggregate welfare is a function of individuals' utilities, each of which depends, in turn, on the bundle of commodities consumed by the individual in question. Let individual h consume the bundle $\mathbf{x}^h$, where individuals are indexed by h ($h = 1, \ldots, H$). For the present, we confine ourselves to the case in which there are only private goods. The absence of any reference to savings implies that each individual's consumption vectors are dated over his or her lifetime. We then have the following form of Eqn (9.1):

$$W = W\{u^1[x^1(q(z), z)], \ldots, u^H[x^H(q(z), z)]\}, \tag{9.1$'$}$$

where it should be noted that (dated) consumer prices will, in general, depend on z. The government may, for example, finance the project by levying higher taxes on commodities or factors. The explicit presence of z in Eqn (9.1$'$) allows for the possibility that lump sum income may also depend on z. Given Eqn (9.1$'$), Eqn (9.3) specializes to

$$dW = \sum_{h=1}^{H} \frac{\partial W}{\partial u^h} \sum_{i=1}^{n} \frac{\partial u^h}{\partial x_i^h} \sum_{j=1}^{n} \frac{\partial x_i^h}{\partial z_j} \cdot dz_j, \tag{9.3$'$}$$

where all derivatives of x^h w.r.t. z are to be understood as

$$\frac{\partial x_i^h}{\partial z_j} = \sum_{k=1}^{n} \frac{\partial x_i^h}{\partial q_k} \cdot \frac{\partial q_k}{\partial z_j} + \frac{\partial x_i^h}{\partial z_j}\bigg|_q. \tag{9.6}$$

In the case where consumer prices are independent of z for some reason or other, the first term on the right-hand side (RHS) of Eqn (9.6) will vanish, only income effects will remain, and life becomes comparatively simple.

If consumers experience no rationing in commodity markets and purchase positive amounts of each and every good, then the first-order conditions for u^h to take a maximum are simply $\partial u^h/\partial x_i^h = \alpha^h q_i$ ($\forall h, i$), where α^h is the marginal utility of the present value of individual h's lifetime income.[2] Rearranging Eqn (9.3$'$), we then obtain

$$dW = \left[\sum_{h=1}^{H} \left(\frac{\partial W}{\partial u^h} \alpha^h\right) \sum_{i=1}^{n} q_i \sum_{j=1}^{n} \frac{\partial x_i^h}{\partial z_j} \cdot dz_j\right]. \tag{9.7}$$

It is helpful to express the distributional considerations that enter into Eqn (9.7) as follows: without loss of generality, let individual 1 have the smallest present value of lifetime income and define

$$\omega^h \equiv \frac{\alpha^h \cdot (\partial W/\partial u^h)}{\alpha^1 \cdot (\partial W/\partial u^1)}. \tag{9.8}$$

---

[2] Recall that α^h is the Lagrange multiplier associated with this individual's lifetime budget constraint.

Thus, ω^h is the ratio of the social values of a unit increase in income accruing to individuals h and 1, respectively. Without loss of generality, we may normalize the marginal effects on $W(\cdot)$ of changes in individual utilities by setting $\partial W / \partial u^1$ to unity, so that the vector $\boldsymbol{\omega}$ may be interpreted as the set of weights for the social valuation of changes in private incomes. In order to make the role of distributional judgements clear, we divide both sides of Eqn (9.7) by α^1 and then rearrange it in the form

$$\frac{dW}{\alpha^1} = \left[\sum_{h=1}^{H} \sum_{i=1}^{n} q_i \sum_{j=1}^{n} \frac{\partial x_i^h}{\partial z_j} \, dz_j - \sum_{h=1}^{H} (1 - \omega^h) \sum_{i=1}^{n} q_i \sum_{j=1}^{n} \frac{\partial x_i^h}{\partial z_j} \, dz_j \right].$$

(9.9)

With the normalization $\omega^1 = 1$ for the poorest individual or group, we now *define* the shadow price of good j as

$$\pi_j \equiv \frac{1}{\alpha^1} \left(\frac{\partial W}{\partial z_j} \right),$$

(9.10)

where the intrusion of the common factor $(1/\alpha^1)$ rescales the social profitability of any project, but without changing its sign. That is to say, the shadow price of good j is the change in welfare resulting from a unit increase in the net supply of that commodity or factor by the public sector, normalized by the marginal utility of lifetime income of the reference individual. Hence, from Eqn (9.9), we obtain

$$\pi_j = \left[\sum_{h=1}^{H} \sum_{i=1}^{n} q_i \frac{\partial x_i^h}{\partial z_j} - \sum_{h=1}^{H} (1 - \omega^h) \sum_{i=1}^{n} q_i \frac{\partial x_i^h}{\partial z_j} \right].$$

(9.11a)

Note that the role of income distribution considerations is clearly defined, these being reflected by the terms $(1 - \omega^h)$. If income distribution is fully optimal (or of no interest to the government), then $\omega^h = 1$ for all h. In that case, we can confine our attention to what happens in aggregate, and Eqn (9.11a) specializes to the compact form

$$\pi = q \cdot (\partial X / \partial z),$$

(9.11b)

where $X = \sum_{h=1}^{H} x^h$, and $\partial X / \partial z$ is the matrix $(\partial X_i / \partial z_j)$. It is sometimes said that Eqn (9.11b) defines 'efficiency' (shadow) prices for cost–benefit analysis. It hardly needs remarking that this definition rests on a particular notion of what constitutes efficiency. Yet it should be emphasized that this is precisely the notion that underpins the widespread use of the willingness-to-pay in units of money as a measure of a project's benefits or costs. In such a scheme, one rupee accruing to one of the well-to-do counts for exactly the same as one rupee accruing to a landless labourer, a value judgement that can certainly be contested.

9.3. Shadow Prices in a Simple Model

While the reasoning that leads to Eqn (9.11a) is clear enough, the prospect of having to derive the matrix $\partial X/\partial z$ is a daunting one, so it is natural to ask whether there is some other way of arriving at π. It is also far from obvious how Eqn (9.11a) relates to the 'cookbook' rules discussed in Chapter 8. We address these questions by employing the envelope theorem to derive the set of shadow prices for a particular economy, the characteristics of which have been chosen so that the reader will be able to see the technique at work in a transparent way. The setting is a purely static one, the extension to two or more periods being deferred to Chapter 10. The model chosen for this purpose is Bell and Devarajan (1983), but shorn of intermediate inputs in production. The assumptions are as follows:

Assumption 1. There is only one non-produced input, namely labour, which is supplied completely inelastically and traded in a perfect market.

Assumption 2. All goods are produced by means of labour alone under CRS.

Assumption 3. There are three private goods, the markets for which are perfectly competitive. Goods 1 and 2 are tradable in world markets at parametric prices p_i^* $(i = 1, 2)$; the third is a non-tradable. Since there is only one factor, only one tradable will be produced domestically. Without loss of generality, let the technology and world prices be such that it is good 1.

Since the entire labour endowment is offered completely inelastically, a proportional tax on all goods would be equivalent to a lump sum tax. Without loss of generality, therefore, let good 1 be non-taxable. Since A1–A3 imply that there will be no pure profits, we have the following restriction:

Assumption 4. The only instruments available to the government are a tariff on good 2 (the importable) and a commodity tax on the non-tradable.

The other sources of revenue are an endowment of foreign exchange, F, and the profits (or losses) of public sector enterprises, which accrue to the Treasury.

Assumption 5. Public sector enterprises trade at market prices.

Assumption 6. The government raises revenue to finance the provision of a public good, which is denoted by good 0. The amount provided is assumed to be fixed and to require L_0 units of labour.

In time-honoured fashion, we solve the system by proceeding from the world prices of tradables to their respective domestic prices, thence to factor prices, and finally to the prices of non-tradables. If the only taxes on tradable goods are taxes on trade, their domestic prices will be

$$p_i = q_i = p_i^* + t_i, \quad i = 1, 2, \tag{9.12}$$

where p_i^* is the world price and $t_i > 0$ implies a subsidy on an exportable and a tariff on an importable. By virtue of A3, domestic producers in sector 1 are competitive at the world price p_1^*, and since $t_1 = 0$, we have

$$p_1 = q_1 = p_1^*. \tag{9.13}$$

As price equals unit cost in domestic production, the wage rate follows from Eqn (9.13):

$$w = p_1^*/l_1, \tag{9.14}$$

where l_1 is the labour–output ratio in sector 1; and hence also the producer price of the non-tradable:

$$p_3 = wl_3 = p_1^*(l_3/l_1). \tag{9.15}$$

The consumer price of good 3 is simply $q_3 = p_3 + t_3$.

This does not quite complete the picture. For any given configuration of world prices and taxes (p^*, t), Eqns (9.12)–(9.15) yield (p, w), and hence consumer prices. Observe, however, that under the above assumptions, the vector of producer prices is not (p, w), but rather $(p_1^*, p_2^*, p_1^*(l_3/l_1), p_1^*/l_1)$. For by assumption, it is not profitable to produce good 2 at home, even with the help of the protective tariff t_2, so that $wl_2 > p_1^* + t_2$. The alternative actually used is to 'produce' good 2 by exporting good 1 at the fixed exchange ratio (p_1^*/p_2^*), which is also the efficient thing to do given that $wl_2 > p_1^* + t_2$. Note also that producer prices are fixed for any given vector of world prices and labour–input coefficients in domestic production.

A1, A2, and A6 imply that private production possibilities in aggregate are given by

$$l_1y_1 + l_2y_2 + l_3y_3 = \bar{L} - L_0, \tag{9.16}$$

where it should be recalled once more that, by assumption, good 2 will not actually be produced domestically in the setting described by (p^*, t, l). Public production must be introduced into the market-clearing equations for goods, and the profits (or losses) therefrom must be incorporated into the public sector's accounts. The market-clearing equations are

$$y_1 + z_1 = x_1 + e_1, \tag{9.17}$$

$$z_2 = x_2 + e_2, \tag{9.18}$$

and

$$y_3 + z_3 = x_3, \tag{9.19}$$

where e_i $(i = 1, 2)$ is the net export of good i. Multiplying each of Eqns (9.17)–(9.19) by the domestic price of the good in question and then adding them together, we get the following accounting identity for private goods:

$$p_1 y_1 + p_3 y_3 + \sum_{i \neq 0} p_i z_i = \sum_{i \neq 0} p_i x_i + (p_1 e_1 + p_2 e_2). \tag{9.20}$$

Since all private incomes are spent and labour is the only factor of production, we also have

$$w\bar{L} = \sum_{i \neq 0} q_i x_i = \sum_{i \neq 0} p_i x_i + t_2 x_2 + t_3 x_3. \tag{9.21}$$

The government's total net revenue from taxation and the profits of public enterprises yield public income in the amount of $(-t_2 e_2 + t_3 x_3 + \sum_{i \neq 0} p_i z_i)$. Together with the endowment of foreign exchange F, these receipts must cover the cost of producing the public good, namely, wL_0. Multiplying Eqn (9.16) by w, and noting that $y_2 = 0$, we obtain a further national accounting identity in the form:

$$p_1 y_1 + p_3 y_3 + wL_0 = w\bar{L}.$$

Recalling that the government's budget is balanced, this may be rewritten as

$$p_1 y_1 + p_3 y_3 + \left[\left(-t_2 e_2 + t_3 x_3 + \sum_{i \neq 0} p_i z_i \right) + F \right] = w\bar{L}. \tag{9.22}$$

Combining Eqns (9.21) and (9.22), and using Eqns (9.12) and (9.17)–(9.19), we obtain the familiar result that the trade deficit at world prices is equal to the endowment F:

$$p^*e + F = 0, \tag{9.23}$$

which is a simple consequence of the fact that both the private and public sectors are on their respective budget lines. Equation (9.23) is also, of course, a statement of Walras' law, in which the presence of F turns out to yield a convenient way of deriving the shadow price of foreign exchange (equivalently, of government income).

In general, private incomes, and hence consumption, will depend on the pattern of economic activities, and hence on public policies. Under the above assumptions, however, there is full employment at the constant wage $w = p_1^*/l_1$, so that total private income, M, takes the fixed value

$$M = w\bar{L} \tag{9.24}$$

and consumer demand, x, depends only on consumer prices.

Since producer prices are given, the government's problem is to

maximize $v(q, M)$ subject to: Eqns (9.16)–(9.19) and (9.23).   (9.25)
(q_2, q_3)

Following Drèze and Stern (1987), the Lagrangian associated with problem (9.25) is written as follows:

$$\Phi = v(q, M) + \sum_{i \neq 0} \lambda_i [y_i + z_i - x_i(q, M) - e_i]$$

$$+ \lambda_l [\bar{L} - \sum_{i \neq 0} l_i y_i - L_0] + \mu(F + p^*e), \tag{9.26}$$

where $y_2 = e_3 = 0$ and no condition involving M as an endogenous variable appears in Φ in this particular case. By the envelope theorem, we have

$$\pi_i \equiv \frac{\partial \Phi^0}{\partial z_i} = \frac{\partial v^0}{\partial z_i} = \lambda_i, \quad i = 1, 2, 3, \tag{9.27}$$

$$\pi_l \equiv -\frac{\partial \Phi^0}{\partial L_0} = -\frac{\partial v^0}{\partial L_0} = \lambda_l, \tag{9.28}$$

$$\pi_F \equiv \frac{\partial \Phi^0}{\partial F} = \frac{\partial v^0}{\partial F} = \mu, \tag{9.29}$$

where the superscript '0' indicates that the derivatives in question are evaluated at the optimum. When the problem is written down in this particular form, therefore, the values of the dual variables λ_i, λ_l, and μ at the optimum are indeed the appropriate shadow prices for the public sector. As Drèze and Stern (1987) take pains to point out, however, the form is vital to this result; for otherwise, the dual variables will not be equal to the shadow prices of the system.

A remark on the derivation of the shadow price of labour is also in order. The appearance of L_0 as a parameter in the proceedings, though technically necessary, sits a little awkwardly with its employment in the production of a public good. For changes in such employment should lead to changes in the level of the provision of this good, and hence to changes in welfare. This effect has been ruled out in the above derivation, as the definition of a shadow price indeed requires. Hence, a unit increase in L_0 is to be interpreted here as the employment of an additional worker who whiles away his time in idleness but still draws his salary—a thought experiment that should not unduly tax the imagination.

Now, at the optimum, $\Phi(\cdot)$ must be stationary with respect to all of the endogenous variables in the system, whether they be chosen by the government (q), or whether they adjust to bring about equilibrium in the economy ($y, e, x(q)$). Inspection of the Lagrangian reveals that its derivatives with respect to e and y hold out the promise of obtaining the multipliers.

$$\frac{\partial \Phi}{\partial e_i} = -\lambda_i + \mu p_i^* = 0, \quad i = 1, 2, \tag{9.30}$$

$$\frac{\partial \Phi}{\partial y_i} = \lambda_i - l_i \lambda_l = 0, \quad i = 1, 3. \tag{9.31}$$

Rearranging, we obtain the vector of shadow prices:

$$\boldsymbol{\pi} \equiv (\lambda_1, \lambda_2, \lambda_3, \lambda_l) = \mu(p_1^*, p_2^*, p_1^*(l_3/l_1), p_1^*/l_1), \tag{9.32}$$

from which it is seen at once that shadow prices are proportional to producer prices,[3] the factor of proportionality, μ, being the shadow price of public income. It follows that, in this setting, any public project that turns a profit at producer prices will also turn a social profit, in the sense of increasing $v^0(\cdot)$, and hence should be adopted. Observe, in particular, that the relative shadow price of the tradables, (λ_2/λ_1), is equal to their

---

[3] Recall that the public sector is able to 'produce' one tradable by means of another by trading at the ruling world prices p^*.

respective relative world price, (p_2^*/p_1^*): suitably reinterpreted, this is the 'border price' rule. Note also that the multiplier μ is the increase in v^0 that would result if the government were to receive an external gift of one unit of foreign exchange.

The above derivation, though formally clear, is rather wanting where intuition is concerned, so it may be helpful to invoke a geometric argument. Recalling the Diamond–Mirrlees (D–M) diagram in Chapter 4, we begin by deriving the consumption possibility set for private goods in a form where the influence of the vector (z, L_0, F) thereon is clearly seen. Multiplying Eqns (9.17)–(9.19) by p_1^*, p_2^*, and p_3, respectively, adding them together, and noting Eqn (9.23), we obtain

$$p_1^* y_1 + p_3 y_3 + (p_1^* z_1 + p_2^* z_2 + p_3 z_3 + F) = p_1^* x_1 + p_2^* x_2 + p_3 x_3.$$

Multiplying Eqn (9.16) by w and recalling Eqns (9.14) and (9.15), where $y_2 = 0$, we obtain

$$p_1^* y_1 + p_3 y_3 = p_1^* (\bar{L} - L_0)/l_1,$$

and hence the consumption possibility frontier in private goods:

$$p_1^* x_1 + p_2^* x_2 + p_1^* (l_3/l_1) x_3 = (p_1^*/l_1) \cdot \bar{L} + \chi, \tag{9.33}$$

where

$$\chi \equiv [p_1^* z_1 + p_2^* z_2 + p_3 z_3 + F - (p_1^*/l_1) \cdot L_0)].$$

This frontier is a plane in the space of x whose normal is the producer price vector $[p_1^*, p_2^*, p_1^* (l_3/l_1)]$. Since consumption is non-negative, the relevant subset of this plane is depicted in Fig. 9.1 as ABC. The RHS of Eqn (9.33) is the private sector's income from supplying factors to production, augmented by the algebraic sum of the profits of public sector production at producer prices, the endowment F, and the cost of producing the public good. If negative, the latter sum must be covered by net taxes on commodities, and if positive, by net subsidies thereon; for direct transfers have been ruled out. A unit increase in z_1 alone will increase the RHS by the world price of good 1, namely p_1^*, without disturbing the prices on the left-hand side (LHS) of Eqn (9.33). The effects of unit increases in the other elements making up χ can be read off in the same way. All involve parallel shifts of ABC. Since the government's optimal choice of consumer prices, q^0, will leave the consumer on that frontier, it follows that the shadow prices of goods, labour, and foreign exchange must be proportional to the sizes of the (small) shifts they induce, that is, to the vector $[p_1^*, p_2^*, p_1^* (l_3/l_1), (p_1^*/l_1), 1]$, whose last element refers to a unit increase in F.

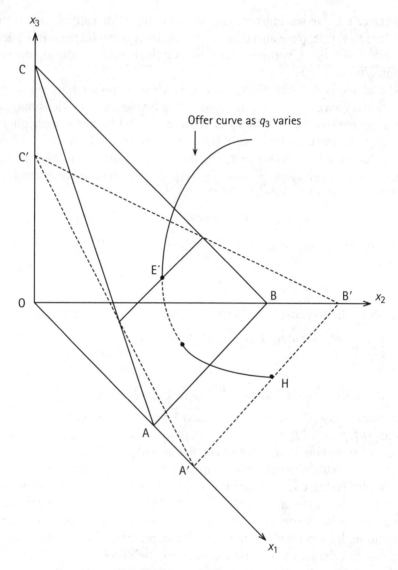

Figure 9.1. A tax on good 3 alone. The normal to $A'B'C'$ at E' is q, where $q = \nabla u(x^{E'})$, $q_1 = p_1, q_2 = p_2$

9.4. Shadow Prices and Policies

The result just derived prompts the important question of whether shadow prices depend on the particular policies pursued by the government. If this proves to be so, then a project that is socially profitable under one set of policies may be unprofitable under another. There is more at stake, however, than ascertaining what current policies are in order to analyse projects, vital though this is. For evaluating a project also offers the opportunity to assess whether the policies themselves should be reformed as part of the evaluation process, a matter that will arise in Section 9.7 and later chapters.

In the setting analysed in Section 9.3, the shadow price of public income depends on the fact that q is chosen so as to solve problem (9.25). In order to see this, we examine the associated first-order conditions:

$$\frac{\partial \Phi}{\partial q_i} = \frac{\partial v}{\partial q_i} - \sum_j \lambda_j \frac{\partial x_j}{\partial q_i} = 0, \quad i = 2, 3, \tag{9.34}$$

which, using Roy's identity and Eqn (9.32), yield the familiar form

$$\alpha x_i = -\mu[p_1^*(\partial x_1/\partial q_i) + p_2^*(\partial x_2/\partial q_i) + p_3(\partial x_3/\partial q_i)], \quad i = 2, 3. \tag{9.35}$$

In this case, we have the full D–M solution, in which there are no restrictions on the magnitudes of taxes or subsidies on commodities, subject, of course, to the overall revenue constraint being satisfied. As already noted, in this case, μ simply scales the vector of producer prices, and so has no effect on whether a particular project should be undertaken.

Now suppose that, instead of all consumer prices being completely flexible, either q_2 or q_3 were fixed for some reason. In that case, the government would have no real choices (degrees of freedom), for the other consumer price would have to be set at a level that would raise the required amount of revenue or return the surplus of revenues over the cost of supplying the public good. In a qualitative sense, a different policy would be pursued, relative to the D–M case.

Returning to the consumption possibility frontier (9.33), observe that this equation can also be interpreted as the government's revenue constraint, a claim that is established as follows. The total revenue from taxation and other sources is

$$(q_1 - p_1^*)x_1 + (q_2 - p_2^*)x_2 + (q_3 - p_3)x_3 + F + p_1^*z_1 + p_2^*z_2 + p_3z_3.$$

Since $qx = M$ and the government's total outlays are wL_0, substituting for M from Eqn (9.24) and rearranging, we obtain the revenue constraint in the form

$$(p_1^*/l_1) \cdot \bar{L} + \chi - [p_1^* x_1 + p_2^* x_2 + p_1^*(l_3/l_1) x_3] \geq 0,$$

which is Eqn (9.33), extended to allow for the possibility that revenue may exceed outlays. With this point settled, we consider restrictions on the taxation of goods 2 and 3. Without loss of generality, suppose that good 2 is also non-taxable, so that $p_i = q_i = p_i^* (i = 1, 2)$ and q_3 must vary freely in response to changes in (z, L_0, F). Then Eqn (9.35) would hold only for $i = 3$, and μ would not, in general, take its D–M value. This case is depicted in Fig. 9.1, where the plane A'B'C' depicts the first part of Eqn (9.21), which is the individual's income–expenditure identity at consumer prices under this additional restriction on taxes:

$$p_1^* x_1 + p_2^* x_2 + q_3 x_3 = (p_1^*/l_1)\bar{L}. \tag{9.21'}$$

The line segment A'B' is drawn farther from the origin than AB, the difference being the term χ, which is assumed to be negative for the purposes of drawing the diagram. When q_3 is arbitrarily large, C' will lie arbitrarily close to the origin; and if good 3 is not necessary in consumption, the individual will choose some bundle on A'B', say point H. As the tax on good 3 falls, C' will move in the direction of C. The optimum lies at E', where, proceeding from H, the offer curve induced by progressive changes in q_3 (given $q_i = p_i^*, i = 1, 2$) intersects the plane ABC for the last time. E' will not, in general, coincide with the D–M optimum; it certainly does not do so in this particular model.

There is, however, one central result in Section 9.3 that is unaffected by this additional restriction on taxes, namely, that the vector of shadow prices remains proportional to the vector of producer prices $[p_1^*, p_2^*, p_1^*(l_3/l_1), (p_1^*/l_1), 1]$; for ABC is unaffected by the choice of q.[4] The additional restriction on q makes itself felt only through a change in the marginal value of public income.

The dependence of the consumer's welfare and μ on the government's opportunity set is nicely revealed in the space of (q_2, q_3). Since $q_1 = p_1^*$ and private income is constant, at $(p_1^*/l_1)\bar{L}$, the demand vector may be written as $x(q_2, q_3)$. From Eqn (9.33), we then obtain the revenue constraint as a function of q_2 and q_3. If the individual's preferences are smooth and convex, the indifference contours will be convex to the origin in this space, as depicted in Fig. 9.2, whereby a contour closer to the origin is preferred

---

[4] This result is also seen by noting that Eqns (9.30) and (9.31) continue to hold at E'.

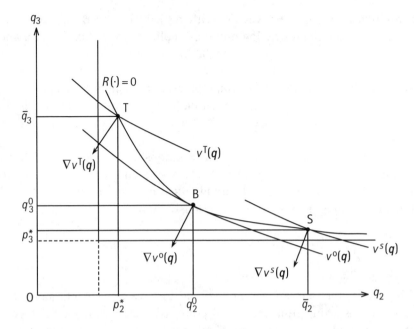

Figure 9.2. Gradient vectors for different policies in the space of consumer prices

to one lying farther out. The revenue constraint holds with equality on the curve labelled $R(\cdot) = 0$, and is also satisfied for all (q_2, q_3) above the same. $R(\cdot)$, too, is drawn as convex to the origin, but it need not be so. Observing from Eqns (9.27) and (9.28) that the vector of shadow prices is simply the gradient of $u(\cdot)$ with respect to z at the optimum, we have

$$\frac{\partial v^0}{\partial z_i} = \frac{\partial v^0}{\partial q_2} \cdot \frac{\partial q_2}{\partial z_i} + \frac{\partial v^0}{\partial q_3} \cdot \frac{\partial q_3}{\partial z_i}, \quad i = 1, 2, 3, l. \tag{9.36}$$

The gradient vector with respect to q at the D–M optimum, $\nabla v^0(q) \equiv (\partial v^0 / \partial q)$, is the vector drawn perpendicular to the indifference contour at the optimum, which is labelled as point B. Hence, if we can find the reduction in taxes that is induced by a unit increase in z_i, we can then obtain the shadow price of good i using Eqn (9.36). In fact, that is precisely what we did in Section 9.3 when using the envelope theorem.

Now suppose, instead, that the required amount of revenue must be raised by means of a tax levied exclusively on either good 2 or good 3. Denote these points by S and T, respectively. Both are inferior to B, which is a consequence of the additional restriction on taxes to which each corresponds. The gradient vectors with respect to q at B, S, and T are all different, and the restriction on taxes implies that $\partial q_3/\partial z = 0$ at S and $\partial q_2/\partial z = 0$ at T. It follows from Eqn (9.36) that the vector of shadow prices is different in each case; but as we noted above, only up to a scalar multiple, namely, the value of μ. It would be very convenient if this last result were robust to changes in the other assumptions set out in Section 9.3. As we are about to see in connection with the labour market, however, this is not always the case.

To close this section, we take up the relationship between π as defined in Eqn (9.11) and π as derived in Sections 9.3 and 9.4, which leads to Eqn (9.32). Since all individuals are identical by assumption, Eqn (9.11b) holds, which may be written in the extensive form

$$\pi_i = \sum_{j=1}^{3} q_j \frac{\partial x_j}{\partial z_i}.$$

Observe that the derivatives $(\partial x_j/\partial z_i)$ all involve movements along the offer curve, starting from the initial point associated with the price vector q. For small movements, the change in welfare will be proportional to the size of the movement. As we just have proved, however, the size of the movement induced by a change in z_i is proportional to the producer price of good i. It follows that Eqns (9.11b) and (9.32) are quite consistent—though the latter is much more appealing where both intuition and practical computation are concerned.

9.5. A Regulated Wage

The shadow wage rate is among the most important of all shadow prices, and its magnitude depends heavily on how the labour market works. A central feature of this market in most developing countries is that the wage in certain sectors of the economy is effectively regulated above its market-clearing level, either directly, or indirectly through a political compact with the trades union. In the remainder of the economy—peasant agriculture, much of the service sector, and unorganized industry—the wage adjusts fairly flexibly in textbook fashion. As a step towards greater realism, we now modify the model of Section 9.3 to accommodate such a distortion in the light of the fact that workers are usually mobile.

Since the export sector is usually agriculture and much of the sector producing non-tradables is urban, and hence easier to regulate, we assume that w_3 is fixed above the level ruling in sector 1, which is set by the requirement that sector 1 be internationally competitive, namely, Eqn (9.14). We deal with two extreme variants. In the first, there is no open unemployment: those who fail to find one of the plum jobs in sector 3 return at once to work in sector 1. The second is the simplest Harris–Todaro model, in which only those actually dwelling in towns can obtain urban jobs, so that they must forgo the sure thing in the form of their alternative earnings in sector 1 in order to do so.

9.5.1. Full Employment

We assume, plausibly enough, that if an additional job is created in the public sector, it will pay the regulated wage. Under conditions of full employment, the gap in wage rates between the two sectors makes the level of private income dependent on the distribution of employment, so that Eqn (9.24) is replaced by

$$M = w_1 \bar{L} + \Delta w \cdot (l_3 y_3 + L_0), \tag{9.37}$$

where the wage 'gap' is $\Delta w \equiv w_3 - w_1$. Observe that even if w_1 is constant, M now depends not only on L_0, but also on y_3, which is endogenous. The Lagrangian (9.26) must therefore be augmented to include Eqn (9.37), whose associated Lagrange multiplier is denoted by ϕ. It is seen at once from the augmented Lagrangian that Eqns (9.27), (9.29), and (9.30) remain unchanged, whereas Eqn (9.28) and that part of Eqn (9.31) dealing with the derivative of Φ w.r.t. y_3 need to be modified. These now read, respectively,

$$\pi_l \equiv -\frac{\partial \Phi^0}{\partial L_0} = -\frac{\partial v^0}{\partial L_0} = \lambda_l + \phi \cdot \Delta w, \tag{9.38}$$

and

$$\frac{\partial \Phi}{\partial y_3} = \lambda_3 - l_3(\lambda_l + \phi \cdot \Delta w) = 0, \tag{9.39}$$

so that the product $\phi \cdot \Delta w$ intrudes as an additional term in both. It remains the case, however, that the shadow price of good 3 is equal to the marginal (equals unit) cost of producing it, calculated at shadow prices.

Since M is now endogenous, the associated first-order condition is also required:

$$\frac{\partial \Phi}{\partial M} = \frac{\partial v}{\partial M} - \sum_{i=1}^{3} \lambda_i \frac{\partial x_i}{\partial M} + \phi = 0. \tag{9.40}$$

Substituting for ϕ from Eqn (9.40) in Eqn (9.38) yields the following expression for the shadow wage rate:

$$\pi_l = \lambda_l + \left[\sum_{i=1}^{3} (\lambda_i/q_i)b_i - (\partial v/\partial M) \right] \Delta w, \tag{9.41}$$

where $b_i \equiv q_i(\partial x_i/\partial M)$ is consumers' marginal propensity to spend on good i. Since Eqns (9.30) and (9.31) continue to hold for good 1, we have

$$\lambda_l = \mu \cdot (p_1^*/l_1), \tag{9.42}$$

which is formally the same as in Section 9.3. It should be recalled, however, that the value of μ depends on how the economy functions in all respects. Combining Eqns (9.41) and (9.42), we obtain

$$\pi_l = \mu \cdot \left\{ (p_1^*/l_1) + \left[\sum_{i=1}^{2} (p_i^*/q_i)b_i + (\lambda_3/q_3)b_3 - \frac{\partial v/\partial M}{\mu} \right] \Delta w \right\}. \tag{9.43}$$

Since μ is the shadow price of public income when $v(\cdot)$ is to be maximized, dividing both sides of Eqn (9.43) by μ is equivalent to choosing public income as the numeraire. Let us do so, defining the shadow wage rate as

$$w^* \equiv \frac{\pi_l}{\mu} \equiv -\frac{1}{\mu} \cdot \frac{\partial v^0}{\partial L_0} = (p_1^*/l_1)$$

$$+ \left[\sum_{i=1}^{2} (p_i^*/q_i)b_i + (\lambda_3/q_3)b_3 - \frac{\partial v/\partial M}{\mu} \right] \Delta w. \tag{9.44}$$

The intuition for this expression is as follows. If an additional worker is employed in the public sector, the direct effect thereof in the present setting is that one worker must be drawn out of sector 1, employment in sector 3 being determined endogenously by domestic demand. As a result, the economy suffers a direct loss of output, valued at world prices, in the amount (p_1^*/l_1). A further direct effect is that private income will also rise by the amount Δw, which is spent in the proportions b. Each additional rupee thereof commits the economy to additional consumption of resources, whose value at shadow prices (normalized by μ) is the consumption conversion factor

$$\text{CCF} \equiv \sum_{i=1}^{2} (p_i^*/q_i)b_i + (\lambda_3/q_3)b_3.$$

At the same time, each additional rupee of private income is socially valuable: to be precise, its value in terms of the numeraire is $(\partial v/\partial M)/\mu$, which duly appears in Eqn (9.44), with a negative sign in view of the benefit it confers on the representative individual. Comparing Eqn (9.44) with (8.8) in Chapter 8, we see that we have derived the 'cookbook' rule, where the social opportunity cost of labour is $\pi_0 m_0 = (p_1^*/l_1)$ and θ is interpreted as the marginal value of private income when public income chosen as the numeraire, namely, $(\partial v/\partial M)/\mu$. With this numeraire, the shadow price of the non-tradable is simply $w^* l_3$.

We now return to the question of whether, and if so, how, shadow prices depend on the government's policies. Comparing Eqns (9.38) and (9.39) with their counterparts in Section 9.3, namely, Eqns (9.28) and (9.31), respectively, it is immediately clear that shadow prices will be proportional to producer prices if and only if either $\Delta w = 0$ or $\phi = 0$. Since, by hypothesis, there is indeed a wage gap, we turn to ϕ. From Eqn (9.40), ϕ vanishes if and only if

$$\left[\sum_{i=1}^{2} (p_i^*/q_i)b_i + (\lambda_3/q_3)b_3 - \frac{\partial v/\partial M}{\mu} \right] = 0,$$

that is to say, if and only if the consumption conversion factor is equal to the ratio of the marginal utility of private income to the shadow price of public income. While this possibility cannot be completely ruled out in advance, it will hold only by fluke. In this setting, therefore, the whole structure of shadow prices is influenced by the policies actually pursued in the labour market.

9.5.2. Open Unemployment

In the simplest version of the Harris–Todaro (1970) model, there are only two locations: the family farm and the city, which we interpret here as sectors 1 and 3, respectively. All urban jobs are assumed to turn over in every period, but an individual must actually be present there in order to get such a job. All urban residents are also assumed to have the same chance of landing a job in each period. As a further simplification, suppose that everyone can move without cost between village and town at the start of each period. Once having chosen a location for the current period, however, an individual must remain there until the beginning of the next; for otherwise we would be back in the world of Section 9.5.1, in which there is no unemployment.

The allocation of labour in the system satisfies

$$L_0 + L_1 + L_3 + U = \bar{L}, \tag{9.45}$$

where L_i is the amount of labour employed in sector i ($i = 0, 1, 3$) and U is the number of the unemployed, all of whom reside in the urban sector. The urban unemployment rate is

$$u \equiv U/(L_0 + L_3 + U). \tag{9.46}$$

In each period, a migrant forgoes the 'sure thing' w_1 from staying on the family farm in exchange for a risky prospect that yields either the prize of an urban job paying w_3 with some prior probability, or unemployment, and hence no income. How do would-be migrants arrive at a prior probability of landing a job? It is plausible that they base their priors on the current rate of open urban unemployment, a decent estimate of which ought to be available from the reports of relatives or friends who are resident there. Given the above assumptions about how jobs turn over and are obtained, the well informed, rational migrant would take the going unemployment rate as his prior probability of failing to land an urban job.

In order to complete the picture, we need an assumption about individuals' preferences over lotteries. We suppose here that individuals are risk neutral, the case of risk aversion being deferred to Chapter 12. Given the lottery described above, an individual will be indifferent between staying at home on the family farm and going off to the city to earn his fortune if, and only if,

$$w_1 = (1 - u)w_3. \tag{9.47}$$

In equilibrium, therefore, the creation of an additional job paying w_3 will induce $[1/(1 - u)]$ migrants to leave the family farm in the hope of getting it. This 'excess' migration turns out to have an important effect on the shadow wage.

With both a wage gap and open urban unemployment, Eqn (9.24) must be modified once more. Total income is now

$$M = w_1 L_1 + w_3(L_0 + L_3) = w_1 \bar{L}, \tag{9.48}$$

where the last part follows from Eqns (9.45)–(9.47). Hence, total income takes the constant value $w_1\bar{L}$, as in Section 9.3. Observe, however, that the system now possesses the endogenous variable U. In deriving the shadow prices, it turns out to be convenient to rewrite Eqn (9.48), using Eqn (9.45), as follows:

$$w_3 U - (w_3 - w_1)(\bar{L} - L_1) = 0; \tag{9.49}$$

for L_0 then appears only in connection with the overall labour constraint (9.45). Proceeding as in Section 9.5.1, the Lagrangian (9.26) is now augmented by condition (9.49) instead of Eqn (9.37), with the full-employment condition (9.16) being replaced by Eqn (9.45). Observing that U is an endogenous variable, we have the corresponding first-order condition

$$\partial\Phi/\partial U = -\lambda_l + \phi \cdot w_3 = 0, \tag{9.50}$$

where ϕ denotes the multiplier associated with Eqn (9.49). The envelope theorem yields Eqn (9.28), as in Section 9.3. Hence, from Eqn (9.50), the shadow price of labour is proportional to the regulated wage:

$$\pi_l \equiv \lambda_l = \phi \cdot w_3. \tag{9.51}$$

Substituting for $L_i = l_i y_i$ ($i = 1,3$) in Eqn (9.45), it is also readily checked that whereas Eqn (9.30) continues to hold, Eqn (9.31) for $i = 1$ is replaced by

$$\partial\Phi/\partial y_1 = \lambda_1 - l_1\lambda_l + \phi \cdot \Delta w = 0, \tag{9.52}$$

which, together with Eqn (9.51), yields

$$\lambda_1 = \phi \cdot w_1 l_1 = \phi p_1^*, \tag{9.53}$$

where the last part follows from Eqn (9.13). Comparing Eqns (9.30) and (9.53), we have $\mu = \phi$, so that

$$\lambda_2 = \phi p_2^*. \tag{9.54}$$

For good 3, Eqns (9.31) and (9.51) yield

$$\lambda_3 = \phi \cdot w_3 l_3. \tag{9.55}$$

In this case, therefore, the vector of shadow prices is

$$\pi = \mu(p_1^*, p_2^*, w_3 l_3, w_3). \tag{9.56}$$

Observe that this is proportional to the vector of producer prices only in the artificial sense that the regulated wage is construed as the producer price of labour. It certainly departs from Eqn (9.32).

Equation (9.51) is indeed a striking result which was first derived, rather informally, by Harberger (1971). The underlying intuition for it is as follows: In equilibrium, total private income is constant, so that it is only the social opportunity cost of labour that matters. By the individual rationality constraint (9.47), the creation of one more job paying the regulated wage will attract $1/(1 - u)$ additional rural migrants into the towns, the shadow value of whose output is $\mu(p_1^*/l_1)/(1 - u)$, or, from Eqn (9.53), $\phi \cdot w_1/(1 - u)$. By Eqn (9.47), the latter is just $\phi \cdot w_3$. The reader should be aware, however, that the assumptions employed here have been chosen, in part, for the sake of expositional clarity. If the output of the source sector is subject to taxation, or if labour inputs therein are subject to diminishing marginal returns, then this beguilingly simple result, which invites us to do our calculations at market prices, will be invalid. Readers should attempt exercises 2 and 3 if they want to be sure to understand the point about the absence of diminishing returns.

9.6. Tax Reform When There are Distortions in Production

In Section 5.3, we analysed the reform of commodity taxes using a model in which producer prices were fixed and there were no distortions in production. As proved in Sections 9.3 and 9.4, shadow prices are then proportional to producer prices. This result has the convenient feature that the λ_i defined in Eqn (5.23) in Section 5.3 can be calculated without reference to the effects of changes in taxes on the resources used to produce final consumption. In view of the highly distortionary nature of taxation in most LDCs, however, it seems strongly desirable to relax this implicit assumption, a step that involves an important generalization of the basic model. This is set out in Drèze and Stern (1987).

Let $s = (s_1, \ldots, s_k)$ denote the vector of all policy variables which can be freely chosen by the government, and $r = (r_1, \ldots, r_l)$ those which are fixed at some set of predetermined values. The latter may include tax rates as well as quotas and rations of various sorts. A *reform* is defined to be a change in the vector r. The government's problem is to choose s so as to

$$\text{maximize } V(s; r) \quad \text{subject to } E(s; r) = z, \tag{9.57}$$

where $E(s;r)$ is the vector of net excess demands for goods by the private sector: that is,

$$E(s;r) = X(s;r) - Y(s;r), \tag{9.58}$$

where $X(s;r)$ is the vector of households' net demands for goods and $Y(s;r)$ is the vector of firms' net supplies. The associated Lagrangian is

$$\Phi = V(s;r) + \pi[z - E(s;r)], \tag{9.59}$$

with first-order conditions

$$\partial V/\partial s_j - \sum_{i=1}^{n} \pi_i \cdot \partial E_i/\partial s_j = 0, \quad j = 1,\ldots,k. \tag{9.60}$$

Now the change in V induced by a small change in r is

$$dV = (\partial V/\partial s) \cdot \mathbf{ds} + (\partial V/\partial r) \cdot \mathbf{dr}$$

or, from Eqn (9.60),

$$dV = \pi(\partial E/\partial s) \cdot \mathbf{ds} + (\partial V/\partial r) \cdot \mathbf{dr}. \tag{9.61}$$

Since $E(s;r) = z$, total differentiation thereof yields

$$(\partial E/\partial r) \cdot \mathbf{dr} + (\partial E/\partial s) \cdot \mathbf{ds} = 0, \tag{9.62}$$

where $\partial E/\partial r = (\partial E_i/\partial r_j)$ and $\partial E/\partial s = (\partial E_i/\partial s_j)$. Combining Eqns (9.61) and (9.62), we obtain the following general result:

$$dV = [(\partial V/\partial r) - \pi(\partial E/\partial r)] \cdot \mathbf{dr}. \tag{9.63}$$

This says that the change in social welfare induced by a change in r is the partial effect thereof on $V(\cdot)$, that is, holding the endogenous variables s fixed, minus the associated cost of the increase in net private excess demands, valued, of course, at shadow prices.

In order to modify the λ_i derived in Section 5.3, we need to introduce the concept of *shadow revenue*. Given that X and Y represent the vectors of aggregate net households' demands and net outputs of firms, respectively, it follows from Eqn (9.58) that

$$-\pi \cdot E = \pi \cdot (Y - X)$$
$$= (\pi - p)Y + (q - \pi)X + (pY - qX). \tag{9.64}$$

The expression $(\pi - p)Y$ is the difference between firms' profits valued at shadow and producer prices, respectively. Similarly, $(q - \pi)X$ is the difference between households' net demands valued at consumer and shadow prices, respectively. The third term, $(pY - qX)$, is the profits of firms at producer prices less the total expenditures of households (including *supplies* of labour to firms and the government) at consumer prices. Ahmad and Stern propose that the RHS of Eqn (9.64) may therefore be thought of as the shadow revenue R^π, that is,

$$-\pi \cdot E \equiv R^\pi; \tag{9.65}$$

for the difference between what the private sector produces and consumes must accrue to the government. An alternative, and perhaps more transparent, interpretation of the RHS of Eqn (9.65) arises from the observation that $E = z$; so that $-\pi \cdot E$ is the negative of the value of public sector firms' profits at shadow prices.

For their empirical analysis of tax reform in Pakistan, Ahmad and Stern (1991) collapse the eighty-seven sector-classifications of the input–output table into thirteen goods, as set out in their Table 7.2 (ibid.: 204–5), along with the accounting ratios corresponding to various values of the shadow prices of labour and assets. What they call the 'shadow consumption tax' on good i is simply the difference between its consumer price, q_i, and its shadow price, π_i: the equivalent rate is one minus the accounting ratio. These rates are sharply different from the effective rates of taxation discussed in Section 4.6, the calculation of which makes no allowance for possible differences between the market and shadow prices of factors.

The effects of distortions in production on desirable directions of reform can be seen by comparing the λ_i in Section 5.3, which are calculated on the basis of the effective taxes derived in Section 4.6, with their counterparts at shadow revenue, λ_i^π, which are defined by replacing R with R^π in Eqn (5.23). These are set out in Ahmad and Stern (1991: Tables 7.3 and 7.4, respectively), a comparison of which reveals that the ranks are indeed somewhat different. We conclude, therefore, that the distortionary effect of the tax system on production was in some sense substantial, so that the evaluation of reforms should be carried out at shadow prices.

9.7. Shadow Prices and Tax Reform

If world prices are parametrically given, the (relative) shadow prices of tradables will be invariant with respect to small changes in domestic taxes.

Such changes will, however, have an effect on the social cost of private consumption, and hence on the shadow prices of non-tradables and labour. Indeed, we have established in Section 9.5 that shadow prices are not, in general, invariant with respect to the level of taxes in the presence of distortions in production.

The next step, therefore, is to demonstrate that if a desirable tax reform can be made, projects must be evaluated at the shadow prices corresponding to the tax structure after the reform has been introduced, and independently of the gains ensuing from the reform alone. The latter are given by,

$$dV = [(\partial V/\partial t) - \pi(\partial E/\partial t)] \cdot dt = -\sum_i (\lambda_i^{\pi} - 1) (\partial R^{\pi}/\partial t_i) \cdot dt_i,$$

where

$$\lambda_i^{\pi} = -\frac{\partial V}{\partial t_i} \bigg/ \frac{\partial R^{\pi}}{\partial t_i}$$

is to be interpreted as the cost of increasing shadow revenue by one unit by taxing good i more heavily. In general, there will exist a set of reforms that yield both $dV > 0$ and $dR^{\pi} > 0$.

The following example illustrates an associated potential pitfall. A proposal is developed to undertake the project $\mathbf{dz}$, which yields a net social profit, at pre-reform shadow prices, of $\pi(t) \cdot \mathbf{dz}$. Suppose this profit is negative. It so happens, however, that the minister in whose constituency the project would be built insists that it be undertaken all the same. A clever expert in the central office of project evaluation comes up with the following idea. He explains to the minister that social welfare can be improved by the reform $\mathbf{dt}$. This reform also happens to make sense in the context of the project, inasmuch as the latter's financial statements at market prices will be improved thereby. The minister in question then approaches other ministers and lobbies, correctly, for the reform, but takes good care not to mention the project. He succeeds in mustering enough support, and the cabinet is presented with the proposal to reform the tax structure accordingly. Attached to the proposal, however, is a rider that the project $\mathbf{dz}$ be undertaken. The interested minister argues, again correctly, that its 'financial viability' is assured by the reform. To seal his case, in a technical tour de force prepared by the expert in COPE, he also explains that social welfare will be improved if the project and the reform are undertaken jointly. As put formally in the private memorandum, but not to the cabinet,

$$dV + \pi(t + \mathbf{dt}) \cdot \mathbf{dz} > 0,$$

where $\pi(t + dt)$ denotes the set of shadow prices corresponding to the post-reform tax structure. Observe that if $dV > 0$ and the project design is sufficiently flexible, then this result can always be obtained by choosing a suitable scale for the project. The cabinet congratulates itself on this wise piece of legislation and adjourns.

What, if anything, is wrong with this manoeuvre? Nothing at all—provided the project is socially profitable at the new shadow prices $\pi(t+dt)$. Unless the project were just marginal in the absence of the reform, however, it is rather unlikely that a small, welfare-improving reform would pull it out of the red through changes in shadow prices alone. There is, for example, no particular reason to suppose that a reform that improves the 'financial viability' of a project should also confer upon it a more favourable structure of shadow prices. In most circumstances, therefore, it is plausible that, taken by itself, the project will remain socially unprofitable in the presence of the reform. In the above example, the minister and his adviser have smuggled a bad project past the usual procedures for scrutinizing decisions by attaching it to a socially desirable tax reform. The moral of this story is clear: if a desirable reform is politically feasible, the central office of project evaluation should press for it, and only then turn its attention to the evaluation of projects—at the appropriate shadow prices, of course.

9.8. Summary

The starting point is to agree on how to define social welfare, for the test of a project is whether it will improve welfare. This is a formidable hurdle; for the scope for dispute, even within the fraternity, seems endless, and one recoils at the prospect of trying to elicit a clear and usable statement from politicians. Faced with the necessity of proceeding on some basis, many, if not most, economists will opt for a Bergson–Samuelsonian social welfare function, whose arguments are individuals' utilities. The family of such functions accommodates various schools of thought as special cases; but to some, the whole approach is anathema. It is the approach adopted here, though not without some misgivings.

The second step is a purely positive one; namely, to obtain the response of each and every argument entering the social welfare function to a unit, net increase in the public sector's supply of each and every commodity separately. Substituting the vector of such responses associated with a particular commodity into the social welfare function yields its shadow price, which is defined as the resulting change in the value of the said function.

Now, for all its conceptual simplicity, this is a tall order in practice. In order to skirt this burdensome task, it is natural to look for a method that shortcuts the process of derivation, while yielding the correct result. Better still, of course, would be to find valid rules that are also robust. The method involves formulating a suitable but simplified model of the entire economy, specifying the social welfare function and the instruments available to the government, and writing out the Lagrangian in an appropriate way. Applying the envelope theorem will then yield expressions for the shadow prices, and the system of first-order conditions can be solved to obtain the values of the endogenous variables—still computationally burdensome, but much less so today than two decades ago.

Before resorting to brute-force computation, however, the clever thing to do is to examine the expressions for the shadow prices in the light of the first-order conditions, in the hope of discovering some structure, or rule, therein, whose application makes much of the computation superfluous. This is exactly what we did in connection with the models in Sections 9.3–9.5. In all variations of this small open economy, the 'border price' rule holds: the shadow prices of tradable goods are proportional to their respective world prices, a rule that turns out to be pretty robust. In those variants where all producers pay the same wage rate (recall that labour is the only input), a still stronger rule emerges, even with restrictions on some tax rates: shadow prices are proportional to producer prices, where relative producer prices for tradables are set by the CRS 'technology' defined by their relative world prices. This elegant result breaks down in the presence of a regulated wage that is enforced in some sectors, but not others. The shadow price of a non-tradable is still equal to its marginal cost of production at shadow prices, but the shadow wage rate now depends on how the labour market functions in the presence of the regulation. This is ultimately an empirical matter, and one that demands careful investigation.

In practice, there are various reasons why shadow prices may not be proportional to producer prices, and when the two do diverge, some revision to the procedures for evaluating economic reforms is called for. In contrast to Section 5.3, desirable directions of reform must now be established at shadow prices, using the concept of shadow revenue. Reforms and projects can also form part of a joint agenda. In that case, it is essential that their evaluation be separated in the following way, particularly if the reform will affect shadow prices. The reform is analysed first. If it is desirable, shadow prices are calculated anew, and only then are the projects assessed for their social profitability. A failure to keep them apart can allow bad projects to slip past under the mantle of a good reform.

Recommended Reading

A good place to start is Squire (1989), which strikes a nice balance between theory and practice. The next step, for those wishing to specialize in this field, is to gird one's loins and prepare to wrestle with Drèze and Stern (1987), which is authoritative and exhaustive. Both surveys contain extensive, if now rather dated, lists of references. For a revealing discussion of distributional considerations in relation to the choice of numeraire, see the exchange among Brekke (1997, 1998), Drèze (1998), and Johansson (1998). A fairly accessible treatment of the relationship between policies and shadow prices can be found in Bell and Devarajan (1983). Two leading approaches to the estimation of the shadow wage rate are synthesized by Dinwiddy and Teal (1994).

Exercises

1. A three-sector economy can produce an exportable (1), an importable (2), and a non-tradable (3), all by means of CRS Leontief technologies. The unit activity vectors are, respectively,

$$a_1 \equiv (a_{11}, a_{21}, a_{31}; l_1) = (0, 0, 0; 1),$$

$$a_2 \equiv (a_{12}, a_{22}, a_{32}; l_2) = (0.1, 0.4, 0.2; 0.2),$$

$$a_3 \equiv (a_{13}, a_{23}, a_{33}; l_3) = (0.1, 0.2, 0.2; 0.3).$$

There is perfect competition in all domestic product markets, but the wage rate in sectors 2 and 3 is regulated and lies above the competitively determined rate in sector 1. The economy's endowment of labour is offered completely inelastically and all labour is fully employed. The economy faces parametrically given world prices, p_1^* and p_2^*, for tradables. Exports of good 1 are subject to an export tax at the *ad valorem* rate of 25 per cent.

(a) If $p_1^* = p_2^* = 1$, the regulated wage rate in sectors 2 and 3 takes the value two, and there are no other taxes or regulations, then show that good 2 will not be produced domestically.

(b) Suppose instead that a binding import quota protects sector 2 and that domestic demand is sufficiently great that good 2 is produced domestically.

What will be the values of the wage rate in sector 1 and the domestic prices of goods 2 and 3?

(c) Households spend any additional income on the three goods in the proportions $b = (0.3, 0.3, 0.4)$. If the premium on uncommitted public income is 25 per cent, find the shadow prices of all goods and labour in cases (a) and (b). In case (b), begin by using the border price rule for good 2, and having done so, assess the validity of this shortcut critically. Given that the government seems determined to hold fast to the quota, what is the correct procedure? Comment on the differences among all three vectors of shadow prices in the light of the possible dependence of shadow prices on economic policy.

(d) There is a proposal to expand the production of good 2 with the above technology. Should it be accepted? Another proposal is made to replace the quota with an *ad valorem* tariff of 20 per cent. Does it have any merit? Give an intuitive account to support any calculations you perform.

2. A small open economy produces two fully traded goods, each by means of labour and a fixed factor specific to the industry concerned. The fixed factors are privately owned. Households supply their labour completely inelastically, and the economy's total endowment thereof is normalized to unity. Production in each industry takes place under competitive conditions, except that the wage rate in sector 2, w_2, is fixed above its market-clearing level. Migration between the two sectors is governed by a Harris–Todaro process, whereby all agents are risk neutral and migrants from sector 1 retain their claims to the rents attributable to the fixed factor employed therein when they go in search of work in sector 2.

The only private good consumed by households is good 1. Good 2 is subject to an exogenous export tax in the amount t_2 per unit shipped. The employment of labour in the provision of public goods is also fixed, at L_0, such labourers being paid at the regulated wage rate. The budget is balanced by means of a *variable* lump-sum tax in the amount T.

(a) If the government is not concerned with distributional objectives, show that the Lagrangian of the system may be written as

$$\Phi = p_1^* x_1 + \lambda_1 [f_1(L_1) + z_1 - x_1 - e_1] + \lambda_2 [f_2(L_2(w_2)) + z_2 - e_2]$$
$$+ \lambda_l [\bar{L} - L_0 - L_1 - L_2(w_2) - U] + \mu (F + p_1^* e_1 + p_2^* e_2)$$
$$+ v[p_1^* f_1(L_1) + p_2 f_2(L_2(w_2)) + w_2 L_0 - p_1^* x_1 - T]$$
$$+ \phi \left[p_1^* \frac{\partial f_1}{\partial L_1} - \frac{L_0 + L_2(w_2)}{1 - L_1} \cdot w_2 \right],$$

where x_1 is the total consumption of good 1, e_i and z_i ($i = 1, 2$) denote, respectively, the net exports and net public production of good i, $f_1(L_1)$

is the output produced in sector 1 when L_1 units of labour are employed therein and $f_2(L_2)$ is analogously defined. Justify each step in your argument carefully.

(b) Using the envelope theorem and the first-order conditions, show that: (i) the shadow prices of goods 1 and 2 are equal to their respective border prices, (ii) $\mu = 1$ and $\lambda_l = \nu = 0$, and (iii) the shadow wage rate for workers employed at the regulated wage is

$$\frac{\partial f_1/\partial L_1}{[(\partial f_1/\partial L_1) - (1 - L_1)(\partial^2 f_1/\partial L_1^2)]} \cdot w_2.$$

Interpret your findings briefly. What conclusion do you draw from the result that $\lambda_l = \nu = 0$ where the specification of the Lagrangian is concerned?

3. A small, open economy produces two goods, both of them fully tradable. The rural sector produces good 1; workers employed therein are paid the value of their marginal product. There are no distortions, except a regulated wage, w_2, in the manufacturing sector, which lies above its market-clearing level. Migration from the rural sector is governed by a Harris–Todaro process.

(a) If rural output is given by

$$y_1 = L_1^{\beta_1},$$

where L_1 is the amount of labour employed in rural production, prove that the shadow wage rate for workers employed in the public sector at the regulated wage is

$$w_2/[1 + (1 - \beta_1)L_u/L_1],$$

where L_u is the number of workers present in the urban sector. Comment on this result in the light of Harberger's claim that the shadow wage rate is equal to w_2.

[Hint: in the absence of any distortions other than the regulated wage, government spending must be financed by lump-sum taxation. This fact should be used in formulating the Lagrangian. A short-cut derivation is also possible after careful reflection on the cookbook rule in Chapter 8.]

(b) Suppose that instead of a regulated wage, the wage rate in the urban sector is set by a monopolistic trade union that views the rural wage as a parametric. The union seeks to maximize the product of the wage gap and the number of workers actually employed in the regulated sector. A formal statement of its problem is

$$\max_{w_2|w_1} (w_2 - w_1)L_2(w_2).$$

If the production function in the urban sector is

$$y_2 = L_2^{\beta_2},$$

show that the union's optimal policy is to set w_2 equal to w_1/β_2, and hence find an expression for the shadow wage. What can be concluded about the shadow wage rate in this case in comparison with that where w_2 is set exogenously by the government? Comment briefly on the reasons for the difference.

10. Time: The Social Discount Rate

The approach adopted in Chapter 9 is quite general, but in the interests of keeping matters comparatively simple, it was developed in detail in a static setting. A project's life usually stretches over many years, however, so that two problems must be dealt with. First, some way must be found to aggregate costs and benefits arising at different points in time. We noted in Chapter 8 that the private firm should do this by discounting future costs and returns at an appropriate rate, which may vary from period to period. We also argued that assessing the social profitability of a project required the same procedure, which leads to the question: what is the appropriate discount rate in this case, and how can it be estimated? The importance of this task can scarcely be stressed too much; for the discount rate is the key to comparisons of projects which have different inter-temporal patterns of costs and benefits. As in Chapter 9, we begin with a formal definition, which involves the choice of numeraire, and then proceed to discuss how the discount rate can be estimated. The discussion in Sections 10.2 and 10.3 is deliberately intuitive, with the emphasis firmly on practical estimation. A more rigorous treatment follows in Section 10.4.

Second, the structure of the shadow prices of goods and labour may vary over time. Here, we begin by recalling that the estimation of the shadow prices of non-tradables and labour at any point in time requires knowledge of the following: the world prices of tradables; the changes in consumers' expenditures generated by changes in private income; the technology for producing non-tradables; how the labour market works; and the social value of private relative to public income. As projects are long-lived, this requirement implies knowledge of, or 'educated' guesses about, the future. Forecasting aside, it also turns out that movements in the premium on public income are intimately linked to the difference between the rates at which the values of public income (the numeraire) and the marginal utility of private consumption, respectively, are falling. The behaviour of the said premium and the problems of estimating it are discussed in Section 10.5, and with that much settled, changes in the inter-temporal structure of shadow prices are taken up in Section 10.6.

10.1. Defining the Social Discount Rate

The use of the definite article in this connection is, strictly speaking, mis-leading; for in a general model, there is no role for *the* discount rate. Physically identical goods appearing at different dates are treated as different goods, and each will have its own, appropriately dated shadow price, a point already made in Section 9.1. In practice, building models that feature both many sorts of goods and many periods is a very time-consuming business, so that the practitioner may be forgiven for regarding this approach as yet another of the theorist's counsels of perfection. Before we consider what is to be done in practice, however, it is still necessary to start with theory.

We begin by choosing a numeraire. In principle, this poses no great difficulty, since any commodity possessing a set of strictly positive, dated shadow prices will do nicely. Observe that, by definition, the 'spot' price of the numeraire at any point in time is unity. The discount rate is therefore related to the set of 'forward' shadow prices. Let the shadow price of commodity i with availability at time τ be denoted by $\pi_{i\tau}$, there being K physically identical commodities altogether. Then the shadow discount rate for period τ, treating i as numeraire, is

$$\rho_{i\tau} \equiv \frac{\pi_{i\tau} - \pi_{i,\tau+1}}{\pi_{i,\tau+1}}. \tag{10.1}$$

That is to say, we have:

Definition 1. The discount rate at time τ is the rate at which the present value of a unit of the numeraire that becomes available at time τ is falling.

It follows that the discount factor for period τ, relative to period 0, is

$$\beta_{i\tau} \equiv 1/[(1+\rho_{i1})(1+\rho_{i2})(1+\rho_{i3}),\ldots,(1+\rho_{i\tau})]. \tag{10.2}$$

If $\rho_{i\tau}$ is constant, as is usually assumed to be the case in practical work, then $\beta_{i\tau} = 1/(1+\rho_i)^\tau$.

The net shadow value of a project dz may be written in the following equivalent ways:

$$\Pi \equiv \boldsymbol{\pi} \cdot \mathbf{dz} \equiv \sum_{\tau=0}^{T} \boldsymbol{\pi}_\tau \, \mathbf{dz}_\tau \equiv \sum_{\tau=0}^{T} \sum_{j=1}^{K} \pi_{j\tau} \, dz_{j\tau}, \tag{10.3}$$

where $\boldsymbol{\pi}_\tau = (\pi_{1\tau}, \pi_{2\tau}, \ldots, \pi_{K\tau})$ denotes the vector of shadow prices at time τ, and $\mathbf{dz}_\tau$ is analogously defined. Without loss of generality, we can normalize each of the vectors $\boldsymbol{\pi}_\tau$ by the corresponding scalar $\pi_{i\tau}$, where good i is the numeraire. Let $\boldsymbol{\pi}_\tau$ so normalized be denoted by

$$\bar{\boldsymbol{\pi}}_\tau(i) \equiv [(\pi_{1\tau}/\pi_{i\tau}), \ldots, (\pi_{i-1,\tau}/\pi_{i\tau}), 1, \ldots, (\pi_{K,\tau}/\pi_{i\tau})],$$

from which is clear that the said vector depicts the structure of relative shadow prices, with the spot shadow price of commodity i being unity, as must be the case when i is chosen as numeraire. Then, using (10.1) and (10.3), we have

$$\Pi = \sum_{\tau=0}^{T} \pi_{i\tau}[\bar{\boldsymbol{\pi}}_\tau(i) \cdot \mathbf{dz}_\tau]$$

$$= \pi_{i0}[\bar{\boldsymbol{\pi}}_0(i)\mathbf{dz}_0 + (\pi_{i1}/\pi_{i0})\bar{\boldsymbol{\pi}}_1(i)\mathbf{dz}_1$$

$$+ (\pi_{i1}/\pi_{i0}) \cdot (\pi_{i2}/\pi_{i1})\bar{\boldsymbol{\pi}}_2(i)\mathbf{dz}_2 + \cdots]$$

$$= \pi_{i0} \sum_{\tau=0}^{T} \beta_{i\tau}\bar{\boldsymbol{\pi}}_\tau(i)\mathbf{dz}_\tau. \tag{10.4}$$

We note three features of this scheme: first, whether a project is socially profitable is completely independent of the choice of numeraire. Second, the discount rate is not, in general, independent of the choice of numeraire. This applies even to the set of all tradables not subject to quotas. For although the shadow prices of such goods are proportional to their respective border prices under quite general conditions, it is a fact of life that the vector of relative border prices of such goods will change over the course of time. Third, there is no particular reason to expect the discount rate to stay constant from one period to another—quite the contrary, in fact.

Recall that in the Little–Mirrlees (L–M) system, the numeraire is uncommitted public income that is freely convertible into foreign exchange, and that net benefits are measured in units thereof. In a many-period setting, the corresponding social discount rate at time τ is the rate at which the present value, viewed from period zero, of an additional unit of public income received at time τ is falling. L–M refer to this rate as the accounting rate of interest (ARI). This is, of course, only a definition, but it yields a valuable clue as to how we should proceed.

10.2. Estimating the Social Discount Rate

The approach in this section is intuitive, with the emphasis on general principles and particular methods that can be readily employed in practice.

10.2.1. No Capital Movements

As a benchmark, it will be useful to begin with the case where there is no foreign borrowing or lending, but the economy is free of distortions. In this case, the future returns yielded by abstaining from consumption in the present will depend on the productivity of investment at home. The essentials are captured by the usual two-period formulation (today and the future), in which there is a single physical commodity. In the absence of foreign borrowing and lending, the consumption possibility frontier (CPF) is the set of efficient consumption pairs (x_1, x_2) generated by all possible combinations of investment activities. The CPF is drawn in Fig. 10.1 in the usual way, that is, as smooth and concave to the origin.[1]

The plausible assumptions that consumption is a necessary good in both periods, and that preferences are smooth and convex, will ensure that there is a unique, interior first-best optimum, at point A say, where the CPF is tangent to a member of the family of indifference contours. That is to say, at A, the usual condition $MRS_{12} = MRT_{12}$ holds. Denoting the rate of interest by r, we have

$$|MRS_{12}| = |MRT_{12}| = (1 + r).$$

In this case, the social discount rate is simply the market rate of interest.

Suppose now that there is a single distortion in the form of a tax on interest income, with the proceeds being rebated to households as lump-sum transfers. The tax in question will drive a wedge between the rates of interest faced by producers and consumers, respectively, with the former rate exceeding the latter but without undermining efficiency in production. Since the relative price of consumption in the two periods is simply one plus the (net) rate of interest on the aggregate commodity, and since the CPF is concave and preferences are convex, the resulting equilibrium must lie on the CPF and to the SE of the first-best allocation at point A, at point B, say. The assumption that there is only one physical produced commodity implies that capital is measured in terms of output, so that the marginal product of capital will be equal to the rate of return thereon. At point B, we have

$$|MRT_{12}| = (1 + f') \quad \text{and} \quad |MRS_{12}| = [1 + (1 - t)f'],$$

---

[1] Note that with a single good and with foreign borrowing and lending ruled out by assumption, the economy is completely closed.

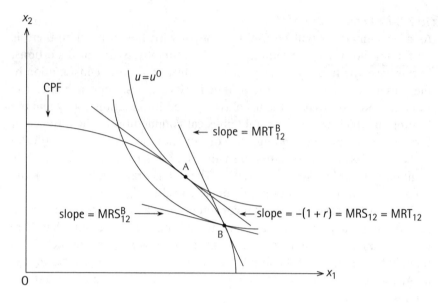

Figure 10.1. First-best and distorted equilibria compared: the closed economy

where t is the rate at which interest income is taxed and f' is the marginal product of capital when the savings and investment choices of households and firms yield the consumption point B. In this case, it is often argued that the social discount rate is a weighted average of the rate of return to capital, f', and the consumer rate of interest, $(1 - t)f'$, with the weights being determined by the extent to which a project displaces current investment and current consumption, respectively, with B as the starting point. The basis of this claim is exactly analogous to the argument underlying Harberger's method of estimating the shadow prices of goods at a point in time, as set out in Section 8.3.

10.2.2. Foreign Borrowing at a Parametric Rate of Interest

The opportunity to borrow or lend without limit in world capital markets at a parametric rate of interest is exactly analogous to the opportunity to trade in goods at parametric prices. Just as the latter is a way for the economy to transform one good into another at a point in time, so the former permits the economy to transform consumption today into consumption in the future. As the shadow price of a tradable is (proportional to) its world price, the analogy suggests that, under the conditions in question, the

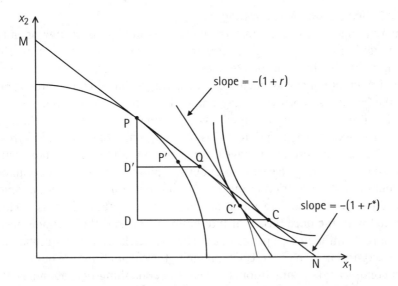

Figure 10.2. Foreign borrowing with and without a borrowing constraint

social discount rate (ARI) is none other than the rate of interest at which the government can borrow or lend abroad.

It is instructive to examine the case where the level of foreign borrowing is optimally chosen. Here, the opportunity to borrow or lend freely at the parametric rate of interest r^* expands the set of feasible consumption bundles, as depicted in Fig. 10.2. By investing an amount such that the marginal product of capital is r^*, the economy can produce the dated bundle represented by point P, where $|MRT_{12}| = (1 + r^*)$. This bundle may be traded inter-temporally with foreigners on terms represented by the availability line through P with slope $-(1 + r^*)$, which is denoted by MN. The production plan that yields point P maximizes the present value of the consumption stream (discounted at the rate r^*). Maximum utility is attained at point C, where $|MRS| = (1 + r^*)$, on the associated budget line MN. Hence, the economy borrows the amount DC in period 1 and repays the amount DP in period 2,[2] where $DP = (1 + r^*)DC$. The story is exactly analogous to that demonstrating the gains from contemporaneous international trade in goods at parametric terms of trade.

---

[2] It is assumed here, perhaps unrealistically, that borrowing countries never default on their foreign debt. The more diplomatic term renegotiation is often used to cover such cases.

10.2.3. Limits on Foreign Borrowing

It may happen, of course, that the country is unable to borrow as much as it would like from foreign sources at a given rate of interest, rationing being pervasive in credit markets, especially in the presence of sovereign risk. The marginal cost of such borrowing, that is, the effective interest rate on the last dollar borrowed, may rise with the total amount borrowed or the level of outstanding indebtedness. It is sometimes argued that in these circumstances, the appropriate ARI is the marginal cost of foreign borrowing. This is not correct, however; for if the marginal cost of borrowing is rising, the country has some monopsony power, which the government should exploit by restricting the amount borrowed below the point where marginal cost is equal to marginal return. Once again, there is a close parallel with the pure theory of international trade: if the economy has a measurable influence on prices in a particular market, then an optimal tariff or export tax is in order. Unfortunately, the calculations are quite tricky and complicated, so practitioners are left in something of a quandary if a quick answer is needed.

There is one case in which it is fairly straightforward to demonstrate the principles involved, namely, a binding ration on how much can be borrowed, a case depicted in Fig. 10.2. The CPF in the presence of this constraint is made up of two segments. The first corresponds to the regime comprising all levels of lending together with all levels of borrowing up to the limit. These options are depicted by the linear subsegments MP and PQ, respectively, where D'Q is equal to the ration and PQ has slope $-(1 + r^*)$. The second section of the augmented CPF, to the SE of Q, corresponds to the case where the country has borrowed up to the limit, so that further increases in consumption in period 1 must be obtained through domestic transformation alone. This second section is simply a rigid shift, with magnitude and direction $\overrightarrow{PQ}$, of that part of the autarky-CPF lying to the SE of P. Any such point on the said section of the augmented CPF is generated from a point on the autarky-CPF by the (vector) movement $\overrightarrow{PQ}$. As the ration is binding, the optimal consumption point in the absence of any other distortions, C', will lie to the SE of Q. Hence, the |MRT| at C' exceeds $(1 + r^*)$, and the appropriate discount rate exceeds r^*. Both income and substitution effects make for a lower value of consumption in the present, relative to that at the non-rationed bundle C. Future consumption could be greater, however, if the substitution effect is strong enough. The point P' on the autarky-CPF depicts the dated bundle produced domestically in the face of the credit ration in world capital markets, where the vectors $\overrightarrow{PQ}$

and $\overrightarrow{P'C'}$ are parallel and equal in length. Note that, by construction, the MRS at C' is equal to the MRT at the point P'.

Two remarks on this analysis are in order. First, if the ration were increased by one unit, the optimal adjustment would involve an increase in current consumption as well as in saving (investment). Second, it is tempting to draw the conclusion that the appropriate discount rate in this case is simply the going rate of interest in domestic capital markets. That is indeed so—provided there are no other distortions in the economy and the government accepts private preferences over dated consumption. If there are other distortions, however, then the point C' will not be attained, and the actual allocation will lie elsewhere on the CPF, or even inside it. In that case, it becomes necessary to ask why C' is unattainable. Only when the source of this non-feasibility is identified will it be possible to establish what will happen when the government undertakes more investment. At this point, the analysis becomes much harder and the resort to short-cuts more frequent. Some rules-of-thumb which feature in practical work are now discussed in turn.

10.2.4. Practical Rules
We consider four basic cases. Suppose, first of all, that the government obtains an extra unit of income in year τ and has no difficulty converting this income into foreign exchange. In that case, the government can invest this income abroad, either directly, by purchasing foreign assets such as US bonds, or indirectly, by reducing its outstanding foreign liabilities by one unit. As a project's net benefits are measured in terms of public income, it follows at once that the rate of interest at which the government can lend or borrow abroad, depending upon the particular financial instrument of its choice, places an appropriate lower bound on the ARI; for such transactions are always an alternative use of public funds. Symmetrically, the argument also holds if the government responds to the loss of a unit of public income by increasing its net foreign liabilities by one unit, if that is possible.

The above argument does not depend in any way on whether the economy is borrowing abroad at an optimal level or whether there is perfect mobility of capital. It requires only that within the range of options considered by the government, the economy will be able to trade in world capital markets at a parametric rate of interest and that the government will actually respond to changes in public income in the manner just described. What should be said in this connection, however, is that the argument in the preceding sections is set out in a world without money, so that the discount rate therein is a 'real' (own) one, as opposed to the nominal rates in which financial instruments are almost invariably denominated. Given that the forecasts of the future world prices of tradables are made in nominal dollars (see Section 10.6), the relevant nominal interest rate in world capital markets is the appropriate choice in this case.

A second possibility is that one government project simply displaces others, so that the appropriate comparison is between the new proposal 'on the desk' and a 'representative' public project. The implicit assumption here is that the government's investment budget is fixed, so that new projects displace representative projects of the same size. As the acceptance criterion for a project is that it should have a non-negative net present value, the only characteristic of the representative project that is relevant in this context is its internal rate of return (IROR), which may (with luck) be unique.[3] Hence, the problem boils down identifying a representative public project and then calculating its IROR, with inputs and outputs valued at shadow prices of course. This is the approach chosen by Squire *et al.* (1979) in their study of Pakistan, who take as the representative project the average IROR of a set of existing public sector projects. As we shall see in the sections that follow, a problem of circularity intrudes here; for it turns out that without the ARI, one cannot estimate θ, and, as we have seen in Chapters 8 and 9, without θ, one cannot estimate the shadow prices (π_τ, w_τ^*) needed to calculate the IROR of the 'representative project'. In any event, the authors' estimate that the ARI lay in the very low range of 1–2 per cent came in for some heavy criticism from Guisinger (1979), though largely on other grounds.

A third possibility is that one unit of public sector investment displaces exactly one unit of private sector investment. In this case, the opportunity cost of the former is the marginal rate of return in the private sector, measured, of course, at shadow prices. In order to estimate it, the composition of the private investment thus displaced must be identified; for even if private rates of return at market prices are identical everywhere, they may well differ at shadow prices. In practice, this is very troublesome; for while financial data on the performance of private projects may be available, the exact nature of the projects that would be displaced is necessarily a matter of conjecture.

---

[3] Recall that 'the' IROR associated with the stream of net benefits $(b_0, b_1, \ldots, b_T)$ is a real root of the polynomial equation $\sum_{\tau=0}^{T} b_\tau/(1 + r)^\tau = 0$, which has, of course, T roots altogether. In practice, there is usually one 'sensible' root thereof, but a multiplicity of sensible roots cannot be ruled out in advance.

The fourth possibility considered here is that one unit of public investment displaces exactly one unit of private consumption. Leaving aside distributional considerations, this suggests that the appropriate discount rate is the consumption rate of interest (CRI). If, however, savings are socially more valuable than consumption at the margin and some of the additional income stemming from the investment in question will be reinvested, then use of the CRI will not be correct.

After careful consideration, the analyst may well decide that none of the above possibilities is an exact description of the economy's response to a public project. It is likely, in practice, that some combination of these 'pure' cases will hold, so that the social discount rate will be an appropriate weighted average of those identified above. It is then the analyst's task to estimate the weights in question.

10.3. The Consumption Rate of Interest

There are two important reasons for discussing the CRI in some detail. First, aggregate consumption is the numeraire in some systems of cost–benefit analysis, notably in UNIDO's (Dasgupta *et al.*, 1972). Second, as we shall see in Section 10.5, the ARI, the CRI, and θ are linked up together. It also turns out that estimating the CRI is a task that can be accomplished without resort to a whole bevy of assumptions (of varying degrees of implausibility) and horrendously complicated procedures.

Recall that the CRI is defined to be the rate at which the marginal utility of consumption is falling. Let preferences be additively separable in the consumption enjoyed at various dates, so that in the two-period framework

$$u(x_1, x_2) = v(x_1) + v(x_2)/(1 + \delta),\tag{10.5}$$

where δ is the rate of 'pure impatience' and $v(\cdot)$ is to be interpreted as the representative individual's felicity function. Since the marginal utilities yielded by an additional unit of x_1 and x_2 are $v'(x_1)$ and $v'(x_2)/(1 + \delta)$, respectively, the CRI is given by

$$\text{CRI} \equiv \gamma = \frac{v'(x_1)(1 + \delta)}{v'(x_2)} - 1.\tag{10.6}$$

Let $v(\cdot)$ take the isoelastic form:

$$v(x) = \frac{x^{\eta+1}}{\eta + 1},\tag{10.7}$$

where $\eta(\leq 0)$ is the elasticity of the marginal utility of consumption. From Eqn (10.6), we obtain the CRI as

$$\gamma = [(1+\delta) \cdot (x_1/x_2)^{\eta}] - 1. \tag{10.8}$$

Let per capita consumption be growing at the rate g_c, so that $(x_1/x_2) = 1/(1+g_c)$. Substituting into Eqn (10.8), we get

$$\gamma = [(1+\delta)/(1+g_c)^{\eta}] - 1.$$

If g_c is sufficiently small, we have the approximation

$$\gamma \cong (1+\delta)(1 - \eta g_c) - 1 \cong \delta - \eta g_c, \tag{10.9}$$

since δ and g_c are both small. Thus, if we can lay our hands on estimates of δ, η, and g_c, we are home.

As indicated earlier, following Ramsey's (1928) lead, some scholars are persuaded that it is immoral to discount the welfare of future generations simply because they arrive on the scene later. If this position be accepted, the right value for δ will be zero—unless there is some positive probability of a general catastrophe, such as nuclear war or a drastic change for the worse in the global climate. In a spirit of determined optimism about the future of the world, one might make a case that δ should be set no higher than 1 per cent per annum.

In this connection, there is also the consideration that the population may be growing, at the rate n say; so that there are $(1+n)$ persons enjoying a consumption level of x_2 in period 2 for each person receiving x_1 in period 1. Additive separability and a radical interpretation of Benthamite doctrine then imply that the welfare function should take the form:

$$u = v(x_1) + v(x_2)[(1+n)/(1+\delta)], \tag{10.5'}$$

and (10.9) would become

$$\gamma \cong (\delta - n) - \eta g_c, \tag{10.9'}$$

with a strong presumption that $(\delta - n)$ is non-positive in most poor countries.

The growth of consumption will, of course, depend on the economy's resources and public policy (including the profitability of projects). One presumes that the government has a 'plan' in the general, if not specific, sense of the word, in which g_c should feature. The analyst should beware

Table 10.1. Typical values* of the
CRI (per cent p.a.)

g_c	η		
	−1	−2	−3
0.01	0.01	0.02	0.03
0.02	0.02	0.04	0.06
0.04	0.04	0.08	0.12

*These values assume that $(\delta - n) = 0$.

of the optimism of public pronouncements, however, and a more cautious estimate of g_c may often be in order.

Finally, there is the matter of determining η. Stern (1977) provides an excellent discussion of how this parameter may be estimated. There are fairly persuasive arguments that its value will normally lie between −1 and −3, which correspond, respectively, to moderate and strong tastes for equality in the distribution of consumption. Based on the foregoing discussion, Table 10.1 summarizes the range of values the CRI is likely to take in practice.

10.4. A Simple Inter-temporal Model

We draw together various elements in the preceding discussion by examining a simple model of a closed economy, with aim of showing how the techniques of Chapter 9 can be employed in such a setting. We revert, in part, to mnemonic notation.

An aggregate private good is produced by private firms under CRS by means of capital and labour, in each of two periods. The economy's initial factor endowments, $(\bar{K}_1, \bar{L}_1)$, are given, as is the endowment of labour in period 2. Capital is produced by public sector firms by means of labour alone. It depreciates fully in one period, so that the stock thereof in period 2, K_2, is equal to whatever amount is produced in period 1. The public sector also produces a non-durable public good in the amount G_τ ($\tau = 1, 2$), again by means of labour alone. Without loss of generality, let one unit of labour be needed to produce any of these goods in the public sector. The available stocks of factors in each period are supplied completely inelastically. Suppose, to start with, that the representative household does not save in any form, so that the entire output of the aggregate good in each period is consumed. All firms trade at producer prices, any losses (profits) from public production being financed by means of taxes (subsidies). It is assumed that the government cannot resort to issuing debt, so it must balance its books in each period taken separately. All markets are perfect, with full employment of both factors in both periods.

The output of the private good in period τ is

$$y_\tau = f_\tau(K_\tau, L_\tau), \quad \tau = 1, 2, \tag{10.10}$$

where $f_\tau(\cdot)$ is assumed to have the usual 'nice' properties and $K_1 = \bar{K}_1$. Full employment of labour implies that

$$L_\tau + G_\tau + I_\tau = \bar{L}_1, \quad \tau = 1, 2, \tag{10.11}$$

where I_τ denotes the level of employment in the production of capital in period τ. Since the world comes to an end at the close of period 2, $I_2 = 0$. Given G_τ and I_1, the output of the private good in period 1 follows at once:

$$y_1 = f_1(\bar{K}_1, \bar{L}_1 - G_1 - I_1).$$

Only relative market prices are determined, and it will be convenient to choose the private good as numeraire, with the spot producer price thereof set equal to unity in each period. Under the above assumptions, factors are paid the values of their respective marginal products:

$$r_\tau = \partial f_\tau / \partial K_\tau, \quad \tau = 1, 2, \tag{10.12}$$

and

$$w_\tau = \partial f_\tau / \partial L_\tau, \quad \tau = 1, 2, \tag{10.13}$$

where it should be noted that r_τ is the price that firms pay the government for the use of capital in period τ. Aggregate private income before tax in each period is, therefore,

$$Y_\tau = w_\tau \bar{L}_\tau, \quad \tau = 1, 2. \tag{10.14}$$

It is clear that a suitably chosen flat tax on income will effectively raise the revenue needed to finance G_τ in lump-sum fashion; for under the above assumptions, private income cannot be altered by changes in private decisions.

10.4.1. A First-best Allocation

Suppose that only lump-sum taxes are levied, the amount thereof in period τ being denoted by T_τ. The household's income–expenditure identities will then take the form

$$Y_\tau = p_\tau x_\tau + T_\tau, \quad \tau = 1, 2, \tag{10.15}$$

where p_τ is the producer price of the private good in period τ.[4] Turning to the finances of the public sector, income is also equal to expenditure in each period:

$$p_\tau z_\tau + r_\tau K_\tau + T_\tau = w_\tau (G_\tau + I_\tau). \tag{10.16}$$

Substituting for G_τ, I_τ, and T_τ from Eqns (10.11), (10.14), and (10.15), (10.16) may be written as the national income identity

$$p_\tau z_\tau + (r_\tau K_\tau + w_\tau L_\tau) - p_\tau x_\tau = 0.$$

By virtue of constant returns to scale (CRS) and competitive factor markets, as expressed in Eqns (10.12) and (10.13), this equation yields, in turn, the condition that the market for the private good clear in both periods:

$$y_\tau + z_\tau - x_\tau = 0. \tag{10.17}$$

It follows that, in specifying the Lagrangian of the system, the appearance of Eqn (10.17) makes Eqn (10.16) redundant. It is also clear that with lump-sum taxes being free to take any value, private consumption in each period can be set at any level consistent with the economy's endowments and technology, the wage rate being independent of T_τ and the household's endowment of labour being supplied wholly inelastically.

The Lagrangian corresponding to this first-best case therefore takes the following form

$$\Phi = u(x_1, x_2) + \lambda_1 (f_1 + z_1 - x_1) + \lambda_2 (f_2 + z_2 - x_2)$$
$$+ \lambda_{l,1}(\bar{L}_1 - L_1 - G_1 - I_1) + \lambda_{l,2}(\bar{L}_2 - L_2 - G_2 - I_2), \tag{10.18}$$

where it should be noted that $K_2 = I_1$ and that the vector G is taken to be exogenously given. The envelope theorem yields

$$\pi_\tau \equiv \frac{\partial \Phi^0}{\partial z_\tau} = \lambda_\tau, \quad \tau = 1, 2 \tag{10.19}$$

[4] Our choice of numeraire implies that $p_\tau = 1$ in both periods; but in order to facilitate the comparison with the second-best case that will follow, the normalization is not used here.

and

$$\pi_{l,\tau} \equiv -\frac{\partial \Phi^0}{\partial G_\tau} = \lambda_{l,\tau}, \quad \tau = 1, 2. \tag{10.20}$$

The assumption that preferences are such that consumption will be positive in both periods hardly needs justification, and the lower Inada condition will see to it that employment in private production and the capital stock in period 2 are likewise positive. Given an interior solution, therefore, the first-order conditions are

$$\frac{\partial \Phi}{\partial x_\tau} = u_\tau - \lambda_\tau = 0, \quad \tau = 1, 2, \tag{10.21}$$

$$\frac{\partial \Phi}{\partial L_\tau} = \lambda_\tau \frac{\partial f_\tau}{\partial L_\tau} - \lambda_{l,\tau} = 0, \quad \tau = 1, 2, \tag{10.22}$$

and

$$\frac{\partial \Phi}{\partial K_2} = \lambda_2 \frac{\partial f_2}{\partial K_2} - \lambda_{l,1} = 0, \tag{10.23}$$

where $u_\tau = \partial u_\tau / \partial x_\tau$. By definition, we have

$$\begin{aligned} \text{CRI} &\equiv |\text{MRS}| - 1 \equiv (u_1/u_2) - 1 \\ &= (\lambda_1/\lambda_2) - 1, \end{aligned} \tag{10.24}$$

from Eqn (10.21). By definition, λ_τ is the shadow price of public income in period τ; for an increase in z_τ permits T_τ to be reduced by the same amount. This result yields

$$\text{ARI} = (\lambda_1/\lambda_2) - 1, \tag{10.25}$$

so that the CRI is equal to the ARI, as required in a first-best allocation.

To complete the picture, observe that Eqns (10.22) and (10.23) yield

$$\frac{\lambda_1}{\lambda_2} = \frac{\partial f_2/\partial K_2}{\partial f_1/\partial L_1}, \tag{10.26}$$

where the right-hand side (RHS) is simply the |MRT|, given the assumption that one unit of labour employed in producing investment in period 1 yields one unit of capital in period 2. We have therefore derived the condition depicted in Fig. 10.1.

10.4.2. A Second-best Allocation

A second-best setting requires not only that lump-sum taxes as such be ruled out, but also that private agents have some means of escaping at least part of the burden of taxation by changing their behaviour. Suppose, therefore, that they have access to a simple 'storage' technology, whereby one unit of the private good can be saved in period 1 and consumed in period 2. Denoting the level of such savings in period τ by s_τ, we have

$$s_1 + s_2 = 0. \qquad (10.27)$$

In the absence of any stocks at the beginning of period 1 and in view of the assumption that there is only one sort of household, it must be assumed that households choose $s_1 > 0$ under the conditions that rule. The basis of taxation is assumed to be consumption, so that a tax thereon in period 1 can be avoided by the expedient of saving for consumption in period 2. Let the consumer price in period τ be denoted by q_τ. The presence of a wedge between the producer and consumer prices of the private good implies that, unless the consumption levels thereof in the two periods are strict complements, the said taxes will be distortionary. Equation (10.15) becomes

$$Y_\tau = q_\tau x_\tau + s_\tau, \quad \tau = 1, 2. \qquad (10.15')$$

Since the storage technology yields no interest, as indicated in Eqn (10.27), Eqns (10.14) and (10.15') imply that the individual's lifetime budget constraint can be written as

$$M \equiv w_1 \bar{L}_1 + w_2 \bar{L}_2 = q_1 x_1 + q_2 x_2, \qquad (10.28)$$

where M is the present value of lifetime income and the RHS is the present value of lifetime expenditures. It is clear from Eqn (10.28) that the CRI is given by

$$\text{CRI} = (q_1/q_2) - 1. \qquad (10.29)$$

The representative household's problem is to choose (x_1, x_2) so as to

$$\text{maximize } u(x_1, x_2) \quad \text{subject to Eqn (10.28)} \qquad (10.30)$$

while taking (q, w), and hence M, as parametrically given. Observe that since the price vector (q, w) is dated, it is assumed either that households have perfect foresight, or that the government makes a credible announcement of its plans at the very start. Let $x^0 = x^0(q, M)$ solve (10.30). In the case of an interior solution, the first-order conditions yield the familiar form

$$\frac{\partial u / \partial x_1}{\partial u / \partial x_2} = \frac{q_1}{q_2},$$

(10.31)

which corresponds to Eqn (10.29).

In order to complete the system, we need both the market-clearing conditions for the private good and the government's revenue–expenditure identities. The former are

$$y_\tau + z_\tau - x_\tau^0 - s_\tau = 0, \quad \tau = 1, 2.$$

(10.32)

The latter read

$$p_\tau z_\tau + (q_\tau - p_\tau) x_\tau^0 + r_\tau K_\tau - w_\tau (G_\tau + I_\tau) = 0, \quad \tau = 1, 2,$$

(10.33)

where $I_2 = 0$ and the choice of numeraire implies that $p_\tau = 1$. It turns out that Eqns (10.32) and (10.33) are not independent. Substituting for $(G_\tau + I_\tau)$ from Eqn (10.11) in Eqn (10.33), we obtain

$$(q_1 - p_1) x_1^0 = w_1 \bar{L}_1 - (r_1 \bar{K}_1 + w_1 L_1) - p_1 z_1.$$

Recalling that there are CRS and perfect markets, we also have

$$p_1 y_1 = w_1 L_1 + r_1 \bar{K}_1,$$

so that

$$(q_1 - p_1) x_1^0 = w_1 \bar{L}_1 - p_1 y_1 - p_1 z_1.$$

Together with Eqns (10.14) and (10.15'), this yields Eqn (10.32). An analogous argument establishes the same result for period 2.

It will be helpful to summarize thus far. Upon reduction, the system contains fourteen endogenous variables, namely, $(I_1, L, M, q, s, w, x^0, y)$, and fourteen equations, namely, Eqns (10.10)–(10.13), (10.27), (10.28), (10.32), and the solution to problem (10.30), namely, $x^0 = x^0(q_1, q_2, M)$, where it should be noted that the property $q_1 x_1^0 + q_2 x_2^0 = M$ makes the second part of Eqn (10.28) redundant, and that the redundancy of Eqn (10.33) has been established above. The system is therefore just determined, so that given the parametric variables $(G_1, G_2, \bar{K}_1, \bar{L}_1, \bar{L}_2, z_1, z_2)$, the government has no real choices (degrees of freedom). To repeat, given any set of values of the parametric variables, the tax rates on consumption will be the same in both periods only by the merest fluke.

The final step is to write down the government's problem. In this second-best setting, the government effectively chooses a consumer price vector q, so that its goal is to maximize the representative individual's indirect utility, $v(\cdot)$, subject to the above constraints. In order to spare the reader the tedious task of writing out the associated Lagrangian, it is given here:

$$
\begin{aligned}
\Phi = {} & v(q_1, q_2, M) + \lambda_1(f_1 + z_1 - x_1^0 - s_1) + \lambda_2(f_2 + z_2 - x_2^0 - s_2) \\
& + \lambda_{l,1}(\bar{L}_1 - L_1 - G_1 - I_1) + \lambda_{l,2}(\bar{L}_2 - L_2 - G_2 - I_2) \\
& + v_{r,1}(r_1 - \partial f_1 / \partial K_1) + v_{r,2}(r_2 - \partial f_2 / \partial K_2) \\
& + v_{w,1}(w_1 - \partial f_1 / \partial L_1) + v_{w,2}(w_2 - \partial f_2 / \partial L_2) \\
& + \mu[M - w_1 \bar{L}_1 - w_2 \bar{L}_2] + \phi(s_1 + s_2),
\end{aligned} \tag{10.34}
$$

where Eqn (10.10) has been used to substitute for the production vector y. Using the envelope theorem, we obtain the shadow prices of (dated) goods and labour as the dual variables associated with Eqns (10.32) and (10.11), respectively,

$$
\pi_\tau \equiv \partial \Phi^0 / \partial z_\tau = \lambda_\tau, \quad \tau = 1, 2, \tag{10.35}
$$

and

$$
\pi_{l,\tau} \equiv -\partial \Phi^0 / \partial G_\tau = \lambda_{l,\tau}, \quad \tau = 1, 2. \tag{10.36}
$$

Since an additional unit of net public supply of the private good can be sold on the open market at the producer price (of unity), it follows from Eqn (10.32) that λ_τ is also the shadow price of public income. Hence the ARI is

$$
\rho = (\lambda_1 / \lambda_2) - 1, \tag{10.37}
$$

from which it follows at once that the CRI and the ARI will be equal if, and only if, $q_1/q_2 = \lambda_1/\lambda_2$, that is, if and only if consumer prices are proportional to shadow prices. This result conforms to expectations; for consumption taxes are, in general, distortionary. In the present setting, however, the tax rates must be set so as to finance the government's expenditure plan (G_1, G_2), so that consumer prices will be proportional to shadow prices only by the merest chance.

10.5. The Premium on Government Income

Having discussed the estimation of the ARI and CRI, we are now in a position to tackle derivation of the premium on government income—equivalently, the parameter θ, which has featured prominently in Chapters 8 and 9. For simplicity, let us assume that all private income is spent. Recalling Eqn (10.5), the value, in terms of utility, of an additional unit of such income at time τ is $v'(x_\tau)/(1 + \delta)^{\tau-1}$. By definition, the value of an additional unit of public income at time τ is λ_τ. Since the latter is the numeraire, θ_τ is defined as follows:

$$\theta_\tau \equiv \frac{v'(x_\tau)/(1 + \delta)^{\tau-1}}{\lambda_\tau}. \tag{10.38}$$

Taking logarithms, treating time as continuous, and differentiating with respect to time, we obtain

$$\frac{\dot{\theta}_\tau}{\theta_\tau} = -\frac{\dot{\lambda}_\tau}{\lambda_\tau} + \left(\frac{\dot{v}'(x_\tau)}{v'(x_\tau)} - \delta\right). \tag{10.39}$$

Recalling Definition 1 and Eqn (10.6), (10.39) may be written as

$$\dot{\theta}_\tau/\theta_\tau = \text{ARI}_\tau - \text{CRI}_\tau, \tag{10.40}$$

that is to say, at time τ, θ_τ is rising at a rate equal to the excess of the ARI over the CRI. This accords with intuition; for if the ARI is high, the value of public income must be falling rapidly, and if the level of the CRI is modest, the *relative* value of private income must be rising.

The result set out in Eqn (10.40) is valuable; but although it tells us the direction and rate of change of θ, it does not tell us the level of θ, which is what we need to estimate the shadow prices of non-tradables and labour. Little and Mirrlees (1974: 283–6) offer the following intuitive approach, which is quite attractive. In the poorest countries, in which skills, managerial capacity, and infrastructure are usually wanting, the rate of return on public and private sector projects alike is likely to be low. Consumption is also very low and will not soon start to grow rapidly under these conditions. Hence, the marginal utility of consumption is high, and it will remain so for some time. Given that the yield from investment is rather meagre, it is then hard to make a strong case that, at the margin, saving is much more valuable than consumption. In other words, θ will be close to unity and the ARI will be roughly equal to the CRI. In extreme cases, investing abroad might be better than investing at home, if that were politically possible.

In the next phase, as skills and experience grow, projects become increasingly profitable. If the government cannot raise sufficient taxes to exploit most of these opportunities, however, the value of public income will not be falling sharply—it may even rise slightly at the onset of this phase. On the other hand, the growth of consumption per head may have begun to pick up a little, and with it the CRI. Thus, θ will tend to fall early on in this phase, and it will continue to do so until the ARI catches up with the CRI. This, the ARI will surely do, since the government's ability to raise taxes efficiently should improve over the longer run, even though a period of high-yielding investment will eventually induce a more rapid growth in consumption. At length, therefore, θ will settle down to a steady value somewhat less than unity—perhaps much less than unity.

There should follow an extended period of fairly rapid and steady growth, in which there is a substantial, but roughly constant, premium on public income and savings. As the economy matures, however, consumption will begin to grow more sluggishly, and the CRI will fall accordingly. The ARI will eventually fall, too, both because the returns on prospective investment begin to decline and because the government's capacity to raise taxes efficiently will largely do away with the savings constraint. When full economic maturity has been attained, one would expect the premium on government income to be rather small, so that as maturity sets in, θ must eventually begin to rise and the ARI and CRI will converge to their common, very long-run value. The trajectories of these variables, as they emerge from the above account, are depicted schematically in Fig. 10.3.

Helpful though it is in gaining a general insight into the problem, this account still lacks a certain specificity. In particular, the practitioner may be forgiven for asking: exactly where is the economy right now? Although the CRI can be estimated independently of θ, the only case in which this is also true of the ARI is that in which the government faces unconstrained foreign borrowing opportunities at a parametric rate. The other cases discussed in Section 10.2 require knowledge of θ. One possibility is to resort to the results yielded by models of optimal growth (see Newbery, 1972; Stern, 1972 for examples of aggregate models, and Bell and Devarajan, 1987, for a many-commodity variant). This approach is so demanding of special assumptions and technique, however, that it is not likely to be attractive in most practical settings.

A rough-and-ready approach is to ask whether there is any way of inferring at what level of consumption per head the government places no

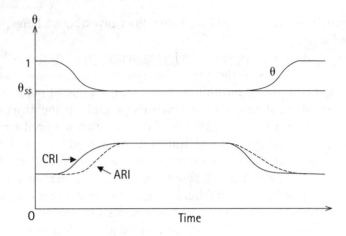

Figure 10.3. The behaviour of the ARI, the CRI, and θ over time

premium on its own income. It could be argued, for example, that if the tax code excludes individuals with incomes below a certain level from income taxation, then θ is equal to one for individuals with that level of income. An alternative measure is the 'poverty level', a (subsistence) standard of living which many governments define fairly precisely and announce as the socially acceptable minimum. In view of the fact that most developing countries have very loose and incomplete systems of income taxation, and also take care not to offend urban workers, the taxation of whose incomes poses few administrative difficulties, there is much to be said for taking θ to be equal to one at the poverty level. Granted this much, the value of θ corresponding to any level of income can be inferred from Eqn (10.7). This is the method adopted by Bell and Devarajan (1982) in their evaluation of the Muda irrigation project, which will be discussed in detail in Chapter 13.

It must not be concluded that the adoption of this method makes (10.38) redundant. At the going urban wage, there will be a particular value of θ, which will enter into the calculation of the ARI if the second or third methods of Section 10.2 are adopted. There is no particular reason to suppose that the resulting value of the ARI will be equal to the going value of the CRI; and if it does not, θ will be changing. If the difference between the ARI and CRI is small, the loose nature of the above argument suggests that the difference may be ignored; so that θ may be taken to be constant. If the difference is large, however, then serious consideration must be given to the construction of a sequence of shadow prices, $\{\pi_\tau, w_\tau^*\}$, that reflects the analyst's best guess as to the trajectory of θ_τ. As projects of various kinds are sufficiently long-lived to straddle several phases of an economy's development as outlined above, such an undertaking seems largely unavoidable. There follows a sketch of what is involved.

10.6. The Inter-temporal Structure of Shadow Prices

The process of estimating the normalized shadow price vector $\bar{\pi}_\tau(i)$ involves a number of steps, starting with the world prices of tradables at time τ, namely, p_τ^*. These are forecast for all years up to the close of a long planning horizon, perhaps with the help of projections published by international agencies, such as the World Bank or the United Nations. Recall that by definition, the normalized shadow price of a tradable good at time τ is simply its spot world price in dollars. The next step is to derive the corresponding shadow prices of non-tradables and labour using the methods described in Chapters 8 and 9, treating each year as if it were a stationary state. In principle, this involves forecasts of the following: (i) the technologies for the production of non-traded goods, (A_{TN}, A_{NN}); (ii) the marginal propensities to consume out of additional private income, b_τ; (iii) the change in private income generated by additional employment, ΔM_τ; (iv) the value of an additional unit of private income in terms of the numeraire, θ_τ; and the social opportunity cost of labour. In effect, a fairly detailed assessment of how the economy is likely to develop over the long run is needed, however speculative such a task might appear to be.

It should be emphasized once more that forecasting θ_τ involves a problem of circularity; for as we have seen in Section 10.5, its value cannot be derived independently of the ARI. Hence, if the ARI is jointly determined with shadow prices that involve θ, as is normally the case, then obtaining a solution to the problem appears to face formidable difficulties. In practice, it is often assumed that an educated guess about the trajectory of θ_τ will suffice to set the ball rolling where estimation is concerned. Refinements, if deemed necessary, can be made through an iterative procedure. If that much be granted, estimates of the trajectories of all shadow prices, in normalized form, $\{\bar{\pi}_\tau, w_\tau^*\}$, can be made. In any event, that is the approach advocated here.

10.7. Summary

It is arguable that, in a purely formal sense, what most clearly distinguishes one project from another is the difference between their time-profiles of net benefits—given that net benefits at any point in time can be satisfactorily estimated. Except in those exceedingly rare cases where one such profile dominates another, establishing whether one time-profile is 'better' than another therefore requires some metric. The appropriate measuring rod here is a profile's net present value (NPV), the calculation of which requires, in turn, the social discount rate in each and every period. The task of estimating this sequence of rates is therefore of central importance, and the resources and effort devoted to it should be correspondingly large. It also greatly widens the scope of the analysis to include the manner and speed with which the economy will develop over a time span that encompasses short- and long-lived projects alike.

As is usually the case, the right way to start is with a clear definition of the concept in question, namely, the social discount rate at any point in time is the rate at which the value of the numeraire is falling at that moment. Given that uncommitted public income is the choice of numeraire, we then know what sequence of values is to be estimated to yield the so-called ARI.

How is this to be accomplished in practice? Various alternative ways of arriving at the ARI present themselves. The simplest is to assess the rate at which the country can borrow or lend (as appropriate) in world capital markets. The next up is the so-called CRI, which is the rate at which the value of private consumption is falling. In order to calculate it, one needs a forecast of how per capita consumption will grow over the entire time-horizon and an estimate of both the inter-temporal elasticity of substitution in consumption and the rate of pure impatience. The remaining candidates are the realized rates of return, calculated at shadow prices of course, of public and private sector projects to date; estimating these involves much more work. None of these methods necessarily commits the analyst to the assumption that the ARI is constant, though the temptation to do so may be well-nigh irresistible. None, however, is particularly watertight. Faced with such difficulties, there is always the possible resort to sensitivity analysis: if a project has a positive NPV at all ARI's between 0 and 20 per cent, then the case is sealed; otherwise, we are forced to come up with a defensible estimate.

This is not, sadly, the end of the story. For to estimate a project's net benefits at a point in time, we need the vector of shadow prices at that date, which depends on θ—equivalently, on the premium on public income. It turns out that θ, the ARI, and the CRI are not independent: the rate of change of θ is equal to the excess of the ARI over the CRI. Hence, there is a fundamental problem of circularity where the use of short-cut methods is concerned, for even if θ is estimated by another route, with reference to the official poverty line for example, the internal consistency of all the estimates must be carefully checked. In any event, the point so frequently emphasized in Chapter 9 that shadow prices depend on the policies pursued now reappears in another guise, namely, that the trajectory and structure of shadow prices depend on the development path of the economy over the long run.

All this must seem rather complicated, and to involve a great deal of work; it is, and it does. Practitioners must use judgement and experience when deciding between what needs careful attention and what can be dealt with fairly quickly.

Recommended Reading

The formal treatments of the social discount rate are not for the faint-hearted. Perhaps the best place to start is Sen (1967), followed by Newbery (1972) and Stern (1972). Applications of computable, multisectoral models are Bell and Devarajan (1987) and Martin and Van Wijnbergen (1988).

Exercises

1. Per capita consumption in Belindia is currently growing at the annual rate of 2 per cent, and it is generally expected that this rate will be maintained for some time into the future. The government's policies suggest some, but not a strong, desire for equality.

   (a) What is the CRI? (Give reasons for your answer.)

   The source of labour to the rest of the economy is agriculture, which produces an export crop on which an export tax is levied at the rate of 25 per cent. The agricultural labour market is competitive, and the wage rate is currently 160. Although the wage rate in the rest of the economy is set by regulation at twice this level, there is full employment. The Central Office of Project Evaluation (COPE) has estimated the consumption conversion factor (CCF) to be 0.9 and the current premium on public income to be 33 per cent.

   An examination of the government's behaviour in making and financing investments indicates that new projects displace a bundle of alternative projects with the following aggregate characteristics. The investment phase lasts for two years, in each of which one unit of labour and one unit of a non-competitive import are needed. The domestic price of the latter is 125, the *ad valorem* tariff thereon being 25 per cent. This investment yields an output of one unit per year for twenty years, beginning in the third year. The 'factory' then falls apart, with no salvage value. The only current input needed to produce this annual output is one unit of labour. The output in question is a tradable good which is subject neither to taxes nor to quantitative restrictions. Its domestic price is 350.

(b) Arrive at a 'quick', approximate value of the ARI, stating the simplest possible assumptions you need to make for this purpose. Given this initial estimate, at what rate is θ, the value of private income relative to public income, changing?

(c) Startled by this result, you decide to investigate matters more thoroughly, paying special attention to how certain key variables, which you treated as fixed in parts (a) and (b), are likely to change over the longer run. This involves a very complicated set of calculations if great precision is needed, but you must report to your Minister the next morning, so a short cut is unavoidable. For this purpose, the one thing you may assume is that the economy will develop in such a way that the ARI will remain constant for at least the next two decades. Estimate its value once more, and then assess whether any of the above forecasts need to be revised. Having done so, discuss briefly both whether your second estimate of the ARI might need to be modified and how θ is likely to evolve over the long run. Give careful reasons for your procedure and justify, to the extent possible, the assumptions you have made.

(d) Based on all your analysis, judgements, and knowledge of Belindia, write a short memorandum to your minister on the appropriate discount rate for public sector projects. (You should need no reminder that the Minister will need persuasive, intelligible arguments rather than the gory details of your technical calculations.)

2. A labour-surplus economy produces a single good, which can be exported or consumed. Output may be written as a function of the capital stock alone:

$$y_\tau = f(K_\tau).$$

The capital stock is to be interpreted as public infrastructure, which does not depreciate and is provided to the private sector free of user fees. The investment needed to augment the capital stock takes the form of an importable, which cannot be produced domestically. The economy faces parametric world prices p_c^* and p_m^* for the two goods, respectively. In order to finance capital formation, the government imposes a value added tax at the rate t on domestic production.

Consider a two-period setting. The private sector's felicity function is $v(x_\tau)$, where x_τ is aggregate consumption of the domestic good. The welfare function is

$$W = v(x_1) + [v(x_2)/(1 + \delta)] + \zeta K_3,$$

where K_3 is the capital stock bequeathed to the future at the beginning of period 3, K_1 is the capital stock inherited from the past, δ is the private sector's rate of pure time preference, and ζ is the marginal social value of the capital stock at the beginning of period 3.

(a) Show that the Lagrangian of this problem may be written as

$$\begin{aligned}
\Phi = {} & W(K_1, K_2, K_3) + \lambda_{c1}[z_{c1} + tf(K_1) - e_{c1}] + \lambda_{m1}[z_{m1} - I_1 - e_{m1}] \\
& + \lambda_{c2}[z_{c2} + tf(K_2) - e_{c2}] + \lambda_{m2}[z_{m2} - I_2 - e_{m2}] \\
& + \mu_1[F_1 + p_c^* e_{c1} + p_m^* e_{m1}] + \mu_2[F_2 + p_c^* e_{c2} + p_m^* e_{m2}] \\
& + \phi_1[K_1 + I_1 - K_2] + \phi_2[K_2 + I_2 - K_3],
\end{aligned}$$

where $z_{i\tau}$ is the net public supply of good i in period τ, $e_{i\tau}$ is the net export of good i in period τ, F_τ is the economy's endowment of foreign exchange in period τ, and I_τ is the investment in capital in period τ.

(b) Interpret the terms of the Lagrangian.

(c) Does the border price rule hold? Give the intuition for your answer.

(d) Use the remaining first-order conditions to derive expressions that involve world prices, the instantaneous marginal utility of consumption, the marginal product of capital in period 2, and the shadow price of public finance. Interpret them, derive expressions for the ARI and CRI, and explain why they are valid.

3. A small open economy produces a single tradable good 1 by means of a CRS technology using capital and labour:

$$y_1(\tau) = f_1[K_1(\tau), L_1(\tau)],$$

where $K_1(\tau)$ and $L_1(\tau)$ denote the inputs of capital and labour, respectively, in that sector in period τ. The industry is competitive. The capital stock is owned by the government, and all of it is leased to firms at no charge. The stock can be augmented through investment, the production of each additional unit of the capital good requiring one unit of good 1 and b units of a non-competitive import (good 2). The production process is undertaken by state-owned firms. Workers in the public sector receive the regulated wage rate $w^r(\tau)$, whose level is set above the competitively determined rate in sector 1. The only form of tax revenue is a fixed, *ad valorem* tax on consumption at the rate t.

Households are endowed with $\bar{L}(\tau)$ units of labour in period τ, which they supply completely inelastically. They consume only good 1, and their preferences over present and future consumption thereof can be represented by the form

$$W = v[x_1(1)] + v[x_1(2)]/(1 + \delta) + V[K(3)],$$

where $x_1(\tau)$ is the level of consumption in period τ, $V(\cdot)$ is a smooth, increasing, and concave function, and $K(3)$ is the total capital stock available at the start of period 3. If the government respects private preferences, show that the Lagrangian of the system can be written as

$$
\begin{aligned}
\Phi = W &+ \lambda_1(1)[y_1(1) + z_1(1) - x_1(1) - \Delta K(1) - e_1(1)] \\
&+ \lambda_2(1)[z_2(1) - b\Delta K(1) - e_2(1)] \\
&+ \lambda_1(2)[y_1(2) + z_1(2) - x_1(2) - \Delta K(2) - e_1(2)] \\
&+ \lambda_2(2)[z_2(2) - b\Delta K(2) - e_2(2)] \\
&+ \lambda_l(1)[\bar{L}(1) - L_0(1) - L_1(1)] + \lambda_l(2)[\bar{L}(2) - L_0(2) - L_1(2)] \\
&+ \mu(1)[F(1) + \boldsymbol{p}^*(1) \cdot \boldsymbol{e}(1)] + \mu(2)[F(2) + \boldsymbol{p}^*(2) \cdot \boldsymbol{e}(2)] \\
&+ v(1)[w^r(1)L_0(1) + p_1^*(1)y_1(1) - (1 + t)p_1^*(1)x_1(1)] \\
&+ v(2)[w^r(2)L_0(2) + p_1^*(2)y_1(2) - (1 + t)p_1^*(2)x_1(2)],
\end{aligned}
$$

where $p_i^*(\tau)$ denotes the world price of good i ($i = 1, 2$) in period τ, the stock $K(1)$ is inherited from the past, $\Delta K(\tau) \equiv K(\tau + 1) - K(\tau)$, and the notation in the text is otherwise employed, with all variables suitably dated.

Derive expressions for all shadow prices, examine all the first-order conditions, and interpret them. Hence, or otherwise, derive an expression for the ARI and interpret it. Discuss this expression in relation to other 'rules' for the social discount rate that have been suggested in the literature.

11. Space: Transportation Costs

That physically identical goods at different locations are different commodities is a familiar fact of life. A tonne of maize in a silo in rural Illinois, for example, is not at all the same thing as a tonne of maize in a small town somewhere in the interior of Mozambique. One way of producing the latter is to transport one tonne of maize from the first location to the second, a process which, in this particular case, involves both internal and foreign trade. The first stage of its journey takes it to a port in the Gulf of Mexico, where its free-on-board (f.o.b.) price includes the insurance and freight charges incurred up to that point. On arrival in the port of Beira, the price of the tonne of maize has become the cost-insurance-and-freight (c.i.f.) import price, and when augmented once more to reflect the costs of unloading and the final leg up-country, it becomes the price in the interior. Obtaining clearance through customs at both ports will necessarily add to these costs, as will any duties that are payable.

Several aspects of this story will concern us in this and the following two chapters. First, the difference between the prices at the points of origin and final destination may be so large that no trade actually takes place. Thus, while a good may be tradable in principle, high transport costs can render it non-traded in practice. Second, a salient component of this difference is the cost of the international leg of the journey. Summarizing the findings from a variety of studies, Hummels (1999: 4) voices the opinion that this component alone constitutes a barrier to trade that is usually every bit as substantial as, and quite often even larger than, that posed by tariffs. A still more recent report by the World Bank (2001) provides further support for this claim in the form of a scatter-plot of the share of transport costs in the total value of export trade against the (trade-weighted) nominal tariff rate on goods exported by 216 countries to the United States in 1998. Only in forty-eight cases was the tariff the higher of the two, and in the rest, the index of transport costs tended to be much the larger.[1]

Third, and most importantly for the purposes of this chapter, we need to extend the framework of Chapter 9 with the aim of deriving all shadow prices in the presence of significant internal transportation costs for tradables. For such costs imply that what is normally thought of as a (pure)

---

[1] The picture could be quite different for imports, of course, but this is tantalizingly omitted, perhaps because the data are not available.

tradable good has, in fact, a significant non-tradable component at the point of final use or sale; and on the empirical evidence, these costs can be substantially higher than those associated with the international leg, even for countries that are not landlocked. As the transportation sector produces an intermediate good, introducing it necessarily involves another extension of the framework used in Chapter 9; for in the interests of simplifying the exposition, all intermediate uses of goods were ruled out of that account. This aspect of the extension is conceptually rather minor, but it is of great practical importance, which is motivation enough to cover the case in which all goods may have intermediate uses.

Fourth, the extension to cover internal transportation costs also introduces other issues. In the severe droughts in Southern Africa during the 1990s, for example, many countries that are normally exporters had to import food grains for a year or more. The transportation system being as poor as it is, this led to a substantial increase in domestic prices, even though the governments concerned struggled to offset the rise with additional subsidies. When, moreover, the c.i.f. price does exceed the f.o.b. price by a substantial margin, and fluctuations in the weather and growing conditions result in the good in question being exported in some years and imported in others, its shadow price will fluctuate in sympathy (though not necessarily *pari passu*). The question of how to deal with risk when estimating shadow prices naturally arises in this connection, a topic that will be taken up in Chapter 12.

Finally, transportation projects usually have the effect of reducing transportation costs, and hence of increasing the producer prices of exportables. While the analysis of the general case in which market prices change in response to a project will be deferred until Chapter 13, some progress can be made in certain special cases, as we shall see in Section 11.3, after the model has been set out in Section 11.1 and the corresponding shadow prices derived in Section 11.2.

11.1. The Model

We extend Bell and Devarajan (1983) to cover the case described above. The economy produces three goods, two of which are tradable in world markets at parametrically given prices. Good 1, which may be thought of as a composite primary commodity, is an exportable. When exported, a considerable transport cost must be incurred to get the commodity to the port. Good 2, which may be thought of as manufactures, is an importable;

and when imported, it, too, must be hauled from the port into the interior. Good 3 is the non-tradable; it may be thought of as transportation, storage, and wholesale services. In effect, therefore, domestic producers and consumers reside in the interior of the country, with a small contingent manning the port.

Let a_{ij} denote the input of the ith commodity needed to produce one unit of the jth commodity, with availability at the farm or factory gate; and let a_{3i}^t $(i = 1, 2)$ denote the input of good 3 needed to haul one unit of good i from the interior to the port and once there to load it onto a ship, or the reverse operation, as the case may be, where a_{3i}^t can be thought of as a specific number of tonne-kilometres for good i. The market-clearing equations (or supply–demand balances) for the three goods are

$$y_i + z_i = \sum_j a_{ij} y_j + x_i + e_i, \quad i = 1, 2, \tag{11.1}$$

and

$$y_3 + z_3 = \sum_j a_{3j} y_j + x_3 + [a_{31}^t e_1 - a_{32}^t e_2], \tag{11.2}$$

where it should be observed that the volume of imports is $-e_2$.[2] Equation (11.1) is in the standard form: it is a minor generalization of Eqns (9.12) and (9.13), in that intermediate uses of all three goods in production now make an appearance. Equation (11.2), however, is less familiar: here, the demand for good 3 depends not only on domestic production and consumption, but also on the level of foreign trade. The introduction of this last fact makes the model more realistic—and matters more complicated.

The next step is to specify how prices are determined. As in Chapter 9, let perfect competition rule everywhere. In the absence of any quantitative restrictions on trade, the domestic producer prices of the two tradables at the point of use follow from a simple arbitrage condition in the case where the good is actually traded:

$$p_i = \begin{cases} p_i^* - t_i - p_3 a_{3i}^t & \text{if } e_i > 0, \\ p_i^{**} - t_i + p_3 a_{3i}^t & \text{if } e_i < 0, \end{cases} \quad i = 1, 2, \tag{11.3}$$

[2] In general, which goods are imported and which are exported is determined endogenously, so that strictly speaking, $|e_i|$, with a positive sign for all i, should be employed in Eqn (11.2). For the sake of expositional simplicity, however, the direction of trade has been fixed by assumption.

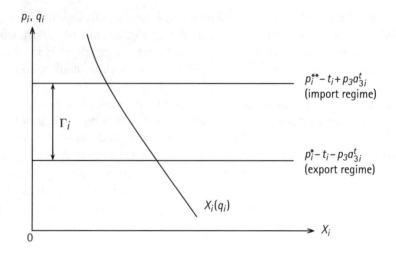

Figure 11.1. Trade regimes in the presence of transportation costs

where p_i denotes the domestic producer price of good i, and p_i^* and p_i^{**} are, respectively, the f.o.b. and c.i.f. world prices of a tradable good ($i = 1, 2$). It has also been assumed that there is an export tax of t_i on good i if it is exported (or a subsidy of t_i if imported),[3] whereby a simple change of sign will deal with the case of an export subsidy and an import tariff.

It is also possible that a good designated as tradable is not actually traded, in which case, its price must lie within the interval set by world prices and transportation costs:

$$p_i \in (p_i^* - t_i - p_3 a_{3i}^t, p_i^{**} - t_i + p_3 a_{3i}^t) \quad \text{if } e_i = 0, \tag{11.4}$$

where the size of the interval

$$\Gamma_i \equiv (p_i^{**} - p_i^*) + 2 p_3 a_{3i}^t, \quad i = 1, 2, \tag{11.5}$$

is a measure of the 'natural' protection enjoyed by the good if it is produced at home in competition with imports. If the domestic market for the good in question clears at a price within the band defined by Eqn (11.4), then the good will not, in fact, be traded. This recalls the switch of regime depicted in Fig. 8.5 in Chapter 8, which is partly reproduced here, but with some additional details, as Fig. 11.1. If the good is exported, the inland price is $p_i^* - t_i - p_3 a_{3i}^t$; if imported, $p_i^{**} - t_i + p_3 a_{3i}^t$, the wedge between them being Γ_i.

---

[3] Asymmetric variations are also possible; the details are left as an exercise for the reader.

The presence of the wedge Γ_i appears to introduce the possibility that all three goods will be produced domestically. The assumptions of perfect competition and constant returns to scale (CRS) then imply that their domestic prices would be equal to their respective unit costs: that is,

$$p_i = \sum_j a_{ji} p_j + w_i l_i, \quad i = 1, 2, 3, \tag{11.6}$$

where l_i is the input of labour needed to produce one unit of good i and w_i is the wage rate in industry i.

We begin with the case where the wage rate is the same everywhere ($w_i = w$). It then follows that in the absence of all transportation costs, internal and external alike, only one tradable will be produced domestically—except in a degenerate case that arises by pure fluke. This well-known result is proved as follows: the absence of all transportation costs implies that $p_i^* = p_i^{**}$ ($i = 1, 2$), and hence that Eqn (11.3) and (11.4) specialize to $p_i = p_i^* - t_i$ ($i = 1, 2$). It follows that if the technology vectors (a_j, l_j) are fixed independently of prices, the system (11.3), (11.4), and (11.6) will be over-determined, there being five equations in the price vector (p, w), which has only four elements. Since the arbitrage conditions (11.3) hold in the form $p_i = p_i^* - t_i$ ($i = 1, 2$) and good 3 must be produced domestically, Eqn (11.6) cannot hold simultaneously for both tradables, unless the values of the parameters are such that the system of equations is not of full rank, a case that normally arises only by the merest chance. In general, therefore, the unit cost of production of one of the tradables will exceed its price, so that the good in question will not be produced domestically.

This result clearly carries over to a wide class of cases in which there is substitution in the production of each good. With perfect competition and CRS, for example, firms in industry j ($= 1, 2, 3$) will choose (a_j, l_j) so as to minimize unit costs, and these choices will depend only on relative prices. Once more, therefore, the system will be over-determined in general, in which case Eqn (11.6) cannot hold simultaneously for both tradables. In the presence of any transportation costs, however, there will be a positive wedge of magnitude Γ_i between the domestic prices of good i in the cases where it is exported and imported, respectively. Condition (11.4) then comes into play, at least potentially.

At this juncture, it will be helpful to anchor the analysis to some empirical orders of magnitude. Beginning with the difference between c.i.f. and f.o.b. prices, Hummels (1999) reports that the ratios of aggregate expenditures on freight (typically excluding port charges) to total imports for the

United States, New Zealand, and five Latin American countries lay in the range of 4–13 per cent. Many of the unweighted rates were considerably higher, 15 per cent or so being usual. Some idea of the magnitude of the costs of both the international and inland legs of transportation is vividly conveyed by the cost of shipping a 40-foot container from Baltimore to various destinations in the developing world (Limao and Venables, 2001). A good benchmark is provided by the port of Dar es Salaam in Tanzania, some 12,500 km away, for which the bill is a modest $1000. If the destination is Durban (South Africa), however, the charge for the same distance is $2500, and from there a mere 1000 km further inland to Mbabame in Swaziland will add no less than $9500 to the bill, at which point the total cost is only $1000 less than that of sending the container to Kathmandu in Nepal. A more detailed breakdown can be given for 'door-to-door containerized imports' in Brazil through the port of Samtos (World Bank, 2001: 109).[4] In round figures, the items making up the total of $4400 (excluding insurance charges) are as follows: ocean freight, $1300; port charges, $400; inland transport, $700; bonded warehouse, $300; and administration and customs clearance, $1700. This last item is particularly striking. In this connection, one usually thinks of public administration as being a hurdle to be surmounted rather than an intermediate input into the production process; but it is still an activity that belongs in what has been called sector 3 in the model set out above.

11.1.1. Trade

With these rather sobering figures before us, we shall concentrate on the usual case in which both of the tradables are actually traded. Thus, (11.4) does not apply, but Eqns (11.3) and (11.6) combined remain over determined, with the exception of the unlikely case where the system is not of full rank. How, then, is this difficulty to be resolved? One possibility is to invoke the Ricardo–Viner assumption that each sector producing a tradable possesses a specific factor. The alternative pursued here, in keeping with common practice in developing countries, is to assume that in order to have the manufacturing sector in business, the government imposes a suitably stiff protective tariff on imports. The magnitude of this tariff is found by treating t_2 as an additional endogenous variable when solving Eqns (11.3) and (11.6) for p and w; so that the system now has full rank. With prices so determined, the actual pattern of resource allocation

---

[4] Precisely which 'doors' is not specified.

in general, and the volume of trade in particular, will then depend on the government's needs for revenue and the private sector's demand for goods.

In the interests of realism, we shall go a step further and assume that the wage rate in sectors 2 and 3 is regulated by the government, at a level exceeding that in sector 1, which is freely and endogenously determined by the condition that price be equal to unit cost, as set out in Eqn (11.6). Given the regulated wage $\underline{w}$, Eqns (11.3) and (11.6) can be solved as before, where it is now to be expected that the protective tariff on good 2 may need to be very stiff. If the solution satisfies $(p, w_1; \underline{w}) \gg 0$ and if, in equilibrium, $e_1 > 0$ and $e_2 < 0$, then the desired configuration will hold. Recalling Fig. 11.1, equilibrium is established on the lower horizontal for good 1 and on the upper for good 2, whereby the wedge in the latter case will be augmented by the protective tariff, it being most unlikely in practice that the government would make the 'symmetric' offer of an export subsidy, were the good to be exported instead. It should be noted that, as long as this qualitative configuration indeed holds and taxes are fixed, the assumption of constant returns to scale implies that all prices will be independent of quantities, a point illustrated by Fig. 11.1. It would be misleading, however, to label the model as fixed-price in nature, for prices are constant by virtue of other assumptions.

We now turn to the determination of income. Labour, the only factor, is supplied by households. In the absence of direct taxes, aggregate household income is therefore given by

$$Y_h = w_1 l_1 y_1 + \underline{w}(l_2 y_2 + l_3 y_3 + L_0), \tag{11.7}$$

where L_0 denotes the level of employment in the public sector, which is assumed to pay the regulated wage.

In addition to employing labour, the government produces the (net) bill of goods z, so that the total value of its domestic expenditures is $(\underline{w}L_0 - pz)$, the negative of which is effectively the profits from production in the public sector. Recalling that there is an export tax on good 1 and a protective tariff on good 2, the government's budget surplus is the algebraic sum of tax revenues, the value of grants from abroad, F, and the profits from public production:

$$Y_g = (t_1 e_1 - t_2 e_2) + F + (pz - \underline{w}L_0).$$

For present purposes, it turns out that there is a more convenient expression for Y_g. In the absence of private borrowing from abroad, it follows at once from Walras' law that Y_g is equal to the algebraic sum of economy's net trade surplus at world prices and F, a sum which is also the net addition to the economy's reserves of foreign exchange. Thus,

$$Y_g = p_1^* e_1 + p_2^{**} e_2 + F, \tag{11.8}$$

which, as we have seen, corresponds to what Little and Mirrlees (1974) call uncommitted foreign exchange in the hands of the government. Observe that GDP in this setting is simply $Y_h + (pz - \underline{w}L_0)$.

Although we have now established how prices are determined, we are still lacking a complete statement of the behaviour of its institutions. Let the economy be endowed with $\bar{L}$ units of labour, whose supply is assumed to be completely inelastic. Hence, the full-employment condition is

$$\bar{L} = \sum_i l_i y_i + L_0. \tag{11.9}$$

Turning to households' expenditure decisions, it is implicitly assumed in Eqns (11.1) and (11.2) that there is no private investment. Hence, the private consumption of good i depends on prices and current income, with all income being spent. Since, by assumption, the only taxes are those on trade, consumer prices will be equal to domestic producer prices, and we may write

$$x_i = x_i(p, Y_h), \quad i = 1, 2, 3, \tag{11.10}$$

where $Y_h = px$. Under the assumptions of this section, prices will be constant, so that changes in private consumption will be induced only by changes in private income. Let the marginal propensity to spend on good i be denoted by

$$b_i \equiv p_i \cdot \partial x_i(p, Y_h)/\partial Y_h, \tag{11.11}$$

where, since all private income is spent, $\sum_i b_i = 1$.

It remains to discuss the government's behaviour, especially where its response to perturbations in the economy is concerned; for as we saw in Chapter 9, the nature of such responses has an important influence on the structure of shadow prices. For present purposes, we choose a policy regime that is analytically tractable. In order to keep market prices constant, let tax rates be fixed. The vector of public production $(z, -L_0)$ is also assumed to be exogenously given. Hence, the export vector e is endogenous, and so too is the government's budget surplus, Y_g. Recalling Eqn (11.8), it is seen that this result involves the implicit assumption that the government is able to balance its books by adjusting its (net) borrowing abroad at a parametrically given rate of interest.

We now have a complete statement of the social accounts of this simple economy, which are set out in the usual form in Table 11.1. Some brief comments are in order. The entries involving z in the column labelled 'Government' have negative signs, net output values being negative expenditures. In the same column, the term Y_g appears on the row 'Rest of the World' in keeping with the assumption that any budget surplus is invested abroad. The sum of the entries in the column 'Rest of the World' is simply $p_1^* e_1 + p_2^{**} e_2 + F$, as can be seen from Eqn (11.3). Where each unit of good 1 is concerned, foreigners pay the inland price p_1 to domestic firms in sector 1, $p_3 a_{31}^t$ in transport charges to domestic firms in sector 3, and t_1 in export duties to the government of the exporting country, the sum being the f.o.b. price p_1^*.

The final element of the model is the social welfare function. Since prices are constant, its arguments are taken to be private income and the public sector's budget surplus, respectively:

$$W = W(Y_h, Y_g). \tag{11.12}$$

Although the setting is static, $W(\cdot)$ can be thought of as implicitly encompassing the inter-temporal considerations analysed in Chapter 10, including a possible premium on savings. That an increase in Y_g implies a smaller burden of financing in the future, and hence, in all likelihood, a smaller deadweight loss in relation to the revenue that must be raised, suggests that $W(\cdot)$ is strictly quasi-concave. It should also be remarked that in the above setting, public production involves only private goods, with state-owned firms trading at market prices and the Treasury pocketing their profits (or picking up their losses). Any variations in the vector $(z, -L_0)$ are therefore valuable only to the extent that they result in increases in Y_h and Y_g. If public goods were produced, the levels of their provision would have to be introduced into $W(\cdot)$, with appropriate valuations in terms of the consumption of private goods.

11.1.2. Autarky

For completeness, we deal briefly with the case where (11.4) holds for both tradables, whereby it should be noted that if (11.4) holds for one, then balanced trade at world prices implies that it must hold for the other. In this particular setting, the price of any good is proportional to the total (direct and indirect) input of labour needed to produce one unit of the good

Table 11.1. A schematic social accounting matrix for the basic model

Incomes	Expenditures								
	Households	Govt.	Factors	Activities/Goods 1	2	3	Taxes	ROW	Total
Households			Y_h						Y_h
Government							T		$F + T$
Factors		wL_0		wL_1	wL_2	wL_3		F	Y_h
Activities/Goods									
1	$p_1 x_1$	$-p_1 z_1$		$p_1 a_{11} y_1$	$p_1 a_{12} y_2$	$p_1 a_{13} y_3$		$p_1 e_1$	$p_1 y_1$
2	$p_2 x_2$	$-p_2 z_2$		$p_2 a_{21} y_1$	$p_2 a_{22} y_2$	$p_2 a_{23} y_3$		$p_2 e_2$	$p_2 y_2$
3	$p_3 x_3$	$-p_3 z_3$		$p_3 a_{31} y_1$	$p_3 a_{32} y_2$	$p_3 a_{33} y_3$		$p_3 \cdot a^t_{31} e_1 - p_3 \cdot a^t_{32} e_2$	$p_3 y_3$
Taxes								$t_1 e_1 - t_1 e_2$	T
Rest of the world		Y_g							Y_g

in question, the factor of proportionality being the uniform wage rate. This fact is seen by writing (11.6) in the form

$$p = w[(I - A')^{-1}I] \equiv w \cdot \xi,$$ (11.6')

where A' is the transpose of the technology matrix (a_{ij}). Observe that as the individual demand functions are homogenous of degree zero in prices and income, the aggregate private demand for good i may be written as $x_i(\xi, \bar{L})$. With p so defined, we desire to show that the following system of inequalities may have a non-negative solution:

$$p_1^* - t_1 - w\xi_3 a_{31}^t < p_1 = w\xi_1 < p_1^{**} - t_1 + w\xi_3 a_{31}^t$$

and

$$p_2^* - t_2 - w\xi_3 a_{32}^t < p_2 = w\xi_2 < p_2^{**} - t_2 + w\xi_3 a_{32}^t.$$

These may be rearranged into the more transparent forms

$$\frac{p_1^* - t_1}{\xi_1 + \xi_3 a_{31}^t} < w < \frac{p_1^{**} - t_1}{\xi_1 - \xi_3 a_{31}^t}$$

and

$$\frac{p_2^* - t_2}{\xi_2 + \xi_3 a_{32}^t} < w < \frac{p_2^{**} - t_2}{\xi_2 - \xi_3 a_{32}^t},$$

respectively. In the presence of transportation costs anywhere in the system, both of these intervals will be strictly positive, and if they overlap, then there will exist a continuum of vectors (p, w) such that no trade actually takes place. Such a case is depicted in Fig. 11.2, where the wage rate must be chosen such that $w\xi_i$ ($i = 1, 2$) lies within the relevant band.

11.2. Shadow Prices

We are now in a position to state the problem formally in the case where the tradable goods are actually traded in equilibrium. The government's

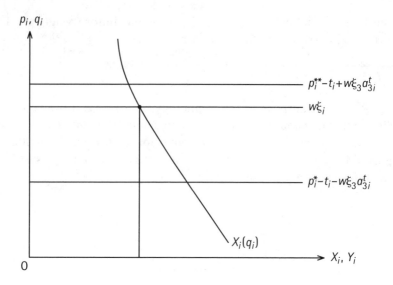

Figure 11.2. Autarky in the presence of transportation costs

problem is to

$$\text{maximize } W(\cdot) \quad \text{subject to Eqns (11.1), (11.2), and (11.7)–(11.10),}$$

$$(11.13)$$

where the vector of domestic prices $(p, w_1, \underline{w})$ is determined independently of all quantities, as described above, and the endogenous variables of the system are y, x, e, Y_g, and Y_h, making ten in all. Against this, the set of constraints is made up of nine equations. With the system thus specified, the government has just one real degree of freedom.

Although it is not necessary for the argument that follows, it will be convenient to make the system just-determined, in the sense of possessing at most one feasible point. This will be done by assuming that the output of manufactures is fixed, so that changes in the demand for the non-tradable will be accommodated by solely by changes in employment in sector 1. Thus, the exogenous variables of the system are world prices, p^*, tariffs, t, the domestic output of manufactures, y_2, and the public (net) production vector $(z, -L_0)$. It should be recalled that a public sector project will take the form of a perturbation to the vector $(z, -L_0)$, with net inputs having a negative sign. As we saw in Chapter 9, when the Lagrangian of the system is set up in a particular way, the Lagrange multipliers associated with the supply–demand balances will be equal to the shadow prices for goods (Drèze and Stern, 1987).

With this preamble, the Lagrangian of the system is written as follows:

$$\Phi = W + \sum_{i=1}^{2} \lambda_i \left[y_i + z_i - \sum_{j=1}^{3} a_{ij}y_j - x_i(q, Y_h) - e_i \right]$$

$$+ \lambda_3 \left[y_3 + z_3 - \sum_j a_{3j}y_j - x_3(\cdot) - a_{31}^t e_1 + a_{32}^t e_2 \right]$$

$$+ \lambda_l \left[\bar{L} - \sum_i l_i y_i - L_0 \right]$$

$$+ \phi_g [F + p_1^* e_1 + p_2^{**} e_2 - Y_g]$$

$$+ \phi_h \left[\sum_i (w_i l_i y_i) + \underline{w} L_0 - Y_h \right]. \tag{11.14}$$

The advantage of this formulation is that the Lagrange multipliers for goods, namely, the λ_i, are the correct shadow prices for the system, each being the improvement in social welfare that would result from a unit increase in the net public supply of the good in question. This claim follows at once from the envelope theorem. For at the optimum (or, in the case of a just-determined system, simply the solution), we have

$$\pi_i \equiv \frac{\partial W^0}{\partial z_i} = \frac{\partial \Phi^0}{\partial z_i} = \lambda_i, \quad i = 1, 2, 3. \tag{11.15}$$

Observe that the shadow wage rate for workers employed in the regulated sectors is given by

$$w^* \equiv \pi_l \equiv -\frac{\partial W^0}{\partial L_0} = -\frac{\partial \Phi^0}{\partial L_0} = \lambda_l - \phi_h \underline{w}. \tag{11.16}$$

That is, w^* depends on both the dual variable associated with the full-employment constraint and that associated with private income. The dual variable λ_l is the opportunity cost of labour to the economy, whereas the term $\phi_h \underline{w}$ measures the net social benefit generated by paying the worker in question the going wage in the regulated sectors of the economy. The counterpart of w^* in sector 1 is similarly defined at the wage rate w_1.

In order to obtain expressions for the shadow prices of goods and labour, we examine the first-order conditions. Assuming that $e_1 > 0$ and $e_2 < 0$, we have

$$\frac{\partial \Phi}{\partial e_1} = \phi_g \cdot p_1^* - \lambda_1 - \lambda_3 a_{31}^t = 0 \qquad (11.17)$$

and

$$\frac{\partial \Phi}{\partial e_2} = \phi_g \cdot p_2^{**} - \lambda_2 + \lambda_3 a_{32}^t = 0. \qquad (11.18)$$

The first-order condition with respect to Y_g is

$$\frac{\partial \Phi}{\partial Y_g} = \frac{\partial W}{\partial Y_g} - \phi_g = 0. \qquad (11.19)$$

Since we are concerned in this section with small projects, we may, without loss of generality, normalize $\partial W / \partial Y_g$ to unity, which implies that $\phi_g = 1$. This is equivalent to treating uncommitted government income as the numeraire, as in Little and Mirrlees (1974). Hence, Eqns (11.17) and (11.18) may be rewritten as

$$\lambda_1 = p_1^* - \lambda_3 a_{31}^t \qquad (11.17')$$

and

$$\lambda_2 = p_2^{**} - \lambda_3 a_{32}^t. \qquad (11.18')$$

In keeping with intuition, the shadow price of the exportable is its f.o.b. world price less the shadow cost of transportation to the ports; and, for the importable, it is the c.i.f. world price plus the shadow cost of transportation from the ports. If internal transport costs were zero, the classic 'border price' rule would hold: the shadow price of a tradable would then be its world price, f.o.b. or c.i.f. as appropriate.

In principle, Eqns (11.17) and (11.18) do not involve a fundamental departure from the classic result. In practice, however, some care is needed. The standard procedure is to invoke the 'border price' rule to get a first estimate of the shadow prices of tradables, and then to use these estimates to arrive at the shadow prices of non-tradables and labour. As a final step, Eqns (11.17') and (11.18') are then used to arrive at the shadow prices of tradables—when the relevant transportation costs are thought to be high enough to warrant the refinement. No further rounds of computation are usually attempted.

It is clear from the first-order conditions, however, that if either of the terms a_{3i}^t is positive, then the entire system of shadow prices is not thus decomposable, and hence the recursive procedure described above, even with successive rounds of computation, is not strictly valid. Instead, all shadow prices must be derived mutually and simultaneously. This will now be done, so that the results of the two procedures can be compared.

Recalling Eqn (11.11), and the fact that $p = q$ under the assumptions made here, the first-order condition w.r.t. Y_h is

$$\frac{\partial \Phi}{\partial Y_h} = \frac{\partial W}{\partial Y_h} - \sum_i \left(\frac{\lambda_i}{q_i}\right) \cdot b_i - \phi_h = 0. \tag{11.20a}$$

Let $\partial W / \partial Y_h = \theta$, that is, let an additional unit of private income be worth θ units of uncommitted government income, which is the numeraire. Rewriting Eqn (11.20a) as follows, we obtain the dual variable associated with the equation defining private income:

$$\phi_h = \theta - \sum_i \left(\frac{\lambda_i}{q_i}\right) \cdot b_i \equiv \theta - \text{CCF}. \tag{11.20b}$$

This result states that if the private sector receives one unit of income, the net benefit to the economy will be the social value of the increase in income itself, less the shadow cost of the additional private consumption that results (i.e. the CCF), all measured in terms of the numeraire. Combining Eqns (11.16) and (11.20b), the origins of, and reasoning behind, the 'cookbook' rule in Chapter 8 should now be clear.

The remaining first-order conditions of interest are

$$\frac{\partial \Phi}{\partial y_j} = \lambda_j - \sum_i \lambda_i a_{ij} - (\lambda_l - \phi_h w_j) l_j \leq 0, \quad j = 1, 2, 3, \tag{11.21}$$

where (11.21) holds as an equality only if the good in question is actually produced at home. If y_2 can be freely chosen, then under the assumptions of Section 11.1, good 2 will not be produced domestically. If, on the other hand, y_2 is fixed exogenously at a positive level, as is the case here, then (11.21) will hold as a strict inequality for good 2, indicating that it should not, in fact, be produced at home. In the case of good 3, which must be produced domestically, (11.21) will indeed hold as an equality. Hence, from Eqn (11.16), we have

$$\lambda_3 = \sum_i \lambda_i a_{i3} + w^* l_3. \tag{11.22}$$

Interpreted in this way, Eqn (11.21) states that the shadow price of a good whose output is *endogenously* determined at a positive level, which will always hold in the case of a non-tradable, is equal to its marginal social cost of production. That is to say, such activities just break even at shadow prices.

Using Eqn (11.20b) and (11.21), it is also instructive to write w^* as follows:

$$w^* = (1/l_1)\left(\lambda_1 - \sum_i \lambda_i a_{i1}\right) + \left(\sum_i \left(\frac{\lambda_i}{q_i}\right) \cdot b_i - \theta\right) \cdot (\underline{w} - w_1).$$

$$(11.16')$$

The first term is the loss of net output (valued at shadow prices) that results from the withdrawal of one worker from employment in sector 1. This is the value of the social opportunity cost of labour in alternative employment. The second term is the net social cost of the increase in consumption that he enjoys as a result of getting a job in the regulated sector.

It is important to note that the improvement in social welfare resulting from the arbitrary project $(\Delta z, -\Delta L_0)$ is $[\boldsymbol{\lambda} \cdot \Delta z - \lambda_l \Delta L_0]$. This can be thought of as the social 'profit' of the project.

In this chapter, we are particularly concerned with the shadow price of the non-tradable, the value of which will determine the magnitude of the departure from the so-called 'border price' rule for tradables. As a final step, therefore, we derive an expression for λ_3 in closed form. Substituting for ϕ_h from Eqn (11.20b) in Eqn (11.16), Eqns (11.17'), (11.18'), (11.20a), and (11.22) may be solved to yield the complete vector of shadow prices. Some rather tedious algebra yields the following result:

$$\lambda_3 = m\{(p_1^* a_{13} + p_2^{**} a_{23}) + [p_1^* - (p_1^* a_{11} + p_2^{**} a_{21})](l_3/l_1)$$
$$+ [(p_1^*/q_1)b_1 + (p_2^{**}/q_2)b_2 - \theta](\underline{w} - w_1)l_3\}, \qquad (11.23)$$

where

$$1/m = \{(1 - a_{33}) + (a_{31}^t \cdot a_{13} - a_{32}^t \cdot a_{23}) - [(b_3/q_3)$$
$$- a_{31}^t \cdot (b_1/q_1) + a_{32}^t \cdot (b_2/q_2)](\underline{w} - w_1)l_3\}$$
$$+ (l_3/l_1) \cdot [a_{31} + a_{31}^t(1 - a_{11}) - a_{32}^t \cdot a_{21}]. \qquad (11.24)$$

The expression in braces in Eqn (11.23) is the direct absorption of foreign exchange which results from the production of a unit of good 3. This absorption takes three forms: (i) the use of tradable inputs in its production, (ii) the net direct loss of foreign exchange in sector 1, from which additional labour would be drawn, and (iii) the net social cost of any additional payments to labour. The term m is simply the closed-loop multiplier of the system, which here incorporates not only the usual inter-industry and consumption effects, but also those stemming from the internal transportation of exports and imports and from the ensuing reallocations of a fully employed workforce. Observe that m is a pure number.

A notable feature of Eqn (11.23) is that the terms a_{3i}^t, which are the salient parameters of the system for present purposes, appear only in m. If these parameters were all zero, the system would specialize to that in Bell and Devarajan (1983), and Eqn (11.22) would, in turn, specialize to Eqn (24) therein (ibid.: 465). Thus, $1/m$ contains the following additional term:

$$Q \equiv [a_{31}^t \cdot (b_1/q_1) - a_{32}^t \cdot (b_2/q_2)](\underline{w} - w_1)l_3$$
$$+ [a_{31}^t \cdot (a_{13} + (1 - a_{11})(l_3/l_1)) - a_{31}^t \cdot (a_{23} + a_{21}(l_3/l_1))],$$
$$(11.25)$$

the sign of which is, a priori, unclear. It will now be argued that Q is very likely to be positive in practice.

Primary commodities are usually more bulky in relation to their unit values at the point of production than are manufactures; and in poor countries, it is also the case that $b_1 > b_2$, even allowing for the fact that some primary commodities are used as raw materials. Hence, it is plausible that $[a_{31}^t \cdot (b_1/q_1) - a_{32}^t \cdot (b_2/q_2)] > 0$. This difference will only be of any account, however, if there is a gap in wage rates between the primary sector, which is the source of labour to rest of the economy, and the sector producing non-tradables. In that case, the effect of such differences will be to increase Q, and hence to reduce m. Thus, the shadow price of the non-tradable will be somewhat smaller, ceteris paribus, than in the absence of such specific internal transport costs associated with foreign trade. The intuition here is that spending out of extra private income will reduce exports and increase imports. Under the above assumptions, this will lead to a contraction in the derived demand for transportation, and hence also in the employment of resources in that activity.

The second set of terms arises from changes in the inputs of tradables in sectors 1 and 3 (by assumption, the domestic output of good 2 is fixed), and hence in the derived demand for transportation. Given that $a_{31}^t > a_{32}^t$, and that sector 1 is almost certainly more labour intensive than sector 3, it is probable, but not certain, that the second set of terms is positive too.

On balance, it seems very likely that Q will be positive, so that 'multiplier effects' will be correspondingly weaker than in the case where there are no internal transport costs.

11.3. Transportation Projects

Thus far, we have been concerned with the effects of transport costs on all prices, market and shadow alike, and on the pattern of international trade. Yet when transportation projects are proposed or mooted, their advocates almost invariably emphasize that their proximate aim is to reduce these costs, relative to some counterfactual. There is nothing intrinsically wrong with this aim, of course; for, all else being equal, lower costs are the source of the benefits generated by transportation projects. This very effect significantly complicates the task of evaluating of such projects, however, precisely because they cause changes in one or more market prices, an effect which we have been at pains to rule out in the preceding analysis.

   In order to see what is involved, consider once more the example with which we began this chapter. Suppose the port in Beira and the rail network into the interior were substantially improved. In the absence of any other changes in policy, the domestic prices of goods that were previously exported (imported) would rise (fall), and some goods might switch from the category of non-traded to traded, or conversely. Conditions (11.3) and (11.4) supply the exact formulation, where the improvements in infrastructure can be thought of as a project that reduces the market price of good 3. If the resulting change in any price is not negligible, firms' choices of technique in production, namely, $(a_j; l_j)$, will also change, in general, as will the unregulated wage rate. Private welfare and consumption, moreover, will respond to the changes in prices too, so that it will no longer be valid to use Y_h as a direct argument of $W(\cdot)$. The tidy expression in Eqn (11.16), $[\sum_i (\lambda_i/q_i) \cdot b_i - \theta] \cdot (\underline{w} - w_1)$, which arises from the changes in consumption induced by changes in income alone, will also be invalid: instead, the complete consumption vector x must be estimated both in the absence and in the presence of the project, and each then valued at the corresponding vector of shadow prices. Projects that induce changes in prices on this scale will be called 'large', and dealing with them is a rather tall order. This task we defer until Chapter 13.

   Can anything be said without going into the whole gamut of these complications? Strictly speaking, not much; yet there is a pressing need for shortcuts in practical work. The following proposal seems defensible under the conditions about to be described. Consider a small part of the transportation network, say a rural road, and let it be improved or extended. Such a project will certainly have some effect on market prices in the immediate neighbourhood, and hence also on local output, incomes, and consumption. The changes it induces in all of the latter are essential to its description as a project, properly defined, and so must be estimated. Let the resulting changes in (net) outputs be denoted by $\Delta z \equiv z^2 - z^1$, where it should be recalled that these will usually arise mainly in the private sector. The trick here, as we saw in Section 8.7, is to treat Δz as a project in the public sector, with the changes in private after-tax incomes being viewed as transfers from the Exchequer to the households concerned. Turning to private consumption, let the bundle chosen in the absence of the project be denoted by x^1 and that in the event that the project is undertaken by x^2.

There remains the central task of evaluating these changes without going through the rigmarole of a full general equilibrium analysis. The vector of shadow prices in the absence of the project, π^1, is estimated in the manner set out in Section 11.2. Given that the project involves only a small part of the transportation network, it is plausible that *ratio* of the shadow price of transportation services to their market price will change little, if at all. If this be granted, then we obtain the said shadow price in the presence of the project, which is denoted by π_3^2. The corresponding shadow prices of tradables follow at once from Eqns (11.17′) and (11.18′), and those of all other non-tradables from the usual rules. With the vector π^2 thus derived, we can value the vectors (z^1, x^1) and (z^2, x^2) at their respective shadow prices—provided the market prices of the goods entering the consumption basket do not change appreciably. Since θ is also plausibly constant in the face of small perturbations to the economy, the evaluation of the project is, in principle, complete.

11.4. Summary

Distance, like protective tariffs and quotas, is a barrier to trade, but with an important difference: overcoming it requires the direct use of resources, whereas tariffs and quotas, which involve only transfers (albeit accompanied by deadweight losses), can be abolished at the stroke of a pen. From the viewpoint of the home country, the costs of overcoming this barrier can be broken down into two components, namely, the difference between the c.i.f. and f.o.b. price of the good in question, and the unit cost of the internal leg of the journey between the point of production or final use and the port. The sum of the first component and twice the second is the size of the 'natural' protection afforded by distance to domestic producers who compete with imports (or of the 'natural' tax on those seeking to export), and it may be so large as to deter trade in particular goods altogether. The empirical evidence suggests that for goods that are actually traded, natural protection is generally as great as, if not larger than, that afforded by tariffs.

The international leg poses no difficulties where the estimation of shadow prices is concerned—provided no good makes a switch among the categories of exports, imports, and non-tradables, for whatever reason. In the absence of such switches, exports and imports are associated with their corresponding f.o.b. and c.i.f. prices, respectively, and if world prices are parametrically given, the system of domestic prices is firmly anchored. Should such switches occur, however, domestic prices will move in sympathy, and on the empirical evidence, some of these movements will not be negligible. We have now entered more difficult terrain, the exploration of which will be taken up in Chapters 12 and 13.

The internal leg, in contrast, introduces inherent difficulties. For in its presence, all traded goods are, in effect, mixtures of pure traded goods and the (non-tradable) transport services needed to move them internally: the pure traded good becomes a mere theoretical ideal. An immediate casualty is the so-called border price rule: the shadow price of an exportable is now lower than its f.o.b. world price in the amount of the unit shadow cost of getting it from the producer to on board the ship; that of an importable is now higher than its c.i.f. world price in the amount of the unit shadow cost of getting it off the ship to the point of final use in the interior. At first glance, this may seem to involve no more than a simple calculation using the shadow prices derived in earlier chapters, in which space made no explicit appearance whatever. This is almost invariably what is done in practice. It is also invalid; for as we have demonstrated in this Chapter, the whole system of shadow prices is mutually and simultaneously determined in a manner that is incompatible with such recursive calculations. Indeed, the central purpose of this chapter has been to show how to derive all shadow prices when internal transport costs are not negligible—and the resulting errors from the practical short cut could be serious.

There remains the awkward conclusion that these shadow prices are not, in general, satisfactory for the evaluation of transportation projects themselves, when these projects would bring about significant reductions in transportation costs. It has been argued in Section 11.3 that one can skirt this difficulty if there are compelling reasons for supposing that the accounting ratio for transportation services will remain roughly constant in the face of such projects and that the changes in the market prices of the goods entering the consumption basket are small. Otherwise, there is nothing for it but to employ some apparatus for evaluating 'large' projects, a task which will be taken up in Chapter 13.

Recommended Reading

As noted above, the spatial dimension of shadow pricing has been almost wholly neglected as a subject in its own right, being widely viewed as a minor variation of the general case; so there is little to recommend. The later arrival on the scene of the topic known as 'Economic Geography', on which there is now a vast and growing literature, has done little to change matters. Limao and Venables (2001) is well worth reading, both as general background and as a serious attempt to come to grips with the empirical importance of spatial factors.

Exercises

1. A small, open economy comprises two regions, namely, the capital city, which is also the only port, and its rural hinterland. The rural sector produces a single tradable good 1 by means of land and labour, the form of economic organization being the family farm. Field studies of this sector have revealed that the marginal and average physical products of labour are one-half and unity, respectively. The cost of transporting one unit of good 1 from the farm to the port is 20 per cent of the farm-gate price. The f.o.b. world price of good 1 is unity, and exports thereof are subject to an *ad valorem* tax at the rate of 10 per cent. Exports of good 1 finance imports of good 2, which are subject to a tariff at the *ad valorem* rate of 25 per cent, the parametric c.i.f. world price being unity. The costs of transporting good 2 into the hinterland are negligible.

Good 3 is not tradable internationally, but it is freely tradable internally; the costs of transporting it into the hinterland are also negligible. It is produced in the capital city under conditions of perfect competition by means of a CRS Leontief technology whose unit activity vector is

$$a_3 \equiv (a_{13}, a_{23}, a_{33}; l_3) = (0.1, 0.3, 0.3; 1).$$

The government so regulates the wage rate in sector 3 that its level is twice that ruling in the rural hinterland.

Studies of households' budgets have yielded the finding that rural house-holds spend their entire incomes on goods 1, 2, and 3 in the proportions 0.5, 0.2, and 0.3, respectively, whereas the proportions for urban households are 0.3, 0.3, and 0.4, respectively. Studies of migrants' behaviour suggest that for every additional job created in the city, one labourer leaves the rural sector.

If the premium on public income is 25 per cent, find the shadow prices of all goods and labour, and justify any approximations you employ. (You should assume that the sector producing transportation services is a rep-resentative subsector of sector 3.) Is the so-called 'border-price' rule valid in this setting? State the reasons for your answer carefully.

2. Consider the following special case of the model in Section 11.1.

(a) To avoid the burden of unnecessary calculations, let $a_{ij} = 0$ for all i,j. The values of the remaining parameters are: $p_1^* = p_2^{**} = 1; l_1 = 1, l_2 = 2, l_3 = 1; a_{31}^t = 0.2, a_{32}^t = 0.1$. The labour market is perfectly competitive. Find all domestic prices in the case where $t_1 = 0.2$ and the value of the protective tariff on good 2 is chosen such that the domestic production thereof is barely profitable. (Assume that the gap between p_i^{**} and p_i^* ($i = 1, 2$) suffices to induce the configuration so described.)

(b) Turning to resource allocation, let the economy be endowed with 10 units of labour and assume that consumers' preferences can be represented by

$$u(x) = 0.3 \ln x_1 + 0.3 \ln x_2 + 0.4 \ln x_3.$$

If $(z, L_0) = 0$, then verify that $y = (3, 3/2, 4)$ and $e = (0, 0)$ is an equilibrium and explain why it is so.

(c) Now suppose that the government desires to employ one unit of labour to produce a public good. Find the corresponding quantity vector (x, y, e) in equilibrium, and verify that exactly the right amount of revenue will be raised to finance the said one unit of labour.

(d) If no protective tariff were imposed on the import of good 2, verify that insufficient revenue would be raised to finance the public good. Given that the value of t_1 must be held at 0.2, find the smallest value of t_2 that is needed for this purpose and the associated price and quantity (x, y, e) vectors. Is this allocation superior to that in (c), and if so, why?

3. A remote village has n identical households, each of which has three adults of working age. These family farms are specialized in the produc-tion of an exportable cash crop using land and family labour. Production possibilities on each farm are given by

$$y = L^{1/2},$$

where y denotes output and L inputs of labour.

Each individual is endowed with one unit of time. Whatever time is left after cultivating the cash crop is spent in leisure, whereby each household places the constant monetary value of 50 on each unit of time its members spend in this pursuit. All cash income is spent on a basket of manufactured consumer goods, which are purchased in the nearest town. These tradable goods sell at a retail price of 100. The protective tariff is 33 per cent, transport costs are negligible, and the retail margin is 25 per cent.

The f.o.b. world price of the cash crop is 250, but the government levies an export tax thereon at 25 per cent. The nearest town is a marketing centre for the crop. Thanks to a rail link, the cost of transporting each unit of the crop from the town to the port is a modest 20. The road between the village and the town, however, is a dirt track. Trucks are used to transport the crop from the village, but they often get stuck and/or damaged, and the round-trip time is great. Even though the trucking industry is competitive and the supply of transport services is highly elastic, farmers pay 80 per unit transported.

Angered by this state of affairs, the villagers press the government to build an all-weather road, which would reduce unit transport costs to 30. The government puts a 25 per cent premium on public income relative to the incomes of peasants such as the villagers. COPE has estimated the accounting ratios for construction, retail services, and transportation to be 0.7, 0.6, and 0.8, respectively, and the social discount rate to be 10 per cent p.a. If the road can be built in one year, requires no maintenance, and lasts forever, what is the most that the government should be prepared to pay for its construction?

[Hint: First, establish what farmers do now and what they would do if the road were built. Second, compare the economy with and without the project at market prices. Finally, value all outcomes at shadow prices.]

12. Risk and Uncertainty

Thus far, we have proceeded as if everything relevant to a project's profitability were known with perfect certainty, even into the far future. A little reflection suggests that this involves an unusually strong 'willing suspension of disbelief'; for experience tells us that things rarely work out exactly as expected. On the technical side, a factory may not function with the productivity claimed by the consulting engineers, especially if the process is new and untried. Prices also have a disconcerting habit of changing unexpectedly. Indeed, some think that world prices are especially given to springing surprises. Be that as it may, any uncertainty about the future course of world prices will necessarily introduce uncertainty into the structure of shadow prices—of tradable and non-tradable goods alike.

The existence of such uncertainty raises three important questions. First, how does uncertainty about both a particular project's technical performance and the vector of shadow prices translate into uncertainty about its social profitability? Second, how are shadow prices to be estimated when the economy is subject to uncertainty? Third, in the event that the social profitability of a project is uncertain, is the use of a decision criterion based on expected values justifiable? The first question is separate from, and obviously logically prior to, the second, so we will consider them in that order. The second and third are closely related, whereby the case for a decision rule based on expected values will be subjected to close scrutiny.

12.1. The Risk Profile of a Project

We begin with a simple example. Consider a project in which a tradable good is produced by means of unskilled labour alone. According to the technical 'blueprint', one unit of labour is required to produce one unit of output; but there is a nagging suspicion that two units of labour might be needed instead. After an examination of past experience with such projects (including those in foreign countries), consultation with experts (and/or astrologers), and private contemplation, the members of COPE arrive at a subjective prior probability that the project will work according to the blueprint. Let it be 90 per cent.

Suppose, to start with, that there is no uncertainty about market or shadow prices. Then the social profit yielded by the project is

$$\Pi^* = \begin{cases} \pi_0 - w^* & \text{with probablity } 0.9, \\ \pi_0 - 2w^* & \text{with probablity } 0.1, \end{cases}$$

where π_0 is the shadow price (= world price) of the output and w^* is the shadow wage rate. Hence, the expected social profit yielded by the project is

$$E\Pi^* = 0.9(\pi_0 - w^*) + 0.1(\pi_0 - 2w^*) = \pi_0 - 1.1w^*,$$

where E denotes the expectations operator.

Now suppose, instead, that at the time of deciding whether to undertake the project, the world price of the output is not known with certainty. According to COPE, the world price will take either the 'normal' value π_0 with probability 0.75, or the low value $0.8\pi_0$ with probability 0.25. If the world price turns out to be only $0.8\pi_0$, however, the shadow wage rate will no longer be w^*: deferring the matter of how to calculate it until Section 12.2, let its value be $0.95w^*$ in this case. There remains the question of whether the occurrences of low productivity and a low world price are statistically independent events. Unless the country is a large player in the world market in question, it seems highly plausible that they should be independent, and it greatly simplifies matters in the general case if they are so.

There are four possible cases, or states of the world ($s = 1, 2, 3, 4$), to be considered:

(1) normal productivity, normal world prices;
(2) normal productivity, low world prices;
(3) low productivity, normal world prices;
(4) low productivity, low world prices.

Under the assumption that the movements in productivity and world prices are indeed statistically independent, the probabilities that these states will occur are, respectively:

$$p(1) = 0.9 \times 0.75 = 0.675,$$
$$p(2) = 0.9 \times 0.25 = 0.225,$$
$$p(3) = 0.1 \times 0.75 = 0.075,$$
$$p(4) = 0.1 \times 0.25 = 0.025.$$

Hence, the social profit yielded by the project is:

$\pi_0 - w^*$ with probability 0.675,
$0.8\pi_0 - 0.95w^*$ with probability 0.225,
$\pi_0 - 2w^*$ with probability 0.075,
$0.8\pi_0 - 1.9w^*$ with probability 0.025.

The expected social profit yielded by the project is, therefore,

$$E\Pi^* = 0.675(\pi_0 - w^*) + 0.225(0.8\pi_0 - 0.95w^*) + 0.075(\pi_0 - 2w^*)$$
$$+ 0.025(0.8\pi_0 - 1.9w^*)$$
$$= 0.95\pi_0 - 1.086w^*.$$

Observe that this is simply the expected value of output less the expected value of costs, all measured at shadow prices.

The above example shows how a probability distribution of possible outcomes is constructed. To make the example numerically complete, let $\pi_0 = 3$ and $w^* = 2$. Then the probability distribution of social profits, which is a set of four mass points, is as shown in Fig. 12.1a, and the associated distribution function is depicted in Fig. 12.1b.

To close this section, we lay out the general case. The entire set of outcomes must be enumerated and the probability that each will occur must be specified. Let the set of possible states of the world in each period be denoted by S. Then the set of possible states of the world for a project that spans T periods is the T-fold Cartesian product $S^T = S \times S \times \cdots \times S$. Let $p(s)$ denote the probability that state $s = (s_1, \ldots, s_T) \in S^T$ will occur, where $s_\tau \in S$. Now consider the project

$$\Delta z(s) = [\Delta z(1, s), \Delta z(2, s), \ldots, \Delta z(\tau, s), \ldots, \Delta z(T, s)],$$

where the presence of s makes it clear that the technical performance of the project in each period may depend on the state of nature. Given that state s is realized, the present value of the project at shadow prices is

$$\text{NPV}^*(s) = \sum_\tau \beta(\tau, s) \cdot [\pi(\tau, s) \cdot \Delta z(\tau, s)], \qquad (12.1)$$

where $\beta(\tau, s)$ is the (social) discount factor and $\pi(\tau, s)$ is the vector of shadow prices in period τ, both in the event that state s is realized. If S^T has very many elements, as is usually the case in practice, then the probability distribution of the NPV^* can be constructed by Monte Carlo methods.

As the number of possible outcomes increases, this distribution, which is composed of a few mass points in the discrete case presented above,

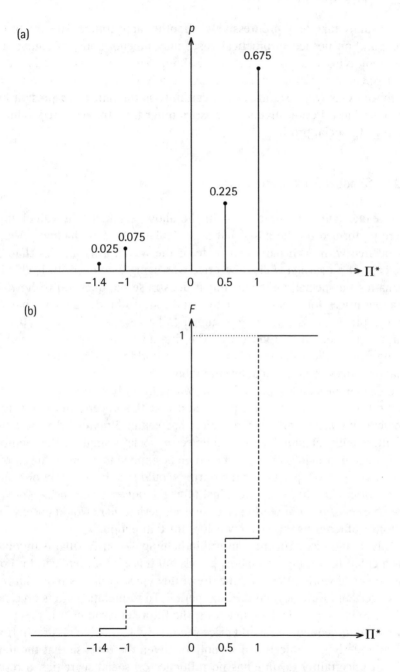

Figure 12.1. (a) The probability distribution of social profits. (b) The distribution function of social profits

will usually take on a progressively smoother appearance. The amount of computation needed in practical cases may be enormous, of course, but the underlying principle is that used above. With the advent of low cost, high-speed computing, moreover, there really is no excuse not to pursue such analyses when significant uncertainty is thought to be present and the decision criterion involves statistics other than the expected value of a project's social profit.

12.2. Shadow Prices Under Risk

The reader will have noted that in the above example, the calculations were performed on the basis that a particular vector of shadow prices is associated with each particular state of the world. This implies that the concept of a *contingent* shadow price was being employed. In itself, this demands no special comment; but it does raise the question of how the shadow prices for each state of the world are to be calculated. That the border price rule is implicitly assumed to be valid should also cause no surprise in view of its robustness. The first awkward step, then, involves going from a particular set of values of the world prices of tradables to the shadow prices of non-tradables and labour.

Consider the simplest possible case, where the only source of uncertainty is the future course of world prices and that this uncertainty is resolved immediately after work on the project has begun. Provided the mere fact of uncertainty *ex ante* has no influence on social scarcities, the methods developed in previous chapters may then be applied to estimate the associated set of shadow prices; for the setting would then be a certain one once world prices had been revealed, just after the outset, so to speak. To each possible realization of world prices in each period there would correspond a vector of (contingent) shadow prices for that period.

This thought experiment is useful in helping to clarify what is involved in calculating contingent shadow prices, but it is a bit far fetched; for both the course of world prices and the life of the typical project stretch out into an uncertain future beyond the next period. To formulate matters precisely with an eye on practical applications, the future environment is described by a random sequence of world price vectors, $\{p_\tau^*\}_{\tau=1}^T$, which is drawn from some underlying subjective distribution. Given the premise that the mere fact of uncertainty *ex ante* has no influence on social scarcities, a resort to the methods of previous chapters to compute the associated sequence of shadow prices, $\{\pi_\tau\}_{\tau=1}^T$, seems justifiable, provided the economy moves more or less without friction from one momentary equilibrium to another as the course of world prices is progressively revealed. The latter is admittedly a strong supplementary assumption, but it is not clear that there is a practicable alternative.

There remains the question of whether the existence of uncertainty *ex ante* has any bearing on social scarcities, as one might expect if individuals are risk averse and insurance markets are incomplete. If, in a sense to be defined in Section 12.3, society's preferences over lotteries *effectively* exhibit risk neutrality,[1] then the procedure just described, which yields shadow prices that are free of any notion of a risk premium, will permit the calculation of expected values that are internally consistent. It is therefore of the utmost importance to establish conditions under which such effective risk neutrality will hold, a task to which we now turn.

12.3. A Decision Rule

Once the risk profile is in hand, the next step is to use it to establish whether the project in question should be accepted. In the light of Section 12.2, the rule which suggests itself at once is based on a project's *expected* net present value.

Decision Rule 1: If

$$E(NPV^*) \equiv \sum_{s \in S^T} p(s) \cdot NPV^*(s) \geq 0, \tag{12.2}$$

accept the project; otherwise, reject it.

This expected value can be found from the project's risk profile, but it is worth investigating whether there is a short cut. We have, from Eqns (12.1) and (12.2),

$$E(NPV^*) = \sum_{\tau=1}^{T} \sum_{s \in S^T} p(s)[\beta(\tau, s) \cdot \pi(\tau, s) \cdot \Delta z(\tau, s)]. \tag{12.3a}$$

If the dated vector of (discounted) shadow prices $[\beta(\tau, s) \cdot \pi(\tau, s)]$ and the dated vector $\Delta z(\tau, s)$ are statistically independent in each period, then

---

[1] To illustrate, consider the simple lottery $(1, y_1, y_2, p)$, in which one dollar is staked and the outcomes y_1 and y_2 occur with probabilities p and $1 - p$, respectively. The lottery is actuarially fair if the expected value of the winnings is equal to the stake money: $py_1 + (1 - p)y_2 = 1$.

Eqn (12.3a) specializes to the very convenient form

$$E(\text{NPV}^*) = \sum_{\tau=1}^{T} E_{s \in S^T}[\beta(\tau, s) \cdot \pi(\tau, s)] \cdot E_{s \in S^T} \Delta z(\tau, s)$$

$$= \sum_{\tau=1}^{T} E_{s_\tau \in S}[\beta(\tau, s_\tau) \cdot \pi(\tau, s_\tau)] \cdot E_{s_\tau \in S} \Delta z(\tau, s_\tau). \qquad (12.3b)$$

That is to say, in each period, one calculates the average value of each and every (discounted) shadow price, and then uses the resulting vector of such averages to value the vector of average net outputs. In this case, therefore, there is no need to undertake the much more arduous task of calculating the project's risk profile.

Now the use of expected values in decision making under risk is usually associated with risk-neutrality—equivalently, with the willingness to accept actuarially fair bets. If (12.2) is adopted as the decision rule, therefore, it seems that the underlying social preferences where risk bearing is concerned must exhibit risk-neutrality. Yet this leads to an immediate difficulty. As individuals, especially poor ones, are commonly unwilling to accept an actuarially fair bet, it is natural to ask whether, and if so, how, private risk aversion should enter into calculations of the social profitability of public sector projects. Hirschleifer's (1965) view is that since such considerations enter into the determination of market parameters, particularly the rate of interest, to disallow this implicit risk premium in the evaluation of public sector projects is to encourage excessive investment by the public sector, at the expense of higher yielding projects that would be favoured by the private sector.

Others argue to the contrary. First, it is plausibly claimed that the government can deal with risk better than the private sector through a more extensive pooling of risks. It is also sometimes claimed, though less frequently, that the state's collective arrangements leave fewer opportunities for the operation of moral hazard, a claim that seems less immediately convincing. Second, individuals' preferences need not be respected, either on the grounds of paternalism, or because private subjective probabilities and attitudes towards risk bearing are veiled by the operation of very imperfect informational and market structures.

In this connection, Arrow and Lind (1971) prove that in the 'complete markets' setting, the additional assumption that the returns from any particular investment are independent of other components of national income suffices to establish that expected returns should be discounted at a rate appropriate for projects yielding perfectly certain returns. That is to say, no premium for risk should be allowed into the reckoning. In view of the character of the Arrow–Debreu world, this result is not wholly surprising.

In the real world, of course, we cannot appeal to a complete set of contingent markets to extricate ourselves from these practical difficulties, so we are led to ask: is there some other, more plausible way of giving rigorous justification to (12.2) as a decision rule? Arrow and Lind provide an ingenious argument based on risk-spreading over a large pool of individuals, some or all of whom may be risk averse. Informally, the argument runs as follows. Let an individual have preferences over lotteries that conform to the expected utility hypothesis, where the utility function $u(y)$ is strictly concave in realized income, y, if the individual is risk averse. Suppose now that a project producing a random return is undertaken and that all individuals have the same share therein. If the number of people sharing in the return is large, each individual's share will be small, so that his total income will depart very little from his draw y, however well or badly the project in question turns out. The upshot is that the marginal utility of realized income, $u'(y)$, will also be virtually independent of the performance of the project, so that the concavity of $u(\cdot)$ can be ignored for the purposes of evaluating it. As the 'shareholders' in public sector projects are the taxpayers, and taxpayers are numerous relative to the size of any individual project, the argument for using (12.2) seems to be complete—provided, of course, that the returns from different projects are statistically independent.

One step remains, however. Although the cost of risk to each individual ensuing from the randomness of the project's return may be negligible, the aggregate cost of risk summed over all individuals could still be significant. To show that it is not, a formal proof of Arrow and Lind's result is now given.

Consider a public sector project yielding a random return, Z, which is distributed in the form of lump-sum transfers to the population at large. (The government's budget is balanced, and lump-sum transfers are the easiest case to deal with.) With n identical individuals, each taxpayer can be thought of as having a share $\zeta = 1/n$ in the project in question.[2] Since we are interested in what happens as n becomes large, it will be convenient

---

[2] Although individuals are identical, they may make different i.i.d. draws from the distribution of y. That is to say, the individuals are identical *ex ante*, but not necessarily so *ex post*. For a fairly extensive treatment of this matter in a related context, see Bell (1991).

to write the welfare index of an individual as

$$v(\zeta) = Eu(y + \zeta Z), \tag{12.4}$$

$y + \zeta Z$ being the individual's total income from all sources. Hence,

$$v'(\zeta) = E[u'(y + \zeta Z) \cdot Z], \tag{12.5}$$

from which it follows that, given the assumption that Z is independent of y,

$$v'(0) = [Eu'(y)] \cdot EZ. \tag{12.6}$$

That is to say, as the population of individuals becomes indefinitely large, the improvement in any individual's expected utility brought about by a small increase in the share ζ is the product of the expected value of the marginal utility of income and the project's mean return. No risk premium in connection with the project appears here.

Recalling the definition of a derivative[3], and noting that E is a linear operator, Eqn (12.4) yields the following expression for $Eu'(y)$:

$$Eu'(y) = \lim_{n \to \infty} E\{[u(y + Z/n) - u(y)]/(Z/n)\}, \tag{12.7}$$

to which we shall return shortly.

If the individual is risk-averse ($u'' < 0$), then there will exist a certain sum $k(n) > 0$ such that he is indifferent between the lotteries yielding the random payoffs $(y + Z/n)$ and $[y + (\bar{Z}/n) - k(n)]$, respectively: that is,

$$Eu(y + Z/n) = Eu[y + (\bar{Z}/n) - k(n)], \tag{12.8}$$

where $EZ = \bar{Z}$ is the mean value of the project's return and the term $(\bar{Z}/n) - k(n)$ is non-stochastic. Intuitively, $k(n)$ is the cost to the individual of the additional risk introduced by the project. As $\lim_{n \to \infty}(\bar{Z}/n) = 0$, it follows at once from Eqn (12.8) that $\lim_{n \to \infty} k(n) = 0$, that is, the cost of the said risk to an individual goes to zero as n becomes arbitrarily large.

This is not enough, however. We also need to prove that $\lim_{n \to \infty}[nk(n)] = 0$, that is, the *aggregate* cost of the risk associated with the project also goes to zero as the population becomes very large. By the definition of a derivative, we have

$$Eu'(y) = \lim_{\alpha \to 0} E\{[u(y + \alpha) - u(y)]/\alpha\}.$$

---

[3] That is, $f'(x) = \lim_{h \to 0}[f(x + h) - f(x)]/h$.

Recalling Eqn (12.8), let $\alpha = (\bar{Z}/n) - k(n)$, so that $\alpha \to 0$ as $n \to \infty$. Substituting for α, we obtain

$$Eu'(y) = \lim_{n \to \infty} n\{E[u(y + (\bar{Z}/n) - k(n)) - u(y)]\}/[\bar{Z} - nk(n)].$$

Substituting for $E[u(y + (\bar{Z}/n) - k(n)]$ from Eqn (12.8) then yields

$$Eu'(y) = \lim_{n \to \infty} n\{E[u(y + Z/n) - u(y)]\}/[\bar{Z} - nk(n)]. \qquad (12.9)$$

We now return to Eqn (12.7), which has not been used in the derivation of Eqn (12.9). Multiplying both sides of Eqn (12.7) by Z and recalling that Z is independent of y, we obtain

$$[Eu'(y)] \cdot \bar{Z} = \lim_{n \to \infty} nE[u(y + Z/n) - u(y)],$$

or

$$Eu'(y) = \lim_{n \to \infty} nE[u(y + Z/n) - u(y)]/\bar{Z}, \qquad (12.10)$$

a comparison of which with Eqn (12.9) yields

$$\lim_{n \to \infty} [nk(n)] = 0,$$

which is the required result. It follows that when deciding whether or not to undertake the project in question, EZ tells us all we need to know about it.

It may be helpful to approach this question in a somewhat different way. Suppose the social welfare function is the sum of individuals' expected utilities, so that

$$W^1 = nEu(y) \qquad (12.11)$$

in the absence of the project, and

$$W^2 = nEu(y + Z/n) \qquad (12.12)$$

if it is undertaken. If n is sufficiently large, the project will yield the social 'profit'

$$\Delta W \equiv W^2 - W^1 = nEu(y + Z/n) - nEu(y) = nE[u'(y) \cdot (Z/n)]. \qquad (12.13a)$$

Given the assumption that y and Z are independent, Eqn (12.13a) specializes to

$$\Delta W = Eu'(y) \cdot EZ, \tag{12.13b}$$

so that the sign of the project's expected return reveals whether it will improve or diminish welfare, $Eu'(y)$ (> 0) being the expected marginal utility of income in the absence of the project.

12.4. Some Reservations

Lest the decision rule defined in condition (12.2) be accepted too hastily, two general grounds for caution need to be discussed.

12.4.1. The Concentration of Benefits

It is rare for the benefits of a public project to be spread evenly over the entire population of taxpayers. In the nature of things, most projects produce rather specific and geographically local effects, even though the costs of constructing and maintaining them are often borne by the population as a whole. The main beneficiaries of a dam, for example, are usually the farmers in its command area, even though farm prices may fall following the introduction of irrigation and those farmers may pay more in taxes, directly or indirectly, and so reduce the net burden on the rest of society. In any event, the concentration of a project's benefits on a rather small proportion of the entire population will undermine the main result of Section 12.3 because the resulting additional random element in the beneficiaries' incomes will no longer be necessarily small. That being so, the aggregate cost of risk almost certainly cannot be ignored. The only refuge from this awkward conclusion is the hope that the government's current portfolio of projects is such that there is something in it for everyone. Unless the horizon in question is quite long—at least a generation—that hope seems rather forlorn, however, and the fact that many will have to wait their turn introduces other difficulties.

In order to pursue this point formally, consider the case in which all individuals in the economy share equally in the cost, C, of establishing the project, but only a limited number, n_2, share in its stream of benefits, Z, where Z now denotes the project's gross return. The number of individuals who do not receive benefits is therefore denoted by $n_1 = n - n_2$. Extending the notation of Section 12.3, we define the shares in costs and benefits as

$\zeta \equiv 1/n$ and $\zeta_2 \equiv 1/n_2$, respectively. Also, let the functions

$$v_1(\zeta) = Eu(y_1 - \zeta C) \qquad (12.14)$$

and

$$v_2(\zeta, \zeta_2) = Eu(y_2 - \zeta C + \zeta_2 Z), \qquad (12.15)$$

denote the expected utilities of individuals belonging to groups 1 and 2, respectively, in the event that the project is undertaken, and let the social welfare function be additively separable:

$$W = n_1 v_1 + n_2 v_2. \qquad (12.16)$$

Proceeding as in Section 12.3, we have

$$\frac{\partial v_1}{\partial \zeta} = -C \cdot Eu'(y_1 - \zeta C), \qquad (12.17)$$

$$\frac{\partial v_2}{\partial \zeta} = -C \cdot Eu'(y_2 - \zeta C + \zeta_2 Z), \qquad (12.18)$$

$$\frac{\partial v_2}{\partial \zeta_2} = E[u'(y_2 - \zeta C + \zeta_2 Z) \cdot Z]. \qquad (12.19)$$

The change in W induced by the project is

$$\Delta W = n_1 [Eu(y_1 - \zeta C) - Eu(y_1)] + n_2 [Eu(y_2 + \zeta_2 Z - \zeta C) - Eu(y_2)]. \qquad (12.20)$$

Now let n become arbitrarily large, while n_2 is kept fixed, so that n_1 will also become arbitrarily large and the benefits of the project will be increasingly concentrated on group 2, relatively speaking. Then, using the definition of a derivative and noting that $\zeta \to 0$ as $n \to \infty$, we have

$$\lim_{n \to \infty} \Delta W$$
$$= -\lim_{n \to \infty} n_1 (C/n) \cdot Eu'(y_1) + \lim_{n \to \infty} n_2 [Eu(y_2 + Z/n_2)$$
$$- (C/n) \cdot Eu'(y_2 + Z/n_2) - Eu(y_2)]$$
$$= -C \cdot Eu'(y_1) + n_2 [Eu(y_2 + Z/n_2) - Eu(y_2)], \qquad (12.21)$$

where a first-order Taylor expansion about $(y_2 + \zeta_2 Z)$ has been used to evaluate the expression $Eu(y_2 + \zeta_2 Z - \zeta C)$. It is clear that a potential problem has arisen in connection with the term $n_2[Eu(y_2+Z/n_2)-Eu(y_2)]$. If the random benefit accruing to each individual in group 2, Z/n_2, is not always negligible, relative to y_2, the use of a linear approximation of $Eu(y_2 + Z/n_2)$ in the neighbourhood of $Eu(y_2)$ to yield the expression

$$n_2[Eu(y_2 + Z/n_2) - Eu(y_2)] \cong n_2 E[u'(y_2) \cdot Z/n_2] = Eu'(y_2) \cdot \bar{Z}$$

will be invalid. In this case, the concavity of $u(\cdot)$ will indeed matter, and the results of Section 12.3 will cease to hold.

It is enlightening to investigate the case where $Eu(y)$ can be represented as a linear function of the mean and variance of income:[4]

$$Eu(y) = Ey - \gamma \cdot \sigma_y^2,$$

for it is then possible to obtain a closed-form expression for ΔW. We have

$$Eu(y_2 + Z/n_2) = Ey_2 + (\bar{Z}/n_2) - \gamma[\sigma_{y_2}^2 + (\sigma_Z^2/n_2^2) + 2\,\mathrm{cov}(y_2, Z/n_2)].$$

Hence,

$$Eu(y_2 + Z/n_2) - Eu(y_2) = (\bar{Z}/n_2) - \gamma[(\sigma_Z^2/n_2^2) + 2\,\mathrm{cov}(y_2, Z/n_2)].$$

Since $u(\cdot)$ is unique up to affine transformations, we may normalize $Eu'(y_1)$ to unity. Substituting for $[Eu(y_2+Z/n_2)-Eu(y_2)]$ in Eqn (12.21), we then obtain

$$\lim_{n\to\infty} \Delta W = (\bar{Z} - C) - \gamma[(\sigma_Z^2/n_2) + 2n_2\,\mathrm{cov}(y_2, Z/n_2)].$$

The term $(\bar{Z} - C)$ is simply the expected net return yielded by the project. The term

$$-\gamma[(\sigma_Z^2/n_2) + 2n_2\,\mathrm{cov}(y_2, Z/n_2)]$$

does not, however, appear in Section 12.3. It arises from both the concentration of benefits in the hands of the group numbering n_2 and the possibility that y_2 and Z are not independent. Even if n_2 is large enough to render the former effect negligible, the latter effect, when summed over n_2 individuals, may be too large to be ignored.

---

[4] A necessary and sufficient condition for this representation is that y be normally distributed and that $u(\cdot)$ be a negative exponential: after normalization, $u = 1 - a \cdot \exp(-\gamma y)$. In this case, preferences over lotteries exhibit constant absolute risk aversion.

12.4.2. Risk Aversion and Shadow Prices

The second note of caution concerning condition (12.2) as a decision rule stems from the fact that if individuals are risk averse, the very presence of risk will influence equilibrium in the labour market. How, if at all, is this to be reconciled with Arrow and Lind's result? In particular, one is prompted to ask: is the shadow wage rate free of any risk premium, even when workers are risk averse? The following example, which is drawn from Drèze and Stern (1987: 978–9), suggests that risk is indeed likely to make an appearance in the shadow wage rate.

Suppose peasant farmers consume out of stocks in period 0, which are denoted by y_0, and supply a fixed amount of labour (L, say) to own cultivation and public sector employment combined in period 1. The economy produces just one physical commodity, and both peasant farming and public production are risky. Let all peasant households share equally in the returns from public projects.

The peasant farmer is assumed to make no active choices where labour supply is concerned; he simply complies with the demands of public sector employment, the rest of his time being devoted to the cultivation of his own farm, with all labour inputs in both lines of employment being committed before the state of nature is revealed. His sole decision is how much of the stock y_0 to consume in period 0, the rest being carried over to period 1. In this setting, the level of expected utility attained by a representative peasant is arguably the appropriate indicator of social welfare:

$$W = \sum_s p(s)u[x_0, x_1(s)], \tag{12.22}$$

where x_0 is his consumption in period 0. As the outcomes of public sector production activities accrue ultimately to the peasant, his consumption in period 1 in the event that state s is realized is

$$x_1(s) = F(L + z_l; s) + z_1(s) + y_0 - x_0, \tag{12.23}$$

where $F(L + z_l; s)$ is the output on the peasant's farm, $-z_l$ is the amount of labour demanded of him by the public sector, and $z_1(s)$ is the per capita level of public production. (Recall that there is only one physical commodity.)

We now employ the envelope theorem in the usual way to derive shadow prices. Substituting for $x_1(s)$ from Eqn (12.23) in Eqn (12.22), the shadow wage rate is

$$\pi_l \equiv \partial W^0/\partial z_l = \sum_s p(s) \cdot [\partial u[x_0^0, x_1(s)]/\partial x_1(s)] \cdot F'(\cdot; s), \tag{12.24}$$

where $x_0^0 \equiv \arg\max_{x_0} W$. Similarly, the shadow price of output in state s is

$$\pi_l(s) \equiv \partial W^0 / \partial z_1(s) = p(s) \cdot [\partial u(x_0^0, x_1(s))/\partial x_1(s)] \equiv p(s)u_1(s),$$

(12.25)

that is, the said shadow price is the marginal utility of consumption in state s in period 1 multiplied by the probability with which state s occurs. Observe that $\pi_l(s)$ is a *contingent* shadow price, for the additional unit of output is delivered only in state s. The marginal social value of obtaining an additional unit of public output *with certainty* in period 1 (that is, $dz_l(s) = 1 \; \forall s$) is

$$\pi_1 = \sum_s \pi_1(s) = \sum_s p(s)u_1(s) \equiv Eu_1(s).$$

(12.26)

From Eqns (12.24) and (12.26), we obtain the shadow wage rate relative to the shadow value of the certain delivery of an additional unit of public output per head in period 1:

$$\frac{\pi_l}{\pi_1} = \frac{E[u_1(s) \cdot F'(\cdot\,;s)]}{Eu_1(s)}$$

$$= \frac{[Eu_1(s)] \cdot [EF'(s)] + \text{cov}[u_1(s), F'(s)]}{Eu_1(s)} < E[F'(s)]$$

(12.27)

if cov[·] < 0. Equation (12.27) may be rewritten as

$$\frac{\pi_l}{\pi_1} = \left[1 + \rho\left(\frac{\sigma_{u_1}}{E_s u_1(s)}\right) \cdot \left(\frac{\sigma_{F'}}{E_s F'(s)}\right)\right] \cdot E_s[F'(s)],$$

(12.28)

where ρ is the correlation coefficient between the marginal product of labour (MPL) in state s, $F'(\cdot\,;s)$, and the marginal utility of consumption in period 1 in the event that state s is realized, $u_1(s)$. The terms multiplied by ρ are the coefficients of variation of the marginal utility of consumption in period 1 and the marginal product of labour in private production, respectively. It is certainly plausible that ρ is negative in some circumstances. A drought, for example, results in a low MPL and, hence, in the absence of sufficiently strong offsetting movements in public production, a high marginal utility of income, where it should be remarked that public production in this context includes programmes of disaster relief, if they exist. If ρ is indeed negative, then the social cost of labour in terms of the 'sure thing' in period 1 is lower than the expected value of the MPL in private production. It follows that the more risky is private production, the bigger is the divergence between (π_l/π_1) and the expected value of the MPL, a result which accords with good sense in this setting.

Now consider a risky project $(dz_1, -dz_l)$, where the elements of the vector dz_1 are the state-contingent deliveries $(dz_1(s))$ of the aggregate good. Given the definition of the shadow prices, the appropriate decision rule is

Decision Rule 2: If

$$\sum_s \pi_1(s)dz_1(s) - \pi_l dz_l \geq 0, \tag{12.29}$$

accept the project; otherwise reject it.

Recalling Eqns (12.24) and (12.25), it is seen that condition (12.29) can be rewritten as

$$\sum_s p(s)[u_1(s)dz_1(s) - u_1(s)F'(\cdot\,; s)dz_l] \geq 0. \tag{12.30a}$$

What, then, is the difference between Decision Rules 1 and 2? Formally speaking, none at all—apart from a possible change of numeraire from uncommitted public income to the expected utility of private income. Where the shadow prices themselves are concerned, some care is needed. Consider once more the special case where the marginal utility of consumption in period 1 is independent of both the project's payoff and the marginal product of labour on the family farm. Here, condition (12.30a) will specialize to

$$E_s u_1(s) \cdot [E_s dz_1(s) - E_s F'(\cdot\,; s) \cdot dz_l] \geq 0, \tag{12.30b}$$

from which it is seen that the project's expected net return is the right yardstick for judging its social profitability. This case corresponds to Arrow and Lind's assumption that public projects produce returns which are independent of the rest of the peasant's income. If this assumption is violated, however, the shadow prices derived in previous chapters cannot be taken over wholly as they stand to yield suitable averages. Rather they must be modified to reflect the costs of the additional risks that the project in question will generate.

12.5. Summary

Any undertaking that stretches into the future is necessarily an uncertain one, so the first task is to identify the sources of uncertainty. In the present context, these are, first, the technical performance of the project itself and, second, the economic environment in which the project will function, an environment whose character is heavily influenced, in turn, by the course of world prices and the development of the domestic economy. The approach adopted here involves enumerating the possible states of the world in each period and attaching a probability—no doubt a subjective one—to each. This is a rather daunting task, but a sensible list should emerge from meetings of experts in the various fields and a resort to independent judgement. The probability that a particular sequence of states over any given time horizon will be realized can then be calculated, allowing for possible departures from statistical independence both within and across periods. Suppose, for the moment, that the vector of shadow prices in each state of the world is known, so that the project's net present value in each sequence of realized states over its lifetime can be calculated accordingly. It is then a straightforward, albeit tedious, matter to derive the project's risk profile in the form of the distribution function of its net present value at shadow prices (NPV*), whereby a resort to Monte Carlo methods will cut down on the tedium.

In formulating a decision rule that will govern whether a project should be undertaken, we start with the question: is the only relevant statistic of the distribution function of the project's NPV* its mean value? Given that the shadow prices have been correctly derived in the risky environment in which resources are allocated, the answer is surely in the affirmative. Yet this answer merely pushes the problem one stage back; for nothing has been said about how the shadow prices are to be 'correctly' derived. It is here that Arrow and Lind's celebrated result comes to the rescue. If, in a numerous society, all members thereof share equally in the project's net returns and these returns are statistically independent of the other components that make up national income, then it turns out that the cost of the risk associated with the project is negligible, not only to each member but also to society as a whole. The underlying intuition is that as the returns are spread over a ever larger number of individuals, the pooling effect progressively eliminates the project's risks—provided they are independent of those associated with other activities. That being so, the use of (state-contingent) shadow prices derived without reference to risk, as set out in previous chapters, will be valid.

This elegant simplification is subject to two potentially important reservations in practice. The first is that the benefits generated by projects often accrue to relatively small groups, even when allowance is made for the fact that, over a stretch of time, the government will have a portfolio of diverse undertakings, whereas the costs of projects are typically widely spread. The second reservation is that the returns from public sector projects may not be independent of private incomes, especially in agrarian economies or those otherwise subject to external shocks. To the extent that the government is willing and able to mount fairly effective schemes of relief in the event of disasters, this latter reservation loses much of its force. Otherwise, there is nothing for it but to derive (state-contingent) shadow prices that reflect the costs generated by a project's risks—and to make a mental note that this is yet another example of the dependence of shadow prices on the choice of policies.

Recommended Reading

The classic contribution is Arrow and Lind (1971), which readers should follow up with Graham (1981).

Exercises

1. A small, open economy produces a single exportable good, which may be thought of as a primary good, and a single non-tradable. These are labelled goods 1 and 3, respectively. Both are produced by means of labour alone under CRS, and good 1 is subject to a fixed *ad valorem* export tax of 10 per cent. Producers in sector 1 are confronted with two, stochastically independent sources of risk: output per worker varies with the state of the weather and growing conditions at home, and the world price of the good fluctuates with conditions in the global economy. To be precise, the output–labour ratio $(1/l_1)$ takes the values (1, 0.8) with probabilities (0.8, 0.2), respectively, and p_1^* the values (1, 0.75) with probabilities (0.9, 0.1).

The wage rate in sector 3 is fixed by the government at the value $w_3 = 1.5$, but no Harris–Todaro mechanisms are at work. The labour market always clears at full employment, with households offering their endowments of labour completely inelastically, and the wage rate in sector 1 being perfectly flexible. If $(1/l_1)$ and p_1^* are revealed before producers make their input decisions, what will be the market wage rate in sector 1 in each state of the world?

Let the world prices of imported consumer goods be perfectly steady. Will the CCF and θ nevertheless depend on the state of the world, and if so, why? In what follows, we shall assume that the value of the expression $[CCF(s) - \theta(s)]$ is 0.1 in all states of nature.

A project to produce an imported consumer good (2) domestically is put on the table. Its construction would require 10 units each of labour and another importable (good 4), and would last one year–if all goes according to plan. The consulting engineers note that difficulties could arise, however, in which case 15 and 12 units, respectively, would be needed for the timely execution of the work. The chances of such a setback are reckoned to be 30 per cent. The world price of good 4 is also uncertain: it takes the values (1, 1.25) with probabilities (0.8, 0.2), respectively, and is independent of the engineering risks. When completed, the factory would produce good 2 by means of labour and good 1. If it functions as designed, 10 units of output will be produced from 1 unit each of labour and good 1. Otherwise, only 8 units will be produced, and only then when the input of good 1 is double that specified in the blueprint. Experience suggests that the probability that the factory will operate according to plan is 0.75 and that this probability is independent of construction costs. All labour employed on the project is paid the regulated wage rate.

If the world price of good 2 is perfectly steady, at $p_2^* = 3$, construct the risk profile of the project's undiscounted net benefits in the investment and output phases, respectively. Should the project be undertaken? (You must give a clear statement of any additional assumptions you need in arriving at a decision.)

[Hint: observe that the four possible states of the world where the macro-economic setting is concerned must be suitably extended to deal with the additional uncertainties that would arise if the project were undertaken. In order to keep the total number of cases within manageable bounds, you should assume that all uncertainty is resolved immediately after the decision to proceed or not has been made.]

2. Consider the following specialization of the model of Drèze and Stern (1987), as presented in Section 12.4. The peasant is assumed to be endowed with one unit of labour and to carry no stocks from period to period, so that all output, whether privately or publicly produced, is consumed. The peasant supplies his endowment of labour completely inelastically. Thus, Eqn (12.22) specializes to

$$W = \sum_s p(s)u[x_1(s)],$$

and Eqn (12.23) to

$$x_1(s) = F(1 + z_l; s) + z_1(s).$$

Let risk affect private production multiplicatively, and let the technology be Cobb–Douglas:

$$F(1 + z_l; s) = \phi(s) \cdot [1 + z_l]^{1/2}.$$

There are just two states, namely, 'good' 1 and 'bad' 2, whereby the scalar $\phi(s)$ takes the values (1.1, 0.6) with probabilities (0.8, 0.2), respectively. The public production vector, $(z_1(s), z_l(s))$, takes the values (0.20, −0.1) and (0.15, −0.1) with the same probabilities as $\phi(s)$. Is this probability structure plausible?

If $u(\cdot)$ takes the form $u(x_1) = \log_e x_1$, what is the shadow wage rate relative to that of the aggregate good when the latter is delivered with certainty? Interpret your finding.

3. A backward region is populated by identical peasant farmers, who produce a single crop, which cannot be stored. Output varies with the weather, one year in four being on average poor, and the rest being normal. The technology can be represented as follows: when L units of labour are applied to a peasant's holding, output will be $L^{3/4}$ in a bad year and $1.25L^{3/4}$ in a normal one. Each family is endowed with one unit of labour and has preferences over lotteries that can be represented by the von Neumann–Morgenstern utility function

$$u(x) = 1 - 1/x,$$

where x denotes the family's annual consumption.

The region is so cut off from the rest of the economy that the only transactions it has with the outside take the form of transfers from the central government. These amount to 0.25 units of output per family in bad years and 0.15 in good ones.

The government now considers the possibility of introducing small projects that would employ the local people to produce the same crop, and whose proceeds would be distributed solely to the region's households. Find the shadow prices of labour and the *contingent* shadow prices of output, and compare them in an appropriate fashion. What conclusions do you draw concerning the role of risk in this setting? Give reasons for your answer. How would the possibility of temporary migration out of the region affect the analysis?

13. Large Projects

Apart from a brief excursion in Chapter 11, we have thus far carefully avoided cases in which market prices change in response to projects. This was ensured by the assumptions that: (i) there are no quantitative restrictions on international trade; and (ii) there are constant returns to scale (CRS) and constant costs in the production of non-tradables. Unfortunately, these conditions are not always satisfied in practice, and it is essential that we find ways of evaluating projects when they are violated. The problem arises most frequently in connection with 'lumpy' projects that produce non-tradables, especially those dealing with communications, utilities, and infrastructure. In the presence of such indivisibilities, supply cannot be increased continuously at constant costs, but rather must be expanded in discrete steps; so that price (or user cost) at first falls sharply following the completion of each project and then rises with growing demand until the next lumpy project comes on stream. It should be remarked that the completion of such a project usually entails a reduction in the *effective* price of the good it produces, either because the new tariff schedule is set below the price ruling beforehand, or because the quality of the good improves. For example, a new power plant and transmission system may greatly improve the reliability of power supply and reduce the waiting time for would-be customers to get connections, even if the rate schedule does not change for existing customers. Similarly, a new or expanded port will relieve congestion, and hence reduce users' real costs, even if port charges are unaltered or even modestly increased.

The first step is to accommodate changes in market prices within the framework of shadow pricing that has been built up in the preceding chapters. This is done in Sections 13.1 and 13.2, whereby the former is largely concerned with what are called the 'direct' effects of changes in prices induced by a project, and the latter sets out and draws together all effects relevant to the calculation of the project's social profitability. The apparatus at hand is then applied, in Section 13.3, to a classic example, namely, a proposal to reduce the cost of travel within a region by constructing a bridge over an estuary that divides it. An extension to cover the case where congestion is important follows in Section 13.4, which also introduces the topic of user charges, thereby emphasizing once more the intimate connection between policy and project appraisal. Sections 13.5 and 13.6 deal with the case where a project has a significant effect on factor prices, and hence on the full incomes of the households owning those factors, the illustrative example chosen for this purpose being an irrigation project in Malaysia.

13.1. The Approach

We begin by returning to fundamentals, as set out in Section 9.1. Consider the project Δz, where it is no longer assumed that all the elements of Δz are 'sufficiently small', in a sense that will be made precise below. In the event that the project is undertaken, let the ensuing vector of the arguments of the social welfare function $W(\cdot)$ take the value S^2. The alternative is to reject the project, in which case, the vector S^1 will be realized. The decision rule is simple: the project should be undertaken if $W(S^2) > W(S^1)$; otherwise, it should be rejected. If we had a sufficiently detailed and well-specified computable general equilibrium (CGE) model of the economy, whose parameters had been estimated in such a way as to induce us to lay serious wagers on the outcomes of our decisions, then there would be no need to estimate shadow prices as measures of social scarcity in connection with small perturbations of the individual elements of z, and then to calculate the social profit $\pi \cdot \Delta z$. Instead, we could proceed directly, by using the model, first, to obtain the vector S^1, and then, by perturbing the system by Δz, to arrive at S^2, without, moreover, having to assume that Δz is sufficiently small to justify the 'local' analysis that is needed to produce valid estimates of shadow prices.

The problem with such a direct, or 'primal', approach in practice is two-fold: first, by their very nature, applied models of this sort can rarely accommodate the extensive detail concerning goods, activities, households, and institutions usually needed to evaluate a project. Second, their 'global' span involves much stronger assumptions than the 'local' approach employed here, so that, in general, such models are also likely to be a good deal less robust. If a project is large, therefore, we are left in something of a quandary. The direct approach is theoretically sound, but apt to be fragile in practice—assuming that the resources are available to build the CGE model in the first place. The 'dual', shadow pricing approach, on the other hand, is invalid if a project causes significant changes in consumer or producer prices.

Is there some way of combining them, thereby enjoying the flexibility, comparative robustness, and economy of the dual approach, while retaining the theoretical tightness of the primal approach? It will now be argued in the next two sections that there is—provided very few market prices would be significantly affected by the project in question. This claim is of the first practical importance; for, in practice, a lumpy project usually affects only the price of the output it produces and perhaps those of one or two inputs that it requires, unskilled labour in a regionally heterogeneous economy being a notable example. In such cases, an attractive line of attack is to employ a 'direct' approach to deal with the goods whose prices would change significantly, and the dual, shadow-price approach to deal with the rest. We set out the elements of the direct approach, including possible changes in shadow prices, in this section. The task of showing how to combine them with the latter approach in order to assess a project's social profitability is taken up in Section 13.2.

13.1.1. The Direct Effects on the Private Sector

The essentials are captured in the trusty price–quantity diagram depicting equilibrium in a single market. For the present, it is assumed that the good in question is not taxed, so that $p_i = q_i$. It is further assumed that the aggregate demand schedule, $D(q)$, is independent of the project under consideration. The aggregate supply schedule, however, would shift to the right, being $y_i^1(p_i)$ in its absence and $y_i^2(p_i)$ if it were undertaken. In Fig. 13.1, equilibrium is established at point A in the former case and at B in the latter. Defining welfare as the sum of net consumers' and producers' surpluses, the project would yield a gain in welfare equal to the shaded area CABD. Since the project would result in a fall in price, net consumers' surplus would increase, whereas producers' surplus might go either way.

Armed with this preliminary intuitive account, we now lay out the analysis more formally with an eye on two essential considerations that must be dealt with when evaluating social profitability: first, shadow prices will normally differ from market prices, and second, the welfare weights are not all necessarily equal. For expositional purposes, it will be helpful to examine a pair of 'pure' cases: in one, a project brings about a change in the prices of final goods to households without disturbing the prices received or paid by producers; in the other, the converse holds. They are taken up in turn.

Given that only the consumer prices of final goods change, a household's so-called 'full income', which is the scalar product of the ruling factor price vector and its endowment of factors, will be constant. Let q^1 and q^2 denote, respectively, the consumer price vectors ruling before and after the project is completed. For a household possessing full income M, therefore, the

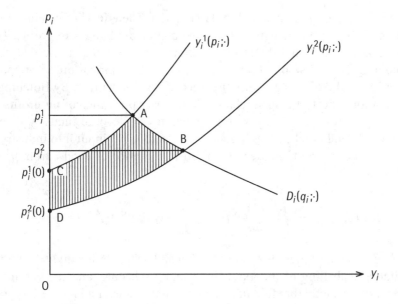

Figure 13.1. A shift in the aggregate supply schedule

change in utility arising directly from the project is $[v(\boldsymbol{q}^2, M) - v(\boldsymbol{q}^1, M)]$, which may be expressed in money metric utility as the equivalent variation $EV(\boldsymbol{q}^2, \boldsymbol{q}^1, M)$. In principle, this is splendidly simple; but there remains the awkward problem that consumers' utility functions are needed to calculate it. Equivalently, one needs a reliable estimation of a complete system of consumer demand equations which has been derived from a well-defined preference structure. There is, fortunately, one case where this difficulty can be skirted, namely, that where only one price changes and expenditures on the good in question make up a small part of total income. For one may then resort to the familiar concept of net consumers' surplus, with the great advantage that knowledge of the ordinary demand function for that commodity will yield a good approximation to the EV. As noted above, this case arises frequently in practice, the good in question being that produced by the project itself. In what follows, this reference good will be denoted by good i, and vectors whose ith element has been deleted will carry the subscript $-i$ (e.g. $\boldsymbol{q}^1_{-i}$ denotes the vector of all consumer prices bar q_i in the absence of the project).

We now address the second setting, in which both the prices of inputs into production and output prices may change. Let all industries face the parametric output and input prices $\boldsymbol{p}$ and $\boldsymbol{q}$, respectively, and let the profits made by industry j, which employs fixed factors, $\bar{\boldsymbol{K}}_j$, and variable inputs to produce good j, be denoted by $\Pi_j(p, q, \bar{K}_j)$. The effects of changes in p and q accrue to the owners of the fixed factors as changes in profits. The immediate snag is that the profit functions for all sectors are needed, and obtaining them, like obtaining the EV, is a tall empirical order. Suppose once more, therefore, that only the price of good i changes. By Hotelling's lemma, the effect of a small change in the user price thereof on profits in industry j is $\partial\Pi_j/\partial q_i = y_{ij}$, where y_{ij} denotes the level of industry j's net output of good i and $y_{ij} < 0$ if good i is actually a net input into industry j. The change in profits induced by a fall in the price of good i from q_i^1 to q_i^2 is, therefore,

$$\Delta\Pi_j(p, q, \bar{K}_j) = \int_{q_i^1}^{q_i^2} \frac{\partial\Pi_j}{\partial q_i}\,\mathrm{d}q_i = -\int_{q_i^2}^{q_i^1} y_{ij}(q_i; \cdot)\,\mathrm{d}q_i, \quad (j \neq i), \quad (13.1)$$

$-y_{ij}(q_i; \cdot)$ being industry j's derived demand schedule for input i. With a suitable relabelling of the axes, the demand schedule, and the variables, the story is exactly that told in Fig. 13.1. Summing over all industries but i, we obtain

$$\sum_{j \neq i} \Delta\Pi_j(p, q, \bar{K}_j) = -\sum_{j \neq i} \left(\int_{q_i^2}^{q_i^1} y_{ij}(q_i; \cdot)\,\mathrm{d}q_i \right), \quad (13.2)$$

which is simply the change in producers' surplus in the industries that use good i as an input.

For industry i itself, on the other hand, the change in producers' surplus will result from the effect of the project on the industry's supply schedule, as depicted in Fig. 13.1. The change in producers' surplus in that industry is

$$\Delta\Pi_i(p, q, \bar{K}_i) = \int_{p_i^2(0)}^{p_i^2} y_i^2(p_i; \cdot)\,\mathrm{d}p_i - \int_{p_i^1(0)}^{p_i^1} y_i^1(p_i; \cdot)\,\mathrm{d}p_i, \quad (13.3)$$

where $p_i^1(0)$ is the minimum price that will call forth production in the absence of the project, and $p_i^2(0)$ is analogously defined in its presence. Thus, estimates of industry i's supply function in the two cases are needed in order to calculate the desired quantity. The algebraic sum of the changes in producers' surpluses in all industries is the additional income accruing to the owners of fixed factors when the price of good i changes.

Combining the two 'pure' cases, in the event that both the consumer and the producer price of a good change in response to a project, the direct benefits thereof comprise the sum of the equivalent variations (EVs) for households and the said algebraic sum of the changes in producers' surpluses in all industries.

The remaining 'direct' effect on households that must be brought into the reckoning arises from the substitution in consumption induced by changes in prices. When shadow prices diverge from market prices, such a switch in expenditures will alter the social cost of private consumption, and so must be taken into account. Let X^1 and X^2 denote, respectively, the vectors of households' aggregate demands for all goods, including leisure, in the absence of the project and in the event that it be undertaken. If an estimate of a complete system of consumer demand equations is available, these vectors can be derived at once, given the price vectors q^1 and q^2. Failing this happy circumstance, an approximation is needed. In any event, given that full incomes are constant, the aggregate expenditure on goods and leisure is the same in both cases. The social cost of the switch from X^1 to X^2 will be taken up in Section 13.2, after we have discussed the possibility that the shadow prices of goods other than i will change in response to the project in question.

To complete the picture, observe that if firms and households pay the same prices for good i, then the aggregate domestic demand function is

$$D_i(q_i) = X_i(q_i) - \sum_{j \neq i} y_{ij}(q_i; \cdot).$$

As a rule, good i is non-tradable in the present setting, so that the market clears when

$$y_i^k(p_i; \cdot) = D_i(q_i), \quad k = 1, 2. \tag{13.4}$$

13.1.2. The Direct Effects on Government Revenues

In the present context, government revenue is directly affected by a project in two ways: the difference between the consumer and producer prices of the reference goods may change, and the quantities consumed thereof will normally change significantly too. Suppose, as before, that only the price of good i changes significantly. Then the direct change in government revenues resulting from the project, defined as the change in revenue arising from the consumption of good i alone, is

$$\Delta R_i \equiv (q_i^2 - p_i^2)y_i^2(p_i^2) - (q_i^1 - p_i^1)y_i^1(p_i^1).^1 \tag{13.5}$$

---

[1] It is possible that firms that use good i pay a different price from households, as in the case of a VAT. That being so, Eqn (13.5) must be modified accordingly.

This term is represented by the difference in the areas of two rectangles in the standard price–quantity diagram, the associated extension of Fig. 13.1 being left as an exercise to the reader.

The changes in revenue resulting from expenditure-switching will be dealt with by using shadow prices, as will be explained in Section 13.2. Whether the government should alter the wedge between producer and consumer prices in the event that the project is undertaken is a question that will be addressed in Sections 13.3 and 13.4.

13.1.3. Shadow Prices

In order to complete the preliminaries, we turn to the question of whether shadow prices are sensitive to the changes induced by the project in question. It is vital to the whole approach that the shadow prices of all goods other than i are unaffected; for both the elements of Δz that are associated with them and the expenditure-switching effects remain to be valued, and it is precisely for this purpose that shadow prices are needed.

As the validity of the border price rule does not hinge on whether a project is large in the sense used here, we confine our attention to non-tradables and labour. We begin with good i, the change in whose market price will usually be the result of the change in its technique of production that the project brings about. To give an example that will be pursued in some detail below, a new bridge will reduce travel-times for some set of destinations, thereby saving not only travellers' time, but also expenditures on running and maintaining vehicles. In doing so, it will reduce not only the private cost of a particular trip, but also the shadow cost thereof, and the latter must be brought into the reckoning. Let the unit activity vector for the production of good i in the presence of the project be denoted by (a_i^2, l_i^2). If all other shadow prices remain unchanged, then the (social) marginal-cost rule for non-tradables yields the following shadow price of good i in that case:

$$\pi_i^2 = \pi_i^2 a_{ii}^2 + \pi_{-i}^1 a_{-i}^2 + w^* l_i^2. \tag{13.6}$$

This is straightforward enough, but if the whole procedure is to have a firm foundation, we are still left with the task of justifying the assumption that all other shadow prices are invariant with respect to the project, at least to a close approximation. Suppose, to start with, that the prices at which producers buy and sell do not change. Then changes in shadow prices will arise only through the changes in the shadow wage rate induced by changes in the appropriate consumption conversion factor (CCF) and θ.

Changes in the latter are almost surely second order in magnitude, and we shall ignore them. As for the CCF, the ith element thereof is $(\pi_i/q_i) \cdot b_i$, changes in which will certainly be small if the expenditure parameter b_i is small, as will normally be the case for a single non-tradable, and if the accounting ratio (π_i/q_i) changes little, as one might also expect. Under these conditions, therefore, it seems defensible to proceed on the basis that the shadow prices of all goods other than i are indeed insensitive to changes in the market price of good i.

To complete matters, we must also deal with the case where the prices faced by firms would be significantly affected by a project. Changes in the shadow prices of other goods can arise either through a change in the shadow price of good i, or through changes in the technique with which other non-tradable goods are produced, that is, through changes in the unit input vectors (a_j, l_j) for all $j \neq i$. The possibility that a change in the shadow price of good i will have an effect of the same order on the shadow prices of other non-tradables cannot be wholly ruled out, but is rather unlikely, as can be seen from Eqn (13.6). Whether changes in the market price of good i will have a significant effect on other shadow prices depends on whether the relevant elasticities of substitution in production are sufficiently large as to yield significant changes in the unit input vectors employed in producing non-tradables. If the said elasticities are modest, then the associated shadow prices will be little affected. Under these (sufficient) conditions, therefore, we are in a position to combine the two approaches, whereby we shall employ a suitably revised shadow price of good i in the event that the project is undertaken, but leave all other shadow prices unaltered.

13.2. The Social Profitability of a Large Project

Recall that in the case of a small project, we simply calculate the scalar product $\pi \cdot \Delta z$. In order to make it clear how the 'direct' and 'dual' approaches will be combined, it will be helpful to partition $\pi \cdot \Delta z$ into the form $(\pi_i, \pi_{-i}) \cdot (\Delta z_i, \Delta z_{-i})$, where good i is the reference good in the sense used in Section 13.1. In calculating the social profit yielded by a *large* project Δz, the approach set out above involves replacing the term $\pi_i z_i$ with a set of terms covering the changes in consumers' and producers' surpluses, the divergence between the market and shadow prices of good i, and the switches in consumers' expenditures, all with reference to a change in the market price of good i.

Some care is also needed where the term $\boldsymbol{\pi}_{-i} \cdot \Delta \boldsymbol{z}_{-i}$ is concerned. For reasons that will become clear shortly, the elements making up $\Delta \boldsymbol{z}_{-i}$ should be restricted to those needed just to construct and run the project, viewed as a facility, independently of the level of the output it produces. The variable costs are dealt with separately. In the case of a new power plant, for example, kilowatt-hours are produced principally by means of fuel and operating personnel, which comprise the variable costs. In the case of a new road, the situation is essentially the same, with the slight twist that the services the road provides must be combined with other resources to produce the commodity called a trip, which is labelled good i. The costs of trips, which involve time, fuel, the use of vehicles, tolls, wear and tear, and so forth, are not included in $\Delta \boldsymbol{z}_{-i}$, being variable in nature.

Recall that although private agents purchasing good i make their decisions and reap their rewards at the going consumer price, the latter will almost surely differ from the shadow price, which, according to Eqn (13.6), is the marginal social cost of producing good i. An appropriate allowance for this divergence must be made when calculating the project's social profitability. We proceed as follows. The social value of the changes in households' EVs and producers' surpluses is

$$\sum_{h=1}^{H} \theta^h \mathrm{EV}^h(\boldsymbol{q}^1, \boldsymbol{q}^2, M^h) + \theta_K \cdot \left[\sum_{j \neq i} \Delta \Pi_j(\boldsymbol{p}, \boldsymbol{q}, \bar{K}_j) + \Delta \Pi_i(\boldsymbol{p}, \boldsymbol{q}, \bar{K}_j) \right].$$

These, of course, must be 'produced'. Consider household h's ordinary demand function for good $i, x_i^h(q_i; \cdot)$, and construe the household's total willingness to pay for $x_i^h(q_i^k; \cdot)$ units of good i as the area under its demand curve between zero and $x_i^h(q_i^k; \cdot), k = 1, 2$. If the household experiences a fall in the price of good i from q_i^1 to q_i^2, the change in its net consumer's surplus will be

$$\Delta \mathrm{CS}^h(q_i^2, q_i^1) = \int_{x_i^{1h}}^{x_i^{2h}} q_i(x_i^h) \mathrm{d}x_i^h - \left[q_i^2 x_i^h(q_i^2) - q_i^1 x_i^h(q_i^1) \right],$$

where $q_i(x_i^h)$ is the household's inverse demand function for good i. This result is depicted in Fig. 13.2, in which the change in the household's net consumer surplus is the shaded area. Observe, however, that whereas the household will choose to spend $q_i^k \cdot x_i^h(q_i^k; \cdot)$ on good i when faced with the consumer price q_i^k, the social cost of the resources needed to satisfy that demand is actually $\pi_i^k \cdot x_i^h(q_i^k; \cdot)$. Assuming that the change in the

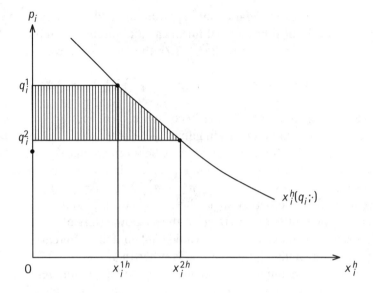

Figure 13.2. The change in household h's net consumers' surplus

net consumer's surplus is a close enough approximation to the EV, the improvement in social welfare that arises when household h experiences a fall in the price of good i from q_i^1 to q_i^2 is, therefore,

$$\theta^h \cdot \Delta CS^h \left(q_i^2, q_i^1 \right) - \left[\left(\pi_i^2 - q_i^2 \right) x_i^h \left(q_i^2 \right) - \left(\pi_i^1 - q_i^1 \right) x_i^h \left(q_i^1 \right) \right].$$

Thus, not only is the change in consumer's surplus appropriately weighted, but there is also a 'correction' to reflect any departure of the good's shadow price from its consumer price. An analogous argument applies in the case of the change in the producers' surpluses of firms using good i. Summing over all such firms and all households, and recalling Eqn (13.4), define

$$\Phi \equiv \sum_{h=1}^{H} \theta^h \cdot \Delta CS^h \left(q_i^2, q_i^1 \right) + \theta_K \left[\sum_{j \neq i} \left(\Delta \Pi_j(\boldsymbol{p}, \boldsymbol{q}, \bar{K}_j) \right) + \Delta \Pi_i(\boldsymbol{p}, \boldsymbol{q}, \bar{K}_i) \right]$$

$$- \left[(\pi_i^2 - q_i^2) y_i^2 (p_i^2) - (\pi_i^1 - q_i^1) y_i^1 (p_i^1) \right]. \tag{13.7}$$

Note that Φ, like all other elements of the project, is normally a vector of dated flows.

A related consideration where all other goods are concerned is that households consume the bundle $\boldsymbol{X}_{-i}^1$ in the absence of the project and

X^2_{-i} if it is undertaken. Again, any departure of shadow prices from consumer prices will must be allowed for in calculating the social profit, ΔW, generated by the project. From Eqn (13.7), therefore, we have,

$$\Delta W = \Phi - \left[\left(\pi^2_{-i} - q^2_{-i} \right) X^2_{-i} - \left(\pi^1_{-i} - q^1_{-i} \right) X^1_{-i} \right] + \pi^1_{-i} \cdot \Delta z_{-i}. \quad (13.8)$$

Observe that the effects of switches in consumers' expenditures on government revenue are fully reflected in Eqn (13.8). The term ΔR_i in Eqn (13.5) is implicitly accounted for in any divergence between the market and shadow prices of good i, as can be seen from Eqn (13.7). In the absence of changes in other market prices, the term $-[(\pi^2_{-i} - q^2_{-i})X^2_{-i} - (\pi^1_{-i} - q^1_{-i})X^1_{-i}]$ captures everything else, where it has been argued in Section 13.1 that the project will have little or no effect on the shadow prices of other goods.

It is instructive to examine what would happen if the differences between the market and shadow prices of goods other than i were simply ignored and changes in incomes were accorded the same weight, regardless of to whom they accrued. Recalling Eqn (13.4), we would then have the following specialization of Eqn (13.8):

$$\Delta W = \sum_{h=1}^{H} \Delta CS^h(q^1_i, q^2_i) + \sum_{j \neq i} \Delta \Pi_j(p, q, \bar{K}_j) + \Delta \Pi_i(p, q, \bar{K}_i)$$
$$- \left[(\pi^2_i - q^2_i)y^2_i(p^2_i) - (\pi^1_i - q^1_i)y^1_i(p^1_i) \right] + p^1_{-i} \cdot \Delta z_{-i}. \quad (13.9)$$

Even so, this does not immediately yield the basis of Harberger's rule, as derived and discussed in Section 8.3. The first three terms comprise the sum of the changes in consumers' and producers' surpluses, as required; but the term $-[(\pi^2_i - q^2_i)y^2_i(p^2_i) - (\pi^1_i - q^1_i)y^1_i(p^1_i)]$ is potentially awkward. For it specializes to ΔR_i, as given by Eqn (13.5), if and only if the shadow price of good i is equal to its producer price in both settings. As we saw in Chapter 9, this condition will hold only in particular circumstances. Thus, not only is Eqn (13.9) itself invalid—except in the uninteresting case where the starting point is first-best—but an additional, arguably strong, assumption must be made if it is to yield the basis of Harberger's rule.

In this connection, it should be remarked that the simple aggregation of households is standard practice, but problematic—unless they are homogeneous, though even here, the social value of the direct benefits accruing to households is θ times the sum of the individual EVs. When households' full incomes differ and income distribution matters, the use of a single value of θ will certainly be incorrect; so that the convenient short-cut of using the change in net consumers' surplus will be flawed too.[2] If resort to this short-cut is made, the hope is that one will not go far wrong in choosing the value of θ that is used in the derivation of the vector of shadow prices. The social value placed on an additional unit of profits, θ_K, will not, moreover, necessarily be equal to such an 'average' value of θ, and if it is not, then the net demands of households and firms must be separated when estimating the social value of the change in consumers' surplus from the market demand function. As noted above, such a separation may be hard to bring off in practice.

To close this section, we take up the social cost of the switch from the bundle X^1 to X^2. If a complete system of demand equations is available, calculating the expenditure-switching terms in Eqn (13.8) is trivial. Otherwise, it is useful to provide an approximation based on more limited information. The said terms may be written as

$$
\begin{aligned}
&\left[(\pi^2_{-i} - q^2_{-i})X^2_{-i} - (\pi^1_{-i} - q^1_{-i})X^1_{-i}\right] \\
&= \sum_{j \neq i}\left[\left(\frac{\pi^2_j}{q^2_j} - 1\right)q^2_j X^2_j - \left(\frac{\pi^1_j}{q^1_j} - 1\right)q^1_j X^1_j\right].
\end{aligned}
\tag{13.10}
$$

Recalling that full incomes are assumed to be constant and noting the definition of the consumption conversion factor, Eqn (13.10) becomes

$$
\begin{aligned}
&\left[(\pi^2_{-i} - q^2_{-i})X^2_{-i} - (\pi^1_{-i} - q^1_{-i})X^1_{-i}\right] \\
&= \sum_{h=1}^{H}\left[(1 - b^{2h}_i)(\mathrm{CCF}^{2h}_{-i} - 1) - (1 - b^{1h}_i)(\mathrm{CCF}^{1h}_{-i} - 1)\right]M^h,
\end{aligned}
\tag{13.11a}
$$

where $b^{kh}_i \equiv q^{kh}_i x^{kh}_i / M^h$ is the proportion of household h's full income spent on good i ($k = 1, 2$). The consumption conversion factors for the bundles of all other goods in the absence of the project are calculated in the usual way, that is to say, with the expenditure on each good expressed as a proportion of the total expenditure on the bundle in question. In order to estimate their counterparts in the event that it is undertaken, however, some assumptions have to be made about substitution in consumption, the vectors b^{2h} being needed. If preferences are separable in the form that the marginal rate of indifferent substitution (MRS) between any pair of

---

[2] In this connection, see once more the exchange among Brekke (1997, 1998), Drèze (1998), and Johansson (1998).

goods other than i is independent of how much of good i is consumed, then, given that only the shadow price of good i changes, it follows that $\text{CCF}^1_{-i} = \text{CCF}^2_{-i}$; so that Eqn (13.11a) specializes to

$$\left[(\pi^2_{-i}-q^2_{-i})X^2_{-i}-(\pi^1_{-i}-q^1_{-i})X^1_{-i}\right] = \sum_{h=1}^{H}\left[(b_i^{1h} - b_i^{2h})(\text{CCF}^{1h}_{-i} - 1)\right]M^h.$$

(13.11b)

It is clear that one should be wary of simply invoking Cobb–Douglas preferences as a short cut; for the right-hand side (RHS) would then vanish, and we would be back in the familiar territory of a small project, in this respect at least.

13.3. An Example: A Bridge

The method laid out above looks rather dry and abstract, so we shall try to enliven it by means of an example. In order to cover the main points, the choice should involve a good which possesses the following characteristics: (i) it is purchased by both households and firms; (ii) its consumer price can be directly altered by taxation or regulation; and (iii) its quality depends, in general, on the number of users. Consider, therefore, a proposal to construct a bridge that would reduce the effective distance between two towns, A and B, which lie on opposite sides of a wide estuary and are presently connected by a road that makes a longish detour to a crossing well upstream. Such a bridge would yield savings of the time, fuel, and other resources expended on travel between them. It might also relieve congestion at the existing crossing, albeit at the possible cost of causing additional congestion elsewhere in the system as new traffic is generated.

13.3.1. The Direct Benefits
The total cost of a trip to a traveller comprises the value she places on her time and the monetary outlay on getting from A to B, be it by foot, bullock cart, bicycle, bus, or car, where the latter outlay will be the marginal cost of the trip by the mode of transport she chooses. In order to keep matters simple, it is assumed that all users are identical. Let the time taken to travel from A to B be h^1 in the absence of the bridge and h^2 if it were built, and let the private value placed a unit of time be w. The latter is not necessarily the wage rate, but for the present, we shall think of it as such. In general,

the (marginal) monetary cost of a trip in the two cases, c^1 and c^2, will depend on the total number of travellers (or trips), n^k $(k = 1, 2)$; for at some point, congestion will appear, though this is a complication that we will defer until Section 13.4. In the absence of congestion, h^k and c^k will be independent of n^k, and the 'price' of a trip will be written as

$$q_i^k = c^k + wh^k, \quad k = 1, 2. \tag{13.12}$$

While h^1, c^1, and n^1 can be observed by means of traffic surveys in the planning phase, h^2, c^2, and n^2 must be forecasted, a task whose importance in the context of evaluating such projects can hardly be overestimated. Given such forecasts, we have two points on the demand schedule for trips between A and B, the number of trips being the quantity variable. In the absence of any other information, it seems reasonable to assume that the demand schedule, $D(q_i)$, is linear over the interval (n^1, n^2), and it is thus drawn in Fig. 13.3.

It is plausible that the only market price that would change appreciably in the event that the bridge were built is the cost of a trip between A and B, so that the direct benefits that would accrue to users (both households and firms) will be satisfactorily measured by the change in consumers' surplus associated with travel between the two towns. The change therein is the

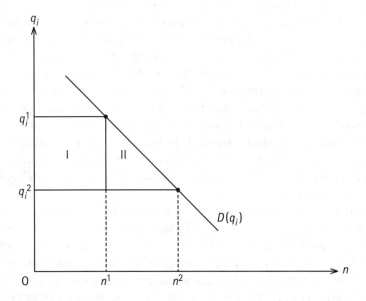

Figure 13.3. The bridge lowers costs and generates additional traffic

sum of the areas I and II, which are, respectively, the gains to existing travellers and the gains arising from the new traffic generated by the reduction
in costs. Hence, the direct private benefits generated by the bridge in each
period are

$$B = \left(q_i^1 - q_i^2\right)\left(n^1 + n^2\right)/2. \tag{13.13}$$

As noted in Section 13.2, the aggregation implicit in Eqn (13.13) is problematic if users of the bridge are heterogeneous. In practice, they will
include not only households supplying labour or enjoying leisure, but also
firms producing transportation services. In principle, we can deal with this
difficulty by assigning a different value of θ to each class of user, as was
done in deriving Eqn (13.17). This would entail deriving a separate demand
schedule for each such class; but this is implicit anyway in the process of
measuring current, and forecasting future, traffic.

13.3.2. User Charges

In view of these benefits to the private sector, we digress briefly by asking
whether the government should impose user charges in the form of a toll, in
order to cover the wear and tear caused by traffic or even to raise revenue
to help finance the bridge's construction. To answer this question, we keep
the two issues separate by beginning with the assumption that no wear
and tear occurs. Let a toll of t be charged, so that the price of a trip that
involves the use of the bridge rises to $(q_i^2 + t)$ and the number of trips
falls to $n^2(t) = D(q_i^2 + t)$. Figure 13.4 shows that although this charge
generates revenue in the amount of $t \cdot n^2(t)$, it also results in a loss of
consumers' surplus in the amount of $t \cdot [n^2 + n^2(t)]/2$. Hence, if private
income is just as valuable as public income, the toll will result in an excess
burden of $t \cdot [n^2 - n^2(t)]/2$, which leads to the immediate conclusion that
no toll should be charged—provided the bridge can be financed by means
of lump-sum taxation. If there is a substantial premium on public income,
however, the excess burden may be more than offset by the social premium
placed on the toll revenues.

Turning to the very real possibility that each trip causes wear and tear
on the bridge and its approaches, the monetary value of this damage is a
perfectly tangible element of the cost of a journey, and as such, it belongs
in c^k. Setting aside the fact that market prices may diverge from shadow
prices, users should, therefore, pay a toll in that amount, to reflect in full
the real resources needed to make good the damage resulting from a trip.
Having resolved the matter in the present context, we continue the analysis

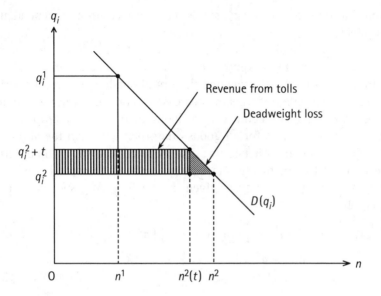

Figure 13.4. The effects of a toll in the absence of congestion

by assuming away wear and tear, so that no toll should be levied on that account.[3]

13.3.3. Social Benefits and Costs

The remaining terms in ΔW, as defined in Eqns (13.7) and (13.8), deal with the difference between the market and shadow costs of all trips and the net shadow cost of changes in the aggregate expenditure bundle induced by changes in the cost of a trip. We begin by calculating the shadow cost of a trip. From Eqn (13.12), this is

$$\pi_i^k = (\pi_c^k/q_c^k) \cdot c^k + w^* h^k, \quad k = 1, 2, \tag{13.14}$$

where (π_c^k/q_c^k) is the accounting ratio of a unit of transportation services, a ratio that is unlikely to be particularly sensitive to the presence or absence of the project in question. In the case of a bridge, the relevant unit of measurement of such services is arguably a passenger- or tonne-kilometre, c^k being the unit cost thereof at market prices multiplied by the number of kilometres travelled in case k. It is clear from Eqn (13.14) that the

---

[3] As we shall see in Section 13.4, if there is congestion then an (optimal) toll will be necessary to bring about a first-best allocation, even in the absence of other distortionary taxation or a premium on public income.

accounting ratio of a trip, (π_i^k/q_i^k), is most unlikely to be independent of the project.

In order to calculate the expenditure-switching term, we employ Eqn (13.11a). For this purpose, we need the aggregate bundles X^1 and X^2, together with their associated vectors of shadow and market prices. Obtaining the number of trips in each case is (comparatively) unproblematic, estimates thereof being central items in the project proposal. The vector of shadow prices for all goods other than good i in the absence of the project is known, whence the shadow price of a trip is then derived from Eqn (13.14). In the setting considered here, the social profit yielded by the bridge is therefore given by the following specialization of Eqn (13.8):

$$\Delta W = (\theta/2) \cdot \left(q_i^1 - q_i^2\right) \left(n^1 + n^2\right) - \left[\left(\pi_i^2 - q_i^2\right) n^2 - \left(\pi_i^1 - q_i^1\right) n^1 \right]$$
$$- \left[\left(\pi_{-i}^2 - q_{-i}^2\right) X_{-i}^2 - \left(\pi_{-i}^1 - q_{-i}^1\right) X_{-i}^1 \right] + \pi_{-i}^1 \cdot \Delta z_{-i},$$
$$(13.15)$$

where a trip between locations A and B is denoted by good i and it will be recalled that the vector $-\Delta z_{-i}$ denotes the bundle of net inputs needed to construct and maintain the bridge. Since $\pi_i^2 < \pi_i^1$, the savings per trip find clear expression at shadow prices. Weighing against this effect is the fall in the private cost of a trip, which generates extra traffic and so demands additional resources. Hence, the change in the total expenditure on trips at shadow prices, $(\pi_i^2 n^2 - \pi_i^1 n^1)$, may take either sign, depending on the elasticity of the demand for trips and the change in π_i induced by the project.

It has been argued that the shadow and market prices of other goods are unlikely to change, in which case the term

$$\left(\pi_{-i}^2 - q_{-i}^2\right) X_{-i}^2 - \left(\pi_{-i}^1 - q_{-i}^1\right) X_{-i}^1 = \left(\pi_{-i}^1 - q_{-i}^1\right) \left(X_{-i}^2 - X_{-i}^1\right).$$

The fall in q_i may, of course, bring about measurable reductions in the prices of other goods, to the extent that transport costs are important; but even with lump-sum income unchanged, the sign of the expenditure-switching term is unclear a priori.

13.4. Congestion and Tolls

Casual observation of traffic conditions in most towns of any size, and the fact that the hypothetical bridge discussed here will generate additional traffic, force us to introduce the possibility of congestion. By definition, congestion implies the presence of an externality. For when the route is congested and an additional car or bus joins the stream of traffic, this vehicle will increase the cost of a journey to all existing users, not through the price mechanism but directly, by increasing h and the unit input requirements entering into c at given prices. The newcomer does not, of course, consider these external effects on others, so that the signal provided by the market, in the form of the 'price' q_i, does not lead to a social optimum. That these effects are large in practice is an established fact: for city traffic during rush hours, they are commonly at least 50 per cent of the private cost of the trip (Walters, 1987).

A natural way to combat this market failure is to impose a toll on users. It is intuitively clear that a toll is desirable in these circumstances, even if the bridge could be financed by lump-sum taxes. For by imposing a cost on the user, the toll makes good her ignorance, or disregard, of the fact that her decision to make a trip imposes an (external) cost on others. A discussion of tolls in this context is also valuable in that it provides an example of a case in which the social profitability of a project may depend on changes in the structure of taxation, a matter we have already addressed generally in Chapters 5 and 9.

Suppose, therefore, that both the time taken to journey from A to B and the direct monetary cost of a trip depend on the total number of trips (users). Reformulating Eqn (13.12) accordingly, the private cost of a trip is now written as

$$q_i^k(n) = c^k(n) + wh^k(n), \quad k = 1, 2. \tag{13.16}$$

If n is sufficiently large, the functions $h^k(n)$ and $c^k(n)$ will be increasing in n, that is, congestion will have set in. In Fig. 13.5, the functions $q_i^1(n)$ and $q_i^2(n)$ are accordingly drawn, first, as horizontal lines, and then as upward sloping. As depicted, they intersect the demand schedule at points A and B, respectively, where both are rising. The associated values of n are the number of trips that will be undertaken in each case. In these free-entry equilibria, however, $q_i^k(n)$ will not be the marginal social cost of a trip, even if we disregard the presence of distortionary taxation and the possibility of a premium on government income. For as just noted, when an additional trip is made under congested conditions, the individual in question increases q_i^k slightly for everyone else by *directly* increasing both h^k and the inputs making up the monetary costs. Hence, the increase in the total private cost of all trips when an additional trip is made (equivalently,

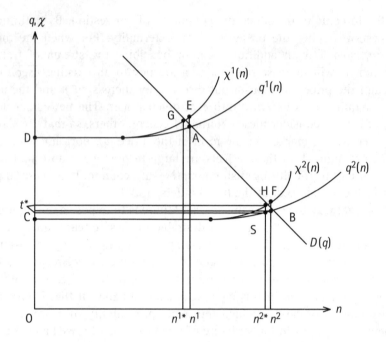

Figure 13.5. Congestion and a Pigouvian toll

the total cost of an extra trip when summed over all users) is

$$\chi^k(n) \equiv \frac{d[nq_i^k(n)]}{dn} = q_i^k(n) + n\left(\frac{dc^k(n)}{dn} + w\frac{dh^k(n)}{dn}\right), \quad k = 1, 2.$$

(13.17)

Although the terms $dc^k(n)/dn$ and $w(dh^k(n)/dn)$ may be very small, the aggregate external cost, $n\cdot[dc^k(n)/dn+w(dh^k(n)/dn)]$, may still be significant under congested conditions, as depicted in Fig. 13.5. In the absence of a toll, the actual numbers of trips taken are n^1 and n^2, respectively, these being the values at which the cost schedules $q_i^1(n)$ and $q_i^2(n)$ intersect the demand schedule; but the numbers of trips at which χ^k would be equal to the corresponding marginal willingness to pay for a trip are n^{1*} and n^{2*}, respectively.

This prompts the question: how big should the toll be in order to induce the optimal volume of traffic n^{2*}? For simplicity, we ignore the presence of other distortionary taxes and any premium on public income. Suppose also that we have the necessary information to estimate $\chi^2(n)$ and $q^2(n)$. Then, knowing the demand schedule $D(q_i)$, we can calculate t^* as follows. If a toll in the amount

$$t^* = n^{2*} \cdot [dc^2(n^{2*})/dn + w(dh^2(n^{2*})/dn)]$$

is charged, users will face a trip-price of $\chi(n^{2*})$, and will therefore undertake n^{2*} trips, as required. The toll in question is an example of a Pigouvian tax.

Let us now evaluate the benefits accruing to users of the bridge. We calculate the total willingness to pay for n^1 and n^2 trips, respectively, and then subtract from each the associated total costs incurred. For any n, the total cost of travel is the area from zero to n under the associated marginal cost schedule $\chi^k(n)$, which is depicted as DGE in the absence of the bridge, and as CHF if it were built. In the absence of tolls, there will be 'excess congestion' in the amounts $(n^1 - n^{1*})$ and $(n^2 - n^{2*})$, respectively, associated with which are net social costs represented by the areas AEG and BFH, respectively. Hence, in the absence of a toll, the benefits (net of total travel costs) generated by the bridge are

$$B = \int_0^{n^2} [D^{-1}(n) - \chi^2(n)]\, dn - \int_0^{n^1} [D^{-1}(n) - \chi^1(n)]\, dn, \qquad (13.18)$$

which corresponds to the area (DGHC − BFH + AEG) in Fig. 13.5, $D^{-1}(n)$ denoting the inverse demand schedule for trips.

If the toll t^* were imposed, the government would collect revenues in the amount $n^{2*}t^*$, but the costs of 'excess congestion' in the event that the bridge were built, namely, BFH, would be removed thereby. Since the toll can be levied only if the bridge is built, the removal of 'excess congestion' at the old upstream crossing also remains as a benefit. Hence, the accounting thus far would run as follows:

net benefits to users   DGHC − $n^{2*} \cdot t^*$ + AEG,
increase in government revenue from tolls $n^{2*} \cdot t^*$.

Note that the amount $n^{2*} \cdot t^*$ corresponds to the RHS of Eqn (13.5).

It remains to deal with the term $[(\pi_i^2/q_i^2) - \theta] q_i^2 n^2 - [(\pi_i^1/q_i^1) - \theta] q_i^1 n^1$. The only twist here arises from the fact that congestion has adverse effects on the 'technology' for producing passenger- or tonne-kilometres. Recalling Eqn (13.14), we have the generalization:

$$\pi_i^k(n) = [\pi_c^k(n)/q_c^k(n)] \cdot c^k(n) + w^* h^k(n), \quad k = 1, 2, \qquad (13.14')$$

where not only the cost $c^k(n)$ at market prices, but also the accounting ratio $[\pi_c^k(n)/q_c^k(n)]$, is now plausibly dependent on whether the project is undertaken. The latter claim follows at once from the generalization of Eqn (13.6) in the presence of congestion:

$$\pi_i^k(n) = \pi_i^k(n)a_{ii}^k(n) + \pi_{-i}^1 a_{-i}^k(n) + w^* l_i^k(n), \quad k = 1, 2. \qquad (13.6')$$

With this extension, we have furnished the last element needed to estimate ΔW.

13.5. Changes in Factor Prices: An Irrigation Project

The assumption that full income is constant is largely innocuous if households are endowed solely with labour and can trade in perfect markets. For a household's lump-sum income is then zero, its wage earnings being equal to its expenditure on all goods but leisure. If, however, households possess endowments of two or more factors of production, then changes in relative factor prices will result in changes not only in full income, but also in lump-sum income. The prime factor in question in the context of development policy is land, which usually accounts for at least a quarter of value added in agriculture. In order to evaluate projects that raise agricultural productivity and incomes, it follows that an extension of the analysis in earlier sections is needed. The obvious choice of example in this context is a large-scale irrigation project, to which we now turn.

13.5.1. The Muda Project in Outline

One of the largest agricultural development projects ever undertaken in Malaysia, the Muda scheme was designed to bring just over 100,000 hectares of paddy land under double cropping, where previously only a single rain-fed crop could be cultivated. Some 55,000 agricultural households lived in the command area at the time, about 4000 of which earned their livelihoods almost exclusively from wage labour. When the scheme was planned in the early 1960s, imports of rice were large, the balance of payments was under serious strain, and achieving national self-sufficiency in rice was high on the government's list of priorities. It seems likely that the farming community's poverty also played an important part in the political reckoning behind the project.

Construction work began in 1966 and proceeded with commendable speed, the first release of irrigation water taking place in the off-season

(March–August) of 1970. By 1974, the scheme was fully operational. Total outlays on the capital account, including interest charges, had reached US $270 million, of which about US $100 million were financed by a loan from the World Bank to cover the project's direct foreign exchange costs.

The project brought about striking changes in output and techniques of cultivation. Its construction also coincided with the introduction of high-yielding varieties of paddy, which quickly displaced the traditional varieties farmers had grown earlier. The gross cropped area expanded from 97,000 hectares in 1967 to 188,000 hectares in 1974, and output grew faster still, from 278,000 tonnes in 1967 to 671,000 tonnes in 1974. The increase in the level of average yield from each net hectare sown stemmed from the near universal adoption of high-yielding varieties and a doubling of fertilizer application rates. The stringent rhythm of farming operations under double cropping had a further consequence: buffaloes were largely displaced, first, by four-wheel tractors owned by non-farm contractors, and then by two-wheel tractors, which the farmers themselves purchased. Less than a decade after ground-breaking on the project, therefore, Muda's farmers were producing on a wholly different scale, and with quite different techniques from those ruling beforehand.

To complete this sketch, a word about price policy is needed. Although the marginal source of rice supplies was always imports, the degree of nominal protection enjoyed by Malaysia's paddy farmers varied a good deal between 1967 and 1975, the accounting ratio of rice ranging from a low of 0.72 in 1973 to a high of 1.11 in the following year (in which there was a worldwide boom in commodity prices), with an average of about 0.87. The policy makers appeared to be aiming for a good measure of stability in the domestic price, which entailed a variable tariff in the face of fluctuations in world prices. In any event, there is little evidence that the surge in Muda's output put much downward pressure on the domestic price of rice.

13.5.2. The Project's Direct Effects

From the foregoing account, it is clear that the project had a dramatic impact on output and incomes, and hence on factor prices, in the command area. That account does not, however, tell us exactly what we need to know in order to estimate its direct effects. For that purpose, we require the answer to a counterfactual question: what would have happened had the project not been undertaken? In order to answer this question, we need a model of the farming economy. What follows is very much a stripped-down version of that set out in Chapter 3 of Bell *et al.* (1982), to which those keen to learn all the details are referred.

In order to avoid any confusion with earlier sections, we revert, in part, to mnemonic notation. Let paddy be produced under CRS by means of land (H), labour (L), and fertilizer (N).[4] All markets are perfect, endowments of land are supplied completely inelastically, and all households have a common reservation wage rate, which is denoted by w_0. Under these assumptions, all cultivators will choose the same technique of production, and since a household's (full) income will be just the scalar product of its endowment vector and the factor price vector that rules in equilibrium, who leases in labour or land from whom is indeterminate. Hence, we may treat the paddy sector as one large farm, albeit one that takes all prices as parametrically given.

The output of paddy (good i) is given by

$$y_i^k = F^k(H^k, L^k, N^k), \quad k = 1, 2, \tag{13.19}$$

where the superscript k on the production function $F(\cdot)$ is a reminder that the technology under double-cropping differs from that under single-cropping, even if the same set of crop varieties is available under both. Given the price vector (p_i^k, w^k, v^k), the producers' surplus accruing to cultivating households is

$$\Pi_i^k = p_i^k y_i^k - w^k L^k - v^k N^k, \quad k = 1, 2. \tag{13.20}$$

Labour is supplied not only by the cultivating households themselves and landless farm households within the command area, but also by migrants, who come from villages on the project's periphery, from elsewhere in Malaysia, and even from southern Thailand. The aggregate (inverse) labour supply function is assumed to take the form

$$w(L) = \begin{cases} w_0, & \text{if } L < \bar{L}, \\ w_0 + \beta(L - \bar{L}), & \text{otherwise,} \end{cases} \tag{13.21}$$

as depicted in Fig. 13.6, where $\bar{L}$ is the aggregate endowment of labour of all cultivating households and the parameters (w_0, β) are indexed to the consumer price index for landless farm households.

Given the price vector (p_i^k, w^k, v^k), the representative household chooses (H^k, L^k, N^k) so as to

$$\text{maximize } \Pi_i^k \quad \text{subject to} : 0 \leq H^k \leq \bar{H}^k, \ L^k \geq 0, \ N^k \geq 0, \tag{13.22}$$

---

[4] In the full model, all inputs are dated fortnightly over the two growing seasons.

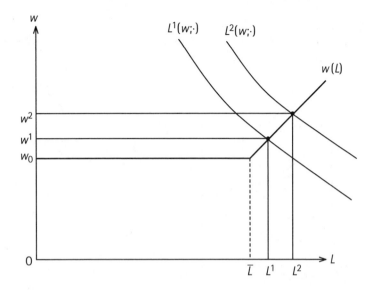

Figure 13.6. Equilibrium in the labour market with and without the project

where $\bar{H}^k$ is the total area available for cultivation. The choice of labour inputs at the optimum, $L^k\left(p_i^k, w^k, v^k; \bar{H}^k\right)$, is the derived demand for labour. Both $L^1(\cdot)$ and $L^2(\cdot)$ are drawn in the space of (L, w) depicted in Fig. 13.6. Their respective intersections with the (inverse) labour supply function are the equilibria that would rule in the absence and in the presence of the project, respectively, at the same prices of paddy and fertilizer.

By the envelope theorem, the (imputed) rent per hectare of land is the value of the dual variable associated with the constraint $H \leq \bar{H}$. If the latter binds at the optimum, then the rent will be the value of the marginal product of land in that allocation:

$$R^k = p_i^k \frac{\partial y_i^k(p_i^k, w^k, v^k; \bar{H}^k)}{\partial \bar{H}^k}. \tag{13.23}$$

If the said constraint does not bind, then land will command no rent in equilibrium.

The next step is to derive the household's full income and the EV associated with the project. The former is spent on a basket of goods and leisure:

$$M^k \equiv w^k \bar{L}^k + R^k \bar{H}^k = q^k x^k + w^k l^k, \quad k = 1, 2, \tag{13.24a}$$

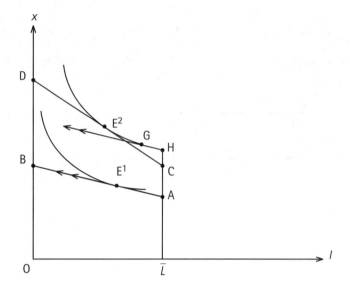

Figure 13.7. The household's feasible sets and optima with and without the project

where l^k denotes the amount of the endowment of labour (time) devoted to the pursuit of leisure and $q^k x^k$ is the total nominal expenditure on (final) goods other than leisure. If goods are chosen as the numeraire, we have

$$(w^k/q^k) \cdot \bar{L}^k + (R^k/q^k) \cdot \bar{H}^k = x^k + (w^k/q^k) \cdot l^k, \quad k = 1, 2. \quad (13.24b)$$

The feasible sets in the space of (l, x) are depicted in Fig. 13.7, in which it is plausibly assumed that both the real wage, (w/q), and the real rent per hectare, (R/q), rise as a result of the project. An important restriction is that the household's members cannot trade non-wage income for leisure beyond the point at which all of their time is spent at ease. Thus, confronted with the prices (q^k, w^k, R^k), the household's members could take their ease in full by choosing the bundle $[\bar{L}^k, (R^k/q^k)\bar{H}^k]$, which is depicted as points A and C, for $k = 1, 2$, respectively. At the other extreme, they could work from morning until night by choosing the bundle $(0, M^k/q^k)$, which is depicted as points B and D, for $k = 1, 2$, respectively. By assumption, all commodities are divisible, so that all bundles lying on AB and CD, respectively, are also feasible in each case.

Superimposing the indifference map onto these feasible sets, we obtain the household's optimum in each case, which is depicted as the points E^1 and E^2, respectively. The EV is derived by finding a point on the indifference curve passing through E^2 where that curve is supported by a line parallel to AB, namely, a line with slope $-(w^1/q^1)$. If the indifference map is smooth and strictly convex, there will be just one such point, which is denoted by point G in Fig. 13.7. Let the said line with slope $-(w^1/q^1)$ through G intersect the vertical through AC at point H. Then the EV associated with the project, measured in units of the aggregate commodity x, is AH. Observe that since CD is steeper than AB, the difference in the consumption of the aggregate commodity arising from the project, $(x^2 - x^1)$, is necessarily greater than the EV if any substitution between goods and leisure is possible.

So much for the technical preliminaries. We turn now to the empirical estimates, which are laid out in Table 13.1. Before discussing them, however, a few remarks are in order. First, Bell *et al.* (1982) did not take the final step of deriving the EV; rather, they left the treatment of preferences in the implicit form of the reservation wage rate w_0. What is labelled 'aggregate net income' in Table 13.1 is the nominal value of output in paddy farming less the nominal outlays on purchased inputs, both deflated by the consumer price index.[5] In the above notation, this is simply

$$\{p_i^k y^k - w^k[L^k - (\bar{L}^k - l^k)] - v^k N^k\}/q^k = [R^k \bar{H}^k + w^k \bar{L}^k - w^k l^k]/q^k = x^k.$$

(If $\bar{L}^k > L^k$, it is assumed that all labour is supplied by cultivating households.) As noted above, $x^2 - x^1$ is an overestimate of the EV, but the error is arguably small. Second, the average (nominal) wage rate is obtained by dividing the total outlays on day (hired) labour by the total number of person-days hired. Third, the results correspond to the steady state that would rule under each set of prices and technologies, so that there are inevitably departures from the state of the world as it was actually observed in the years 1967 and 1974, when the two surveys were carried out. The corresponding columns are labelled 0 and 2. All other columns relate to counterfactual cases, which are needed to establish the project's payoffs under various assumptions. Here, it should be noted that the project had just about reached maturity in 1974, so that comparisons of columns for that year yield defensible estimates of its steady-state effects.

The effects of the project *ex post* are as follows: given that prices turned out as they did in 1974, and assuming that the new varieties of rice would have been introduced even if the project had not been undertaken, one takes the difference between the columns labelled 2 and 1. *Ex ante*, however, when the decision to begin construction was taken, prices were quite

---

[5] The increase in the consumer price index is reflected exactly in the ratio of the reservation wage rates in the two years, namely, $1.85/1.15 = 1.61$.

Table 13.1. The effects of the Muda project on output, inputs, net incomes, and factor prices, 1967–74 (nominal Malaysian dollars)

	Model Solution							Impact of Project	
	1967	1974		1967	1974		Project	1967 prices	1974 prices
		No project	Project		Project	No Project		$\frac{(4)-(5)}{(4)-(0)} \times 100$	$\frac{(4)-(5)}{(4)-(0)} \times 100$
	(0)	(1)	(2)	(3)[a]	(4)[b]	(5)[b]	(6)[c]		
Aggregate net income ($ thousands)	43,526	89,958	187,240	71,442	112,352	55,235	75,932	83	84
Total paddy production (thousands of piculs)	3826	4751	9584	3750	9594	4775	7534	83.5	82.8
Aggregate Inputs:									
Nitrogen (thousands of pounds)	7212	9747	19,740	6065	20,517	10,570	13,705	74.8	73.1
Family labour (thousands of days)	12,878	13,664	19,586	12,794	50,532	13,796	14,138	88	87.5
Day labour (thousands of days)	1562	1649	4566	1393	5997	1930	7064	91.7	91.9
Total labour (thousands of days)	14,440	15,293	24,152	14,187	26,529	15,726	21,202	89.4	88.9
Stock of 4-wheel tractors	39	185	1526	91	640	39	1736	100	93.4
Stock of pedestrian tractors	0	0	0	0	0	0	0	0	0
Stock of buffaloes	15,736	13,806	0	15,064	10,708	15,924	0	103.7	91.6

Land Rents ($/relong):									
Nonacid soil	85	194	453	143	258	117	159	81.5	83.5
Acid soil	64	147	349	109	200	89	119	81.6	84.2
Monthly wages ($/day)									
Nov. 26–Dec. 23	1.15	2.53	1.85	1.85	1.15	1.60	1.15	—	—
Dec. 24–Jan. 20	1.15	2.35	2.05	1.85	1.21	1.47	1.15	—	—
Jan. 21–Feb. 17	1.35	1.98	2.73	2.10	1.64	1.26	1.15	—	—
Feb. 18–Mar. 17	1.20	2.01	2.85	1.93	1.94	1.28	2.07	—	—
Mar. 18–Apr. 17	1.28	1.85	1.85	2.03	1.34	1.15	2.52	—	—
Apr. 18–May 12	1.16	1.85	1.93	1.85	1.35	1.15	2.52	—	—
May 13–Jun. 7	1.15	1.83	2.01	1.85	1.32	1.15	1.28		
Jun. 8–Jul. 7	1.15	1.85	1.85	1.85	1.15	1.15	1.15	—	—
Jul. 8–Aug. 4	1.15	1.85	3.50	1.85	2.39	1.15	1.15	—	—
Aug. 5–Sep. 1	1.49	2.16	3.50	2.35	2.31	1.37	1.67	—	—
Sep. 2–Sep. 29	1.37	2.06	3.48	2.18	2.46	1.32	1.93	—	—
Sep. 30–Oct. 27	1.65	2.49	1.89	2.59	1.40	1.61	3.15	—	—
Oct. 28–Nov. 25	1.28	1.90	1.91	2.01	1.28	1.22	1.53	—	—
Average wage ($/day)	1.46	2.34	3.20	2.31	2.09	1.47	2.23	98.4	96.6
Annual wage payments ($ thousands)	2285	3855	14,615	3221	12,563	2846	16,842	94.5	94.4

[a] 1974 prices, [b] 1967 prices, 1974 varieties [c] 1967 prices, 1967 varieties

Source: Bell *et al.* (1982)

different, so that using these particular columns to assess the project's profitability is valid only if the prices that actually ruled in 1974 were fully anticipated at the time of the decision, in 1967. The simplest alternative basis for evaluating the project *ex ante* involves static expectations, that is, the prices ruling in 1967 were expected to rule in the future, too. In this case, the right comparison is between columns 4 and 5, the difference between which is then construed as the expected impact of the project *ex ante*. In this connection, it is helpful to express the project's impact in relation to the changes that would have occurred between 1967 and 1974 had the project not been undertaken. That is to say, for the *ex ante* impact with static expectations, one divides the difference between any pair of corresponding elements of columns 5 and 4 by the difference between the same pair of elements of columns 5 and 0. For the *ex post* impact, the relevant pairs are taken from columns 2 and 1 and columns 2 and 3, respectively. It is reassuring that, when so normalized, the *ex ante* and *ex post* impacts of the project differ little. The project accounted for almost 85 per cent of the total gains in aggregate net income, output, and rents, almost 90 per cent of the increase in aggregate employment in paddy production (slightly more for hired hands), and almost 95 per cent of the total payments to hired workers. At 1967 prices, it would have reduced the stock of buffaloes by just over a third; as things turned out, at 1974 prices, it brought about their demise as a working animal.[6]

Turning to comparisons of levels, for the year 1974, when it had reached maturity, the project had brought about a doubling of output and of cultivators' aggregate net income, and almost a quadrupling of payments to hired workers. Given the modest levels of protection against imports of rice, all this augurs well for the project in the final reckoning of its social profitability, to which we now turn.[7]

13.6. Evaluating Muda

Despite the wealth of detailed results reported in Section 13.5, two additional matters must be dealt with before the final accounting can be completed. First, it is not the crop paddy itself that is normally internationally traded, but rather the milled product rice. The project therefore

---

[6] There were, of course, thousands of buffaloes still at work in 1974; as emphasized earlier, the model's results relate to the associated steady state.

[7] It is clear from a comparison of columns 5 and 6 that the introduction of new, short-maturing varieties had a substantial impact on the project's profitability.

produces a non-traded intermediate good, whose shadow price must be estimated, as opposed to being lifted out of a suitable report on international trade in primary commodities. Second, it is clear from Table 13.1 that all groups of households in the command area enjoyed very large gains in income within a few years, so large that the assumption that the associated premia on public income are constant is simply indefensible, even in the short run. These complications are taken up in turn.

13.6.1. The Paddy–Rice Complex

It should be clear from Section 13.5 that in order to value the output of this particular project, one cannot appeal to the standard rule that the shadow price of a non-tradable be equal to its marginal cost of production at shadow prices. The solution, however, is not far to seek. Since rice is a fully traded good and rice milling is arguably a CRS production activity, at least over the medium run, it follows that by combining the paddy farming and rice milling sectors, one has an analytically manageable 'production complex', which produces a fully traded good. For completeness, we now describe the features of this complex in a little detail.

Agricultural land within the command area and, to a good approximation, the labour of cultivating households are fixed factors that are wholly employed within the complex. Paddy is a purely intermediate good, and is not traded across the complex's boundaries. The inputs that go into the complex in connection with the production of paddy are the following: fertilizers, the services of tractors, the labour supplied by migrant workers, the operations and maintenance of the irrigation system, financial and transportation services, and the extension and related services supplied by the government. All of the corresponding quantities are known, either from direct observation or from experiments using the model described in Section 13.5. Where the corresponding shadow prices are concerned, fertilizers are tradable, and the changes in the scale of output of the remainder are sufficiently modest that one need have few reservations about using the marginal cost rule. The paddy farming sector's associated final 'output', so to speak, is the vector of farming households' incomes, the relevant estimates of which are also known.

Turning to the milling sector of the complex, as noted above, this is a CRS activity with a known technology, whereby the associated unit activity vector includes a full allowance for the expansion of capacity and the balancing investments (e.g. in dryers) needed to mill the additional output produced by the paddy sector. The shadow pricing of this activity involves no particular difficulties, being an example of the sort treated in detail in Chapters 8 and 9. Its contribution to the complex's final output is the tradable good rice.

13.6.2. Valuing Changes in Income

In order to estimate θ, two parameters are needed: the level of private consumption at which an additional unit of income (valued at market prices) is just as socially valuable as a unit of uncommitted public income; and η, the elasticity of the marginal utility of consumption. As argued in Section 10.5, the former level is taken to be the official poverty line. That being so, and given the choice of government income as the numeraire, it follows that we should specify the utility function such that it takes the value of income at the poverty line, with an associated slope of unity there. Bell and Devarajan choose two values for η, namely, 1 and 2, in which case the foregoing normalizations yield the forms

$$u(M) = \begin{cases} M_0 \cdot [1 + \ln(M/M_0)], & \eta = 1, \\ M_0 \cdot [2 - (M_0/M)], & \eta = 2, \end{cases} \tag{13.25}$$

where M denotes here the level of real income and M_0 the poverty line.[8] The 'average' value of θ associated with a change in income from M^1 to M^2 is, therefore

$$\theta = \left[u(M^2) - u(M^1) \right] / (M^2 - M^1). \tag{13.26}$$

As can be seen from a glance at Table 13.2, the value of $\theta(\eta)$ varies sharply, both over households in any particular year and over the course of time for each household group.

13.6.3. Calculating the Social Profit

We employ the now familiar device of treating the paddy–rice complex as a public sector undertaking, with transfers of income to farming households in the command area and of the profits from rice milling to mill owners, as set out in Section 8.7. At time τ, let Δy_τ^k denote the vector of net outputs crossing the paddy–rice complex's boundaries $(k = 1, 2)$, M_τ^k the vector of households' real incomes, and $\Pi_{i\tau}^k$ the profits of the rice milling sector.

---

[8] The actual calculations excluded leisure, first, in order to maintain consistency with the official definition of M_0, and second, because the data was patchy for some groups.

Table 13.2. Social weights for household consumption at market prices

Household group	1967		1970		1972		1974	
	$\theta(1)$	$\theta(2)$	$\theta(1)$	$\theta(2)$	$\theta(1)$	$\theta(2)$	$\theta(1)$	$\theta(2)$
Landless paddy workers	3.25	10.53	2.62	6.9	2.29	5.39	2.14	4.70
Labour-abundant paddy farms	2.37	5.63	2.11	4.45	1.83	3.41	1.61	2.63
Land-abundant paddy farms	1.54	2.36	1.38	1.92	1.19	1.43	1.03	1.08
Non-project farms	1.75	3.09	1.59	2.55	1.39	1.94	1.26	1.42
Non-farm	0.78	0.61	0.73	0.53	0.63	0.41	0.53	0.29

Source: Bell *et al.* (1982)

Then the social profit generated by the project in that period is

$$\Delta W_\tau(\eta) = (\pi_\tau^2 y_\tau^2 - \pi_\tau^1 y_\tau^1) - \sum_h [1 - \theta_\tau^h(\eta)](M_\tau^{2h} - M_\tau^{1h})$$

$$- (1 - \theta_{K\tau})\left[\Pi_{i\tau}^2 - \Pi_{i\tau}^1\right] - (\pi_\tau^2 X_\tau^2 - \pi_\tau^1 X_\tau^1), \quad \eta = 1, 2.$$

$$(13.27)$$

Comparing Eqn (13.27) with its counterpart when the price of a project's output changes, namely Eqn (13.8), it is seen that the trials and tribulations of calculating the EV are replaced by those of estimating output and incomes, both with and without the project.

13.7. Summary

The core of any good long-term plan of public expenditure will include a set of infrastructure projects, broadly conceived. Yet the task of determining exactly which ones should be on the list is greatly complicated by the fact that such projects, being usually 'lumpy' in nature, bring about a significant reduction in the effective price of the good or service they provide, thereby undermining the basis on which shadow prices are derived. The central problem of this chapter, therefore, has been to find a way of fitting a set of non-local changes into the 'local' framework that underpins previous chapters.

The approach chosen here rests on the plausible assumption that projects of this kind usually have a measurable effect on just one or two prices. Granted this much, one begins by identifying the goods in question and then proceeds to analyse the markets for them in a partial equilibrium framework. This yields essential components of what are termed the project's 'direct' effects, in the familiar form of the associated changes in households' consumers' surpluses, producers' surpluses, and the government's revenues arising from transactions in that good. At the same time, allowance must be made for the fact that while private decisions are taken at market prices, the resulting use of resources should be valued at shadow prices. Thus, the sum of consumers' and producers' surpluses, even when the individual elements are weighted in terms of public income to reflect a desire for equity, must be corrected for any divergence between market and shadow prices. Here, the procedure becomes effectively 'local' once more. It is argued, first, that the only shadow prices that are likely to change appreciably are those of the goods in question, and second, that the said shadow prices are equal to the respective marginal costs of production, measured at shadow prices.

With the 'direct' effects so corralled, and all shadow prices at hand, it remains only to deal with the fact that the changes in market prices will normally induce changes in the composition of final expenditures. All relevant effects, including those on government revenue, arising from such expenditure-switching will be taken into account as follows. The values at shadow prices of the aggregate consumption baskets of all other goods before and after the introduction of the project, respectively, measure the social cost of the resources so committed to consumption. The difference between these values is an additional cost attributable to the project.

The approach is put to work in the context of two examples, namely, a bridge and an irrigation project. The bridge provides what can be thought of as a service which is combined with other inputs—the services of vehicles, fuel, and time—to produce a commodity called a trip, for which there is a well-defined demand, at a reduced cost. The irrigation project's immediate output is water, but again it is best not to stop there. Farmers combine water with other inputs to produce crops, and it often happens that productivity rises so strongly that factor prices, and hence incomes, increase substantially. The crops may, moreover, need processing before they become internationally tradable. In that case, the trick is to treat the project as a public sector undertaking within a production 'complex' made up of an agricultural and a processing sector. The net outputs of goods and services crossing the complex's boundaries are valued at shadow prices, whereby consumption is viewed as a net input. The changes in incomes are treated as transfers from the public sector to the private parties concerned, as set out in Section 8.7. If a project is large, both in the sense used in this chapter and in the tangible sense of being very expensive, such refinements are not only intellectually unavoidable, but also a necessary part of practice; for the ultimate aim is to reduce the chances of wasting valuable resources on a vast scale.

Recommended Reading

In the nature of things, large projects do not readily lend themselves to brief treatments. Flowerdew (1972) gives a useful and compact account of the approach adopted by the Roskill Commission to the evaluation of alternative sites for London's third airport three decades ago. For an assault on both the Commission's Report and the presumed need for the airport itself, see Mishan (1970). Neither employs shadow prices, though Mishan is deeply concerned with equity and damage to the environment. Where the use of shadow prices in the context of large changes in incomes is concerned, Bell *et al.* (1982) conveys what is involved and is technically fairly accessible.

Exercises

1. We consider a setting of the type described in Sections 13.3 and 13.4. The travellers may be thought of as workers, who commute from their homesteads on one side of the river to urban activities on the other, in which they earn Rs. 5 an hour. In the absence of the bridge over the estuary, the round-trip by bus takes an hour and costs Rs. 5; and 10,000 commuters make the round-trip daily. Were the bridge to be built and no toll charged, the journey time would be cut in half and the fare would fall to Rs. 3. The consultants estimate that the number of commuters would rise to 30,000 daily.

Bus services are produced by means of diesel fuel, labour, and depreciation and maintenance of the vehicles. The unit cost shares are 0.50, 0.30, and 0.20, respectively, and the corresponding accounting ratios are 0.5, 0.8, and 0.9. The CCF in the absence of the bridge is 0.85. Commuters presently spend 10 per cent of their incomes on commuting. If the premium on public income is 25 per cent, what is the value of the daily, direct net benefits that the bridge would generate?

Central Office of Project Evaluation (COPE) now reflects on the desirability of a toll, purely for the purpose of financing the running costs of the project. The minister of transport suggests the round figure of Rs. 1 per round-trip. Would this be an improvement over no toll at all? What is the value of the optimal toll?

2. A homogeneous village of n households lies at some distance from a river, which is its only source of drinking water. The task of fetching water falls to married women, who are observed to make two trips daily, each trip lasting h hours and yielding L litres of water. Some otherwise similar villages in the region are fortunate enough to have wells. In such villages, households are observed to consume L_0 litres a day.

The village produces a single crop, which is imported subject to a protective tariff of 20 per cent. The regional labour market is competitive, hours of work are flexible, and the hourly wage is w.

(a) The villagers press the government to sink a well, the construction and indefinite maintenance of which would cost K at shadow prices. Derive the condition on which the government should base its decision.

(b) You now learn from a chance meeting with an anthropologist that married women are prevented by social custom from doing any work in the fields. How would this knowledge affect your analysis in part (a)?

(c) A subsequent chat with her yields the information that the villagers practise exogamy, and that bridegrooms' families in the village in question obtain much lower dowries than their counterparts in similar villages that already have wells. She puts the difference at D rupees. How, if at all, does this additional information help you in part (b)?

3. A fully traded good is produced by private firms under conditions of increasing marginal cost. The world price is parametrically given, and the domestic industry enjoys a protective tariff in the amount of t per unit imported. A public sector project is now proposed, which would induce additional output in the said industry.

(a) Show that, ignoring any effects on consumption, the change in the value of the industry's output net of variable costs, all valued at shadow prices, due to the project is

$$\Delta PS - (AR_c - 1)\Delta TVC + t(y^1 - y^2),$$

where ΔPS denotes the change in producers' surplus, ΔTVC the change in total variable costs, AR_c the accounting ratio for variable inputs, y^1 the level of output in the absence of the project, and y^2 if it were undertaken.

(b) Let the industry's cost functions in the absence and presence of the project be

$$C^1(y) = y + y^2/2$$

and

$$C^2(y) = (y + y^2)/2,$$

respectively. Ignoring consumption effects, find the net social pay-off of the project if the world price of the good is two, $t = 0.5$, $AR_c = 0.8$, and the premium on public income is one-third. Illustrate the main elements of your analysis in a diagram.

(c) If the value of the CCF is 0.8, do you now possess enough information to find the social cost of the additional consumption induced by the project and to assess its social profitability? State your reasons succinctly and carefully.

4. An unirrigated plain is cultivated by farmers with family labour and the aid of migrant workers from neighbouring regions. The technology exhibits CRS in land and labour, the output produced from one unit of land and L units of labour being given by

$$y = AL^{1/2}.$$

(a) If the supply of migrant workers is perfectly elastic at the wage rate w and the producer price of agricultural output is p, prove that the supply schedule of a farmer who cultivates one unit of land is

$$y(p, w; A) = A^2(p/2w).$$

(b) Under unirrigated conditions, $A = 1$. A project is now proposed, whereby all farms would be served by canals, which would have the effect of increasing the value of A to $\sqrt{2}$. The world price of the crop is unity, but farmers enjoy the protection of an *ad valorem* tariff of 10 per cent. Were the project to be built, the same tariff would remain in force and the crops in question would continue to be imported, as they are at present. Field studies indicate that the wage rate for migrant workers in their home regions is one-half.

There are n units of land altogether, and n farming families. Each of the latter is endowed with one unit of labour (time), which it allocates between work on the farm and leisure (l). All families have identical preferences, which can be represented in the form

$$u = x_1^{\beta_1} x_2^{\beta_2} l^{1-\beta_1-\beta_2},$$

where x_1 denotes the consumption of the crops produced in the region and x_2 the consumption of all other goods. Econometric studies suggest that $\beta_1 = \beta_2 = 0.4$. The market price of the basket labelled good 2 is unity.

COPE estimates the accounting ratios for good 2 and migrant workers to be 0.9 and 0.8, respectively. Calculate all relevant quantities for the evaluation of the project and present them in a table, together with their accounting ratios. If the premium on public income is 10 per cent, what is the value of the annual social profit the project would yield at maturity (gross of operations and maintenance charges)?

14. Land Reform and Tenancy

In the middle of the twentieth century, the great majority of less developed countries (LDCs) were agrarian economies by any reasonable definition of the term, with agriculture accounting for 40–70 per cent of gross national product and 50–80 per cent of total employment. Something of a structural shift has taken place since then—in those that have grown fairly rapidly, as a matter of course. Among the current group of some fifty low-income countries,[1] however, the mean values of these shares still stand at about one-third and two-thirds, respectively. In such economies, land is a central factor of production, with actual and imputed land rents combined accounting for at least one-third and sometimes over one half of agricultural value added. Hence, not only does the general level of rural incomes depend heavily on the efficiency with which land is used in combination with other factors of production, but its distribution is also strongly influenced by the distribution of the rents so generated. That such a high proportion of the population continues to depend directly on agriculture is therefore a compelling reason to examine what can be called the 'land question' in some detail.

The level and distribution of rents depend on the nature and allocation of property rights in land, which specify who can make claims on each particular use of it and on the ensuing output. Direct access to land can come about either through individual ownership or, at the other extreme, through membership in a community that holds all land in common. When land is individually owned, the property rights therein usually permit usufructuary rights to be transferred to other parties under tenancy contracts; when it is collectively held, usufructuary rights may not be individual, and even if they are, individuals may not have the right to transfer them.

Yet for all the variety and complexity of such rights, most discussions of land reform begin—and often end—with proposals to transfer individual property rights in land from the relatively affluent to the poor. One important recent variation deals with the transformation of collective rights into individual ones, collectivism of virtually any stripe having gone out of fashion with peasants, governments, and most academics alike. A

---

[1] Defined by the World Bank as those with a per capita GNP of less than $755 in 1999. Successor states of the former Soviet Union and some small islands have been excluded from the calculations, leaving a group of about fifty such economies.

closely related question is whether self-cultivation should be promoted at the expense of tenancy, the debate over which also revolves about the distribution of land rents, actual or imputed. In practice, a strong concern with equity has often led to legislation that, perhaps unintentionally, obstructs tenancy in the performance of its role as a mechanism for allocating resources. Reforms of these kinds also have fiscal consequences, especially when compensation for expropriated holdings is to be paid out of tax revenues. While it is fair to say that the potential direct fiscal burden of such reforms has certainly exercised some of those who advocate them, the workings of the whole array of distortions in the economy, which will surely influence how any reform affects welfare, has received very little attention. An important task of this chapter is to remedy that neglect.

The chapter begins with a discussion of the nature of property rights in land and how land is distributed in selected countries. This is followed, in Section 14.2, by an analysis of the effects of a redistribution of individual landholdings by *fiat* on output and incomes. Section 14.3, in contrast, deals with the so-called 'market' approaches to bring about a redistribution of holdings. The analysis is further extended in Section 14.4 to take into account the presence of pervasive distortions, whereby the use of shadow prices to evaluate a land reform plays a central role. Section 14.5 takes up the potential functions of tenancy, both as a response to shortcomings in other markets and as an avenue of opportunity for individual mobility, and then assesses what interventions are desirable. The discussion then moves on to the political economy of agrarian reforms, drawing on the experience of the twentieth century, in which social upheaval played a crucial part. Looking forward, Section 14.7 assesses the prospects for reformist policies in 'normal' times, when the social and political order is fairly secure. It is argued that the general need for fiscal austerity opens the door to specific tax reforms that improve the chances of pushing through land reform measures at a later stage.

14.1. Property Rights in Land

In essence, property rights involve three separate issues: (i) who may use the asset and how much of the resulting output he or she may claim; (ii) whether such uses and claims may be transferred to another party, temporarily or permanently; and (iii) if transfers are permitted in principle, whether there are restrictions on how or to whom they may be made. These forms of rights can appear in various combinations. For example, an owner may enjoy an exclusive claim to the standing crops on the plots he or she has cultivated, but everyone in the community may have the right to graze their cattle on the stubble that is left after the harvest has been brought in. Customary grazing rights of this sort are widespread in India, where individual property rights in land are normally thought of as being strong.

Purely individual and purely collective forms of property rights are, therefore, simply polar cases. Where the rights are purely individual, the owner has complete and exclusive claims to all uses and outputs, and may dispose of the land as, and to whom, he or she sees fit. Land is then a purely commercial commodity. Where the rights are purely collective, all members of a community have claims on the output of land held in common (usually to the exclusion of outsiders), but they have no rights of transfer, except (perhaps) to bequeath membership to their children. Many intermediate forms are found between these extremes, sometimes as a result of local initiatives in the face of changing circumstances and an indifferent central state, and sometimes as a result of central initiatives over local opposition.

In Africa, for example, usufructuary rights to farmland were normally acquired by initial clearing and then maintained by cultivation, with suitable fallowing practices. When it is not under crops, such land is open to secondary use by members of the owner's social group. Once cultivation is resumed, however, the plots in question cease to be a common property resource (Blarel et al., 1993). Where alienation of rights is concerned, in certain regions of Ghana and Rwanda, for example, one survey in the 1980s revealed that 59 and 62 per cent, respectively, of all parcels could be alienated outside their holders' lineage (ibid.). For all parcels that could be alienated in some form, the proportions that could be alienated outside the lineage were higher, at 75 and 83 per cent, respectively. This evidence appears to support the hypothesis that commercialization and population pressure encourage the emergence of individual rights, Rwanda being much more densely settled. Be that as it may, this traditional form of tenure is evidently more open, to insiders at least, than that based on pure individual rights.

Statistics on the average size of holding and the distribution of holdings by size and tenure status for selected countries in Africa, Asia, and Latin America (Tables 14.1 and 14.2) reveal great variations across countries and regions, which reflect profound differences in demographic, social, and economic history. Average holdings are small in Africa and Asia, with a somewhat more egalitarian pattern in Africa (notwithstanding a certain dualism in Kenya and Zambia, where there are a few very large holdings

Table 14.1. Distribution of landholdings by size, for selected countries, about 1970 (per cent)

Region and country	Average size of holdings (hectares)	Distribution of holdings by number of hectares								
		0–1	1–2	2–5	5–10	10–20	20–50	50–100	100–500	500+
Africa										
Cameroon	1.6	42.7	30.5	23.3	3.2	0.3	...	—	—	—
Ghana	3.2	37.7	24.2	24.0	8.8	3.5	1.8	...	—	—
Kenya	4.1	31.8	26.9	31.1	9.9	...	—	—	0.1	...
Malawi	1.5	39.1	34.6	26.3	...	—	—	—	—	—
Sierra Leone	1.8	37.8	26.9	29.7	5.6	—	—	—	—	—
Zambia	3.1	50.4	28.6	17.2	3.8	1.4	0.5	—	0.1	—
Asia										
India	2.3	50.6	19.1	19.0	7.4	3.0	0.8	0.1	...	—
Indonesia	1.1	70.4	18.1	9.4	1.5	0.6	—	—	—	...
Iraq	9.7	20.1	11.2	18.1	21.5	18.6	9.0	1.0	0.5	—
Korea Rep. of	0.9	66.9	26.4	6.7	...	—	—	—	—	—
Pakistan	5.3	13.8	14.3	39.9	21.1	7.7	2.5	0.6	...	—
Philippines	3.6	13.6	27.4	43.8	10.4	3.6	1.0	0.2	...	—
Sri Lanka	1.2	71.2	16.9	9.9	1.3	0.4	0.2	...	—	—
Latin America										
Brazil	59.7	8.1	10.0	18.7	14.7	15.7	16.7	7.0	7.5	1.8
Colombia	26.3	22.9	15.1	21.6	13.6	10.0	8.5	4.1	3.6	0.7
Costa Rica	38.1	22.9	9.8	15.9	11.0	11.0	14.6	7.3	6.2	1.0
El Salvador	4.6	23.2	18.6	13.5	5.0	2.8	2.2	0.6	0.5	0.1
Mexico	137.1	56.6	11.1	15.1	10.0	7.8	8.1	4.8	6.0	3.6

Source: FAO 1981.

Table 14.2. Distribution of landholdings by form of tenure, for selected countries, about 1970 (per cent)

Region and country	Holdings under one form of tenure								Holdings under mixed tenure		Proportion of area rented	Proportion of area rented under share tenancy
	Owned		Rented		Squatter		Communal and other					
	Number	Area	Number	Area	Number	Area	Number	Area	Number	Area		
Africa												
Cameroon	2.4	2.5	5.2	2.7	7.5	6.1	59.5	58.4	25.4	30.2	7.5	0
Ghana	–	–	–	–	–	–	–	–	–	–	–	–
Kenya	–	–	–	–	–	–	–	–	–	–	–	–
Malawi	–	–	–	–	–	–	–	–	–	–	–	–
Sierra Leone	–	85.6*	–	6.3*	–	0.5*	–	7.6*	(+)	(+)	6.3	0
Asia												
India	92.0	91.5	4.0	2.4	...	...	...	...	4.0	6.1	–	–
Indonesia	74.8	76.2	3.2	2.1	...	...	...	0.2	22.0	21.5	–	–
Iraq	–	52.4*	–	40.9*	–	4.8*	–	1.9*	(+)	(+)	40.9	–
Korea Rep. of	65.9	66.1	9.5	6.7	...	...	...	...	23.8	27.2	17.2	–
Pakistan	41.7	39.5	34.5	29.6	...	...	...	...	23.8	30.9	46.1	83.4
Philippines	58.0	65.6	29.0	21.4	...	...	1.5	1.5	11.4	11.4	–	–
Sri Lanka	–	64.9*	–	22.4*	–	4.0*	–	8.7*	(+)	(+)	22.4	–
Latin America												
Brazil	60.4	82.6	20.4	6.1	16.5	7.2	0	0	2.7	4.1	7.1	24.6
Colombia	68.7	74.6	14.1	5.3	4.0	9.5	6.0	4.5	7.1	6.2	6.5	48.0
Costa Rica	85.4	90.8	4.7	1.2	...	...	0.2	0.2	9.7	7.8	3.0	–
El Salvador	35.3	77.1	24.0	7.2	...	...	12.0	5.8	13.9	9.9	11.3	1.5
Mexico	–	44.5*	–	2.6*	–	1.2*	–	51.7*	(+)	(+)	2.6	17.0
Peru	62.2	82.1	8.6	4.5	5.5	2.6	5.8	1.7	18.0	9.1	6.0	–

*Includes holdings under mixed tenure; [+]Included under communal and other tenure;_ = Not available; ... = Less than 0.1 per cent.

Source: FAO 1981.

owned by settlers of European descent). Average holdings are much larger in Latin America, and inequality is much more extreme. Size is not, of course, the only natural determinant of a holding's productivity. Soils, climate, and access to water are also very important, and they typically vary a good deal within a country or even within a region. To the extent that they do so systematically, any account based on area alone may be seriously misleading: fertile regions are usually densely settled, whereas arid ones are thinly populated. Bhalla (1988), for example, finds a strong negative correlation between an econometrically estimated index of land quality and farm size in India. Whereas the bottom 40 per cent of farms possess only 7 per cent of the total area, that share rises to 15 per cent or more when the sizes of holdings are adjusted for their quality.

Owner-operated holdings are the largest category in both number and area, except in Cameroon and Mexico, where tribal and communal forms are dominant. In all cases the average owner-operated holding is larger than the average pure tenancy. Holdings comprising more than one form of tenure are relatively numerous, especially in Asia, where peasants frequently lease land to augment their own holdings and such operational holdings are at least as large, on average, as owner-operated holdings. The proportion of the entire area under tenancy is rather small, except in some Asian countries, notably Iraq and Pakistan. The extent of tenancy is surely underreported in most national censuses, however, because legislation prohibiting or regulating tenancy discourages truthful reporting. Evidence on the form of contract is available for only a few countries. The dominant form is sharecropping in most of South Asia and fixed rent (in cash or kind) elsewhere.

14.2. Redistributing Private Holdings

Consider the classic setting in which property rights in land are individually held and concentrated in the hands of a few, as would be the case where economic organization takes the form of plantations, estates, or a strongly differentiated peasantry. A redistribution of existing property rights in favour of erstwhile workers, tenants, and marginal farmers will make them independent landholders. The first-order economic effect of such a reallocation of rights will be to redistribute land rents, actual and imputed, in the latter's favour. Its effects on the levels of inputs, outputs, and factor prices in general equilibrium, which are essential elements in evaluating any reform, are less clear. In particular, a careful distinction must be drawn between differences in factor intensities across farms in a given equilibrium and differences therein across equilibria. Although much attention has been lavished on the former, we shall begin our theoretical discussion with the latter, precisely in order to draw out this distinction.

14.2.1. Theory

Suppose that a single agricultural output is produced under constant returns to scale (CRS) by means of land and labour, both of which are homogeneous in quality. Under the assumption that all markets are perfect, all producers will choose the same ratio of labour to land and all will obtain the same yield per hectare. If agriculture is the only sector of the economy, let its output be the numeraire; if there are other sectors, let the (relative) price of agricultural output be set by parametrically given trading opportunities in world markets. For simplicity, intersectoral migration is ruled out in the latter case. Let there be two types of agrarian households, with n^h of each type ($h = 1, 2$) and n households altogether. Each household of type h is endowed with H^h hectares and one unit of labour (time). Land is supplied completely inelastically; but time is allocated between work and leisure so as to maximize utility. Without loss of generality, let $H^1 < H^2$ at the outset, so that a reform will involve an increase in H^1. Observe that the setting is purely static, so that a redistribution of existing endowments will have no effect on future endowments, for example, by influencing investment in land or the accumulation of human capital through experience.

Denoting the total area of land by $\bar{H}$, we have the identity

$$n^1 H^1 + n^2 H^2 \equiv \bar{H}. \tag{14.1}$$

Since all producers will choose the same labour–land ratio in cultivation, it follows that, on the production side, the system may be treated as one big farm. Total output is, therefore,

$$Y = f(n^1 L^1 + n^2 L^2, \bar{H}), \tag{14.2}$$

where the production function $f(\cdot)$ is well-behaved and L^h denotes the amount of labour supplied by each household of type h. In a competitive equilibrium, the prices of factors will be equal to the values of their respective marginal products:

$$w = f_1(n^1 L^1 + n^2 L^2, \bar{H}) \tag{14.3}$$

and

$$R = f_2(n^1L^1 + n^2L^2, \bar{H}), \tag{14.4}$$

where f_j denotes the derivative of $f(\cdot)$ with respect to its jth argument. Since the total area is fixed, the wage rate w is decreasing in $(n^1L^1 + n^2L^2)$, whereas the rent per hectare, R, is increasing in the same.

The full income of a household of type h is

$$M^h = w + RH^h, \quad h = 1, 2. \tag{14.5}$$

The amount of labour it chooses to supply depends on w and M^h:

$$L^h = L^h(w, M^h).$$

Define the aggregate input of labour as

$$L \equiv n^1L^1(w, M^1) + n^2L^2(w, M^2). \tag{14.6}$$

Recalling Eqn (14.1), it is seen from Eqn (14.6) that the effects of redistributing land among households can be found by establishing how such a redistribution affects L. Differentiating Eqn (14.6) with respect to H^1 and noting that w and R satisfy Eqn (14.3) and (14.4), we obtain:

$$\frac{\partial L}{\partial H^1} = \left(n^1 \frac{\partial L^1}{\partial w} + n^2 \frac{\partial L^2}{\partial w} \right) \frac{\partial w}{\partial H^1} + \left(n^1 \frac{\partial L^1}{\partial M^1} + n^2 \frac{\partial L^2}{\partial M^2} \right) \frac{\partial w}{\partial H^1}$$
$$+ \left(n^1 H^1 \frac{\partial L^1}{\partial M^1} + n^2 H^2 \frac{\partial L^2}{\partial M^2} \right) \frac{\partial R}{\partial H^1} + \left(\frac{\partial L^1}{\partial M^1} - \frac{\partial L^2}{\partial M^2} \right) (n^1 R).$$

$$\tag{14.7}$$

The first expression on the right-hand side (RHS) of Eqn (14.7) is the substitution effect, which arises from the possible dependence of the wage rate on the distribution of holdings. The remaining terms comprise the income effect, where (full) income depends on w, R, and H^h, as given by Eqn (14.5). From Eqns (14.3) and (14.4), we have

$$\frac{\partial w}{\partial H^1} = f_{11} \frac{\partial L}{\partial H^1} \tag{14.8}$$

and

$$\frac{\partial R}{\partial H^1} = f_{12} \frac{\partial L}{\partial H^1}. \tag{14.9}$$

Substituting into Eqn (14.7) and rearranging, we obtain

$$\left\{ 1 - \left[\left(n^1 \frac{\partial L^1}{\partial w} + n^2 \frac{\partial L^2}{\partial w} \right) + \left(n^1 \frac{\partial L^1}{\partial M^1} + n^2 \frac{\partial L^2}{\partial M^2} \right) \right] f_{11} \right.$$

$$\left. - \left(n^1 H^1 \frac{\partial L^1}{\partial M^1} + n^2 H^2 \frac{\partial L^2}{\partial M^2} \right) f_{12} \right\} \frac{\partial L}{\partial H^1}$$

$$= \left(\frac{\partial L^1}{\partial M^1} - \frac{\partial L^2}{\partial M^2} \right) (n^1 R). \tag{14.10a}$$

A special case, which serves as a valuable benchmark, is that where all households have the same, quasi-homothetic preferences. In that case, $\partial L^1 / \partial M^1 = \partial L^2 / \partial M^2$, and Eqn (14.10a) specializes to

$$\left\{ 1 - \left[\left(n^1 \frac{\partial L^1}{\partial w} + n^2 \frac{\partial L^2}{\partial w} \right) + \frac{\partial L^1}{\partial M^1} \right] f_{11} - nH \cdot \frac{\partial L^1}{\partial M^1} f_{12} \right\} \frac{\partial L}{\partial H^1} = 0,$$

$$\tag{14.10b}$$

from which it follows that $\partial L / \partial H^1 = 0$. That is to say, in the benchmark case, any redistribution of land will leave factor prices and aggregate output unchanged, and so result in a pure redistribution of aggregate full income.

The intuition for this result is as follows. Consider two households, whose preferences are identical and quasi-homothetic. If both are at an interior optimum where the allocation of their time is concerned, and if factor prices are constant, then any reallocation of land between them will leave unchanged not only their combined full income, but also their combined supply of labour. Hence, with all land supplied inelastically, both factor markets would continue to clear at the originally prevailing factor prices, so validating the initial hypothesis that they do so. In this benchmark case, therefore, the effects of the reform are purely redistributive. Observe also that the distribution of operational, as distinct from ownership, holdings is indeterminate: a household's full income depends only on its endowments, and is quite independent of whether it is a net supplier of labour or land in the equilibrium that rules.

Departures from this benchmark case generally result in output becoming sensitive to the distribution of endowments. From Eqn (14.10a), it is clear that the key to whether a redistributive reform affects prices and aggregate output is the term $(\partial L^1 / \partial M^1 - \partial L^2 / \partial M^2)$. If, as is often asserted to be the case, the rich (group 2) will take their ease anyway—unless

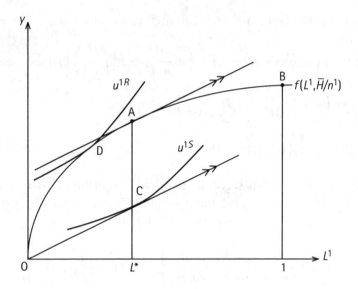

Figure 14.1. An egalitarian reform

they are relatively impoverished by a radical reform—then the normality of leisure for the poor implies that this term will be negative, so that aggregate labour supply, and hence aggregate output, will fall following such a reform. Gersovitz (1976), for example, analyses the case where there are initially landowners, who do not work at all, landless agricultural labourers, and a very small group of peasant farmers, hereinafter denoted by type 3, to serve as a benchmark. Let the landless take some leisure, at least after the reform has been implemented. Then, as noted above, any redistribution of land in their favour will cause a reduction in aggregate labour supply and hence in aggregate output.

A geometric argument makes the intuition underlying this result—and the associated changes in factor prices—more transparent. Consider Fig. 14.1, in which the upper boundary of the set of all efficient bundles of leisure, namely $l^1 \equiv 1 - L^1$, enjoyed by each initially landless household and the aggregate output generated by its labour is depicted by OB, this frontier being just the function $f(L^1, H/n^1)$ over the interval $0 < L^1 < 1$.[2]

Before the reform, equilibrium is established at the pair (A, C) such that the tangent to $f(\cdot)$ at A is parallel to the line through OC, where

---

[2] Observe that since landowners are assumed not to work at all, the assumption of CRS allows us to base the analysis on what happens on a holding of size H/n^1 both before and after the reform.

C lies vertically below A and OC is also tangential to the indifference curve passing through C, which is labelled u^{1S}. Their common slope is the product wage, at which profit-maximizing producers choose L^* units of labour and the household, being endowed solely with labour, chooses to supply the same amount. Following a completely egalitarian reform, there will be no trade in the resulting equilibrium, which will be established at that point on OB where this frontier is tangential to an indifference curve, at D say. It is clear that D must lie to the left of A if leisure is a normal good. The strict concavity of $f(\cdot)$ implies that the (imputed) product wage will be higher, and the rent per hectare lower, than their respective levels before the reform. Less radical reforms, in which the landless receive only a portion of the total endowment, will yield the same qualitative result, again by virtue of the income effect stemming from the receipt of some rental income (actual or imputed) after the reform.[3]

Consider next the case where there is a substantial group of small family farms and a 'segmented' labour market for hired and family labour, in the sense that family farms do not trade in the labour market at all. Given such autarky, there will be differences in the technique of cultivation on large and small farms, with the latter 'exploiting' family labour, in the sense that its marginal product is lower than the ruling wage rate for hired hands on large farms. As depicted in Fig. 14.2, a small-farm household has an opportunity set whose upper boundary is the curve OE, which is just the production function $f(L^3, H^3)$, and it chooses the allocation depicted by the point G, where the indifference curve labelled u^{3S} is tangential to OE. Let these small farms be the sole direct beneficiaries of a radical reform, with agricultural workers left to fend for themselves in the labour market, as has commonly been the case in contemporary history. Each small farm will now possess a holding of size $\bar{H}/n^3$, and hence a larger opportunity set under autarky, as depicted by OF. In order that the labour market be active in the post-reform equilibrium, of course, the family farms must be hiring in some labour, so it is assumed that they have no aversion to doing so, whatever may have deterred them from working off the farm before the reform. The reform's effect on output and the wage rate is unclear. Although the income effect of the redistribution in favour of family farm households, whose magnitude depends on the pre-reform distribution of land, will induce them to supply less labour, the direction of the substitution effect is unclear, because where the wage rate settles

---

[3] The details of the argument, which also appeals to the substitution effect, are left as an exercise for the reader (see Exercise 1).

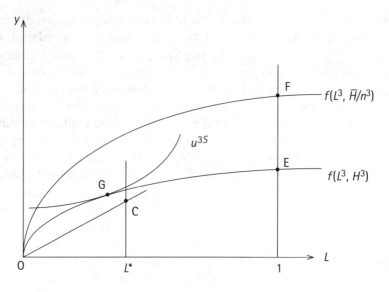

Figure 14.2. A reform that excludes the landless

will also depend on landless households' preferences. If the wage rate is higher, then aggregate output will be lower after the reform; but if the wage rate falls, output could go in either direction.

Other possible variations are that large landowners are simply inefficient, in the sense that they fail to operate on the production possibility frontier, or that they are monopsonists in the labour market (each, presumably, in his own village). In these cases also, a radical egalitarian reform may cause output to rise or fall.

Factor–use ratios may vary across farms for reasons other than segmentation of the labour market or monopsony, and some are arguably of much greater practical importance. One limitation of both the 'benchmark' case and Gersovitz's variants is that they ignore the fact that employers need to ensure that hired hands put their backs into their work, an agency problem that pure family farms do not face. Another is the neglect of other factors of production such as draught animals and managerial and husbandry skills, the markets for which are often thin or even absent. The allocation of land among households is crucial to the efficiency with which these specific factors are used. If a reallocation of property rights brings about a more efficient use of such factors or improves the system of incentives, simple intuition suggests that, following a reform, both the

level of aggregate output and that on the plots now farmed by the beneficiaries will be higher than the above analysis suggests. Some caution is
in order, of course, because one is dealing here with comparative statics
in a general equilibrium setting with incomplete markets, which is still far
from fully charted theoretical territory—and possibly a minefield for the
unwary. What can be said on the basis of the results obtained above is
that a redistributive reform's effects depend on the initial configuration of
property rights and on the reasons why the ratios of output and labour to
land vary across farms of different types—if, indeed, they do vary. Stronger
claims are unwarranted without further assumptions.

14.2.2. Evidence

The empirical evidence in favour of the claim that such reforms will yield
the happy combination of improvements in both equity and efficiency is
largely indirect. Most earlier studies of the status quo revealed an inverse
relation between farm size and productivity, stemming largely from an
inverse relation between farm size and inputs of labour per hectare (see
e.g. Bhagwati and Chakravarty, 1969; Berry and Cline, 1979). This finding
is consistent with agency problems or monopsonistic power in the labour
market, either of which would result in an intensification of labour inputs
on small family farms. A quite different explanation is that small farms,
which usually predominate in densely settled regions, enjoy the advantages
of both better climatic conditions and better soils than larger farms, which
predominate in less favourable natural environments. The difference in
yields arises not only directly, but also indirectly, if land quality and other
inputs are complements in production. For India, at least, Bhalla and Roy
(1988) provide evidence that this competing explanation must be taken
very seriously. Based on a very large sample of farms drawn from 176 districts, they find strong support for the hypothesis that farm size and yield
are inversely related when the observations are grouped by state, even con-
trolling for soil quality, fragmentation, and 'exogenous' irrigation (canals
and tanks). When the observations are disaggregated by district, however,
the null hypothesis that there is no relationship between farm size and yield
cannot be rejected in 125 districts (ninety-three if soil quality, fragmentation, and yield are omitted). Since redistributive reforms are normally
intra-district affairs, this finding ought to put a damper on expectations
that they would result in an appreciable improvement in yields.

This does not quite clinch the argument, however, for there are at least
two other factors at work that do not appear explicitly in Bhalla and Roy's

reduced-form analysis, namely, large farmers' superior access to credit and rationed inputs, and their higher costs of agency in employing labour. These pull in opposite directions, and so leave unresolved the question of what would happen to yields following a redistributive reform. The agency problem is probably sufficiently serious to warrant cautious optimism, but certainly not the headier claims based on the sharp inverse relationship found in most earlier studies.

14.3. The 'Market' Solution

The market for land, where one exists, provides a mechanism for redis-tributing property rights in land, inasmuch as those who want more land can, in principle, buy it from those who want to sell. If, for example, the reservation price a big landowner places on part of his holding is lower than a poor household's willingness to pay for it, then a mutually profit-able deal can be struck, however the market is organized. It is often argued that since the poor enjoy the advantage of cheap family labour, the gains from trade are potentially there, especially when ownership is very con-centrated. Advocates of a so-called 'market' solution to the land reform problem have proposed making voluntary trade the basis of land redistribu-tion, with suitable inducements to make such trade feasible and attractive, including the payment of substantial subsidies to qualified purchasers.

This approach runs into various difficulties, one of which is funda-mental: one can appeal to a 'market' solution only when the market in question functions reasonably well. Now it is one thing when cadastral surveys are up-to-date, legal titles are secure, and there is a steady stream of sales whose terms are on the public record, so that sellers and buyers can form fairly confident estimates of what a parcel of land with particular characteristics is likely to fetch. It is quite another matter when surveys are antediluvian, the legal system is shaky, the market is thin, and the terms of transactions may remain private information. The problem would seem to be especially acute when land ownership is concentrated in the hands of a few. How often, for example, is a small part of a hacienda sold and the terms of sale put on the public record? For those who advocate a 'market' solution, therefore, every recorded sale has the character of a public good, in that it may provide valuable information to other potential transactors. In the absence of a 'thick' record of transactions, the buyer's and seller's reservation limits are bound to be rather subjective, and strik-ing a deal may prove to be difficult. With a land reform agency in the background, ready to grant a subsidy and finance the sale, moreover, the temptation for the private parties to settle on a high price for official purposes, coupled with a private side-payment to divide up the subsidy, will be well-nigh irresistible. Deininger (1999) points to precisely this pitfall in the case of a pilot scheme to promote a 'market' solution to the land reform problem in Colombia, where INCORA, the official reform agency, had already established a well-earned reputation for inefficiency and bureaucracy, having spent most of its budget on self-administration during the 1980s. In extreme cases, where the market is very thin, advocates of the market approach therefore find themselves in the unenviable position of needing the results of the reform, so conceived, in order to make its realization feasible.

Let it be granted that this potentially fundamental difficulty can be overcome. Other difficulties remain, all serious and all having to do with finance in one form or another. First, the poor will not be able to finance the purchase of land unless the capital market functions fairly well, which it does not, or a special credit programme is introduced for the purpose at hand, which will unleash other problems (see Chapter 15). Second, if finance were available on such a scale that all who desired to hold land as an asset could acquire it, the notional demand for land as an asset would be fully realized and its price would almost certainly rise, to the advantage of those who held it at the outset. Any net benefits that the ensuing general equilibrium realignment of wages, rents, and commodity prices might bring to the poor as a group would most likely be rather small. Third, although the prime objective is to secure significant gains for the poor, this must be brought about without placing an intolerable burden on the Treasury, a condition that requires, in turn, that some way be found to reduce large landholders' reservation prices of land below the levels prevailing before the intervention is attempted. For the poor to gain, therefore, it is virtually certain that some other group must lose, so that an appeal to the principle of voluntary trade yields no escape from the general problem of political economy that besets all redistributive reforms, direct and indirect alike.

The third point—that the reform must be undertaken in conditions of fiscal austerity—highlights once more the desirability of thinking carefully about policy as a whole. To give an example, ending the heavy subsidies that are often directed towards large farms would be a good move in itself, and it would also surely please international agencies. Its further, incidental effect of lowering land values would also reduce the scale of any compensation based on fair market value—provided, of course, that the tax reform were undertaken first. De Janvry and Sadoulet (1993) draw attention to this sequence in connection with legislation in Colombia (Law 15 of 1961). Some at the World Bank must have fastened onto the same idea; for the terms of a recent structural adjustment loan to that country included reductions in subsidies to large farms, a measure that provoked strong lobbying for its reversal (Deininger, 1999). In any event, it is clear that a systematic evaluation of land reform in the wider context of economic policy is essential, to which we now turn.

14.4. Land Reform as a 'Large' Project

Advocates of land reforms are usually keenly concerned with equity, though they take good care to buttress their case with arguments that such reforms will also promote efficiency. Where solving the potential fiscal problem is concerned, those wedded to the classical approach rely on a political stroke—in the form of confiscation—whereas those who extol the virtues of a 'market' approach implicitly appeal to the generosity of the Treasury or outside donors. What all almost invariably fail to do, however, is to take into account the effects of the plethora of distortions that would still be at work should a land reform be carried out. The apparatus of shadow pricing developed in previous chapters will serve admirably for this purpose, whereby a radical land reform should clearly be viewed as a 'large' project in the sense of Chapter 13.

14.4.1. The 'Benchmark' Case

As we saw in Section 14.2.1, in the benchmark case, a reform has no effect on aggregate output or factor prices in the agricultural sector, so that it is unlikely that the full vectors of market and shadow prices will be much affected either. That being so, there are only two effects to consider: the social value of the redistribution of full income among households and the social value of the change in the aggregate consumption bundle of all rural households. Given that consumer prices are constant, it suffices to examine what happens to full incomes when H^1 is increased at the expense of group 2. Recalling Eqns (14.1) and (14.5), we have

$$\frac{\partial M^1}{\partial H^1} = R \quad \text{and} \quad \frac{\partial M^2}{\partial H^1} = -\frac{n^1}{n^2} \cdot R.$$

Hence, summing over all households, the social value of the pure redistribution of full incomes induced by a 'small' reform dH^1 is $[(\theta^1 - \theta^2)n^1R] \cdot$

dH^1, whereby the beneficiaries' comparative poverty implies that $\theta^1 > \theta^2$. This is the standard argument in favour of a reform from the standpoint of equity.

Turning to consumption, we need to extend the notation of Section 14.2 somewhat in order to accommodate a variety of goods, including those produced outside the agricultural sector. The demand vector of a household of type h is denoted by $x^h(q, M^h)$. If preferences are both identical and homothetic, then a pure redistribution of (full) incomes will leave the aggregate demand vector

$$X(q, M) \equiv n^1 x^1(q, M^1) + n^2 x^2(q, M^2) \tag{14.11}$$

unaltered. Hence, the improvement in welfare induced by a small reform will be simply

$$dW = (\theta^1 - \theta^2) n^1 R \cdot dH^1. \tag{14.12}$$

Equation (14.12) corresponds to the case of pure confiscation. Suppose now that the Treasury is persuaded to help out by allocating some revenues (presumably from sources outside agriculture) to ease the losses of group 2 and so, perhaps, secure their acquiescence. Let this budgetary allocation suffice to finance compensation in the amount of α (<1) for each rupee of income transferred through the reallocation of landholdings. Then Eqn (14.12) becomes

$$dW = [(\theta^1 - \theta^2) - \alpha(1 - \theta^2)] n^1 R \cdot dH^1, \tag{14.13}$$

and since θ^2 is surely less than unity, the scheme of compensation is seen to be a political necessity that reduces the gains from the reform.

The next step is to relax the assumption that preferences are identical, though in order to preserve the benchmark case, we still need to ensure that the aggregate input of labour is independent of the allocation of landholdings. Consider, therefore, the case where preferences over leisure and all other goods can be represented by the additively separable form

$$U^h(l^h, x^h_{-l}) = \beta \cdot \ln l^h + \phi^h(x^h_{-l}), \quad h = 1, 2, \tag{14.14}$$

where $\phi^h(\cdot)$ is a homogeneous function of degree γ, but is otherwise free to vary across groups. Observe that the marginal rate of indifferent substitution (MRS) between any pair of goods other than leisure is independent of the amount of leisure taken. By writing down the household's consumer problem, summing over the first-order conditions, and appealing to Euler's theorem, it can be shown that the household will spend a fixed fraction of its full income on leisure: to be precise

$$l^h(q_{-l}, w, M^h) = \frac{\beta}{\beta + \gamma} \cdot \frac{M^h}{w}.$$

Given the hypothesis that factor prices are independent of the distribution of landholdings, aggregate labour supply is, from Eqn (14.6),

$$L \equiv n^1 L^1 + n^2 L^2 = \frac{\beta}{\beta + \gamma} \cdot \frac{n^1 M^1 + n^2 M^2}{w},$$

which is indeed independent of the allocation of landholdings, and so confirms the hypothesis that the benchmark case is in force.

With this point established, we turn to the effects of a small reform on the social cost of aggregate consumption. Recalling Eqn (14.12) and the argument that shadow prices are unlikely to be affected by a land reform in the benchmark case, we have

$$\pi \cdot [\partial X(q, M)/\partial H^1] = \pi \cdot [n^1 \partial x^1(q, M^1)/\partial H^1 + n^2 \partial x^2(q, M^2)/\partial H^1]$$

$$= \pi \cdot \left(\frac{\partial x^1}{\partial M^1} - \frac{\partial x^2}{\partial M^2} \right) n^1 R, \qquad (14.15)$$

where use has been made of Eqns (14.1) and (14.5). Since aggregate labour supply does not change, we can re-express this effect in terms of the consumption conversion factors as follows:

$$\pi \cdot \left(\frac{\partial x^1}{\partial M^1} - \frac{\partial x^2}{\partial M^2} \right) n^1 R = (\text{CCF}^1_{-l} - \text{CCF}^2_{-l}) n^1 R, \qquad (14.16)$$

from which it is apparent that the attendant expenditure-switching effect may run either way, depending on the differences between shadow and market prices and on the tastes for goods other than leisure, as expressed by the difference between $\phi^1(\cdot)$ and $\phi^2(\cdot)$. Taking all effects together and recalling Eqn (14.12) once more, we may write the improvement in welfare ensuing from a small reform as

$$dW = \left[(\theta^1 - \text{CCF}^1_{-l}) - (\theta^2 - \text{CCF}^2_{-l}) \right] n^1 R \cdot dH^1. \qquad (14.17)$$

The intuition underlying this expression should now be familiar: the transfer of a rupee to a household of type h is socially valuable, but the resulting claim on resources through the associated increase in consumption is socially costly. Whether, in fact, $CCF^1_{-l} < CCF^2_{-l}$, thereby reinforcing the gains from a pure redistribution of income, depends very much not only on differences in tastes, but also on the government's choice of policies in general, a choice which lies at the root of the divergence between shadow prices and market prices.

In order to complete this discussion, we need to go beyond a 'small' reform to a more radical redistribution of land. This is easily accomplished in the benchmark case. For under the assumptions needed to support it, the consumption conversion factors will be independent of the distribution of landholdings and the changes in the vector of weights θ can be dealt with as in Section 13.6.2. The details are as follows. Let the utility function, construed as a social evaluation function of full income, take the isoelastic form

$$u(M) = \begin{cases} M_0 \cdot \left[\dfrac{(M/M_0)^\eta}{\eta + 1} - \eta \right], & \eta \neq 1, \\ M_0 \cdot [1 + \ln(M/M_0)], & \eta = 1, \end{cases} \tag{14.18}$$

where M_0 denotes the poverty line. This form yields the convenient normalization $u(M_0) = M_0$ and the value of θ corresponding to any M:

$$\theta(M) \equiv u'(M) = (M/M_0)^\eta, \tag{14.19}$$

so that $\theta(M_0) = 1$, as desired. Let the reform increase H^1 from H^1 Eqn (14.1) to H^2 Eqn (14.2). Recalling Eqn (14.5), we obtain the improvement in welfare resulting from such a redistribution by changing variables (to M) and integrating Eqn (14.17) over the associated limits of full income:

$$\begin{aligned} \Delta W &= n^1 \int_{w+RH^1(1)}^{w+RH^2(2)} \left[\theta(M^1) - CCF^1_{-l}\right] \cdot dM^1 \\ &\quad + n^2 \int_{w+R(H-n^1H^1(1))/n_2}^{w+R(H-n^1H^1(2))/n_2} \left[\theta(M^2) - CCF^2_{-l}\right] \cdot dM^2 \\ &= \frac{n^1 M_0}{\eta + 1} \cdot \left[\left(\frac{M^1(2)}{M_0}\right)^{\eta+1} - \left(\frac{M^1(1)}{M_0}\right)^{\eta+1} \right] \\ &\quad + \frac{n^2 M_0}{\eta + 1} \cdot \left[\left(\frac{M^2(2)}{M_0}\right)^{\eta+1} - \left(\frac{M^2(1)}{M_0}\right)^{\eta+1} \right] \\ &\quad + (CCF^1_{-l} - CCF^2_{-l}) \cdot n^1 R \cdot [H^1(2) - H^1(1)], \end{aligned} \tag{14.20}$$

where $M^h(k)$ denotes the income of a type-h household ($h = 1, 2$) before ($k = 1$) and after ($k = 2$) the reform, respectively, these being the limits of integration in Eqn (20).

14.4.2. Changes in Output

In the light of Section 14.2, the main reason for supposing that a reform might affect output is that factor intensities vary with the size of farm, and here it seems most promising to concentrate on the possibility that the costs of keeping hired hands to their tasks induce big farms to use less labour per hectare than small ones, which are likely to rely heavily on family labour. In order to keep matters very simple, we assume that the cultivator must spend some of his time supervising hired hands in such a way that they perform their jobs as well as family workers, and that this demand on his time grows with the number he hires. The total input of labour on his farm, given that he chooses l units of leisure and hires L_0 workers, is

$$L = \begin{cases} 1 - l & \text{if } L_0 = 0, \\ 1 - l + L_0 - s(L_0) & \text{if } L_0 > 0, \end{cases} \tag{14.21}$$

where the supervision function $s(\cdot)$ is assumed to be strictly increasing, strictly convex, and twice differentiable in L_0.

Let the household's preferences be defined over its net income from production,

$$x \equiv y - wL_0, \tag{14.22}$$

measured in terms of output (the numeraire) and leisure; and suppose, for simplicity, that these preferences are additively separable:

$$U(x, l) = \phi(x) + v(l), \tag{14.23}$$

where ϕ and v are both strictly increasing, strictly concave, and twice differentiable functions. Assume also that both functions satisfy the lower Inada condition, which ensures that both goods will be consumed in strictly positive quantities. The household's problem is to choose $l \in [0, 1]$ and $(x, L, L_0) \geq 0$ so as to

$$\text{maximize } U \quad \text{subject to: } y = f(L, H) \text{ and Eqn (14.21).} \tag{14.24}$$

Assuming an interior solution with respect to l, but not necessarily with respect to L_0, the first-order conditions may be written as

$$-\phi' \cdot f_1 + v' = 0 \tag{14.25}$$

and

$$(1 - s')f_1 - w \leq 0, \quad L_0 \geq 0 \text{ complementarily.} \tag{14.26}$$

By virtue of CRS, the MPL is decreasing in the labour–land ratio, so that in the case of an interior solution, the strict convexity of s in L_0 implies that L/H and L_0 will move in opposite directions in response to a change in the size of the holding: that is to say, labour intensity will decline with the size of holding. This conforms to intuition, for the marginal cost of hired labour is effectively $w/(1 - s')$, which is increasing in L_0. In the case where the household does not trade in the labour market, we have $(1 - s'(0)) \cdot f_1(1 - l, H) - w \leq 0$, so that in this regime an increase in H will bring about an increase in leisure (as argued in Section 14.2), and hence a fall in labour intensity.

With these preliminaries established, we turn to the effects of a redistribution of holdings, beginning with a full interior solution. We have, by the envelope theorem,

$$\mathrm{d}r = -f_1 \cdot \mathrm{d}l + f_2 \cdot \mathrm{d}H$$

and

$$\mathrm{d}L = -\mathrm{d}l + (1 - s') \cdot \mathrm{d}L_0.$$

Differentiating Eqn (14.25) and (14.26) totally, and then substituting for $\mathrm{d}r$ and $\mathrm{d}L$ as needed, some tedious algebra yields

$$(\phi'' \cdot f_1 + v'') \, \mathrm{d}l - [s''\phi'/(1 - s')] \, \mathrm{d}L_0 = (\phi'' \cdot f_1 f_2) \cdot \mathrm{d}H \tag{14.27}$$

and

$$-f_{11} \cdot \mathrm{d}l + [(1 - s')f_{11} - s''f_1/(1 - s')] \, \mathrm{d}L_0 = -f_{21} \cdot \mathrm{d}H. \tag{14.28}$$

Cross multiplying and rearranging to eliminate $\mathrm{d}H$, we obtain

$$\frac{\mathrm{d}l}{\mathrm{d}L_0} = \frac{f_{21}(s''/(1 - s')) \cdot \phi' + [(1 - s')f_{11} - s''f_1/(1 - s')]f_1 f_2 \cdot \phi''}{-f_{21}(\phi'' \cdot (f_1)^2 + v'') + f_{11}f_1 f_2 \cdot \phi''}, \tag{14.29}$$

from which it is seen that the assumptions on the technology and preferences imply that l and L_0 move in the same direction, and hence, from Eqn (14.27), that both are increasing in H. It is also clear from Eqn (14.29) that if s is not too strongly convex, then $dl/dL_0 < 1$. Recalling Eqn (14.26), the finding that L_0 is increasing in H yields the result that labour intensity, L/H, decreases as the farm becomes bigger, as the advocates of reform are keen to argue.

Now suppose that some land is redistributed from the 'commercial' farms making up group 2 to the 'family' farms comprising group 3, with land-less households continuing to supply their labour perfectly elastically at the wage rate w. A 'small' reform dH^2 (<0) of this sort will induce the following changes in the output produced by a member of each group, respectively:

$$dy^2 = \left[f_1^2 \cdot \left(-\frac{\partial l^2}{\partial H^2} + (1-s') \frac{\partial L_0^2}{\partial H^2} \right) + f_2^2 \right] \cdot dH^2 \tag{14.30}$$

and

$$dy^3 = -\frac{n^2}{n^3} \left[-f_1^3 \frac{\partial l^3}{\partial H^3} + f_2^3 \right] \cdot dH^2. \tag{14.31}$$

Hence, the resulting change in aggregate output will be

$$dY = n^2 \left[\left(f_1^3 \frac{\partial l^3}{\partial H^3} - f_1^2 \frac{\partial l^2}{\partial H^2} \right) + (1-s') \frac{\partial L_0^2}{\partial H^2} + (f_2^2 - f_2^3) \right] \cdot dH^2. \tag{14.32}$$

That the labour–land ratio on large farms is lower than on small ones implies that the marginal product of land is also lower on large farms: $f_2^3 - f_2^2 > 0$. Since the reform reduces the difference in holding sizes somewhat, it will induce an increase in aggregate output on this account. Its effect on labour inputs, however, is unclear a priori. The employment of hired hands on the commercial farms will certainly fall, as will the inputs of family labour on family farms; the only offsetting factor is a less leisured existence for the members of households owning commercial farms. As in the rather different setting analysed in Section 14.2, further assumptions are needed if one is to reach the unambiguous conclusion that aggregate output will surely rise as a result of such a reform.

The next step is to evaluate the reform's effects on social welfare. The changes in the households' consumption bundles are, respectively,

$$(-f_1^2 dl^2 + f_2^2 dH^2, dl^2) \quad \text{and}$$
$$(-f_1^3 \cdot (\partial l^3/\partial H^3) + f_2^3, \partial l^3/\partial H^3) \cdot (-(n^2/n^3) \cdot dH^2).$$

Noting from Eqn (14.25) that the MRS is f_1, and neglecting the (small) change therein induced by the reform, the corresponding equivalent variations are seen to be $f_2^2\, dH^2$ and $-(n^2/n^3)f_2^3\, dH^2$, respectively. In order to calculate the change in welfare, we resort to the now familiar device of treating the reform as a public sector undertaking that trades at shadow prices and makes transfers to the private sector. As in the analysis of the Muda project in Section 13.6, the endowments of farming households are treated as fixed factors, which are not traded outside the undertaking. Assuming that shadow prices do not change in response to a small reform, and recalling that the changes in consumption must also be allowed for, we then obtain

$$\Delta W = (\pi \cdot dY - \pi_L \cdot dL_0) + [(\theta^2 - \pi)f_2^2 - (\theta^3 - \pi)f_2^3]n^2 \cdot dH^2, \quad (14.33)$$

where π is the shadow price of output, π_L is the shadow wage rate, and $\theta^3 > \theta^2$. Comparing this expression with Eqn (14.17), its benchmark counterpart, observe that the difference between the marginal products of land reinforces the higher social weight accorded to group 3 than to group 2. The extension to cover the case where net income is spent on a bundle of commodities is readily accomplished along the lines laid out in Section 14.4.1, and is left as an exercise to the reader.

If the reform is large, the approximations used in deriving Eqn (14.33) will no longer be defensible, and a full-scale model of the agrarian sector will be needed to estimate the changes in inputs, outputs, and consumption, as in the case of the Muda project. The possibility that the rural wage rate will change significantly cannot be ruled out, and if it does so, the shadow wage rate and hence the shadow prices of non-tradables must be re-estimated.

14.5. Tenancy

In regulating individual tenancies, it is essential to distinguish between the reallocation of rents associated with ownership and the function played by tenancy in allocating resources. Consider, for example, the imposition of a ceiling on market rents that results in, or intensifies, excess demand for tenancies. Ignoring general equilibrium effects, this intervention will redistribute income in favour of those who are fortunate enough to obtain tenancies on regulated terms. By inducing landlords to resume some of their tenancies for direct cultivation, however, the measure will cause at least some erstwhile tenants to suffer as a result—unless they were receiving the same utility they could have obtained in alternative employment. If both tenancies and tenants turn over frequently, this will even out in the long run, though the effects of exacerbated excess demand will still be at work in the background. In any event, there is no direct abridgement of property rights in this case.

Suppose, however, that the aim of legislation is to redistribute income in favour of incumbent tenants in proportion to the rents that they currently pay. Then a binding ceiling on rents must be accompanied by the granting of security of tenure to all those who hold tenancies. Since this security yields a stream of economic rents to the tenant, granting it is tantamount to giving him limited ownership rights in the tenancy, the value of which is measured by how much the landlord is willing to pay him to quit the lease or, if subtenancy can be practised without much risk, how much others would be prepared to pay to assume the lease themselves. If such rights are also inheritable, the landlord's original rights will be further eroded, and the regulation of contracts between landlords and tenants will more closely approach the ideal of a redistribution of pure individual rights in land.

The problem with a great deal of tenancy legislation is precisely that it has sought to transfer ownership-like rights to tenants by the back door, without heed to its potentially harmful effects on the functioning of the market for tenancies. Occasionally, as in the Philippines (Hayami and Otsuka, 1993), or more recently in West Bengal (Subbarao, 1985), there has been some success on the first score. More often than not, however, such legislation has been honoured mainly in the breach, for reasons that should now be clear. Evasion and avoidance of these provisions of the law have also affected the functioning of the market for tenancies, usually for the worse. Since tenancy is a potentially useful institution, any discussion of how to reform and regulate it should therefore draw a sharp distinction between its role as an allocative mechanism and its potential as an instrument for redistributing individual rights to land and the rents land generates.

In order to establish how, if at all, tenancy should be regulated, it is necessary to understand what function tenancy performs and how well it does so in the various circumstances in which it is found. It will be argued that tenancy is a response to particular economic conditions and that its existence may provide important opportunities for the poor to improve their lot, not only statically, when endowments and skills are given, but also dynamically, as opportunities to enhance endowments and skills arise. The analysis that follows is almost unswervingly partial equilibrium in character: 'second-best' considerations remind us, however, that if other markets are imperfect or absent, then interventions in the market for tenancies need not reduce welfare, and may even improve it. At present, the analysis of general equilibrium systems with incomplete markets has yielded rather little in the way of practical guidance as to how erroneous partial equilibrium analysis of particular configurations is likely to be, so that the conclusions drawn below should be viewed with some caution.

14.5.1. The Static Argument

Consider, as a benchmark, a competitive economy with a complete set of contingent markets. In this case, loosely speaking, it does not matter whether land hires labour (wage employment) or labour hires land (fixed rent tenancy). The economy will be productively efficient and the distribution of income will be independent of the leasing arrangements under which production is organized.

In practice, of course, there are egregious departures from this case, many markets being imperfect or wholly absent, usually for reasons stemming from asymmetric information. Notable among them are the markets for insurance, but sometimes also those for husbandry and managerial skills, and even the services of draught animals. If the market for land as an asset were well developed, which would surely require that capital markets function well, sales and purchases would move land to the complementary factors that are very imperfectly, if at all, tradable, thereby tending to reduce differences in marginal products across farms. In reality, however, the market for land as an asset is often thin (Binswanger and Rosenzweig, 1986), to which the emergence of tenancy is a natural response.

The absence of insurance and other markets encourages tenancy in various forms. By itself, an active spot market for land sales will not be fully equivalent to a system of fixed rent tenancies if there is risk. For such an equivalence to hold, there must also be a set of futures markets for the sale of land, in which case renting a hectare of land will be effectively the same as purchasing a hectare of land for cultivation on the spot market and selling it forward for delivery after the harvest at a known price. In the absence of insurance markets, moreover, fixed rent tenancies will not always permit the exploitation of all opportunities for spreading the risks arising from production. If, for example, wages are risky and imperfectly correlated with output (Newbery, 1977), or if the markets for farming skills or the services of draught animals are absent (Bell, 1989), then sharecropping will emerge alongside fixed rent tenancy.

Thus, contractual diversity is a response to a risky environment when direct arrangements for the provision of insurance are not available.

This line of reasoning implicitly emphasizes the possibility that tenancy may promote (constrained) efficiency in second-best environments. Note, however, that there is no direct redistribution of economic rents in this story. Nor can there be any general presumption that the poor, who usually have little land, will rent land from the rich, who usually have a lot. For tastes for risk bearing may be distributed in such a way as to induce small farmers to rent out their land to large farmers. If poorer households do benefit from the existence of tenancy in such settings, they will do so because there are more extensive and remunerative opportunities for risk spreading and a fuller utilization of family resources under tenancy than under wage employment or the cultivation of their (relatively) small plots alone.

Turning to the empirical evidence concerning how well tenancy performs as a mechanism for allocating resources, one notable study is that of Palanpur village in north-west India by Bliss and Stern (1981) in 1974–5, with a follow-up by Drèze and Mukherjee (1989) in 1983–4. To sum up their findings, first, there were no significant differences in yields and input intensities between land under owner cultivation and land under tenancy, a result consistent with resource allocation being (constrained) efficient. Second, the form of tenancy was sharecropping (with cost sharing for some inputs), an arrangement which is inherently susceptible to incentive problems where the use of variable inputs as a whole is concerned. That households chose sharecropping despite this potential drawback suggests that tenancy in Palanpur is a response to the lack of full insurance as well as other markets, since long term, fixed rent tenancy would avoid incentive problems altogether. Third, in the face of changing conditions, fifty-fifty sharecropping (with provisions for cost sharing) was nevertheless flexible enough for mutually profitable trade to occur. Tenancy had an equalizing effect on the distribution of operational landholdings in 1974–5, but a concentrating effect in 1983–4, when some smaller owners were renting out their land to more efficient and often larger landholders (Lanjouw and Stern, 1993).

The evidence from South Asia as a whole concerning the efficiency of resource allocation under share tenancy is mixed, in part because the influence of other factors affecting farming technique and performance, such as access to credit, willingness to bear risk, and farming and husbandry skills, is not always properly controlled for. The best way of doing so is to compare input intensities and yields on owned and leased plots farmed by the same individual, so that these fixed effects can be removed. Among such studies, Bell (1977) for Bihar, Hossain (1977) for Bangladesh, and Shaban (1987) for the Deccan plateau found significant differences, whereas Chakravarty and Rudra (1973) found none in the case of West Bengal. Another survey of more recent studies of Asian economies (Otsuka and Hayami, 1988) also reveals rather mixed findings. It seems fair to conclude that the performance of share tenancy is quite often constrained efficient, but occasionally a bit dismal, when landlords cannot find a cheap solution to the incentive problem. Whether there is constrained efficiency or not, however, the role of share tenancy in a static system of incomplete markets appears to be useful. For it provides an inducement to risk-averse individuals to supply family resources and skills to cultivation, as opposed to unskilled wage employment, in which such skills and resources are of no account, and which is usually less remunerative. It is still possible, however, that such simple intuition is undermined by the reallocation of resources elsewhere that exploiting sharecropping opportunities brings about.

14.5.2. The Dynamic Argument

Tenancy can also serve as a vehicle for the accumulation of assets and skills by those who start out with little of either. In principle, therefore, it provides opportunities for individual mobility. Contracts are sometimes struck, for example, between the aged (as landlords) and mature, successful owner cultivators, who wish to take on additional land. Earlier in their careers, the latter may have worked on the family's farm as unpaid labourers and supplemented their incomes by taking on small tenancies from relatives. These patterns point, therefore, not only to a potentially concentrated pattern of operational holdings, but also to a life-cycle process (Chayanov, 1966). The life-cycle process, in turn, brings to mind the 'agricultural ladder' hypothesis suggested by studies of US agriculture in the nineteenth century (Spillman, 1919; Reid, 1974). Young, relatively poor individuals begin as labourers and acquire sufficient skills and capital through experience, work, and saving to progress through the succeeding stages of share tenancy, fixed rent tenancy, and, with good fortune, outright ownership. Although it cannot be claimed that full mobility on this scale is open to all individuals in all agrarian systems, this hypothesis points to the opportunities created by tenancy, not only for the employment of existing family factors, but also for the accumulation of human and physical capital by those individuals who begin with little but labour power and some promise as farmers. These arguments support the contention that tenancy, as a market response, is neither inherently nor inevitably damaging to the interests of the poor. For some, indeed, it may offer the best avenue out of poverty. That avenue can, however, be blocked, if, as in the Philippines and West Bengal, one cohort of tenants is granted ownership-like rights; for owners will then resume land to cultivate themselves, thereby excluding later cohorts of would-be tenants. In West Bengal, the reform has further exacerbated this problem by specifically prohibiting the subleasing of registered tenancies. Tenancy legislation in some other countries has arguably had similar effects for similar reasons.

14.5.3. Policy

What scope does this conclusion leave for public intervention in tenancy markets? The impulse to regulate stems in part from the perception that individual landlords possess market power, which they use to exploit their tenants. This raises a second question: what can, and should, be done to improve the bargain struck by tenants? Taking these questions in turn, it should now be clear that attempts to redistribute property rights through the back door by regulating the terms of tenancy are often doomed to failure. They are also harmful to the extent that they impede tenancy in the performance of its proper functions—albeit with the usual second-best caveat. Turning to the second question, in the nature of things the market for tenancies is local, in the sense that the actual and potential participants are drawn from a limited area, usually the village in which the land is located and perhaps its neighbours. If, as in Palanpur, the ownership of land is not very heavily concentrated, the market for tenancies may work rather well, and no intervention seems called for. If, however, village life is dominated by one or two rural tyrants, who ruthlessly wield their market power and engage in various forms of extra-economic coercion, then something should be done to curb them.

The discussion of the political economy of land reform in Section 14.6 suggests that while getting rid of rural tyrants by an assault on their property rights is usually possible only in rather special circumstances, an indirect approach may favour tenants at their expense, and even improve efficiency into the bargain. Suppose tenants (and labourers) are pushed down to their reservation levels of utility by landlords who make astute use of the instruments available to them. These reservation levels may be set by employment opportunities outside the village or the needs of mere subsistence. In either case, guaranteed public employment at remunerative wages in, say, rural works programmes would improve tenants' bargaining power and hence the terms of their tenancy contracts. Landlords might respond by resuming some of their land for self-cultivation, but this is not certain, since wage rates will rise. At any rate, they would have no particular incentive to refuse to offer tenancy contracts at all, as they would in the case where threatening but incompletely enforceable legislation promising 'rights to the tiller' is enacted. They might attempt to subvert rural works programmes to their own advantage by capturing the mechanisms of job recruitment and using recruitment as a source of patronage. That possibility cannot be dismissed, but neither is it a certainty. Under the right circumstances, therefore, intervention in the labour market may weaken the power of rural tyrants while leaving substantially intact the improvements in resource allocation and individual mobility that the existence of a market in tenancies makes possible.

14.6. The Political Economy of Land Reform in Historical Perspective

Much of the discussion thus far savours of the deliberations of the Platonic 'guardians of the state'. In fact, land reform is an intensely political matter, involving as it does sharply conflicting interests. Indeed, the ownership of land reflects and underpins social power and structure in agrarian economies, so that changes in the pattern of ownership necessarily involve changes in society itself. The very notion of public intervention as an autonomous action is, therefore, deeply problematic.

14.6.1. War, Revolution, and Liberation

Most important land reforms in the twentieth century occurred in rather special and often catastrophic circumstances. In the Soviet Union and China, foreign invasion preceded and paved the way for social revolution and the destruction of the old agrarian order. The peasant mode of production intensified in the immediate wake of these upheavals, and the central authorities imposed wholesale collectivization only when power had been completely secured. In Eastern Europe, social revolution and the remaking of the agrarian structure were imposed by an army of occupation; but wholesale collectivization was not the rule. Instead, a substantial sector of private holdings, distributed in an egalitarian pattern, emerged to create a dual structure of private and collective forms. Defeat in war or occupation also led to land reforms in some notable capitalist countries. In Japan, the Republic of Korea, and Taiwan, a redistribution of individual rights was imposed on a landed class rendered impotent by the collapse of a state that had reflected its power and interests. In these societies, foreign armies did much to bring about the initial conditions favourable to the rapid growth with equity that followed.

The remaining instances of social revolution in smaller countries—Cuba, Egypt, Ethiopia, Nicaragua, and Vietnam—are interesting in that revolution was brought about by indigenous forces. Except for Vietnam, the regimes overthrown were also indigenous and reflected societies marked by great inequality in the holdings of land and wealth. With the exception of Egypt, all followed the example of the Soviet Union and China in collectivizing land substantially or completely, sometimes in the form of state farms, whose workers received a regulated wage. The revolution that overthrew the Egyptian monarchy in 1952 was more nationalist than socialist; more than half of the land expropriated was formerly in the possession of the monarchy (Warriner, 1969: 413), all of it in the form of large estates. Although individual rights were assigned to the beneficiaries, some collective features were retained with a view to improving efficiency.

Elsewhere, nationalist movements began their successful struggles to throw off colonial rule in much of Asia and Africa in the aftermath of the Second World War. These successes created opportunities to remake the agrarian order, particularly in countries in which there were significant European settlements (Kenya and Zimbabwe) or foreign plantations (Indonesia, Malaysia, and Sri Lanka), or in which some domestic landed classes were perceived to be allied with colonial rulers (India). These opportunities were sometimes fleeting, being the products of turmoil and a temporary loss of confidence and power on the part of landed interests, and were not always fully seized. In India, for example, the abolition of *zamindari* (tax intermediary) interests worked to the advantage of the upper and middle sections of the peasantry, which had provided the base of support for the nationalist movement. One result was a strongly differentiated peasantry, the upper strata of which have been able to block most subsequent efforts at more radical reform. The overthrow of Marcos's regime in the Philippines also created the conditions of fluidity and turmoil that would have made a bold stroke politically possible. In the event, the opportunity was squandered, and landed interests soon began to reassert themselves in the new government.

What these cases have in common is that the opportunities to redistribute property rights in land, whether they were seized or not, arose from social upheavals that are not normally thought of as policy interventions by an autonomous and stable central authority. The same applies, moreover, to the full-scale reversals of collectivization that followed the fall of the Soviet Union.

14.6.2. 'Normal' times

What happens when the social and political order is fairly secure? The following experiences—in Colombia, the Philippines, and Peru—illustrate some important aspects of the political economy of agrarian reformism,[4] the diverse forms intervention may take, and the responses of those directly affected.

The first is the failure of such reform in Colombia, as described and analysed by de Janvry and Sadoulet (1993). Under a law passed in 1936, potentially productive but poorly cultivated or abandoned land on large holdings was to be expropriated after a grace period of ten to fifteen years. Under the goad of this threat, land productivity rose for a time, to the satisfaction of the urban interests that had pressed for the law, and little land was expropriated. Shortly after the Second World War, there began a period of strife and virtual civil war known as 'La Violencia', which hastened the destruction of traditional social relations on the haciendas and greatly weakened the old agrarian oligarchy.

The power-sharing pact between the liberals and conservatives that brought about peace ushered in a new phase of land reform, which envisaged the creation of a family farm sector, with payment of full compensation to existing landholders in the event of expropriation. Implementation turned out to be very limited. One important reason was political pressure from landed interests and certain urban groups, which saw to it that subsidized inputs were captured by large-scale farms. As a result, their land values increased so much that large-scale expropriation with full compensation became fiscally impossible. Whether landed interests anticipated this consequence of selective subsidies is unclear. In any event, by 1972, only 1.5 per cent of the area of all large farms had been redistributed, and shortly thereafter there was a return to the principle of Law 200 of 1936.

---

[4] Reformism is the doctrine that social change can be pursued and achieved short of a social revolution. Perhaps its most eloquent advocate is Hirschman (1963).

In this third phase, the complementary, and perhaps more important policy was an ambitious rural development program, which was intended to serve family farms (whose numbers had grown somewhat) as well as the large-scale sector. While rural development had apparently become the basis for a coalition of urban, landlord, and family farming interests, the landless and marginal farmers remained excluded, both politically and economically. Continued guerrilla warfare and land invasions by these groups was the predictable and enduring outcome.

The Philippines provides a case involving the transfer of property rights through tenancy legislation. Under the proclamation (and partial enforcement) of Presidential Decree 27 in 1972, sharecroppers were converted into leaseholders or owners. The land rent or amortization payment was fixed at 25 per cent of annual rice yields, averaged over three normal years preceding the year in which the programme went into effect. In itself, the limitation of rents below market-clearing levels transferred ownership-like rights and economic rents to those tenants who managed to get their claims registered. As it turned out, the redistributive force of the decree was greatly increased by a more or less simultaneous development. Public investment in irrigation in central Luzon had induced a shift from single to double cropping in the 1970s. The shift was accompanied by the diffusion of new varieties and a more intensive use of farm chemicals, both promoted by public policies. As a result, paddy yields more than doubled, from less than two tons per hectare in the early 1970s to about four tons in the mid-1980s (Hayami and Otsuka, 1993). Such an improvement in land productivity would almost certainly have led to a considerable increase in market rents. For registered tenants, therefore, the fact that Decree 27 was followed by public investment produced a large extra windfall, though it seems doubtful that this was part of the government's design.

The landlords' failure to get the terms of the decree changed as these additional and, for them, adverse consequences became clear is puzzling: 25 per cent of two tons per hectare is only 12.5 per cent of four tons per hectare, a difference that seems too large for the outcome to be assigned to inertia. Whatever be the reason, landlords took defensive action: they began to substitute permanent labourers for sharecroppers in order to protect their ownership rights in the lands that remained to them (ibid.). Thus, an important repercussion of this particular legislation and technical change on property rights was to inhibit tenancy over the longer run, which, as has been argued in Section 14.5, was probably damaging to the rest of the poor.

The third case is notable for a sequence of reforms that, first, col-
lectivized individual property rights, which had been concentrated in
very few hands, and then, a decade or so later, distributed all collective land to members in the form of individual properties. This happened
in Peru, starting in 1969, after a revolutionary government had come to
power through a coup. In the coastal zone, which was well developed
and productive, nearly all private holdings of more than 150 hectares
were eliminated and replaced by labour-managed agricultural production
co-operatives. The typical co-operative had 200 members and close to
1000 hectares.

Carter (1993) argues that there were reasons besides mere ideology for
maintaining the original scale of the enterprises. The beneficiaries of the
reform were not tenants but workers, whose managerial and husbandry
skills were probably too limited at the outset for them to farm individual
holdings well. He also hints at, but does not decisively establish, the
existence of technical economies of scale. As it turned out, however,
most of the enterprises were unable to induce their members to work
hard, and they resorted so heavily to hiring permanent workers that, by
1981, the ratio of land to (permanent) labour had fallen by a quarter.
The problem of securing sufficient effort, according to Carter, was not
so much the difficulty of monitoring the length and intensity of individuals' efforts, as the lack of authority to enforce the rules of payment.
In any event, although some enterprises did elicit adequate effort from
their members, most did not, with dismal consequences for productivity.
Parcelacion, or the breaking up of larger holdings into smaller parcels,
was apparently their members' collective response to this unsolved problem of collective organization, and the move went unchallenged by the
central state.

This rapid disintegration of a collective form of organization has paral-
lels elsewhere. In China, the peasants began to farm individually on their
own initiative in the early 1980s and met with no serious resistance from
the government. They have since become individual leaseholders from the
state on terms close to outright ownership, and subleasing is also beginning to appear. In Tanzania, following the failure of the *Ujamaa* villages,
and in Vietnam, governments have made efforts to grant long-term leases
to individual farmers. Similar proposals were openly debated in the Soviet
Union before its collapse, and limited steps were taken to implement them
even before the successor states emerged. Three generations have passed
since Stalin's collectivization, however, so it is doubtful whether there are
the specific human capital and skills that are needed to make individual

family farming an initial success. The security offered by the old system may be preferred to the risky prospect of earning a higher expected income as a tenant of the state.

Surveying this turbulent period of history, it can be argued that the path from concentrated individual property rights to collective farms and thence to a fairly egalitarian distribution of individual rights may have entailed an unnecessary, or at least unnecessarily protracted, detour into collectivism. Even so, the fact remains that many of those who had little or no land at the outset are now actual or virtual owners, with an exclusive claim on the economic rents yielded by their new holdings.

14.7. The Prospects for Reformism

If reform—or the failure to reform—is an endogenous outcome, what scope is left for reformism? This question appears to be especially nettlesome in the case of land reform, for some kind of social upheaval preceded a remaking of the agrarian order in virtually all of the examples just discussed. In this domain, therefore, the outlook for reformist policies in normal times is not immediately encouraging. We begin by examining the political economy of the status quo, and then turn to how it might be undone to the advantage of the poor.

As usually conceived, redistributive land reforms do not provide for compensation at current market value to the original owners, who therefore understandably oppose them. If this group is numerically small, its power to resist must derive from its control over the apparatus of the state, including the legislature, the army, the police, and the judiciary. Such cases are not unknown. Some scholars claim, however, that it is more common for the dominant landed class to form an (uneasy) alliance with certain urban groups (Lipton, 1977). Urban capitalists and workers in the organized sector have a common interest in cheap and assured supplies of food and raw materials. So does the government, whose hold on power a disaffected urban populace can readily threaten. Since the marketed surplus (in the form of food and commercial crops) per hectare is usually higher on large farms than on small ones, these groups benefit in some measure from an unequal distribution of landholdings. This, the argument runs, is the basis for a coalition of the rural well-to-do with a fairly wide sector of urban society. The deal usually involves relatively low agricultural prices coupled with highly selective subsidies to large farms, the main fiscal burden of which falls on the groups outside the coalition.

In this situation, the opposition to redistributive reforms is much broader than a rural oligarchy, although it has several potential lines of fissure. Colombia, as de Janvry and Sadoulet (1993) describe it, is a good exemplar. In Asia and parts of Africa, the reformers' problem appears even less tractable because the dominant landed class is not a rural oligarchy, but a large group of relatively rich peasants who are politically active and who 'secure' the countryside for the parties they support. They, too, would appear to have considerable power to resist expropriation without full compensation.

The prospects of pushing though a reform against such opposition have drawn widely differing assessments. Binswanger and Elgin (1988), for example, view the status quo coalition as so stable as to constitute an almost insuperable obstacle to any reform with an element of confiscation. They also point to the effects of selective subsidies to large farms on the price of land, which allegedly exceeds the capitalized value of the services the land would produce in the hands of the poor if the subsidies were discontinued as part of the reform. This, they argue, makes its purchase at current values either unattractive to the poor or, if the purchase is sufficiently subsidized, intolerably burdensome to the exchequer. The contrary view points to the acute pressure on land arising from population growth, particularly in those densely settled regions where technical change in agriculture is sluggish and not especially labour-intensive. Lipton (1995) argues that this will generate strong political pressures and reinstate redistributive reform to a prominent place in discussions of how to improve the lot of the poor.

This latter prognosis is open to dispute on several grounds. First, there is no conclusive evidence that population growth concentrates the ownership of land in fewer hands even as the size of the average holding shrinks. In India, for example, the distribution of ownership holdings became somewhat more equal over the period 1955–72, and the proportion of households without any land fell strikingly, from 23 to 10 per cent, even while the rural population was growing at an annual rate of about 2 per cent (Sanyal, 1988: 150). If such inequality does not increase, it is not clear why political and social unrest stemming from land hunger should necessarily intensify. Second, population growth may be fully offset by technical progress in agriculture, as has happened in many countries. Indeed, if technical progress has a sufficiently land-augmenting character and urbanization proceeds fairly rapidly, the effective supply of land may increase more rapidly than the rural population. Although technical progress can also be labour-saving, which would be damaging to the rural poor, such a bias is not inevitable and its character may be influenced by public policy. Third, there is the simple fact that populations have been swarming for at least half a century, in densely and sparsely settled regions alike. Yet the agrarian structures and economies of most countries have managed to accommodate the pressures thus generated, and land reform has failed to re-emerge as a pressing political issue. Fourth, many governments have become wary of making a direct assault on property rights in any form, for fear of its potentially adverse effects on investment and growth in the long run. This appears to be a weighty consideration, even in South Africa, with its history of large-scale and illegal dispossession of black farmers almost a century ago and the subsequent oppression of Apartheid (Deininger, 1999).

If, therefore, population growth does not make land reform inevitable, are any reformist policies feasible? Property rights might be considered sacrosanct, but the citizenry of most countries accepts the need for taxation, however grudgingly. Thus, taxes on factors, for example, are usually viewed as legitimate, whereas 'confiscation' of property is not. Yet there is no formal difference between having to pay taxes on the value of a property and having the same proportion of the property confiscated. That such a distinction rules in the public's mind happily opens the door to land reform through taxation, to the extent that the price of land is influenced by tax policy. There is a parallel here between the political economy of so-called structural adjustment programmes and that of land reform. For both, the trick is to find a way of distributing the burden in a manner acceptable to the contending parties.

A clear conclusion to be drawn from the foregoing account is that dismantling the systems of selective subsidies and other tax provisions favourable to large landholders is an essential first step, which would make land a less attractive asset to them but not to the poor. A programme of land reform, whether of the classic kind or mediated through the market, would be announced and launched only after the effects of the tax reform were largely realized. This tax reform could, and should, be advocated on the grounds that the distortionary losses resulting from these policies is large and the need for additional (net) public revenue is pressing. A more courageous government could, and should, impart a further turn to the screw by introducing a progressive land tax, whereby a flat rate with an exemption limit has the virtue of simplicity and leaves fewer opportunities for wrangling over loopholes.

A rather conservative programme might stipulate the following. All land in excess of a certain ceiling, adjusted for quality, would be subject to compulsory purchase at fair market value, that is, at the relatively depressed prices prevailing after the tax reform. In order to finance the purchase, the beneficiaries of the land reform would make annual payments to the government, which, in turn, would issue bonds to those whose land was subject to compulsory purchase. In order to secure the value of these compensatory payments, especially if the secondary market for government paper is not well developed, the bonds could be indexed. At the same time, the payments by the beneficiaries need not equal the payments to the former landholders; for the tax reform will have generated additional net public revenues. This is not quite the end of the story, however, for the removal of subsidies on inputs may increase the price of food and so arouse the opposition of many sections of the urban population. In view of the losses sustained by the rural rich, this outcome may be barely acceptable politically. If it is not, some or all of the savings from dismantling the system of selective subsidies to the rural rich will have to be used to placate the urban interests in question. To that extent, the transfer of land to the beneficiaries of the land reform would be on somewhat less favourable terms.

Under the 'market' solution, there would, of course, be no compulsory purchases. Instead, the fiscal savings flowing from the tax reform would be used to subsidize purchases of land by qualified beneficiaries, either directly, or indirectly through the schedule of their mortgage payments. The area of land transferred would be determined by the particular provisions of the tax reform and the schedule of subsidies for beneficiaries. Under a system of compulsory purchase, in contrast, the ceiling must be chosen such that it can be financed from the revenues yielded by the tax reform and other sources.

At the first round, the losses sustained by the rural rich would be limited to the capital losses on their landholdings induced by the tax reform. As emphasized in Sections 14.2 and 14.4, however, there are also general equilibrium effects to be considered; for any changes in taxes and subsidies, coupled with a redistribution of ownership rights, will have an effect on factor and goods prices. Hence, it is not so clear who will bear the ultimate burden of the tax.

Similar considerations would arise if the sequence were supported by a structural adjustment loan from an international agency. Part of the loan could be used to cover certain hidden costs of the land reform, for example, those arising from the need to carry out surveys, register new titles, and build new infrastructure. If the beneficiaries were not charged for these services, they would receive a covert subsidy. On the other side, payments of debt service would be made out of general tax revenues, again with a pattern of economic incidence which is unclear a priori. Indeed, the fact that it is unclear and may depart strongly from the statutory incidence of the tax system is something of a virtue. For it may be possible to find an outcome that is acceptable as presented to the contending parties, yet in reality favours those who are comparatively poor.

14.8. Summary

The principal impulse behind programmes of land reform has been, and remains, the worthy goal of reducing rural poverty. The classic route is the enactment of legislation under which individual property rights in land would be transferred from well-to-do landholders to small family farms, tenants, and landless workers. In recent years, a so-called 'market' approach has been increasingly promoted, under which a like pattern of transfers would arise from voluntary trade, with the (poor) purchasers receiving large subsidies to enable them to complete the deal. Conscious of the potential costs of such programmes, advocates of both approaches argue that output and efficiency would also rise in the wake of such a redistribution, thereby sealing the case for it. The latter claim has certainly not gone uncontested, however. First, it is not difficult to construct plausible, a priori arguments that aggregate output might fall, leisure being almost surely a normal good in consumption, even for beneficiaries who are poor. Second, the empirical evidence, when carefully scrutinized, is also far from generally compelling.

If the claim that such reforms invariably promote improvements in output and efficiency is thrown into doubt, concerns about their fiscal effects become all the sharper, especially when the losers are to receive compensation at full market value. Yet these are but some of the elements, albeit important ones, of a full welfare analysis of any reform in a distortion-ridden economy, in which claims about efficiency require support from calculations at shadow prices. In the literature dealing with land reform, very little attention has been paid to this central point, a neglect that this chapter has sought to redress by treating a land reform as a project to be evaluated using the apparatus developed in earlier chapters.

Turning to the vexed political economy of such reforms, history suggests that a substantial redistribution of individual property rights is most likely to occur in the wake of a social upheaval. Such opportunities should, therefore, be seized at once, or the chance will be lost. In normal times, the prospects for reform look far less promising, and bringing them off will require luck as well as skill in finding an acceptable distribution of burdens among the contending parties. Here, an indirect approach through the tax system has much to commend it. The idea is to begin with a tax reform that dismantles the distortionary provisions favouring large farms in order to bring about a fall in the price of land, and only then to announce the land reform. The terms of the latter could be more or less closely tied to 'fair' market prices ruling after the tax reform has been fully implemented, if it is important to fend off the charge that land reform is an attack on property rights. A courageous government should also introduce a progressive land tax in order to give the whole process a further shove in the same direction, while raising valuable revenue into the bargain.

As for tenancy, there are strong arguments that it is a socially useful institution, even if no direct redistribution occurs. The widespread attempts to use tenancy legislation as a camouflaged means of redistributing individual ownership rights have generally failed for the very reasons that direct redistribution has generally failed. These attempts have, moreover, been positively harmful, by discouraging tenancy and otherwise distorting the way in which the markets for tenancies function. If landlords possess market power, other forms of intervention to curb it, such as the provision of improved employment opportunities, are probably superior to most current tenancy legislation, and they would also be a boon to the landless, who rarely benefit directly from the redistribution of property rights.

Recommended Reading

There is a wealth of interesting material on land reform, tenancy, and related aspects of taxation in Hoff et al. (1993), on which this Chapter has liberally drawn. A classic reference on land reform, written in the 'institutionalist' tradition, is Warriner (1969). For a more recent assessment of the experience of land reform, combined with tireless advocacy, see Lipton (1995). A comprehensive treatment of the subject is provided by Binswanger et al. (1995).

Exercises

1. A closed two-class farming community produces grain by means of land (H), labour (L), and a composite input of draught animals and

'management' (m). The technology is Cobb–Douglas:

$$y = H^{\alpha_1} L^{\alpha_2} m^{\alpha_3} \quad (\alpha_1 + \alpha_2 + \alpha_3 = 1),$$

where y denotes the level of output yielded by the input bundle (H, L, m). The endowments of a household of type $h \ (= 1, 2)$ are, respectively,

$$\omega^1 = (1, 1, 1) \quad \text{and} \quad \omega^2 = (3, 1, 2),$$

there being seventy-five households of type 1 and twenty-five of type 2. All endowments are supplied completely inelastically. Let each market, should it exist, be perfect. In the case where $\alpha_1 = 0.5, \alpha_2 = 0.3, \alpha_3 = 0.2$, find outputs, incomes, and factor prices (if any) when:

(a) there is complete autarky within the community;
(b) there is only a labour market;
(c) there are only labour and tenancy markets; and
(d) all factor markets exist.

Repeat for the case where $\alpha = 0.25, \alpha_2 = 0.5, \alpha_3 = 0.25$.

Now suppose, instead, that the community is no longer closed where the labour market is concerned. If employment opportunities are available outside the community at the parametric wage rate of 0.5, repeat the relevant parts of both of the above cases. Discuss the merits of banning tenancy in the light of your results.

15. Small-Scale Credit

The campaign to raise agricultural productivity and alleviate rural poverty through land reform in the broad sense has often been accompanied—or succeeded—by attempts to remake the financial system in such a way as to serve the same ends. In practice, the latter interventions have generally been much more ambitious in scope and scale, but not necessarily more successful. The original characters here are the peasant, the petty producer, the small trader, and their principal antagonist, the traditional moneylender; and the play is about their awkward and tense relationship. The moneylender is almost invariably cast as the villain of the piece. His grasping nature, his usurious terms, his envious eye for any of his client's goods or forms of wealth that might serve as collateral—all these are the stuff of both literature and popular folklore. In the course of successful economic development over the long run, he disappears from the scene anyway. Yet a salient feature of public policy towards credit markets in many countries has been a determined attempt to speed up his departure.

Various means have been employed for this purpose. The direct interventions include ceilings on interest rates, restrictions on the use of collateral to secure loans, prohibitions on lending to particular groups, and even an outright ban on moneylending. The indirect ones fall under the general rubric of financial development, and some of them belong in a programme of financial repression:[1] accelerated development of the deposit banking system, its forced spread into rural areas, and credit and interest rate controls designed to channel funds (and subsidies) to particular groups and undertakings. Given the predictable difficulties of enforcing the direct measures, the task of putting the moneylender in his place—and ultimately out of business—has perforce fallen to the indirect ones.

The snag in all this is that the moneylender has not kept to the script, at least as governments have written it. The principal reason for this is that formal credit institutions, which are supposed to displace him, are rarely up to the role envisaged for them. Weighed down by regulations, inefficient in their operations as intermediaries, plagued by high rates of default, and forced to resort to rationing in the face of heavy excess demand for

---

[1] The memorable phrase 'financial repression' was coined by McKinnon (1973) to describe how governments in most LDCs have, in his view, abused the financial system in order to generate resources for state activities in particular and to influence resource allocation in general.

loans, formal lenders have generally failed to push traditional lenders to the margins of the market. The traditional lender, indeed, has usually accommodated quite successfully to the arrival of a local branch of a bank. He often obtains its cheap credit to augment his own loanable funds, and when his clients have also obtained a bank loan, he often enjoys implicit debt seniority. Hence, any discussion of public policy in this domain must proceed from an understanding of the interplay between the formal and informal segments of the market for credit.

This stricture applies with equal force to initiatives in the field of what is known as 'microfinance', in which NGOs and other institutions seek to serve the special financial needs of the poor, that is, for small loans that are unsecured by the usual forms of collateral and are flexibly disbursed without procedures that drive the effective cost of funds beyond reasonable limits. Meeting these needs has called for various innovations, the success of which is still not completely clear. What should not be forgotten in evaluating such initiatives, moreover, is that in many parts of the world there are important alternatives to lenders as a source of funds—for the wealthy and poor alike. One of them is the traditional institution known as the rotating savings and credit association, or Rosca, which shows no sign of withering away in the face of the expansion of organized banking.

The plan of the chapter is as follows: Section 15.1 deals with the demand for credit, beginning with the case when there is no uncertainty and then extending the argument to a risky setting. Lenders' costs are taken up in Section 15.2, with particular emphasis on the differences between the cost structures of formal and informal lenders. With the basis thus laid, Section 15.3 is devoted to the question of how to evaluate a formal credit programme that would offer an alternative to self-finance. In keeping with the message relentlessly propagated in earlier chapters, the outcomes of decisions taken at market prices must be valued at shadow prices. There follows a discussion of competition between formal and informal lenders in Section 15.4, together with an analysis of the effects of such competition on borrowers' welfare. The chapter concludes by pulling together the various findings in the form of some proposals for the reform of public policy.

15.1. The Demand for Credit

We begin with a simple case, in which there is no uncertainty, producers can buy and sell as much as they please in perfect markets, finance is available in unlimited amounts at the parametric rate of interest r, and borrowers always repay their loans when these fall due. A single output is produced by means of a bundle of inputs, which must be committed to production at the start of each period. The amount of output yielded by the input bundle x is given by

$$y = f(x), \tag{15.1}$$

where the production function $f(\cdot)$ is assumed to possess all the usual convenient properties. Faced with the output price p and the vector of input prices q, a producer who chooses the input bundle x commits working capital in the amount of qx at the beginning of the period and will obtain a profit at its close of

$$\Pi = py - R \cdot qx, \tag{15.2a}$$

where the interest factor $R \equiv (1 + r)$, and it is assumed that all working capital is financed by means of loans. Substituting for y from Eqn (15.1) and dividing through by p, Eqn (15.2a) becomes

$$\Pi/p = f(x) - (R/p) \cdot qx. \tag{15.2b}$$

The associated first-order conditions for profits to be maximized are

$$\partial f/\partial x_i - (R/p)q_i = 0 \quad \forall i, \tag{15.3}$$

where an interior solution, $x^0(p, q, R)$, is ensured by the Inada conditions. Given that $f(\cdot)$ is homothetic, it follows at once from Eqn (15.3) that any set of changes in the rate of interest, the output price, or input prices that yield the same scalar change in the vector $(R/p)q$ also yield the same optimal input bundle. By the envelope theorem, it follows from Eqn (15.2b) that such changes in prices yield the same change in profit (measured in units of output) at the producer's optimum. In this setting, therefore, we draw the following conclusion: if the aim is to improve producers' incomes, then access to finance is necessary for production to be undertaken, but subsidies on output or on all inputs at the same rate are perfectly good substitutes for subsidized credit.

The analysis is now extended in various ways, with the primary aim of establishing whether the above conclusion is robust. Particular attention is paid to the case where the producer is a family enterprise, such as a peasant farm, a workshop, or a small-scale factory. Let such a business be endowed with an initial stock ω of goods and factors, including inventories of inputs and finished goods, cash and other financial instruments, durable producer goods, and family labour. If all these items are fully tradable at parametric prices (rental rates in the case of durables), then self-finance up to the amount $q\omega$ is feasible, albeit with possibly painful restrictions on consumption within the production period. The family enterprise's full income at the close of the period is

$$Y = \Pi + R \cdot q\omega, \tag{15.4}$$

and since $q\omega$ is a constant by assumption, the introduction of the endowment ω has no effect on production decisions. There is, however, an effect on the demand for external finance. The value of working capital committed to production at the optimum is qx^0, which is also the demand for credit in the absence of any endowments of the kind described above. With such an endowment, the demand for credit at the prices (p, q, R) is

$$K(p, q, R; \omega) = \max[q \cdot (x^0 - \omega), 0]. \tag{15.5}$$

It might be objected that some of the family's endowments, such as child and female labour and certain fixed factors, are imperfectly, if at all, tradable. This is readily conceded; but as long as such factors are good substitutes for their tradable counterparts and the net input demand vector $(x^0 - \omega)$ is non-negative, the argument leading to Eqn (15.5) will go through as before. While the condition $x^0 \geq \omega$ will not always hold, it will do so for most producers, even quite small ones.

What does have a bearing on the above claim that subsidies on output, inputs, and interest are equivalent where production and profits are concerned, is the administrative feasibility of taxing or subsidizing all inputs, fully tradable or otherwise. While inputs such as fertilizers, electricity, and other mass-produced intermediate goods lend themselves to this intervention, it is practically impossible to tax or subsidize employment in the unorganized sectors of the economy. With a simple scaling of the input price vector q thus ruled out, the equivalence between (uniform) subsidies on input prices and subsidies on interest is lost. As long as producers are actually trading their outputs, however, output subsidies remain fully equivalent to interest subsidies, even under the heroic assumption that all producers have unlimited access to credit at the same parametric rate of interest.

We now examine more critically the preliminary conclusion that access to external finance is necessary. In the setting defined by the technology $f(\cdot)$ and prices (p, q, R), the demand for working capital is qx^0, which can be satisfied by taking on loans at the rate r, or by resort to self-finance out of the endowment ω. In a steady state, let the family enterprise choose some production-cum-consumption plan that yields ω at the start of each period, the interest on, and principal of, external finance being paid off in full at the close of the preceding one. Now suppose that an improved technology becomes available, whose profitable exploitation, at unchanged prices, involves much heavier demands for inputs. The associated rise in the value of qx^0 implies a like rise in the demand for finance, part of which can surely be met out of ω, albeit with some temporary belt tightening where consumption is concerned. With such divisibility, therefore, the new steady state can be attained, in time, without resort to additional external finance along the way. This is not to claim that such a path of accumulation would be efficient, but rather to emphasize that the term 'necessary' should not be used lightly in this context.

A further consideration when weighing the advantages and drawbacks of intervention in the markets for credit, inputs, and outputs is the fact that transacting in the credit market is relatively more costly and onerous, even for borrowers. Application fees must be paid, several trips to the bank may be necessary, and, if credit is subsidized, bribes may be needed to grease the wheels of the application process. The borrower must incur these costs at the start of the period; for simplicity, they are assumed to be independent of the size of the loan. The household now has two options: either to pursue the production plan x^0, which yields full income in the amount of $\Pi(x^0) + R \cdot q\omega$, or to rely wholly on self-finance, thereby avoiding the (fixed) transactions cost C. Suppose the whole of $q\omega$ is used in the latter case, and that the optimal input bundle associated therewith is x^a, where x^a satisfies $qx^a = q\omega$. Then the alternative, second option yields a full income of $pf(x^a)$. The household chooses the first or the second according as

$$pf(x^0) - R \cdot [q(x^0 - \omega) - C] \gtrless pf(x^a). \tag{15.6}$$

For any given (p, q, C), there will exist an R, R^a say, such that both options yield the same full income. For all higher values of R, the demand for external finance will be zero; for all lower values, it will be $K(R; \cdot)$; and there will be a discontinuity at $R = R^a$.

The results derived thus far can be set out in the usual price–quantity diagram, as in Fig. 15.1. The demand for credit is the curve DD', which is made up of the vertical axis for all $R > R^a$, and the downward-sloping section $K(R; \cdot)$ for all $R < R^a$. Given the market interest factor R_1, an interest subsidy yielding the interest factor R_2 to borrowers induces the demand $K(R_2; \cdot)$ for credit. In doing so, it raises the producer's (borrower's)

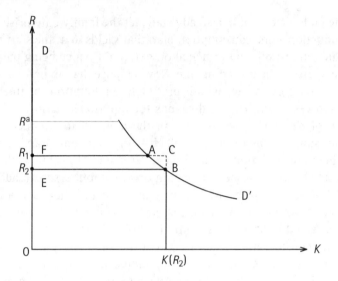

Figure 15.1. The demand for credit at a parametric rate of interest

full income by the trapezoidal area ABEF, at a direct cost to the Treasury of BEFC, the residual triangle ABC being the associated deadweight loss.

At this juncture, it will be useful to give some idea of the empirical values of borrowers' costs. As noted above, the formal and lengthy processing procedures adopted by institutions impose heavier transactions costs on borrowers than does the traditional lender's way of doing business. Just how powerfully the former can affect the borrower's effective cost of funds is brought home by Adams and Nehman (1979), who drew on studies of farmers in Bangladesh, Brazil, and Colombia. In Bangladesh, which was then known as East Pakistan, the nominal rate of interest charged by the Agricultural Development bank in the early 1960s was 7 per cent a year; yet even for the largest category of loans, interest charges comprised just over one-half of the total costs of borrowing on a twelve-month loan. The transactions costs ranged from about Rs. 17 on a loan of Rs. 50 to Rs. 69 on one of Rs. 1300, implying an effective annual rate on a six-month loan of 74 per cent on the former and a relatively modest 18 per cent on the latter. What makes these figures even more telling is that most of the farmers in question had some previous experience of dealing with formal credit institutions; first-time borrowers undoubtedly faced higher transactions costs, on average. In the Brazilian sample, which was canvassed in the early 1970s, the effective rate on a six-month loan varied from 44 to 18 per cent, against an average nominal rate of about 13 per cent a year.

In the Colombian one, the average effective rate on a one-year loan was no less than 42 per cent, also against an average nominal rate of about 13 per cent. In this connection, it would be useful to have estimates of the effective cost of credit from competing private sources, but the studies in question did not take up this comparison. A somewhat more recent survey of farming households in the southern Indian state of Andhra Pradesh in 1982 revealed the following picture: the average nominal rates charged by institutions and private lenders were a little over 11 and 18 per cent per annum, respectively; but the difference of 7.3 per cent was reduced only modestly to 5.8 per cent when transactions costs were brought into the reckoning, so that institutional credit still looked decidedly cheap—if a farmer could get his hands on it (Bell *et al.*, 1997).

We now introduce uncertainty into the analysis. Let the set S of all possible states of nature be finite. In each production period, the realized state, $s \in S$, is revealed only after all inputs have been committed, so that when production decisions are made both the resulting output and the price it will fetch are unknown. What is assumed to be known, however, is the probability, $\gamma(S)$, that state s will occur, the output, $f(x, s)$, that a given bundle of inputs will then yield, and the output price, $p(s)$, that will then rule. Natural uncertainty of this kind can, of course, translate into uncertainty about the fulfilment of contractual obligations. Let the costs to lenders of verifying which state has occurred be prohibitively high, but those of observing the level of output and of appropriating payment from it be negligible. In the absence of any collateral other than the output itself, a credit contract in which the amount K is borrowed at the rate of interest r can stipulate that if the borrower does not repay the amount RK at the end of the period, then the lender will be entitled to the entire output. Lenders will clearly insist upon such a clause. For simplicity, it is assumed that the 'game' lasts for just one period, so that the borrower enjoys limited liability, in as much as he cannot be forced to repay more than the value of the realized output, however large RK may be. Moral hazard arises because lenders are unable to ascertain whether a failure to repay in full is due to bad luck or lack of diligence (in the sense that insufficient inputs were committed to production); but the contract is still such that if a borrower can repay in full, he will choose to do so.

The position can now be set out formally. If the borrower chooses the bundle x and state s is realized, his limited liability with respect to the loan (K, R) implies that his full income will be

$$Y(x, s) = \max\{p(s)f(x, s) - Rq(x - \omega), 0\}. \tag{15.7}$$

Let the borrower's preferences over lotteries be representable by the von Neumann–Morgenstern utility function $u(Y)$, where u is strictly concave if the borrower is risk averse. Given the probabilities γ $(s \in S)$, the choice of the bundle x yields the expected utility

$$E_s u[Y(x, s)] = \sum_{s \in S} \gamma(s) \cdot u[Y(x, s)]. \tag{15.8}$$

Analogously to the case of perfect certainty, the first-order conditions are

$$\frac{\partial Eu}{\partial x_i} = \sum_{s \in S} \gamma(s) \cdot u' \cdot \frac{\partial Y}{\partial x_i} = 0, \tag{15.9}$$

where, from Eqn (15.7),

$$\frac{\partial Y}{\partial x_i} = \max \left\{ p(s) \frac{\partial f}{\partial x_i} - Rq_i, 0 \right\}. \tag{15.10}$$

Recalling the envelope theorem, inspection of Eqns (15.7) and (15.8) reveals that a given improvement in the borrower's expected utility at the optimum can be accomplished by a suitable choice of a subsidy on output, a uniform subsidy on all inputs, or a subsidy on the rate of interest. Inspection of Eqns (15.9) and (15.10) reveals that each induces the same choice of input bundle at the new optimum. Thus, the equivalence established in the case of perfect certainty continues to hold, which, in view of the linearity of Eqn (15.8) in the probabilities γ $(s \in S)$, should come as no great surprise.

To sum up, a case can be made for the importance of access to adequate external finance to realize efficiency in production, especially where the adoption of new technologies is concerned, these being often associated with significant indivisibilities. There is no compelling case, however, that such finance should be made available on subsidized terms if the aim is to improve producers' (borrowers') welfare. For such improvements can be accomplished perfectly well, in principle at least, by means of output or (uniform) input subsidies, and in practice, output subsidies have clear advantages. Having treated the demand side of the story in some detail, it is now time to turn to the lending side.

15.2. Lenders' Costs

Lenders' costs fall into four broad categories. First, there is the cost of funds, which can be thought of as the raw material for their loans. Second, there are the costs of evaluating applicants for loans and the projects they propose to undertake. Third, and closely related to the second, there are the costs of securing and disbursing loans, a task that often involves the evaluation of collateral, if any, used as security. Fourth, there are the costs of recovering loans when they fall due. These categories are taken up seriatim, whereby the cost structures of formal and informal lenders will be compared in some detail as a preliminary to Sections 15.4 and 15.5.

Informal lenders, who often combine lending with retail or wholesale trade, pawnbroking, and farming, tend to rely on own capital as a source of funds; but they may also be able to borrow from other lenders, including banks and other formal institutions. Only rarely do they take in deposits. It is most unlikely that their marginal cost of funds is the rate at which the banks lend to one another; generally speaking, it will be much higher. The banks tap their depositors' savings, of course, but they can also issue bonds and they enjoy access to the central bank's lending window. This latter access yields a crucial advantage in financially repressed systems; for by definition, the discount rate will be artificially low. Thus, not only do banks enjoy a lower cost of funds than informal lenders by the very fact of taking in deposits on a large scale, but they are also the beneficiaries of specific regulations, which are often designed to limit informal lenders' operations, if not to drive them out of business altogether. Round one, therefore, goes to the banks and other formal institutions such as co-operatives.

Evaluating borrowers and their project proposals requires specialized knowledge, and in certain sectors of the economy, such as peasant farming and small-scale enterprise, the established informal lender usually has a clear advantage over competing formal institutions. He carefully builds up a clientele over a period of years; he is sometimes a member of the same community (village or social); he knows about his clients' lines of business and is often in a related line himself; and, above all, he has a clear incentive to make his clients' business and doings his own business. All this stands in stark contrast to the position of the banks, which often lend to such sectors not out of choice, but rather in order to comply with government regulations, and whose loan officers are petty bureaucrats without incentives to perform such tasks well. True, informal lenders are not in a position to finance steel mills, automobile plants, or microchip factories; but on their own chosen turf, they are patently better at the task of evaluation than are formal institutions.

Such evaluation would not matter so much, of course, if borrowers could tender readily marketable forms of collateral, whose worth is relatively straightforward to assess, in order to secure their loans. Indeed, if the value of the collateral were large enough in all states of nature to cover the principal and all other associated costs of the loan in full, then there would be no lender's risk at all, and assessing borrowers' creditworthiness and the prospective profitability of their projects would be superfluous if the lender chose to conduct his operations in that particular way. Two difficulties beset this 'solution' in practice. First, many would be borrowers have little or nothing in the way of marketable collateral to offer. They might be able, industrious, honourable, and in possession of at least one good plan or project; but if the lender cannot be so persuaded, the only collateral they can offer is what the loan itself yields, namely, output, inventories, and the durable producer goods so financed. By its very nature, such collateral has a very uncertain market value, to the extent that it is marketable at all, and it may be hard to appropriate in the event of default. Second, governments sometimes place restrictions on the kinds of collateral that may be used to secure particular sorts of loans. The most important example involves agricultural land, the use of which as collateral to secure private loans is legally banned in a number of countries, for fear that peasants' holdings will wind up in the hands of 'usurers'. This restriction is at least understandable. Less so is the fact that it also applies, in places, to organized financial lenders in connection with short-term loans for production, even when these institutions are in the public sector itself. The obvious means for them to overcome their profound disadvantages in gathering and assessing information are therefore denied them by regulation.

The final stage is to recover the loan. If the borrower wants to take out a new loan, he will have every incentive to find the money to repay the old one when it falls due, and should he succeed in doing so, the lender will not need to exert himself until the new loan application is filed. Before issuing a new loan, the lender would ideally like to know whether the repayment of the old loan was financed by a loan from another source, but until that point is reached, the cycle is closed. The lender's problems begin, of course, when the loan becomes overdue. If the borrower appears, probably because he wants to roll over the debt or even to obtain additional credit, then the situation must be assessed anew. If he does not turn up of his own accord, however, he must be sought out, cajoled, badgered, threatened, and ultimately subjected to the execution of such threats until he pays up, with the lender's costs escalating at each step. Even so, the outcome is by no means a certain one. The borrower may have absconded with an unsecured loan, or may remain unmoved by persuasion and threat, so that there is nothing left but to write off the loan in question.

Here, too, the informal lender is usually better placed than a bank or a co-operative to secure his interests. First, he is more likely to have weeded out 'bad' borrowers and projects at the loan evaluation stage. Second, as noted above, he often has connections to, and in, the borrower's community, and so has access to social influence and sanctions to recover the loan. Third, he can resort to extra-legal coercion, in the form of threats against the borrower's person, family, and property. These specific advantages yield him clear savings in the expected costs of recovering loans. For their part, formal lending institutions occasionally labour under a specific disadvant-age, namely, that formal loans are regarded not as financial obligations, but rather as public grants. This pernicious conception is fostered by gov-ernments themselves, not only indirectly through regulations restricting the use of certain forms of collateral and a permissive attitude towards default where resort to legal process to obtain repayment is concerned, but also directly, in the form of electoral promises to forgive all outstanding debts. When carried out, such promises do more than convert loans into once-and-for-all grants with no strings attached; they also hold out the expectation that there will be similar windfalls to debtors in the future. In so doing, these policies destroy repayment morale, and with it the very basis on which credit markets function; for the demand for credit on such terms is surely unbounded.

There is one particular feature of lenders' costs that works to the dis-advantage of the poor, and so merits attention: a large component of the expected costs of administering a loan is independent of the amount that is lent. All borrowers, their projects, and their applications must be assessed, and in particular sectors of economic activity, the process for a large loan will consume little more time and resources than for a small one. The same holds for securing loans though collateral or third parties and for disbursement itself. Where loan recovery is concerned, however, there is an additional factor at work, namely, whether the borrower's will-ingness to repay when he is able to do so is independent of how much he has borrowed, this amount usually being strongly correlated with his wealth. In this connection, it has been asserted that the well-to-do often have a worse repayment record than poorer borrowers, a fact (when it is a fact) that is attributed to the formers' political connections. Be that as it may, it remains the case that the expected costs of recovering a loan within a given category of loans will have a substantial fixed compon-ent. The cost of funds being common to all loans, therefore, a lender must charge either a higher rate of interest, or a largely invariant specific fee as an element of a two-part tariff, in order to break even on a small loan. If, as is almost invariably the case, the rate of interest charged is independent of the amount borrowed and the specific fees are much smaller than the associated administrative costs, then those borrowers who do succeed in obtaining small loans are effectively cross subsidized. Lenders are, of course, well aware of this aspect of their cost structures, and so avoid making small loans, unless specifically encouraged or forced to do so.

To sum up, formal lenders enjoy a lower cost of funds, in part though their ability to collect deposits, but also though regulations that belong to regimes of financial repression. Their 'administrative' costs, on the other hand, are far higher than those of informal lenders. Once again, regulatory interventions and other policies that have little to do with ensuring prudential standards of lending (some even undermine the latter) play an important role. The upshot is that formal financial institutions in many countries have performed poorly by the usual yardsticks, some being effectively bankrupt, and most being kept afloat with renewed infusions of subsidized funds provided by the Treasury and external donors.

15.3. Evaluating a Credit Programme

We are now in a position to evaluate the social profitability of a proposal to extend credit to borrowers in a particular class, which means a resort to the apparatus of shadow pricing. Since the emphasis here is naturally on the effects of distortions, the assumptions are kept as simple as possible. Let the borrower be faced with a choice between the two alternatives set out in Section 15.2, that is, between self-finance and an elastic supply of credit from a bank at the parametric rate r, where the introduction of the latter alternative constitutes the project. Suppose, to start with, that all loans are paid in full when they fall due, though the recovery of loans may still be costly. In the light of Section 15.2, let the bank's administrative costs of evaluating the application and disbursing the loan at the start of the period, and then recovering what is due at the close, be the fixed amounts C_1 and C_2, respectively.

At the risk of repeating what should now be obvious, the trick in evaluating the project in question is to treat the borrower's family enterprise as a public sector undertaking that transfers its profits at market prices to the household in question. It is the family firm, however, that chooses the production plan and how it is to be financed. In order to make matters interesting, therefore, suppose that condition (15.6) is satisfied in the credit programme's favour, so that if it is indeed introduced, it will find no lack of takers. The result is that the vector of inputs, outputs, and full income $(x^a, f(x^a), pf(x^a))$ will be replaced by $(x^0, f(x^0), pf(x^0) - R[q(x^0 - \omega) - C])$. Recalling the dates on which each of these elements become available, and valuing all inputs and outputs at shadow prices, the social value of this switch at the close of the period is

$$\pi_y(y^0 - y^a) - (1 + \rho)[\pi \cdot (x^0 - x^a) + \alpha_c C] + (\theta - \text{CCF})(Y^0 - Y^a),$$

where $Y^0 = pf(x^0) - R[q(x^0 - \omega) - C], Y^a = pf(x^a), \alpha_c$ denotes the accounting ratio for the borrower's transactions costs and ρ denotes the accounting rate of interest. In order to complete the accounting, the bank's administrative costs must be valued at shadow prices. Let the accounting ratios in question be α_1 and α_2, respectively. When discounted back to the start of the period, the social profit yielded by a single loan of this sort is, therefore,

$$\Delta W = \left[\pi_y(y^0 - y^a) + (\theta - \text{CCF})(Y^0 - Y^a)\right]/(1 + \rho) - [\pi \cdot (x^0 - x^a)$$
$$+ \alpha_c C + \alpha_1 C_1 + \alpha_2 C_2]. \tag{15.11}$$

The elements of Eqn (15.11) are now familiar. The change in the net output vector of the system is valued at shadow prices, and the 'transfer' takes the form of the change in full income, which is weighted by the difference between θ and the CCF. What does merit some comment is the fact that in order to make the programme attractive to borrowers, the rate of interest charged may have to be set some way below ρ. If $\theta < \text{CCF}$, it is seen that the associated subsidy works against the programme's social profitability.

Default is readily incorporated into this scheme by using the formulation in Section 15.2. Without loss of generality, let the states of nature be ordered such that $p(s)f(x, s) < RK$ for all $s \le k$, so that default occurs in states 1 through k and repayment is made in full otherwise. Let the bank's costs of laying claim to whatever output is produced in the case of default be fixed, at C_3. Then the bank's expected net return from a loan (K, R) with a limited liability lause, discounted back to the start of the period, is

$$(1 + r_0) \bigg/ \left\{ \sum_{s=1}^{k} \gamma(s)[p(s)f(x^0) - C_3] + \sum_{s=k+1}^{n} \gamma(s)(RK - C_2) \right\} - (K + C_1),$$

where r_0 denotes the bank's opportunity cost of funds. Recalling the definition of contingent shadow prices in Chapter 12, the (expected) social profit from such a loan is

$$\Delta W = \sum_{s \in S} \gamma(s) \left\{ \pi_y(s)[f(x^0, s) - f(x^a, s)] \right.$$

$$+ [\theta(s) - CCF(s)][u(Y^0) - u(Y^a)] \right\} / (1 + \rho)$$

$$- \left\{ [\pi \cdot (x^0 - x^a) + \alpha_c C + \alpha_1 C_1 + \sum_{s=1}^{k} \gamma(s)\alpha_2 C_2 + \sum_{s=k+1}^{n} \gamma(s)\alpha_3 C_3 \right\},$$

$$(15.12)$$

where $Y^0(s)$ is given by Eqn (15.7) and $Y^a(s) = p(s)f(x^a, s)$. It is quite possible, therefore, that the bank will fail to break even, on average, on a class of loan that is socially profitable.

Self-finance is not, of course, the only alternative to a loan from a bank, there being an active system of informal finance in various forms in most less developed countries (LDCs). In order to extend the evaluation of credit programmes to cover these possibilities, it is necessary to begin by analysing how informal lenders compete with formal institutions.

15.4. Competition Between Formal and Informal Lenders

One of the principal aims of public policy has been to push formal lenders into competing with their traditional counterparts. The stated reason for doing so is usually that traditional lenders' terms of credit are usurious and their practices predatory. An ample supply of cheap formal credit, it was claimed, would release the peasant and small producers from the moneylender's clutches. We now examine this claim in some detail, paying particular attention to the structure of competition among traditional lenders.

In keeping with this view of the traditional moneylender, we begin with the case where he is a monopolist, a position he enjoys by virtue of the isolated character of the small community he serves and the stock of knowledge he has accumulated concerning his clients' characters, possessions, and doings. It is assumed that he can make each would-be borrower a all-or-nothing offer of a loan in the amount K at the rate of interest r. In making and recovering such a loan, he will incur some (small) fixed costs and he must draw on his sources of funds, the marginal cost of which is certainly rising once the loan becomes sufficiently big. As the loan increases in size, it is plausible that the problems of moral hazard also become more pronounced and with them, the chances of default. Thus, his iso-(expected) profit curves in the space of (K, R) are U-shaped, the downward-sloping sections of which arise from the presence of the fixed costs. The locus of the minima of this family of curves is his so-called 'notional' supply curve (though this turns out not to play any role in the proceedings). In choosing a contract (K, R) to maximize his expected profits, he is constrained by the borrower's participation constraint, which is defined by the borrower's alternative option of doing without a loan and relying instead on self-finance. (We ignore, for the present, the incentive constraint arising from the requirement that the terms of the loan be such that the borrower not abscond with the money.)

All these elements are depicted in Fig. 15.2. The borrower's indifference contour passing through the point (K^a, R^a) is, by definition, the set of all loan contracts that yield him the same expected utility as not borrowing at all, namely, V^a, and is so labelled. He strictly prefers all points below the contour in question to this alternative. The lender, however, prefers a higher rate of interest to a lower for any given size of loan and so chooses a contract on $V(K, R) = V^a$. If both parties' indifference maps are smooth, the lender's optimum will be the point of mutual tangency between $V(K, R) = V^a$ and his map of iso-(expected) profit contours. As depicted in Fig. 15.2, this point, M, lies on the downward-sloping sections of V^a and the associated iso-expected profit contour, respectively; but the case where M lies on the upward-sloping sections is also possible.

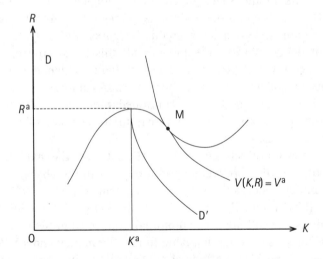

Figure 15.2. The monopolistic moneylender's optimum

This, then, is the state of affairs when a formal institution, hereinafter a bank, enters the picture. Its rules of operation are assumed to be as follows. For each loan applicant, the bank arrives at a credit limit, $\bar{K}_1$, based on those of his readily observable characteristics as are set out in the book of regulations. The applicant may borrow as much as he pleases up to this limit, and pays thereon the regulated rate of interest r_1. Public policy being what it is, we can confidently assume that $r_1 < r^a$; and since the bank will have nothing to do with very small loans, it is plausible that the pair $(\bar{K}_1, R_1)$ is preferred to any point on $V(K, R) = V^a$. Hence, if the borrower can obtain a bank loan (i.e. if $\bar{K}_1 > 0$), he will be better off than in the days when the traditional moneylender ruled the roost.

The story is not, however, quite complete. The bank is most unlikely to be able to prevent its borrowers from seeking additional credit from the moneylender, if they so desire; nor, for his part, can the moneylender hinder those fortunate enough to have the offer of a bank loan from taking it up. What he can do, however, is to insist upon debt seniority should they borrow from him. With his superior knowledge of the borrower's circumstances and the means at his disposal to ensure repayment, the moneylender is certainly in a position to enforce such a demand, and it is clearly in his interest to do so. It should also be noted that the (junior) debt the borrower owes to the bank should increase the moneylender's returns from a loan of any given size in all states of nature, so that the moneylender's map of iso-(expected) profit contours in the space of (K, R) will depend, in general, upon $(\bar{K}_1, R_1)$. Hence, although the traditional lender suffers direct losses when his clients gain access to bank credit, he gains indirectly through the exercise of debt-seniority. The loser in all this is, of course, the bank as junior creditor—unless it can secure its loan by demanding marketable forms of collateral from its borrowers. As noted above, this it is often unable to do; so that the continued presence of the traditional moneylender poses an additional threat to its chances of successfully recovering its loans.

The essentials are set out in Fig. 15.3. Given the bank's offer of $(\max[\bar{K}_1, 0], R_1)$, the borrower's opportunity set in the absence of a loan from the moneylender is the horizontal segment AB, where $OA = R_1$ and $AB = \bar{K}_1$. If his notional demand for credit, $K(R_1; \cdot)$, is smaller than his credit limit $\bar{K}_1$, he will not seek additional finance from the moneylender, and if the bank has enough loanable funds, the moneylender will go out of business, in line with the aims of public policy. This case is depicted in panel (a) of Fig. 15.3.

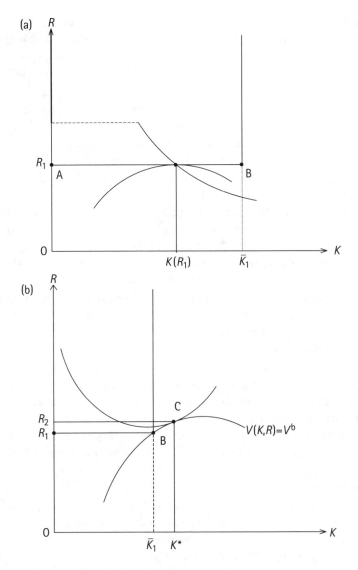

Figure 15.3. (a) The entry of a bank: the borrower experiences no rationing.
(b) The entry of a bank: rationing and spillover

The catch here in practice is that the bank cannot satisfy the entire
demand for loans at the regulated rate of interest, and so is driven to
ration credit in such a way that some would-be borrowers obtain no credit
at all, while the great majority of those who do obtain loans get less than

their notional demand at that rate. This situation is set out in panel (b) of Fig. 15.3. The borrower makes full use of his credit limit with the bank by taking out a loan of size $\bar{K}_1$, and so can obtain at least the expected utility yielded by the exclusive contract $(\bar{K}_1, R_1)$, namely, V^b. By definition, the indifference curve corresponding to V^b is upward sloping at B. It also defines the borrower's participation constraint in connection with a supplementary loan from the moneylender. The point of common tangency between the indifference curve labelled V^b and the map of iso-(expected) profit contours is denoted by the point C. As drawn, C lies on the upward-sloping segments of the two contours; but the optimum could just as well lie on the downward-sloping segments. If, at C, the moneylender's expected profit is non-negative, a mutually acceptable deal is feasible and C will be the outcome. Let C denote the pair (K^*, R_2). Then the moneylender will offer the loan contract $(K^* - \bar{K}_1, R_2)$. Since the moneylender's opportunity cost of funds is higher than the bank's, it is almost certain that $R_2 > R_1$, which is the case depicted in panel (b). Here, the moneylender is not driven out of business, but rather accommodates himself to the bank's entry into his formerly exclusive domain. More likely than not, he continues to enjoy super-normal expected profits.

So much for monopoly. Consider next the case where competition among traditional lenders is so sharp that expected profits are driven down to zero. It is now the borrower who has the upper hand. Suppose, for simplicity, that lenders are able to enforce exclusive contracts. Competitive pressures will induce each lender to offer a menu of contracts such that each will yield an expected profit of zero. This condition defines the lender's participation constraint, and the borrower will select from the menu in question so as to maximize his expected utility. Panel (a) of Fig. 15.4 depicts the case where a mutually acceptable deal is feasible. The iso-expected profit contour labelled W^a depicts the said menu of contracts. The borrower chooses the contract represented by point F, where an indifference curve and W^a have a common tangent.

The entry of a bank can improve the borrower's welfare only if it enlarges his opportunity set. A sufficient condition for this to hold is that the regulated rate of interest be lower than the minimum rate that a moneylender can charge while still breaking even on average. It is plausible that this condition is satisfied in practice, and panel (b) of Fig. 15.4 depicts such a case. The borrower's opportunity set is now the horizontal segment AB as before, supplemented by the lender's isoexpected profit contour W^a, which is drawn with the displaced origin $(\bar{K}_1, 0)$ to reflect the presence of the (junior) debt to the bank. If he is sufficiently tightly rationed in

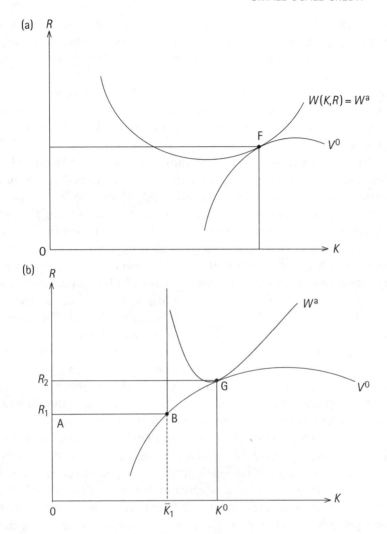

Figure 15.4. (a) Competition among private lenders: no bank. (b) Competition among private lenders: entry of a bank

the formal sector of the market, the borrower will choose supplementary informal finance, his combined optimum being depicted by the point G, which depicts the pair (K^0, R_2), the amount $(K^0 - \bar{K}_1)$ being borrowed from the moneylender.

Spillover of demand and the effects of the moneylender's position as senior creditor when spillover occurs are not the only forms of interaction between the formal and informal segments of the market. It is not uncommon for moneylenders, in their other guises as richer peasants and landholders, traders, and commission agents, to obtain formal loans, and with their loanable funds so augmented, to expand the scale of their own lending operations. When they do so, not only do they enjoy the subsidies presumably intended for the less well-to-do, but they also intensify the degree of rationing the latter experience in the formal sector of the market.

Whether the increased volume of informal finance made possible by on-lending brings compensating advantages to borrowers depends on the structure of competition among moneylenders. Under the form of monopoly assumed here, there will be no such offsetting advantages, the entire gains accruing to the moneylender. If, in contrast, competitive pressures among lenders are so strong as to yield zero expected profits, then the position is rather more complicated. In the absence of entry (or costs of entry), reductions in the lender's cost of funds will be passed on in full to borrowers in the form of more attractive loan contracts. The net outcome of on-lending will actually be advantageous from the borrower's standpoint if moneylenders' greater operational efficiency more than offsets the costs entailed by the additional layer of intermediation. Casual observation suggests that this possibility cannot be ruled out in advance, a point to which we return below. The second subcase of zero expected profits is that of free entry with fixed costs, the latter taking the form mostly of acquiring information about prospective clients and their specific undertakings. If the new entrants into the moneylending business are no more efficient than their long-established competitors, borrowers are unlikely to gain much indirectly from on-lending, the lower cost of funds to lenders being largely, or even wholly, dissipated by the costs of additional entry.

Assessing the social profitability of formal credit programmes in the various settings analysed above is carried out exactly along the lines set out in Section 15.3, where the alternative was self-finance. Establishing the precise details of private responses is evidently more complicated, of course; but that simply makes the task all the more gripping for the interested reader.

15.5. Reforming Public Policy

We now draw together a set of conclusions and proposals concerning public policy in the light of the above arguments. We begin by making three general points, and then take them up in detail in connection with microfinance and conventional lending institutions, respectively.

The first point commands wide agreement: The long-established practice of pumping credit into the formal institutions of the financial sector and then prescribing in detail how it should be allocated, and on what terms it should be lent, has little to commend it and should be ended forthwith (Braverman and Guasch, 1985). Ample credit can be superior to subsidized credit that is strongly rationed, even for those fortunate enough to obtain it in some measure; and subsidies exacerbate the excess demand to which credit markets are prone. If the aim is raise producers' returns and the profitability of investment, then it is far from clear that interest subsidies have compelling advantages over output or input subsidies. As for the oft-stated goal of influencing the distribution of income in favour of the poor by means of carefully selective targeting of interest subsidies, the record suggests that such targeting usually ends in failure: the rich and well-connected find loopholes in, or ways around, the regulations, and wind up capturing a goodly share of the subsidies intended for the needy.

The secondary aim of greatly restricting the traditional moneylender's scale and sphere of operations is also far from being realized. Whatever be the merits of this aim—and they are certainly debatable—the formulation of public policy must come to terms with the fact that traditional lenders have accommodated successfully to the spread of organized financial institutions. The emphasis, therefore, should be on influencing how the private lender conducts his business in the direction of serving the larger good rather than on driving him out of business altogether, at least for the foreseeable future. This involves elements of both competition and cooperation, perhaps tacit, between formal and informal lenders.

Third, the scope for public policy to improve outcomes depends on both market structure and the nature of the informational problems confronting lenders. In the case of free entry into moneylending, lenders' expected profits will be zero; but it does not then follow that there is no scope for intervention. For the welfare of borrowers still depends on lenders' costs, which can be influenced by public policy. The inside knowledge possessed by moneylenders will not be directly available to regulated or state-owned banks, and when there are adverse selection problems, it is implausible that the banks will do a better job of screening applicants. Thus, unless the banks enjoy advantages where other costs are concerned, direct competition prompted by the state is not necessarily the right form of intervention here. If private lenders do possess significant market power, the case for intervention may look stronger; but in a setting of incomplete markets, second-best considerations intrude. There is also the related point that the instruments available to the government may not suffice to bring about full efficiency.

15.5.1. Microfinance

The fact that making separate small loans to individuals who cannot offer readily marketable collateral is a high-cost business has prompted some hard and imaginative thinking about ways to make formal credit accessible to such would-be borrowers. One response is exploit potential economies of scale by lending to groups of individuals in the same line of business, such as farming and petty manufacturing or trading. The advantages of group lending, as it is called, can only be realized, however, when the members of a group are contractually bound by the legal clause known as joint and several liability. That is to say, each member is ultimately responsible for the repayment of the entire loan: if one or more members fails to meet his or her repayment obligations, then the rest must make good the shortfall in full. Such a clause is, of course, effective only when repayment is legally enforceable, and if public policy destroys repayment morale, group loans are doomed like any other.

Given that the clause is effective, group lending does much to ameliorate the informational problems that typically plague institutional lenders. First, each group is formed of individuals who have chosen membership therein willingly. In this respect, a group loan shares a key feature in common with Roscas. Being in the same line of business, and with joint and several liability hanging over her, each member will have the necessary background, social connections, and incentives to seek out capable, reliable, and diligent partners. This is the self-selection aspect of group lending. Second, each has an incentive to monitor what the others are doing, from the moment the loan is obtained, though the course of the production process, and right up to the final sale of output. This peer monitoring within the group should do much to ease the lender's problems with moral hazard. Third, the costs of loan recovery are substantially displaced onto the members of the group, and when any of them fail to repay on time, the rest can bring social and other pressures to bear upon the laggards. Group lending in this form therefore induces a measure of homogeneity within each group with respect to its members' characteristics, the projects they undertake, the diligence with which the projects are pursued, and the willingness to make timely repayments of their loans when the returns are there.

The best known, and in many ways pioneering, example of institutional group lending is the *Grameen* Bank of Bangladesh.[2] This institution started life as a project of the Bangladesh Bank in November 1979, with the object of making loans without collateral to the rural poor, who were defined to be individuals belonging to households owning up to half an acre of land. Borrowers formed groups of five unrelated persons. If any defaulted, the entire group became ineligible for new loans. Additional enforcement was provided by the weekly collection of dues (2 per cent of the loan) at the group's meeting place by the local employee of the Bank, and compulsory contributions to insurance and savings funds against default, death, illness, and acute need. Five years later, the Bank had grown from 2 to 108 branches covering about 2000 villages, with outstanding loans of over 200 million *Taka* to 110,000 clients. A very modest 2.5 per cent of loans were overdue at the end of 1982. The effective annual rate of interest was 20 per cent, excluding transactions costs. Borrowing at the rate of 8.5 per cent from the Bangladesh Bank, the *Grameen* Bank was just able to cover its costs. Since then, its branches have spread throughout much of Bangladesh, reaching hundreds of thousands of clients, most of whom would have virtually no chance of obtaining a loan from a traditional financial institution. Whether this massive expansion has been possible only through the infusion of outside funds on a large scale, and whether there has been a substantial deterioration in the quality of management and supervision provided by the Bank's staff, are questions to which there are, at present, no firm answers. We shall return to this matter below.

One of the *Grameen* Bank's salient features is that its lending is very heavily directed to non-agricultural activities in which the production or turnover process is quite short, with outlays and revenues occurring rather frequently. In consequence, the credit cycle of disbursement is also short, but not necessarily completely regular. In order to overcome these difficulties, the Bank has instituted a system whereby repayments are made with a very short and fixed frequency. These regular payments include modest, but obligatory, contributions to a provident fund, so that each member of the group is insured against the ill health, disability, or death of all. Solidarity is further reinforced by the requirement that the group meet regularly, not only to discuss the members' problems, but also for the purposes of supervision by one of the Bank's field officers. It is interesting to note that the officers' visits are used as the occasion to promote

---

[2] The experience of the early years is described and analysed by Hossain (1985), upon which the following account draws.

and reiterate the Bank's general aims, so that supervision has a distinctly ideological slant to it. In any event, supervision is very intensive, as the Bank's proponents themselves concede, so that the cost advantages of group lending are substantially offset thereby.

Matters are considerably simpler when the borrowers are cultivators, the crop cycle being fixed and predictable, with a single repayment in the case of so-called crop loans used to cover outlays on seed, fertilizers, irrigation, and other variable inputs. The bank's administrative costs can be limited to one visit at the time of loan disbursement, another after the harvest has been brought in, and perhaps another in the interim to gain an idea of how the crops are progressing, this last intelligence gathering being in any case important in the bank's forward planning. Siamwalla *et al.* (1990) describes a successful programme of this sort in Thailand.

Group lending is not the only possible route to formal microfinance for the needy. Producer and consumer durables can, in principle, serve as collateral for the loans that finance them. In practice, of course, matters are not quite straightforward. Animals, such as cows, can be abused in various ways without the resulting damage being apparent upon immediate inspection. The problem is less severe in the case of a refrigerator or a set of hand tools, but it is not negligible. The standard remedy for these difficulties is to require that the borrower make a substantial down payment on the item in question, so that the down payment serves as additional collateral. It has the obvious drawback that even the deposit may be beyond the borrower's means, too. When such goods are readily and easily moved, as is often the case, outright fraud becomes a distinct, even tempting, possibility: the durable is sold off and then reported as stolen when the bailiffs arrive to repossess it. Fraud of this sort is not especially risky for the borrower when the legal system is shaky, and it contributes correspondingly to lender's risk. If these problems of moral hazard are not too grave, loans for the purchase of durables on an instalment payment basis can be 'mass-produced', so to speak, at low administrative costs.

What is the outlook for such initiatives? Their more ardent advocates make the radical claim that they can serve the financial needs of the poor on the basis of a strictly temporary infusion of subsidies to cover start-up and learning costs, with their long-term financial liability being secured by the unswerving application of sound banking principles—underpinned by suitable innovations and experimentation. The *Grameen* Bank is often held up as the canonical example. If the claim is correct, then the alleviation of poverty and an appropriate, efficient development of a component of the

financial system can be accomplished through a single, nicely timed intervention. This claim and the general state of play in the field are admirably
laid out and analysed by Morduch (2000), on which the following draws
in a selective way.

The first point is disarmingly simple: if, in the extreme case, the lot
of the poor can be thus improved at no cost to the Treasury, then the
government's task is to create a friendly but firm legal environment in
which the institutions in question (principally NGOs) can go about their
business. Having done so, the government should then withdraw to the
sidelines, which is what most NGOs would prefer anyway. In practice,
however, the Treasury is always required to make a donation, if only a
temporary one, through one channel or another, whereupon the radical
claim becomes vulnerable.

Suppose, for the sake of argument, that the required financial support
can be exactly ascertained in advance and is proof against all forms of
time-inconsistency *ex post*. It is immediately clear that what is being proposed is a project in the public sector, in just the same way that the
construction of a dam or a rural road is. That being so, the project in
question should be subjected to evaluation at shadow prices, as set out
in Section 15.3. If it will indeed function so as to serve the poor, then
the project's chances of passing muster will be that much greater, *ceteris
paribus*. Yet the test is still necessary. The second point, therefore, is that
an insistence on the use of shadow prices is a potentially valuable antidote
to an excess of ideology. It gains additional force from the fact that very
few of those programmes hold out a realistic chance of becoming truly
self-financing: Morduch (ibid.: 618) gives a widely cited 'speculation' of a
mere 5 per cent.

The near certainty that such programmes will require an unending
stream of subsidies also raises the issue of incentives. It can be argued
that achieving consistency in the allocation of resources requires that those
who run the programmes in general, and disburse loans in particular, make
their decisions at shadow prices. If they do not—as farmers benefiting from
irrigation, for example, do not—then this fact must be taken into account
when evaluating the entire programme as a public sector project. In any
event, the stream of net costs borne by the Treasury will depend on which
rule is followed. A quite different sort of incentive problem arises regardless of whether the decision makers choose at shadow or market prices,
namely, what personal incentives do they have to choose carefully and
well at the prices in question? Shadow prices have many virtues, but they
do not rule out the time-inconsistency problems that arise when the budget

constraint is thought to be 'soft'. If, therefore, public subsidies will be a permanent feature of the microfinance landscape, the government cannot be held wholly at arm's length.

The final point concerning subsidies has to do with targeting. As noted earlier, the cheap credit offered by conventional financial institutions has attracted the interest of rich and poor alike, with the lion's share being captured by the former. Doing away with such subsidies will relieve the burden on the Treasury, while doing relatively little harm to the poor. The funds so released will then be available, in principle, to subsidize microfinance programmes – provided the latter are profitable at shadow prices. To that end, setting the effective cost of funds to borrowers above the level ruling in the credit contracts offered by banks will deter the better-off from attempting to capture funds intended for the poor.

A closing remark: it is important not to lose sight of the fact that microfinance programmes compete, in effect, with traditional institutions, such as Roscas. The latter, like the moneylender, are widespread and flourishing in many parts of the world. They take various forms, some being designed to finance the acquisition of lumpy durable goods and others to provide insurance against idiosyncratic risks. Thus, the poor (but not the destitute) have a real alternative to self-finance, and one that they organize themselves. To appraise 'new' initiatives in the field of microfinance without taking into account the existence of this sort of alternative is to run the risk of making a serious error.

15.5.2. Formal and Informal Lenders

The forms of intervention are taken up seriatim. First, where lender's costs are concerned, it is plausible that the moneylender's inside knowledge and informal style of operation will keep his administrative costs low. That leaves the opportunity cost of his principal and the premium to cover risk as the remaining elements of his costs that might be the object of intervention. In the textbook case, the former is usually treated as a perfectly safe placement yielding r_0, which may be interpreted as the rate on government bonds. Leaving aside reductions in r_0 effected through changes in monetary policy—to the extent that such policies are effective nowadays—bond markets may be so poorly developed that local lenders do not have much access to such placements in practice. More extensive open market operations would lower their costs in these circumstances. It is also argued that the maturities of these instruments, when available, are not always well attuned to the cycle of the moneylender's operations. If his loans are used to finance working capital for cultivation, he will normally receive repayment about six months later. If bonds have a minimum maturity of one year, his funds will be idle for half the year in the absence of a secondary market, unless there is double cropping or a conveniently located bank offering deposit accounts. At worst, the effective rate for arriving at the opportunity cost of his principal would not be r_0, but twice that rate. Here, the creation of new instruments with appropriately short maturities, or a well-organized secondary market, would reduce a significant element of the lender's total costs. It is worth noting, however, that the introduction of double cropping is an agricultural improvement which produces the same effect.

While there may be some scope for the monetary authorities to effect improvements of this sort, the distribution of the gains therefrom will depend on market structure. In the case of free entry for lenders with zero costs of entry, all the gains will go to borrowers, although the rate of interest they pay may not fall *pari passu* with the reduction in lenders' opportunity cost of funds. In the case of monopoly, all the gains will accrue to the lender if the borrower can be pinned down on his reservation frontier. The best that can be said here is that the general improvements in financial intermediation brought about by the monetary authorities or innovations in private instruments may induce more entry into the private segment of the local market. That seems a rather frail and speculative argument to set against a presumptive transfer to local lenders, especially if borrowers are no better off as a result.

Turning to lender's risk, where strategic default is concerned we have already seen that with complete information, this should happen only through a failure of judgement on the lender's part. The risk arising from the borrowers' inability to pay is affected by the riskiness of the projects that they undertake. Improvements here lie more in the province of the ministries of agriculture and irrigation than in that of the central bank, though the latter is certainly capable of affecting the volatility of prices. There is, however, one respect in which such risk could be affected by legal and administrative action: cadastral surveys and registration of land titles together with well defined and formal procedures for the registration of loans could improve the acceptability of land and other assets as collateral to moneylenders.[3] As argued above, this would not necessarily eliminate

---

[3] More ambitiously still, the state could declare that in the event of natural disasters, which would otherwise precipitate a collapse of the prices of assets used as collateral, it would step in as a buyer of last resort, thereby staving off the collapse in question. In view of the administrative difficulties confronting such a policy, it is rather doubtful that it would be credible.

lender's risk entirely; but when there is free entry into moneylending, it would improve the terms obtained by borrowers whose collateral was previously constraining. Under monopoly, of course, all the gains thereof would once more accrue to the lender.

Turning to the banks, these have an overwhelming advantage, absolute as well as comparative, over traditional lenders in the collection and mobilization of deposits. There is much evidence that in many countries, there used to be a large, pent up demand for deposit banking, especially in rural areas, a demand that the spread of branch banking has done much to satisfy. This supply of loanable funds might respond significantly to an increase in deposit rates, as would come about in the course of easing financial repression, so that an easing of excess demand for credit could result.

It is less straightforward to find ways of making formal institutions more efficient lenders of funds. With little incentive to keep costs low and knowing that there are rents to be had from the system, the officers of the bank may pay themselves better salaries financed by suitable adjustments to their offer schedule, as depicted by the L-shaped schedule with horizontal segment AB in Fig. 15.3. In other words, the very existence of the moneylender's pure expected profits may induce the people who run the bank to move in the direction of M in Fig. 15.2 rather than conversely, as assumed above. If a gap remains, borrowers will do better than they would at point M; but that very fact gives individual officers of the bank an incentive to solicit bribes, and borrowers an incentive to pay them. For example, bribes may be tendered when there is excess demand for funds at the announced rate of interest, or the borrower, claiming inability to repay, wishes to roll over a loan. The moneylender will accommodate himself quite happily to such moves, for they will cut into his profits less by limiting the effectiveness of the bank's challenge to his market power. Casual observation of backward areas where commercialization is limited suggests that when traditional moneylenders continue to exercise a good deal of market power, the banks settle for a quiet, even a venal, life.

One clear conclusion that emerged above is the necessity of securing formal loans with marketable forms of collateral, both to overcome institutional lenders' apparent inability to collect and evaluate relevant information on borrowers at tolerable cost and to deny traditional lenders the advantage of debt seniority, with all the drawbacks these entail for the banks. To the usual objection that some borrowers will lose their collateral, there are two simple responses: first, all stand to all gain *ex ante* from the resulting improvement in efficiency; and secondly, general systemic risks from droughts, floods, pests and the like can be covered by specific insurance, and some idiosyncratic ones, such as ill health, by insurance premia payable as part of the loan contract, as demanded of borrowers by the *Grameen* Bank. As for so-called 'predatory' lending, whereby the lender advances a loan with the primary aim of acquiring the collateral that secures it, no one can seriously argue that formal credit institutions hanker after peasants' landholdings, producers' equipment and hand-tools, and traders' inventories and shops for their own sake as tangible possessions. For these reasons, a relaxation of the laws prohibiting or restricting the use of collateral to secure formal loans should be high up on the reform agenda.

The use of such collateral is not, of course, without its drawbacks. First, those with little or no land will get little or no institutional credit, while those with large holdings will do well. Where, as in parts of Africa, individual titles to land are not well established, the adoption of this policy generates pressures to register titles, often when land policy is itself not fully resolved (see Chapter 14). One, possibly unintended, consequence is a transfer of wealth from women to men (see, e.g. Collier and Lal, 1985). Second, given that institutions are usually required to charge the same rate of interest to all borrowers, the only decision left to them is how much to lend to each client, as depicted in Figs 15.3 and 15.4. In the presence of fixed transactions costs for processing loans, that gives them an incentive to lend to clients who seek large loans and have the collateral to make themselves creditworthy.

That moneylenders themselves obtain formal credit and use it for on-lending cannot be prevented, and if the volume of formal credit expands, such financial intermediation is likely to expand in sympathy. The question now arises as to whether this tacit form of agency should be augmented by direct forms, whereby traditional lenders would be explicitly engaged as the banks' agents on terms that are quite different from those of the standard debt contract. The use of agents to evaluate and monitor other agents has already been discussed in connection with group lending. Engaging traditional lenders to broker, disburse, and even collect loans when they fall due is, in principle, no different—though the moneylender's reputation in some circles is such that putting him to work in this way could be likened to letting the fox into the chicken coop. Be that as it may, Miracle (1973) describes a successful scheme of this kind in rural Malaysia.

Such indirect interventions do not look very promising, however, in situations where productivity is very low and conditions are such that a traditional moneylender enjoys a local monopoly. The introduction of a bank branch within easy range of his fief will do something to curb his power if the branch operates efficiently and its officers are incorruptible. A better remedy, however, would be the promotion of general economic development in the community, which would bring about new entry into traditional lending in its train. One cannot expect financial development in general, or specific credit policies in particular, to solve all deep-seated problems of backwardness and poverty. Not infrequently, the chain of causation is exactly the reverse.

15.6. Summary

The traditional moneylender and his system, like many traditional agrarian institutions, is often regarded as a social evil—to be stamped out if possible, to be sternly contained otherwise. This view has clearly coloured the numerous and widespread attempts to build up a network of formal financial institutions to serve rural communities and the unorganized sectors in towns, with a strong emphasis on providing cheap (subsidized) credit in order to raise borrowers' incomes and put the moneylender under heavy competitive pressure. On the positive side, it is also argued that improving the availability of credit on reasonable terms will raise productivity, both by relieving the financial constraint on small producers' use of working capital and by permitting more profitable, but 'lumpy', projects to be undertaken.

In the light of theory and experience, it seems fair to say that the vast majority of these lending schemes have met with mixed success at best, and many must be counted as failures. While the argument that adequate financing potentially improves economic efficiency in such settings is sound, the case for subsidizing credit does not bear close scrutiny. First, the need for fiscal prudence places limits on the subsidies, and hence on the volume of subsidized credit that can be offered. This limits, in turn, the gains that can be realized from greater efficiency. Second, the subsidies attract the interest of the well-to-do, who tend to do very well in capturing them. Thus, subsidized credit has proved to be a poor instrument in combating poverty. Third, if the aim is to raise producers' incomes by means of a subsidy, then a subsidy on output or certain categories of intermediate inputs is simpler and cheaper to administer—and proof against unintended 'leakage' to the better-off. To compound matters, the institutions in question have amassed an unenviable record of high costs, high rates of default on their loans, and losses to match. The Treasury is called upon to bail them out in the interest of maintaining confidence in the financial system—and all the while the moneylender continues to go about his business.

The manifest failings of what might be called these 'first generation' programmes of institutional credit for small producers have prompted a variety of initiatives, some involving procedures and others new institutions. An important example of the former is group lending, whereby peer selection and monitoring are combined with joint and several liability to overcome problems of asymmetric information and to serve as a collateral substitute. The best-known of the new institutions is the *Grameen Bank* of Bangladesh, which seeks to reach only the poor. Group lending is supplemented with compulsory insurance contributions and reinforced by frequent meetings and indoctrination, a regime that surely deters better-off households in search of subsidies. The catch in all this is that the *Grameen Bank*, and other so-called 'microfinance' institutions that have sprung up after it, are all heavily dependent on subsidies, and the prospects they will be able to wean themselves over the long haul are dim.

This brings us to the pitfalls of assessing the social profitability of all such schemes. Two points have received particular emphasis here. First, it is essential to identify the various alternatives borrowers face—self-finance, moneylenders, Roscas, or whatever—if certain of the key effects of introducing a scheme are to be correctly identified and estimated. This step involves the positive analysis of agents' decisions at market prices. The second step is normative, namely, to value all inputs and outputs at shadow prices. This step is a systematic test of social profitability from which no project should be exempt; it is conspicuous in the literature on this subject largely by its absence.

Recommended Reading

This field is a graveyard for optimists. Braverman and Guasch (1985) provide a damning indictment of conventional credit programmes, and Morduch's (2000) measured and incisive assessment of microfinance initiatives should be read as an antidote to the headier claims advanced in their favour. Early, somewhat divergent, accounts of the moneylender's traditional system are Bottomley (1975) and Wharton (1962). A set of more recent contributions with a broader span is to be found in Hoff *et al.* (1993).

Exercises

1. Consider a community of identical peasant farmers, each of whom produces output by means of a bundle of family resources and a variable input that is produced elsewhere in the economy. The output yielded by x units

of the latter input is

$$y = x^{\alpha} \quad (0 < \alpha < 1),$$

there being no natural uncertainty. The peasants live hand-to-mouth and so must resort to borrowing to finance these inputs. If a household chooses not to cultivate in this way, its resources yield the pay-off Y_0.

(a) If credit is available in perfectly elastic supply at the parametric rate r and the variable input at the parametric price q, and if output can be traded at the parametric price p, derive the (notional) demand for finance.

For simplicity, assume that the only cost of moneylending is the lender's opportunity cost of funds, which is denoted by r_2.

(b) If there is free entry into moneylending, find all variables in equilibrium.

(c) Suppose, instead, that a single moneylender held sway and was able to prevent any re-lending among the members of the community, so that take-it-or-leave-it contracts of the form (K, r) would be enforceable. Write down his optimization problem and find the optimum contract.

A regulated bank now enters the scene and offers credit at the rate $r_1 (< r_2)$ up to the limit of $\bar{K}_1$ per household. In the case where

$$\alpha = 1/2, \quad p = 2, \quad q = 1, \quad r_2 = 0.18, \quad r_1 = 0.1, \quad \text{and } \bar{K}_1 = 0.4,$$

find the resulting equilibrium in cases (b) and (c), respectively, and depict your findings in a price–quantity diagram.

(d) Suppose that the bank's officers are self-seeking and corrupt. If farmers approach the bank first, how large a bribe can an officer demand from each applicant? (Recall that farmers have no cash at the start of each season.) What effect does such corruption have on private lenders in cases (b) and (c), respectively? Consider what happens in case (c) if the bank and the single private lender move simultaneously.

Appendix. A Primer in Duality Theory

The purpose of this appendix is to provide a concise account of the main results in duality theory, which are employed extensively in the text. The approach is unswervingly heuristic and most proofs are omitted. Those readers who hanker after a detailed, formal treatment of this topic are referred to textbooks such as Kreps (1990), Mas-Colell *et al.* (1995), and Varian (1992). Much of what follows draws heavily on Kreps and Varian.

A.1. Technology

A feasible process (or activity) is such that the vector of outputs, $y = (y_1, \ldots, y_n)$, can be produced by means of the vector of inputs, $x = (x_1, \ldots, x_n)$. When, by convention, inputs are given a negative sign, the activity may be compactly written as $(y, -x)$. It is sometimes useful to employ the concept of a *netput*, which is the excess of output over the input of the good bearing the same label. A process yields a positive net output of good i if $y_i > x_i$; conversely, it requires a positive net input of good i if $x_i > y_i$. A feasible process is defined by its netput vector

$$z \equiv y - x.$$

The set of all feasible processes, or the *technology set*, is denoted by Z.

It is commonly assumed that Z exhibits the following properties:

Convexity: If z and $z' \in Z$, then $[\alpha z + (1 - \alpha)z'] \in Z \; \forall \alpha \in [0, 1]$.

That is to say, convex mixtures of feasible processes are also feasible.

Free disposal: If $z \in Z$ and $z' \le z$, then $z' \in Z$.

No free lunch: There exists no $z \in Z$ such that $z_i \ge 0 \; \forall i$ with $z_i > 0$ for at least some i.

Inactivity is feasible: $0 \in Z$, which may be interpreted to mean that no lunch at all is free.

Observe that the feasibility of inaction and the convexity of Z together imply that Z exhibits non-increasing returns to scale; for if z is feasible, then so too is αz for all $\alpha \in (0, 1)$. That is to say, a feasible process may be scaled down arbitrarily and yet remain feasible.[1] Non-decreasing returns to scale rule if, for any $z \in Z$ and $\forall \alpha \geq 1$, then also $\alpha z \in Z$. When this condition is added to convexity and the feasibility of inaction, the technology will exhibit:

Constant returns to scale (CRS): If $z \in Z$, then $\alpha z \in Z \; \forall \alpha \geq 0$.

Consider next the property of

Additivity: If $z \in Z$ and $z' \in Z$, then $z + z' \in Z$.

This states that if two processes are feasible separately, then they are also feasible jointly. Observe that additivity follows from convexity and CRS. For CRS implies that the processes z/α and $z'/(1 - \alpha)$ are feasible, and convexity then implies that $[\alpha(z/\alpha) + (1 - \alpha)z'/(1 - \alpha)] = z + z'$ is feasible. In this connection, recall that a *convex cone* is a subset of R^n which is closed under the operations of addition and multiplication by non-negative scalars (Gale, 1960). Hence, convexity and CRS together imply that the technology set is a convex cone.

If a clear division can be made between the inputs and outputs, respectively, of a particular process, in the sense that after a suitable relabelling of goods, $x_i \leq 0$ and $y_i = 0$ for $i = 1, \ldots, k$, and $x_i = 0$ and $y_i > 0$ for $i = k+1, \ldots, n$, then it is sometimes convenient to make the input vector non-negative by writing

$$x = (x_1, \ldots, x_n) = -(z_1, \ldots, z_k, 0, 0, \ldots, 0),$$

where one or more of the elements of the vector $(z_1, \ldots, z_k)$ may also be zero. The output vector is simply

$$y = (y_1, \ldots, y_n) = (0, 0, \ldots, 0, z_{k+1}, \ldots, z_n),$$

where, by the above convention, goods $k + 1$ through n are all produced in strictly positive quantities.

In the case where there is only one output, the assumption of free disposal implies that a firm that maximizes profits will produce as much output as it can from any given bundle of inputs. The relationship between output and inputs under these conditions is called the *production function*: $y = f(x)$. The above properties of Z imply that $f(\cdot)$ possesses the following properties:

(a) f is non-decreasing in x. This follows from the assumption that there is free disposal. For suppose $x \geq x'$ and $y = f(x) < y' = f(x')$. Then $(y', -x')$

---

[1] This result is contradicted by the fact that many processes are subject to a certain minimum scale of operation.

is still feasible by the simple expedient of disposing of the vector of inputs $(x - x')$.

(b) f is concave in x, which is a consequence of non-increasing returns. Since a concave function is also quasi-concave, the associated isoquant map is convex. If the technology exhibits CRS, then f will be homogeneous of degree one: $f(\alpha x) = \alpha f(x)$ for all $\alpha > 0$.

(c) $f(0) = 0$, which follows from the absence of a free lunch and the existence of a free no lunch.

A.2. The Profit Function

We assume that the firm faces parametric prices p, where $p \geq 0$ and $p_i > 0$ for at least one i, and that it seeks to maximize profits at those prices by choosing some (feasible) process. Stated formally, the firm's problem is to

$$\text{maximize}_{(z)} \; pz \quad \text{subject to } z \in Z. \tag{A.1}$$

Since pz is concave in z, this problem will have a solution if Z is strictly convex.[2] The value of the firm's profits at the optimum is a function of p and it is called the *profit function*:

$$\pi(p) = \text{maximum}_{(z)} \; pz \quad \text{subject to } z \in Z. \tag{A.2}$$

The profit function possesses the following properties:

(a) $\pi(p)$ is non-decreasing in output $(z_i > 0)$ prices and non-increasing in input $(z_i < 0)$ prices.

(b) $\pi(p)$ is homogenous of degree one in p.

(c) $\pi(p)$ is convex in p.

(d) $\pi(p)$ is continuous in p.

Observe that the only restriction placed on Z is the requirement that problem (A.1) possess a solution, $z(p)$ say. Observe also that there may be more than one solution.

Property (a) follows from the fact that if the price of a net output $(z_i > 0)$ rises, the original choice of activity, $z(p)$, will yield higher profits; for in this case, $\pi(p) \equiv pz(p) < p'z(p) \leq \pi(p')$. If, instead, the level of that net output is exactly zero, than profits will fail to be larger only if $z(p)$

---

[2] Note that if the technology exhibits CRS, profits may be unbounded, in which case problem (A.1) will have no solution.

continues to be optimal at the new prices p'. An analogous argument establishes that $\pi(p)$ is non-increasing in the prices of net inputs.

In order to prove property (b), observe that, by definition, $\pi(p) \equiv pz(p) \geq pz \; \forall z \in Z$. It follows that $tpz(p) \geq tpz \; \forall z \in Z$ for any positive scalar t. Hence, $z(p)$ also maximizes profits at prices tp; so that $\pi(tp) = tpz(p) = t\pi(p)$.

To establish the convexity of $\pi(p)$, consider two price vectors p and p'. By definition, $pz(p) \geq pz$ and $p'z(p') \geq p'z \; \forall z \in Z$. Hence, for any $\alpha \in [0, 1]$,

$$\alpha\pi(p) + (1 - \alpha)\pi(p') \geq [\alpha p + (1 - \alpha)p']z \quad \forall z \in Z.$$

Since this weak inequality holds, in particular, for $z[\alpha p + (1 - \alpha)p']$, we obtain the desired result.

The intuition for this result is as follows: if the firm does not change its choice of z when prices change to p', its profits will be $p'z(p)$, an expression which is linear in p'. If other feasible processes exist, one or more of them may yield higher profits at p' than does $z(p)$, in which case the profit function will be strictly convex for some subset of the price vectors defined by $[\alpha p + (1 - \alpha)p']$ for any $\alpha \in [0, 1]$. Figure A.1 depicts the case where

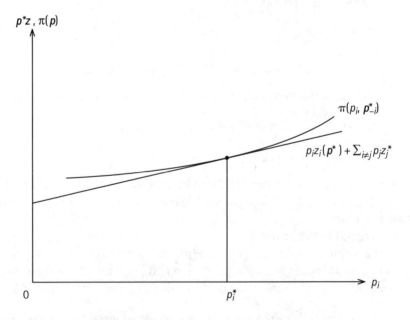

Figure A.1. A depiction of Hotelling's lemma

the price of an output changes and all other prices remain constant. As drawn, $\pi(\mathbf{p})$ is assumed to be differentiable and strictly convex in p_i.

This result leads to

Hotelling's lemma. *If $\pi(\mathbf{p})$ is differentiable at $\mathbf{p}^*$, then*

$$\partial\pi(\mathbf{p}^*)/\partial p_i = z_i(\mathbf{p}^*) \quad \forall i.$$

Proof. Consider Fig. A.1. The linear function in p_i

$$\psi(p_i, \mathbf{p}^*_{-i}) = \left[p_i z_i(\mathbf{p}^*) + \sum_{j\neq i} p_j^* z_j(\mathbf{p}^*) \right]$$

and $\pi(\mathbf{p})$ both pass through the point $[p_i^*, \pi(\mathbf{p}^*)]$. Since $\mathbf{pz}(\mathbf{p}^*) \leq \pi(\mathbf{p})$, with equality at $\mathbf{p} = \mathbf{p}^*$, and $\pi(\mathbf{p})$ is differentiable by assumption, it follows that the functions have a common tangent at $\mathbf{p}^*$. The result then follows from the fact that the linear function has a slope of $z_i(\mathbf{p}^*)$. □

The lemma states that a small change in the price of an output (input) will increase (decrease) profits by the current level of that output (input) multiplied by the said (small) increase in price. Any adjustments in the production process induced by this change in price will have an effect on profits that is second order in magnitude and can therefore be neglected.

A.3. The Cost Function

Suppose, for simplicity, that the firm produces only one (net) output, and let it be charged with producing at least y_0 units of the good in question. Conditional on this requirement, it will maximize profits by minimizing the cost of producing y_0. The firm's problem is, therefore, to

$$\underset{(\mathbf{x})}{\text{minimize}} \; \mathbf{wx} \quad \text{subject to } f(\mathbf{x}) \geq y_0, \tag{A.3}$$

where $\mathbf{w}$ is the vector of parametric input prices. When this problem has a solution, the value of the firm's costs at the optimum will be a function of $\mathbf{w}$ and y_0. This function is called the *cost function*:

$$c(\mathbf{w}, y_0) = \underset{(\mathbf{x})}{\text{minimum}} \; \mathbf{wx} \quad \text{subject to } f(\mathbf{x}) \geq y_0. \tag{A.4}$$

It possesses the following properties:

(a) $c(\cdot)$ is non-decreasing in w for each value of y_0.
(b) $c(\cdot)$ is homogenous of degree one in w for each fixed y_0.
(c) $c(\cdot)$ is concave in w for each fixed y_0.
(d) $c(\cdot)$ is non-decreasing in y_0 for each fixed w.

Remark 1. Observe that there is a certain 'duality' between the profit and cost functions. Although both are homogenous of degree one in prices, the former is convex, whereas the latter is concave.

We shall return to Remark 1 later in this appendix.

The proofs of claims (a)–(c) are similar to those employed to establish the properties of the profit function, and are left to the reader. In order to prove (d), consider Fig. A.2, in which the shaded area bounded from below by the isoquant $f(x) = y_0$ depicts the set of all input vectors yielding at least y_0. If, at any optimum $x(w, y_0)$, production is costly (i.e. $x_i > 0$ and $w_i > 0$ for at least one i), then $f[x(w, y_0)] = y_0$. For if $f[x(w, y_0)] > y_0$, then at least one costly component of $x(w, y_0)$ could be reduced somewhat without violating the requirement that at least y_0 be produced, which would contradict the hypothesis that $x(w, y_0)$ minimizes wx. An increase in y_0 then implies that no minimizer of wx at the initial value of y_0 can yield the higher level of output, so that the cost of producing the latter cannot be smaller than that of producing y_0.

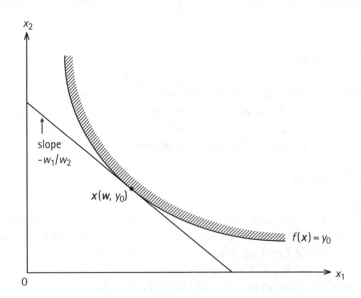

Figure A.2. Cost minimization

Analogously to Hotelling's lemma, we have

Shephard's lemma. *If $c(w, y_0)$ is differentiable at w^* for each y_0, then*

$$\partial c(w^*, y_0)/\partial w_i = x_i(w^*, y_0) \quad \forall i,$$

where $x(w^*, y_0)$ is any solution to problem (A.3).

Interested readers should attempt a proof before proceeding to Section A.4, where those who are anxious to get on with matters will find one awaiting them.

Thus far in this section, we have said nothing about returns to scale. Suppose the technology exhibits CRS, so that $f(\alpha x) = \alpha f(x) \ \forall \alpha > 0$, and let $x(w, y_0)$ be any solution to problem (A.3). Since $\alpha w x(w, y_0) \leq \alpha w x$ for any x satisfying $f(x) \geq y_0$, we choose $\alpha = 1/y_0$ and observe that this choice implies that $w \cdot [x(w, y_0)/y_0] \leq w \cdot (x/y_0)$ for any x satisfying $f(x) \geq y_0$. By CRS, however, the constraint may be written as $f(x/y_0) \geq 1$. Hence, the process $[x(w, y_0)/y_0]$ is a solution to problem (A.3) when the firm must produce at least one unit of output. It follows that

$$c(w, 1) = c(w, y_0)/y_0,$$

so that average cost is constant everywhere, and marginal and average cost are identical.

A.4. The Envelope Theorem

We now turn to a powerful and very useful theorem, particularly in the realm of comparative statics. It must be emphasized, however, that the theorem is applicable only if the objective function and the functions that define the constraint set are continuously differentiable. The following formulation is drawn from Takayama (1974: 160–1).

Consider the constrained optimization problem:

$$\underset{(x)}{\text{maximize}} \ f(x, \alpha) \quad \text{subject to } g_j(x, \alpha) = 0, \ j = 1, \ldots, m, \text{ and } x \in X,$$

$$(A.5)$$

where α is a vector of parameters and X is an open subset of R^n. Observe that all constraints are in the form of strict equalities. What follows will also be valid, however, if there are inequalities, provided the set of binding constraints does not change in a neighbourhood of the particular vector $\boldsymbol{\alpha}$ under consideration. The Lagrangian is

$$\Phi(x, \lambda; \alpha) = f(x, \alpha) + \lambda \cdot g(x, \alpha), \tag{A.6}$$

where $\lambda = (\lambda_1, \ldots, \lambda_m)$ is a vector of multipliers. Let $[x(\alpha), \lambda(\alpha)]$ maximize Φ and define the functions

$$F(\alpha) \equiv f[x(\alpha), \alpha],$$

$$\Psi(\alpha) \equiv f[x(\alpha), \alpha] + \lambda(\alpha) \cdot g[x(\alpha), \alpha].$$

Thus, $F(\alpha)$ and $\Psi(\alpha)$ are the values of $f(\cdot)$ and $\Phi(\cdot)$, respectively, at the optimum.

The Envelope Theorem. *If F and Ψ are continuously differentiable, then*

$$F_\alpha = \Psi_\alpha = \Phi_\alpha, \tag{A.7}$$

where

$$\Phi_\alpha = f_\alpha + (\lambda_1 \cdot \partial g_1/\partial \alpha, \ldots, \lambda_m \cdot \partial g_m/\partial \alpha). \tag{A.8}$$

Remark 2. Equation (A.7) states that the effect of a change in $\boldsymbol{\alpha}$ on the value of the maximand at the optimum is equal to the *total* effect on the Lagrangian at the optimum, which is equal in turn to the *partial* effect of $\boldsymbol{\alpha}$ on the Lagrangian when x and λ are kept fixed. All derivatives in Eqn (A.7) are evaluated at the optimum, namely, $[x(\alpha), \lambda(\alpha); \alpha]$.

In order to show the envelope theorem at work, we return to the cost function. The parameters of problem (A.3) are (w, y_0), and the maximand is $[-wx]$, which is continuously differentiable. Under the weak assumption that at least one input used at the optimum has a positive price, we know that the constraint $f(x) \geq y_0$ will hold as an equality. If f is differentiable, then so is the constraint $f(x) - y_0 = 0$. Hence, assuming that none of the constraints $x_i \geq 0$ switches regime in response to the changes in (w, y_0), we may apply the envelope theorem to problem (A.3).

Write the Lagrangian as

$$\Phi = -wx + \lambda[f(x) - y_0] + vx,$$

where the multiplier v_i is associated with the non-negativity constraint $x_i \geq 0$. Recalling that

$$c(w, y_0) \equiv -\underset{x}{\text{maximum}}[-wx] \quad \text{subject to } f(x) \geq y_0 \text{ and } x \geq 0,$$

Eqns (A.7) and (A.8) yield at once

$$\partial c(\boldsymbol{w}, y_0)/\partial w_i = x_i(\boldsymbol{w}, y_0) \quad \forall i,$$

namely, Shephard's lemma, and

$$\partial c(\boldsymbol{w}, y_0)/\partial y_0 = \lambda(\boldsymbol{w}, y_0),$$

which establishes property (d) in Section A.3 by virtue of $\lambda \geq 0$.

In order to give the reader an intuitive grasp of why the envelope theorem works as it does, we derive these results by totally differentiating the maximand and the side constraint $f(\boldsymbol{x}) \geq y_0$ and then using the first-order conditions to simplify the resulting expressions. Differentiating $-\boldsymbol{w}\boldsymbol{x}$ and $f(\boldsymbol{x}) - y_0 = 0$ totally, we have

$$d(-\boldsymbol{w}\boldsymbol{x}) = -(\boldsymbol{w}\, d\boldsymbol{x} + \boldsymbol{x}\, d\boldsymbol{w})$$

and

$$d[f(\boldsymbol{x}) - y_0] = f_{\boldsymbol{x}} \cdot d\boldsymbol{x} - dy_0 = 0,$$

where $f_{\boldsymbol{x}} \equiv \nabla f$. Assuming an interior solution to problem (A.3), so that $\boldsymbol{v} = 0$, the first-order conditions are

$$\Phi_{\boldsymbol{x}} = -\boldsymbol{w} + \lambda f_{\boldsymbol{x}} = 0, \qquad \Phi_{\lambda} = f(\boldsymbol{x}) - y_0 = 0.$$

Beginning with the case where input prices change with output held constant, $dy_0 = 0$ implies that $f_{\boldsymbol{x}} \cdot d\boldsymbol{x} = 0$. Hence, the 'marginal' condition $\boldsymbol{w} = \lambda f_{\boldsymbol{x}}$ implies that $\boldsymbol{w}\, d\boldsymbol{x}$ $(=\lambda f_{\boldsymbol{x}} \cdot d\boldsymbol{x})$ will vanish at the optimum and so yields the result

$$\partial[\boldsymbol{w}\boldsymbol{x}(\boldsymbol{w}, y_0)]/\partial w_i = x_i \quad \forall i.$$

Consider next the case where output varies at constant input prices ($d\boldsymbol{w} = 0$), so that

$$[d(\boldsymbol{w}\boldsymbol{x})/dy_0]_{\boldsymbol{w}} = \boldsymbol{w} \cdot (d\boldsymbol{x}/dy_0).$$

At the optimum, however, $\boldsymbol{w} = \lambda f_{\boldsymbol{x}}$, and recalling that $f_{\boldsymbol{x}} \cdot d\boldsymbol{x} - dy_0 = 0$, we obtain

$$\partial[\boldsymbol{w}\boldsymbol{x}(\boldsymbol{w}, y_0)]/\partial y_0 = \lambda,$$

which is the desired result.

The essential point to note is that the maximand is locally stationary at the optimum, so that a small change in any choice variable will leave the maximand's value unchanged (the effect is second-order in magnitude). A small change in a parameter, however, will have a direct first-order effect on the maximand, or on the constraints, or on both; but it will have only a second-order effect on the maximand by inducing small changes in the choice variables, and the latter effect can be neglected when the change in the parameter is sufficiently small.

A.5. The Revenue or GNP Function

It will be useful to introduce non-produced goods, or factors, of which the economy is assumed to have a fixed endowment vector $\bar{X} = (\bar{X}_1, \ldots, \bar{X}_m)$. For the economy as a whole, the value of the net output of produced goods is the total return to this endowment, or simply GNP.

In order to avoid an unnecessarily complicated formulation, we specialize the technology to the case where each process can produce a positive net output of only one good, all other goods being net inputs. Given that firms will choose to produce efficiently, that is, on the frontiers of their respective technology sets, the technology available to the economy is therefore described by a set of production functions

$$y_j = f_j(x_j; X_j), \quad j = 1, \ldots, n,$$

where $x_j = (x_{1j}, \ldots, x_{nj})$ and $X_j = (X_{1j}, \ldots, X_{mj})$ are, respectively, the vectors of produced and non-produced inputs used to produce good j ($j = 1, \ldots, n$). We assume that $f_j(\cdot)$ is an increasing, concave, and smooth function for all j.

Suppose that the prices of produced goods $p = (p_1, \ldots, p_n)$ are given parametrically and that the endowment $\bar{X}$ is supplied completely inelastically. If the goal is to maximize GNP, subject to technological and factor availability constraints, the problem may be written as

$$\underset{x_j, X_j}{\text{maximize}} \left[\sum_{j=1}^{n} (p_j y_j - px_j) \right] \qquad (A.9)$$

subject to: $y_j = f_j(x_j; X_j), \ j = 1, \ldots, n,$

$$\bar{X}_k \geq \sum_{j=1}^{n} X_{jk} \quad , k = 1, \ldots, m, \text{ and the non-negativity constraints.}$$

Under the foregoing assumptions, this problem will have a solution. The value of the maximand at the optimum is a function of $(p, \bar{X})$ and is called the *GNP*, or *revenue, function*:

$$\Omega(p, \bar{X}) = \max_{x_j, X_j} \left[\sum_{j=1}^{n} (p_j y_j - px_j) \right] \tag{A.10}$$

subject to the constraints in problem (A.9).

In the case of a closed economy, the net supply of each and every produced good must be non-negative, that is, $y_j \geq \sum_{i=1}^{n} x_{ij}$. Under the above assumptions, the GNP function then possesses the following properties:

  (a) Ω is non-decreasing and concave in $\bar{X}$,
  (b) Ω is non-decreasing and convex in p,
  (c) Ω is homogenous of degree one in p.

The proofs of these claims are left as an exercise to the interested reader.

Suppose that for each and every factor, at least one output, j say, is being produced whose production function, $f_j(\cdot)$, is strictly increasing in that factor; so that all factors will be fully employed and the availability constraints will hold as equalities. Then, given that the production functions are continuously differentiable, the envelope theorem may be applied. Proceeding as in Section A.4, we write the Lagrangian as

$$\Phi = \left[\sum_{j=1}^{n} (p_j y_j - px_j) \right] + \sum_{j=1}^{n} \lambda_j \left[f_j(x_j, X_j) - y_j \right]$$

$$+ \sum_{k=1}^{m} \mu_k \left(\bar{X}_k - \sum_{j=1}^{n} X_{jk} \right) + vx + \xi X,$$

where the vectors v and ξ are the multipliers associated with the non-negativity constraints on x and X. The envelope theorem yields:

$$\partial \Omega(p, \bar{X}) / \partial p_i = y_i(p, \bar{X}) - \sum_{j=1}^{n} x_{ij}(p, \bar{X}) \tag{A.11}$$

and

$$\partial \Omega(p, \bar{X}) / \partial \bar{X}_k = \mu_k(p, \bar{X}), \tag{A.12}$$

where $y_i(p, \bar{X})$ is the supply of good i at prices p and the endowment $\bar{X}$, and $x_{ij}(p, \bar{X})$ is the derived demand for good j in the production of good i

at $(p, \bar{X})$. Since the RHS Eqn of (A.11) is the net supply of good j, it follows at once that the first part of (b) above holds.

From Eqn (A.12), the multiplier $\mu_k(p, \bar{X})$ is the increase in the maximand at the optimum that would result if the endowment of factor k were to increase by one unit. In a perfectly competitive economy, the vector $\mu = (\mu_1, \ldots, \mu_m)$ would be the vector of factor prices.

As a variation, consider the classic example in which the prices of all produced goods are parametrically given, that is, where all goods are tradable and the country is small. In keeping with the assumption that factors are supplied completely inelastically, let them be internationally immobile. In this case, it is seen from Eqn (A.11) that the GNP function is increasing in p_i if the economy is a net producer (exporter) of good i; conversely, Ω is decreasing in p_i if the economy is a net consumer (importer) thereof.

A.6. The Indirect Utility Function

In the final two sections, we deal with the rational consumer's choices. We assume that her preferences are complete, transitive, locally non-satiated, continuous, and convex, so that they can be represented by a continuous, increasing, and quasi-concave function $u(x)$, whose arguments are the consumption bundle $x = (x_1, \ldots, x_n)$.

Consider the standard consumer's problem: choose x so as to

$$\text{maximize } u(x) \quad \text{subject to } M - qx \geq 0 \text{ and } x \geq 0, \tag{A.13}$$

where she faces parametrically given prices q and M denotes her money income. Given that her preferences are not locally satiated, then all income will be consumed:

$$M = qx(q, M).$$

If her preferences are strictly convex, problem (A.13) will have a unique solution, $x(q, M)$.

Remark 3. $x_i(q, M)$ is the consumer's Marshallian demand function for good i.

The value of the maximand at the optimum is a function of q and M, a function which is called the *indirect utility function*:

$$v(q, M) = \underset{x}{\text{maximum }} u(x) \quad \text{subject to } M - qx \geq 0 \text{ and } x \geq 0.$$

$$\tag{A.14}$$

The properties of the indirect utility function are as follows:

    (a) v is non-increasing in q and non-decreasing in M,
    (b) v is homogenous of degree zero in q and M,
    (c) v is quasi-convex in q and M,
    (d) v is continuous in q and M for all $q > 0$ and $M \geq 0$.

The proofs of claims (a)–(c) are left as an exercise to the reader. The proof of part (d) is rather technical (see, e.g. Kreps, 1990: 45).

    Since $u(x)$ and px are differentiable, and $M = qx$ in the absence of satiation, we may apply the envelope theorem to problem (A.13) to obtain

Roy's identity: $[\partial v(q, M)/\partial q_i]/[\partial v(q, M)/\partial M] = -x_i(q, M)$.

Proof. By writing the Lagrangian as

$$\Phi = u(x) + \lambda(M - qx) + vx,$$

we obtain

$$\Phi_q = -\lambda x \quad \text{and} \quad \Phi_M = \lambda.$$

Recalling Eqn (A.7), the desired result follows at once.   □

A.7. The Expenditure Function

In the 'dual' to problem (A.13), the consumer chooses a bundle so as to attain any given level of utility as cheaply as possible. Formally, this may be stated as

$$\underset{(x)}{\text{maximize}} \; (-qx) \quad \text{subject to } u(x) - u_0 \geq 0 \text{ and } x \geq 0. \tag{A.15}$$

The additional assumption of strictly convex preferences ensures that this problem has a unique solution $x(q, u_0)$, which is known as the *Hicksian*, or *compensated*, demand function. The value of the minimand (qx) at the optimum is a function of the parameters (q, u_0) and is known as the *expenditure* function:

$$e(q, u_0) = \underset{x}{\text{minimum}} \; qx \quad \text{subject to } u(x) - u_0 \geq 0 \text{ and } x \geq 0.$$

$$\tag{A.16}$$

The properties of the expenditure function are as follows:

     (a) e is non-decreasing in q,
     (b) e is homogenous of degree one in q,
     (c) e is concave in q,
     (d) e is continuous in q for $q > 0$,
     (e) if e is continuously differentiable at the optimum corresponding to the pair (q, u_0), then

$$\partial e(q, u_0)/\partial q_i = x_i(q, u_0).$$

Observe that the indirect utility and expenditure functions are dual to one another in a way that is exactly analogous to the profit and cost functions. Parts (a)–(d) are proved in just the same way as in their counterparts in Section A.3. Part (e) follows from the envelope theorem. For

$$\Phi_q = -x,$$

and at the optimum, Eqn (A.7) yields

$$\Phi_q = \partial[-qx(q, u_0)]/\partial q \equiv -\partial e(q, u_0)/\partial q$$

and hence establishes the claim. This property of $e(q, u_0)$ is analogous to Shephard's lemma, but it appears to lack the dignity of a formal title.

References

Adam, C., Ndulu, B., and Sowa, N. K. (1996), 'Liberalisation and Seigniorage Revenue in Kenya, Ghana and Tanzania', *Journal of Development Studies*, 32: 531–53.

Adams, D. W. and Nehman, G. I. (1979), 'Borrowing Costs and the Demand for Rural Credit', *Journal of Development Studies*, 15(2): 165–76.

Ahmad, E., Leung, H.-M., and Stern, N. H. (1984), 'Demand Response and the Reform of Indirect Taxes in Pakistan', Discussion Paper no. 50, Development Economics Research Centre, University of Warwick.

— and Stern, N. H. (1984), 'The Theory of Tax Reform and Indian Indirect Taxes', *Journal of Public Economics*, 25: 259–98.

— and — (1989), 'Taxation for Developing Countries', in Chenery, H. B. and Srinivasan, T. N. (eds), *Handbook of Development Economics*, vol. 2, Amsterdam: North-Holland.

— and — (1991), *The Theory and Practice of Tax Reform in Developing Countries*, Cambridge: Cambridge University Press.

Arrow, K. J. (1962), 'The Economic Implications of Learning by Doing', *Review of Economic Studies*, 28(3): 155–73.

— and Lind, R. C. (1971), 'Uncertainty and the Evaluation of Public Investment Decisions', *American Economic Review*, 60: 364–78.

Atkinson, A. B. and Stiglitz, J. E. (1980), *Lectures on Public Economics*, New York: McGraw-Hill.

Auerbach, A. A. (1985), 'The Theory of Excess Burden and Optimal Taxation', in Auerbach, A. A. and Feldstein, M. (eds), *Handbook of Public Economics*, Amsterdam: North-Holland.

Bahmani-Oskooee, M., Mohtadi, H., and Shabsigh, G. (1991), 'Exports, Growth and Causality in LDCs: A Re-examination', *Journal of Development Economics*, 36(2): 405–15.

Balassa, B. (1971), *The Structure of Protection in Developing Countries*, Baltimore: Johns Hopkins University Press.

— (1978), 'Exports and Economic Growth', *Journal of Development Economics*, 5(2): 181–9.

Bell, C. (1977), 'Alternative Theories of Sharecropping: Some Tests Using Evidence from Northeast India', *Journal of Development Studies*, 13 (July): 317–46.

— (1989), 'The Choice of Tenancy Contract', in Irma Adelman and Sylvia Lane (eds), *The Balance between Industry and Agriculture in Economic Development*, vol. 5, *Social Effects*, London: Macmillan.

— (1991), 'Shadow Prices, Migration and Regional Heterogeneity', *Journal of Public Economics*, 36: 1–27.

Bell, C. and Devarajan, S. (1982), 'A Social Cost-Benefit Analysis of the Project', in Bell, C., Hazell, P., and Slade, R. (eds), *Project Evaluation in Regional Perspective*, Baltimore: Johns Hopkins University Press.

— and — (1983), 'Shadow Prices for Project Evaluation under Alternative Macroeconomic Specifications', *Quarterly Journal of Economics*, 97: 454–77.

— and — (1987), 'Intertemporally Consistent Shadow Prices in an Open Economy: Estimates for Cyprus', *Journal of Public Economics*, 32: 263–88.

— Hazell, P., and Slade, R. (1982), *Project Evaluation in Regional Perspective*, Baltimore: Johns Hopkins University Press.

— Srinivasan, T. N., and Udry, C. (1997), 'Rationing, Spillover, and Interlinking in Credit Markets: The Case of Rural Punjab', *Oxford Economic Papers*, 49: 557–85.

Berry, R. A. and Cline, W. R. (1979), *Agrarian Structure and Productivity in Developing Countries*, Baltimore: Johns Hopkins University Press.

Bhagwati, J. N. (1971), 'The Generalized Theory of Distortions and Welfare', in Bhagwati, J. N. (ed.), *Trade, Balance of Payments, and Growth: Papers in Honour of Charles P. Kindelberger*, Amsterdam: North-Holland.

— (1978), *Foreign Trade Regimes and Economic Development: Anatomy and Consequences of Exchange Control Regimes*, Cambridge, MA: Ballinger.

— and Chakravarty, S. (1969), 'Contributions to Indian Economic Analysis: A Survey', *American Economic Review*, 59, supp. (July): 1–73.

— Panagariya, A., and Srinivasan, T. N. (1998), *Lectures on International Trade*, 2nd edn, Cambridge, MA: MIT Press.

Bhalla, S. S. (1988), 'Does Land Quality Matter? Theory and Measurement', *Journal of Development Economics*, 29 (July): 45–62.

— and Prannoy Roy (1988), 'Misspecification in Farm Productivity Analysis: The Role of Land Quality', *Oxford Economic Papers*, 40 (March): 55–73.

Binswanger, H. P. and Elgin, M. (1988), 'What are the Prospects of Land Reform?' in Maunder, A. and Valdes, A. (eds), *Agriculture and Governments in an Interdependent World, Proceedings of the Twentieth International Conference of Agricultural Economists*, Buenos Aires.

— and Rosenzweig, M. (1986), 'The Behavioral and Material Determinants of Production', *Journal of Development Studies*, 22 (April): 503–39.

— Deininger, K., and Feder, Gershon (1995), 'Power, Distortions, Revolt and Reform in Agricultural Land Relations', in Behrmann, J. and Srinivasan, T. N., *Handbook of Development Economics*, Amsterdam: North Holland.

Black, S. (1992), 'Seigniorage', in Newman, P., Milgate, M., and Eatwell, J. (eds), *The New Palgrave Dictionary of Money and Finance*, London: Macmillan.

Blarel, B., Hazell, P. B. R., Migot-Adholla, S., and Place, F. (1993), 'Land Tenure Reform and Agricultural Development in Sub-Saharan Africa', in Hoff et al., *The Economics of Rural Organization*, Oxford: Clarendon Press.

Bliss, C. (1987), 'Taxation, Cost-Benefit Analysis and Effective Protection', in Newbery, D. M. G. and Stern, N. H. *The Theory of Taxation for Developing Countries*, New York: Oxford University Press.

— and Nicholas, H. Stern (1981), *Palanpur: The Economy of an Indian Village*, Oxford: Clarendon Press.

Bottomley, A. (1975), 'Interest Rate Determination in Underdeveloped Areas', *American Journal of Agricultural Economics*, 57: 279–91.

Braverman, A. and Guasch, L. (1985), 'Rural Credit Markets and Institutions in Developing Countries: Lessons for Policy Analysis from Practice and Modern Theory', *World Development*, 14: 1253–67.

Brekke, K. A. (1997), 'The Numéraire Matters in Cost-Benefit Analysis', *Journal of Public Economics*, 64: 117–23.

— (1998), 'Reply to J. Drèze and P.-O. Johansson', *Journal of Public Economics*, 70: 495–6.

Buffie, E. F. (1995), 'Trade Liberalization, Credibility and Self-fulfilling Failures', *Journal of International Economics*, 38: 51–73.

— (2001), *Trade Policy in Developing Countries*, Cambridge: Cambridge University Press.

Buiter, W. H. and Patel, U. R. (1992), 'Debt, Deficits and Inflation: An Application to the Public Finances of India', *Journal of Public Economics*, 47: 171–205.

Burgess, R. and Stern, N. H. (1992), 'Taxation and Development', *Journal of Economic Literature*, 31(2): 762–85.

Calvo, G. A. (1987), 'On the Costs of Temporary Policy', *Journal of Development Economics*, 27: 245–61.

Carter, M. (1993), 'A Microeconomic Chronicle of the Evolution of Land Reform in Peru: Implications for Agrarian Theory and Policy', in Hoff *et al.*, *The Economics of Rural Organization*, Oxford: Clarendon Press.

Cass, D. (1965), 'Optimum Growth in Aggregate Model of Capital Accumulation', *Review of Economic Studies*, 32: 233–40.

Chakravarty, A. and Rudra, A. (1973), 'Economic Effects of Tenancy: Some Negative Results', *Economic and Political Weekly*, 13(28) (July 14): 1239–46.

Chayanov, A. V. (1966), *The Theory of Peasant Economy*, Kerblay, B., Thorner, D., and Smith, R. E. F. (eds), Homewood, Ill.: American Economic Association.

Collier, P. and Lal, D. (1985), *Labour and Poverty in Kenya*, London: Oxford University Press.

Dasgupta, P., Marglin, S. A., and Sen, A. K. (1972), *Guidelines for Project Evaluation*, New York: United Nations.

Deaton, A. S. (1987), 'Econometric Issues for Tax Design in Developing Countries', in Newbery, D. M. G. and Stern, N. H., *The Theory of Taxation for Developing Countries*, New York: Oxford University Press.

— and Stern, N. H. (1986), 'Optimally Uniform Commodity Taxes, Taste Differences, and Lump-Sum Grants', *Economic Letters*, 20: 263–6.

Deininger, K. (1999), 'Making Negotiated Land Reform Work: Initial Experience from Colombia, Brazil and South Africa', *World Development*, 27 (April): 651–72.

De Janvry, A. and Sadoulet, E. (1993), 'Path Dependent Policy Reforms: From Land Reform to Rural Development in Colombia', in Hoff et al., *The Economics of Rural Organization*, Oxford: Clarendon Press.

Devarajan, S. and Rodrik, D. (1991), 'Pro-Competitive Effects of Trade Reform: Results from a CGE Model of Cameroon', *European Economic Review*, 35: 1157–84.

Diamond, P. A. and Mirrlees, J. A. (1971), 'Optimal Taxation and Public Production, Part I: Production Efficiency', and 'Part II: Tax Rules', *American Economic Review*, 60(1) and 61(3).

Diewert, W. E. (1988), 'Index Numbers', in Eatwell, J., Milgate, M., and Newman, P. (eds), *The New Palgrave*, London: Macmillan.

Dinwiddy, C. and Teal, F. (1994). 'The Shadow Wage Rate: Theory and Application', *Journal of Public Economics*, 53: 309–17.

Dixit, A. (1985), 'Tax Policy in Open Economies', in Auerbach, A. J. and Feldstein, M. (eds), *Handbook of Public Economics*, vol. 1, Amsterdam: North-Holland.

—— and Norman, V. (1980), *Theory of International Trade*, Cambridge: Cambridge University Press.

Dornbusch, R. and Reynoso, A. (1993), 'Financial Factors in Economic Development', in Dornbusch, R. (ed.), *Policymaking in the Open Economy*, New York: Oxford University Press.

Dréze, J. (1998), 'Distribution Matters in Cost-Benefit Analysis: Comment on K. A. Brekke', *Journal of Public Economics*, 70: 485–8.

—— and Mukherjee, A. (1989), 'Labor Contracts in Rural India: Theories and Evidence', in Sukhamoy Chakravarty (ed.), *The Balance between Industry and Agriculture in Economic Development*, vol. 3, *Manpower and Transfers*, London: Macmillan.

—— and Stern, N. H. (1987), 'The Theory of Cost-Benefit Analysis', in Auerbach, A. J. and Feldstein, M. (eds), *Handbook of Public Economics*, vol. 2, Amsterdam: North-Holland.

Emery, R. F. (1967), 'The relation of exports and economic growth', *Kyklos*, 20: 470–86.

FAO, Food and Agriculture Organization (1981), *1970 World Census of Agriculture: Analysis and International Comparison of Results*. Rome.

Feder, G. (1983), 'On Exports and Economic Growth', *Journal of Development Economics*, 12(1–2): 59–73.

Feenstra, R. C. (1992), 'Money in the Utility Function', in Newman, P., Milgate, M., and Eatwell, J. (eds), *The New Palgrave Dictionary of Money and Finance*, London: Macmillan.

Fel'dman, G. A. (1928), 'K teorii tempov narodnogo dokhoda' ('On the Theory of National Income Growth'), *Planovoe Khoziaistvo* (*The Planned Economy*), 11–12: 146–70, 151–78. [For a full and critical exposition, see E. D. Domar (1957),

Essays in the Theory of Economic Growth, ch. 4, New York: Oxford University Press.]

Fischer, S. (1982), 'Seigniorage and the Case for a National Money', *Journal of Political Economy*, 90: 295–313.

Flowerdew, A. D. J. (1972), 'Choosing a Site for the Third London Airport: The Roskill Commission's Approach', in Layard, R. (ed.), *Cost-Benefit Analysis*, Harmondsworth: Penguin Books, 431–51.

Gale, D. (1960), *The Theory of Linear Economic Models*, New York: McGraw-Hill.

Gersbach, H. and Haller, H. (2001), 'Hierarchical Trade and Endogenous Price Distortions', Alfred Weber Institute, Heidelberg University.

Gersovitz, M. (1976), 'Land Reform: Some Theoretical Considerations', *Journal of Development Studies*, 13 (October): 79–92.

Graham, D. A. (1981), 'Cost-Benefit Analysis under Uncertainty', *American Economic Review*, 71: 715–25.

Grossman, G. and Helpman, E. (1991), *Innovation and Growth in the Global Economy*, Cambridge, MA: MIT Press.

Guisinger, S. (1979), 'Calculating Shadow Prices in Pakistan', *Pakistan Development Review*, 18: 117–27.

Habib, I. (1982), 'The Systems of Agricultural Production (Mughal India)', in Raychaudhuri, T. and Habib, I. (eds), *The Cambridge Economic History of India*, vol. I, Cambridge: Cambridge University Press.

Hahn, F. H. (1973), 'On Optimum Taxation', *Journal of Economic Theory*, 6: 96–106.

Harberger, A. C. (1971), 'On Measuring the Social Opportunity Cost of Labour', *International Labor Review*, 103: 559–79.

— (1972), *Project Evaluation: Collected Papers*, London: Macmillan.

— (1993), 'The Other Side of Tax Reform', in Dornbusch, R. (ed.), *Policymaking in the Open Economy*, New York: Oxford University Press.

Harris, J. R. and Todaro, M. (1970), 'Migration, Unemployment and Development', *American Economic Review*, 60(1): 126–42.

Hayami, Y. and Otsuka, K. (1993), 'Kasugpong in Central Luzon: "Indianization" of the Philippine Rice Bowl?' in Hoff *et al.*, *The Economics of Rural Organization*, Oxford: Clarendon Press.

Heller, P. and Porter, R. (1978), 'Exports and Growth: An Empirical Reinvestigation', *Journal of Development Economics*, 5(2): 191–3.

Hicks, J. R. (1959), 'National Economic Development in an International Setting', in *Essays on World Economics*, Oxford: Clarendon Press.

— (1964), *Lectures on International Trade and Development*, Cairo: Bank of Cairo.

— (1965), *Capital and Growth*, Oxford: Clarendon Press.

Hirschleifer, J. (1965), 'Investment Decisions Under Uncertainty–Choice-Theoretic Approaches', *Quarterly Journal of Economics*, 79: 509–36.

Hirschmann, A. O. (1963), *Journeys toward Progress*, New York: Twentieth Century Fund.

Hoff, K., Braverman, A., and Stiglitz, J. E. (1993), *The Economics of Rural Organization*, Oxford: Clarendon Press.

Hossain, M. (1977), 'Farm Size, Tenancy and Land Productivity: An Analysis of Farm Level Data in Bangladesh Agriculture', *Bangladesh Development Studies*, 5 (July): 285–348.

—— (1985), *Credit for the Rural Poor: The Grameen Bank in Bangladesh*, Research Monograph 4, Dhaka: Bangladesh Institute of Development Studies.

Hummels, D. (1999), 'Toward a Geography of Trade Costs', University of Chicago, processed.

Intriligator, M. D. (1971), *Mathematical Optimization and Economic Theory*, Englewood Cliffs, NJ: Prentice-Hall.

Issler, J. V. and Lima, L. R. (2000), 'Public Debt Sustainability and Endogenous Seigniorage in Brazil: Time-Series Evidence from 1947–1992', *Journal of Development Economics*, 62: 131–47.

Jarvis, S. (1987), *Smuggling in East Anglia, 1700–1840*, Newbury: Countryside Books.

Johansson, P.-O. (1998), 'Does the Choice of Numéraire Matter in Cost-Benefit Analysis?' *Journal of Public Economics*, 70: 489–93.

Joshi, V. and Little, I. M. D. (1994), *India: Macroeconomics and Political Economy, 1964–1991*, Oxford: Clarendon Press.

—— and —— (1996), *India's Economic Reforms, 1991–2001*, Oxford: Clarendon Press.

Jung, W. and Marshall, P. (1986), 'Exports, Growth and Causality in Developing Coutries', *Journal of Development Economics*, 18(1): 1–12.

Kaldor, N. (1962), 'Comment', *Review of Economic Studies*, 29: 246–50.

—— and Mirrlees, J. A. (1962), 'A New Model of Economic Growth', *Review of Economic Studies*, 29: 176–92.

Karvis, I. B. (1970), 'Trade as a handmaiden of growth: similarities between the nineteenth and twentieth centuries', *Economic Journal*, 80: 870–2.

Kimbrough, K. P. (1986), 'The Optimum Quantity of Money Rule in the Theory of Public Finance', *Journal of Monetary Economics*, 18: 277–84.

—— (1992), 'Inflation Tax', in Newman, P., Milgate, M., and Eatwell, J. (eds), *The New Palgrave Dictionary of Money and Finance*, London: Macmillan.

Koopmans, T. C. (1965), 'On the Concept of Optimal Economic Growth', *The Econometric Approach to Development Planning*, Amsterdam: North-Holland.

Kreps, D. M. (1990), *A Course in Microeconomic Theory*, Princeton, NJ: Princeton University Press.

Kreuger, A. O. (1983), *Trade and Employment in Developing Countries, vol. 3: Synthesis and Conclusions*, Chicago: University of Chicago Press.

Kumar, D. (ed.) (1982), *The Cambridge Economic History of India*, vol. II, Cambridge: Cambridge University Press.

Kydland, R. E. and Prescott, E. C. (1977), 'Rules Rather than Discretion: The Inconsistency of Optimal Plans', *Journal of Political Economy*, 85: 513–48.

Lahiri, S., Nassim, A., and Ghani, J. (2000), 'Optimal Second-Best Tariffs on an Intermediate Input with Particular Reference to Pakistan', *Journal of Development Economics*, 61(2): 393–416.

Lanjouw, P. and Stern, N. H. (1993), 'Markets, Opportunities and Changes in Inequality in Palanpur, 1957–84', in Hoff *et al.*, *The Economics of Rural Organization*, Oxford: Clarendon Press.

Layard, R. and Glaister, S. (1994), *Cost-Benefit Analysis*, 2nd edn, Cambridge: Cambridge University Press.

Lewis, W. A. (1980), 'The Slowing Down of the Engine of Growth', *American Economic Review*, 70(4).

Limao, N. and Venables, A. (2001), 'Infrastructure, Geographical Disadvantage, Transport Costs, and Trade', *World Bank Economic Review*, 15(3): 451–79.

Lipton, M. (1977), *Why Poor People Stay Poor*, London: Temple Smith.

— (1995), 'Land Reform as Commenced Business: The Case against Stopping', in de Janvry *et al.* (eds), *State, Market and Civil Organizations: New Theories, New Practices and their Implications for Rural Development*, London: Macmillan.

Little, I. M. D., Cooper, R. N., Corden, W. M., and Rajapatinara, S. (1993), *Boom, Crisis, and Adjustment: The Macroeconomic Experience of Developing Countries*, New York: Oxford University Press.

— and Mirrlees, J. A. (1974), *Project Appraisal and Planning for Developing Countries*, London: Heinemann.

— and — (1991), 'Project Appraisal and Planning Twenty Years on', in Fischer, S. *et al.* (eds), *Proceedings of the World Bank Annual Conference on Development Economics 1990*, Washington, DC: World Bank. (Reprinted in Layard and Glaister, 1994.)

— Scitovsky, T., and Scott, M. F. G. (1970), *Industry and Trade in Some Developing Countries*, Oxford: Oxford University Press.

Mahalanobis, P. C. (1955), 'The Approach of Operational Research to Planning in India', *Sankhya: The Indian Journal of Statistics*, 16: 3–62.

Maizels, A. (1968), *Exports and Economic Growth of Developing Countries*, Cambridge: Cambridge University Press.

Maneschi, A. (1998), 'The Dynamic Nature of Comparative Advantage and of Gains from Trade in Classical Economics', *Journal of the History of Economic Thought*, 20(2): 133–44.

Marshall, A. (1920), *Principles of Economics: An Introductory Volume*, 8th edn, London: Macmillan.

Martin, R. and Wijnbergen, S. V. (1988), 'Efficient Pricing of Natural Gas', *Journal of Public Economics*, 36: 177–96.

Martin, W. and Winters, L. (1996), *The Uruguay Round and the Developing Countries*, Cambridge: Cambridge University Press.

Mas-Colell, A., Whinston, M. D., and Green, J. R. (1995), *Microeconomic Theory*, New York: Oxford University Press.

McKinnon, R. I. (1973), *Money and Capital in Economic Development*, Washington, DC: Brookings Institution.

Michaely, M. (1977), 'Exports and Growth: An Empirical Investigation', *Journal of Development Economics*, 4(1): 49–53.

Middlebrook, M. (1985), *The Schweinfurt-Regensburg Mission: American Raids on 17 August, 1943*, Harmondsworth: Penguin.

Miracle, M. (1973), 'Economic Incentives for Loan Agents', *AID Spring Review of Small Farmer Credit*, 19: 223–33.

Mishan, E. J. (1970), 'What Went Wrong with Roskill?' *Journal of Transport Economics and Policy*, 4(3): 241–3.

Morduch, J. (2000), 'The Microfinance Schism', *World Development*, 28(4): 917–629.

Newbery, D. M. G. (1972), 'Public Policy in the Dual Economy', *Economic Journal*, 82: 567–90.

Newbery, D. M. G. (1977), 'Risk Sharing, Sharecropping and Uncertain Labour Markets', *Review of Economic Studies*, 44 (October): 585–94.

— and Stern, N. H. (eds) (1987), *The Theory of Taxation for Developing Countries*, New York: Oxford University Press.

Newman, P., Milgate, M., and Eatwell, J. (1992), *The New Palgrave Dictionary of Money and Finance*, London: Macmillan.

OECD (1968), *Manual of Industrial Project Analysis*, vol. II, Paris: OECD, Development Centre.

Otsuka, K. and Hayami, Y. (1988), 'Theories of Share Tenancy: A Critical Survey', *Economic Development and Cultural Change*, 37 (October): 31–68.

Perron, P. (1989), 'The Great Crash, the Oil Price Shock, and the Unit Root Hypothesis', *Econometrica*, 57: 1361–401.

Phelps, E. S. (1973), 'Inflation in the Theory of Public Finance', *Swedish Journal of Economics*, 75: 67–82.

Prebisch, R. (1951), 'The Spread of Technical Progress and the Terms of Trade', in United Nations, *Economic Survey of Latin America, 1949*, New York: UN Department of Economic Affairs.

Rajaraman, I. and Mukhopadhyay, A. (1999), 'Sustainability of Public Domestic Debt in India', in Sivrastara, D. K. (ed.), *Contemporary Fiscal Issues: Papers for the Eleventh Finance Commission*, New Delhi: Oxford University Press.

Ramsey, F. P. (1928), 'A Mathematical Theory of Saving', *Economic Journal*, 38: 543–59.

Reid, J. D. (1974), 'Sharecropping as an Understandable Response: The Post-Bellum South', *Journal of Economic History*, 33: 106–30.

Rodrik, D. (1991), 'Policy Uncertainty and Private Investment in Developing Countries', *Journal of Development Economics*, 36(2): 229–42.

— (1999), *The New Global Economy and Developing Countries: Making Openness Work*, Baltimore, MD: The Johns Hopkins University Press.

Rowley, C. K. and Peacock, A. T. (1975), *Welfare Economics: A Liberal Restatement*, London: Martin Robertson.

Sandmo, A. (1972), 'Discount Rates for Public Investments under Uncertainty', *International Economic Review*, 13: 287–302.

Sanyal, S. K. (1988), 'Trends in Landholding and Poverty in Rural India', in Srinivasan, T. N. and Bardhan, P. K. (eds), *Rural Poverty in South Asia*, New York: Columbia University Press.

Sen, A. K. (1967), 'Isolation, Assurance and the Social Rate of Discount', *Quarterly Journal of Economics*, 81(1): 112–24.

Shaban, R. A. (1987), 'Testing between Alternative Models of Sharecropping', *Journal of Political Economy*, 95 (October): 893–920.

Sheehey, E. J. (1990), 'Exports and Growth: A Flawed Framework', *Journal of Development Studies*, 27(1): 111–6.

Shoven, J. B. and Whalley, J. (1984), 'Applied General Equilibrium Models of Taxation and International Trade: An Introduction and Survey', *Journal of Economic Literature*, 22: 1007–51.

Siamwalla, A. *et al.* (1990), 'The Thai Rural Credit System: Public Subsidies, Private Information, and Segmented Markets', *World Bank Economic Review*, 4(3): 271–96.

Singer, H. W. (1950), 'The Distribution of Gains between Investing and Borrowing Countries', *American Economic Review*, 40: 473–85.

Spillman, W. J. (1919), 'The Agricultural Ladder', *American Economic Review*, 9 (March): 170–9.

Squire, L. (1989), 'Project Evaluation in Theory and Practice', in Chenery, H. B. and Srinivasan, T. N. (eds), *Handbook of Development Economics*, vol. 2, Amsterdam: North-Holland.

— Little, I. M. D., and Durdag, M. (1979), 'Shadow Pricing and Macroeconomic Analysis: Some Illustrations from Pakistan', *Pakistan Development Review*, 18: 90–112.

— and van der Tak, H. G. (1975), *Economic Analysis of Projects*, Baltimore, MD: The Johns Hopkins University Press.

Subbarao, K. G. K. (1985), 'State Policies and Regional Disparities in Indian Agriculture', *Development and Change*, 15: 523–46.

Srinivasan, T. N. (2000), 'Trade, Development and Growth', *The Graham Lecture*, Princeton University.

Stern, N. H. (1972), 'Optimum Development in a Dual Economy', *Review of Economic Studies*, 39: 171–84.

— (1977), 'Welfare Weights and the Elasticity of the Marginal Value of Income', in Artis, M. and Nobay, R. (eds), *Studies in Modern Economic Analysis*, Oxford: Blackwell.

— (1994), 'From the Static to the Dynamic: Some Problems in the Theory of Taxation', in Bagchi, A. and Stern, N. H. (eds), *Tax Policy and Planning in Developing Countries*, New Delhi: Oxford University Press.

Stiglitz, J. E. and Dasgupta, P. S. (1971), 'Differential Taxation, Public Goods and Economic Efficiency', *Review of Economic Studies, 38*.

A Symposium on the OECD Manual of Social-Cost Benefit Analysis (1972), *Oxford Bulletin of Economics and Statistics*.

Takayama, A. (1974), *Mathematical Economics*, Hinsdale, IL: The Dryden Press.

Varian, H. R. (1992), *Microeconomic Analysis*, 3rd edn, New York: W.W. Norton.

Walters, A. A. (1988), 'Congestion', in Eatwell, J., Milgate, M., and Newman, P. (eds), *The New Palgrave*, London: Macmillan.

Warriner, D. (1969), *Land Reform in Principle and Practice*, Oxford: Clarendon Press.

Whalley, J. and Clarete, R. L. (1987), 'Comparing the Marginal Welfare Costs of Commodity and Trade Taxes', *Journal of Public Economics*, 33: 357–62.

Wharton, C. (1962), 'Marketing, Merchandising and Moneylending: A Note on Middleman Monopoly in Malaya', *Malayan Economic Review*, 7: 24–44.

World Bank (1987), *World Development Report 1987*, New York: Oxford University Press.

— (1995), *Development Indicators*, New York: Oxford University Press.

— (1997), *Development Indicators*, New York: Oxford University Press.

— (1998), *Development Indicators*, New York: Oxford University Press.

— (2001), *Global Economic Prospects*, Washington, DC.

Index